Psychodrama in Counsellin and Education

Volume 1

Series Editors

Jochen Becker-Ebel, Psychodrama and Geriatric Palliative Care, Yenepoya University, Mangalore, India

Scott Giacomucci, Social Work and Social Research, Bryn Mawr Graduate School of Social Work, Philadelphia, USA

The series situates psychodrama studies and research in Asia and beyond in a global context. It provides a unique and innovative resource for the latest developments in the field, nurturing a comprehensive and encompassing publication venue for humanistic psychodrama and sociodrama in therapy and coaching. The series publishes peer-reviewed volumes related to therapy, psychotherapy, counselling, coaching, HRD, team development and education including training. The series reflects on cultural creativity and new developments beyond J L Moreno in the second century of the existence of Psychodrama. The editor, with the assistance of distinguished scholars from Asia and elsewhere specializing in a variety of disciplinary and thematic areas, welcomes proposals that are related to the above-mentioned wide-ranging psychodrama studies. The series promotes the understanding of psychodramatic tools which are relevant in education, coaching, and team development. The series will appeal to researchers, clinicians/practitioners, and graduate students in the behavioral, social, medical, psychological and MBA sciences as well as leaders in Education, Corporate world and politics. It accepts monographs, edited volumes, and textbooks.

More information about this series at http://www.springer.com/series/16448

Scott Giacomucci

Social Work, Sociometry, and Psychodrama

Experiential Approaches for Group Therapists, Community Leaders, and Social Workers

 Springer

Scott Giacomucci
Phoenix Center for Experiential Trauma Therapy
Media, PA, USA

Graduate School of Social Work and Social Research
Bryn Mawr College
Bryn Mawr, PA, USA

ISSN 2662-5490   ISSN 2662-5504 (electronic)
Psychodrama in Counselling, Coaching and Education
ISBN 978-981-33-6344-1   ISBN 978-981-33-6342-7 (eBook)
https://doi.org/10.1007/978-981-33-6342-7

This Springer imprint is published by the registered company Springer Nature Singapore Pte Ltd.
The registered company address is: 152 Beach Road, #21-01/04 Gateway East, Singapore 189721,
Singapore

To the future generations of psychodramatists and social workers

may the contents of this book enliven your practice

and enhance the lives of those you serve

Series Preface

We are pleased to introduce you to this New Springer Nature psychodrama book series titled, *Psychodrama in Counselling, Coaching and Education,* edited by Jochen Becker-Ebel and by Scott Giacomucci (who is also the author of the first book in the series).

The series situates psychodrama practice and research in Asia and beyond in a global context. It provides a unique and innovative resource for the latest developments in the field, nurturing a comprehensive and encompassing publication venue for humanistic psychodrama and sociodrama in therapy, coaching, and education. The series publishes peer-reviewed volumes related to therapy, psychotherapy, counselling, coaching, human resource development, organizational dynamics, education, and training. This series will annually publish two monographs, edited volumes, and/or textbooks.

The rich tradition of Dr. Moreno's methods, including sociometry, psychodrama, and sociodrama, has been primarily disseminated through private post-graduate training institutes over the past 100 years of its existence. This academic book series brings the creativity and innovation of these experiential approaches more fully into academia with publications included in academic databases freely accessible to thousands of individual students, researchers, and professors.

The series reflects on cultural creativity and new developments beyond Dr. Jacob L. Moreno in the second century of the existence of psychodrama. The editors, with the assistance of distinguished scholars from Brazil, Germany, Indonesia, India, Taiwan, Turkey, and USA specializing in a variety of disciplinary and thematic areas, welcome proposals that are related to the above-mentioned wide-ranging psychodrama studies. Books in this series will also emphasize the unique histories and methodologies emerging in international psychodrama communities. The platform created by this series highlights psychodrama practice wisdom from around the world in the English language, making it more accessible for a wide audience. Additionally, this book series will include books that systematically integrate psychodrama philosophy and practice into other established fields of group psychotherapy, social work, counseling, psychology, coaching, trauma theory, education, and organizational development.

The series promotes the understanding of psychodramatic and sociometric tools which are relevant for counselors, supervisors, trainers, educators, creative arts therapists, group workers, and community or organizational leaders. The series will appeal to researchers, practitioners, and graduate students in the behavioral, social, medical, psychological, and business sciences as well as leaders in education, the corporate world, and politics.

As series editors, we would like to extend our gratitude to Springer Nature, Mrs. Satvinder Kaur, and her team, for believing in the creativity and strength of psychodrama. This series will serve to promote the methods of sociometry and psychodrama in multidisciplinary contexts to ultimately enhance the provision of social services, psychotherapy, education, scholarship, and research throughout the world.

Chennai, India/Hamburg, Germany   Jochen Becker-Ebel
Philadelphia, USA   Scott Giacomucci
January 2021

Foreword

Ours is a nation built upon trauma. We are a nation of immigrants. The original trauma of all immigrants who voluntarily come here is that they wrenched themselves from their families, communities, and countries. Many immigrants traveled here with only their hopes and dreams of creating a better life for themselves and their descendants.

One such immigrant was Dr. Jacob L. Moreno who migrated from Vienna to New York City in 1925, bringing with him new ideas of sociometry, psychodrama, and a vision of healing society. Zerka Toeman Moreno was also an immigrant who migrated from the Netherlands, via London to New York City in 1939. They both championed the isolated and rejected. His causes were the destigmatization of prostitutes, prisoners, and delinquents; hers were gay, lesbian, bisexual and transgender persons, and later those living with HIV and AIDS.

The original colonists established this great country by inflicting unspeakable trauma that continues even today upon the indigenous Native Americans. Our country's greatest wealth was created on the back, blood, sweat, and tears of slaves (1619–1865). After the Civil War and until the civil rights movement in the 1960s, most African Americans still lived in a nation of systemic oppression and legalized discrimination. Today, we still find vestiges of systemic oppression and social injustice in the ways in which we treat our African American citizens. These past traumas may have been denied or repressed from our conscious minds, but the pernicious and persistent aftershocks of these traumas live on in our unconscious, our bodies, and the body politic. This book offers a variety of action-based tools to address trauma with individuals, groups, and communities.

Now, the winds of change, fanned by the COVID-19 pandemic, and social, political, economic, and environmental unrest, are rapidly sweeping across our nation and the globe. Some have exploited these dramatic changes to achieve or retain power. They sow discord and distrust. Some have used their words and deeds to demean and demonize others and even to marginalize and criminalize minorities. When people are fearful, ignorant, and prejudiced, they are more likely to believe anti-science, anti-Semitic, political, racial, and religious conspiracies that create divisions within families, communities, and countries.

These divisions and separations are largely caused by a social phenomenon that Moreno terms "the sociodynamic effect" which underlies social inequality in society.

The reversal of the sociodynamic effect and movement toward social justice are tasks of utmost importance at this specific point in history.

Social workers and psychodramatists embody the hope that "A truly therapeutic procedure can have for its objective no less than the whole of mankind." Together we can bridge the divides that separate us and, once again, respect and honor the differences between us. We agree that what binds us together is greater than what separates us. We all hope for a brighter future, a happy and healthy family, a good job with good pay, and an opportunity for our children to have a better life than we have had.

Jacob Levy Moreno, M.D. (1889–1974), along with Jung, Freud, and Adler, was one of the last great psychiatrists of the twentieth century. Dr. Moreno is the founder of psychodrama and sociometry and one of the co-founders of group psychotherapy and role theory.

Dr. Moreno and his colleagues and followers since his death have created and refined a complex and comprehensive body of knowledge encompassing a philosophy of spontaneity and creativity, a theory of human development, a theory of personality, a body of historic and voluminous scientific research (1920–1970), current worldwide research, and over 800 assessment, intervention and evaluation tools and techniques. It is quite remarkable that so few have contributed so much and have had such an enormous impact on the social sciences.

Dr. Scott Giacomucci, DSW, LCSW, BCD, FAAETS, PAT, is at the forefront of the next generation of Moreno's followers, and he spans the intersection of social work, group work, trauma treatment, and psychodrama, sociometry, and group psychotherapy. He is uniquely positioned to teach and train others how to mend the cleavages of gender, race, religion, gender, socio-economic status, and cultures. He has developed his gifts of intellect, courage, curiosity, and charisma into talents that he has faithfully and consistently used on behalf of the isolated, forgotten, marginalized, and oppressed. He has boundless affection, love, and fealty to the family of humans and not just for the family of his birth.

Dr. Giacomucci is also that rare and exceptional academic author with a deep reservoir of clinical practice who weaves history, theory, research, best practices, and practical applications into a cohesive narrative that is clear and practical. One book does not lead to mastery of any field, but this book launches us on a journey that inspires us, imbues us with passion and purpose, and provides us with strategies and tools to move forward. While this book is best read from cover to cover, the sections stand alone and offer specific guidance for history, theory, assessment, intervention, and evaluation. As you read this book, you may find that some of the terms, theoretical constructs, and intervention tools are familiar to you and many more that offer new, exciting, and practical ways to heal relationships.

The Reverend Dr. Martin Luther King, Jr., reminded us that the arc of history bends toward justice. Yet the arc cannot bend unless there are sufficient people dedicated to bringing about that change. Social workers and psychodramatists can help make the arc of history bend toward justice. When we are trained in the art, science, and craft of creativity and spontaneity, we can bring healing and reconciliation to our families, our communities, our country, and the world. As Dr. Moreno once asked,

"How can we expect there to be peace in the world when there is not peace within in our own social and cultural atoms (networks)?"

In the final pages of this book, Dr. Giacomucci shares his future vision of social work, psychodrama, and sociometry. He does this by combining several psychodrama techniques, "The Letter," "Role Reversal," and "The Future Projection Technique."

Now, I ask you the reader to future project to the end of your professional career and write a letter from your future self to your present self. In the letter, list some of the most important lessons you learned on your way and some positive results of having learned those lessons. End your letter with telling your present self one thing that you did today that made it possible for your best future self to come true.

Dr. Giacomucci has shared his vision. You have shared your vision.

At this moment and every moment, your world is at an intersection. Which path will you choose?

Dale Richard Buchanan, Ph.D., L.I.C.S.W., T.E.P.
Director
Clinical Therapies (Retired)
Saint Elizabeths Hospital
Washington, DC, USA

Acknowledgements

The completion of this book requires acknowledgments to many who have supported me in the writing process. The warming-up process for this book began with my psychodrama training and graduate social work education. My foundational understanding of Moreno's methods is attributed to my training with Edward Schreiber, David Moran, and Kate Hudgins. I would like to recognize the faculty at the University of Pennsylvania and Bryn Mawr College for the superb graduate social work education and scholarly mentorship that I received as a student—and later as an adjunct professor at Bryn Mawr College. The initial idea for this book emerged in the summer of 2019 after completing my DSW program—a small portion of this book is republished from my dissertation. I owe much gratitude to my dissertation committee for their guidance—Marcia Martin, Sari Skolnik, and Cathy Nugent.

The writing process of this book has been largely influenced by Jochen Becker-Ebel who has offered much encouragement, guidance, advocacy, editing, and insight. Jochen's contributions have helped me refine the book text, enhance its international readability, and navigate the publishing process. I also extend my appreciation to Satvinder Kaur and Springer Nature for their publishing support and promotion of psychodrama through this new book series. I would like to also recognize Georgie Klotz for her many of hours of work producing the beautiful images and figures throughout this text. The historical photographs within the book have been made available for reprint (from The JL Moreno Memorial Photo Album) due to the careful historical research conducted by Sérgio Guimarães and with the permissions of Zoli Figusch and Jonathan Moreno. I also extend my gratitude to Leticia Nieto for generously helping with editing and proofreading, while also helping me to see the importance of this book being accessible to all—which warmed me up to the idea of publishing open-access.

The inspiration that fueled my writing came from my admiration for leaders in the social work, group work, and psychodrama communities—especially Jacob and Zerka Moreno. I am indebted to Adam Blatner who helped me to frame writing as an act of creating through the lens of Moreno's Canon of Creativity—this insight created an internal shift from which the role of writer emerged within me. My brief encounter with Zerka Moreno in April 2016 resulted in a deep commitment to help carry psychodrama to the next generation. Motivation for this project has come in large part from my current clients, students, and trainees at the Phoenix Center for Experiential Trauma Therapy, Mirmont Treatment Center, and Bryn Mawr College. Witnessing them access their own internal autonomous healing centers, spontaneity, and genius through psychodrama fortifies my commitment to help ensure Moreno's methods are available for future generations of students and clients.

Finally, I'd like to acknowledge my family, especially my wife Maria, for their support throughout my writing process. The production of this book proved to me much more than I expected and has regularly occupied my thoughts and discussions at home for many months. Maria has engaged with me in countless conversations about the book content and the emotional highs and lows of the writing process. Her patience, grace, and insights as a partner and fellow social worker have in large part created the holding environment from which this book has emerged.

Acknowledgement Sections of content throughout this book were initially published in the author's dissertation: Giacomucci, S. (2019). *Social Group Work in Action: A Sociometry, Psychodrama, and Experiential Trauma Therapy Curriculum.* Doctorate in Social Work (DSW) Dissertations. 124. https://repository.upenn.edu/cgi/viewcontent.cgi?article=1128&context=edissertations_sp2.

Praise for *Social Work, Sociometry, and Psychodrama*

"Scott Giacomucci has written an excellent and very important book locating psychodrama, sociometry and sociatry alongside social work. This book lays out the history, philosophy, and practice of Moreno's triadic system clearly for the reader offering a more complete understanding of not only the methods but the mission behind them. This is truly an important contribution to the literature that firmly establishes the connection between Moreno's triadic system and the social work field today."

—Tian Dayton, Ph.D., TEP, *Senior Fellow at The Meadows, Director of The New York Psychodrama Training Institute, Developer of the Relational Trauma Repair Model (RTR), and author of fifteen books including, Neuropsychodrama (2015) and The Living Stage (2005)*

"This wonderful book brings Moreno vividly back to life in front of us! I got hooked and could not put it down until the very last page. It presents a panoramic view on the broad and unlimited possibilities of psychodrama, while placing it within cultural and systemic perspectives."

—Nien-Hwa Lai, Ph.D., TEP, *Professor, Department of Psychology and Counseling, National Taipei University of Education*

"This book is aptly dedicated to the future generations of psychodramatists and social workers. It is the most comprehensive book to recount in meticulous details the history, philosophy and underlying theories of both psychodrama and social work. This scholarly work should be required reading for both faculty and students of these disciplines, and will be the best resource for psychodrama trainees studying for their certification exam. The book is well-written, its style is accessible, making it a page-turner, which not a common phenomenon in academic writing."

—Jacob Gershoni, LCSW, CGP, TEP, *Co-Director of the Psychodrama Training Institute at The Sociometric Institute, New York, NY; Editor of Psychodrama in the 21st Century (2003)*

"Dr. Scott Giacomucci's book takes a much-needed new look at the intersection between psychodrama, sociometry, and social work that will be of great interest to practitioners, students, trainers, and researchers. He presents the theory and practice of psychodrama in depth and provides a comprehensive account of contemporary applications in individual, group, and community settings. State of the art research findings are discussed clearly and insightfully throughout. This innovative book will certainly be a timely and invaluable resource for readers in many human service fields."

—Hod Orkibi, Ph.D., *Tenured Senior Lecturer and Researcher, Psychodrama and Dramatherapy Graduate Program, School of Creative Arts Therapies, University of Haifa, Israel*

"This book takes psychodrama beyond the therapeutic consultation room, to the crossroads where it meets social work and community practice. It explores and integrates the theory and philosophy underpinning these disciplines, and offers an experiential perspective of using action methods, psychodrama and sociometry within these settings, with particular focus on trauma work. A great addition to the library of all professionals working in any of these areas!"

—Zoli Figusch, *British psychodrama psychotherapist/trainer, Series Editor at North-West Psychodrama Association, Editor of two texts on Brazilian psychodrama—Sambadrama (2005) and From One-to-One Psychodrama to Large Group Socio-psychodrama (2009/2019)*

"When Bruce Springsteen's album, "Born to Run" was released, critics wrote that Springsteen was the 'future of rock and roll.' Dr. Giacomucci's text will be required reading for generations of group therapists to come. This book conveys to the reader— experienced or novice, the fundamentals that are elusive to capture, but can clearly be understood and utilized by everyone. Scott Giacomucci is this generation of group therapists' Bruce Springsteen."

—Richard Beck, LCSW, BCD, CGP, FAGPA, *President, International Association of Group Psychotherapy and Group Processes; Lecturer, Columbia University School of Social Work; Lecturer of Social Work in Psychiatry (Voluntary), Weill Cornell Medicine*

"Dr. Scott Giacomucci has taken the task of integrating the essentials of the history, practices, and complex theories of Dr. J. L. Moreno—incorporated with a similarly complex set of ideas, theories, practices of Social Work. Through extensive research, diligence, and skill Scott has succeeded in offering a new view of Moreno's work within the context of Social Work. This book serves to advance both fields in a scholarly and remarkable way. I intend to use this book as a core text for the Psychodrama class I teach at Lesley University in Cambridge, MA."

—Edward Schreiber, DD, Ed.M, MSW, TEP, *Director of the Zerka Moreno Foundation; Co-Editor of the Autobiography of a Genius by Jacob Moreno, The*

Quintessential Zerka and To Dream Again by Zerka Moreno; Adjunct Professor,
Lesley University Drama Therapy Program

"Dr. Scott Giacomucci is a real pioneer and revolutionary with great creativity and productivity. This is a brilliant and quite interesting book that provides innovative resources for social work, sociometry and psychodrama. His creativity for experiential approaches cultivates an important culture of therapy and leadership which gives courage to trainees, practitioners, and educators in the field to go forward for a better world."

—Caner Bingöl, MD, Ph.D., TEP, LCFT, LCTP, *Founding member of Dr. Ali Babaoğlu Psychodrama Institute; Istanbul, Turkey; Interim Chair of Trauma/Disaster Task Force, International Association of Group Psychotherapy*

"This scientific book is comprehensive, easy to read, and depicts the state of the art of social work and psychodrama. Chapters include practical content for direct use in social work, psychodrama, and beyond. This book is an essential read and is valuable for a variety of fields."

—Jochen Becker-Ebel, Ph.D., *Owner PIB Germany and Adj. Prof. f. Psychodrama, Medical Faculty, Yenepoya University, India*

"Dr. Giacomucci has been committed to integrating psychodrama into social work. This well-written book is not only grounded in theory, but also very practical. The book content is excellent, insightful, and surely a milestone in the process of the integration of psychodrama and social work. With the rapid development of social work in China, sociometry and psychodrama have great potential application in competence-based social work education."

—Xiaohui Wang, Ph.D., *Associate Professor, China University of Labor Relations*

Contents

About the Author

Dr. Scott Giacomucci, DSW, LCSW, BCD, FAAETS, PAT is the director/founder of the Phoenix Center for Experiential Trauma Therapy in Pennsylvania and the director of Trauma Services at Mirmont Treatment Center. He is a research associate and adjunct professor at Bryn Mawr College Graduate School of Social Work teaching a course on psychodrama and experiential trauma therapy. He completed his Doctorate in Clinical Social Work (DSW) from the University of Pennsylvania and is recognized as a board-certified diplomate of clinical social work. He is also a fellow of the American Academy of Experts in Traumatic Stress and certified EMDR Consultant. He serves on the Executive Council of the American Society of Group Psychotherapy and Psychodrama (ASGPP), the Advisory Board of the International Society of Experiential Professionals, and the Trauma and Disaster Task Force of the International Association of Group Psychotherapy. He is currently co-chair of ASGPP's research committee and professional liaison committees and was a founding member of ASGPP's Sociatry and Social Justice Committee.

He is the recipient of various national and international awards, most recently as the first recipient of the National Association of Social Workers' (NASW) Emerging Social Work Leader Award, the 2019 Group Practice Award from ACA's Association of Specialists in Group Work (ASGW), and his dissertation received a 2018 SPARC endorsement from the International Association of Social Work with Groups (IASWG). He presents regularly at regional, national, and international events. He has published multiple peer-reviewed articles and co-edited the newly published *Autobiography of a Genius* in 2019 by psychodrama's founder, Jacob Moreno. He also serves as co-editor of the first international psychodrama book series recently announced by Springer Nature titled *Psychodrama in Counselling, Coaching, and Education.*

List of Figures

List of Tables

Chapter 1
Introduction to Social Work, Sociometry, and Psychodrama

Abstract This introductory chapter provides context for the content covered in the rest of the book. Background on the evolution of the book and increased social work attention to psychodrama is offered while also defining the basic concepts of sociometry, psychodrama, and social work with groups. The importance of considering differences between cultures, populations, and countries is highlighted, especially as it relates to scope of practice of the social work field which varies between countries. Specifics of chapter topics are overviewed with suggestions to the reader on how to approach this book. Though the book explicitly focuses on social work, many other professionals will find this publication useful including group therapists, counselors, psychologists, creative arts therapists, psychodramatists, community workers, supervisors, and professors.

Keywords Social work · Sociometry · Psychodrama · Group work · Experiential therapy

This book aims to integrate Moreno's methods into the social work field. Social work and Moreno's methods, specifically sociometry and psychodrama, remain largely unintegrated. An attempt is made throughout this book to outline the congruent histories, philosophies, theories, and practices of social work, sociometry, and psychodrama. Both sociometric and psychodramatic processes will be presented with emphasis on their usefulness in clinical social work practice with individuals, groups, communities, organizations, supervision, and education. Though this book will explicitly address social workers, it is also applicable for group therapists, community leaders, drama therapists, creative arts therapists, psychologists, counselors, coaches, supervisors, and educators.

The idea for this book emerged from my own professional journey. After completing my master's in social work, I threw myself into intensive psychodrama training. Upon completion of my psychodrama certification, I returned to pursue a doctorate in clinical social work. Tasked with assignments about social work history, philosophy, and theory, I hunted through the academic literature for publications about the connection between sociometry, psychodrama, and social work but found nearly nothing had been written on the topic in English. There are several related German publications on the topic however (Böcker, 2004; Dannheiser, 2007;

© The Author(s) 2021

S. Giacomucci, *Social Work, Sociometry, and Psychodrama*, Psychodrama in Counselling, Coaching and Education 1,
https://doi.org/10.1007/978-981-33-6342-7_1

Engelke, 1981; Müller, 2009; Neudorfer, 2014; Niepenberg, 2017; Ramsauer, 2007; Schwinger, 2014, 2016; Stimmer, 2004; Zwilling, 2004). It seemed I had unexpectedly encountered a major gap in the (English) literature base. I decided to devote my doctoral dissertation to the topic and created an MSW course curriculum to disseminate my findings on the overlap between social work with groups and Moreno's methods (Giacomucci, 2019b). My dissertation is the foundation of this book concept, though the majority of the content in this book is new.

In the past few years, the social work field seems to have a newfound interest in the creative arts therapies, *non-deliberative* or action-based approaches, and psychodrama (Giacomucci, 2019b; Heinonen, Halonen, & Krahn, 2018; Sulman, Sullivan, & Nosko, 2016). This is evidenced in multiple ways including an increased number of psychodrama presentations at social work conferences at the state, national, and international levels. Perhaps a more objective measure of this is the *social work with groups* journal hosting special issues focused on non-deliberative social work in 2016, social work and the arts in 2018, and psychodrama in 2020. Moreno's methods would fall within each one of these categories which shows an increased receptibility and interest within the social work with groups community. The number of English publications specific to social work, sociometry, and psychodrama has increased each year since 2017. The International Association of Social Work with Groups (IASWG) has created a new annual event at their symposium focused on non-deliberative social work (a category that psychodrama would fall within). Furthermore, in 2017 there was not a single course devoted to sociometry and psychodrama taught within a social work department in the USA (though many existed decades ago). As of 2020, at least two psychodrama courses are being taught in graduate social work programs in the USA (Bryn Mawr College and Yeshiva University). This book was written to serve as a textbook for a psychodrama course for social workers or other professionals.

The number of social workers with certification in sociometry, psychodrama, and group psychotherapy has also increased significantly in the past decade. In 2011, 11% of certified psychodramatists were social workers (Konopik & Cheung, 2013); however, in 2020 that has jumped to almost 30% (ABESPGP, 2020). Although social work is one of the most represented mental health fields within the USA psychodrama community, sociometry and psychodrama receive very little attention within the social work field in the USA. In other countries too, it seems that many psychodramatists hold degrees or licenses in social work; however, there has not been much attention given to a systematic exploration of the social work and psychodrama intersection, especially at a theoretical level. The richness of psychodrama remains mostly unharvested by social workers today. This book delivers social workers with a historical, theoretical, and practical understanding of how to use the theory and experiential processes from sociometry and psychodrama in social work practice.

1.1   USA and International Contexts

This book is primarily presented from my perspective as a US-based social worker and psychodramatist attempting to incorporate an awareness of how the fields of both social work and psychodrama have fundamental differences in other countries. This book is also partially limited by my inability to read non-English languages. I have done my best to access sources relevant to this book in other languages and include reference to them when appropriate.

In the USA, it is common practice for social workers to provide clinical services and psychotherapy, but this may not be the case in every part of the world. Although this book depicts the use of sociometry and psychodrama methods for social workers in clinical settings, it is important that each reader practices within the scope of their licensure and understands the boundaries of their practice based on the governing bodies and codes of ethics of their own countries.

It is my belief that the social work and psychodrama communities in the USA have much to offer professional communities in other countries—and that we have much more to learn from our international colleagues. This is especially true when it comes to psychodrama. Although psychodrama initially took root and developed in the USA, the US psychodrama community has failed to grow and professionalize in many ways (Giacomucci, 2019a). International psychodrama communities in Europe, South America, Asia, and Australia have outgrown psychodramatists in the USA in the areas including numbers of members, psychodrama research, embedding psychodrama in academia, and integrating psychodrama into mainstream group therapy, psychology, social work, and counseling fields. Internationally, there are entire graduate degrees awarded in the study of sociometry, psychodrama, and group psychotherapy, including in Israel, England, Spain, and Bulgaria; and at the same time, it is difficult to find mention of sociometry or psychodrama academic institutions in the USA. In some countries, Moreno's methods are widely accepted but in the USA they remain largely unknown.

1.1.1   Cultural Contexts

The practice of any method is embedded within a specific cultural context. Regardless of one's approach, it is important to consider the cultural context and contemplate ways that the approach can be modified when working with different cultural groups or multicultural groups. Zerka Moreno states that "warming-up to psychodrama may proceed differently from culture to culture and appropriate changes in the application of the method have to be made" (1965/2006, p. 108). Culture has a considerable impact on communication (verbal and non-verbal), social norms, belief, physical contact, value systems, politics, religion, gender roles, power, and meaning making. Both social work and Moreno's methods initially emerged within the framework of western perspective (European/USA). Although psychodrama was primarily developed in the USA, it seems that the highly individualistic and medicalized culture may have significantly contributed to the decline of psychodrama's popularity (among other factors). However, at the same time, it appears that psychodrama's popularity has greatly increased in continents that have a more collective and communal culture—especially in Asia, the Middle East, and Latin America. It also seems that the practice of psychodrama in the USA and Western Europe is more focused on psychotherapy while psychodrama practice in other countries encompasses psychotherapy and non-clinical contexts including public community sessions, social activism, and politics (Fürst, 2006).

The psychodramatic approach honors the perspectives and experiences of each participant while supporting individuals in their own process of meaning making. Psychodrama is inherently focused on process, creativity, spontaneity, and largely rooted in a postmodern framework (Oudijk, 2007)—all of which make it more easily adaptable for different content, populations, and cultural contexts (Fürst, 2006). At the same time, because of its emphasis on action and group work, it may be even more important in group therapy and psychodrama to consider cultural contexts than with other approaches (Bustamante, 1961). Nieto (2010) presents an anti-oppression approach to inform psychodrama which emphasizes the need for awareness and respect of differences in social identity. Specific aspects of psychodrama practice that may need to be modified for different cultures include the use of physical touch, religion or spirituality, expressions of anger or conflict (especially toward parents), disclosing family issues, and recognizing personal strengths (Fürst, 2006; Gong, 2004; Hudgins & Toscani, 2013; Lai, 2011, 2013; Lai & Tsai, 2014; Ottomeyer, 2003).

I believe it is important for me to acknowledge my own cultural bias and limited experience in most cultural systems around the world. This book is written based on my own experience practicing in the USA, learning primarily from psychodramatists in the USA, and teaching primarily in the USA with occasional presentations for international audiences. While this book may be a source of new learning related to the theory and practice of Morenean methods, I urge readers to critically consider the applicability of each process in this book to the cultural context(s) in which you work. Readers are encouraged to develop new adaptations of sociometry and psychodrama methods to better meet the needs of diverse populations.

1.2   What Are Sociometry and Psychodrama?

Though future chapters will provide extensive descriptions of sociometry (Chap. 155) and psychodrama (Chap. 6), I will introduce the concepts briefly here. Throughout this book, the founder of sociometry and psychodrama will be referred to with various names including "Moreno," "Jacob Moreno," Jacob L. Moreno," "Dr. Jacob L. Moreno," "J.L. Moreno," and "J.L." (See Fig. 1.1). These names are used interchangeably within the psychodrama community when talking about Moreno, and I

Fig. 1.1 Jacob Moreno ascending the psychodrama stage. Reprinted with permission from Figusch (2014)

have also used each of them when referencing Moreno throughout the book. Both sociometry and psychodrama exist within the triadic system developed by Dr. Jacob L. Moreno—sociometry, psychodrama, and group psychotherapy. Quite often, the term "psychodrama" is used when referring to the entire triadic system. From a Morenean perspective, each element of the triadic system is intimately connected and emerged from Moreno's existential philosophy (Moreno, 2019). Though he is often neglected in the group therapy literature, J.L. Moreno actually coined the terms "group therapy" and "group psychotherapy" in 1932 (Moreno, 1957). His approach to group therapy emphasizes action over analysis and was based on his early mystical experiences, his development of the Theater of Spontaneity, and the sociometric ideas—all of which emerged in the early 1900s.

Sociometry is defined as the study of group dynamics, the evolution of groups, and the network of relationships within groups (Moreno, 1953). Moreno's sociometric system offers a theory of society and interpersonal relations, a research methods for studying the nature of groups and relationships, and experiential practices for assessing and promoting change within and between individuals and groups (Hale, 2009; Nolte, 2014). Sociometry facilitates both written and/or action-based group assessment using a variety of novel instruments. While psychology and psychodrama are focused on psychodynamics, sociometry emphasizes the sociodynamic realm of experience. Most psychodrama group sessions begin with action-based sociometry processes to initiate a warm-up, explore group dynamics, and establish the topic of the psychodrama enactment (Giacomucci, 2020).

Psychodrama is most often described as an experiential approach that integrates aspects of psychotherapy and role playing techniques to externalize intrapersonal or interpersonal issues. Psychodrama is primarily recognized as a form of psychotherapy, but it is also used extensively outside of clinical settings. Psychodrama sessions generally involve a protagonist, a director, role players, a stage of some sort, and an audience. The story of a protagonist is dramatized using unique role playing techniques including doubling, soliloquy, self-presentation, mirroring, and role reversal. Psychodramas vary greatly in their size, length, number of scenes, goals, topics, settings, orientation to time (past, present, and/or future), and the nature of the roles (intrapsychic, interpersonal, spiritual, axiological, etc.).

After the completion of a psychodrama, participants de-role and return to the group as themselves. The final group phase is focused on personal sharing related to the psychodrama enactment. This sharing phase almost resembles more traditional talk therapy group sessions, however during the sharing phase of a psychodrama group, analysis or intellectualization is discouraged in favor of authentic sharing about one's own experience.

Moreno's methods have largely been separated from each other, from their underlying philosophy, and from their founder. Moreno (see Fig. 1.2) published his first nine books anonymously, inspired by his spiritual beliefs. As a result, it was easy for others to take his ideas and claim them as their own. Morenean philosophy directly challenges and contradicts psychoanalysis, the medical model, individualism, and capitalism. It seems that these philosophical differences may have contributed to the separation of Moreno's philosophy from his methods by many practitioners in the

Fig. 1.2 Jacob Moreno in 1925 in Vienna. Reprinted with permission from Figusch (2014)

USA. Furthermore, as his methods penetrated the larger culture, the triadic system fell apart as some fields absorbed one element but not the others. For example, sociology and social network researchers adopted ideas of sociometry without giving second thoughts to psychodrama or group psychotherapy. Similarly, the group therapy world largely ignores sociometry and psychodrama. And multiple fields, such as education, coaching, organizational leadership, gestalt therapy, encounter groups, and therapeutic communities have incorporated aspects of psychodrama, particularly role playing and the empty chair technique, without also integrating sociometry or Morenean philosophy. Moreno believed that his work had been cannibalized at the expense of its reputation (Moreno, 2014).

1.3   Social Work with Groups

This book will primarily focus on group work, but also contains sections on using sociometry and psychodrama in one-to-one sessions, work with communities or organizations, and social work education and supervision. Throughout the book, the terms "social work with groups," "social group work ," and "group work" will be used interchangeably. "Group therapy" and "group psychotherapy" will also be used interchangeably. While group therapy is focused on clinical applications of group work within a therapeutic context, social group work has a wider orientation that encompasses group therapy, community group work, educational groups, skill-building groups, task groups, social action groups, remedial groups, supervisory groups, and training groups. Clinical applications of sociometry and psychodrama will be primarily emphasized throughout the examples in each chapter, nevertheless these approaches are also used in non-clinical or non-therapeutic social work settings.

Social workers are experiencing increased expectations to facilitate groups in their careers while receiving little to no formal education, training, or supervision specific on group work. Social work students and graduates are being placed in internships and jobs where they are expected to facilitate group psychotherapy without special-ized skills training necessary to work competently in group settings (Knight, 2017). The resulting consequences limit the quality of treatment that clients receive, the preparedness of MSWs to work in their field, and social workers' feelings of compe-tence and confidence in their professional roles (Clements, 2008; Kammerman, 2011; Yalom & Leszcz, 2005). The Council on Social Work Education (CSWE) does not require devoted courses in group work in their accreditation requirements for MSW programs. The CSWE required competencies include "assessing," "intervening," and "evaluating practice" "with individuals, families, groups, organizations, and commu-nities," but do not explicitly highlight the importance of education and training related to group work on its own (CSWE, 2015, p. 8). Renowned existential therapist and group expert Irving Yalom implores that:

> It is abundantly clear that, as time passes, we will rely on group approaches ever more heavily. I believe that any psychotherapy training program that does not acknowledge this and does not expect students to become as fully proficient in group as in individual therapy is failing to meet its responsibilities to the field. (2005, p. 544).

I wholeheartedly agree with Yalom and encourage CSWE to reconsider the place of group work within social work education as its own specialty with unique knowl-edge and skills that differentiate it from work with individuals, families, organi-zations, and communities. My hope is that this book might help embed Moreno's methods in social work academia while also helping to fortify social worker prac-titioners with knowledge, resources, and action-based group work tools. The rich tradition of J.L. Moreno's methods of sociometry and psychodrama, in addition to the many trauma-specific adaptations that have evolved from them, offers social workers the much-needed clinical skills and sociometric understanding to safely and compe-tently facilitate psychotherapy groups (Giacomucci, 2018a, b; Giacomucci & Stone, 2019; Skolnik, 2018). Sociometry and psychodrama methods would fall within the larger category of "non-deliberative" methods of social work practice which seems to be increasing in popularity in the social work with groups community (Lang, 2016; Sulman, Sullivan, & Nosko, 2016).

This book has been written in a way that integrates both the foundational knowledge of a social worker and a psychodramatist. Social work and social group work core concepts have been emphasized including person-in-environment perspective, the biopsychosocial-spiritual model, mutual aid, the centrality of relationships, and social justice. Entire chapters have been devoted to outlining Moreno's methods within the essential social work themes of trauma (Chap. 7), neurobiology (Chap. 8), the strengths-based approach (Chap. 9), and evidence-based practice (Chap. 10).

1.4 Social Workers and Beyond

This book will predominately focus on integrating Moreno's methods into the social work field. Nevertheless, the philosophies, theories, and practices of social work, sociometry, and psychodrama are each relevant and adaptable for other fields including psychology, counseling, group therapy, marriage and family therapy, drama therapy, the other creative arts therapies, community organizing, and education. Psychology, counseling, and marriage and family therapy, dominated by traditional talk therapies or cognitive behavioral therapy, can benefit from the experiential approaches offered by sociometry and psychodrama. The creative arts therapies, which already are based on expressive and experiential methods, will find sociometry and psychodrama to be complimentary to their practices. At the same time, social work's emphasis on relationships, person-in-environment, biopsychosocial-spiritual perspectives, mutual aid, social justice, and the integration of clinical, group, and community practices can all serve to enhance the practice of non-social work professionals.

As an expert in traumatic stress, I have also included considerable content related to using psychodrama for both trauma-informed ways and trauma-focused practices. Trauma is not the primary focus of this book, nevertheless, a trauma-informed perspective is incorporated throughout each chapter. The use of a trauma-informed clinical map and trauma-focused psychodrama models are emphasized. It has been my experience that many veteran social workers (and other professionals) have had adverse experiences or misconceptions about psychodrama specifically related to its use in ways that were harmful or not very trauma-informed (Giacomucci, 2018c). By emphasizing trauma throughout the book, my hope is to renegotiate some of psychodrama's reputation in the social work community.

Though this publication attempts to present the fullness of psychodramatic philosophy, theory, and practice, pieces of it can be easily integrated into the repertoires of other professionals. It is expected that a minority of readers of this book will be implementing the psychodrama as a comprehensive system. But instead, most readers will be interested in adapting various aspects of sociometry and psychodrama into their work. The chapters of this book have been written in a way to speak to both types of readers. Furthermore, the experiential processes of sociometry and psychodrama are applicable in a range of spaces beyond psychotherapy and clinical settings. Chapter 2020 is devoted to the use of sociometry and psychodrama by supervisors, educators, and leaders as experiential teaching processes.

1.5   Concerning Psychodramatists

This book includes the foundations of sociometry and psychodrama, as well as advanced content for psychodramatists. Psychodrama trainees preparing for their written exam will find this book a valuable resource as it encompasses each of the areas on the board of examiner's examination. In the production of the book, I have attempted to create content that would not only be useful for social workers, but for psychodrama students and advanced psychodrama practitioners. New contributions to the psychodrama literature base have been offered throughout each chapter of this book. Psychodramatists will also find the underlying philosophy, theory, and core values of social work as complimentary to their psychodrama praxis.

Drawing from Jacob Moreno's newly published *Autobiography of a Genius* (2019), I have infused novel content on psychodrama history and sociatry throughout this book. The early history chapters (Chaps. 2 and 3) of this publication contain a comprehensive timeline of psychodrama, social work, and group therapy in the contexts of the larger fields of medicine, psychology, and social history. This is perhaps the most comprehensive timeline of psychodrama that has been created. Furthermore, the chapter devoted to Morenean philosophy (Chap. 4) is one of the most complete summaries of sociatry and Moreno's mystical tradition. Little has been written about sociatry or Moreno's mysticism beyond the writings of Zerka and Jacob Moreno. Unaware of the existential philosophies from which psychodrama and sociometry emerged, many professionals, including psychodramatists, unintendedly utilize Morenean methods while divorcing them from the philosophy that they originated from.

1.6   How to Read This Book

This book has been written in a way that each section and each chapter might stand on their own. Some readers may choose to read isolated chapters or sections within this book that speak to their specific research or practice interests. My only caution to these readers is related to the unintended consequence of perpetuating the further separation of Moreno's methods from his philosophy and theory. I encourage readers to consider Chaps. 4–6 as an essential foundation to fully understanding the later sections devoted to the practice of sociometry and psychodrama with groups, individuals, and communities.

The first section of the book (Chaps. 2 and 3) is devoted to the histories of social work and psychodrama. Historians of group work, social work, and psychodrama will find these chapters of interest. The second section of the book (Chaps. 4–6) orients itself upon the philosophical and theoretical intersections of sociometry, psychodrama, and social work. Chapter 4 also includes significant content related to the codes of ethic of social workers. Section 3 (Chap. 7–10) dissect major themes in social work practice (trauma, neurobiology, strengths-based, and evidence-based practice and explore them within the contexts of social work, group therapy, and psychodrama. Sections 4–6 are primarily practice-oriented and include case depictions, vignettes, and example prompts of using sociometry and psychodrama within social work practice with individuals, groups, and communities. Section 4 (Chaps. 11–15) outlines the use of sociometry and psychodrama within group work. A subsection devoted to Yalom's therapeutic factors of group therapy is included in Chap. 12—I hope this might help provide common language for psychodramatists and group therapists. Chapter 14 offers advanced psychodrama directing strategies that experienced psychodramatists will find of great interest. And the final chapter of this section (Chap. 15) offers short descriptions of other experiential approaches that are similar to psychodrama. This includes approaches that are directly emerged from psychodrama (sociodrama, social microscopy, axiodrama, etc.), as well as approaches similar to psychodrama with varying degrees of overlap (drama therapy, Playback Theater, Theater of the Oppressed, Gestalt Therapy, Internal Family Systems, etc.). Section 5 (Chap. 16–16) is devoted to one-to-one work using sociometric and psychodramatic methods. Practitioners that primarily provide individual psychotherapy services will find this section most helpful. The sixth section (Chap. 18–20) includes chapters on community, organizational, and educational applications of sociometry, sociodrama, and role training. This section is written with community organizers, organizational leaders, supervisors, and educators in mind. The final chapter of this book is a psychodramatic letter inspired by my vision of a future where the social work field has fully integrated Moreno's methods into its professional repertoire. In this future projection, I have role reversed with a social work leader in 2074, on the 100th anniversary of Jacob Moreno's death, reflecting on the concretized potentialities of Moreno's methods absorbed within all aspects of the social work field (see Fig. 1.3).

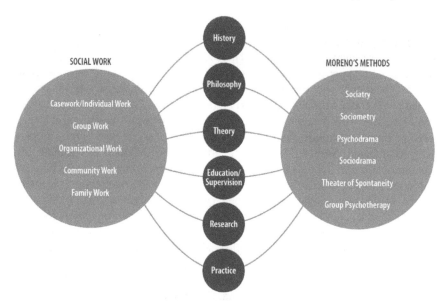

Fig. 1.3 Intersecting aspects of social work and Moreno's methods

References

American Board of Examiners in Sociometry, Psychodrama, and Group Psychotherapy (ABESPGP). (June 1, 2020). Member Directory. Retrieved from www.PsychodramaCertificat ion.org.

Böcker, I. (2004). Psychodramatische Schulsozialarbeit. *Zeitschrift Für Psychodrama Und Soziometrie, 3*(1), 47–68.

Bustamante, J. A. (1961). Importance of cultural patterns in group psychotherapy and psychodrama. *Acta psychotherapeutica et psychosomatica*, 262–276.

Clements, J. (2008). Social work students' perceived knowledge of and preparation for group-work practice. *Social Work with Groups, 31*(3–4), 329–346.

Council on Social Work Education. (2015). *Educational Policy and Accreditation Standards for Baccalaureate and Master's Social Work Programs*. The Commission on Accreditation & Commission on Educational Policy. Retrieved from CSWE.org.

Dannheiser, S. (2007). Das Psychodrama als Methode der psycho-sozialen Therapie. Analyse von Möglichkeiten und Grenzen im Bereich der Klinischen Sozialen Arbeit mit Suchtkranken (Diploma Thesis). Available from https://www.diplomarbeiten24.de/document/87597.

Engelke, E. (Ed.). (1981). *Psychodrama in der Praxis: Anwendung in Therapie, Beratung und Sozialarbeit*. Stuttgart: Klett-Cotta Verlag.

Figusch, Z. (2014). The JL Moreno memorial photo album. London: lulu.com.

Fürst, J. (2006). Psychodrama... Psykodrama... psicodrama... psicodramma... Психодрама... פסיכודרמה. *Zeitschrift für Psychodrama und Soziometrie, 5*(2), 207–223.

Giacomucci, S. (2018a). Social Work and Sociometry: An Integration of Theory and Clinical Practice. *the Pennsylvania Social Worker, 39*(1), 14–16.

Giacomucci, S. (2018b). Social work and sociometry: Integrating history, theory, and practice. *The Clinical Voice*. Richboro, PA: Pennsylvania Society for Clinical Social Work.

Giacomucci, S. (2018c). The trauma survivor's inner role atom: A clinical map for post-traumatic growth . *Journal of Psychodrama, Sociometry, and Group Psychotherapy, 66*(1), 115–129.

Giacomucci, S. (2019a). Moreno's methods in academia (or the lack of): A call to action. *Psychodrama Network News*. Fall 2019, p. 20. American Society of Group Psychotherapy and Psychodrama.

Giacomucci, S. (2019b). Social group work in action: A sociometry, psychodrama, and experiential trauma group therapy curriculum. *Doctorate in Social Work (DSW) Dissertations*, 124. Retrieved from https://repository.upenn.edu/cgi/viewcontent.cgi?article=1128&context=edisse rtations_sp2.

Giacomucci, S. (2020). Experiential sociometry in group work: mutual aid for the group-as-a-whole. *Social Work with Groups*, Advanced online publication. https://doi.org/10.1080/01609513.2020. 1747726.

Giacomucci, S., & Stone, A. M. (2019). Being in two places at once: Renegotiating traumatic experience through the surplus reality of psychodrama. *Social Work with Groups, 42*(3), 184–196. https://doi.org/10.1080/01609513.2018.1533913.

Gong, S. (2004). *Yi Shu: The art of living with change: Integrating traditional Chinese medicine, psychodrama and the creative arts*. St. Louis: F. E. Robbins & Sons Press.

Hale, A. E. (2009). Moreno's sociometry: Exploring interpersonal connection. *Group, 33*(4), 347–358.

Heinonen, T., Halonen, D., & Krahn, E. (2018). *Expressive arts for social work and social change*. Oxford University Press.

Hudgins, M. K., & Toscani, F. (2013). *Healing World Trauma with The Therapeutic Spiral Model: Stories from the Frontlines*. London: Jessica Kingsley Publishers.

Kammerman, D. (2011). A new group workers struggles and successes in a host school. *Social Work with Groups, 34*(3/4), 233–245.

Knight, . (2017). Social Work Students' experiences with group work in the field practicum. *Journal of Teaching in Social Work, 37*(2), 138–155.

Konopik, D. A., & Cheung, M. (2013). Psychodrama as a social work modality. *Journal of Social Work, 58*(1), 9–20.

Lai, N. H. (2011). Expressive arts therapy for mother-child relationship (EAT-MCR): A novel model for domestic violence survivors in Chinese culture. *The Arts in Psychotherapy, 38*(5), 305–311.

Lai, N. H. (2013). Psychodrama in Taiwan: Recent developments and history. *The Journal of Psychodrama, Sociometry, and Group Psychotherapy, 61*(1), 51–59.

Lai, N. H., & Tsai, H. H. (2014). Practicing psychodrama in Chinese culture. *The Arts in Psychotherapy, 41*(4), 386–390.

Lang, N. C. (2016). Nondeliberative forms of practice in social work: artful, actional, analogic. *Social Work with Groups, 39*(2–3), 97–117.

Moreno, J.D. (2014). *Impromptu man: J.L. Moreno and the origins of psychodrama, encounter culture, and the social network*. New York, NY: Bellevue Literary Press.

Moreno, J. L. (1953). *Who shall survive? Foundations of sociometry, group psychotherapy and sociodrama* (2nd edn.). Beacon, NY: Beacon House.

Moreno, J. L. (1957). *The first book on group psychotherapy* (3rd edn.). Beacon, NY: Beacon House.

Moreno, J.L. (2019). *The autobiography of a genius* (E. Schreiber, S. Kelley, & S. Giacomucci, Eds.). United Kingdom: North West Psychodrama Association.

Moreno, Z. T. (1965/2006). Psychodramatic rules, techniques, and adjunctive methods. In T. Horvatin & E. Schreiber (Eds.), *The Quintessential Zerka* (pp. 104–114). New York: Routledge.

Müller, J. (2009). Psychodrama in social work. In F. von Ameln, R. Gerstmann, & J. Kramer (Eds.), *Psychodrama* (2nd ed., pp. 519–531). Berlin: Springer.

Neudorfer, M. (2014). Soziale Arbeit und Psychodrama. Eine zielführende Methode in der Sozialen Arbeit? (Bachelor's Thesis). Available from https://pub.fh-campuswien.ac.at/obvfcwhs/content/ titleinfo/1784207.

Niepenberg, K. (2017). Gesellschaftlicher Wandel in der Sozialen Arbeit. *Zeitschrift Für Psychodrama Und Soziometrie, 16*(1), 171–183.

Nieto, L. (2010). Look behind you: Using anti-oppression models to inform a protagonist's psychodrama. In E. Leveton (Ed.), *Healing collective trauma using sociodrama and drama therapy* (pp. 103–125). New York: Springer Publishing Company.

Nolte, J. (2014). *The philosophy, theory, and methods of J.L. Moreno: The man who tried to become god.* New York, NY: Routledge.

Ottomeyer, K. (2003). Psychodrama in Südafrika. *Zeitschrift Für Psychodrama Und Soziometrie, 2*(1), 189–202.

Oudijk, R. (2007). A postmodern approach to psychodrama theory. In C. Baim, J. Burmeister, & M. Maciel (Eds.), *Psychodrama: Advances in theory and practice* (pp. 139–150). London: Routledge.

Ramsauer, S. (2007). Psychodramatische Supervision in der Sozialen Arbeit: Kleine Interventionen mit großer Wirkung. *Zeitschrift Für Psychodrama Und Soziometrie, 6*(2), 293–302.

Schwinger, T. (2014). Die Rolle des Psychodramas in der Sozialarbeit. *Zeitschrift Für Psychodrama Und Soziometrie, 13*(1), 257–273.

Schwinger, T. (2016). Das Soziale Atom in der Sozialen Arbeit: Begriff und Untersuchungsmethoden. *Zeitschrift Für Psychodrama Und Soziometrie, 15*(2), 275–289.

Skolnik, S. (2018). A Synergistic Union: Group work meets psychodrama. *Social Work with Groups, 41*(1–2), 60–73.

Stimmer, F. (2004). Psychodrama – Soziale Arbeit – Netzwerke. *Zeitschrift Für Psychodrama Und Soziometrie, 3*(1), 17–27.

Sulman, J., Sullivan, N. E., & Nosko, A. (2016). Not your usual special issue about activities. *Social Work with Groups, 39*(2–3), 94–96.

Yalom, I. D., & Leszcz, M. (2005). *The theory and practice of group psychotherapy* (5th ed.). New York, NY: Basic Books.

Zwilling, M. (2004). Methodisches Handeln in der Sozialen Arbeit—Psychodrama als Basismethode. *Zeitschrift Für Psychodrama Und Soziometrie, 3*(1), 5–15.

Part I
History of Social Work with Groups and Moreno's Methods

The histories of social work with groups and Moreno's methods appear to have emerged independently but on parallel timelines. Both trace their early histories to European religious traditions in the late 1800s before becoming popular in the United States in the 1900s. Since their inception, they have both spread quickly around the world. Social work and psychodrama originated separate from psychology but have integrated aspects of mainstream psychology into their fields in their attempts to professionalize.

The initial practices of social work and Moreno's methods were primarily oriented on work with the most underserved, oppressed, and marginalized of society. Early approaches in each fields emphasized work with immigrants, refugees, youth, schools, and populations involved in the criminal justice system. As they developed, they seemed to also offer services to the upper classes of society. Moreno's methods and social work arose with multiple areas of practice including individual work, group work, and community work. Social justice and the promotion of a better society became central tenents—as embodied in Moreno's vision of Sociatry and a therapeutic society. Core philosophies integrated the importance of human relationships, group work, family dynamics, and affirmed the dignity and worth of each person.

This part provides a detailed history of social work with groups and psychodrama as they relate to both practice and education in the United States. Similarities in historical trajectories are emphasized while depicting their parallel and concurrent chronicles. Within this evaluation of overlapping histories, Jacob Moreno will also be framed as a social worker due to his philosophy and practice orientations.

Chapter 2
History of Social Work with Groups in Practice and Education

Abstract This chapter outlines a brief history of social work with groups including its place within the larger social work field and the landscapes of group work practice and education. Basic theory and concepts in social work with groups are presented including mutual aid, the centrality of relationships, and an introduction to the non-deliberative social work tradition. The presence of group work in social work practice has significantly increased due as research studies have piled up to support its efficacy. Nevertheless, at the same time, the presence of group work in social work education has steadily declined in the past several decades.

Keywords Social work history · Group work · Social work education · Group therapy · Teaching group work

The early histories of group work, social work with groups , and social work education exist within a state of interdependence and intersection. Unfortunately, today these three fields have lost much of their connection. The history of sociometry and psychodrama ran a parallel process with the evolution of group work in general and unfortunately remains mostly segregated from the larger group work world (Giacomucci, 2019). Just as the history of an individual significantly impacts its present-day functioning, so too does the history and development of a model or professional field. For this reason, it is important that we start this exploration of social work, sociometry, and psychodrama at the beginning.

2.1 Brief History of the Social Work Profession

This history of social work is often traced back to the Charity Organization Society and the Settlement House Movement at the end of the nineteenth century in Europe and the United States. In the context of this discussion, it is relevant to note that the many settlement homes included prominent art-based programs, theaters, and/or drama clubs (Bailey, 2006; Hecht, 1982; Kelly & Doherty, 2016, 2017). Social problems became exacerbated and more visible in American society due to industrialization, immigration, and poverty which led to a stronger need for the social work

© The Author(s) 2021   17
S. Giacomucci, *Social Work, Sociometry, and Psychodrama*, Psychodrama in Counselling, Coaching and Education 1,
https://doi.org/10.1007/978-981-33-6342-7_2

profession (Ehrenreich, 2014; VanBreda, 2001). The social work field, like Moreno's methods of sociometry and psychodrama, also traces their origins back to religious communities. Social work as a profession with established schools of training appears to have emerged simultaneously around the world at the turn of the century (de Jongh, 1972; Healy & Link, 2012). By the mid-1930s, schools of social work had emerged on every inhabitable continent (Healy & Link, 2012).

The social work tradition of casework arose from the "friendly visitors" programs of charitable organizations in the late 1800s (Ehrenreich, 2014). Because of its early roots in religion, charity, and volunteer work, social workers experienced difficulty in being recognized by others as their own profession. In the 1930s, the social work field attempted to professionalize and enhance its status in the mental health field by adopting the popular psychanalytic theory (Bendor, Davidson, & Skolnik, 1997; Ehrenreich, 2014; Weick & Chamberlain, 1997; Weick, Rapp, Sullivan, & Kisthardt, 1989). While many social workers welcomed psychoanalytic theory as core knowledge of the profession, others rejected it. With this change in social work's orientation came also a change in the social worker's clientele—"by turning toward the inner life, social work escaped its previously almost exclusive concern with the problems of the poor" (Ehrenreich, 2014, p. 75). Because psychoanalysis is time-consuming and thus expensive, social workers began working more with the middle and upper classes.

Due to challenges to the legitimacy of social work as a profession, Ehrenreich explicitly writes that "the solution was psychoanalytic theory" (2014, p. 60). This major shift in the social work profession also created a shift toward intrapsychic understandings of human suffering and more congruence with the medicalized pathology models of mental illness (VanBreda, 2001). In doing so, social work as a field shifted away person-in-environment and ecological perspectives on human suffering. This alliance with psychoanalysis could be seen as a pivotal moment in the future absence of Moreno's methods in the social work field. Had social work not succumbed to the pressures of professionalizing and adopting psychoanalytic perspectives in an effort to increase its status, it is much more likely that the social work field would have aligned itself with Moreno's philosophy, sociometric theory, and group work—all of which appear to philosophically compliment social work more so than psychanalytic theory.

2.2 History of Group Work in Social Work

Social group work was introduced as a method of social work practice in the first quarter of the twentieth century, emerging in the midst of a renewed dichotomy between casework and community/policy work (Wilson, 1956). In some ways, group work serves as a happy medium between individual work and community work . Papell (2015) suggests that social group work provided the social work profession with a method for operationalizing its ideology and social mission. Since its inception, group work practice has been grounded in "social reform; social responsibility, democratic ideals, and social action as well as social relatedness and human attach-ment" (Lee, 1991, p. 3). Though the term social justice may be relatively new, its underlying principles—highlighting inequality, advocacy, and empowerment for disenfranchised and oppressed communities—are the historically core elements of group work (Singh & Salazar, 2010, 2011).

As early as 1920, Mary Richmond , the founder of social casework , indicated her belief in social group work as "the future of social treatment" (Richmond, 1930 as cited in Northen & Kurland, 2001, pp. 3–4). In response to the growing popularity of group work, Emory Bogardus outlined the "Ten Standards for Group Work" in 1936 which serves as one of the earliest set of standards for group practice. In the same year, the National Association for the Study of Group Work was formed (later renamed the American Association of Group Work—AAGW to promote professional standards for social group work (Andrews, 2001). In 1948, The American Association of Group Workers (AAGW) issued the following statement regarding the function of the group worker:

> Through his participation the group worker aims to affect the group process so that decisions come about as a result of knowledge and a sharing and integration of ideas, experiences and knowledge rather than as a result of domination from within or without the group. (as cited in Wilson, 1956)

Group work first formally associated with social work practice in 1935 when the National Conference on Social Work created a group section. Later, in 1944, Trecker stated that "group work is a method in social work... not a profession—social work is the profession" (p. 4). The 1955 merger of AAGW into the NASW symbolized the experience of most group workers at the time who professionally identified with the social work profession (Andrews, 2001). Group work existed as one of the five primary practice sections within NASW until the 60 s when the practice sections were disbanded in exchange for a generalist approach which was followed a few years later by a similar policy change in the CSWE . Considering the NASW and CSWE structural changes in the 1960s that marginalized group work within social work education , it is important to note that it flourished at this time in clinical practice—especially after its usefulness was recognized during World War II (Northen & Kurland, 2001). In 1979, the Association for the Advancement of Social Work with Groups (AASWG) formed and later in 1999 released the first edition of Standards Social Group Work. More recently, in 2013, the second edition was released (AASWG , 2013) providing a clinical framework for social group work moving forward.

While much of the social work field has emphasized the importance of evidence-based practice (EBP), in the group work arena, there is growing evidence against the efficacy of manualized EBP group work (Rivera & Darke, 2012; Sweifach, 2014; Yalom & Leszcz, 2005). Instead, attention to the group process is emphasized with its ability to "move beyond the constraints of method and technique and respond imaginatively and creatively to the impromptu, unrehearsed nature of the special human relationship" (Goldstein, 1998, p. 247).

Group work has been increasingly marginalized within the social work profession, while at the same time, it is in high demand in social work practice and the greater psychotherapy arena (Skolnik-Basulto, 2016). One might argue that as the social work profession moved toward professionalization and medicalization , it focused more on how psychopathology existed within the individual and thus treated mental illness in an individual psychotherapy context. Conrad takes this very stance, "Medicalization also focuses the source of the problem in the individual rather than in the social environment; it calls for individual medical interventions rather than more collective or social solutions" (2007, pp. 7–8). He goes on to discuss how instead of looking at the social sources of individual problems, medicalization focuses on the individual manifestations of the social malady—he calls this "the individualization of social problems" (2007). Group work exists within a *paradox of individuality*, as described by Smith and Berg (1997), "the only way for a group to become a group is for its members to express their individuality… and that the only way for individuals to become fully individuated is for them to accept and develop more fully their connections to the group" (pp. 99–100). Group work challenges popular sociopolitical discourses in the United States around medicalization, individualism, competition, dualism, and authoritarianism, which may be contributing to its marginalization (Drumm, 2006). This depreciation of social work with groups is evidenced by its invisibility in most social work educational programs. This gap in social work education only continues to fuel the marginalization of group work as social worker practitioners and educators enter the field without specialized group work training (Knight, 2017).

2.3 Social Group Work Defined

Social group work has been defined as a major component of social work practice with the focus of enhancing group members' social functioning, social connections, social support, coping skills, personal fulfillment, providing psychoeducation, or stimulating community-action (Gitterman & Shulman, 2005; Hartford, 1964; Northern & Kurland, 2001). In the social group work practice literature, there are several essential ingredients of group work outlined, including inclusion and respect, mutual aid, group cohesion, conflict resolution, interpersonal communication, and group development.

Mutual aid is the linchpin of social work with groups (Gitterman & Shulman, 2005; Glassman & Kates, 1990; Northen & Kurland, 2001; Skolnik-Basulto, 2016; Steinberg, 2010). Mutual aid is a group phenomenon by which the group heals itself—each group member supporting and helping another (Giacomucci, 2020). Kurland and Salmon, when describing the role of the social worker in group work, state that "the worker's role is to set in motion a process of mutual aid in the group" (2005, p. 131). In order to access the power of mutual aid within the group, the group must be treated as a group-as-a-whole rather than just one individual at a time (Kurland & Salmon, 2005).

Although the mutual aid concept was first introduced to social work by William Schwartz in 1961, many others had written about it earlier (Dewey , 1916; Kropotkin, 1922; Mead, 1934; Moreno, 1945, 1947, 1955a, 1963, 2019). The mutual aid group recognizes that all participants have inherent strengths, valuable information and experiences, a common goal and common needs, the potential to help each other and in doing so, help themselves (Cicchetti, 2009; Gitterman & Shulman, 2005; Skolnik-Basulto, 2016; Steinberg, 2010). Shulman (2015) discusses how the essential ingredient of mutual aid helps group members to "use the group to integrate their inner and outer selves and to find more adaptive mechanisms to cope with oppression , including personal and social action" (p. 548). Different evidence highlights mutual aid's capacity to increase self-esteem, improve problem-solving ability, and relieve shame and isolation (Gitterman & Shulman, 2005; Knight, 2006; Steinberg, 2010). A recent article in the Journal of *Social Work with Groups* highlighted the use of expressive interventions to promote mutual aid for trauma survivors (Neuschul & Page, 2018).

Alissi (1982) states that "the hallmark of social group work process is evidenced in the ability to recognize the power that resides in the small group, to help members harness this power to meet personal needs and to achieve socially constructed purposes" (p. 15). Social group work practice operationalizes social workers' belief in the significance of interrelations between humans and the importance of contextualizing clients within their social reality (Carey, 2016). Some theorists have even claimed that all social work is group work based on the premise that a group is defined as "two or more persons in a relationship of functional dependence, one upon the other" (Deutschberger, 1950, p. 12).

Social group work can take many different forms with a variety of different personal and/or social goals. Groups may be open-ended or time-constrained, open to new members or closed to only existing members, task-centered and/or growth-oriented, large or small, specific to a particular experience or aspect of identity—group work is adaptable to suit the needs of any population, setting, issue, or content (Alissi, 1982). Group work is commonly used throughout the entire treatment continuum, from inpatient/residential programs to outpatient groups.

In the social work with groups practice arena, the dominant approach is a "cognitively-focused, verbally articulated, contemplative, and reasoned problem-solving model"; however, there are also many practitioners integrating action methods (Lang, 2016, p. 97). Lang (1979a; b) even suggests that other group therapy traditions were more focused on cognitive approaches while social group work prioritized the use of action methods and activity in groups (Kelly & Doherty, 2016, 2017). Lang (2010, 2016) proposes a "nondeliberative " form of social group work which encompasses non-verbal, expressive, and action methods (art, dance, music, games , activity, drama, play , role-play , intuitive processes, etc.) tracing its history to previous social work authors (Middleman, 1968, 1983; Middleman & Goldberg Wood, 1990; Shulman, 1971; Vinter, 1985; Whittaker, 1985).

Non-deliberative social work practice is operationalized through experiential problem-solving methods and characterized by the paradigm of "do, then think" (Shapiro, 2016; Sulman, Sullivan, & Nosko, 2016). Norma Lang's "do, then think" philosophy mirrors Moreno's action theory—"however important verbal behavior is, *the act is prior to the word* and 'includes' it" (Moreno , 1955b, p. 17). Similar to J.L. Moreno 's statement, Zerka Moreno later writes that "even when interpretation is given, action is primary. There can be no interpretation without previous action" (1965, p. 77). In this approach, the non-deliberative group worker's role is to "identify activities that further the work of the group and facilitate the group process" (Kelly & Doherty, 2016, p. 222). Based on Lang's (2016) definition of non-deliberative forms of social work practice, sociometry and psychodrama would fall within this larger category of social work practice. In their accepted proposal for a new IASWG symposium invitational on non-deliberative practice, Sullivan, Sulman, & Nosko (2019) advocate for non-deliberative approaches with the following arguments:

1. Non-deliberative practice is uniquely allied with social group work .
2. Non-deliberative practice gives leverage and visibility to group work within the social work profession and among the other helping professions.
3. Non-deliberative theory offers an opportunity to enhance the profile of social group work in relationship to the other creative arts therapy and experiential fields.
4. Non-deliberative theory offers an avenue for social work to further develop its practice theories.

The integration of the non-deliberative social work practice theory invitational event into the annual IASWG symposium is an indicator of the movement within the social group work community toward experiential and creative arts therapy approaches.

2.4 Group Work's Increased Demand in Practice

The cost-effectiveness of group therapy , along with increasing research demonstrating its treatment efficacy (Callahan, 2004; Kanas, 2005; McDermut, Miller, & Brown, 2001), has both contributed to its rise in popularity. Group therapy is recognized as an effective treatment modality for a variety of mental health disorders, psychosocial problems, social skills training, and personal growth work (Drumm, 2006; Furman, Rowan, & Bender, 2009; Yalom & Leszcz, 2005). Group psychotherapy has been shown to be at least as effective as individual psychotherapy (Wodarski & Feit, 2012; Yalom & Leszcz, 2005). As such, it has been regarded as an essential aspect of social work practice (Carey, 2016; Corcoran, 2020; Garvin, Gutierrez, & Galinskey, 2004; Gutman & Shennar-Golan, 2012; LaRocque, 2017). Although the availability of group work education has steadily diminished over the last 50 years, the utilization of group therapy in clinical practice has increased significantly—both in social work practice (Gutman & Shennar-Golan, 2012; Heinonen & Spearman, 2010; McNicoll & Lindsay, 2002; Skolnik, 2017; Wodarski & Feit, 2012; Zastrow, 2001) and the larger psychotherapy world (Drum, Becker, & Hess, 2010; Yalom & Leszcz, 2005).

According to NASW (as cited in Probst, 2013), clinical social workers now make up the largest group of clinical professionals—totaling about 60% of all clinical mental health professionals. Clinical social workers provide more therapeutic services than psychiatrists, psychologists, counselors, and other therapists. Thus, suggesting that clinical social workers may also make up the majority of clinical group facilitators in the treatment industry, and causing many group work experts to demand that group work be a mandatory component within social work education (Birnbaum & Wayne, 2000; Drumm, 2006; Kurland & Salmon, 2002). Zastrow exclaims that group work is of utmost importance as "every social service agency uses groups, and every practicing social worker is involved in a variety of groups" (2001, p. 2).

2.5 Placing Group Work Within the Historical Context of Social Work Education

Professional social work education has its early roots in the first formal course of Philanthropic Work offered in 1898 by the Charity Organization Society in New York City, foreshadowing the 1908 establishment of the Philadelphia Training School for Social Work (evolving into what is now the University of Pennsylvania's School of Social Policy and Practice) (New York Charity Organization Society, 1903; Lloyd, 2008). Group work was introduced to social work education in the early 1920s (Wilson, 1976) and emerged just years after the formation of professional social case work. The American Association of Group Workers was organized in 1936, which later merged into the National Association of Social Work when NASW was founded in 1955 (Schwartz, 2008).

Until 1969 when the Council on Social Work Education (CSWE) changed its Educational Policy and Accreditation Standards (EPAS), social work education had been organized into three specialization tracts—casework , group work, and community organization (Simon & Kilbane, 2014). This structural shift toward a focus on social work generalist practice is often underlined as the catalyst for the steady decline over the past 40 years of group work from social work education (Goodman & Munoz, 2004; Steinberg & Salmon, 2007). Although the intent of the policy was to promote a more holistic approach and find common ground between the three aforementioned specializations, many social group workers refer to this initiative as "genericide" (Abels & Abels, 1981; Birnbaum & Auerbach, 1994).

In 1994, Birnbaum and Auerbach wrote that "although social work practice with groups is on the rise, social work education has neglected to prepare students for group work practice" (p. 325). In lieu of the consistent outcry from social group workers over the past few decades, the percent of MSW programs offering a concentration in group work has steadily declined from 76% in 1963, to 22% in 1981, 7% in 1992, (Birnbaum & Auerbach, 1994; Drumm, 2006) and only 2% in 2014—with only four MSW programs in the United States offering concentrations in group work

(Simon & Kilbane, 2014). This 2014 study, which is a modified replication of Birnbaum and Auerbach's 1994 study, provides us with alarming figures suggesting a possible future annihilation of the once prevalent group work concentration in social work graduate programs.

Furthermore, Simon and Kilbane's 2014 study of MSW programs found that nearly 1 of 5 programs admittedly did not offer a single (required or elective) course with a primary focus on group work, while 58% offer a required course and 40% offer an elective in group. While many social work programs are providing some form of group work education in abbreviated segments within other courses, such as a course titled "clinical social work practice with individuals, families, communities, and organizations", the teaching faculty and field placement supervisors do not have specialization in group psychotherapy, and it is questionable how much attention is given to group work (Carey, 2016; Goodman & Munoz, 2004; Knight, 2017; LaRocque, 2017; Sweifach, 2014; Tully, 2015). A national survey of first year MSW students found that over half of their field instructors provided little or no information on group theory or practice during their first-year foundations (Sweifach & Heft-LaPorte, 2008). In the same study, two-thirds of these MSW students indicated that they were expected to facilitate groups in their first-year field placement (Sweifach & Heft-Laport, 2008). A survey conducted by Goodman, Knight, and Khudododov (2014) found that of a sample of both clinical and community concentrated MSW students working in a variety of different field placements, more than 80% of them were expected to facilitate groups. Similarly, Clements' (2008) survey of BSW and MSW students found that only 20% of them had never had a group experience in their field placement.

Additionally, research has demonstrated that students who have taken a course specifically devoted to group work consistently demonstrate positive attitudes toward working with groups (Gutman & Shennar-Golan, 2012; Knight, 1999). On a positive note, there has been a slight increase in MSW programs that require group work experience as part of the fieldwork requirement. However, at the same time, many authors have criticized the level of group work competency demonstrated by fieldwork educators/supervisors (Birnbaum & Wayne, 2000; Kurland et al., 2004; LaPorte & Sweifach, 2011; Simon & Webster, 2009; Skolnik, 2017; Steinberg, 1993; Tully, 2015).

While the Council for Accreditation of Counseling and Related Educational Programs (CACREP, 2016) explicitly requires a group therapy course and a practicum including group facilitation in accredited programs, the Council on Social Work Education (CSWE) does not require either in their accreditation requirements. The listed CSWE competencies are generically lumped together to cover working "with Individuals, Families, Groups, Organizations, and Communities" (CSWE , 2015, p. 8). In doing so, the importance of education specific to group work has been lost. Alternatively, CACREP specifically highlights "Group Counseling and Group Work" as one of the eight required curriculum commosn core areas for all students. The skills to facilitate group psychotherapy are equally necessary for counselors and social workers. These skills are essential for clinical social workers who provide direct services in groups, as well as macrosocial workers who regularly work with groups, communities, or organizations.

2.6 Conclusion

In many ways, it seems that there is a missing generation of social group workers in the United States due to the lull of group work education in the past few decades. Some argue that many of today's social work educators and supervisors simply do not have the specialized education and training required to teach or supervise social work students or new graduates in their practice of group work (Carey, 2016; Goodman & Munoz, 2004; Knight, 2017; LaRocque, 2017; Sweifach, 2014; Tully, 2015). As we will explore in future chapters, this reduced number of social group workers mirrors the limited number of psychodramatists in the United States.

References

Abels, S. L., & Abels, P. (1981). Social group work issues. In S. L. Abels & P. Abels (Eds.), *Social work with groups: Proceedings 1979 symposium* (pp. 7–17). Louisville, KY: Committee for the Advancement of Social Work with Groups.

Alissi, A. S. (1982). The social work group method: Towards a reaffirmation of essentials. *Social Work with Groups, 5*(3), 3–17.

Andrews, J. (2001). Group work's place in social work: A historical analysis. *Journal of Sociology and Social Welfare, 28*(4), 45–65.

Association for the Advancement of Social Work with Groups. (1999). *Standards for social work practice with groups* (1st Edn.). Alexandria, VA.

Association for the Advancement of Social Work with Groups, Inc. (2013). *Standards for social work practice with groups. Social work with groups* (2nd ed., Vol. 36(2–3), pp. 270–282).

Bailey, S. (2006). Ancient and modern roots of drama therapy. In S. L. Brooke (Ed.), *Creative arts therapies manual: A guide to the history, theoretical approaches, assessment, and work with special populations of art, play, dance, music, drama, and poetry therapies* (pp. 214–222). Springfield, IL: Charles C. Thomas Publisher.

Bendor, S., Davidson, K., & Skolnik, L. (1997). Strengths-pathology dissonance in the social work curriculum. *Journal of Teaching in Social Work, 15*(1/2), 3–16.

Birnbaum, M., & Auerbach, C. (1994). Group work in graduate social work education: The price of neglect. *Journal of Social Work Education, 30*(3), 325–335.

Birnbaum, M. L., & Wayne, J. (2000). Group work in foundation generalist education: The necessity for curriculum change. *Journal of Social Work Education, 36*(2), 347–356.

Bogardus, E. S. (1936). Ten standards for group work. *Journal of Sociology and Social Research, 30,* 175–183.

Callahan, K. (2004). A review of interpersonal-psychodynamic group psychotherapy outcomes for adult survivors of childhood sexual abuse. *International Journal of Group Psychotherapy, 54*(4), 491–519.

Carey, L. A. (2016). Group work education: A call for renewed commitment. *Social Work with Groups, 39*(1), 48–61.

Cicchetti, A. (2009). *Mutual aid processes in treatment groups for people with substance use disorders: A survey of group practitioners.* City University of New York

Clements, J. (2008). Social work students' perceived knowledge of and preparation for group-work practice. *Social Work with Groups, 31*(3–4), 329–346.

Corcoran, J. (2020). *Case based learning for group intervention in social work*. New York: Oxford University Press.

Conrad, P. (2007). *The medicalization of Society*. Baltimore, MD: John Hopkins Press.

Council for Accreditation of Counseling and Related Educational Programs. (2016). *2016 CACREP Standards*. Retrieved from CACREP.org.

Council on Social Work Education. (2015). *Educational policy and accreditation standards for baccalaureate and master's social work programs*. The Commission on Accreditation & Commission on Educational Policy. Retrieved from CSWE.org.

De Jongh, J. F. (1972). A retrospective view of social work education. In IASSW (Ed.), *New themes in social work education. Proceedings of the XVIth International Congress of Schools of Social Work*, The Hague, Netherlands (pp. 22–36), August 8–11, 1972. New York: IASSW.

Deutschberger, P. (1950). Sociometry and social work. *Sociometry, 13*(1), 8–21.

Dewey, J. (1916). *Democracy and education: An introduction to the philosophy of education*. New York: The Free Press.

Drum, D., Becker, M. S., & Hess, E. (2010). Expanding the application of group interventions: Emergence of groups in health care settings. *The Journal for Specialists in Group Work, 36*(4), 247–263.

Drumm, K. (2006). The essential power of group work. *Social Work with Groups, 29*, 17–31.

Ehrenreich, J. H. (2014). *The altruistic imagination: A history of social work and social policy in the United States*. New York: Cornell University Press.

Furman, R., Rowan, D., & Bender, K. (2009). *An experiential approach to group work*. Chicago, IL: Lyceum Books.

Garvin, C. D., Gutierrez, L. M., & Galinsky, M. J. (2004). *Handbook of social work with groups*. New York: The Guilford Press.

Giacomucci, S. (2019). Social group work in action: A sociometry, psychodrama, and experiential trauma group therapy curriculum. *Doctorate in Social Work (DSW) Dissertations*. 124. Retrieved from https://repository.upenn.edu/cgi/viewcontent.cgi?article=1128&context=edisse rtations_sp2.

Giacomucci, S. (2020). Experiential sociometry in group work: Mutual aid for the group-as-a-whole. *Social Work with Groups, Advanced Online Publication*. https://doi.org/10.1080/01609513.2020. 1747726.

Gitterman, A., & Shulman, L. (2005). *Mutual aid groups, vulnerable and resilient populations, and the life cycle* (3rd ed.). New York, NY: Columbia University Press.

Glassman, U., & Kates, L. (1990). *Group work: A humanistic approach*. New York, NY: Sage.

Goldstein, H. (1998). Education for ethical dilemmas in social work practice. *Families in Society, 79*(3), 241–253.

Goodman, H., Knight, C., & Khudododov, K. (2014). Graduate social work students' experiences with group work in the field and the classroom. *Journal of Teaching in Social Work, 34*(1), 60–78.

Goodman, H., & Munoz, M. (2004). Developing social group work skills for contemporary agency practice. *Social Work with Groups, 27*(1), 17–33.

Gutman, C. & Shennar-Golan, V. (2012). Instilling the soul of group work in social work education. *Social Work with Groups, 35*(2), 138–149.

Hartford, N.E. (1964). *Working papers toward a frame of reference for social group work*. New York: National Association of Social Workers.

Healy, L. M., & Link, R. J. (Eds.). (2012). *Handbook of international social work: Human rights, development, and the global profession*. USA: Oxford University Press.

Hecht, S. (1982). Social and artistic integration: The emergence of hull-house theatre. *Theatre Journal, 34*(2), 172–182.

Heinonen, T., & Spearman, L. (2010). *Social work practice: Problem solving and beyond* (3rd ed.). Toronto, Canada: Nelson Education.

Kanas, N. (2005). Group therapy for patients with chronic trauma-related stress disorders. *International Journal of Group Psychotherapy, 55*(1), 161–166.

Kelly, B. L., & Doherty, L. (2016). Exploring nondeliberative practice through recreational, art, and music-based activities in social work with groups. *Social Work with Groups, 39*(2–3), 221–233.

Kelly, B. L., & Doherty, L. (2017). A historical overview of art and music-based activities in social work with groups: Nondeliberative practice and engaging young people's strengths. *Social Work with Groups, 40*(3), 187–201.

Knight, C. (1999). BSW and MSW student's perceptions of their academic preparation for group work. *Journal of Teaching in Social Work, 18*(1), 133–148.

Knight, C. (2006). Groups for individuals with traumatic histories: Practice considerations for social workers. *Social Work, 51*(1), 20–30.

Knight, C. (2017). Social work students' experiences with group work in the field practicum. *Journal of Teaching in Social Work, 37*(2), 138–155.

Kropotkin, P. A. (1922). *Mutual aid: A factor of evolution.* New York, NY: Knopf.

Kurland, R., & Salmon, R. (2002, October). *Caught in the doorway between education and practice: Group work's battle for survival.* Plenary presentation at the 24th Annual Symposium of the Association for the Advancement of Social Work with Groups, Brooklyn, New York.

Kurland, R., & Salmon, R. (2005). Group work vs. casework in a group: Principles and implications for teaching and practice. *Social Work with Groups, 28*(3–4), 121–132.

Kurland, R., Salmon, R., Bitel, M., Goodman, H., Ludwig, K., Newmann, E., & Sullivan, N. (2004). The survival of social group work: A call to action. *Social Work with Groups, 27*(1), 3–16.

Lang, N. C. (1979). A comparative examination of therapeutic uses of groups in social work and in adjacent human service professions: Part I—The literature from 1955–1968. *Social Work with Groups, 2*(2), 101–115.

Lang, N. C. (1979). A comparative examination of therapeutic uses of groups in social work and in adjacent human service professions: Part II—The literature from 1969–1978. *Social Work with Groups, 2*(3), 197–220.

Lang, N. C. (2010). *Group work practice to advance social competence.* New York, NY: Columbia University Press.

Lang, N. C. (2016). Nondeliberative forms of practice in social work: Artful, actional, analogic. *Social Work with Groups, 39*(2–3), 97–117.

LaPorte, H. H., & Sweifach, J. (2011). MSW foundation students in the field: Reflections on the nature and quality of group work assignments and supervision. *Journal of Teaching in Social Work, 31,* 239–249.

LaRocque, S. E. (2017). Group work education in social work: A review of the literature reveals possible solutions. *Journal of Social Work Education, 53*(2), 276–285.

Lee, J. (1991). Forward. In M. Weil, K. Chau, & D. Sutherland, (Eds.), *Theory and practice in social group work: Creative connections.* New York: Haworth Press.

Lloyd, M. F. (2008). 100 Years: A centennial history of the school of social policy & practice. In *100 Years of Social Work Education.*

McDermut, W., Miller, I. W., & Brown, R. A. (2001). The efficacy of group psychotherapy for depression: A meta-analysis and review of the empirical research. *Clinical Psychology: Science and Practice, 8*(1), 98–116.

McNicoll, P., & Lindsay, J. (2002). Group work in social work education: The Canadian experience. *Canadian Social Work Review, 19*(1), 153–166.

Mead, G. H. (1934). *Mind, self and society* (Vol. 111). Chicago, IL: University of Chicago Press.

Middleman, R. R. (1968). *The non-verbal method in working in groups.* New York, NY: Association Press.

Middleman, R. R. (Ed.). (1983). Activities and action in group work [Special issue]. *Social Work with Groups, 6*(1), 1–105.

Middleman, R. R., & Wood, G. G. (1990). *Skills for direct practice in social work.* New York, NY: Columbia University Press.

Moreno, J. L. (1945). Scientific foundations of group psychotherapy. *Sociometry, 8*(3–4), 77–84.

Moreno, J. L. (1947). *Open letter to group psychotherapists*. Psychodrama Monograms, No. 23. Beacon, NY: Beacon House.

Moreno, J. L. (1955a). *Preludes to my autobiography*. Beacon, NY: Beacon House.

Moreno, J. L. (1955b). The significance of the therapeutic format and the place of acting out in psychotherapy. *Group Psychotherapy, 8,* 7–19.

Moreno, J. L. (1963). Reflections on my method of group psychotherapy and psychodrama. *Ciba Symposium, 11*(4), 148–157.

Moreno, J. L. (2019). In E. Schreiber, S. Kelley, & S. Giacomucci, (Eds.), *The autobiography of a genius*. United Kingdom: North West Psychodrama Association.

Moreno, Z. T. (1965). Psychodramatic rules, techniques, and adjunctive methods. *Group Psychotherapy, a Quarterly Journal XVIII, 1–2,* 73–86.

Neuschul, T., & Page, E. A. (2018). Creating shared worlds: Promoting mutual aid and community-building through expressive intervention. *Social Work with Groups, 41*(1–2), 21–33.

New York Charity Organizational Society (1903, August 29). *Charities: A review of local and general philanthropy* (Vol. 11(9)). New York, NY.

Northen, H., & Kurland, R. (2001). *Social work with groups*. New York: Columbia University Press.

Papell, C. P. (2015). Social work with groups: What, why, and wherefore? *Social Work with Groups, 38*(3–4), 241–246.

Probst, B. (2013). "Walking the tightrope:" Clinical social workers' use of diagnostic and environmental perspectives. *Clinical Social Work Journal, 41,* 184–191.

Richmond, M. E. (1930). *Some next steps in social treatment*. New York: Russell Sage.

Rivera, M., & Darke, J. L. (2012). Integrating empirically supported therapies for treating person-ality disorders: A synthesis of psychodynamic and cognitive-behavioral group treatments. *International Journal of Group Psychotherapy, 62,* 500–529.

Shapiro, B. Z. (2016). Norma Lang's use of nondeliberative approaches: Through a multi-dimensional lens of activity in social work groups. *Social Work with Groups, 39*(2–3), 260–273.

Schwartz, W. (1961). The social worker in the group. *New perspectives on services to groups: Theory, organization, and practice,* 7–34.

Schwartz, W. (2008). The group work tradition and social work practice. *Social Work with Groups, 28*(3–4), 69–89. https://doi.org/10.1300/J009v28n03_06.

Shulman, L. (1971). "Program" in group work: Another look. In W. Schwartz & S. Zalba (Eds.), *The practice of group work* (pp. 221–240). New York, NY: Columbia University Press.

Shulman, L. (2015). *The skills of helping individuals, families, groups, and communities* (8th ed.). Boston, MA: Cengage Learning.

Simon, S., & Kilbane, T. (2014). The current state of group work education in U.S. graduate schools of social work. *Social Work with Groups, 37,* 243–256.

Simon, S. R., & Webster, J. A. (2009). Struggle for survival. In A. Gitterman & R. Salmon (Eds.), *Encyclopedia of social work with groups* (pp. 33–38). New York, NY: Routledge.

Singh, A. A., & Salazar, C. F. (2010). The roots of social justice in group work. *Journal for Specialists in Group Work, 35*(2), 97–104.

Singh, A. A., & Salazar, C. F. (Eds.). (2011). *Social justice in group work: Practical interventions for change*. New York, NY: Routledge.

Skolnik-Basulto, S. (2016). *Coming together: A study of factors that influence social workers' connection to group work practice* (Order No. 10758221). Available from ProQuest Disser-tations & Theses Global. (1988269052). Retrieved from https://proxy.library.upenn.edu/login?url=https://proxy.library.upenn.edu:2072/docview/1988269052?accountid=14707.

Skolnik, S. (2017). Coming together: Factors that connect social workers to group work practice. *Social Work with Groups*. https://doi.org/10.1080/01609513.2017.1384948.

Smith, K. K., & Berg, D. N. (1997). *Paradoxes of group life: Understanding conflict, paralysis, and movement in group dynamics*. San Francisco, CA: Jossey-Bass.

Steinberg, D. M. (1993). Some findings from a study on the impact of group work education on social work practitioners' work with groups. *Social Work with Groups, 16*(3), 23–39.

Steinberg, D. M. (2010). Mutual aid: A contribution to best-practice social work. *Social Work with Groups, 33*(1), 53–68.

Steinberg, D. M., & Salmon, R. (2007, June). *Re-visiting "… joyful noise": Gateways from the blues to the Hallelujah Chorus.* Plenary presentation at the 29th annual symposium of the Association for the Advancement of Social Work with Groups, Jersey City, NJ.

Sullivan, N. E., Sulman, J., & Nosko, A. (2019). *Proposal for an IASWG Symposium Invitational in Honour of Norma C. Lang and Nondeliberative Practice Theory.* International Association of Social Work with Groups (IASWG). Retrieved from: https://www.iaswg.org/Nondeliberative-Invitational.

Sulman, J., Sullivan, N. E., & Nosko, A. (2016). Not your usual special issue about activities. *Social Work with Groups, 39*(2–3), 94–96.

Sweifach, J. (2014). Group work education today: A content analysis of MSW group work course syllabi. *Social Work with Groups, 37*(1), 8–22.

Sweifach, J., & LaPorte, H. (2008). Why did they choose group work: Exploring the motivations and perceptions of current MSW students of group work. *Social Work with Groups, 31*(3/4), 347–362.

Trecker, H. (1944). Group work: Frontiers and foundations—In wartime. *The Compass, 25*(3), 3–8. Retrieved from https://www.jstor.org/stable/23706466.

Tully, G. (2015). The faculty field liaison: An essential role for advancing graduate and undergraduate group work education. *Social Work with Groups, 38*(1), 6–20.

VanBreda, A. D. (2001). *Resilience theory: A literature review.* Gezina, SA: South African Military Health Service, Military Psychological Institute, Social Work and Research Development.

Vinter, R. D. (1985). The essential components of social group work practice. In M. Sundel, P. Glasser, R. Sarri, & R. Vinter (Eds.), *Individual change through small groups* (2nd ed., pp. 11–34). New York, NY: Free Press.

Weick, A., & Chamberlain, R. (1997). Putting problems in their place: Further explorations in the strengths perspective. In D. Saleebey (Ed.), *The strengths perspective in social work practice* (2nd ed., pp. 37–48). New York City, NY: Longman.

Weick, A., Rapp, C., Sullivan, W. P., & Kisthardt, W. (1989). A strengths perspective for social work practice. *Social Work, 34*(4), 350–354.

Wilson, G. (1956, May). *Social group work theory and practice.* Presentation at the 83rd Annual Forum of the National Conference of Social Work, St. Louis, Missouri. Social Welfare History Project. Retrieved January 22nd, 2018 from https://socialwelfare.library.vcu.edu/social-work/social-group-work-theory-and-practice/.

Wilson, G. (1976). From practice to theory: A personalized history. In R. W. Roberts & H. Kurland (Eds.), *Theories of social work with groups* (pp. 1–44). New York: Columbia University Press.

Whittaker, J. K. (1985). Program activities: Their selection and use in the therapeutic milieu. In M. Sundel, P. Glasser, R. Sarri, & R. Vinter (Eds.), *Individual change through small groups* (2nd ed., pp. 237–250). New York, NY: Free Press.

Wodarski, J. S., & Feit, M. D. (2012). Social group work practice: An evidenced based approach. *Journal of Evidence-Based Social Work, 9,* 414–420.

Yalom, I. D., & Leszcz, M. (2005). *The theory and practice of group psychotherapy* (5th ed.). New York, NY: Basic Books.

Zastrow, C. (2001). *Social work with groups: Using the classroom as a group leadership Laboratory* (5th ed.). Pacific Grove, CA: Brooks/Cole.

Chapter 3
History of Sociometry, Psychodrama, Group Psychotherapy, and Jacob L. Moreno

Abstract This chapter presents the histories of sociometry, psychodrama, and group psychotherapy while also outlining the history of Jacob L. Moreno, their founder. Major events from Moreno's life are covered as they relate to the development of his philosophy and the practice of his triadic system, sociometry, psychodrama, and group psychotherapy. The popularity and decline of Moreno's methods throughout their history are highlighted while offering insights into these historical trends in the USA and globally. Connections are drawn between Moreno's history and the history of social work while also framing him as a social worker due to the nature of his philosophy, theory, and practice. A comprehensive timeline is offered which depicts the parallel timelines of psychodrama, social work, group therapy, psychology, and society.

Keywords History · Sociometry · Psychodrama · Group work · Group psychotherapy · Jacob Moreno

A historical analysis of sociometry, psychodrama, and group psychotherapy is incomplete without also presenting the life of Jacob L. Moreno. While there is no disagreement about Moreno being the founder of sociometry and psychodrama, there is controversy about his claim to be the founder of group psychotherapy. At the very least, he was a pioneer of group work and group psychotherapy. His sociometric and psychodramatic approach to group work offered one of the only alternative approaches to psychoanalytic groups at the time of its conception. To understand the marginalization of Moreno's approaches in the larger group work and social work arena, it is essential to get to know Moreno himself.

3.1 History of Group Psychotherapy

Within the group work arena, there is some ambivalence surrounding the development of group therapy. Many attribute the first group therapy session to Dr. Joseph Pratt who, in 1905, brought together 15 of his tuberculosis patients in Boston for an educational meeting and gradually noticed the therapeutic effects of these groups

S. Giacomucci, *Social Work, Sociometry, and Psychodrama*, Psychodrama in Counselling, Coaching and Education 1,
https://doi.org/10.1007/978-981-33-6342-7_3

for his patients (Hadden, 2015). Pratt's approach certainly is group work, but can we call it group therapy? Moreno argues that an educational lecture and discussion cannot by itself be classified as *group psychotherapy*, because first the group (group = patient) must be diagnostically assessed (1947a). Others suggest that J.L. Moreno is the father of the group psychotherapy *movement* which encompassed multiple group *methods* attributed to other individual pioneers—including Pratt's didactic approach and Trigant Burrow's group analysis (Meiers, 1946; Moreno, 1966; Renouvier, 1958; Thomas, 1943). It appears that the emergence of group work field was introduced by a *group* of pioneers.

According to Jacob Moreno (see Fig. 3.1), there have been three psychiatric revolutions. The first was led by Philippe Pinel at the turn of the eighteenth century in France with the rejection of punishment in favor of treatment for the mentally ill. Sigmund Freud led the second psychiatric revolution by shifting the conceptualization of mental illness symptomology from neurological roots to a psychological basis. Jacob L. Moreno, in a 1955 address to the American Society of Group Psychotherapy and Psychodrama (ASGPP), laid claim to group psychotherapy as the third psychiatric revolution with himself as its pioneer (Moreno, 1961, 2006; Nolte, 2014).

The terms "group therapy" and "group psychotherapy" were first formally introduced by Dr. Jacob L. Moreno in 1932 at the annual conference of the American Psychiatric Association in Philadelphia (Moreno, 1945; Moreno & Whitin, 1932). Until 1935, Moreno was the only author to use the terms "group psychotherapy" or "group therapy" (Renouvier, 1958).

Fig. 3.1 Jacob Moreno in the early 1960s. Reprinted with permission from Figusch (2014)

3.1.1 Group Psychotherapy Defined

Moreno's group therapy ideas began in 1913 with his experience organizing a group of sex workers in Vienna—"we began to see then that one individual could become a therapeutic agent of the other and the potentialities of a group psychotherapy on the reality level crystallized in our mind" (1955a, p. 22). Moreno argued that group therapy must include more than an educational lecture, a discussion, a group member sharing their story to the group, or even watching a psychodrama, though group therapy may include one or more of these (1947b). While Moreno also advocated for the use of group work outside of the psychotherapy realm, this question is restricted to that of group psychotherapy. In his *Open Letter to Group Psychotherapists*, Moreno states that "in individual psychotherapy the patient is a single individual. In group psychotherapy the patient is a group of individuals" (1947a, p. 16).

John Nolte, in *The Philosophy, Theory, and Methods of J.L. Moreno*, offers us a striking clarification regarding group psychotherapy:

> Moreno's idea of group psychotherapy meant treating the group; other group therapists remained focused on the individual, and their methods could often be better described as treating individuals in a group setting. Individual psychotherapy, Moreno pointed out, is based on the psychodynamics of the individual. The treatment of a group is based on sociodynamics that involve the interrelationships and interactions of the members of the group, not just the collection of individuals and their personal dynamics. According to Moreno, treatment of groups became possible only after the development of sociometry, which allows the group therapist to identify and characterize the constellation of relationships existing within a group. (2014, p. 122)

Group psychotherapy developed within the context of Moreno's triadic system of sociometry, psychodrama, and group psychotherapy (Moreno, 1946). It is important to note here that many group work experts in the social work profession have also criticized social work practitioners and educators as lacking a basic understanding and competency to engage the group-as-a-whole, instead they do casework or individual therapy in a group setting (Bitel, 2014; Corcoran, 2020; Giacomucci, 2020; Gitterman, 2005; Knight, 2017; Kurland & Salmon, 2005; Shulman, 2015).

According to Carl Whitaker, Jacob L. Moreno "was probably more clearly responsible for the move from individual therapy to the understanding of interpersonal components of psychological living than any other single psychiatrist in the field" (Fox, 1987, p. ix; as cited in Gershoni, 2009). Moreno organized both the first American and International societies of group therapists and served as the first presidents of these societies—now known as the American Society of Group Psychotherapy and Psychodrama (founded in 1942) and the International Association of Group Psychotherapy (founded in 1973).

3.1.2   Moreno's Controversial Personality

Moreno viewed each human as having within them a mirror of the Godhead. He aimed to realize and actualize his own expression of godlikeness, and at the same time, he was not always a saint. In some ways, his actions contributed to the isolation of sociometry and psychodrama and their lack of presence in the social work field. The clinical social work field adopted much of its foundation from psychology, psychoanalysis, and psychodynamic schools in an attempt to professionalize as early as the 1920s (Ehrenreich, 1985). Moreno's philosophical system contradicts with psychoanalytic theory and Moreno himself was an outspoken critic of it. He believed that insight was a product of action—what he called *action insight*. And he believed that creativity and spontaneity were a necessity for change. He harshly criticized Freud's *talking cure*. In an encounter with Freudthat possibly took place at the University of Vienna, Moreno declared:

> Dr. Freud, I start where you leave off. You meet people in the artificial setting of your office. I meet them on the street and in their homes, in their natural surroundings. You analyzed their dreams; I try to give them courage to dream again. (Moreno, Moreno, & Moreno, 1964, pp. 16–17)

Taken from their context, one might have guessed that these words were uttered by a social worker in that they reflect early social work's philosophy and practice.

Moreno's differentiation from Freud and his followers is one of the reasons that sociometry and psychodrama have been marginalized in the larger psychotherapy field (Gershoni, 2009; Moreno, 2014). In 1934, Moreno writes of the conflict between his approaches and psychoanalysis stating "there is no controversy" between the two approaches, "I am the controversy" (Moreno, 1934, p. cviii). Gershoni (2009) indicates two primary reasons for psychodrama's isolation in the larger group therapy field: "One was that Moreno's ideas and methods were wildly divergent from established methods in the fields of psychiatry and psychotherapy, particularly psychoanalysis. The second was that his personality was as controversial as his ideas" (p. 298). J.L. Moreno established the ASGPP in 1942, and within a year of its founding, Samuel Slavson started the American Group Psychotherapy Association (AGPA). AGPA maintained a psychoanalytic focus and much higher professional standards even requiring doctoral degrees for membership (Moreno, 2019). The ASGPP welcomed anyone as a member and was more focused on psychodrama and the other creative arts therapies (until they formed their own associations in the 60s and 70s). Moreno and Slavson developed a rivalry which seems to be continued to this day by the ASGPP and AGPA which remain mostly segregated with their own memberships, journals, theoretical traditions, and histories (Blatner, 2005; Gershoni, 2009). Gershoni (2009) writes that there is only about a ten person overlap in membership and that each organizations' journal includes almost no reference to each other's publications.

While the AGPA and ASGPP continue to remain loyal to their histories, the International Association of Group Psychotherapy and Group Processes (IAGP) operates as an inclusive group work organization with an entire section devoted to

psychodrama and another to group analysis. It seems that the American group organizations became divisive and differentiated themselves from each other while the
IAGP and group workers around the world have done a much better job at integrating
psychodrama into mainstream group work and psychotherapy as a whole.

Moreno's personality also impacted the integration of his ideas into academia in
the USA. Though he initially emerged as one of the most notable social scientists
in the 1930s, his personality got in his way and in the way of the acceptance of his
approaches. One of his critics writes, "his commitment to mysticism, his bombastic
personal style and his megalomania drove most of his early supporters away. These
features of Moreno's persona (see Fig. 3.2) were too much for regular members of
the academic community to bear" (Moreno, 2014, p. 144). Moreno published most
of his work through his own publishing house (Beacon House), which may have also
contributed to the absence of his work beyond the psychodrama community. Perhaps

Fig. 3.2 Jacob Moreno in action. Reprinted with permission from Figusch (2014)

the greatest lost opportunity for integrating his methods into academia came in 1947 when Moreno was nominated by leading professors from multiple universities to head Harvard University's new sociology department laboratory. He writes of his gratitude for the unnamed sociometrist who spoke on his behalf arguing that he would not be a good fit for the role—"I owe him everlasting gratitude for talking in my behalf as an auxiliary ego *in absentia*—remarked that I would hardly accept the job, that I would not fit into academic life, with its formalities and limitations" (Moreno, 2019, p. 87).

3.2 History of Sociometry, Psychodrama, and Jacob L. Moreno

While group work was gaining momentum in the USA, J.L. Moreno's ideas of sociometry, psychodrama, and group psychotherapy were beginning to emerge in Vienna. In the early 1900s, as a university student, he and his friends founded the Religion of the Encounter and opened the House of the Encounter, which seems to mirror the settlement house. It is interesting to note that Jane Adam's settlement house even included drama clubs which were the most popular groups within Hull House (Bailey, 2006). The House of the Encounter provided free support, help completing official applications, job assistance, food, housing, and legal support for refugees and immigrants flooding into Europe (Marineau, 2014; Nolte, 2014). In the evenings at the House of the Encounter, everyone gathered for a community ritual discussing the events, concerns, and problems of the day. Moreno described these mutual aid meetings as the first encounter groups and a "theater of everyday life" in his autobiography (2019, p. 211).

Moreno describes himself as a mystic prior to his education in psychiatry. He studied theology and philosophy and was deeply influenced by his spiritual experiences and beliefs. He wrote of the evolution of an understanding of God, moving from a distant *I-He* God in the Old Testament, to a more personal *I-Thou* God with Jesus in the New Testament. His religion, and one of his early anonymous publications titled *Words of the Father* (1921), pronounces a new philosophy of an *I-I* God. Moreno was declaring that everyone has the capacity of accessing and awakening the Godhead within them. To support his claim, he highlighted creativity as a quality inherent to deities across culture and history and argued that human beings also have the capacity to create. The Religion of the Encounter is the basis for Moreno's conceptualization of human nature through an existential and spiritual framework that recognizes the dignity and worth of each individual. Moreno's sociometry, psychodrama, and group psychotherapy developed from the philosophy that we are "cosmic beings" in addition to our biological, economical, sociological, and psychological nature (Moreno, 2012). Through this conceptualization of human nature, he avoided pathologizing approaches and worked to empower individuals and groups to heal themselves.

Later, in his work at Mittendorf refugee camp, he had proposed that a formal assessment and diagnoses would uncover the social configuration of the refugee camp as the root of its troubles and formally suggested that the camp be restructured "by means of sociometric analysis" (Marineau 2014, p. 55). Moreno's work in Mittendorf, between 1915 and 1918, is identified as a foundational event in the establishment of sociometric theory. Coincidentally, at about the same time, Mary Richmond published her famous book "Social Diagnosis" (1917) as social work practice continued to evolve, emphasizing the social environment of the individual (Giacomucci, 2018a). Moreno originally conceptualized group therapy as the treatment of oppressed, marginalized, or excluded populations (Gershoni, 2013; Nolte, 2014)—he worked with a variety of populations including immigrants, sex workers, prisoners, and the severely mentally ill. Stimmer (2004) claims that because of the context and nature of Moreno's work, sociometry, psychodrama, and group psychotherapy really began as social work—"Die psychodramatische Idee jedenfalls begann als Soziale Arbeit; ihre Wurzel, ihre Basis ist die Soziale Arbeit" ("In any case, the psychodramatic idea began as a social work; its root, its basis is social work"; p. 19).

Moreno's experiments with drama and theater began in the parks of Vienna playing with the children, telling them stories, and experimenting with role-playing. In the refugee camp, he developed *Theater Reciproque* where refugees found relief from their harsh reality by engaging in the surplus reality of drama. Of this time, Moreno writes, "when Theater Reciproque becomes a part of the life of the community it takes on the force of a religious ritual, a ritual of healing." (2019, p. 212) As a mystic studying medicine at the University of Vienna, Moreno seems to conceptualize the healing process from a religious perspective.

Jacob L. Moreno writes that the first psychodrama/sociodrama took place in Vienna on April Fool's Day of 1921, at a decisive time in Austria just after World War I and the dismantling of the Austria-Hungary Empire. Dressed as the king's jester, he called for members of the prestigious audience to come on stage and take the role of "King of the New World Order" and discuss their plans to stabilize the country. Shortly after this historical moment, Moreno organized the Theater of Spontaneity (Stegreiftheater) which enacted spontaneous scenes incorporating the audience, often using events from the local newspaper or suggested topics from the audience. Moreno intended to use the theater as a medium for social change, but in the process, observed that participation had been therapeutic for both the audience and role players (Nolte, 2014; Marineau, 2014; Moreno, 2019). He developed his vision of *sociatry*—or psychiatry for society (1947) which articulated his commitment to healing at the societal level: "A truly therapeutic procedure cannot have less an objective than the whole of mankind. But no adequate therapy can be prescribed as long as mankind is not a unity in some fashion and as long as its organization remains unknown." (1934, p. 3).

In 1925, Moreno immigrated to New York City. This decision was impacted by a number of factors including a vivid dream of living in New York that he had experienced, involvement in conflicts with other Vienna theater leaders, a new invention of a recording device he was working on, and hopes for a new audience that would be more accepting of his ideas. Prior to his migration to the USA, Moreno published his first nine books anonymously, inspired by his spiritual principles which suggest that ideas could not be owned by anyone:

> A name is a form of capital and links the inventions and works of an author to proprietary, priority and other legal rights. Anonymity, on the other hand, begins and ends with the assumption that a work created by an individual or a group is not the property of anyone in particular, it belongs to universality. (Moreno, 1955, p. 29).

However, as a result, many of his early ideas were taken by others. In his move from Austria to the USA, he shifted from primarily religious writing to primarily scientific publications and began to publish using his name.

Upon arrival to New York, Moreno began tirelessly working to promote his ideas offering demonstration at hospitals, churches, prisons, and schools, though he experienced many difficulties as an immigrant. At her suggestion, he married Beatrice Beecher in 1926, largely to be granted US citizenship and a license to practice medicine in New York State. In 1929, he opened *Impromptu Theater* at Carnegie Hall, a re-creation and adaptation of the Vienna *Theater of Spontaneity*. In 1932 at the APA conference in Philadelphia, he presented his sociometric research from Sing Sing Prison coining the terms "group therapy" and "group psychotherapy." It is interesting to note that psychoanalyst Franz Alexander, who coined the term corrective emotional experience, was present at this 1932 APA meeting with Moreno and commented on the potential effectiveness of Moreno's group method to reduce crime (Moreno & Whitin, 1932). Through his work in the early 1930s, Moreno gained the support of Dr. William Alanson White, superintendent of St. Elizabeths Hospital in Washington, DC and former APA president. While supporting Moreno in New York, White was also working with Harry S. Sullivan in DC (Marineau, 2014) who later developed an interpersonal theory of psychiatry (1953) which shows some resemblance to Moreno's interpersonal theory of sociometry.

For an entire year in the early 1930s, Moreno lived at the New York State Training School of Girls at Hudson, New York, and worked as the Director of Research. Here, he conducted extensive sociometric assessments, tests, interventions, and research which led to the 1934 publication of one of his most famous books, *Who Shall Survive?: A New Approach to the Problem of Human Interrelations*. Moreno and his colleagues in Hudson were some of the first social scientists to address racism and racial tensions within communities (Moreno, 2014). By this time, he was lecturing regularly in multiple universities including Columbia University, the New School for Social Research, and New York University. Beginning in 1935, Moreno started predicting boxing match winners through the application of sociometric analysis; for the next 19 years, he never made a wrong prediction and was often in the newspapers because of it. After his short marriage to Beatrice, he married Florence Bridge in 1938. Jacob and Florence had one child, Regina Moreno, and worked together to further the field of psychodrama until their divorce some years later. Florence's contribution to psychodrama theory was primarily on the topic of child development (Moreno & Moreno, 1944).

It was not until 1936 in Beacon, New York, that Moreno began to systematically develop and use psychodrama as a form of psychotherapy at which point, he

Fig. 3.3 Beacon Hill Sanitarium, later renamed Moreno Sanitarium in 1951. Reprinted with permission from Figusch (2014)

developed a reputation for successfully treating psychosis, interpersonal problems, and marital conflicts. In 1936, Moreno opened Beacon Hill Sanitarium in New York State which was later renamed Moreno Sanitarium (see Fig. 3.3). It was here that his group therapy and psychodramatic approaches found a firm foundation and was used routinely with his clients suffering from severe mental illness. This treatment program was in many ways similar to the milieu therapy and therapeutic communities that would emerge later (Moreno, 2014).

Moreno Sanitarium developed a reputation for treating "untreatable" psychiatric cases (Moreno, 2019). In his work with patients with psychosis and schizophrenia, rather than try to convince them that their delusions and fantasies were not real, he encouraged them to act it out on the psychodrama stage. In 1937, the Red Cross Director became interested in psychodrama, and a few years later, a psychodrama stage was built at St. Elizabeths Hospital in Washington, DC, the largest federal mental health institute in the USA. Even President Franklin D. Roosevelt expressed interest in Moreno's ideas in the mid-1930s hoping that they could help the USA through its time crisis (Moreno, 1955).

In 1941, Zerka Toeman traveled from England to Beacon, New York, in hopes of finding effective treatment for her mentally ill sister at Moreno's Sanitarium. Zerka quickly began working for Jacob Moreno, editing and translating his work and later contributing her own additions to sociometry and psychodrama. Later in 1949, they married. In 1941, J.L. Moreno opened the Sociometric Institute and Theater of Psychodrama (later known as the Psychodramatic Institute) in downtown New York City where he began to train other practitioners in his new model—from the late 1940s until the early 70s, six nights a week, a public psychodrama was conducted at J.L.

Moreno's Manhattan theater (Moreno, 2014). Within a few years, dozens of psychiatric hospitals around the USA were using psychodrama in their treatment programs including multiple Veterans Administration hospitals—some of which event built dedicated psychodrama stages on their campuses.

In the USA, Moreno's popularity increased in the 1940s and he was even considered for a department chair role at Harvard University (Moreno, 1955). American Sociologists adopted Moreno's ideas with a passion while American psychiatry remained less interested. The American Sociological Society even created a section on sociometry in 1941 and in 1955 began publishing Moreno's *Sociometry* journal which had been in print since 1937 (Moreno, 2019). The Cold War and World War II sparked a greater reliance upon group therapy due to the influx of soldiers back into society. All three branches of the US military employed Moreno's sociometry concepts along with Lewin's group dynamic analyses to enhance the functioning of military leadership (Moreno, 2014). The US Navy became particularly interested—sociometric studies in the Navy discovered that poor group cohesion and low sociometric choices were correlated with various poor outcomes such as sick days, low morale, accidents, and disciplinary actions (Moreno, 2014). The British sent leaders of the military to study sociometry with the Morenos' to better understand the varying death rates in various military platoons. They attempted to use used sociometry to organize groups of soldiers within the army during the war—"the whole process of induction and basic training in the British Army was restructured along the lines laid down by sociometric theory" (Moreno, 2019, p. 320). By the 1950s, Jacob Moreno and his wife Zerka Moreno had begun traveling six months of the year to provide psychodrama demonstrations around the world. The increasing popularity of psychodrama at the time is evidenced by a 1950 publication which estimated that about one-third of all mental institutions were using psychodrama as a therapy approach (Borgatta, 1950).

In the 1960s–70s, psychodrama techniques became popularized through the encounter movement, T-Groups, sensitivity training, the Human Potential Movement, and humanistic psychology. J.L Moreno's work influenced most of the leaders of these movements who had studied with him previously, including Kurt Lewin, Abraham Maslow, Fritz Perls, Viktor Frankl, and Carl Rogers (Maslow, 1971; Moreno, 2014, 2019; Treadwell, 2016). Within these popular movements, very little credit was given to Moreno's influence. Moreno was friendly with Kurt Lewin, who was a pioneer of group dynamics, T-Groups, action research, and founded the National Training Laboratories (NTL) which had a significant impact on the field of group dynamics and group research. Unfortunately, Lewin died suddenly in 1947 and his followers and Moreno did not get along which further marginalized psychodrama from the emerging T-Group movement and group dynamics research (Moreno, 2014).

The popular magazine *Life* published a 1968 article on the Human Potential Movement (Howard, 1968) which provoked Abraham Maslow, father of humanistic psychology and former APA president, to send the following letter to the editors:

> Jane Howard's article on Esalen and other new developments in education and psychology was excellent. I would however like to add one "credit where credit is due" footnote. Many of the techniques set forth in the article were originally invented by Dr. Jacob Moreno, who is

still functioning vigorously and probably still inventing new techniques and ideas. (Maslow, 1968, p. 15)

Other authorities in the field have made similar comments as it relates to Moreno's influence on the encounter movement, the Human Potential Movement, T-Groups, gestalt therapy, and other experiential techniques. Eric Berne, the founder of transactional analysis, comments on this dynamic which he calls *the Moreno problem*:

Perls, founder of the gestalt movement, shared with other 'active' psychotherapists the Moreno problem: the fact that nearly all known 'active' techniques were first tried out by Moreno in psychodrama, so that it makes it difficult to come up with an original idea in this regard. (Berne, 1970, p. 164)

Similarly, William Schultz, a pioneer in the encounter group movement, notes that "virtually all of the methods that I had proudly compiled or invented [Moreno] had more or less anticipated, in some cases forty years earlier" (as cited in Blatner, 1996, p. 181). And in his book on the history of the encounter movement, Kurt Back (1972) notes that "Moreno can claim, perhaps rightly, that he is the originator of both group therapy and encounter groups" (p. 149).

J.L. Moreno believed that the encounter movement "cannibalized" his work and impacted the reputation of psychodrama (Moreno, 2014, 2019). It was during this time that many developed concerns for the psychological safety of psychodrama techniques and encounter groups which had become more focused on confrontation (Blatner, 2000; Cooper, 1974, 1975; Giacomucci, 2018b; Posthuma & Posthuma, 1973; Yalom & Lieverman, 1971). In a large study on various types of encounter groups, researchers found 7.8–9.1% of participants reported harm related to their participant in the encounter groups (Lieberman, Yalom, & Miles, 1973).As the encounter groups (as well as T-Groups and sensitivity training groups) became more sensationalized in the late 1960s and early 1970s, academic respectability and theoretical connections dissipated leading to a loss in credibility (Spence, 2007). As the evidence-based practice movement began to take root and grow in the 1970s–90s, the encounter movement and psychodrama techniques continued to lose their popularity.

In 1974, Jacob L. Moreno died. He abstained from food and drink after a long battle with illness. Moreno's youthful dream had come true—his methods had been adopted into the larger culture while his influence remained mostly anonymous. When his friend and colleague Lewis Yablonsky visited him just before his death, Moreno whispered in his ear, "I've lived a full life. I've done my job. It's time for me to go on to something else" (1976, p. 284). Although his life on earth ended here, in true psychodramatic fashion, the final chapter of his autobiography describes his future projected journey beyond death—into the afterlife including encounters with God, angels, Freud, and the great philosophers (Moreno, 2019).

3.3 Moreno as a Social Worker and Sociatrist

Jacob Moreno's career reflects that of a social worker. His clinical work was with societies most oppressed and underserved communities including immigrants, refugees, prostituted women, inmates, children, and the severely mentally ill. He explicitly worked to empower these communities and develop systems and tools to help individuals help each other. Early in his career, while his colleagues were practicing psychoanalysis, he was exploring the impact of relationships, society, and the environment on individuals—he even suggested that mental illness was a result of larger social forces (1950). Similar to the social work profession which emerged from charity and settlement house movements with religious influence, Moreno's work began with the House of the Encounter. Moreno's community work to promote exemplifies social work's commitment to social justice, self-determination, and empowerment (Niepenberg, 2017). Moreno even worked several years as Director of Social Research for the New York State Department of Social Welfare. The whole of his work could be seen as a career composed of an integrated blend of case work, group work, and community work—micro, mezzo, and macrosocial work. His work included the entire range of social work practice including with individuals, couples, families, groups, organizations, communities, and even leaving an impact on the larger society. One aspect of social work that makes it unique is its multidisciplinary nature; it integrates psychology, medicine, sociology, criminology, philosophy, education, policy, politics, and activism. Similar to social work, Moreno's work included each of these fields and his methods continue to be used within each of these respective fields.

Interestingly, in 1947, Moreno predicted that a doctoral degree in sociatry will be given in the future, utilizing a synthesis of knowledge from the fields of psychiatry, medicine, psychology, education, and sociology. He writes that "The art and skill of the sociatrist will depend upon a synthesis of knowledge towards which all social and psychiatric sciences will have made their contribution" (Moreno, 1947, p. 10). In the same year, Catholic University began offering the first Doctorate in Clinical Social Work (DSW) degree, though the PhD in Social Work had been around since 1920. By the late 1990s, the DSW degree disappeared until the University of Pennsylvania reintroduced it in 2007 (Hartocollis, Cnaan, & Ledwith, 2014). If Moreno was alive today, he might argue that the DSW is the fulfillment of his prediction—the social worker is fundamentally a sociatrist, one that treats conditions arising from interrelations of individuals, families, groups, and society.

3.4 Sociometry and Psychodrama Since Moreno's Death in 1974

Following J.L. Moreno's death, Zerka continued to spread psychodrama through her leadership, writing, and training—she is affectionately remembered by many as "the mother of psychodrama" (see Fig. 3.4). A year after J.L. Moreno's death, the American Board of Examiners (ABE) in sociometry, psychodrama, and group psychotherapy emerged to provide standards for certification and promote a wave of professionalism in the psychodrama field. While J.L.'s writing was hard to understand and philosophically complex, Zerka translated his methods in a way that made it easier to understand and teach. A collection of Zerka's most popular publications was organized and republished under the title *The Quintessential Zerka* in 2006, making them more available to students and trainees. In her memoir, *To Dream Again* (2012), she mentions around two dozen countries that she repeatedly traveled to teach psychodrama.

In the decades after Moreno's death, the membership of the American Society of Group Psychotherapy and Psychodrama was consistently declining. Other creative arts therapists, who were previously ASGPP members, began to organize and found their own societies including the dance therapists (in 1966), art therapists (in 1969), music therapists (in 1971), drama therapists (in 1979), and the poetry therapists (in 1981). Numerous other humanistic psychologies (including gestalt therapy and transactional analysis) emerged. Concurrently, the counselors (in 1973), psychologists (in 1991), and social workers (in 1979) began to establish their own formal group work divisions or associations. Previously, the ASGPP and AGPA (in addition to AAGW

Fig. 3.4 Jacob and Zerka Moreno in Amsterdam in 1971. Reprinted with permission from Figusch (2014)

until its 1955 merger with NASW) were the only group therapy organizations in the USA—with ASGPP being the only creative arts therapy organization. As such, it attracted a much broader membership of group workers, psychodramatists, and creative arts therapists until they differentiated with their own organizations.

At the same time, many mental health hospitals that had adopted psychodrama were closing due to deinstitutionalization policies. The development of new psychiatric medications led to the further medicalization of mental health treatment and a significant decline in inpatient treatment programs beginning in the late 1950s. While psychiatric hospitals closed and medicalization promoted medication-based treatments for mental illness, it also created conditions for alcoholism and addiction to be recognized as a disease and an increased number of addiction treatment programs became available. Many of these programs integrated psychodrama into their programs tracing their psychodrama lineages to the therapeutic communities, or trainers such as Virginia Satir, Sharon Wegscheider-Cruse, Tian Dayton, and others.

In the first few decades after Moreno's death, it seems that psychodrama's popularity significantly declined overall in the USA while increasing around the world. One of the larger influences related to psychodrama's decline in the USA included the lack of quality research on psychodrama as the psychotherapy field moved toward medicalization and evidence-based practices. Psychodrama's theory of change, spontaneity-creativity theory, makes it nearly impossible to manualize the psychodramatic approach, and thus, it was not eligible for review as an evidence-based practice by the American Psychological Association. As the psychodrama field progressed, it seems to have fallen short in its attempts to professionalize. In the USA, most psychodramatists are in private practice rather than university settings which limits their access to research support and research grants (Orkibi & Feniger-Schaal, 2019). Until the mid-1990s, very little had been done to address psychodrama's potential for re-traumatizing clients. As trauma theory and trauma research progressed (Herman, 1997; van der Kolk, 1996), multiple trauma-focused and trauma-informed psychodrama approached emerged (Dayton, 1994; Giacomucci & Marquit, 2020; Hudgins & Toscani, 2013; Kane, 1992; Kellermann, 2000) but the damage to psychodrama's reputation had already been done. A new wave of cognitive behavioral psychotherapies seemed to monopolize the psychotherapy field with a plethora of empirical research to support their approaches which seamlessly fit within the US medical system.

Although the mental health field in the USA has not embraced psychodrama in the past few decades, it is especially popular in Australia, New Zealand, Europe, Turkey, Israel, Asia, and South America (Nolte, 2014). Many countries have established psychodrama psychotherapy as a scientifically validated evidence-based practice (Orkibi &Feniger-Schaal, 2019). Though it is hard to find psychodrama in US universities, various other countries have entire graduate degree programs in sociometry and psychodrama (Giacomucci, 2019). While psychodrama's popularity declined in the USA, it continued to increase on the international stage. The influence of culture may have been at play in these larger fluctuations as well. The countries that do have robust psychodrama communities also have cultures that place significant value on community, relationships, and expression. Individualism and the medical model in the USA appear at odds with many of Moreno's theories.

In the past few years, it seems that both group psychotherapy and psychodrama are increasing in popularity again. The most recent meta-analysis on psychodrama psychotherapy indicates an increase in psychodrama research from 2008 to 2017 with over a quarter of studies in that decade taking place in 2017 (Orkibi & Feniger-Schaal, 2019). Between 2011 and 2013, the North-West Psychodrama Association in England republished 9 of J. L. Moreno's most popular books which had become difficult to find since they were no longer being printed. In 2018, the American Psychological Association formally recognized group psychology and group psychotherapy as a specialty which creates the possibility of new educational programs in group psychotherapy. In 2018, the *Journal of Social Work with Groups* published two articles emphasizing the usefulness of J. L. Moreno's triadic model—psychodrama, sociometry, and group psychotherapy—for social workers who facilitate groups. The first article explores the "synergistic relationship between group work and psychodrama" while discussing "the convergence of these two approaches as well as ways they can enhance one another and service delivery when used together" (Skolnik, 2018, p. 1). The second article continues the dialogue started by Skolnik and emphasizes the power of psychodrama to renegotiate traumatic experiences (Giacomucci & Stone, 2019). The authors of the two aforementioned articles also teach the only current psychodrama courses within social work graduate programs in the USA at Yeshiva University (Sari Skolnik) and Bryn Mawr College (Scott Giacomucci) which both emerged in the 2019 Spring semester.

Moreno died in 1974 before he could finish organizing his complete autobiography. In 2019, the completed *Autobiography of a Genius* was published—just a year after the 100th anniversary of Moreno's*Daimon* journal publication in Vienna. Social worker's interest in the creative arts therapies continues to increase (Heinonen, Halonen, & Krahn, 2018). In 2020, the *Social Work with Groups* journal published a special edition titled *The Creative Practitioner: An Introduction to Psychodrama, Sociometry, and Group Psychotherapy*. This appears to be the first social work journal to publish a special edition on psychodrama and is a significant event in the integration of sociometry and psychodrama into the social work field. If this momentum continues, we could see a more dramatic re-emergence of sociometry and psychodrama within the social work field. At this particular point in time, there appears to be newfound interest and growing attention to Moreno's methods in the social work field and the other mental health professions. Perhaps we are at the beginning increased integration and collaboration between psychodramatists and social workers. This book is an attempt to concretize that integration.

3.5   Conclusion

In our work with clients, we engage in a thorough history taking process in order to fully understand the here-and-now presentation of a client. Without this, intervention or future planning is limited. The same is true when considering the future of an organization or a field—in the case of this chapter, the future of the field of psychodrama. An understanding of Moreno's methods is incomplete without considering the historical contexts during which his methods were developed and how the larger socio-cultural forces influenced his work, particularly in the USA where he was living and working. The history of psychodrama emerged in parallel with the history of social work. Both histories intertwine with the fields of group work, psychology, and medicine (see Fig. 3.5).

SOCIAL WORK & GROUP THERAPY TIMELINES

- 1889: Settlement Movement begins with Hull House in Chicago, founded by Jane Addams – drama club were the most popular groups within Hull House
- 1904: Simmons College in Boston becomes first to train social workers
- 1905: Joseph Pratt organized educational groups with tuberculosis patients
- 1917: Beginning of the National Social Workers' Exchange which would later form NASW
- 1917: Mary Richmond Publishes Social Diagnosis, a core text for social workers
- 1918: Trigant Burrow used psychoanalytic methods in group settings
- 1919: Association of Training Schools for Professional Social Workers established (forerunner organization to CSWE)
- 1922: Sigmund Freud wrote on group dynamics - "Group Psychology and the Analysis of the Ego."
- 1928: Milford Conference declares social work as its own profession
- 1928: 1st International Conference of Social Work in Paris
- 1930s: social work adopts psychoanalytic perspective in attempt to professionalize
- 1935: British Federation of Social Workers forms
- 1935: group work formally joins social work field at national conference
- 1936: National Association for the Study of Group Work (NAGSW) founded
- 1940s: Fritz & Laura Perls develop Gestalt Therapy
- 1943: Samuel Slavson founded the American Group Psychotherapy Association (AGPA), began The International Journal of Group Psychotherapy, and publishes An Introduction to Group Therapy
- 1944: Establishment of the Research Center for Group Dynamics by Kurt Lewin & others
- 1946: T-Groups develop
- 1947: First National Training Laboratory in Group Development is held
- 1948: S.H. Foulkes publishes Introduction to Group-Analytic Psychotherapy

JACOB MORENO & PSYCHODRAMA TIMELINE

- 1889: Jacob Moreno is born
- 1908: Moreno helps establish the Religion of the Encounter and the House of the Encounter providing services to immigrants/refugees
- 1911: Moreno experiments with role-playing with children in the parks of Vienna
- 1913: Moreno organizes prostituted women in Vienna and writes of the therapeutic agency of each group member
- 1914: Moreno publishes An Invitation to an Encounter
- 1915-1918: Moreno worked with Tyrolean refugees WWI and first uses the term "Sociometry"
- 1918: Moreno starts the existential journal Daimon (which included working with Martin Buber)
- 1920: Moreno publishes The Words of The Father
- 1921: First psychodrama/sociodrama session in Vienna
- 1921: J. L. Moreno organized the "Theatre of Spontaneity" in Vienna
- 1925: Moreno immigrates to USA
- 1925: Moreno immigrates to USA
- 1929: Moreno started the Impromptu Theater at Carnegie Hall in NYC
- 1932: Moreno coins the term "group therapy" at APA in Philadelphia presenting his work from Sing Sing Prison
- 1934: Publication of Who Shall Survive? outlining his sociometric research in Hudson Valley
- 1936: Moreno founded Beacon Hill Sanitarium and begins to use psychodrama as a treatment approach
- 1937: Moreno starts the journal publication Sociometry: A Journal of Interpersonal Relations
- 1937-1938: Moreno teaches the first university courses on psychodrama and sociometry.
- 1941: St. Elizabeth's Hospital opens a psychodrama stage in DC.
- 1941: American Sociological Association begins a sociometry section
- 1942: Moreno opens the Sociometric Institute
- 1942: First group organization founded – American Society of Group Psychotherapy & Psychodrama (ASGPP)
- 1946: Publication of Psychodrama Vol 1
- 1947: Beginning of the journal Sociatry, later renamed Group Psychotherapy
- 1949: Jacob and Zerka Moreno marry

PSYCHOLOGY, MEDICINE, & SOCIETY TIMELINE

- 1885: Freud travels to Paris to study with Charcot who teaches hypnosis as a treatment for hysteria
- 1885: Automobile is invented
- 1892: American Psychological Association forms
- 1895: Radio is invented
- 1896: Freud first uses term psychoanalysis
- 1906: Pavlov publishes studies on Classical Conditioning
- 1913: Watson establishes Behaviorism
- 1913: Jung separates from Freud
- 1914-1918: World War I
- 1920: 19th Amendment Grants Women the Right to Vote
- 1923: Martin Buber publishes I and Thou
- 1927: First Trans-Atlantic Flight
- 1929-1939: The Great Depression in America
- 1933-1945: The Holocaust
- 1935: Alcoholics Anonymous is formed based on mutual aid principles
- 1935: US president Roosevelt's New Deal expands social services
- 1938: Harry S. Sullivan publishes Psychiatry: Introduction to the Study of Interpersonal Relations
- 1939-1945: World War II
- 1942: Carl Rogers develops client-centered therapy
- 1945: United Nations is established
- 1945: First electronic computer is built
- 1946: National Institute of Mental Health formed

Fig. 3.5 Parallel timelines depicting the intersections between social work, group therapy, Moreno, psychodrama, psychology, medicine, and USA history

1952: Council on Social Work Education formed

1955: National Association of Social Workers (NASW) forms through the integration of 7 professional groups including the American Association of Group Workers

1955: Publication of Social Work Journal begins

1956: International Federation of Social Workers forms

1959: W.R. Bion publishes Experiences in Groups

1960: Mutual aid as social work term - Richard Schwartz 60s

1960s: Empirical Clinical Practice (ECP) movement turns social work's attention to research in attempt to professionalize

1961: Eric Berne publishes Transactional Analysis in Psychotherapy

1966: American Dance Therapy Association forms

1969: American Art Therapy Association forms

1969: NASW Delegate Assembly approves resolution to pursue social work licensure in each state

1971: American Music Therapy Association forms

1973: ACA's Association for Specialists in Group Work is founded

1978: Social Work with Groups Journal begins

2018: APA formally recognizes Group Psychology and Group Psychotherapy with specialty status

2020: Social work with Groups Journal publishes special edition on sociometry & psychodrama

1950: Moreno petitions American Psychiatric Association to start Group Psychotherapy section; in the same year he unsuccessfully runs for president of APA

1950: An estimate suggests 1/3 of mental institutions in USA are using psychodrama

1951: Moreno forms International Committee on Group Psychotherapy in Paris

1954: First International Congress on Group Psychotherapy in Toronto (held every 3rd year)

1959: Moreno publishes Psychodrama Vol 2 in collaboration with Zerka Moreno

1964: Moreno publishes Psychodrama Vol 3

1964: First International Congress on Psychodrama in Paris

1967: Moreno closes his hospital in Beacon. NY to focus on training and writing

1968-1969: Moreno receives Doctor Honoris Causa (Barcelona University) and Golden Doctorate (Vienna University)

1970s: ASGPP conferences have 2000+ attendees (compared to a few hundred today)

1973: International Association of Group Psychotherapy (IAGP) founded by Moreno and others

1974: Death of JL Moreno

1975: American Board of Examiners in Sociometry, Psychodrama, and Group Psychotherapy forms

2011-2013: North-West Psychodrama Association republishes most of Moreno's foundational books, making them available around the world

2016: Death of Zerka Moreno

2019: Moreno's Autobiography of a Genius is published

2019: ABE has record number of applications for certification

2020: Springer begins publishing first international book series on psychodrama

1950-1953: Korean War

1950s: American McCarthyism and Communist fear

1950s: Anti-psychotic medications developed & American deinstitutionalization – closing of many 'insane asylums'

1952: First DSM publication by APA

1954: Maslow publishes his hierarchy of needs theory

1955-1975: Vietnam War

1957: Space Age begins with Russian Sputnik I

1958: Synanon Movement emerges, popularizing therapeutic communities

1960s: Encounter Group Movement gains popularity

1960s: Aaron Beck develops cognitive therapy

1962: Cuban Missile Crisis & Peak of the Cold War

1960s: American Civil Rights Movement

1970s: American Improv movement and Theater of the Oppressed become popular

1970: First Earth Day, Environmental Movement gains influence

1970s: New technology makes Advanced Statistical Analyses more available for quantitative research

1973: First Mobile Phone Call

1975: Playback Theater is developed by Jonathan Fox and Jo Salas

2010-2012: Arab Spring Movements

2011: Occupy Wall Street Movement Against Financial Inequality

2013: DSM-5 released – eliminates "gender identity disorder"

2019: Coronavirus Pandemic

Fig. 3.5   (continued)

References

Back, K. W. (1972). *Beyond words: The story of sensitivity training and the encounter movement* . New York: Russell Sage Foundation.

Bailey, S. (2006). Ancient and modern roots of drama therapy. In S. L. Brooke (Ed.), *Creative arts therapies manual: A guide to the history, theoretical approaches, assessment, and work with special populations of art, play dance, music, drama, and poetry therapies* (pp. 214–222). Springfield, IL: Charles C. Thomas Publisher.

Berne, E. (1970). A review of gestalt therapy verbatim. *American Journal of Psychiatry, 126*(10), 164.

Bitel, M. (2014). Flipping the equation: The need for context-focused group work education. *Social Work with Groups, 37,* 48–60.

Blatner, A. (1996). *Acting-in: Practical applications of psychodramatic methods* (3rd ed.). New York: Springer Publishing Company.

Blatner, A. (2000). *Foundations of psychodrama: History, theory, and practice* (4th ed.). New York City: Springer Publishing Company.

Blatner, A. (2005). Psychodrama. In R. J. Corsini & D. Wedding (Eds.) *Current psychotherapies.* (7th ed.). Belmont, CA, US: Thomson Brooks/Cole Publishing Co.

Borgatta, E. (1950). The use of psychodrama, sociodrama and related techniques in social psychological research. *Sociometry, 13*(3), 244–258.

Cooper, C. L. (1974). Psychological disturbance following T-groups: Relationship between Eysenck personality inventory and family/friends judgements. *British Journal of Social Work, 4,* 39–49.

Cooper, C. L. (1975). How psychologically dangerous are T-groups and encounter groups? *Journal of Human Relations, 28*(3), 249–260.

Corcoran, J. (2020). *Case based learning for group intervention in social work.* New York: Oxford University Press.

Dayton, T. (1994). *The drama within.* Deerfield Beach, FL: Health Communications Inc.

Ehrenreich, J. H. (1985). *The altruistic imagination: A history of social work and social policy in the United States.* Ithaca, New York: Cornell University Press.

Figusch, Z. (2014). The JL Moreno memorial photo album. London: lulu.com.

Fox, J. (Ed.). (1987). *The essential Moreno: Writings on psychodrama, group method, and spontaneity by J. L. Moreno, M.D.* New York: Springer.

Gershoni, J. (2009). Bringing psychodrama to the main stage in group psychotherapy. *Group, 33*(4), 297–308.

Gershoni, J. (2013). Psychodrama. *Encyclopedia of social work.* Retrieved 28 Apr. 2018, from http://socialwork.oxfordre.com/view/https://doi.org/10.1093/acrefore/978019997 5839.001.0001/acrefore-9780199975839-e-316.

Giacomucci, S. (2018a). Social work and sociometry: Integrating history, theory, and practice. In *The clinical voice.* Richboro, PA: Pennsylvania Society for Clinical Social Work.

Giacomucci, S. (2018). The trauma survivor's inner role atom: A clinical map for post-traumatic growth. *Journal of Psychodrama, Sociometry, and Group Psychotherapy., 66*(1), 115–129.

Giacomucci, S. (2019). Social group work in action: A sociometry, psychodrama, and experiential trauma group therapy curriculum. *Doctorate in Social Work (DSW) Dissertations.* 124. Retrieved from https://repository.upenn.edu/cgi/viewcontent.cgi?article=1128&context=edisse rtations_sp2.

Giacomucci, S. (2020). Experiential sociometry in group work: Mutual aid for the group-as-a-whole. *Social Work with Groups, Advanced Online Publication.* https://doi.org/10.1080/01609513.2020. 1747726.

Giacomucci, S., & Marquit, J. (2020). The effectiveness of trauma-focused psychodrama in the treatment of PTSD in inpatient substance abuse treatment. *Frontiers in Psychology, 11,* 896. https://doi.org/10.3389%2Ffpsyg.2020.00896.

Giacomucci, S., & Stone, A. M. (2019). Being in two places at once: Renegotiating traumatic experience through the surplus reality of psychodrama. *Social Work with Groups, 42*(3), 184–196. https://doi.org/10.1080/01609513.2018.1533913.

Gitterman, A., & Shulman, L. (2005). *Mutual aid groups, vulnerable and resilient populations, and the life cycle* (3rd ed.). New York, NY: Columbia University Press.

Hadden, S. B. (2015). Historical background of group psychotherapy. *International Journal of Group Psychotherapy, 5*(2), 162–168.

Hartocollis, L., Cnaan, R. A., & Ledwith, K. (2014). The social work practice doctorate. *Research on Social Work Practice, 24*(5), 636–642.

Heinonen, T., Halonen, D., & Krahn, E. (2018). *Expressive arts for social work and social change*. Oxford University Press.

Herman, J. L. (1997). *Trauma and recovery: The aftermath of violence—From domestic abuse to political terror*. New York: Basic Books.

Howard, J. (1968). Inhibitions thrown to the gentle winds. *Life, 65*(5), 48–65.

Hudgins, M. K., & Toscani, F. (2013). *Healing world trauma with the therapeutic spiral model: Stories from the frontlines*. London: Jessica Kingsley Publishers.

Kane, R. (1992). The potential abuses, limitations, and negative effects of classical psychodramatic techniques in group counseling. *Journal of Group Psychotherapy, Psychodrama & Sociometry, 44*(4), 181–189.

Kellermann, P. F. (2000). The therapeutic effects of psychodrama with traumatized people. In P. F. Kellermann & K. Hudgins (Eds.), *Psychodrama with trauma survivors: Acting out your pain* (pp. 23–40). Philadelphia: Jessica Kingsley Publishing.

Knight, C. (2017). Social work students' experiences with group work in the field practicum. *Journal of Teaching in Social Work, 37*(2), 138–155.

Kurland, R., & Salmon, R. (2005). Group work vs. casework in a group: Principles and implications for teaching and practice. *Social Work with Groups, 28*(3–4), 121–132.

Lieberman, M. A., Yalom, I. D., & Miles, M. (1973). *Encounter groups: First facts*. New York: Basic Books.

Marineau, R. (2014). *Jacob Levy Moreno 1889–1974: father of psychodrama, sociometry, and group psychotherapy*. Princeton, New Jersey: Psychodrama Press.

Maslow, A. H. (1968, August). Letters to editor. *Life*, 15.

Maslow, A. H. (1971). *The farther reaches of human nature*. New York, NY: Viking Press.

Meiers, J. I. (1946). Origins and development of group psychotherapy. In Moreno (Ed.), *Group psychotherapy: A symposium*. Beacon, NY: Beacon House.

Moreno, J. D. (2014). *Impromptu man: J.L. Moreno and the origins of psychodrama, encounter culture, and the social network*. New York, NY: Bellevue Literary Press.

Moreno, J. L. (1921). *Das Testament des Vaters*. Vienna, Austria: Gustav Kiepenheuer Verlag.

Moreno, J. L. (1934). *Who Shall Survive? A new approach to the problems of human interrelations*. Washington, DC: Nervous and Mental Disease Publishing Co.

Moreno, J. L. (1945). *Group psychotherapy: A symposium*. Beacon, NY: Beacon House Press.

Moreno, J. L. (1946). *Psychodrama Volume 1*. Beacon, NY: Beacon House Press.

Moreno, J. L. (1947). The social atom and death. *Sociometry, 10*(1), 80–84.

Moreno, J. L. (1947b). *Open letter to group psychotherapists*. Psychodrama Monograms, No. 23. *Beacon, NY: Beacon House*.

Moreno, J. L. (1950). The sociometric approach to social case work. *Sociometry, 13*(2), 172–175.

Moreno, J. L. (1955). *Preludes to my autobiography*. Beacon, NY: Beacon House.

Moreno, J. L. (1961). The role concept, a bridge between psychiatry and sociology. *American Journal of Psychiatry, 118*(6), 518–523.

Moreno, J. L. (2019). In E. Schreiber, S. Kelley, & S. Giacomucci, (Eds.), *The autobiography of a genius*. United Kingdom: North West Psychodrama Association.

Moreno, J. L., & Moreno, F. B. (1944). Spontaneity theory of child development. *Sociometry, 7*(2), 89–128.

Moreno, J. L., Moreno, Z. T., & Moreno, J. D. (1964). The first psychodramatic family. Group. *Psychotherapy, 16,* 203–249.

Moreno, J. L., & Whitin, E. S. (1932). *Application of the group method to classification.* New York: National Committee on Prisons and Prison Labor.

Moreno, Z. T. (1966). Evolution and dynamics of the group psychotherapy movement. In J. L. Moreno (Ed.), *The international handbook of group psychotherapy.* London: Peter Owen.

Moreno, Z. T. (2006). In T. Horvatin, & E. Schreiber, (Eds.), *The Quintessential Zerka.* New York, NY: Routledge.

Moreno, Z. T. (2012). *To dream again: A memoir.* New York: Mental Health Resources.

Niepenberg, K. (2017). Gesellschaftlicher Wandel in der Sozialen Arbeit. *Zeitschrift Für Psychodrama Und Soziometrie, 16*(1), 171–183.

Nolte, J. (2014). *The philosophy, theory, and methods of J.L. Moreno: The man who tried to become god.* New York, NY: Routledge.

Orkibi, H., & Feniger-Schaal, R. (2019). Integrative systematic review of psychodrama psychotherapy research: Trends and methodological implications. *PLoS ONE, 14*(2), e0212575. https://doi.org/10.1371/journal.pone.0212575.

Posthuma, A. B., & Posthuma, B. W. (1973). Some observations on encounter group casualties. *Journal of Applied Behavioral Sciences, 9,* 595–608.

Renouvier, P. (1958). *The group psychotherapy movement: J.L. Moreno, its pioneer and founder.* Psychodrama and Group Psychotherapy Monographs, No. 33. Beacon, NY: Beacon House.

Richmond, M. E. (1917). *Social diagnosis.* New York: Russell Sage Foundation.

Shulman, L. (2015). *The skills of helping individuals, families, groups, and communities* (8th ed.). Boston, MA: Cengage Learning.

Skolnik, S. (2018). A synergistic union: Group work meets psychodrama. *Social Work with Groups, 41*(1–2), 60–73.

Spence, G. B. (2007). Further development of evidence-based coaching: Lessons from the rise and fall of the human potential movement. *Australian Psychologist, 42*(4), 255–265.

Stimmer, F. (2004). Psychodrama—Soziale Arbeit—Netzwerke. *Zeitschrift Für Psychodrama Und Soziometrie, 3*(1), 17–27.

Sullivan, H. S. (1953). *The interpersonal theory of psychiatry.* New York: W. W. Norton & Co.

Thomas, G. W. (1943). Group psychotherapy, a review of the recent literature. *Psychosomatic Medicine, 5*(2), 166–180.

Treadwell, T. (2016). J. L. Moreno: The origins of the group encounter movement and the forerunner of web-based social network media revolution. *The Journal of Psychodrama, Sociometry, and Group Psychotherapy, 64*(1), 51–62.

Van der Kolk, B. A. (1996). The body keeps the score: approaches to the psychobiology of post-traumatic stress disorder. In B.A. van der Kolk, A.C. McFarlane & L. Weisaeth (Eds.), *Traumatic stress: The effects of overwhelming experiences on mind, body, and society.* New York: Guilford Press.

Yalom, I. D., & Lieverman, M. A. (1971). A study of encounter group casualties. *Archives of General Psychiatry, 25,* 16–30.

Part II
An Integrated Theory and Philosophy of Social Work, Sociometry, and Psychodrama

While social work has integrated group work into its field, sociometry and psychodrama have been mostly excluded from the social work profession. Until 2017, there were very few English publications on social work, sociometry, and psychodrama, though several earlier articles have been published on the topic in German language (including Müller, 1986, 2009; Ramsauer, 2007; Stimmer, 2004; Zwilling, 2004). There have been countless books, article, and courses within social work's history that focus on social work with groups. The social work philosophy has been infused into group work from the start (Giacomucci, 2019). This section intends to promote the same philosophical infusion of sociometry and psychodrama within social work philosophy and theory. In the following chapters, the theory and philosophical systems of sociometry and psychodrama will be presented separately, each with highlighted connections to social work.

The philosophy and theories of any given field are inevitably interlinked and overlap. The social work field and the triadic system of Jacob Moreno are no different. This section aims to uncover the unity between the Morenean philosophical system and social work philosophy—as well as the theoretical connections between social work, sociometry, and psychodrama. While theories shape how we practice and intentionally interact with clients, philosophy is the foundational conceptualization that guides our work. Philosophy provides a framework for defining problems while theories offer strategies for action and movement towards solutions to the problems (Himes & Schulenberg, 2013). Philosophy and theory directly inform all aspects of social work, sociometry, and psychodrama practice.

References

Giacomucci, S. (2019). *Social group work in action: A sociometry, psychodrama, and experiential trauma therapy curriculum*. Doctorate in Social Work (DSW) Dissertations. 124. https://repository.upenn.edu/cgi/viewcontent.cgi?article=1128&context=edissertations_sp2.

Himes, H., & Schulenberg, J. (2013). Theoretical reflections: Theory and philosophy should always inform practice. *Academic Advising Today, 36*(3). Retrieved from www.nacada.ksu.edu.

Müller, J. (1986). Psychodrama in der ambulanten Sozialarbeit im Alkoholbereich. *Gruppenpsychotherapie und Gruppendynamik, 22* (2), 186–197.

Müller, J. (2009). Psychodrama in social work. In F. von Ameln, R. Gerstmann, & J. Kramer (Eds.), *Psychodrama* (2nd ed., pp. 519–531). Berlin: Springer.

Ramsauer, S. (2007). Psychodramatische Supervision in der Sozialen Arbeit: Kleine Interventionen mit großer Wirkung. *Zeitschrift Für Psychodrama Und Soziometrie, 6*(2), 293–302.

Stimmer, F. (2004). Psychodrama – Soziale Arbeit – Netzwerke. *Zeitschrift Für Psychodrama Und Soziometrie, 3*(1), 17–27.

Zwilling, M. (2004). Methodisches Handeln in der Sozialen Arbeit—Psychodrama als Basismethode. *Zeitschrift Für Psychodrama Und Soziometrie, 3*(1), 5–15.

Chapter 4
Social Work Philosophy Encounters Morenean Philosophy

Abstract Core Morenean philosophy is covered in this chapter as it relates to social work philosophy. The existential and spiritual philosophies from which sociometry and psychodrama emerged are comprehensively depicted including his theory of human nature, the encounter, the Godhead, the autonomous healing center within, spontaneity–creativity theory, the here-and-now, action theory, role theory, and psychodrama's developmental theory. Attention is given to the biopsychosocial - spiritual nature of both social work and psychodrama's conceptualizations. The inter-section of Morenean philosophy is presented with each of the six core social work values—the centrality of human relationships, the dignity and worth of each person, social justice , service, competence, and integrity.

Keywords Social work philosophy · Psychodrama · Sociatry · Morenean philosophy · Social work core values

I have had the good fortune to develop three ideas. The first idea, a study of the godhead ,' has remained cryptic and misapprehended. The second, a study of man called psychodrama, has aroused some hope that man can train his spontaneity to overcome many of his shortcomings. My third idea, the study of society called sociometry, has given the greatest promise that a measure can be developed for a deeper understanding of society and a key to the treatment of its ills. Many of my friends consider these three ideas one apart from the other. In my own mind, however, all the three ideas are of one piece. One has developed out of the other. The first idea initiates a cannon of the universe, the second a cannon of the individual, the third a cannon of human society. (Moreno, 1943, p. 299)

4.1 Philosophical Underpinnings of Moreno's Work

While some modern psychotherapists are aware of the contributions of technique from J. L. Moreno (see Fig. 4.1), most are unaware that psychodrama is a comprehensive system of theory, philosophy, and technique.

© The Author(s) 2021
S. Giacomucci, *Social Work, Sociometry, and Psychodrama*, Psychodrama in Counselling, Coaching and Education 1,
https://doi.org/10.1007/978-981-33-6342-7_4

Fig. 4.1 Jacob Moreno in the early 1960s. Reprinted with permission from Figusch (2014)

My philosophy has been misunderstood. It has been disregarded in many religious and scientific circles. This has not hindered me from continuing to develop techniques whereby my vision of what the world could be might be established in fact. It is curious that these techniques—sociometry, psychodrama, group therapy - created to implement an underlying philosophy of life have been almost universally accepted while the underlying philosophy has been relegated to the dark corners of library shelves or entirely pushed aside. (Moreno , 2019, p. 175)

Some suggest psychodrama is one of the most complex psychotherapy systems (von Ameln & Becker-Ebel, 2020). Psychodrama is built upon multiple theories including action theory , role theory , and spontaneity–creativity theory . While psychodrama does come equipped with its own theoretical basis, because it is highly process-driven involving numerous clinical techniques, it can be adapted to contain the theoretical content of any other theoretical system.

Psychodramatists have integrated psychodrama with many other modalities or theoretical systems including: cognitive behavioral therapy (Hammond, 2007; Treadwell, Dartnell, Travaglini, Staats, & Devinney, 2016; Treadwell, 2020), Freudian psychoanalysis (Brown, 2007; Cortes, 2016), Jungian psychology (Gasseau & Scategni, 2007), object relations theory (Holmes, 2015), positive psychology (Tomasulo, 2011), 12-step and addiction frameworks (Dayton, 2005; Giacomucci, 2017, 2020a; Giacomucci, Gera, Briggs, & Bass, 2018; Miller, 2007), trauma therapy (Dayton, 2005, 2015; Giacomucci & Marquit, 2020; Hudgins, 2017; Hudgins & Toscani, 2013; Kellermann & Hudgins, 2000), attachment theory (Baim, 2007), drama therapy (Casson, 2007; Landy, 2017), family systems therapy (Anderson & Carnabucci, 2011; Chimera, 2007; Gershoni, 2003), EMDR therapy (Bradshaw-Tauvon, 2007), music therapy (Moreno, 1999), and art therapy (Peterson, 2003). In the same way, foundational social work theories can be integrated with psychodrama practice. Bitel (2000) writes, "Social group work is an arena for boundless creativity . In viewing the group work setting as a stage for the creation of countless stories, dramas, struggles, and resolutions, the social group worker becomes an artist in her own medium" (p. 79).

This section outlines the core of Morenean philosophy which is essential understanding prior to engaging with his methods of sociometry and psychodrama. Moreno had mixed feelings about his methods being adapted into the mainstream culture , while his philosophy was neglected. Zerka Moreno writes in 1969:

> Substitute theories are false and misleading as they abrogate or abort the complete execution of the methods. Moreno's position was therefore "take my ideas, my concepts, but do not separate them from their parent, the philosophy; do not split my children in half, like a Solomonic judgment, love them in toto, support and respect the entire structure upon which they rest." (p. 5)

4.2 Human Nature, Cosmic Man, and the Godhead

Moreno's philosophy is essentially an existentialist understanding of human nature and human's place within the cosmos. Moreno was strongly influenced by Einstein's inclusion of God consciousness into his mathematical and scientific understandings of the world. Morenean philosophy argues that humans are not only biological, psychological, and social creatures, but also *cosmic creatures*. Moreno's conceptualizations of forces that influence humans go beyond psychodynamics and sociodynamics to include cosmodynamics (von Ameln & Becker-Ebel, 2020). He declared "every man is a genius "—there are only geniuses (Moreno, 2019, p. 12). Moreno's newly published *Autobiography of a Genius* title may sound egotistic and grandiose; however, his intent is to elevate everyone to experiencing themselves and everyone around them as a geniuses.

> In declaring the essential nature of the genius , Jacob Levy Moreno declares that you are a genius – that all humans are genius. He calls upon all human beings to recognize their creative genius and co-create a better world. This call to action comes at a pivotal time in the history of our world: will we survive? (Schreiber, Kelley, & Giacomucci, 2019, pp. 9–10)

Moreno's attempts to empower human's sense of self did not start with the exclamation that everyone is a genius . He began with the even bolder statement the Godhead is within each person.

His early work prior to immigrating to the United States was essentially spiritually and existentially oriented. He was deeply influenced by world religions, saints, Jesus, the Buddha, his family's Jewish heritage, and his mother's spirituality. His idea of a healer was closely related to Jesus, a traveling mystic who goes to meet the people where they are, rather than a doctor psychoanalyzing a patient on a couch. In *Who Shall Survive?* he writes:

> *I did not think that a great healer and therapist would look and act the way Wagner or Freud did.* I visualized the healer as a spontaneous-creative protagonist in the midst of the group.

My concept of the physician as a healer, and that of theirs were very far apart. To my mind, persons like Jesus, Buddha, Socrates, and Ghandi were doctors and healers; for Freud they were probably patients. (1953, p. xxvii)

In studying the evolution of the concept of God, he provided a new evolution of understanding the Godhead . He highlights that the Old Testament concept of God was a distant and invisible deity ("He-God"), and that the New Testament God was human, loving and present ("Thou-God"). He declared the only natural evolution of the God idea to be an understanding of humans as God ("I-God") (Moreno, 1921, 2019). His early work culminated with a 1921 publication titled *The Words of the Father* , which outlined his spiritual views. Moreno attempted to put these views into action by treating everyone as if they were God and possessed the same divinity and capacity for creativity . While some may be deterred by his spiritual views, essentially, he elevated the dignity and worth of each human being to the forefront of his philosophical system and approach to societal problems.

In addition to seeing every human as God, Moreno also wrote of a *Godhead* , the ultimate creator. He writes that his fascination with God began in his childhood—leading to what he described as his first psychodrama at age 4 when he and his friends began to enact a heavenly scene with Moreno in the role of God. Later as a young adult, Moreno could be found encouraging other children in the parks of Vienna to role-play as God through impromptu play and drama. Moreno repeatedly suggests to his readers that his sociometric and psychodramatic systems cannot be fully understood without first understanding his spiritual views. "I had envisioned the Godhead as the Protagonist of the Universe and made the first sociogram , the sociogram of the Godhead." (Moreno, 2019, p. 174).

I tried the sociometric system first on the cosmos. God was a super sociometrist. The genesis of sociometry was the metric universe of God's creation, the science of "theometry". What I know of sociometry I learned first from my speculations and experiments on a religious and axiological plane. (Moreno, 2019, p. 28)

In these quotes from his autobiography, we can see the influence of his spirituality on the development of his thinking about sociometry and society. He goes on to say that in addition to sociometry, "the genesis of psychodrama was closely related to the genesis of the Godhead " (Moreno, 2019, p. 25). The impact of his philosophy of human nature and the universe is inseparable from the methods of sociometry and psychodrama. Zerka Moreno, in her memoir *To Dream Again*, echoes J. L.'s philosophical view when stating, "our instruments are basically spiritual and existential, pointing to and supporting the value of the human spirit" (2012, p. 515). She goes on to indicate that "we are more than biological, economical, sociological, or psychological creatures, that we are first of all cosmic beings" (2012, p. 40). And, "instead of looking at mankind as a fallen being, everyone is a potential genius and like the Supreme Being, co-responsible for all of mankind" (Moreno, 2012, p. 295).

The conceptualization of all people as Gods or geniuses requires a stance that all people are co-responsible and capable of contributing to the enhancement of the world. Moreno thought of humans as auxiliary egos for God and his work in the cosmos—"there is so much misery and suffering in the world, even God seems unable to heal it all alone, so we must share responsibility." (Moreno, 1989, p. 6) Moreno, in the final section of his autobiography describes the cosmic man as:

> A man who is warmed up to himself - to act in accordance with his own moods or designs, unwilling to act by any other law beside his inner voice. He is an individual who is close to all beings, not really apart from them but with them and within them, involved with all men, animals and plants. He believes himself to be a part of the universe and not a member of a family or clan. Everyone is a brother or partner to him, - he does not make any distinction between rich or poor, black or white, man or woman. Everyone is his friend and he wants to help everybody. (2019, p. 339)

Many parallels can be drawn between this description of the cosmic man and a description of a social worker who inherently is motivated to speak difficult truths, to treat all as equals, to prevent injustice and discrimination based on difference, and to help as many people as possible.

4.3 The Encounter Symbol and Autonomous Healing Center

Moreno described the presence of a first universe "which contains all beings and in which all events are sacred" (Moreno, 2019, p. 27) as opposed to the second universe of form, space, and time. It is at the encounter of these two universes that the human being exists (see Fig. 4.2). His philosophy suggests that there is "primordial nature which is immortal and returns afresh with every generation," (Moreno, 2019, p. 27) that the spirit or soul of an infant emerges from the first universe into the second universe through the birth experience. He describes the first few years of an infant's life as existing within the matrix of identity where no sense of self is realized and the infant is one with all (Moreno, 1953). Through the course of socialization and psychosocial development, humans become more integrated within the second universe while experiencing glimpses of the first universe or cosmic reality. Moreno envisioned the surplus reality of psychodrama as an avenue for accessing and living within the first universe and that upon death one returns to this first universe (Moreno, 2012).

Fig. 4.2 The encounter model

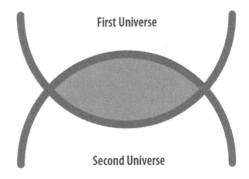

First Universe

Second Universe

In Morenean philosophy , this component of human nature is called the *autonomous healing center* . The Morenos described the activation of one's autonomous healing center as a process that happens quietly within the body, deep within the self, and that it is initiated through action not mere words (Moreno, 2012). Zerka later states explicitly that the intention of all forms of therapy should be to help the client tap into their autonomous healing center and find their own path (2012).

Just as each individual is seen as containing an autonomous healing center , the Godhead within, Moreno also believed every group, community, and even society itself to have an autonomous healing center within and the capacity to heal itself if accessed. All of Moreno's group methods and instruments are mutual aid processes focused on cultivating the power of group members healing and helping each other—or in other words, the group accessing its autonomous healing center which exists within the interpersonal sociometry and collective consciousness of the group (Giacomucci, 2019).

How would our work look if we treated each human as God with the capacity to heal themselves and each group as already possessing everything it needs to self-heal?

The role demand and expectation that this belief puts on others empower them to access their spontaneity and creativity to heal themselves and resolve their own problems. This is essentially the role of the social worker and the role of the psychodramatist.

4.4 Spontaneity–Creativity Theory

J. L. Moreno 's spontaneity –creativity theory is the theory of change within Morenean philosophy and psychodrama as a therapeutic approach. Prior to his medical training, Moreno studied theology and philosophy with the intent of developing a religion (see the Religion of Encounter in Nolte, 2014) and was described by many as a mystic. In defining his concept of the *Godhead* , he described its most defining quality as the function as creator—its creativity. Thus, he believed that the ability to create something new—art, music, an idea, a new response, a child—was inherently godlike (Moreno, 1921, 2019). At the same time, Moreno suggested that as a culture we overemphasized the products of creation without giving attention to the process of the creative act itself. He believed both spontaneity and creativity to be foremost spiritual qualities and emphasized the 'godlikeness' of all humans (Moreno, 2019). He writes that "spontaneity is the constant companion of creativity. It is the existential factor 'intervening' for creative processes to be released" (1956, p. 103). For Moreno, the twin principles of spontaneity–creativity are the ultimate force underpinning all human progress and all human activity (Nolte, 2014). He defined spontaneity as the ability to "respond with some degree of adequacy to a new situation or with some degree of novelty to an old situation" (Moreno, 1964, p xii).

He also identified "forms of pathological spontaneity that distort perceptions, dissociate the enactment of roles, and interfere with their integration on the various levels of living" (Moreno, 1964, p. xii); one might think of pathological spontaneity as a novel response without adequacy (Dayton, 2005). He believed that emotional or psychological problems were either related to a lack of healthy spontaneity or some type of pathological spontaneity. Furthermore, he observed that anxiety and spontaneity are inversely proportional in that as one increases, the other decreases— "Anxiety sets in because there is spontaneity missing, not because 'there is anxiety', and spontaneity dwindles because anxiety rises" (1953, p. 337). This observation was later confirmed through quantitative research on panic disorder and spontaneity (Tarashoeva, Marinova-Djambazova, & Kojuharov, 2017).

Interestingly, Daniel Siegel 's definition of health and wellness seems to reflect Moreno's spontaneity theory decades later. Siegel suggests that all mental illness and social dysfunction are a result of too much chaos or too much rigidity—and that a state of health exists at the balance between these two extremes (Siegel, 2010). In Morenean philosophy , chaos is a function of pathological spontaneity , and rigidity is a function of the lack of spontaneity. Moreno argues that spontaneity is essentially an indicator of health and the ability to respond with competence.

J. L. Moreno described the *warming up process* as essential for the generation of spontaneity —"spontaneity is generated in action whenever an organism is found in the process of warming-up" (1956, p. 110). While spontaneity is associated with the *readiness* of the creative act, creativity is associated with the *act* itself. The created product, after the moment it is produced, is no longer spontaneous; this is referred to as a *cultural conserve* . J. L. Moreno developed a visual chart, the Canon of Creativity (1953) to visualize the creative process and depict his theory of spontaneity–creativity (see Fig. 4.3). It is through this process that all intrapsychic, interpersonal, and social change takes place.

4.5 The Moment, the Situation, and the Here-and-Now

Moreno emphasized the here-and-now and the sacredness of the moment. Action, spontaneity , and creativity are only accessible in the here-and-now. The present moment has a different type of quality and is the bridge between the past and the future. Moreno's philosophy considers the past as "memory-in-the-moment of past experiences" and the future as "here and now anticipation-in-the-moment of what might be eventually experienced" (Nolte, 2020, p. 131). The present is a transition between past and future. When spontaneity and creativity are accessed in the present, new dynamic meaning is created which transforms the *present* into a *moment* (Moreno & Moreno, 1969). In psychodrama, the protagonist puts a scene into action in the here-and-now as if it was currently happening. The protagonist's subjective truth is honored and enacted on the psychodrama stage. Zerka Moreno notes that the concretization of an old event in the here-and-now of psychodrama allows one to find a new truth from an old event (1994).

Moreno's existential philosophy positions each moment and each situation as an opportunity for change through spontaneity and creative action. In this way,

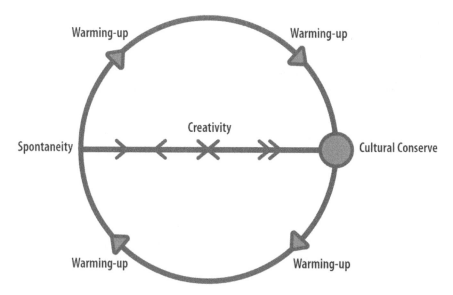

Fig. 4.3 Canon of creativity, depicting the warming up process and the relationship between spontaneity, creativity, and the cultural conserve

each human is an initiator, a creator, and an active agent in the world rather than a victim of predeterminism. Psychodrama provides one with the opportunity to revisit moments of the past and enact another possibility; or to fast forward time in the here-and-now to experience a moment yet to come. Psychodrama allows one to become unchained from their reality and experience the freedom of creating a new drama through surplus reality (Moreno, 1946).

> At first sight it looks as if the psychodramatic function and the reality function would exclude one another. This is in fact only an outward appearance, the stage is not a stage in a theatrical sense, it is a social platform, the actors are not actors but actual people and they do not "act" but present their own selves. (Moreno, 1943, p. 333)

Human beings are fundamentally meaning makers—psychodrama is used to explore, deconstruct, and construct meaning through the creative process in action (Oudijk, 2007). Moreno operated from a postmodern framework as evidenced by psychodrama's emphasis on the perspective of the protagonist (Blatner, 2000). In enacting a psychodrama scene, the protagonist portrays the scene, the roles, and the action *from their perspective*—Moreno even held to this principle when working with psychotic and schizophrenic patients providing them with a space to literally act out their fantasies and realities. He emphasized the importance of meeting the client where they were at and in the here-and-now .

4.6 Action Theory

J.L. Moreno believed that we were all improvising actors in the play of life that each human was an auxiliary ego for one another (Moreno, 2013). He integrated aspects of theater to create psychodrama, believing that "what was learned in action, must be unlearned in action" (Dayton, 2005, p. xxvii). The very term *psychodrama* means "Psyche in action" (Carnabucci, 2014). He believed in the power of action to create change and challenged Freud 's "talking cure". In encountering Freud at the University of Vienna, J. L. Moreno exclaimed:

> Dr. Freud , I start where you leave off. You meet people in the artificial setting of your office. I meet them on the street and in their homes, in their natural surroundings. You analyzed their dreams; I try to give them courage to dream again. (J. L. Moreno, Z. T. Moreno, & J. D. Moreno, 1964, pp. 16–17).

Psychodrama is one of the first body-oriented forms of psychotherapy, moving beyond just words and narrative (Carnabucci & Ciotola, 2013). J. L. Moreno 's action theory rests on the idea that talking alone severely limits the client–therapists' ability to explore an issue or produce change. "However important verbal behavior is, *the act is prior to the word* and 'includes' it" (Moreno, 1955, p. 17). Zerka Moreno later states that "even when interpretation is given, action is primary. There can be no interpretation without previous action" (1965, p. 77).

Neuroscience research has demonstrated that we are "beings of action and the stories of our lives are literally written on our neural systems" (Dayton, 2005, p. 55). It has been declared by the neuroscientists thast experience changes the brain and has the corrective potential to reverse the impact of previous adverse experiences (Cozolino, 2014; Siegel, 2012). The surplus reality of psychodrama offers possibilities for corrective emotional experiences that would have been otherwise impossible (Giacomucci, 2018c; Giacomucci & Stone, 2019).

Action theory is complimentary with experiential learning theories which have become embedded within social work education . Experiential education proposes an embodied learning experience where the teaching content is interfaced with in action rather than simply talked about. Moreno was inspired by John Dewey , the father of experiential education , and even proposed his own *Spontaneity Theory of Learning* (1949) which emphasized spontaneity training in education rather than memorizing facts or information. Moreno's action-based education ideas reflect those of Freire (2013), as well as Kolb & Kolb who describe the approach as "an integrative approach to learning that balances feeling, thinking, acting and reflecting" (Kolb & Kolb, 2005, p. 200). Social work education describes its *signature pedagogy* as the field placement experience which is essentially an experiential learning structure emphasizing role training (Giacomucci, 2019).

4.7   Role Theory

Moreno's ·theory of personality is based on role theory (Telias, 2018). The term *role* does not originate from sociology , psychology , or psychiatry , but instead comes from the theater . In ancient Greek and Roman drama productions, an actor's character or lines would often be written on "rolls" and memorized. J. L. Moreno claims that role theory transcended the limitations of psychoanalysis and behaviorism with a systematic exploration of social phenomenon, thus serving as a major bridge between psychiatry and the social sciences (1961). The concept of the role integrates cognitive, affective, and behavioral states for simple categorization (Buchanan, 1984) while demystifying psychiatric labels and connecting them with the client's experience of self (Hudgins, 2002).

J. L. Moreno viewed each human being as a role-player (Fox, 1987). He states that the self, or the personality, is composed of all the roles that one plays in their life— "roles do not emerge from the self, but the self emerges from roles" (1953, p. 76). He outlines three categories of roles—somatic, psychodramatic, and social roles . Somatic roles develop first, in the preverbal stages of life, and represent physical or bodily aspects of the self—including eater, breather, sleeper, crawler, etc. Later, psychodramatic and social roles develop—but all three types of roles are intimately connected. Psychodramatic roles , or roles played out in the psyche, represent the internal dimensions of the self—the thinker, feeler, fantasizer, dreamer, etc. And, finally social roles , which are embedded within a cultural context, are the roles that we hold in relationship to others and society, such as father, sister, teacher, and student. (Moreno, 1934). Moreno writes that the collection of all of one's somatic or physiological roles equals their somatic or physiological self. Similarly, the cluster of all of one's psychodramatic roles and social roles represent their psychodramatic self and social self. These three clusters of roles allow an individual to fully experience their body, psyche, and society (Moreno, 1972).

> Operational and contact links must gradually develop between the social, the psycholog-
> ical, the physiological role clusters in order that we can identify and experience after their
> unification, that which we call the "me" or the "I"... Body, psyche, and society are then the
> intermediary parts of the entire self. (Moreno, 1972, p. III–IV)

In this way, Moreno's role theory is inherently a biopsychosocial-spiritual conceptualization of self which fits nicely within the social work philosophy framing an individual within a larger social context.

Furthermore, he outlines three stages of role-development , beginning with *role-taking* or *role training* . In this phase, an individual is learning a new role and the process of stepping into the role including working through any ambivalence about the role and connecting with role models. Once a culturally conserved role is learned, it is *role-played*. During the role-playing stage of development, an individual starts to naturally bring parts of themselves to the role. The final stage of development is that of *role creation* , which describes the process of transforming the once learned role into a new, unique role (Dayton, 2005). This process of role creation or role transformation often bring one back to the role-taking stage as they learn to hold the newly created role.

Role theory proposes that an individual with a wide role repertoire, or the ability to adequately transition to diverse roles based on the situational context (spontaneity) will demonstrate healthy personality and social functioning (Fox, 1987). Role theory provides a non-pathologizing alternative to traditional theories of personality and psychopathology. For example, J. L. Moreno conceptualized regression as a type of role-playing :

> In a paranoiac behavior, the repertory of roles is reduced to distorted acting in a single role. The deviate is unable to carry out a role in situ. He either overplays or underplays the part; inadequate perception is combined with distorted enactment. Histrionic neurosis of actors is due to the intervention of role fragments "alien" to the role personality of the actor. (1961, p. 521)

This passage points to his understanding of roles as being in ascendance or descendance based on how much, or how little, one has developed the role and how accessible the role is to the ego. "The ego must have roles in which to operate" (Hale, 1981, p. 8).

As role-players, we do not exist in social isolation—instead, each of our roles develops and exists in relationship with others. Roles are linked to counter-roles demonstrating the phenomenon of *role reciprocity* . "There are no parents without children, no teachers without students, no therapists without clients, no slaves without masters, etc. In other words, we are all inter-actors with one another" (Moreno, 2013, p. 38). Role reciprocity emphasizes the person-in-environment perspective by conceptualizing roles, or aspects of self, as inherently in relation to others. In a future Sect. (5.4), the cultural atom will be presented as a diagram of role relationships between an individual and their social circle.

4.8 Developmental Theory

Moreno's philosophy includes its own unique developmental theory and stages of development which reflect and guide the interventions used in a psychodrama enactment. The developmental theory is intricately linked to Morenean philosophy of human nature and the cosmic man—this link is explicit in article 27 of the Quintessential Zerka titled *The Eight Stages of Cosmic Being in Terms of Capacity and Need to Double and Role Reverse* (2006). As noted previously, Moreno suggested that an infant is given birth into this world from the first universe and exists in a state of undifferentiated identity. In the first few weeks after birth, infants live within the *matrix of identity* during which they experience themselves as one with not only their mothers, but all objects and their surroundings (1952). Through appropriate doubling , mirroring , and role reversal , the child develops a sense of self and a sense of others.

Doubling is the first stage of J. L. Moreno 's psychodramatic development theory . Zerka Moreno (2006) indicates that doubling is essential to healthy attachment in that the caregivers put words to what is unspoken and unlabeled for the non-verbal infant (as cited in Hudgins & Toscani, 2013). In this developmental stage, doubling creates a holding environment for the infant (or client) to feel seen and understood from the inside out (Dayton, 2005). This stage of development is characterized by the significance of attachment between infant and caregiver(s) and sets the framework for the infant's ability to self-regulate in the future (Cozolino, 2014). Dayton outlines the importance of attachment from J. L. Moreno 's developmental theory in the following passage:

> If the parent is an attuned 'double' for the child's experience, the child feels a sense of place and belonging. If, on the other hand, she leaves the infant to a world without doubling , the child may feel that he is incomprehensible to others and a sort of fissure may occur within the self due to feeling misunderstood or out of sync with his external representations of self since, from a child's point of view, parents and some siblings are part of his own self. (2005, p. 161)

In this first developmental stage, doubling is essential for the healthy formation of identity. If the mother's attempts to double and meet the needs of the infant are inaccurate, the infant will surely let her know through non-verbal communication. In a similar way, the protagonist will correct inaccurate doubling statements from other group members—thus strengthening their ego identity. The double intervention, or role, in a psychodrama helps with the exploration of the inner reality of the protagonist and serves as a bridge between the director and protagonist (Hudgins & Toscani, 2013; Moreno, 2006).

Developmentally speaking, the mirror stage is when the child begins to recognize himself as a separate individual (Moreno, 1952). This stage, which starts around nine months of age, includes the infant's capacity for "joint attention" and "secondary intersubjectivity" (Dayton, 2005). The infant is now able to shift attention between person and object by aligning their visual attention with their caregiver's, thus beginning to develop awareness of a shared, but separate experience (Hobson, 1989; Trevarthen, 1998). This is, as Dayton states: "the dawning of an awareness of self as differentiated from the world outside the self" (2005, p. 163).

Moreno's developmental theory outlines *role reversal* as the third phase. One does not have the ability to reverse roles until they have first established a basic sense of self. An infant in a previous stage of development, before about the age of two or three, will not have this capacity, though most adults do (Moreno, et al., 1955). J. L., Zerka , and Jonathan Moreno published an article about the use of role reversal to aid in raising a child and emphasizing its therapeutic potential. Role reversal resembles the process of separation and individualization outlined by Mahler, Pine, and Bergman (1975). This stage of development represents a true sense of separateness and the ability to empathize with others. It is a state of intersubjectivity, being in relationship with dual awareness of one's self and the other within a dynamic relationship (Dayton, 2005). "In role reversal the sense of self is intact enough so that we can temporarily leave it, stand in the shoes of another, and return safely home" (Dayton, 2005, p. 439). Through psychologically role reversing with others, the child develops a greater responsibility for their actions, for their self, and enhances their capacity for empathy with others in the social world.

As the child progresses into adulthood, the parent continues to double and role reverse with them to achieve separation and independence. The adult child then becomes an auxiliary for the aging parent who is declining in health and preparing to reenter the cosmos (Moreno, 2006). Now, the caregiver roles have reversed, and the adult child is doubling and role reversing the parent as they live out their final years in the second universe and fully transition back into the first universe.

4.9 Biopsychosocial-Spiritual Existence

Most credit the development of the biopsychosocial approach to George Engel in the late 1970s. Nevertheless, Moreno had written of the biopsychosocial contexts of individual experience, relationships, and society decades prior in *Who Shall Survive?* (1953). In discussing his sociometric system and the distribution of choice, preference, and connection within groups, he writes: "these attractions and repulsions must be related to an index of biological, social, and psychological facts" (1953, p. 611). While traditional conceptualizations of human nature place the psyche within the body, Moreno argues that the psyche exists outside of the body.

> The biological picture of an individual places the psyche within the body (as an epi phenomenon). In the sociometric picture of the individual (person), the psyche appears as outside the body, the body is surrounded by the psyche and the psyche is surrounded by and interwoven into the social and cultural atoms. (Moreno, 1943, p. 319)

He argues that the traditional perspective is that feelings emerge within the individual organism and are projected toward others in the social environment. His conceptualization of human beings challenges this idea and instead suggests that the psyche largely emerges and is influenced by social relationships and social forces. Figure 4.4 depicts the interconnectedness of body, psyche, social, and cultural in Moreno's philosophy. The direction of influence travels from the larger culture and social forces to the interpersonal relations which impact the development of the psyche and the body. The same image depicts the direction of influence for cultural change beginning within the body moving to the psyche and relational to impact the larger social and cultural structure. This framework (see Fig. 4.4), outlining the relationships between the body, psyche, social, and cultural, makes clear the necessity of involving the body in the therapeutic process.

Modern neuroscience offers us further insight into the potential of understanding the body as engulfed within the psyche. The work of Bessel van der Kolk (2014), Levine (2010), Perry (2006), and Cozolino (2014) point to the significant impact of psychological and relational trauma upon the body and the nervous system. We now know that psychological trauma and relational adversity, especially in childhood, creates lasting imprints in non-verbal and primal parts of the body and brain. The trauma healing process in most contemporary trauma therapies involves the body within the intervention as an essential vehicle for creating psychological and relational change. The field of interpersonal neurobiology highlights the interdependence

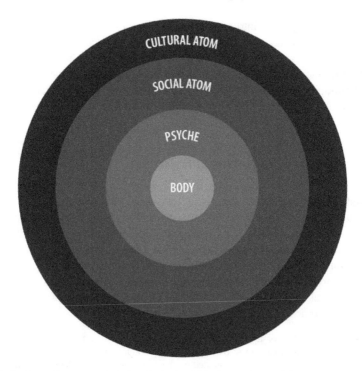

Fig. 4.4 Sociometric concept depicting the body within the psyche, social atom, and cultural atom

of brain, psyche, and social relationships especially as it relates to the developing brain. Moreno's role theory even explicitly articulates the presence of a physiological self, psychodramatic self, and social self (1972). Previously accepted psychotherapy approaches focused solely on healing the psyche and isolating the mind from the body, the social, and the cultural—most would accept this way of working as faulty today. It is fitting to credit the social work profession for promoting an understanding of the psyche–social–cultural influence as it relates to the core values of social justice and the centrality of relationships.

There is more unknown than known when it comes to the brain–mind relationship and thus the body–psyche relationship. New neuroscience findings give us an enhanced, but still incomplete, understanding of the entire picture. In future decades, our knowledge of the position of the body and the psyche will become more evident and clearer. Most recently, Wang and Liu (2020) published an article in a Chinese social work journal emphasizing the complimentary nature between social work with Moreno's emphasis on (1) the goodness of each person, (2) the importance of relationships , and (3) the structure of society.

Fig. 4.5 Social work core values

4.10 Social Work Values Relationship to Moreno's Work

Social work philosophy and Morenean philosophy have many shared values and elements. The field of social work upholds six distinct core values—importance of relationships , dignity and worth of each human being, social justice , service, competence, and integrity (see Fig. 4.5). These six social work values are echoed throughout the body of Moreno's work, his philosophy, and his 1957 *Code of Ethics of Group Psychotherapists*.

4.11 The Importance and Centrality of Relationships

This is a shared core value that makes both social work and Moreno's work unique. This core value was key for social work's differentiation process in relation to the field of psychology . While the psychologists were more focused on the individual and the internal drives, feelings, and thoughts of the individual, social work positioned itself emphasizing the relationships of the individual within their social environment. Similarly, Morenean philosophy developed with emphasis on the sociodynamics of interpersonal relationships, in opposition to psychoanalysis which was oriented on the individual's psychodynamics. Truedley (1944) goes as far as writing that psychodrama "often does succeed in treating the relationship rather than the individual" (p. 171).

While the traditional psychologist conducts Rorschach tests and diagnostic assessments, the social worker assists the client in drawing genograms and ecomaps, and the psychodramatist facilitates the production of social atoms , sociograms , and role diagrams. The differences in assessment tools utilized between from the start of treatment demonstrate the philosophical variations between fields. The social worker and psychodramatist are assessing the person in their environment because of the fields' philosophical emphasis and value of relationships. The fact that the development of the social atom assessment (Moreno, 1934) preceded the emergence of the genogram and ecomap in the 1970s-80s (Hartman, 1978; McGoldrick, Gerson, & Petry, 2008) has caused some to argue that Moreno's work had a larger influence than he is given credit for. Schwinger (2016) highlights the social atom as a useful tool for the field of social work. While the psychologist and analyst exclusively met with clients in their offices, social workers and psychodramatists emphasized the importance of meeting clients within their communities and neighborhoods.

The therapeutic relationship occupies a central component in social work philosophy , while psychology and psychoanalysis place less emphasis on use of self and the here-and-now relationship in the office. Psychoanalysis and psychology seem to emphasize the therapeutic relationship as it relates to transference and projection much less than the here-and-now relational experience. Psychodrama and sociometry are inherently here-and-now approaches in that even when the past is being explored, it is often done so through enactments where everyone acts as if it were happening in the here-and-now. The social worker and the psychodramatist seem much more likely to utilize self-disclosure and use of self than a traditional psychoanalyst or psychologist. Moreno advocates for the importance of the therapeutic relationship in the following quote, "I believe that the doctor's warmth and caring, the touch of his hand, his compassion for his patients are the most decisive elements in a doctor's success or failure in treating people" (2019, p. 238).

The importance of relationships is also considered from a macro and mezzoapproach in social work and Morenean philosophy in that both also concern themselves with a larger picture of social groupings, social networks , and society (Giacomucci, 2018a, b). Social work often uses the language of micro, mezzo, and macro to describe its attentions to clinical work (micro), group work (mezzo), and community work (macro). Similarly, Moreno's triadic and sociatric system attends to each level in that psychodrama enacts an individual's experience (micro), group psychotherapy is group work (mezzo), and sociometry and sociatry offer approaches to community work and society (macro). The attention given to each of these three domains is unique to social work and Moreno's methods. The psychology and counseling fields have integrated more focus on relationships in contemporary times; however, they remain almost entirely micro/mezzoapproaches in that they are only concerned with the impact of society and social forces upon their clients. Other macrophilosophies exist in sociology , anthropology, and philosophy; however, they remain overly focused on society at the macrolevel without intervention at the micro or mezzospheres. Both social work and Morenean philosophies integrate micro, mezzo, and macroperspectives as they take into consideration the impact of society on the individual clients they treat while also concerning themselves with intervening and creating change on a larger societal level. Blatner (2000) writes that Moreno saw individual and social psychology as inseparable and that healing had to be oriented not only at "those in the 'sick role' but equally to the cultural matrix which often revealed its own pathological features" (p. 77). Few other fields are driven by philosophies as encompassing and integrative as social work and Morenean philosophy.

In addition to the macro and microconnections, social work and Morenean philosophies place much more emphasis on the mezzoaspect of group work than other fields. As noted previously (see Sect. 2.2), mainstream group work essentially aligned itself with the social work profession (Andrews, 2001; Trecker, 1944). Although social work's emphasis on group work has declined tremendously, some graduate social work degree programs offer concentrations in group work, unlike master's degrees of psychology , counseling , or marriage and family therapy . Moreno's philosophy embedded within his triadic system of sociometry, psychodrama, and group psychotherapy which explicitly aligns itself with group work.

Moreno's philosophy of group work perceives each group member to possess therapeutic power and agency—the ability to contribute to the healing of other group members. Social workers refer to this as mutual aid (Northen & Kurland, 2001; Steinberg, 2010). Moreno's *Code of Ethics for Group Psychotherapists* (1957) suggests that because not only the physician has therapeutic agency, but that it resides with each group member—that the *Hippocratic Oath* extends to each group participant. He writes specifically in terms of each participant upholding the ethical principles of confidentiality, do no harm , and contributing to the welfare of the group. This principle within his code of ethics formalizes and concretizes commitments to the centrality of mutual aid relationships, dismantling the power dynamic within the therapist–patient relationship, and honoring the dignity and worth of each human being.

4.11.1 Dignity and Worth of Each Human Being

Unique to both social work with groups and psychodrama is the emphasis on mutual aid (Giacomucci, 2019, 2020b). For both social group workers and psychodramatists, the goal of the facilitator is to help participants to support, heal, and educate each other. Other fields implicitly emphasize the therapeutic power of the professional, while social workers and psychodramatists explicitly emphasize the therapeutic potential within each group member. The mutual aid approach cannot operate without placing considerable value in each individual's strengths, dignity, and worth.

Both fields began with a focus entirely on working with the most oppressed, stigmatized, and vulnerable populations; in doing so, they demonstrated their value of acknowledging and enhancing the recognized worth and dignity of each person regardless of their race, ethnicity, culture, country of origin, religion, gender, sexuality, social status, physical ability, finances, and other histories. Social workers advocate for society's outcasts and underserved, believing in their inherent worth. Moreno went as far as elevating the dignity and worth of each person to that of a potential genius with the Godhead within (2019). Psychodrama's emphasis on helping a client access their autonomous healing center is based on the belief that each individual has the power and capacity to solve their own problems and heal themselves. Moreno's (1957) code of ethics states that group psychotherapists are expected "to render service to groups of patients with full respect for the dignity of every patient" (p. 143).

Empowerment is an unspoken value that social workers and psychodramatists demonstrate through their work based on their faith in the worth of others. Both fields, though forced to work within the medicalized mental health industry, attempt to avoid and even challenge pathologizing norms and practices. The valued dignity and worth of each person is strongly related to social work's commitment to social justice .

4.11.2 Social Justice

Some argue that this is the value that significantly differentiates social workers from other mental health practitioners, including psychologists, counselors, and marriage and family therapists. Social workers attempt to avoid falling into the trap of only helping their clients adjust to social injustice and instead work to change unjust policies and systems that are causing many of the interpersonal and psychological problems that clients present with. The NASW Code of Ethics states that "Social workers are cognizant of their dual responsibility to clients and to the broader society" (2017, p. 6). Jacob Moreno , originally trained as a psychiatrist, developed a socially just vision of *Sociatry* —or "healing for society" (Moreno, 2019). He wrote that "a truly therapeutic procedure must have no less objective than the whole of mankind" (Moreno, 1953, p. 1)—suggesting that seeing clients in an individual or group setting was not enough. Moreno envisioned a therapeutic society and worked to create tools that had the potential for societal change including using the theater , radio, film, and music.

J. L. Moreno 's own experiences as a Jewish man, a refugee in Europe, and an immigrant to the United States likely impacted his sense of social justice . He writes in his autobiography about how the discrimination he experienced as a Jew influenced him to create his own professional society. Moreno, along with his colleagues, developed *Ethnodrama* as an approach to resolving ethnic problems. Moreno's methods are inherently aligned with social constructionism and postmodern theory in that they consider the client and the group to be the experts of their experience. Rather than attempt to convince others of an objective reality or truth, the psychodramatist puts into action the subjective truth of the protagonist or the collective truth of the group. Heinonen, Halonen, and Krahn (2018) note that, "As social workers (or representatives of any other professional discipline), expressive artforms such as psychodrama can also support us in deconstructing our own cultural location and its historical legacies, which may be unconsciously influencing our relationships with others" (p. 14). Through the integration of anti-oppressive frameworks and psychodrama, Nieto (2010) proposes a new approach to practice in an anti-oppressive and culturally-informed way.

Moreno's methods have been absorbed into community work , community organizing , social activism, and cultural diversity work (see Chaps. 18 and 19). Many community organizers and activists use sociometry processes such as the spectrogram, step-in sociometry , and locograms, as well as role-playing techniques or simulations to empower the communities that they work with or promote social change. Some of this integration may have been influenced by Boal's *Theater of the Oppressed* (1985) or *Playback Theater* (Salas, 1993) both of which emphasize a social justice approach and share considerable philosophical and practical overlap with z's work (Landy, 2008) (see Sects. 15.5.2 and 15.5.3). Interestingly, it seems that psychodramatists in the United States are, as a whole, more focused on therapeutic applications while psychodramatists of other countries are also oriented on social justice and community applications.

Social group workers are expected to use a social justice framework to contextualize their group work experience and create a fair and just group experience for each participant. Similarly, Moreno writes in his code of ethics for group psychotherapists that "therapeutic groups should be so organized that they represent a model of democratic behavior. Regardless of the economic, racial, and religious differences of the patients they should be given "equality of status" inside the therapeutic group" (1957, p. 143). Without this objective, our groups will simply reenact the systems of oppression, discrimination, privilege, and social injustice that exist within the larger society because of the sociodynamic effect. From a Morenean perspective, group workers are expected to prioritize the active reversal of the sociodynamic effect within the groups they facilitate. Both social workers and psychodramatists emphasize their role as being of service to individuals, groups, communities, and society (Niepenberg, 2017).

4.11.3 Service

The NASW Code of Ethics describes the core value of service stating "social workers' primary goal is to help people in need and to address social problems" (2017, p. 5). Many social workers provide psychotherapy and operate as *therapists*—a word that has ancient Greek etymological roots meaning "service" (Wronka, 2016). Being in service to individuals and to society is an explicit mission of all social workers. Social workers provide services in a variety of contexts including psychotherapy services, child and family services, government services, military services, prison services, medical services, case management services, organizational services, educational services, research services, social services, and policy services. The social worker is one who is in service to individuals, groups, families, organizations, communities, and society. Similarly, Moreno writes that.

"the world at large needed a doctor more urgently than the sickest individual... I began to think in earnest that I had a special mission, that there was an important service to be rendered to the world, and that there was no reason why I shouldn't undertake that mission. (2019, p. 233)

Moreno challenges psychodramatists to be of service not only to their clients or groups, but also to the society as a whole—to be world therapists. Of all the professions, the field of social work is most closely related to the praxis of serving the world and operating as world therapists.

4.11.4 Competence

This core value dictates that social workers practice within their area of competence and training. The NASW Code of Ethics states "social workers practice within their areas of competence and develop and enhance their professional expertise" (2017, p. 7). In order to practice competently, one must be aware of their strengths and limitations, as well as personal issues that may impact professional competence.

Licensure and certification are designed to be stamps of competence for practitioners who have completed extensive training, supervision, and practice requirements. In the United States, the process of becoming a licensed clinical social worker takes several years between degree programs and post-graduate practice under supervision. Similarly, the American Board of Examiners in sociometry, psychodrama, and group psychotherapy offers certification after rigorous training, supervision, and practice. The entry level psychodrama certification requires a graduate degree, 780 training hours, a year of supervised practice, a written exam, and an on-site examination. These requirements generally take many years to fulfill which helps to ensure the competency of the practitioner.

Most social workers are expected to facilitate groups in their careers with little or no education in group work through their degree programs. The lack of group work training for social workers makes social workers' level of competence in facilitating groups questionable. Pursuing training in sociometry, psychodrama, and group psychotherapy fills the gaps in group work competencies for social workers. In the past decade, it seems that the Council on Social Work Education has given more attention to the core value of competency by adopting a new "competency-based framework" for Education Policy and Accreditation Standards (EPAS) (CSWE , 2015). The new EPAS standards outline the nine social work competencies (see Fig. 4.6).

Competencies 6–9 focus on social workers' relationships to "individuals, families, groups, organizations, and communities" through engagement (competency 6), assessment (competency 7), intervention (competency 8), and evaluation (competency 9). Unfortunately, there is little to no differentiation offered by the CSWE when it comes to each of these competencies and the differences between engaging

COMPETENCY 1 Demonstrate Ethical and Professional Behavior	COMPETENCY 2 Engage Diversity and Difference in Practice	COMPETENCY 3 Advance Human Rights and Social, Economic, and Environmental Justice
COMPETENCY 4 Engage In Practice-informed Research and Research-informed Practice	COMPETENCY 5 Engage in Policy Practice	COMPETENCY 6 Engage with Individuals, Families, Groups, Organizations, and Communities
COMPETENCY 7 Assess Individuals, Families, Groups, Organizations, and Communities	COMPETENCY 8 Intervene with Individuals, Families, Groups, Organizations, and Communities	COMPETENCY 9 Evaluate Practice with Individuals, Families, Groups, Organizations, and Communities

Fig. 4.6 Coucil on social work education's (CSWE) nine competencies outlined in the educational policy and accreditation standards (EPAS)

(assessing, intervening, or evaluating) with individuals, families, groups, organizations, and communities. The knowledge, skills, and approaches to engaging individuals are quite different than those needed to engage groups or communities. It seems that the lack of differentiation between approaches to individual work and work with groups is perpetuated by the new CSWE EPAS. If we are to increase the group work competence level of social workers, we must differentiate individual work (psychodynamics) from group work (sociodynamics). The practices of group-as-a-whole engagement, assessment, intervention, and evaluation simply require different knowledge, understanding, and competencies than working with individuals. Moreno's (1957) code of ethics explicitly states that the designation group psychotherapist should not be used by anyone unless they have obtained specialized formal training in group therapy .

The ability to uphold social work's value of competence requires one to demonstrate humility and an awareness of their scope of practice and the areas outside their scope of practice. Attempting to work outside the scope of one's knowledge and skill set is a violation of this value and potentially harmful for clients. The value of competence is also closely related to social work's final core value of integrity.

4.11.5 Integrity

Social workers are expected to uphold the core value of integrity in all that they do including working in a trustworthy manner. Interestingly, in Aristotle 's philosophical system, integrity is presented as the glue that holds together all the other virtues or values (Banks, 2012). NASW Code of Ethics state that "social workers are continually aware of the profession's mission, values, ethical principles, and ethical standards and practice in a manner consistent with them" (2017, p. 6). Maintaining professional integrity requires a social worker to uphold the values and mission of the field.

Banks (2004) writes that "'Integrity' is literally about 'wholeness'" and has multiple layers including moral integrity, professional integrity, personal integrity, and intellectual integrity (p. 22). Banks touch upon the idea of integrity for the social worker as being related to integrating a personal identity and professional identity with congruent values. For many, social work is a vocation or a calling which allows for unity between personal and professional life. In a similar way, Moreno hoped his methods would be experienced as a way of life rather than just a therapy practice (Moreno, 2012). The experiential learning process one undertakes to become certified as a psychodramatist requires extensive experience and participation in psychodramas. In order to become a psychodramatist, one is expected to engage in their own personal work through the experiential training process. For both the social worker and the psychodramatist, the personal and the professional are married.

4.11.6 Conclusion

Morenean philosophy and social work philosophy exist with considerable overlap. The emergence of both fields took place around the same historical time and in similar sociocultural contexts. Both philosophical systems are rooted in and influenced by postmodernism, social constructionism, and existentialism. The underlying philosophical framework of social work and Moreno's methods provide a basis for understanding individuals, groups, and society. Moreno's philosophy of human nature , mental illness, relationships, groups, and society have much in common with core social work philosophy . In both systems, the individual is conceptualized within their environment while considering biological, psychological, social, and cultural influences. Both systems are truly interdisciplinary or transdisciplinary in that their philosophies encompass psychology , sociology , anthropology, theology, and medicine. While Morenean and social work philosophies offer a framing of the nature of human problems, their theories offer strategies for action and intervention—which will be outlined in the following chapters.

References

Anderson, R., & Carnabucci, K. (2011). *Integrating psychodrama and systemic constellation work: New directions for action methods, mind-body therapies and energy healing*. London: Jessica Kingsley Publishers.

Andrews, J. (2001). Group work's place in social work: A historical analysis. *Journal of Sociology and Social Welfare, 28*(4), 45–65.

Baim, C. (2007). Integrating psychodrama with attachment theory: Implications for practice. In P. Holmes, M. Farrall, & K. Kirk (Eds.), *Empowering therapeutic practice: Integrating psychodrama into other therapies* (pp. 125–156). London: Jessica Kingsley Publishers.

Banks, S. (2004). Professional integrity, social work, and the ethics of distrust. *Social Work & Social Sciences Review, 11*(2), 20–35.

Banks, S. (2012). *Ethics and values in social work* (4th ed.). Basingstoke & New York: Palgrave Macmillan.

Bitel, M. C. (2000). Mixing up the Goulash: Essential ingredients in the "Art" of social group work. *Social Work with Groups, 22*(2–3), 77–99.

Blatner, A. (2000). *Foundations of psychodrama: History, theory, and practice* (4th ed.). New York City: Springer Publishing Company.

Boal, A. (1985). *Theatre of the oppressed*. New York: Theatre Communications Group.

Bradshaw-Tauvon, K. (2007). Psychodrama informed by adaptive information processing (AIP): The theory underpinning eye movement desensitization reprocessing (EMDR). In P. Holmes, M. Farrall, & K. Kirk (Eds.), *Empowering therapeutic practice: Integrating psychodrama into other therapies* (pp. 203–226). London: Jessica Kingsley Publishers.

Brown, T. M. (2007). Psychoanalysis and psychodrama. In P. Holmes, M. Farrall, & K. Kirk (Eds.), *Empowering therapeutic practice: Integrating psychodrama into other therapies* (pp. 227–250). London: Jessica Kingsley Publishers.

Buchanan, D. R. (1984). Psychodrama. In T. B. Karasu (Chair), *The psychiatric therapies*. Washington, DC: American Psychiatric Press, Inc.

Carnabucci, K. (2014). *Show and tell psychodrama: Skills for therapists, coaches, teachers, and leaders*. Racine Wisconsin: Nusanto Publishing.

Carnabucci, K., & Ciotola, L. (2013). *Healing eating disorders with psychodrama and other action methods: Beyond the silence and the fury*. London: Jessica Kingsley Publishers.

Casson, J. (2007). Scenes from a distance: Psychodrama and dramatherapy. In P. Holmes, M. Farrall, & K. Kirk (Eds.), *Empowering therapeutic practice: Integrating psychodrama into other therapies* (pp. 157–180). London: Jessica Kingsley Publishers.

Chimera, C. (2007). Passion in action: Family systems therapy and psychodrama. In P. Holmes, M. Farrall, & K. Kirk (Eds.), *Empowering therapeutic practice: Integrating psychodrama into other therapies* (pp. 83–108). London: Jessica Kingsley Publishers.

Cortes, E. (2016). *Psicodrama Freudiano: Clinica y Practica [Kindle Version]*. Antonio Luis Maldonado Cervera Publishing Retrieved from Amazon.com.

Council on Social Work Education. (2015). *Educational policy and accreditation standards for baccalaureate and master's social work programs.* The Commission on Accreditation & Commission on Educational Policy. Retrieved from CSWE.org.

Cozolino, L. J. (2014). *The neuroscience of human relationships* (2nd ed.). New York: W.W. Norton & Company.

Dayton, T. (2005). *The living stage: A step-by-step guide to psychodrama, sociometry, and experiential group therapy* . Deerfield, FL: Health Communications Inc.

Dayton, T. (2015). *NeuroPsychodrama in the treatment of relational trauma: A strength-based, experiential model for healing PTSD* . Deerfield Beach, FL: Health Communications Inc.

Figusch, Z. (2014). *The JL Moreno memorial photo album.* London: lulu.com.

Fox, J. (Ed.). (1987). *The essential Moreno: Writings on psychodrama, group method, and spontaneity by J. L. Moreno, M. D.* New York: Springer.

Freire, P. (2013). *Education for critical consciousness.* London: Bloomsbury.

Gasseau, M., & Scategni, W. (2007). Jungian psychodrama: From theoretical to creative roots. In C. Baim, Clark, J. Burmeister, & M. Maciel, Manuela (Eds.) *Psychodrama: Advances in theory and practice* (pp. 261–270). New York: Routledge/Taylor & Francis Group.

Gershoni, J. (2003). The use of structural family therapy and psychodrama: A model for a children's group. In J. Gershoni (Ed.), Psychodrama in the 21 Century: Clinical and educational applications (pp. 49–62). New York: Springer Publishing Company.

Giacomucci, S. (2017). The sociodrama of life or death: Young adults and addiction treatment. *Journal of Psychodrama, Sociometry, and Group Psychotherapy, 65*(1), 137–143. https://doi. org/https://doi.org/10.12926/0731-1273-65.1.137.

Giacomucci, S. (2018a). Social work and sociometry: An integration of theory and clinical practice. *The Pennsylvania Social Worker, 39*(1), 14–16.

Giacomucci, S. (2018b). Social work and sociometry: Integrating history, theory, and practice. In *The clinical voice.* Richboro, PA: Pennsylvania Society for Clinical Social Work.

Giacomucci, S. (2018c). The trauma survivor's inner role atom: A clinical map for post-traumatic growth. *Journal of Psychodrama, Sociometry, and Group Psychotherapy., 66*(1), 115–129.

Giacomucci, S. (2019). *Social group work in action: A sociometry, psychodrama, and experiential trauma therapy curriculum.* Doctorate in Social Work (DSW) Dissertations. 124. https://reposi tory.upenn.edu/cgi/viewcontent.cgi?article=1128&context=edissertations_sp2.

Giacomucci, S. (2020). Addiction, traumatic loss, and guilt: A case study resolving grief through psychodrama and sociometric connections. *The Arts in Psychotherapy, 67,* 101627. https://doi. org/10.1016/j.aip.2019.101627.

Giacomucci, S. (2020b). Experiential sociometry in group work: Mutual aid for the group-as-a-whole, *Social Work with Groups,* Advanced online publication. https://doi.org/https://doi.org/10. 1080/01609513.2020.1747726.

Giacomucci, S., Gera, S., Briggs, D., & Bass, K. (2018). Experiential addiction treatment: Creating positive connection through sociometry and therapeutic spiral model safety structures. *Journal of Addiction and Addictive Disorders, 5,* 17. http://doi.org/https://doi.org/10.24966/AAD-7276/ 100017.

Giacomucci, S., & Marquit, J. (2020). The effectiveness of trauma-focused psychodrama in the treatment of PTSD in inpatient substance abuse treatment. *Frontiers in Psychology, 11,* 896. https://dx.doi.org/https://doi.org/10.3389%2Ffpsyg.2020.00896.

Giacomucci, S., & Stone, A. M. (2019). Being in two places at once: Renegotiating traumatic experience through the surplus reality of psychodrama. *Social Work with Groups., 42*(3), 184–196. https://doi.org/10.1080/01609513.2018.1533913.

Hale, A. E. (1981). *Conducting clinical sociometric explorations: A manual for psychodramatists and sociometrists.* Roanoke, VA: Royal Publishing Company.

Hammond, B. (2007). Cognitive behavioural therapy and psychodrama. In P. Holmes, M. Farrall, & K. Kirk (Eds.), *Empowering therapeutic practice: Integrating psychodrama into other therapies* (pp. 109–124). London: Jessica Kingsley Publishers.

Hartman, A. (1978). Diagrammatic assessment of family relationships. *Social casework, 59*(8), 465–476.

Heinonen, T., Halonen, D., & Krahn, E. (2018). *Expressive arts for social work and social change.* Oxford University Press.

Hobson, J. A. (1989). *The dreaming brain: How the brain creates both the sense and nonsense of dreams.* New York: Basic Books Inc., Publishers.

Holmes, P. (2015). *The inner world outside: Object relations theory and psychodrama.* London: Routledge.

Hudgins, M. K. (2002). *Experiential treatment of PTSD: The therapeutic spiral model .* New York, NY: Springer Publishing.

Hudgins, M. K. (2017) PTSD Unites the World: Prevention, intervention and training in the therapeutic spiral model. In C. E. Stout & G. Want (Eds.), *Why global health matters: Guidebook for innovation and inspiration.* Self-Published Online.

Hudgins, M. K., & Toscani, F. (2013). *Healing world trauma with the therapeutic spiral model: Stories from the frontlines.* London: Jessica Kingsley Publishers.

Kellermann, P. K., & Hudgins, M. K. (Eds.). (2000). *Psychodrama with trauma survivors: Acting out your pain.* London: Jessica Kingsley Publishers.

Kolb, D. A., & Kolb, A. Y. (2005). Learning styles and learning spaces: Enhancing experiential learning in higher education. *Academy of Management Learning & Education, 4*(2), 193–212.

Landy, R. J. (2008). *The couch and the stage: Integrating words and action in psychotherapy.* Lanham, MD, US: Jason Aronson.

Landy, R. J. (2017). The love and marriage of psychodrama and drama therapy. *The Journal of Psychodrama, Sociometry, and Group Psychotherapy, 65*(1), 33–40.

Levine, P. A. (2010). *In an unspoken voice: How the body releases trauma and restores goodness.* Berkeley, CA: North Atlantic Books.

Mahler, M. S., Pine, F., & Bergman, A. (1975). *The psychological birth and the human infant.* New York: Basic Books.

McGoldrick, M., Gerson, R., & Petry, S. S. (2008). *Genograms: Assessment and intervention.* WW Norton & Company.

Miller, C. (2007). Psychodrama, spirituality, and souldrama. In C. Baim, Clark, J. Burmeister, & M. Maciel, Manuela (Eds.) *Psychodrama: Advances in theory and practice* (pp. 189–200). New York: Routledge/Taylor & Francis Group.

Moreno, J. D. (1989). *The autobiography of J. L. Moreno, M.D. (Abridged).* Berkeley, CA: Copy Central.

Moreno, J. J. (1999). *Acting your inner music: Music therapy and psychodrama.* Barcelona: Barcelona Publishers.

Moreno, J. L. (1921). *Das Testament Des Vaters.* Vienna, Austria: Gustav Kiepenheuer Verlag.

Moreno, J. L. (1934). *Who shall survive? A new approach to the problems of human interrelations.* Washington, DC: Nervous and Mental Disease Publishing Co.

Moreno, J. L. (1943). Sociometry and the cultural order. *Sociometry, 6*(3), 299–344.

Moreno, J. L. (1946). *Psychodrama volume 1.* Beacon, NY: Beacon House Press.

Moreno, J. L. (1949). The spontaneity theory of learning. In R. B. Hass (Ed.), *Psychodrama and sociodrama in American education.* Beacon, NY: Beacon House Press.

Moreno, J. L. (1952). Psychodramatic production techniques. *Group Psychotherapy, Psychodrama, & Sociometry, 4,* 273–303.

Moreno, J. L. (1953). *Who shall survive? Foundations of sociometry, group psychotherapy and sociodrama* (2 ed.). Beacon, NY: Beacon House.

Moreno, J. L. (1955). The significance of the therapeutic format and the place of acting out in psychotherapy. *Group Psychotherapy, 8,* 7–19.

Moreno, J. L. (1956). System of spontaneity and creativity. In J. L. Moreno (Ed.), *Sociometry and the science of man.* Beacon, New York: Beacon House Press.

Moreno, J. L. (1957). Code of ethics of group psychotherapists. *Group Psychotherapy, 10,* 143–144.

Moreno, J. L. (1961). The role concept, a bridge between psychiatry and sociology. *American Journal of Psychiatry, 118*(6), 518–523.

Moreno, J. L. (1964). *Psychodrama, first volume* (3 ed.). Beacon, NY: Beacon House Press.

Moreno, J. L. (1972) *Psychodrama Volume 1* (4th ed.). Beacon, NY: Beacon House Press.

Moreno, J. L. (2019). In E. Schreiber, S. Kelley, & S. Giacomucci, (Eds.), *The autobiography of a genius*. United Kingdom: North West Psychodrama Association.

Moreno, J. L., & Moreno, Z. T. (1969). *Psychodrama: Third volume, action therapy and principles of practice*. New York: Beacon House.

Moreno, J. L., Moreno, Z. T., & Moreno, J. D. (1955) The discovery of the spontaneous man with special emphasis upon the technique of role reversal, *Group Psychotherapy, 8,* 103–29. (Reprinted in 1959, Psychodrama, vol. 2, New York: Beacon House, pp. 135–58.)

Moreno, J. L., Moreno, Z. T., & Moreno, J. D. (1964). The first psychodramatic family. Group. *Psychotherapy, 16,* 203–249.

Moreno, Z. T. (1965). Psychodramatic rules, techniques, and adjunctive methods. *Group Psychotherapy, A Quarterly Journal XVIII, 1–2,* 73–86.

Moreno, Z. T. (1969). Moreneans: The heretics of yesterday are the orthodoxy of today. *Group Psychotherapy, 22,* 1–6.

Moreno, Z. T. (1994). Foreword. In P. Holmes, M. Karp, & M. Watson (Eds.). *Psychodrama since Moreno*. London: Routledge.

Moreno, Z. T. (2006). In T. Horvatin & E. Schreiber (Eds.), *The Quintessential Zerka*. New York, NY: Routledge.

Moreno, Z. T. (2012). *To dream again: A memoir*. New York: Mental Health Resources.

Moreno, Z. T. (2013). A life in psychodrama. In K. Hudgins & F. Toscani, (Eds.), *Healing world trauma with the therapeutic spiral model: Psychodramatic stories from the frontlines*. London: Jessica Kingsley Publishers.

National Association of Social Workers. (2017). *Code of ethics*. Washington, D.C.: NASW.

Niepenberg, K. (2017). Gesellschaftlicher Wandel in der Sozialen Arbeit. *Zeitschrift Für Psychodrama Und Soziometrie, 16*(1), 171–183.

Nieto, L. (2010). Look behind you: Using anti-oppression models to inform a protagonist's psychodrama. In E. Leveton (Ed.), *Healing collective trauma using sociodrama and drama therapy* (pp. 103–125). New York: Springer Publishing Company.

Nolte, J. (2014). *The philosophy, theory, and methods of J.L. Moreno: The man who tried to become god*. New York, NY: Routledge.

Nolte, J. (2020). *J. L. Moreno and the psychodramatic method: On the practice of psychodrama*. New York: Routledge.

Northern, H., & Kurland, R. (2001). *Social work with groups*. New York: Columbia University Press.

Oudijk, R. (2007). A postmodern approach to psychodrama theory. In C. Baim, J. Burmeister, & M. Maciel (Eds.), *Psychodrama: Advances in theory and practice* (pp. 139–150). London: Routledge.

Perry, B. D., & Szalavitz, M. (2006). *The boy who was raised as a dog and other stories from a child psychiatrist's notebook: What traumatized children can teach us about loss, love, and healing*. New York, NY, US: Basic Books.

Peterson, J. (2003). The synergism of art therapy and psychodrama: Bridging the internal and external worlds. In J. Gershoni (Ed.), *Psychodrama in the 21 Century: Clinical and educational applications* (pp. 81–102). New York: Springer Publishing Company.

Salas, J. (1993). *Improvising real life: Personal stories in playback theater*. Dubuque, Iowa: Kendall Hunt.

Schreiber, E., Kelley, S., & Giacomucci, S. (2019). Editors Introduction and acknowledgements. In *Autobiography of a genius* (pp. 9–11). United Kingdom: North West Psychodrama Association.

Schwinger, T. (2016). Das Soziale Atom in der Sozialen Arbeit: Begriff und Untersuchungsmethoden. *Zeitschrift Für Psychodrama Und Soziometrie, 15*(2), 275–289.

Siegel, D. J. (2010). *Mindsight: The new science of personal transformation*. New York: Bantam Books.

Siegel, D. J. (2012). *Developing mind: How relationships and the brain interact to shape who we are*. New York: Guilford Press.

Steinberg, D. M. (2010). Mutual aid: A contribution to best-practice social work. *Social Work with Groups, 33*(1), 53–68.

Tarashoeva, G., Marinova-Djambazova, P., & Kojuharov, H. (2017). Effectiveness of psychodrama therapy in patients with panic disorders—Final results. *International Journal of Psychotherapy, 21,* 55–66.

Telias, R. (2018). *Moreno's personality theory and its relationship to psychodrama: A philosophical, developmental and therapeutic perspective*. New York: Routledge.

Tomasulo, D. (2011). *The virtual gratitude visit (VGV): Psychodrama in action*. Retrieved from PsychologyToday.com.

Treadwell, T. (2020). *Integrating CBT with experiential theory and practice: A group therapy workbook*. New York: Taylor & Francis.

Treadwell, T., Dartnell, D., Travaglini, L. E., Staats, M., & Devinney, K. (2016). *Group therapy workbook: Integrating cognitive behavioral therapy with psychodramatic theory and practice*. Outskirts Press.

Trecker, H. (1944). Group work: Frontiers and foundations—In wartime. *The Compass, 25*(3), 3–8. Retrieved from https://www.jstor.org/stable/23706466.

Trevarthen, C. (1998). The concept and foundations of infant intersubjectivity. In S. Bråten (Ed.), *Intersubjective communication and emotion in early ontogeny* (pp. 15–46). Cambridge: Cambridge University Press.

Truedley, M. B. (1944). Psychodrama and social case work. *Sociometry, 7,* 170–178.

Van der Kolk, B. A. (2014). *The body keeps the score: Brain, mind, and body in the healing of trauma*. New York: Viking Press.

von Ameln, F., & Becker-Ebel, J. (2020). *Fundamentals of psychodrama*. Singapore: Springer Nature.

Wang, X. H., & Liu, A. Q. (2020). Psychodrama: A professional method for social work. *Social Work and Management, 20*(2), 65–70.

Wronka, J. (2016). *Human rights and social justice: Social Action and service for the helping and health professions*. Los Angelos, CA: Sage.

Chapter 5
Sociometry and Social Work Theory

Abstract The congruence of sociometry theory and social work theories is covered in detail in this chapter. The social atom, cultural atom, and sociogram are described with visual depictions. Moreno's theories of interpersonal connection, social networks, and society are depicted while introducing sociometry terms such as the sociodynamic effect, tele, and the organic unity of mankind. Sociometry's connection to social work's person-in-environment theories is emphasized while also considering the shared concern for how social forces impact individuals and groups.

Keywords Social work · Sociometry · Social atom · Social network · Person-in-environment

The term sociometry is derived from two parts—"socius" and "metrum." As its etymology suggests, sociometry is concerned with the assessment of groups, social circles, and social networks. Moreno suggested that other social fields were too focused on *measurement* or too focused on *social phenomenon* without balancing and integrating a focus on both. He promoted sociometry as a field of its own that explores the sociodynamics within groups and society. Sociometry is a system composed of three parts: a *theory* of the structure of society and interpersonal relations, a *research* method for studying that structure and relationships, and the clinical *practice* for reorganizing groups for optimal functionality (Hale, 2009; Nolte, 2014). This section will orient itself on the theoretical aspects of sociometry as they relate to social work.

Moreno reflects on the foundational role of sociometry for group psychotherapy in the 25th anniversary edition of his *First Book on Group Psychotherapy*:

> Group psychotherapy, sociometry and psychodrama are like three sons born from one another. They grew together and nourished each other. Group psychotherapy may never have succeeded had sociometry not followed immediately and spread the news about the group and the dynamics of group structure... All three developments are the products of a single germinal idea. (Moreno, 1957, p. xxiv).

This passage underscores the relationship between sociometry and group psychotherapy from Moreno's perspective. Founder of the Sociometric Institute and trainee of Moreno, Bob Siroka notes how Moreno used to remark that "I use psychodrama to get people in the door so that I can teach them sociometry" (personal

S. Giacomucci, *Social Work, Sociometry, and Psychodrama*, Psychodrama in Counselling, Coaching and Education 1,
https://doi.org/10.1007/978-981-33-6342-7_5

communication, May 9th, 2020). While his most known contribution comes from psychodrama and role playing techniques, he frequently reminds us of the essential nature of sociometry for both group work and psychodrama practice.

"A true therapeutic procedure cannot have less an objective than the whole of mankind," this is the motto of the American Board of Examiners in Sociometry, Psychodrama, and Group Psychotherapy and the first sentence of Moreno's 1934 *Who Shall Survive?* (p. 3). They are arguably Moreno's most famous words but are almost always detached from the sentence that follows—"But no adequate therapy can be prescribed as long as mankind is not a unity in some fashion and as long as its organization remains unknown" (1934, p. 3). A psychiatrist by training, Moreno argued that assessment always needed to precede intervention—even with group therapy and society. His sociometric system is the means by which he believed we could uncover the organization and dynamics of groups and society so that they could be improved and enhanced. The quote from *Who Shall Survive?* was inspired by the story of a traveling doctor who travels to meet a patient but comes across many others with the same malady suggesting "no man can be treated singly but all men together" (Moreno, 1953, p.426).

5.1 Sociometric Theory and Research

Sociometry is defined by Moreno as "the inquiry into the evolution and organization of groups and the position of individuals within them" (Moreno, 1953, p. 23). Moreno suggested that sociometry bridges the gap between psychology and sociology, offering a functional theory for exploring interpersonal relations (1949). He referred to sociometry as a science by, for, and of the people (Moreno, 2014); it is both the quantitative and qualitative exploration of the interrelations of humans. Moreno states that the study of sociometry resolves the quantitative versus qualitative dichotomy as "the qualitative aspect of social structure is not destroyed or forgotten, it is integrated into the quantitative operations, it acts from within. The two aspects of structure are treated in combination and as a unit" (p. 23). He writes that the primary task of sociometry has been "the reorientation of the experimental method so that it can be applied effectively to social phenomena" (Moreno, 1948, p. 121).

Sociometric research was first adopted by the sociologists and social scientists who Moreno criticized as being too detached from the lives of the communities they were studying.

> ...the most important influence which sociometry exercised upon the social sciences is the urgency and the violence with which it pushed the scholars from the writing desk into actual situations, urging them to move into real communities and to deal there with real people; urging them to move in personally and directly, with a warm and courageous heart, implemented with a few hypotheses and instruments, instead of using go-betweens as translators and informants; urging them to begin with their science now and here (action research), not writing for the milennium of the library shelves. (Moreno, 1949, p. 244).

Sociometric research is action based and participatory (Moreno, 1942). It insists that research in the social sciences cannot take place within a sterile laboratory or clinic; instead, it must be conducted in real-life situations (1931). In group therapy, Moreno elevated each group member to that of a patient–therapist; in the classroom, students were considered student-teachers; and in research, participants are subject-researchers. Likewise, the leader is considered a part of the group, not a person on the outside. In 1943, he writes, "sociometry has taught us to be pessimistic, critical of all enterprises which try to solve problems of human relations without the most intensive participation of the people involved, and the most intensive knowledge of their psycho-social living conditions" (p. 344).

The social work profession's orientation to social science and research seems highly compatible with sociometry in that it merges the qualitative with the quantitative and considers participants as the experts. In this way, the dehumanization of research participants is avoided, and the communities studied are involved in the design, implementation, and distribution of the research. The social work researcher recognizes their role responsibility of conducting research to empower communities and assess the needs of different social groups—rather than simply for academic prestige or self-promotion. Social work research, like sociometry research, integrates both psychology and sociology into a more complete exploration of the individual within their social environment and of groups within society. "Social work, like sociometry, has its major focus upon those interpersonal and social processes that determine human behavior and make for human adjustment" (Deutschberger, 1950, p. 8).

J.L. Moreno's book, *Who Shall Survive?* (originally published in 1934), provides an in-depth description of his sociometric theory with a large collection of sociometric research, mostly conducted at the New York Training School for Girls, a reformatory school in Hudson where Moreno was invited to serve as the Director of Research. Through the course of his sociometric studies of various communities and groups, he uncovered and labeled multiple social phenomena including the *social atom*, the *cultural atom*, *social networks*, *tele*, and the *sociodynamic effect*.

5.2 Moreno's Interpersonal Theory and the Encounter

A meeting of two: eye to eye, face to face And when you are near I will tear your eyes out and place them instead of mine and you will tear my eyes out and place them instead of yours then I will look at you with your eyes and you will look at me with mine. (Moreno, 1914).

This quote from Moreno's 1914 poem, *An Invitation to an Encounter*, conveys the basis of his interpersonal theory, his psychodramatic theory, and his existential philosophy. He writes that the concept of "encounter" (Begegnung) does not translate well from German into English. That, in English, it loses its depth and becomes sterile, a vague interpersonal relationship. His intended meaning is of a much more meaningful encounter.

> It means that two or more persons meet, but not only to face one another, but to live and experience each other, as actors each in his own right, not like a "professional" meeting (a case-worker or a physician or a participant observer and their subjects), but a meeting of two people. In a meeting the two persons are there in space, with all their strengths and all their weaknesses, two human actors seething with spontaneity..." (Moreno, 1943, p. 310).

Moreno describes this poem as the simplest definition of interpersonal relations (1955). He writes that only through authentic meeting of others do natural groupings and actual societies emerge (1946). Through a genuine encounter, both individuals are changed and impacted by the other. Nolte describes an encounter as "two active individuals who live and experienced each other" (2014, p. 19). Each participant in the encounter comes to a deeper realization of self through total reciprocity with the other while intuitively reversing roles in full spontaneity and autonomy in the here-and-now (Moreno, 1960). He goes on to write that "encounter is also the real basis of the therapeutic process" (1960, p. 16). It is through this lens that Moreno's sociometric and psychodramatic theories developed.

Moreno's interpersonal theory and Martin Buber's *I and Thou* concept (Buber, 1923), published 9 years later, have much in common. Interestingly, Moreno and Martin Buber worked together on the editorial team of a literary journal called *Daimon* in Vienna and clearly had a significant influence on each other's thinking (Moreno, 2019). Moreno's work influenced many others, and because he published his work anonymously for nine years, his name has become distant from many of his creations. Regardless, few would argue against the statement that "Moreno was a pioneer in the exploration of human connection" (Hale, 2009, p. 356).

5.3   The Social Atom

> As the individual projects his emotions into the groups around him, and as the members of these groups in turn project their emotions toward him, a pattern of attractions and repulsions, as projected from both sides, can be discerned on the threshold between individual-and group. This pattern is called his asocial atom. (Moreno, 1941, p. 24).

Moreno described human society as having similar properties to the atomic structure defining matter. He saw that a person is defined by their social relationships and conceptualized this network of close interpersonal relations as one's social atom (Ridge, 2010). The social atom is similar to and influenced the creation of social work's genogram and the ecomap (Dayton, 2005). It can be used to map an individual's perception and experience of the nature of their familial relationships, their social relationships, their relationships to collectives or organizations, their relationships to objects or behaviors (especially in addictions treatment), their desired relationships, and/or the nature of their relationships at different points in time (Hale, 1981). The social atom not only depicts one's relationships, but also the nature of the relationships—attractions, repulsions, indifferences, and the reciprocities of (Hale, 1981). Moreno (1939, p. 3) indicates that an individual's social atom begins as a dyad between self and mother and grows to include "persons who come into [the] child's orbit." He hypothesizes that:

> a) An individual is tied to his social atom as closely as to his body; b) as he moves from an old to a new community it changes its membership but its constellation tends to be constant. Notwithstanding that it is a novel social structure into which he has entered, the social atom has a tendency to repeat its former constellation; its concrete, individual member have changed but the pattern persists. (J.L. Moreno, 1953, p. 703).

As such, the social atom often provides an object relations map for working with clients which can be used to help both the client and clinician understand transference (Dayton, 2005). J.L. Moreno understood the social atom as the smallest of social structures—one that is actively changing as individuals attempt to maintain *sociostasis*, or social balance characterized by an ease of socio-affective experience (1947). Moreno's social atom theory argues that there are few things more important to humans than their position within groups and how others feel about them; thus, the patterns of attractions and repulsions within one's social atom may be responsible for the intrapsychic tensions and problems that human's experience (1941).

Social work's person-in-environment theory reflects the position of the social atom—which visually depicts the individual within their interpersonal environment. Moreno articulates social work's person-in-environment philosophy in the following quote, "every individual man functions in a system which is confined by two boundaries: the emotional expansiveness of his own personality and the socio-emotional pressure exerted upon him by the population." (1953, p. 316). The centrality of human relationships is given significance through the social atom and sociometric theory (Giacomucci, 2018a; b). Moreno's 1950 article, *The Sociometric Approach to Social Case Work*, urges social workers to utilize the social atom, the cultural atom, and the sociogram to develop a clearer social understanding of the individual client.

The social atom is "the sum of interpersonal structures resulting from choices and rejections centered about a given individual" (Moreno, 1987, p. 239). Moreno conceptualized society and the social network as an innumerable series of interlinked social atoms (Moreno, 1937a, b; Nolte, 2014). The social atom is primarily created through a written exercise. It can be used as an assessment tool throughout treatment to measure changes in a client's relational life. It is commonly used as a warm-up for psychodrama and can even be put into action with group members holding the roles of other individuals on one's social atom (Dayton, 2005).

A social atom is created by drawing one's self in the center of a page, surrounded by one's closest relationships. Circles are used to represent females, triangles for males, and squares for non-human entities or objects. In the course of teaching the social atom to social work students, this writer's student (Jordan Briem) suggested the use of a star for transgender or non-binary genders rather than using a square, circle, or triangle. Or, to permit participants to use whichever shapes that they want to use to represent each person on their social atom. A dotted outline of a shape indicates that the person is deceased. Shapes are drawn in proximity to the self on the social

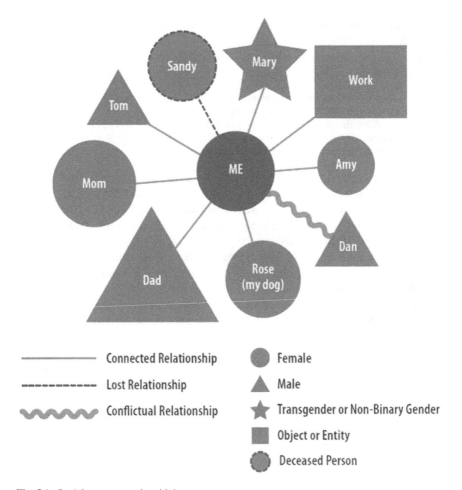

Fig. 5.1 Social atom example with key

atom to represent closeness or distance in the relationship. Finally, lines are drawn between the self and the person or object to represent the nature of the relationship. A solid line represents a secure, connected relationship, dotted line indicates a lost relationship, and a squiggly line depicts a conflicted relationship (see Fig. 5.1 with key).

5.4 Cultural Atom

The cultural atom exists within each social atom. While the social atom depicts the most significant interpersonal relationships within an individual's life, the cultural atom depicts the many roles and role relationships within each of these relationships (Moreno, 1943).

> The pattern of role relations around an individual as their focus is called his cultural atom.
> Every individual, just as he has a set of friends and a set of enemies, -a social atom- also has
> a range of roles facing a range of counter-roles. (Moreno, 1943, p. 331).

The role dynamics and role relationships within the cultural atom can take multiple forms including formal or informal, symmetrical or complementary, reciprocal, triangulated, and/or conflicting (Daniels, 2016). Each individual's personality develops and exists within a matrix of role relationships that give expression to the various aspects of the self.

While the social atom received considerable attention in Moreno's work, the cultural atom has been given very little attention and only a handful of articles exist about it beyond Moreno's original writing. The cultural atom is depicted through first drawing one's social atom and then drawing lines to reflect the role relationships between each individual (see Fig. 5.2). Between the protagonist and each individual in their social atom, there are role relationships that exist and give deeper meaning to the interpersonal relationship while also explaining the patterns of attractions and repulsions between individuals (Moreno, 1941). Moreno considered the social atom to be the smallest functional unit of society and the cultural atom to be the smallest functioning unit of culture (Nolte, 2014). Societal and cultural values are transmitted through the social atom, cultural atom, and role relationships within them. Roles are socially constructed and held, existing in a state of reciprocal interaction between the culture, society, and the individual (Nolte, 2014).

5.5 The Sociogram

While the social atom depicts the attractions and repulsions of individuals within one person's life, the sociogram depicts the interpersonal dynamics within a specific group. The sociogram was one of the first instruments of sociometry to be developed through his work in Mittendorf refugee camp around 1915. He later created sociograms depicting the interpersonal relationships within various groups including prison blocks in Sing Sing Prison, students in classrooms, actors on the stage, military divisions, and organizations. Some argued that with the invention of the sociogram, the first scientific basis for group psychotherapy was born (Renouvier, 1958). Individual psychotherapy techniques are not adequately translatable into group psychotherapy—"a group structure which is more than the sum of the individuals participating in it" (Moreno, 1948, p. 123).

The sociogram made it possible to scientifically assess the sociodynamics within a group in order to appropriately prescribe interventions for better functioning. The functioning of a group, just like an organism or organization is strongly influenced by its structure. "The core of a social structure is the pattern of relationships of all the individuals within the structure" (Moreno, 1941, p. 19). A sociogram is constructed

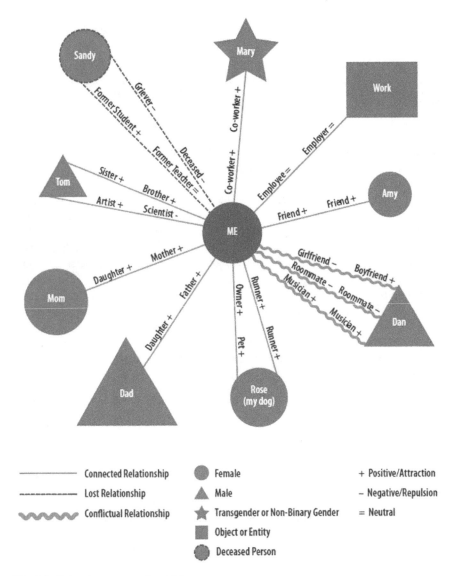

Fig. 5.2 Cultural atom example with key

through the data collected by a sociometric test. A sociometric test measures two-way relations based upon a specific criteria. A simple example of a sociometric test is depicted through the teaching of a psychodrama elective at Bryn Mawr College's Graduate School of Social Work and Social Research. As the instructor, I asked each student to email me the names, in order of preference, of the three classmates that they would most prefer to co-facilitate a class warm-up with later in the semester. Upon receiving the data of this sociometric test, I input it into an online computer

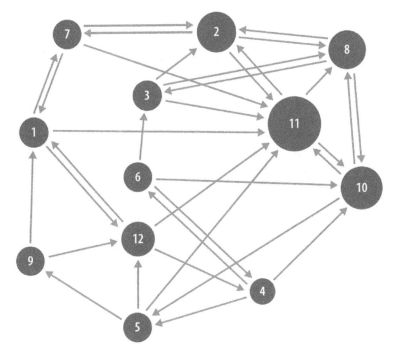

Fig. 5.3 Sociogram from a graduate social work classroom

system that draws the sociogram for me based on the distribution of choices, the attractions and repulsions, within the classroom based on this criteria (see Fig. 5.3).

The resulting sociogram visually shows the choices and preferences of each student. In analyzing the sociogram, we can see that student 11 is the star of the group based on these criteria as they were chosen by five of their peers, more than anyone else. Students 2, 10, and 8 were each chosen four times. Two students (1 and 12) were chosen by three of their peers; four students (3, 4, 5, 7, and 9) were chosen by two classmates; and student 6 was chosen once. Previously, sociograms were drawn by hand, but modern technology has given way to multiple computer programs that can quickly create a sociogram image.

Sociograms can be created for small groups or large groups and give us significant information about the invisible dynamics within the group and between group members. Moreno suggested that the number of mutual choices within a group sociogram is an indicator of its health (Hale, 2009). The organizations of the group, communities, organizations, and agencies could be restructured based on sociometric analysis to determine the best fit for individual members—this was Moreno's original recommendation based on his Mittendorf experience. Through the use of sociograms for sociometric research, it became clear that the social wealth within groups is unequally distributed—there are social stars and social isolates within each group which reflects the structure of society-as-a-whole.

5.5.1   Sociodynamic Effect

The unequal distribution of preferences within a group is a result of the sociodynamic effect which "underlies the development of leadership and isolation" in groups and society (Moreno, 1943, p. 305). Moreno suggested that the sociodynamic effect was the underlying dynamic responsible for every social problem known to humans. The sociodynamic effect "is universally present, appearing like a halo effect, inherent in every social structure" (1941, p. 126).

It was through his systematic study at the Hudson girls reform school that he became more fully aware of this underlying social force. He conducted a sociometric test during which the 505 residents were asked to write down their top five choices of other girls that they would like to live with. It was expected that the distribution of choices would create a normal probability curve where most participants would receive an average amount of choices, few participants would receive above the average, and few participants would receive below the average number of choices. Instead what was found, and replicated in nearly every sociometric test since, was that a handful of girls received many of the choices, the largest number were unchosen or severely under-chosen, and the rest received an average number of choices. The sociodynamic effect is clearly depicted in the sociogram graphic above where a few of the graduate students received an overwhelming majority of choices by the group while others were less chosen.

Social workers are tasked with promoting and developing a more inclusive society where the vulnerable and oppressed are not isolated or unchosen. The creation of a socially just society must take into account the sociodynamic effect and its pervasive impact upon society and groups within society. Many have suggested that the sociometrist and group worker's role responsibilities include reversing the sociodynamic effect (Giacomucci, 2017; Giacomucci et al., 2018; Korshak & Shapiro, 2013; Moreno, 1934; Schreiber, 2018). While a case worker orients around reversing the sociodynamic effect's impact on their client, a social group worker is concerned with reversing the sociodynamic effect in their group, and a macrosocial worker is primarily focused on reversing the sociodynamic effect within society.

This underlying social dynamic which impacts the distribution of social choices leaves many unchosen while others are sociometric stars, is called the sociodynamic effect (Hale, 1981; Moreno, 1934). At the same time, he noticed significantly more mutual choices within his groups than expected. "The trend towards mutuality of attraction and repulsion many times surpasses chance possibility. The factor responsible for this effect is called 'tele'" (Moreno, 1941, p. 24).

5.5.2   Tele

"We could observe that some individuals have for each other a certain sensitivity as if they were chained together by a common soul. When they warm-up to a state, they 'click'" (J.L. Moreno, 1924, p. 57). This quote from J.L. Moreno's *Das Stegreifthe-ater* (Theater of Spontaneity) describes the concept of tele nearly a decade before later naming the term through his sociometric research. The term tele is derived from the Greek word meaning "far" or "at a distance" (Moreno, 1934). J.L. Moreno states that "every wholesome human relationship depends on the presence of tele"; he defines tele as "insight into," "appreciation of," and "feeling for" the "actual make up" of the other person. (1959, p. 37). It is "the socio-gravitational factor, which operates between individuals, drawing them to form more positive or negative pair-relations...than on chance" (J.L. Moreno, 1947, p. 84). Tele may be conceptualized as two-way empathy (J.L. Moreno, 1953). The progress of therapy and the devel-opment of any group depend on tele as a foundation to its advancement (Moreno, 2000). "Tele conveys the message that people are participants in an interpersonal phenomena whereby they contact and communicate and resonate with one another at a distance and that they send emotional messages projected across space" (Keller-mann, 1992, as cited in Dayton, 2005, p. 53). Dayton (2005) suggests that the tele phenomenon operates through what neuroscientists describe as "affectively charged, facially mediated right brain-to-brain communications, at levels beneath awareness" (Lazarus and McCleary, 1951). Similarly, Yaniv (2014) presents a neuropsychology conceptualization of tele as being related to the orbitofrontal cortex's function of tracking emotional valence.

Tele is not transference or countertransference (J.L. Moreno attempted to dismantle the "patient–therapist" power dynamic by referring to countertransference as transference). Transference is a one-way process—a distortion of tele, but tele is a two-way accurate knowing of one another. Both transference and tele are often present in relationships, and the goal over time is to replace transference with tele (J.L. Moreno, 1959). "By definition, transference tends to produce dissociation of interpersonal relations. In contrast, tele strengthens association and promotes conti-nuity, security, stability, reciprocity, and cohesiveness of groups" (Moreno, 1983, p. 164). J.L. Moreno distinguishes tele from transference in the following passage:

> Transference, like tele, has a cognitive as well as a conative aspect. It takes tele to choose the right therapist and group partner; it takes transference to misjudge the therapist to choose group partners who produce unstable relationships in a given activity. (1959, p. 12).

He argued that transference is a fantasy (surplus reality) based on the past expe-rience, while tele is based on feelings into the actuality of another. Transference is based on one's *inner* psychodynamic experience; tele describes the sociodynamics *between* two individuals (1959).

The presence of tele within psychodrama groups is often highlighted when a protagonist chooses another group member (often not knowing their history) to play a specific role—only later to find out that the role directly coincided with that group member's personal work (Nolte, 2014). Tele is at the basis of an individual's ability to fully role reverse with another person (von Ameln & Becker-Ebel, 2020). Tele exists within all groups, and all sociometric, psychodramatic, and group psychotherapy sessions. It is most evident in group sociometry through the development of reciprocal choices or when one's perception toward another matches that person's experience of self (Hale, 1981).

5.6 Social Networks and Society

Moreno's sociograms and sociometric theory serve as the basis for modern social network theories (Moreno, 2014). He suggests that "the discovery that human society has an actual, dynamic, central structure underlying' and determining all its peripheral and formal groupings may one day be considered as the cornerstone of all social science" (Moreno, 1941, p. 15). Within human society, there are "channelized formations, so-called 'psychosocial networks ' which bind individuals and groups together" (1948, p. 125). These social networks are described by Moreno as "the river-bed through which psychological currents flow," and the process by which people educate and impact each other (1943, p. 306). Knowledge and awareness of the structure and organization of human interrelations is an essential foundation for the planning and construction of human society (Moreno, 1941). Society is made up of numerous social networks; social networks are composed of various social atoms; and within social atoms exist a multitude of interpersonal relationships and even more role relationships. "Sociometry, because of the unity of the human group, studies the human group as a totality. It studies every part with a view to the totality and the totality with a view to every part" (Moreno, 1943, p. 317).

In his work at Hudson Valley's girls reform school (1934), Moreno used sociograms to map out the social networks within the community of several hundred girls. He tested his theories and assessments in various ways included spreading information through the community and assessing which sociograms and social networks the information had spread through (Nolte, 2014). His theories of psychosocial networks emerged in the 1930s–40s, decades before social networks became popularized through online social network sites such as Facebook.

Moreno believed in the therapeutic potential of one group member helping another and of one group helping another (1963). Through this framework of mutual aid, he glimpsed the potential of a therapeutic society and healing of all of society. He called this vision *Sociatry*. With an adequate understanding of sociodynamics, social networks, and the social atom, Moreno believed that the assessment and thus enhancement of society were now possible. He places Sociatry, sociodynamics, and sociometry under the umbrella of *socionomy*—which encompasses the science of social laws, sociodynamics, social measurement, and healing society (Hare & Hare, 1996). Like the social worker, Moreno challenged us to create change within the larger social systems which are the source of many interpersonal and emotional problems that we help our individual clients and groups grapple with. He writes "the old adage 'Physician heal thyself' was replaced with a new one '*Community heal thyself*'" (1956, p. 24).

5.7   Organic Unity of Humankind

"Mankind is a social and organic unity."—JL Moreno.

The Organic Unity of Humankind refers to the shared humanness and that binds humanity together as a single group or a single entity. Moreno sometimes called this our primordial nature. Moreno extended his group-as-a-whole approach to the whole of the human species. He writes that the unity of the human group organizes and distributes itself based on a multiple social phenomenon and definite social laws (1953). These social forces are characterized by the systems of attractions and repulsions that exist within all social groupings related to biologic, psychological, and social factors. Considering mankind as a unity, Moreno writes that there are tendencies between parts of mankind which draw it together into unity at times and pull it apart at other times. These integrative and disintegrative forces are detectable within the system of attractions and repulsions within social networks, groups, social atoms, and relationships—"the human group has a science-configuration of its own" (Moreno, 1943, p. 303). He suggests that there exists a common core to all groups or societies that transcends culture or language (Giacomucci, 2018c).

Moreno ends his book *Who Shall Survive?* by proposing over a hundred hypotheses for future sociometric research which are structured in his 1943 *Sociometry and the Cultural Order*, as eight hypotheses about the organic unity of mankind: (1) Sociogenetic Law, (2) Reality Testing of Social Configurations, (3) Reality Testing of Cultural Configurations, (4) The Sociodynamic Effect, (5) The Social Atom, the Smallest Functioning Unit of the Human Group, (6) Psychological Currents and Networks, (7) The Law of Social Gravity, and (8) The Psychosocial Organization and Function of Groups.

(1) *The Sociogenetic Law* describes the idea that the human social structure has evolved from a mostly undifferentiated form at its birth to a more complex and differentiated system of social configurations which correspond to the growth of individuals within society (Moreno, 1943). This law suggests that the complexity of society's evolution and the formation of sub-groups within society will continue to become more differentiated and complicated as society evolves. The sociodynamics within a sub-group of adults will be much more complex than the dynamics within a sub-group of adolescents or children. Just as each individual's socio-emotional expansiveness increase with age, so too does society's (Moreno, 1934). Moreno argued that just as each physical organ evolves and takes on more complex structure and function, so too does society as an organic unity (Moreno, 1953).

(2) *The Reality Testing of Social Configurations* hypothesis states that the social groups formed by humans will always be much more complex and differ from social structures formed by chance, predicted by computer, or imagined. Moreno labeled the socio-gravitational force that underlies this social reality as "tele." (3) Similarly, the *Reality Testing of Cultural Configurations* hypothesis states that the role is the vehicle for cultural exchanges, and that within each relationship within each group, there is a range of role relationships creating a complex web of role relationships

within groups which will also be more sophisticated than what would be predicted by chance. (4) The fourth hypothesis is that of *The Sociodynamic Effect*, which describes the preference system within human groups and society. This underlying social force is the cause of the unequal concentration of social choices which results in social leaders, stars, and isolates. Moreno even states that if we are to change our economic structure, we must take into account the sociodynamic effect because it "effect is underlying unequal distribution of wealth and power" (1943, p. 305).

(5) This hypothesis indicates that the *Social Atom is the Smallest Functional Unit of the Human Group* and that society "consists of an intricate web of social atoms" (Moreno, 1943, p. 305). (6) The idea of Psychological Currents and Networks describes the presences of invisible sociometric connections within larger groups of people within which information flows and impacts each member of the group. (7) *The Law of Social Gravity* declares that there is an intimate relationship between physical proximity/distance and psychological proximity/distance. In the absence of more sophisticated social organs such as technology or even language, social groups are highly characterized by physical proximity (Moreno, 1953). (8) *The Psychosocial Organization and Function of Groups* hypothesis indicates that group dynamics and structures directly impact the behavior of the group and can be measured through sociometric means. Group structure has a determining influence on group functioning and leadership (Moreno, 1943; 1953). Moreno argued that these eight hypotheses were measurable and testable through scientific research and that they would provide proof of an organic unity of mankind.

5.8   Social Work and Sociometry

"There is a striking agreement between the operational framework of theory in social work and the hypotheses basic to sociometry" (Deutschberger, 1950, p. 8). Deutschberger suggests that in both: The focus is on relationships and their impact on individual characteristics, the worker emphasizes the therapeutic relationship, problems are contextualized through a social lens, the process is client-centered and self-determination is emphasized, and the work with an individual also involves working with the larger social systems that they are a part of (1950). Green (1950) also argued that sociometry was a "highly valuable tool for the social worker in the intergroup situation," working at the intersection of different groups.

Sociometry and democracy are intimately connected. Years ago, J.L. Moreno stated that "sociometry can well be considered the cornerstone of a still underdeveloped science of democracy" (Moreno 1953, p. 113). While more recently his son Jonathan echoed his father's words indicating that sociometry is a science by, for, and of the people (Moreno, 2014). A democratic procedure is, in essence, a sociometric exercise. In order to establish a truly democratic society, all voices must be heard and considered—especially oppressed, underserved, and vulnerable populations. J.L. Moreno's methods give us the potential to explore the sociodynamics within society and its sub-groups, reverse the unequal distribution of social wealth, and provide a deeper understanding (and encounter) of difference through the application of Moreno's methods.

In 1950, J.L. Moreno wrote an article titled *The Sociometric Approach to Social Case Work* in which he attempts to integrate sociometric theory into social work practice:

> Man does not live alone and does not get sick by himself. His problems develop in groups....
> the mental and physical equilibrium of an individual depends to a considerable degree upon
> the dynamic interplay of these various individual and social forces. (p. 173).

These words echo social work's person-in-environment theory. He goes on to suggest that "It is obvious that without the knowledge and ability to mobilize the sociometric matrix on behalf of an individual, adequate social case work is not possible or at least greatly handicapped" (p. 173). Moreno's 1934 text *Who Shall Survive?*, outlines much of the micro- versus macrosocial work dichotomy that would play out in the years to follow, "The premise of scientific medicine has been since its origin that the locus of physical ailment is within an individual organism. Therefore, treatment is applied to the locus of the ailment as designated by diagnosis." (p. 60) He goes on to discuss that ailments which arise from within the context of interpersonal relations require interventions on a structural level and/or a group treatment approach (1934). There are countless reflections of social work's person-in-environment perspective in Moreno's writings including the following statement in the foreword to the launch of the 1937 journal *Sociometry: A Journal of Inter-Personal Relations*:

> It becomes evident indeed that the biology of man is, in a thousand ways, a reflection of his
> surroundings, that human evolution is going on apace, that variation, selection, differential
> fecundity and differential death rate are biological realities affected by the social situation....
> Civilized man is an organism forced to make a very exceptional and special type of adaptation,
> and no physiologist, no psychologist, can study man as an organism except in the light of
> his ecology, and his broader social antecedents. (Moreno, 1937a, b, p. 5).

This is perhaps the strongest connection between the field of sociometry and the social work profession.

5.9   Conclusion

One of the J.L. Moreno's colleagues, Helen Jennings, wrote that the task of sociometry is "transforming society to fit man, rather than transforming man to fit society" (1941, p. 512). As indicated by Becker & Marecek (2008), "rather than locating the sources of well-being solely within the individual, the discipline of social work studies individuals in the context of the social environment" (p. 597). This is precisely what sociometry achieves—a contextualization of the individual, and the experience of "mental illness" or "mental health," within the social context. Here, we find a sturdy bridge between clinical social work practice and community praxis of social work. Moreno's work could be seen as an attempt to bridge the gaps between micro-, mezzo-, and macrosocial work (Giacomucci, 2019; Giacomucci & Stone, 2019).

References

Becker, D., & Marecek, J. (2008). Positive psychology: History in the remaking? *Theory & Psychology, 18*(5), 591–604.

Buber, M. (1923). I and Thou, Edinburgh: Clark (English translation, 1970).

Daniels, S. (2016). The social collective and the social and cultural atom in the age of the social network. *Zeitschrift Für Psychodrama Und Soziometrie, 15*(2), 213–229.

Dayton, T. (2005). *The living stage: A step-by-step guide to psychodrama, sociometry, and experiential group therapy*. Deerfield, FL: Health Communications Inc.

Deutschberger, P. (1950). Sociometry and social work. *Sociometry, 13*(1), 8–21.

Giacomucci, S. (2017). The sociodrama of life or death: Young adults and addiction treatment. *Journal of Psychodrama, Sociometry, and Group Psychotherapy, 65*(1), 137–143. https://doi.org/10.12926/0731-1273-65.1.137.

Giacomucci, S. (2018). Social work and sociometry: An integration of theory and clinical practice. *The Pennsylvania Social Worker, 39*(1), 14–16.

Giacomucci, S. (2018b). Social work and sociometry: Integrating history, theory, and practice. *The Clinical Voice*. Richboro, PA: Pennsylvania Society for Clinical Social Work.

Giacomucci, S. (2018). Traveling as spontaneity training: If you want to become a psychodramatist, travel the world! *International Group Psychotherapies and Psychodrama Journal, 4*(1), 34–41.

Giacomucci, S. (2019). *Social group work in action: A sociometry, psychodrama, and experiential trauma therapy curriculum*. Doctorate in Social Work (DSW) Dissertations, 124. https://repository.upenn.edu/cgi/viewcontent.cgi?article=1128&context=edissertations_sp2.

Giacomucci, S., Gera, S., Briggs, D., & Bass, K. (2018). Experiential addiction treatment: Creating positive connection through sociometry and therapeutic spiral model safety structures. *Journal of Addiction and Addictive Disorders, 5*, 17. https://doi.org/10.24966/AAD-7276/100017.

Giacomucci, S., & Stone, A. M. (2019). Being in two places at once: Renegotiating traumatic experience through the surplus reality of psychodrama. *Social Work with Groups, 42*(3), 184–196. https://doi.org/10.1080/01609513.2018.1533913.

Green, H. D. (1950). Sociometry and social intergroup work. *Sociometry, 13*(1), 22–28.

Hale, A. E. (1981). *Conducting clinical sociometric explorations: A manual for psychodramatists and sociometrists*. Roanoke, VA: Royal Publishing Company.

Hale, A. E. (2009). Moreno's sociometry: Exploring interpersonal connection. *Group, 33*(4), 347–358.

Hare, A. P., & Hare, J. R. (1996). *JL Moreno*. London: Sage Publications.

Kellermann, P. F. (1992). *Focus on psychodrama: The therapeutic aspects of psychodrama*. London, UK: Jessica Kingsley.

Korshak, S. J., & Shapiro, M. (2013). Choosing the unchosen: Counteracting the sociodynamic effect using complementary sharing. *Journal of Psychodrama, Sociometry, and Group Psychotherapy, 61*(1), 7–15.

Lazarus, R. S., & McCleary, R. A. (1951). Autonomic discrimination without awareness: A study of subception. *Psychological Review, 58*(2), 113–122.

Moreno, J.D. (2014). *Impromptu Man: J.L. Moreno and the Origins of Psychodrama, Encounter Culture, and the Social Network*. New York, NY: Bellevue Literary Press.

Moreno, J. L. (1914). *Einladung zu einer Begegnung*. Vienna: Anzengruber Verlag.

Moreno, J. L. (1924). *Das Stegreiftheater*. Berlin, Germany: Gustav Kiepenheuer Verlag.

Moreno, J.L. (1931). *Application of the group method to classification*. Beacon, NY: Beacon House Inc.

Moreno, J. L. (1934). *Who shall survive? A new approach to the problems of human interrelations.* Washington, DC: Nervous and Mental Disease Publishing Co.

Moreno, J. L. (1937a). Editorial foreword. *Sociometry, 1*(1/2), 5–7.

Moreno, J. L. (1937b). Sociometry in relation to other social sciences. *Sociometry, 1,* 206–219.

Moreno, J. L. (1939). Psychodramatic shock therapy, a sociometric approach to the problem of mental disorders. *Sociometry, 2,* 1–30.

Moreno, J. L. (1941). Foundations of sociometry: An introduction. *Sociometry, 4*(1), 15–35.

Moreno, J. L. (1942). Sociometry in action. *Sociometry, 5*(3), 298–315.

Moreno, J. L. (1943). Sociometry and the cultural order. *Sociometry, 6*(3), 299–344.

Moreno, J. L. (1946). *Psychodrama Volume 1.* Beacon, NY: Beacon House Press.

Moreno, J. L. (1947). Progress and pitfalls in sociometric theory. *Sociometry, 10,* 268–272.

Moreno, J. L. (1948). The three branches of sociometry: A postscript. *Sociometry, 11*(1/2), 121–128.

Moreno, J. L. (1949). Origins and foundations of interpersonal theory, sociometry and microsociology. *Sociometry, 12*(1/3), 235–254.

Moreno, J. L. (1950). The sociometric approach to social case work. *Sociometry, 13*(2), 172–175.

Moreno, J. L. (1953). *Who shall survive? Foundations of sociometry, group psychotherapy and sociodrama* (2nd edn.). Beacon, NY: Beacon House.

Moreno, J. L. (1955). *Preludes to my autobiography.* Beacon, NY: Beacon House.

Moreno, J. L. (1956). The sociometric school and the science of man. In J. L. Moreno (eds), *Sociometry and the science of man* (pp. 15–35). Beacon, NY: Beacon House.

Moreno, J. L. (1957). *The first book on group psychotherapy* (3rd ed.). Beacon, NY: Beacon House.

Moreno, J. L. (in collaboration with Z.T. Moreno). (1959). *Psychodrama second volume, foundations of psychotherapy.* Beacon, NY: Beacon House.

Moreno, J. L. (1960). The principle of encounter. In J.L. Moreno (Eds.), *The sociometry reader* (pp. 15–16). Beacon, NY: Beacon House.

Moreno, J. L. (1963). Reflections on my method of group psychotherapy and psychodrama. *Ciba Symposium, 11*(4), 148–157.

Moreno, J. L. (2019). In E. Schreiber, S. Kelley, & S. Giacomucci (Eds.) *The autobiography of a genius.* United Kingdom: North West Psychodrama Association.

Moreno, Z. T. (1983). Psychodrama. In H. Kaplan, B. Sadock (Eds.), *Comprehensive group psychotherapy,* 2nd edn. (pp. 158–166). Philadelphia: Lippincott, Williams & Wilkins.

Moreno, Z. T. (1987). Psychodrama, role theory, and the concept of the social atom. In T. Horvatin, E. Schreiber (Eds.) (2006). *The Quintessential Zerka.* New York, NY: Routledge. Originally published in J. Zeig (Ed.), *The Evolution of Psychotherapy.* New York, NY: Brunner/Mazel.

Moreno, Z. T. (2000). The function of 'tele' in human relations. In J. Zeig (Ed.) *The evolution of psychotherapy: A meeting of the minds.* Phoenix, AZ: Erickson Foundation Press.

Nolte, J. (2014). *The philosophy, theory, and methods of J.L. Moreno: The man who tried to become god.* New York, NY: Routledge.

Renouvier, P. (1958). *The group psychotherapy movement: J.L. Moreno, its pioneer and founder.* Psychodrama and group psychotherapy monographs, No. 33. Beacon, NY: Beacon House.

Ridge, R. M. (2010). A literature review of psychodrama. *Journal of Group Psychotherapy, Psychodrama, and Sociometry.* Originally published in Ridge, R. M. (2007). *The body alchemy of psychodrama: A phenomenologically-based qualitative evaluation of a training manual for trainers and practitioners of psychodrama and group psychotherapy.* Union Institute and University, ProQuest Dissertations Publishing. Retrieved from: https://asgpp.org/pdf/Ridge%20Journal.pdf.

Schreiber, E. (2018). Sociatry part 2: Moreno's mysticism. *Psychodrama Network News.* Winter 2018, pp. 24–25. American Society of Group Psychotherapy and Psychodrama.

Yaniv, D. Z. (2014). Tele and the social atom: The oeuvre of J. L. Moreno from the perspective of neuropsychology. *Zeitschrift für Psychodrama und Soziometrie, 13*(1), 107–120.

von Ameln, F., & Becker-Ebel, J. (2020). *Fundamentals of psychodrama.* Singapore: Springer Nature.

Chapter 6
Psychodrama and Social Work Theory

Abstract This chapter includes an overview of foundational psychodrama theories—action theory, catharsis, and surplus reality. The three phases of a psychodrama group (warm-up, enactment, and sharing) and the five elements of a psychodrama (stage, protagonist, director, auxiliary egos, and audience/group) are described. Morenean philosophy and sociometric theory are revisited as they relate to psychodrama. The similar elements of psychodrama theory and social work are underlined including the importance of mutual aid, spontaneity, creativity, empowerment, self-determination, interpersonal skills, relationships, group stages, and roles.

Keywords Social work · Psychodrama theory · Catharsis · Morenean philosophy · Developmental theory

Many definitions of psychodrama have been proposed since its inception. Moreno offers a simple, though ambiguous, definition of psychodrama—"science which explores the 'truth' by dramatic methods" (1972, p. a). Moreno also has defined psychodrama as a theology (1921), a dramatic art form (1924), a socio-political system (1953), a method of psychotherapy (1946), and a philosophy of life (1955) (see Fig. 6.1). It seems that the experiential nature of psychodrama makes it difficult to describe adequately with words. Kellermann (1992) offers us a comprehensive definition of psychodrama:

> Psychodrama is a form of psychotherapy in which clients are encouraged to continue and complete their actions through dramatization, role-playing, and dramatic self-presentation. Both verbal and nonverbal communications are utilized. A number of scenes are enacted, depicted, for example, memories of specific happenings in the past, unfinished situations, inner dramas, fantasies, dreams, preparations for future risk-taking situations, or unrehearsed expressions of mental states in the here and now. These scenes either approximate real-life situations or are eternalizations of inner mental processes. If required, other roles may be taken by group members or by inanimate objects. Many techniques are employed, such the role reversal, the double, the mirror, concretization, maximizing and soliloquy. Usually the phases of warm up, action, working through, closure and sharing can be identified. (p. 20).

Psychodrama is a comprehensive approach that integrates elements of psychology, sociology, religion, and the theater. In the USA, psychodrama seems to be primarily classified as a psychotherapy—internationally, psychodrama seems to be employed

S. Giacomucci, *Social Work, Sociometry, and Psychodrama*, Psychodrama in Counselling, Coaching and Education 1,
https://doi.org/10.1007/978-981-33-6342-7_6

Fig. 6.1 Jacob Moreno seated on the psychodrama stage. Reprinted with permission from Figusch, 2014

more often in a variety of settings beyond psychotherapy including in communities, religion, politics, business, education, training, theater, and research (Nolte, 2020). Though the objectives of psychodrama enactments may vary from setting to setting, most psychodrama sessions consistently include three phases, five elements, and at least a few core psychodrama techniques.

6.1 Healing in Action

The etymology of the word *psychodrama* carries the meaning of "psyche in action" (Moreno, 1946). J.L. Moreno believed that because we are wounded in relationship and in action, healing must also take place in relationship and in action. Moreno suggested that we have various conscious and unconscious drives and urges that move us into action and movement. And that "the hidden dynamics of behavior are better brought to view in action than in words because acting is closer to the deeper levels of that which is unconscious than is language" (Nolte, 2020, pp. 132–133). Prior to verbal language, gesturing is our first mode of communication and serves as "the mind–body connection upon which all subsequent language is built" (Dayton, 2005, p. xvii). Psychodrama's reliance on action helps participants access non-verbal (or preverbal) emotional content in a holistic way. This becomes especially important when working with trauma because of how the body is impacted by adverse experiences and holds implicit memory (Levine, 2010; van der Kolk, 2014).

Psychodrama was the first body-oriented therapy and is operated as a comprehensive biopsychosocial-spiritual approach (Giacomucci, 2019a).

In psychodrama, we are working with roles, which have a physical, psychological, social, and sometimes a spiritual component to them. Moreno argued that the concept of the role provides a bridge between psychology and the social sciences while offering a simplified understanding of the complexities of clustered emotion, cognition, and behavior for clients (Buchanan, 1984; Moreno, 1961). Psychodrama is meant to reflect real life and mirrors the actual behavior of participants in life situations (Nolte, 2020). Psychodrama allows a protagonist to act out situations or events that would have been impossible otherwise. In psychodrama, everything is based on the principle of "*as-if*." The imagination is used to act as if the imaginary aspects of the drama are real and happening in the here-and-now. Moreno writes that "as-if" is the foundation of accessing spontaneity in the moment:

> it is the quality which gives newness and vivacity to feelings, acting, and verbal utterances which are nothing but repetitions of what an individual has experienced a thousand times before…This form of spontaneity has apparently a great practical importance in *energizing* and *unifying* the self. It makes dissociated automaton like acts be felt and look like true self-expression and acts like a 'cosmetic' for the psyche (Moreno, 1972, pp. 89–90, as cited in Kellermann, 1992).

In psychodrama, spontaneity is understood as the curative factor of the therapeutic process. Moreno defined it as the capacity to "respond with some degree of adequacy to a new situation or with some degree of novelty to an old situation" (Moreno, 1964, p xii). Spontaneity allows one to respond in a new way to old behaviors, thoughts, emotions, obsessions, repetitions, re-enactments, and relational experiences. A spontaneous action is characterized by competence, adequacy, and novelty based on the situation at hand—whether it is a social situation or an intrapsychic experience. A psychodramatic scene, infused with spontaneity of its role players acting "as-if", offers unlimited potentials for new experience. This has multiple clinical implications including providing role training for future situations, offering moments developmental repair or corrective emotional experiences, providing the body with the chance to complete survival responses to traumatic events that were interrupted leaving one frozen, and simply establishing an avenue to satisfy various *act hungers*.

Act hunger is a term that describes one's drive to get into action in order to achieve some sort of completion (Dayton, 2005). Act hungers may originate from unrealized roles, dreams, hopes, or goals, from unexpressed thoughts or emotions, from unresolved business, or from unjust circumstances which create oppressive conditions. Psychodrama allows one to embody experiences that have been otherwise absent from their life and experience an *act-completion*, or the satisfaction of resolving the act hunger (Kellermann, 1992). Moreno argued against psychoanalysis's restriction of the client to laying on a couch for interpretation, instead he encouraged them to act out their inner conflicts and joys. While Freud considered "acting out" as a resistance to psychotherapy, Moreno practiced in a way that acting out was the therapy (Nolte, 2014). He believed that acting out through a psychodrama reduced the impulse for acting out inappropriately in real life (Nolte, 2020). A social worker, Treudley, writes of the advantages of psychodrama to case work interviewing:

Psychodrama offers many advantages in fulfilling the functions that case work sets for itself. It makes possible a much clearer understanding of personality patterning than an interview can possibly do…The acting brings back memories that no verbalization would recall. The client is much more in control of an interview than of a play and unconsciously reveals much in acting than he would block from expression in talking." (Treudley, 1944, p. 170).

Moreno believed that through role-playing and action, a participant accesses previously unconscious or suppressed emotions, thoughts, and memories. Acting out issues through psychodrama allows for a deeper, holistic expression, the fulfillment of act hungers, experiences of act completions, and the integration of new *action insights.*

Action insight is defined as experiential learning, or "the integration of emotional, cognitive, imaginary, behavioral, and interpersonal learning experiences" (Kellermann, 1992, p. 86). Action insights are different from intellectual insights or self-awareness in that they are more fully embodied and integrated throughout the self because they are achieved through multidimensional action rather than simply talking or reflecting. Action insights are a function of spontaneity and are most often preceded by an emotional catharsis. Interestingly, some psychologists have highlighted the connections between action and emotion (Nolte, 2020). Even the etymology of the word "emotion" derives the meaning "to stir up" or "to move out." Our emotions prime us for social action through varying experiences of emotion in the body (DeRivera and Dahl, 1977; Pally, 2000). Psychodrama is often associated with emotions because of its power to create intense emotional experiences or catharses for participants. The interconnectedness between mind, body, and relationship is highlighted by the following quote by Pally (2000), "emotion connects not only the mind and body of one individual but minds and bodies *between* individuals" (p. 74, emphasis in original). In psychodrama, the group-as-a-whole emotional experience is palpable as the emotionally charged action of the drama connects the minds and bodies of group members in shared catharsis.

6.2 Catharsis

Breuer and Freud were the first to introduce the concept of catharsis to psychiatry in *Studies on Hysteria* (1895/1957), though the idea was previously used in the medical and theatrical fields. Freud described catharsis as an instinctive and involuntary release of affect associated with a past event (1893). Similarly, catharsis is defined by an influential psychodramatist as an experience of release that takes place when an inner mobilization finds its outlet through action (Kellermann, 1984, p. 1). Psychodrama theory highlights catharsis as a function related to both explicit narrative memory, but also implicit somatic memory. Due to psychodrama's action-based approach, catharsis is quite common because the entire self, physical and mental, is put into action (Nolte, 2014). J. L. Moreno offered significant contributions to the understanding of catharsis in psychotherapy and society (Moreno, 1971).

J.L. Moreno's conceptualization of catharsis was influenced by Aristotle who believed that audience members enjoyed watching Greek tragedies because of the experienced *Katharsis* of fear and pity (1951). Adding to Aristotle's discussion, Moreno noted that "the cathartic effect relies on novelty and surprise" (Nolte, 2014, p. 220). This cathartic effect is most potent on the first viewing, and it gradually diminishes with each viewing—thus catharsis is related to spontaneity (Moreno, 1940). In the traditional theater, actors role-play the same roles with the same scripts lacking spontaneity; the play is a cultural conserve. Psychodrama, on the other hand, is alive with spontaneity. There is no script, everything happens for the first time, and no psychodrama is repeated identically. While Aristotle was focused on spectator catharsis, Moreno was also curious about catharsis of the actors. Psychodrama involves both. He writes "The greater a spectator's social and psychodramatic roles correspond to the symbolic roles portrayed on the stage, the greater is the catharsis produced by the drama" (1940, p. 226).

Moreno also noted the difference between audience catharsis and *action catharsis*, positing that the former could never be entirely adequate by itself (1946). "The greater catharsis achieved through action is undeniable. The patient is able to express kinesthetically many feelings for which he has no words" (Moreno & Enneis, 1950, p. 13). Moreno also considered the relational context of catharsis. In psychodrama and group psychotherapy, catharsis is not taking place in a vacuum; there are other humans in the room. In *Psychodrama Volume 1*, he writes that the catharsis of one group member is dependent upon the catharsis of other group members—"the catharsis has to be interpersonal" (1972, p. 180).

The psychodramatic theory of catharsis includes two primary types of catharsis— *catharsis of abreaction* and *catharsis of integration*. Historically, psychodrama seems to have gained a reputation for its ability to produce catharsis of abreaction – but the goal of psychodrama is actually a catharsis of integration (Hollander, 1969; Hug, 2013; Nolte, 2014). While the catharsis of abreaction could be conceptualized as overcoming or loosening resistance through release, expression, or discharge, the catharsis of integration helps to re-order or transform intrapsychic structure after the release (Kellermann, 1984). Abreaction provides a sense of completion and a release of tension related to the issue; integrative catharsis provides a renewed sense of harmony and equilibrium through a meaningful shift in perception (Nolte, 2014). Kellermann articulately outlines J.L. Moreno's (1924, 1940, 1946, 1953) contribution and enlargement of the original meaning of the term catharsis:

> To include not only release and relief of emotions, but also integration and ordering; not only intense reliving of the past, but also intense living in the here-and-now; not only a passive, verbal reflection, but also an active, nonverbal enactment; not only a private ritual, but also a communal, shared rite of healing; not only an intrapsychic tension reduction, but also an interpersonal conflict resolution; not only a medical purification, but also a religious and aesthetic experience. (1984, pp. 10–11).

While psychodrama may have developed a reputation for being overly focused on catharsis of abreaction, which can be re-traumatizing for trauma survivors, over the past two decades, there has been a deeper sensitivity in considering psychodrama's clinical use with trauma survivors (Dayton, 2015; Giacomucci & Marquit, 2020; Giacomucci & Stone, 2019; Hudgins & Toscani, 2013).

6.3 Surplus Reality and Concretization

A psychodrama enactment almost always takes place through surplus reality. Jacob Moreno defines surplus reality as a mode of subjective experience that is beyond reality and is enhanced through the imagination (1965, pp. 212–213). Surplus reality describes the element of psychodrama during which the subjective reality of the client is put into action using role-playing techniques. "It allows the protagonist to experience physically what has been experienced psychologically" (Watersong, 2011, p. 21). Surplus reality can also be used to describe the inner imaginal space of an individual or the subjective experience of different mental health symptoms that are a distortion of reality—flashbacks, delusions, hallucinations, etc. (Giacomucci, 2018c).

Psychodrama provides a bridge between the intrapsychic reality of the client and the outer objective reality through the technique of concretization (Watersong, 2011). This technique makes the client's inner world tangible by using other group members or objects to represent or symbolize them. The technique of concretization utilizes the vehicle of projection through symbolic representation. A client may choose a group member to play the role of their mother, or a scarf to represent their courage. In these examples, the client is projecting an internalized object relation or intrapsychic quality into another human or object. In an interview, Blatner (2010, as cited in Konopik & Cheung, 2013) emphasized the significance of concretization, stating "it gets past tendencies to distance oneself through narration." The psychodrama stage is seen "as-if" it is a creative and spontaneity space where anything could take place— especially the impossible (Kellermann, 1992). Watersong (2011) states: "Surplus reality in psychodrama addresses our deep hunger to explore creative potential by experiencing and expressing all that we are and expanding into the abundance of life" (p. 26). The use of surplus reality encourages an element of play. Winnicott (1971) writes of the importance of play in that the individual expresses their spontaneity and creativity, engages their whole self, and discovers the new aspects of personality.

Moreno (1939) highlighted the existence of unseen dimensions of life that are not fully explored, processed, expressed, or experienced and that surplus reality of psychodrama was needed to work through these aspects of life. Through the surplus reality of a psychodrama, an experience in the future or a scene from the past could be put into action. A historical moment could be brought into the classroom for students to engage with. In trauma therapy, psychodramatists often create surplus reality moments of developmental repair during which the client is provided with an embodied experience of having their previously unmet needs fulfilled today on the psychodrama stage (Giacomucci & Stone, 2019). Psychodrama techniques permit one to have dialogues with the dead, offering an efficient method for renegotiating unresolved grief and losses (Darrow & Childs, 2020; Giacomucci, 2020a). A protagonist has the capacity in psychodrama's surplus reality to dialogue with ancestors or even an unborn child!

> Psychodrama is a way to change the world in the HERE AND NOW using the fundamental rules of imagination without falling into the abyss of illusion, hallucination or delusion. The human brain is the vehicle of imagination. Psychodrama, in training the imagination, overcomes the differences which hinder communication between the sexes, between the races, the generations, the sick and the healthy, between people and animals, between people and objects, between the living and the dead. The simple methods of psychodrama give us courage, return to us our lost unity with the universe, and re-establish the continuity of life. (Moreno, 1972, p. 131)

Concretization and surplus reality provide the psychodramatist with tools for enactment and assisting the protagonist toward achieving their goal. Zerka Moreno (2000) observed that the most healing catharses emerge from psychodrama scenes that could not, did not, or are unlikely to play out in reality.

6.4 Three Phases of a Psychodrama

A standard psychodrama group includes three essential stages—warm-up, enactment, and sharing (see Fig. 6.2). In many ways, these three stages mirror J.L. Moreno's triadic system of sociometry, psychodrama, and group psychotherapy. Furthermore, these three group phases also reflect the beginning, middle, and ending phases depicted in social work with groups theory (Shulman, 2015).

6.4.1 The Warm-Up

The warm-up stage often includes an action-based sociometric exploration of the group which serves to both warm-up participants to physical action and internally to

Warm-Up   Enactment   Sharing

Fig. 6.2 Three phases of a psychodrama session (Shulman, 2015)

warm up to a psychodrama. The warm-up phase of a group may include introductions, group norms, discussion, check-ins, and/or sociometry explorations. In the warm-up stage, a protagonist is selected—often by sociometric process of the group. Moreno strongly emphasizes the importance of warming-up in his writing—"the chief point of the technique was to get the patient started, to get him warmed up so that he might throw his psyche into operation and unfold the psychodrama" (1972, p. 182). The warm-up is an essential phase of the group; further phases are incomplete without adequate warm-up. Many role-plays attempted by social workers in therapeutic, educational, or community settings fail due to a lack of attention to warm-up.

6.4.2 The Enactment

The enactment phase involves bringing the protagonist's intrapsychic or interpersonal life onto the stage through role-playing and other psychodramatic techniques. Dayton (2005) describes it as externalizing and concretizing the protagonist's inner world of object relations. She states that "the psychodramatic stage becomes a path into another world, where it allows a protagonist to time-travel out of the narrow dimensions of her everyday life" (2005, p. 24). This is the phase during which the group moves onto the stage and into surplus reality. The enactment may be a psychodrama, sociodrama, or other action-based process.

6.4.3 Sharing

After the enactment, group members de-role and the sharing phase begins. During this phase, group members share about their own experience of playing a role or observing the psychodrama with the intent of identifying with and connecting to the protagonist. This serves as an integration period for group members as they apply the theme and experience to their own lives, but also for the protagonist who is re-integrating himself intrapsychically and interpersonally after the enactment. Sharing in psychodrama generally does not include feedback or giving advice; instead, it emphasizes the sharing of personal insight and identification based on the psychodrama enactment. Participants may also provide broader perspectives from the experience in their role (role feedback) (von Ameln & Becker-Ebel, 2020). The psychodrama director often will also participate in the sharing process of a psychodrama with clients while taking into consideration professional boundaries.

6.5 The Five Elements of a Psychodrama

There are five ingredients to any psychodrama; they are the stage, a director, a protagonist, at least one auxiliary ego, and the audience (see Fig. 6.3).

6.5.1 Stage

The *stage* provides a place for the action to be held and contained within space. Moreno (1953, p. 81) states that "the stage space is an extension of life beyond the reality test of life itself. Reality and fantasy are not in conflict, but both are functions within a wider sphere—the psychodramatic world of objects, persons, and events." On the psychodrama stage, anything is possible. Moreno describes it as a multidimensional living space in contrast to the restraints of reality (Nolte, 2020). Moreno designed his own unique stage in the 1920s for the Theater of Spontaneity in Vienna, which he later built in New York at his sanitarium in Beacon. His stage design was circular with three levels and a balcony which was recreated multiple times at psychodrama institutes or hospitals around the world (see Fig. 6.4).

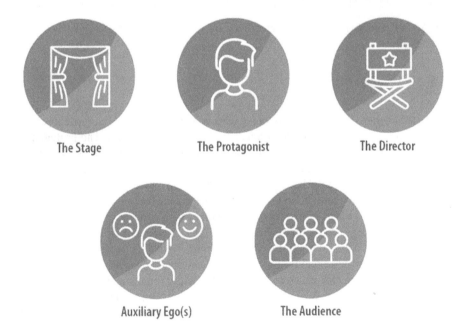

The Stage   The Protagonist   The Director

Auxiliary Ego(s)   The Audience

Fig. 6.3 The five elements of a psychodrama enactment

Fig. 6.4 Psychodrama stage with its three levels and balcony. Reprinted with permission from Figusch (2014)

6.5.2 Protagonist

The second ingredient is a *protagonist* who is a member of the group chosen to provide the content of the psychodrama based on his or her goals. The protagonist emerges from the group and becomes the center of attention for the psychodrama enactment. The protagonist may be selected by the group, self-selected, scheduled, or chosen by the therapist/director. Dayton (2005) says that offering a protagonist the stage is offering them an opportunity to meet themselves on an inward journey. Simultaneously, the protagonist is embarking on a "hero's journey" for themselves, the group, and the larger community (Mosher, 2009). The scene of the psychodrama is primarily based on the experience, perception, and action of the protagonist. They are externalizing their inner reality through the psychodrama process. The protagonist, together with the director, co-creates the psychodramatic enactment on the stage with the support of the group. Moreno notes that the goal is "not to turn the patients into actors, but rather to stir them up to be on the stage what they are, more deeply and explicitly than they appear to be in life reality" (Moreno, 1946, p. 251).

6.5.3 Director

The *director* is the person facilitating the session and guiding the protagonist toward the completion of their goal in the psychodrama. The director uses a variety of techniques which will be discussed further in the next section. In classical psychodrama, the protagonist leads the way as the director helps to concretize and produce the psychodramatic scene. The director's responsibilities also include keeping the enactment physically and emotionally safe. The psychodrama director is an integration of four roles—therapist, sociometrist/group leader, analyst, and producer (Kellermann, 1992). Though psychodrama directing may seem like a straight-forward and simple task, a skilled psychodrama director is incorporating a wealth of philosophy, theory, and interventions within the directing process. The director is faced with countless choices within each moment of the enactment and carefully discerns which intervention might best facilitate movement toward the overall goals of the protagonist, the psychodrama, and the group-as-a-whole. It is not suggested that any professional attempt to direct a full psychodrama until they have completed at least 100 h of psychodrama training—though the process of becoming certified as a practitioner in psychodrama includes a total of 780 training hours.

6.5.4 Auxiliary Egos

The fourth element is that of one or more *auxiliary egos*. These auxiliary roles are most often held by other group members but could also be staff members or students. Moreno writes that the auxiliary ego has three functions: (a) as an actor, (b) as a therapeutic agent, and (c) as an active social investigator, rather than a passive audience member (1972). Utilizing auxiliaries is a tool of the director, but once enrolled, they are an extension of the protagonist (Moreno, 1947). Most often the protagonist selects the auxiliaries who will hold the roles necessary for the enactment to take place. At times, the director may make clinical role assignments based on his knowledge of group members' needs. The auxiliary plays a role based on role training from the protagonist and in service of the needs of the psychodrama scene. At the same time, the auxiliaries may experience a dormant role within their own self-system awaken as they bring themselves to the role (Dayton, 2005; Hudgins & Toscani, 2013).

Auxiliary egos initially play their role in the scene through the role training of the protagonist and director. Often, they are initially role reversed into the protagonist role so they can observe the protagonist demonstrate their role for them. A skillful director will have auxiliaries bring their own emotional content into their roles, so they are playing roles not just for the protagonist, but also for themselves. In most psychodramas, it seems that the protagonist chooses group members for auxiliary roles based on their telic connection which results in the role player having a meaningful connection to the role they are playing. Tele may also active when a group member spontaneously doubles for the protagonist in the scene. The role of the double can be taken by the director, an audience member, an auxiliary ego, or sometimes multiple auxiliary egos.

6.5.5 The Audience or the Group

The *audience* (the group) is the final element in psychodrama and provides the protagonist with an important function by bearing witness to their story. The action of a psychodrama has a catching force that stirs up powerful emotions in audience members, just as observing an emotional movie scene. "The audience sees itself, that is, one of its collective syndromes portrayed on the stage" (Moreno, 1946, p. 251). Group members in the audience have the opportunity to identify with the protagonist's story while watching it from a distance. Most frequently, audience members experience both catharsis of abreaction and integration through their observer role in the drama, which Hug (2007) attributes to the mechanisms of mirror neurons (Sect. 8.4.4 for a more complete description of mirror neurons).

Moreno writes that the audience (or group) has two functions: (a) observing the psychodrama and protagonist on stage, and (b) serving as the patient or a learner (1972). In Moreno's group psychotherapy system, the group is the patient (1947). When the group is the patient, the work becomes "with the group, by the group, and for the group" (von Ameln & Becker-Ebel, 2020, p. 7). The protagonist, auxiliary egos, and the topic of the psychodrama emerge from the group and return to the group through de-roling. In the sharing process of the psychodrama, group members share about how they relate to the protagonist's psychodrama and the roles or themes within it. A skillful psychodrama director facilitates the selection of a psychodrama topic and protagonist that represents the group-as-a-whole. This ensures that audience members are also benefiting from the psychodrama enactment. When a psychodrama is enacted that does not represent the group-as-a-whole, the group session becomes an individual session in a group setting—which Moreno and others have cautioned against (Moreno, 1947; Nolte, 2020).

6.6 Morenean Philosophy and Sociometric Theory Within Psychodrama

Although many have segregated psychodrama from Moreno's philosophy and his sociometric system, they are part of the same whole. So, although this chapter is devoted to psychodrama theory, it is incomplete without also outlining the intersection and integration of Morenean philosophy and sociometry within psychodrama.

6.6.1 Sociometry

Moreno's approach to group psychotherapy begins with assessing the sociodynamics within the group. He used to say that "psychodrama without sociometry is blind." Sociometry is often used as a warm-up to the psychodrama enactment. In some cases, an individual group member's social atom or role atom may be enacted through psychodrama. The sociometric assessment and exploration of the group allows the psychodramatist to help the group uncover a central concern and open tensions systems within the group with a topic that most represents the group-as-a-whole. The topic and protagonist of a psychodrama are often chosen through sociometric selection by the other group members. This ensures that the topic is relatable to the rest of the group and that the psychodrama does not become individual therapy in a group setting. Innumerable sociograms could be created from infinite criteria within one group. While the social atom and cultural atom depict the individual's social life, the sociogram depicts the sociodynamics within the group. Just as a pattern of role relations exists within each social atom, so too does a pattern of role relations exist within each sociogram and within each psychodrama group. An exploration of the complexities of these social and role relationships is further explored in Chap. 14.

Tele is the glue that keeps the group together and cohesive allowing for helpful relationships. Acting as a socio-gravitational force within the group, tele enhances the warm-up process and brings participants together upon a core issue. Tele often expresses itself through the protagonist's choice for role players. Through the intimate experience of psychodrama, transference and projection dissolve and are often replaced by stronger telic connections between group members. "The telic relationships between protagonist, therapist, auxiliary egos, and the significant dramatis personae of the world which they portray are crucial for the therapeutic progress." (Moreno, 1972, p. XI).

The sharing portion of a psychodrama group functions to re-integrate the protagonist back from the surplus reality of the psychodrama stage into the sociometry of the group itself. In the sharing, group members often give voice to previously undiscovered sociometric connections between themselves and the protagonist. At this time, the protagonist takes a less active role while others have a chance to share. This provides the protagonist with a chance to internally integrate and digest their experience while being held by the group. This is when the newfound tele is labeled and relationships between group members further strengthened. In these ways, sociometry is consistently present throughout each of the three phases of a psychodrama group—warm-up, enactment, and sharing.

6.6.2 Role Theory, Role Relations, and Role-Playing

Psychodrama uses drama to express the psyche or the self. The vehicle from which the self is expressed both in life and in psychodrama is through roles. Every psychodrama uses roles and role-playing techniques. The psychodramatic enactment may include intrapsychic roles, interpersonal roles, social roles, psychodramatic or fantasy roles, spiritual roles, or a mix of various types of roles. The protagonist chooses other group members to play the roles needed for the scene. The relationships between the protagonist and the roles on the stage are enacted and often transformed through the psychodrama process. In addition to the role dynamics between the psychodrama roles, each role player also has role relationships to the protagonist, the other group members, the director, the actual role that they are playing, and the roles within their social atom which are symbolically represented through the protagonist's psychodrama. There are layers upon layers of role dynamics actively engaged, some more explicitly than others, within a psychodrama experience. A skillful psychodrama director can bring to consciousness these multiple layers of role relations for each participant and weave them through the psychodrama process—effectively making each participant a protagonist.

While traditional role-plays are often scripted or hypothetical, psychodrama role-plays are spontaneous real-life simulations (von Falko & Becker-Ebel, 2020). Many psychodramas are entirely focused on helping a protagonist adopt a new role, let go of an old role, role train for future situations, feel more competent or spontaneous in their current roles and role relationships (role-playing), or transform an old role into something new (role creation). Many psychodramas even have different scenes that can be connected to the three different phases of role development. At the end of each psychodrama enactment, participants are asked to de-role as they return to the role of themselves for sharing. The essentiality of roles to psychodrama is clearly depicted in that four of the five core elements of a psychodrama are roles (director, protagonist, auxiliary egos, and audience members).

6.6.3   Theories of Change

Psychodrama's theories of change include action theory and spontaneity-creativity theory which are core to every psychodrama enactment. Every psychodrama is spontaneously put into action without a script. Moreno's *Canon of Creativity* provides the psychodrama director with a map for change at the intrapsychic, interpersonal, and social levels. The group begins in the warming-up phase—circling the outside of the canon. A spark of spontaneity emerges from the group process and is met with creativity, giving birth to a new cultural conserve within the group process. This Canon of Creativity is activated multiple times by each group member throughout a psychodrama while also serving as the overarching clinical map for the psychodrama itself.

In psychodrama, the healing does not come from the therapist to the protagonist, but instead from relationships between the protagonist and the enacted roles and other group members. Zerka Moreno states that the purpose of psychodrama is to help the protagonist remove barriers to healing themselves by accessing their autonomous healing center within (Moreno, 2012). Psychodrama leverages the mutual aid between group members, effectively helping the group-as-a-whole to access its autonomous healing center (Giacomucci, 2019b).

6.6.4 Developmental Theory

As noted in a previous chapter (see Sect. 4.8), Moreno's developmental theory reflects core psychodrama interventions—the double, the mirror, and role reversal (Moreno, 1952). Although it is not often considered, these three phases of Moreno's developmental theory can be used as a clinical map to inform which psychodramatic interventions are clinically appropriate for the group and the protagonist in any given moment. Doubling explores the *subjective* experience of the protagonist, the mirror attempts to increase *objectivity* in approaching the situation, and role reversal aims to provide insight into the *intersubjectivity* of the experience. Developmentally speaking, doubling from parents provides a labeling of the infant's experience, stabilization in this universe, and a beginning of differentiation of the self. These developmental goals are also clinical goals that the intervention of doubling can be used to achieve.

Doubling from the director or other group members not only creates connection but also helps to articulate something unspoken for the protagonist. The double provides a stabilizing force for the protagonist within their role in surplus reality of the psychodrama. When a protagonist is unable to fully see themselves and their behavior within relationships in the psychodrama, the mirror intervention may be clinically necessary to assist with the developmental task of accurately seeing one's self in the world. This could be used for helping a protagonist identify problematic behavior or positive aspects of self that they have not fully owned. Role reversal is the third developmental stage during which the individual has the capacity to step into the shoes of another and see the world through their eyes. Once the therapeutic and developmental tasks of doubling and mirroring have been given attention, role reversal can be employed as a clinical intervention for new action insights and catharsis of integration.

In psychodrama work with trauma, it is especially important to consider the role of developmental trauma and how the developmental theory might offer both diagnostic information and direction for corrective experiences (Giacomucci, 2018c). Many survivors of childhood trauma were not adequately doubled or mirrored by their caregivers; thus, they struggle with a sense of self, codependency, individualization, and tasks related to these phases of development. It has been this writer's experience that a client's here-and-now presentation is often indicative of which of the three developmental stages they experienced neglect or trauma and thus which corresponding psychodrama intervention needs to be focused on (see Table 6.1 for more info). A client with a destabilized or lacking sense of self may have experienced a lack of attuned doubling in childhood which would have promoted self-expression and self-understanding. A client with a distorted or undifferentiated sense of self is likely to have suffered from the absence of mirroring or misattunement in the mirror

Table 6.1 Psychodrama developmental phases and interventions—double, mirror, and role reversal

Intervention	Double	Mirror	Role reversal
Developmental tasks	Stabilization, expression, understanding self	Differentiation, individualization, sense of self	Sense of others, perspective, empathy, expansion of self
Focal point	From within	From afar	From the other
Perspective	Subjectivity	Objectivity	Intersubjectivity
Vehicle of change	Group members, auxiliary egos, or director	Seeing self role	Becoming other roles
Awareness	Being seen by others; seeing or sensing aspects of self	Seeing self	Seeing others and self

phase of development. And a client presenting with a distorted sense of others or lack of awareness of others is likely to have suffered adversity or neglect in the role reversal phase. In this way, Morenean developmental theory provides both a diagnostic framework and a prescriptive guide for intervention. This is a new idea and still needs to be further researched and tested.

When working with trauma-based roles (especially the victim and perpetrator roles) in a psychodrama scene with a trauma survivor, it is important that the double and mirror interventions be used prior to the role reversal. This allows the protagonist to stabilize, express (doubling), and accurately see themself and the situation (mirror) prior to being role reversed into a trauma-based role. If role reversal with a trauma-based role is attempted prematurely, it may result in re-traumatization, dissociation, uncontained catharsis, or further role training the protagonist in trauma-based roles. Hudgins & Toscani (2013) suggest that it is unsafe to role reverse a protagonist into a victim or perpetrator role (regardless if it is an intrapsychic or interpersonal role) until they have demonstrated the ability to spontaneously interact with the trauma-based role as themselves. For the victim role, this would mean rescuing, nurturing, and validating the victim role from their adult ego state; for the perpetrator roles, this would mean tolerating, standing up to, and setting boundaries with the perpetrator role from their adult ego state. Using the three phases of developmental theory as a map of clinical interventions within a psychodrama provides a guide to the director.

Furthermore, the three phases of a psychodrama group seem to also reflect the three phases of development. In the warm-up phase, group members are actively doubling each other through sociometry while giving voice to the central concerns of the group-as-a-whole. In the warm-up peer identification, connection, cohesion, and the stability of the group within the session take place. When a protagonist is chosen sociometrically by the group based on identification with a shared topic, the psychodrama enactment becomes relatable to everyone. The scene is essentially a double and a mirror for each group member to see themselves through the protagonist's psychodrama. The role relationships on stage shine light on the similarities in dynamics for each participant in their own lives. Each audience member is in the mirror position, seeing themselves in the protagonist. Each participant intuitively and intrapsychically role reverses with the protagonist through seeing themselves mirrored in the psychodrama process. They are imagining they are on the stage as protagonist, imagining what they would say or do next. The completion of the final phase of the group, sharing, is the completion of this inner role reversal for partici-pants; they de-role from being an auxiliary role or audience member and step into the role of themselves again. The sharing provides the participants with the opportunity to return to the role of self while labeling what they integrated through experiencing the psychodramatic reality of the protagonist. One could argue that even a seem-ingly uninvolved audience or group member is being implicitly doubled, mirrored, and role reversed throughout the process of a psychodrama group. Though there are some parallels between doubling, mirroring, and role reversals with the three phases of a group, it is important to note that these interventions are primarily, and often exclusively, employed in the enactment group phase. The idea of using Moreno's developmental theory as a clinical map to guide the interventions of the director is still a new idea and needs more research and exploration—nevertheless, it can be helpful for directors to consider the various elements of the double, mirror, and role reversal (see Table 6.1). A future chapter (see Sect. 13.1) will dive further into the actual implementation of the aforementioned psychodrama interventions.

6.7   Psychodrama and Social Work Theory

Social work and psychodrama exist with considerable overlap (Zwilling, 2004). Both share emphasis on the significance of mutual aid, non-judgmental acceptance, spontaneity, creativity, meeting the client where they are, roles, group phases, inter-personal skills, communication, empowerment, and human relationships (Gershoni, 2013; Giacomucci, 2018a, b; 2019b; Giacomucci & Stone, 2019; Konopik & Cheung, 2013; Skolnik, 2018; Wang & Liu, 2020). Skolnik's 2018 publication exclaims that social work and psychodrama form "a synergistic union." Social work and psychodrama are both employed in a variety of settings with different group types, including educational groups, training groups, supervision groups, support groups, treatment groups, self-help groups, therapeutic communities, community groups, social activism, policy work, and organizational groups.

Social work and psychodrama hold many core values in common and empha-sizes the significance of human relationships and mutual aid. Moreno believed that change was a result of the interaction between the group members playing roles in a psychodrama, not from the therapist (Moreno, Blomkvist, & Rutzel, 2000). He argued that each participant in the group had therapeutic potential and that group members could collectively act as therapists for each other.

Both psychodrama and social work emphasize the importance of role theory. The IASWG group standards explicitly state that "role theory and its application to members' relationships with one another and the worker" is "required knowledge" for the social worker (IASWG, 2015, p. 14). Similarly, psychodrama is based on

Moreno's role theory. The role of the psychodrama facilitator reflects the role of the social group worker as a guide, ally, or facilitator of the group with the intent to cultivate mutual aid (Carey, 2016; Drumm, 2006; Giacomucci, 2017; Skolnik, 2018). The social worker, within the group, operates as another human being, often sharing personal ideas, perceptions, beliefs, and emotions. The use of self is highlighted as an essential tool for social work practice with groups (Bitel, 2000; Northen & Kurland, 2001). Similarly, the psychodrama director often discloses from self in the sharing and processing stage of the psychodrama. This more active use of self is more common in the social work field and the psychodrama fields than in other fields.

Social work with groups and psychodrama each operates from a phasic model of group development and process (Skolnik, 2018). Social group work's phases of group development describe the tasks of the group over the course of its existence—from the preliminary stage, to a beginning stage, middle stage, and ending stage (Northen & Kurland, 2001; Shulman, 2015). On the other hand, psychodrama theory offers a three-phase conceptualization of each group session—beginning with the warm-up stage, then the action stage, followed by the sharing and integration stage (Wysong, 2017). Shulman (2015) suggests that the social group work stages are also applicable as a framework for each individual session. While these models of group process and development describe different aspects of group experience, they are often integrated and used concurrently by social group workers and psychodramatists.

Both social workers and psychodramatists conceptualize the individual within their social environment and look to increase clients' interpersonal skills. As Bendel's (2017) systematic review indicates, psychodrama research consistently points to its efficacy in improving interpersonal skills (Dogan, 2010, 2018; Karabilgin et al., 2012; Karatas & Gokcakan, 2009; Li et al., 2015; McVea & Gow, 2006; McVea et al., 2011; Smokowski & Bacallao, 2009) and that "psychodrama applications for social work may find aptitude in client development of interpersonal skills" (Bendel, 2017, p. 47). Nolte (2020) compares *organism in an environment* perspective of psychology as slightly different than the *being in a situation* of psychodrama. He writes that the behaviorist psychology perspective, at its extreme, portrays human behavior as predetermined and controlled by its environment. Nolte writes that psychodrama's position is opposite to predetermined behaviorism in that it considers the individual within the environment as a holistic being, actor, and initiator within a situation. He states that "the conventional psychological model is a deterministic, mechanical model of human behavior. The existential psychodramatic one is a non-deterministic (spontaneous), dynamic one." (Nolte, 2020, p. 124) At the same time, one's ability to access spontaneity may be limited due to oppression related to marginalized social group assignments (or identity) within society or within the group itself (Nieto, 2010; Nieto, Boyer, Goodwin, Johnson, & Smith, 2010). Privilege and oppression certainly play a role in the warming up process to spontaneity.

Interpersonal skills and social interaction are based on the foundation and essence of communication (Shaw, 1981). While ideas are primarily expressed through verbal communication, emotional content is conveyed through non-verbal gestures such as facial expression, posture, and subtle body movements (Northen & Kurland, 2001). Though many social group work modalities seem to solely focus on verbal processing, the non-verbal is emphasized in Lang's non-deliberative social work model (2010, 2016) as well as the psychodramatic approach. J.L. Moreno is quick to highlight how action precedes words in human development and often convey messages that words could not (1955). Psychodramatists even use action, body posture, and movement without words as a form of communication or sharing about an experience. Role training effective communication is the objective of some psychodrama groups, during which group members offer various spontaneous demonstrations of communication styles for a given situation. The protagonist is then provided with an opportunity to try these different communication approaches and/or experience them from the role-reversed position. Psychodrama as a process is used in a variety of fields to teach communication skills to clients (Corsini, 2017; Dayton, 2005), students (Joyner & Young, 2009), social workers (Konopik & Cheung, 2013), lawyers (Cole, 2001), medical professionals (Baile & Blatner, 2014; Walters & Baile, 2014), and others.

Just as social workers utilize a systems approach to group and individual treatment, psychodrama uses the social atom to examine the social system in which the client operates, while utilizing the sociogram to see the group as its own sociodynamic system. Sociometry-based warm-up exercises are most commonly used leading up to a psychodrama with the intent of developing group cohesion (Dayton, 2005; Haworth & Vasiljevic, 2012). The International Association of Social Work with Groups Standards of Practice highlights group cohesion as a beginning task of the social worker who "aids the group members in establishing relationships with one another so as to promote group cohesion" (IASWG, 2015, p. 11). In social work research with groups, it has been shown that the greater the group cohesion, the stronger the influence of the group upon its members (Northen & Kurland, 2001). Yalom & Lesczc (2005) reference the importance of group cohesion in group work to that of the therapeutic relationship in individual work.

Social work with groups and psychodrama each place significance on tension and conflict within the group process. Social workers conceptualize both tension and conflict as essential components of human development and group development while offering multiple strategies for working through them (Northen & Kurland, 2001). Similarly, psychodramatists assess tension and conflict in the group with sociometric tools and use a variety of psychodramatic interventions to resolve the conflict—including the encounter (Hale, 1981). The psychodramatic encounter provides participants with an opportunity to explore, label, and concretize transference/countertransference in the conflict and experientially remove projections from the group member. In the psychodramatic encounter, conflicting group members have an opportunity to role reverse with each other to fully see things from the other's perspective which often relieves the conflict. Psychodramatists also pay considerable attention to tension in the group and are trained to assess open tension systems within group members and the group-as-a-whole. Dayton (2005, p. 453) defines open tension systems as "unresolved situations that live inside the psyche in an unfinished state and produce internal tension."

In group treatment, psychodrama and social work approaches complement each other by treating the group-as-a-whole, while also being aware of each individual that make up the group itself (Carey, 2016; Giacomucci, 2020b; Giacomucci & Stone,

2019; Indagator & Chung, 2014). Frequently in a psychodrama group, the topic of the psychodrama is chosen democratically by group members which promotes the group-as-a-whole experience. J.L. Moreno compared the psychodynamics of the individual with the sociodynamics of the group and their interplay in the psychodrama process. The locus of social work has been described by Viglante et al. (1981) as the "psychosocial interface" which seems to capture Moreno's thinking. Both social work and psychodrama focus their work on marginalized populations and work to empower individuals, groups, and communities (Skolnik, 2018).

Skolnik (2018) highlights the overlap between social work and psychodrama in the emphasis on spontaneity and creativity with the group process as a collective and creative endeavor. Both the social worker and the psychodramatist are artists who "integrate knowledge, intuition, experience, and theory in the moment to act spontaneously and creatively to produce an intervention" (Skolnik, 2018, pp. 62–63). The social group work environment of mutual aid cultivates spontaneous and creative action in the group experience (Steinberg, 2010). As outlined in a Sect. 4.4, psychodrama practice developed from, and depends on, Moreno's spontaneity–creativity theory.

6.8 Conclusion

Theoretically, almost all of psychodrama's core theories are reflected in social work theory. Figure 6.5 provides a depiction of the multiple overlapping theories and philosophies between Moreno's system and social work (see Fig. 6.5). As Skolnik

Social Work with Groups	Sociometry, Psychodrama, GP
Person In Environment	Sociometry
Emphasis on relationships	Social Atom; Social Network
Group-as-a-whole	Group as Protagonist/Client
Mutual Aid	Therapeutic agents for each other
Group/family roles	Role theory
Group development stages	Group stages
Inherent worth/dignity	Non-pathologizing
Social Justice	Sociatry - healing society
Meet client where they are at	Follow the protagonist
Creativity and spontaneity	Spontaneity-creativity theory

Fig. 6.5 Similarities between social work with groups and Moreno's triadic system. Reprinted with permission from Giacomucci (2019a, b).

noted, psychodrama and social group work form a synergistic union (2018). The social worker's role in their relationship with individuals, groups, and communities can be enhanced through the integration of psychodrama. Konopik and Cheung's research (2013) outline three major areas of social work that could be enhanced by the integration of psychodrama—clinical social work or psychotherapy, the training of social workers or training of others, and the use of psychoeducation.

References

Aristotle. (1951). *Poetics* (S.H. Butcher, Trans.), Mineola, NY: Dover Publications.

Baile, W. F., & Blatner, A. (2014). Teaching Communication Skills: Using Action Methods to Enhance Role-play in Problem-based Learning. *Simulation in Health Care, 9*(4), 220–227.

Bendel, K. E. (2017). Social work and Moreno: A systematic review of psychodrama methods and implications. *ProQuest Dissertations and Theses*. Retrieved from https://proxy.library.upenn.edu:7450/docview/1920065271?accountid=14707

Breuer, J., & Freud, S. (1895/1957). *Studies on hysteria*. New York: Basic Books.

Bitel, M. C. (2000). Mixing up the Goulash: Essential ingredients in the "art" of social group work. *Social Work with Groups, 22*(2–3), 77–99.

Buchanan, D.R. (1984). Psychodrama. In T.B. Karasu (Chair), *The psychiatric therapies*. Washington, DC: American Psychiatric Press, Inc.

Carey, L. A. (2016). Group work education: A call for renewed commitment. *Social Work with Groups, 39*(1), 48–61.

Cole, D. K. (2001). Psychodrama and the training of trial lawyers: Finding the story. *Northern Illinois University Law Review, 21*(1), 1–35.

Corsini, R. (2017). *Role-playing in psychotherapy*. New York, NY: Routledge.

Darrow, L. S., & Childs, J. (2020). *Experiential action methods and tools for healing grief and loss-related trauma: Life, death, and transformation*. New York: Routledge.

Dayton, T. (2005). *The living stage: A step-by-step guide to psychodrama, sociometry, and experiential group* . Deerfield, FL: Health Communications Inc.

Dayton, T. (2015). *NeuroPsychodrama in the treatment of relational trauma: A strength-based, experiential model for healing PTSD* . Deerfield Beach, FL: Health Communications Inc.

DeRivera, J., & Dahl, H. (1977). *A structural theory of the emotions*. New York: International Universities Press.

Dogan, T. (2010). The effects of psychodrama on young adults' attachment styles. *The Arts in Psychotherapy, 37*(2), 112–119.

Dogan, T. (2018). The effects of the psychodrama in instilling empathy and self-awareness: A pilot study. *Psych Journal, 228*. https://doi.org/10.1002/pchj.228

Drumm, K. (2006). The essential power of group work. *Social Work with Groups, 29,* 17–31.

Figusch, Z. (2014). The JL Moreno memorial photo album. London: lulu.com.

Freud, S. (1893). In Strachey, J. (Ed.). *Standard edition of the complete psychological works of Sigmund Freud* (Vol. 2). London: Hogarth Press.

Gershoni, J. (2013). Psychodrama. *Encyclopedia of Social Work*. Retrieved 28 Apr. 2018, from https://doi.org/10.1093/acrefore/9780199975839.001.0001/acrefore-9780199975839-e-316.

Giacomucci, S. (2017). The sociodrama of life or death: Young adults and addiction treatment. *Journal of Psychodrama, Sociometry, and Group Psychotherapy, 65*(1): 137–143. https://doi.org/10.12926/0731-1273-65.1.137.

Giacomucci, S. (2018). Social work and sociometry: An integration of theory and clinical practice. *The Pennsylvania Social Worker, 39*(1), 14–16.

Giacomucci, S. (2018b). Social work and sociometry: Integrating history, theory, and practice. *The clinical voice*. Richboro, PA: Pennsylvania Society for Clinical Social Work.

Giacomucci, S. (2018). The trauma survivor's inner role atom: A clinical map for post-traumatic. *Journal of Psychodrama, Sociometry, and Group Psychotherapy, 66*(1), 115–129.

Giacomucci, S. (2019a). Bio-psycho-social-spiritual integration through experiential trauma therapies. In *Beykent 1st International Health Sciences Research Days Congress*, Istanbul, Turkey. Retrieved from https://earsiv.beykent.edu.tr:8080/xmlui/bitstream/handle/123456789/1120/1.Beykent%20IHSRDC%20Abstract%20Book_31.07.19.pdf?sequence=1.

Giacomucci, S. (2019b). *Social group work in action: A sociometry, psychodrama, and experiential trauma therapy curriculum*. Doctorate in Social Work (DSW) Dissertations, p. 124. https://repository.upenn.edu/cgi/viewcontent.cgi?article=1128&context=edissertations_sp2

Giacomucci, S. (2020). Addiction, traumatic loss, and guilt: A case study resolving grief through psychodrama and sociometric connections. *The Arts in Psychotherapy, 67,* 101627. https://doi.org/10.1016/j.aip.2019.101627.

Giacomucci, S. (2020b). Experiential sociometry in group work: mutual aid for the group-as-a-whole. *Social Work with Groups*. Advanced Online Publication. https://doi.org/10.1080/01609513.2020.1747726.

Giacomucci, S., & Marquit, J. (2020). The effectiveness of trauma-focused psychodrama in the treatment of PTSD in inpatient substance abuse treatment. *Frontiers in Psychology, 11,* 896. 10.3389%2Ffpsyg.2020.00896.

Giacomucci, S., & Stone, A. M. (2019). Being in two places at once: Renegotiating traumatic experience through the surplus reality of psychodrama. *Social Work with Groups, 42*(3), 184–196. https://doi.org/10.1080/01609513.2018.1533913.

Hale, A. E. (1981). *Conducting clinical sociometric explorations: A manual for psychodramatists and sociometrists*. Roanoke, VA: Royal Publishing Company.

Haworth, P., & Vasiljevic, L. (2012). Psychodrama and action methods in education. *Andragoške Studije, 1,* 113–127.

Hollander, C. E. (1969). *A process for psychodrama training: The Hollander psychodrama curve*. Denver, CO: Snow Lion Press.

Hug, E. (2007). A Neuroscience perspective on psychodrama. In C. Baim, J. Burmeister, & M. Maciel (Eds.), *Psychodrama: Advances in theory and practice*. London: Routledge.

Hug, E. (2013). A neuroscience perspective on trauma and action methods. In K. Hudgins, & F. Toscani (Eds.), *Healing world trauma with the therapeutic spiral model*. London: Jessica Kingsley Publishers.

Hudgins, M. K., & Toscani, F. (2013). *Healing world trauma with the therapeutic spiral Model: Stories from the frontlines*. London: Jessica Kingsley Publishers.

Indagator, Y., & Chung, S. (2014). A review of psychodrama and group process. *International Journal of Social Work and Human Services Practice, 1*(2), 105–114.

International Association of Social Work with Groups. (2015). *Standards for social work practice with groups* (2nd ed.). Retrieved from: https://www.iaswg.org/assets/docs/Resources/2015_IASWG_STANDARDS_FOR_SOCIAL_WORK_PRACTICE_WITH_GROUPS.pdf.

Joyner, B., & Young, L. (2009). Teaching medical students using role-play: Twelve tips for successful role-plays. *Medical Teacher, 28*(3), 225–229.

Karabilgin, Ö., Gokengin, G., Doganer, I., Gokengin, D. (2012). The effect of psychodrama on people living with HIV/AIDS. *European Journal of Psychotherapy & Counseling, 14*(4), 317–333.

Karatas, Z., & Gokcakan, Z. (2009). A comparative investigation of the effects of cognitive-behavioral group practices and psychodrama on adolescent aggression. *Educational Sciences: Theory and Practice, 9*(3), 1441–1452.

Kellermann, P. F. (1984). The place of catharsis in psychodrama. *Journal of Group Psychotherapy, Psychodrama, and Sociometry, 37*(1), 1–13.

Kellermann, P. F. (1992). *Focus on psychodrama: The therapeutic aspects of psychodrama*. London, UK: Jessica Kingsley.

Konopik, D. A., & Cheung, M. (2013). Psychodrama as a social work modality. *Journal of Social Work, 58*(1), 9–20.

Lang, N. C. (2010). *Group work practice to advance social competence: A specialized methodology for social work.* New York: Columbia University Press.

Lang, N. C. (2016). Nondeliberative forms of practice in social work: artful, actional, analogic. *Social Work with Groups, 39*(2–3), 97–117.

Levine, P. A. (2010). *In an Unspoken voice: How the body releases trauma and restores goodness.* Berkeley, CA: North Atlantic Books.

Li, J., Wang, D., Guo, Z., & Li, K. (2015). Using psychodrama to relieve social barriers in an autistic child: A case study and literature review. *International Journal of Nursing Sciences, 2*(1), 402–407.

McVea, C., & Gow, K. (2006). Healing a mother's emotional pain: Protagonist and director recall of a Therapeutic Spiral Model (TSM) session. *Journal of Group Psychotherapy, Psychodrama and Sociometry, 59*(1), 3.

McVea, C. S., Gow, K., & Lowe, R. (2011). Corrective interpersonal experience in psychodrama group therapy: A comprehensive process analysis of significant therapeutic events. *Psychotherapy Research, 21*(4), 416–429.

Moreno, J. L. (1921). *Das Testament Des Vaters.* Vienna, Austria: Gustav Kiepenheuer Verlag.

Moreno, J. L. (1924). *Das Stegreiftheater.* Berlin, Germany: Gustav Kiepenheuer Verlag.

Moreno, J. L. (1939). Psychodramatic shock therapy, a sociometric approach to the problem of mental disorders. *Sociometry, 2,* 1–30.

Moreno, J. L. (1940). Mental catharsis and the psychodrama. *Sociometry, 3,* 209–244.

Moreno, J. L. (1946). *Psychodrama* (Vol. 1). New York: Beacon House.

Moreno, J. L. (1947). *Open letter to group psychotherapists.* Psychodrama monographs, No. 23. Beacon, NY: Beacon House.

Moreno, J. L. (1952). Psychodramatic production techniques. *Group Psychotherapy, Psychodrama, & Sociometry, 4,* 273–303.

Moreno, J. L. (1953). *Who shall survive? Foundations of sociometry, group psychotherapy and sociodrama* (2nd ed.). Beacon, NY: Beacon House.

Moreno, J. L. (1955). The significance of the therapeutic format and the place of acting out in psychotherapy. *Group Psychotherapy, 8,* 7–19.

Moreno, J. L. (1958). Fundamental rules and techniques of psychodrama. In J. H. Masserman & J. L. Moreno (Eds.). *Progress in psychotherapy, Volume III: Techniques of Psychotherapy* (pp. 86–131). New York: Grune and Stratton.

Moreno, J. L. (1961). The role concept, a bridge between psychiatry and sociology. *American Journal of Psychiatry, 118*(6), 518–523.

Moreno, J. L. (1964). *Psychodrama, first volume* (3rd ed.). Beacon, NY: Beacon House Press.

Moreno, J. L. (1965). Therapeutic vehicles and the concept of surplus reality. *Group Psychotherapy, 18,* 211–216.

Moreno, J. L. (1972). *Psychodrama volume 1* (4th ed.). New York: Beacon House.

Moreno, J. L., & Enneis, J. M. (1950). *Hypnodrama and psychodrama.* New York: Beacon House.

Moreno, Z. T. (1971). Beyond Aristotle, Breuer and Freud: Moreno's contribution to the concept of catharsis. *Group Psychotherapy & Psychodrama, 24,* 34–43.

Moreno, Z. T. (2000). The function of 'tele' in human relations. In J. Zeig (Ed.) *The evolution of psychotherapy: A meeting of the minds.* Phoenix, AZ: Erickson Foundation Press.

Moreno, Z. T. (2012). *To dream again: A memoir.* New York: Mental Health Resources.

Mosher, J. R. (2009). *Cycles of healing: Creating our paths to wholeness.* Seattle, WA: Blue Sky Counselors.

Nieto, L. (2010). Look behind you: using anti-oppression models to inform a protagonist's psychodrama. In E. Leveton (Ed.), *Healing collective trauma using sociodrama and drama therapy* (pp. 103–125). New York: Springer Publishing Company.

Nieto, L., Boyer, M. F., Goodwin, L., Johnson, G. R., & Smith, L. C. (2010). *Beyond inclusion, beyond empowerment: a developmental strategy to liberate everyone.* Olympia, WA: Cuetzpalin.

Nolte, J. (2014). *The philosophy, theory, and methods of J.L. Moreno: The man who tried to become god*. New York, NY: Routledge.

Nolte, J. (2020). *J.L. Moreno and the psychodramatic method: On the practice of psychodrama*. New York: Routledge.

Northen, H., & Kurland, R. (2001). *Social work with groups*. New York: Columbia University Press.

Pally, R. (2000). *The mind-brain relationship*. New York: Karnac Books.

Shaw, M. E. (1981). *Group dynamics: The psychology of small group behavior* (3rd ed.). New York: McGraw-Hill.

Shulman, L. (2015). *The skills of helping individuals, families, groups, and communities* (8th ed.). Boston, MA: Cengage Learning.

Skolnik, S. (2018). A synergistic union: Group work meets psychodrama. *Social Work with Groups, 41*(1–2), 60–73.

Smokowsky, P., & Bacallao, M. (2009). Entre Dos Mundos/Between two worlds youth violence prevention: Comparing psychodramatic and support group delivery formats. *Small Group Research, 40*(1), 3–27.

Steinberg, D. M. (2010). Mutual aid: A contribution to best-practice social work. *Social Work with Groups, 33*(1), 53–68.

Truedley, M. B. (1944). Psychodrama and social case work. *Sociometry, 7,* 170–178.

Van der Kolk, B. A. (2014). *The body keeps the score: Brain, mind, and body in the healing of trauma*. New York: Viking Press.

Vigilante, J. L., et al. (1981). *Searching for a theory: Following hearn*. Paper presented at the annual program meeting of the Council on Social Work Education.

von Ameln, F., & Becker-Ebel, J. (2020). *Fundamentals of psychodrama*. Singapore: Springer Nature.

Walters, R., & Baile, W. F. (2014). Training oncology professionals in key communication skills: Adapting psychodrama and sociodrama for experiential learning. *The Journal of Psychodrama, Sociometry, and Group Psychotherapy, 62*(1), 55–66.

Wang, X. H., & Liu, A. Q. (2020). Psychodrama: A professional method for social work. *Social Work and Management, 20*(2), 65–70.

Watersong, A. (2011). Surplus reality: The magic ingredient in psychodrama. *Journal of the Australian and Aotearoa New Zealand Psychodrama Association, 20,* 18–27.

Winnicott, D. W. (1971). *Playing and reality*. Middlesex, UK: Penguin Books.

Wysong, W. H. (2017). *The psychodrama companion*. (N.P.): Author.

Yalom, I. D., & Leszcz, M. (2005). *The theory and practice of group psychotherapy* (5th ed.). New York, NY: Basic Books.

Zwilling, M. (2004). Methodisches Handeln in der Sozialen Arbeit—Psychodrama als Basismethode. *Zeitschrift Für Psychodrama Und Soziometrie, 3*(1), 5–15.

Part III
Social Work and Moreno's Methods Informed by Trauma, Neuroscience, Strengths, and Research

This part explores movements within the field of social work as they relate to the practice of sociometry, psychodrama, and group psychotherapy. The specific movements that will be explored include trauma-informed practice, neurobiology-informed practice, strengths-based practice, and evidence-based practice. This part serves to feature the integrations of movements within the social work field and the field of psychodrama. The fields of social work, sociometry, psychodrama, and group psychotherapy, are largely operating within the same systems and are subject to similar forces and trends within society and the culture. These larger trends represent the directed consciousness of the culture and have led to the creation differentiated specializations of knowledge within each field. The structure of this part will transition from parts on trauma to neurobiology and strengths-based practices, ending in a summary of the evidence-base of research for sociometry, psychodrama, and group psychotherapy. Each subsection will follow the format will address the impact of this trend in the field of social work, group psychotherapy, and psychodrama. It is important to note that these four themes—trauma, neurobiology, strengths-based, and evidence-based are tightly linked, integrated, and inseparable. However, due to the limitations of the writing format, these pieces will be presented in linear form below.

Chapter 7
Trauma, Social Work, and Psychodrama

Abstract The history and principles of trauma-informed practice in social work are presented while differentiating trauma-informed and trauma-focused practices. The practice of trauma-focused group therapy and trauma-focused psychodrama is outlined while acknowledging the recent calls for increased trauma content in graduate curriculums. Safety, play, and spontaneity are elevated as core elements in psychodrama's effectiveness in working with trauma survivors. Psychodrama's unique capacity for treating post-traumatic stress disorder (PTSD) is presented while outlining two trauma-focused psychodrama models—the Therapeutic Spiral Model and the Relational Trauma Repair Model.

Keywords Trauma · Trauma-informed social work · Trauma-focused psychodrama · Therapeutic spiral model · Relationship trauma repair model

7.1 Trauma-Informed Practice

It seems that the term *trauma-informed* is thrown around by programs without much care or recognition of what it means to be trauma-informed. For some, being trauma-informed seems to mean that they had their staff attend a single training workshop on trauma, while other agencies identify themselves as trauma-informed only after taking careful consideration in developing their policies, procedures, designing their physical space, training staff, and operationalizing a philosophy that holds trauma-informed principles at its core. So, what exactly does trauma-informed mean? The Substance Abuse and Mental Health Services Administration (SAMHSA) published the following trauma-informed principles (2014a) (see Fig. 7.1):

The National Center for Trauma-Informed Care (NCTIC), established by SAMHSA in 2005, indicates that every aspect of an organization should be trauma-informed and:

> assessed and potentially modified to include a basic understanding of how trauma affects the life of an individual seeking services. Trauma-informed organizations, programs, and services are based on an understanding of the vulnerabilities or triggers of trauma survivors that traditional service delivery approaches may exacerbate, so that these services and programs can be more supportive and avoid re-traumatization (National Center for Trauma Informed Care, 2012, as cited in Wilson, Pence, & Conradi, 2013).

© The Author(s) 2021
S. Giacomucci, *Social Work, Sociometry, and Psychodrama*, Psychodrama in Counselling, Coaching and Education 1,
https://doi.org/10.1007/978-981-33-6342-7_7

Fig. 7.1 SAMHSA'S trauma-informed principles

According to SAMSHA's NCTIC, "trauma-informed" is a philosophy that can be applied to health care, organizations, systems, treatment, prisons, education, and other settings, which is based on six core principles and critically examines the provision of services to avoid re-traumatization and support healing for trauma survivors.

7.2 History of Trauma-Informed Practice

Our understanding of trauma and PTSD has increased significantly in the past 40 years. PTSD was not recognized by the American Psychiatric Association until 1980 when it was added to the third edition of the Diagnostic and Statistical Manual of Mental Disorders (DSM). This recognition was the result of multiple larger social forces including the return of soldiers from the Vietnam War and the women's movement (Herman, 1992; Ringel & Brandell, 2011; van der Kolk, 2014). Since then, trauma-informed practice in social work and other professions has continued to evolve to where it is today. Trauma-informed practice has become the norm rather than a specialty in the field today.

Some major events in the emergence of trauma-informed care included the 1994 Dare to Vision conference hosted by the Substance Abuse and Mental Health Services Administration (SAMHSA) during which the prevalence of trauma was highlighted in addition to acknowledging the re-traumatization experienced by patients during their treatment experiences (Wilson, Pence, & Conradi, 2013). In the late 1990s, the Adverse Childhood Experiences study (ACE) revolutionized the field by highlighting the relationship between childhood trauma, adversity, and family dysfunction as they relate to negative adult health and mental health outcomes (Felitti et al., 1998). By the late 1990s and early 2000s, multiple professionals were writing about the importance of trauma-informed care and trauma-informed organizations (Bloom, 1997; Covington, 2002; Harris & Fallot, 2001; Rivard, Bloom, & Abramovitz, 2003).

While the term *trauma-informed* in social work is relatively new, social work practice has been informed and focused on trauma, neglect, and adversity from the inception of the field. Social workers historically worked with neglected and oppressed communities, survivors of trauma and family violence, medical trauma, prostitution, human trafficking survivors, poverty, and protecting children, the elderly, and disabled from abuses. The trauma-informed philosophy serves as a bridge between clinical social work, social group work, and macrosocial work practice. Trauma plays a significant role in many social justice concerns, societal or community problems, family conflicts, and individual psychosocial ailments.

7.3 Trauma-Informed Practice Versus Trauma-Focused Practice

The difference between *trauma-informed* treatment and *trauma-focused* treatment is the difference between process and content. Trauma-informed describes a focus on the process of providing services, while trauma-focused treatment describes treatment in which the content of services is trauma-focused. Trauma-focused therapy orients itself on the treatment of PTSD and trauma-related conditions.

Initially, treatments for trauma and PTSD were almost exclusively focused on military veterans, while other trauma survivors seemed to be neglected (van der Kolk, 2014). As a result of this, others have advocated for new trauma-related diagnoses including Complex Traumatic Stress Disorder (Courtois, 2004; Courtois & Ford, 2009; Herman, 1992) and Developmental Trauma Disorder (van der Kolk, 2005, 2014) to describe the specific impact of childhood trauma, attachment ruptures, and family separation caused by immigration or forced displacements.

The current state of trauma-focused social work in clinical settings includes a variety of different approaches. These approaches can be loosely categorized into the following categories: psychodynamic-based, relational, cognitive behavioral, mindfulness-based, body-based, and the creative arts therapies. Psychodynamic-based trauma approaches are oriented around the emotional conflicts and reenactments caused by the traumatic event and early childhood experiences (Horowitz, 1997; Krupnick, 2002). Similarly, relational therapies such as attachment-based approaches focus on the here-and-now therapeutic relationship as a corrective and healing experience for past trauma (Banks, 2006). Cognitive behavioral approaches make up one of the largest categories of trauma-focused treatment approaches which include cognitive behavioral therapy (CBT), cognitive processing therapy (CPT), dialectical behavioral therapy (DBT), eye movement desensitization and reprocessing (EMDR), and prolonged exposure (PE). These approaches focus on changing maladaptive thoughts and behaviors related to the trauma and desensitizing the connection between trauma and present-day triggers (Dass-Brailsford, 2007). It is important to note that EMDR therapy, while often considered a cognitive-based approach, also is a mindfulness-based and body-based approach. Mindfulness-based approaches have also become popular for trauma treatment which are based on Eastern philosophy and the practice of mindfulness-based meditation (Briere & Scott, 2006; Kabat Zinn, 1990, 2003, 2005; Siegel, 2010). Body-based approaches, such as somatic experiencing and sensory-motor therapy, as well as the creative arts therapies, such as art therapy, music therapy, drama therapy, dance therapy, poetry therapy, and psychodrama, have become increasingly utilized in trauma treatment in recent times (Dayton, 2015; Foa, Keane, Friedman, & Cohen, 2008; Gene-Cos, Fisher, Ogden, & Cantrell, 2016; Giacomucci, 2018; Giacomucci & Marquit, 2020; Hudgins & Toscani, 2013; Johnson & Sajnani, 2014; Levine, 2010; Schouten et al., 2015; van de Kamp et al., 2019; van der Kolk, 2014). In addition to the aforementioned methods, many providers or programs utilize an eclectic approach which integrates multiple of the modalities above (SAMHSA, 2014b).

This is by no means a comprehensive list of trauma-focused interventions used by social workers, but most of the popular psychotherapy modalities for trauma and PTSD are included here. It is important to note that the treatment of PTSD and trauma is a specialty which requires specialized knowledge and training for social workers to competently work with traumatized populations. Many have written about the potential for re-traumatization, reenactment, and causing more harm in trauma therapy if not done properly (Giacomucci, 2018; Hudgins & Toscani, 2013; Levine, 2015; Ogden, Minton, & Pain, 2006; SAMHSA, 2014b, van der Kolk, 2014). There is a very real potential for treatment providers and programs to provide *trauma-focused* services in a way that is not *trauma-informed*. Unfortunately, this happens often when providers begin offering services specifically for trauma survivors without formal training or fueled by significant countertransferential issues. In a similar way, many trauma-informed programs do not adequately nor directly address the impacts of trauma. A trauma-informed program suggests that staff and administration are educated on the impacts of trauma but does not guarantee their ability to directly treat PTSD or other trauma-related issues. To mitigate these risks, we turn to the role of social work education.

7.4 Culture, Oppression, and Social Justice

In the discussion of trauma-informed practice, it is essential to highlight the importance of culture, history, gender, oppression, diversity, and social justice. A practitioner who fails to consider the impact of these socio-cultural forces within the group is not fully trauma-informed. Every participant and group leader brings with them their own cultural values, beliefs, assumptions, experiences, biases, and prejudices (Corey, Corey, & Corey, 2018). It is important to develop self-awareness of how one's culture and aspects of identity may impact their group facilitation or participation. Moreno suggests that cultural values are conveyed through role relationships which are contained within interpersonal relationships (Nolte, 2014). The matrix of relationships within any group setting lends itself to the constant transmission of cultural values between group participants (and the facilitator). Furthermore, when a protagonist offers a psychodrama scene, the interactions between psychodrama roles are also saturated with cultural meaning. Participants belonging to diverse cultures could witness the same scene and have very different feelings, assumptions, or conclusions based on their own system of cultural beliefs, values, and norms. This means that the psychodrama director must be aware of the multiplicity of cultural understandings that exist within one scene or one role relationship and avoid interventions that neglect the protagonist's subjective cultural experience in favor of the director's cultural assumptions, values, or norms (Nieto, 2010). Without considering these cultural contexts, a facilitator risks reenacting trauma or neglect through misattunement to the protagonist's (or other group members') aspects of identity that have been socially marginalized or privileged. This also includes the responsibility for the facilitator to be attuned to how their own identities (marginalized or privileged) may impact the experience for participants.

7.5   Trauma and Social Work Education

The past two decades have seen a call to action for social work programs, as well as other helping professionals, to integrate trauma-informed training into their academic programs (Courtois, 2002; Courtois & Gold, 2009; McKenzie-Mohr, 2004; O'Halloran & O'Halloran, 2001; Strand, Abramovitz, Layne, Robinson, & Way, 2014). The growing body of literature highlighting the significance of trauma prevention and trauma treatment has led to this call to action. Social workers are frequently working directly with populations exposed to trauma (Strand et al., 2014). Over the past two decades, research has indicated a strong correlation between trauma and a multitude of mental health, behavioral health, and medical problems (Bloom, 2013; Courtois & Ford, 2016; Dong et al., 2004; Felitti et al., 1998; Putnam, 2006; van der Kolk, 2014). Joseph and Murphy (2014) have even declared trauma to be a "unifying concept for social workers."

In 2012, a Task Force on Advanced Social Work Practice in Trauma published a set of guidelines on integrating trauma content into social work education (CSWE, 2012). The social work education field has responded as a growing number of MSW programs have begun integrating trauma courses into their curriculum (Abrams & Shapiro, 2014; Bussey, 2008; Strand et al., 2014). Gitterman & Knight (2016) also advocate for the inclusion of education on resilience and post-traumatic growth in social work education. Preliminary research has demonstrated that students indicate an increase in self-efficacy around trauma work after taking an MSW trauma course

(Wilson & Nochajski, 2016). To date, the overwhelming majority of social work trauma courses has focused on individual trauma work or the impacts of collective/societal trauma—in contrast, social work education has given very little focus to training social workers to provide group psychotherapy with traumatized groups (Giacomucci, 2019).

7.6 Trauma-Focused Group Work

Trauma is often experienced at the hands of other humans and in the context of relationships, groups, or communities—making group work a potentially healing and corrective emotional experience for trauma survivors. Group psychotherapy is frequently used with trauma survivors as it provides an efficient alternative to individual therapy and the opportunity for interpersonal support between group members (Klein & Schermer, 2000). In the group psychotherapy field, various studies have highlighted the efficacy of various group therapy approaches for trauma and PTSD with various populations (Avinger & Jones, 2007; Davies, Burlingame, & Layne, 2006; Sloan, Bovine, & Schnurr, 2012).

Social work with groups experts has highlighted the value of group work for trauma survivors through the conceptual framework of mutual aid (Knight, 2006). The benefits of group work for trauma survivors include sharing experience, being with others with similar experiences, decreased isolation, increased self-esteem and self-efficacy, challenging distorted views, enhancing capacity for trust, reducing stigma, and practicing emotional regulation (Gitterman & Knight, 2016; Knight, 2006). Mendelsohn, Zachary, and Harney (2007) write that "group [membership] counteracts the isolating effects of [adversity] and enables survivors to connect with sources of resilience within themselves and others" (p. 227). Conceptually, social group work, mutual aid, and trauma-informed principles exist in congruence. Rosenwald and Baird (2019) write that "mutual aid is characterized by trauma-informed principles of peer support, collaboration and mutuality, and empowerment, voice and choice." (p. 8). Social workers often work with traumatized communities in which group work skills and knowledge also become applicable. Most social justice oriented community work centers around a collective trauma, neglect, or injustice. Community organizers and social activists are routinely working with traumatized communities with a focus on the content of collective trauma; nevertheless, they rarely have any training or education on the impacts of trauma or trauma-informed practices. The implementation of a trauma-informed approach in community work is essential to prevent re-traumatization of community members. Further information on this subject will be presented in Chaps. 18 and 19.

7.7 Trauma-Focused Psychodrama

Although Moreno rarely used the term *trauma*, most of his work was with trauma survivors, including youth at a reform school, people of color, immigrants, refugees, prostituted women, inmates, and severely mentally ill patients at his sanitarium in New York. During Moreno's lifetime, dozens of Veterans' Administration Hospitals in the USA integrated psychodrama into their clinical programs (Moreno, 2019). Some even built dedicated psychodrama stages on their campuses. One of the most prestigious and competitive psychodrama internship programs in the world was housed at St. Elizabeths VA Hospital which provided services to US military veterans (Buchanan & Swink, 2017). Moreno died in 1974, six years before PTSD was recognized as by the American Psychiatric Association in the third edition of the Diagnostic and Statistical Manual of Mental Disorders. Nevertheless, Moreno's methods were widely used in the treatment of trauma-related issues.

Classical psychodrama has been, and continues to be, extensively employed with trauma survivors including in various VA hospitals, addiction treatment centers, psychiatric hospitals, mental health settings, youth programs, immigrant/refugee groups, correctional facilities, and community spaces. The person-centered and strengths-based Morenean philosophy is particularly congruent with most trauma approaches as it recognizes the inherent worth of each person and allows the client to control the pace of the session. Role theory's non-pathologizing and user-friendly conceptualizations provide trauma survivors with new ways of conceptualizing their experiences of self and others (Giacomucci, 2018). The experiential and highly relational nature of sociometry, psychodrama, and group psychotherapy offers rich opportunities for corrective emotional experiences and moments of healing. Psychodrama's body-oriented and action-based methodology allows for participants to express themselves through avenues beyond cognition and words while renegotiating their somatic and affective experiences (Kellermann, 2000). Zerka Moreno highlights how the warming-up process moves from the periphery to the center, and as such, the director should not begin psychodrama work with the most traumatic events of the protagonist before warming-up properly (1965/2006). The basic psychodrama interventions of doubling, mirroring, and role reversal are uniquely beneficial for trauma survivors who often struggle with articulating their feelings or sensations, labeling an experience, integrating new perspectives, and connecting with an accurate sense of self or others (Dayton, 2005). Psychodramatic role training is an avenue of simulating real-life experiences and rehearsing new possibilities, especially related to handling future situations related to trauma or present-day triggers.

The rise of trauma-informed care, neurobiology research on trauma, and the increased attention to the pervasiveness of trauma in society brought with it challenges to the practice of classical psychodrama with trauma survivors. The application of psychodrama to traumatized populations requires precise knowledge and slight modification of techniques to avoid re-traumatization (von Ameln & Becker-Ebel, 2020). A growing body of the literature and clinical practice oriented to trauma-specific services prompted the development of the Therapeutic Spiral Model by Kate

Hudgins and Francesca Toscani, and the Relational Trauma Repair Model by Tian Dayton (Giacomucci & Marquit, 2020).

7.7.1 Safety, Play, and Spontaneity

Psychodrama has some inherent advantages to working with trauma survivors, one of which is its experiential nature and emphasis on spontaneity and play. Moreno describes spontaneity as the curative agent in psychodrama—the capacity for an adequate response to a new situation or a new response to an old situation (Moreno, 1946). In many ways, psychodrama is about developing competency and mastery in life through practicing or rehearsing intrapsychic and interpersonal situations on the stage. Moreno theorized that anxiety and spontaneity are inversely related—"anxiety sets in because there is spontaneity missing, not because 'there is anxiety', and spontaneity dwindles because anxiety rises" (1953, p. 337). In recent psychodrama research, spontaneity has demonstrated positive correlations with intrinsic motivation, self-efficacy, self-esteem (Davelaar, Araujo, & Kipper, 2008), creativity (Kipper, Green, & Prorak, 2010), well-being (Kipper & Shemer, 2006; Testoni et al., 2016), and social desirability (Kipper & Hundal, 2005). Research has also shown spontaneity to have an inverse relationship with obsessive–compulsive tendencies, stress, anxiety (Christoforou & Kipper, 2006), depression (Testoni et al., 2016), impulsivity (Kipper, Green, & Prorak, 2010), and panic disorder symptoms (Tarashoeva, Marinova, & Kojuharov, 2017). I hypothesize a similar inverse correlation between spontaneity and PTSD. The results of these studies suggest the important role that spontaneity plays in mental health and well-being.

Post-traumatic stress disorder is a *stress disorder* characterized by states of hyperactivity (hyperarousal, hypervigilance, irritability, anxiety, etc.), and hypoactivity (avoidance, dissociation, loss of interest, etc.). Post-traumatic stress, dissociation, and the tendency toward reenactment decrease a trauma survivors' ability to respond with spontaneity or playfulness. Spontaneity, play, and safety are intricately connected and perhaps interdependent on each other. In order to help a trauma survivor access their spontaneity again, safety must first be established. Safety is found within the window of tolerance (Siegel, 2010). According to Goldstein, the use of playful interventions in group therapy helps promote safety within the group (2018). Gross (2018) offers the following insight into the relationship between play and trauma:

> In many ways, play is the opposite experience of trauma. While play brings about feelings of joy, trauma brings about feelings of hopelessness and despair. While play serves to unite us, trauma serves to isolate us. While play motivates us to actively engage in the moment, trauma motivates us to fight and flee from it. And while play allows us to control our environment, trauma occurs when our environment controls us… play has the potential to serve as an antidote and powerful corrective emotional experience to trauma when integrated into treatment (p. 369).

Play, similar to fight or flight responses, activates the sympathetic system which provides a neurobiological intersection between play and trauma (Kestly, 2018).

Playfulness and *joie de vivre* (zest for life) are necessary to restoring resilience according to Trevarthan and Panksepp (2016). Additionally, the use of the imagination, closely related to play, is associated with resilience in that imagination is required to envision a future self different from a past self (Marks-Tarlow, 2018). Trauma affects imagination resulting in a tendency for trauma survivors to superimpose the trauma upon the world around (van der Kolk, 2014). Through the surplus reality of psychodrama, a trauma survivor can envision a positive future utilizing their imagination and spontaneity. The psychodramatic process places emphasis on both playfulness, imagination, and spontaneity which make it a useful intervention for working with post-traumatic stress. In Chap. 8, the neurobiological underpinnings of psychodrama's effectiveness will be explored further, especially as it relates to trauma.

7.8 Therapeutic Spiral Model

TSM is a clinically modified psychodrama model rooted in clinical psychology, attachment theory, and neurobiology; it underlines the importance of safety, containment, and strengths (Hudgins & Toscani, 2013). TSM comes equipped with a comprehensive clinical map called the Trauma Survivor's Inner Role Atom (TSIRA) which provides a framework for working with trauma using the simplicity of role theory (Giacomucci, 2018; Hudgins, 2019). It facilitates the safety needed to establish a therapeutic alliance and group cohesion while keeping clients in their window of tolerance and transforming internalized trauma-based roles into roles of posttraumatic growth (Giacomucci, 2018; Hudgins, 2017). Over the past two decades, TSM has increased in popularity in the psychodrama world and contributed to the movement toward trauma-focused and strengths-based approaches in psychodrama (Giacomucci & Marquit, 2020).

While classical psychodrama most often explores interpersonal roles and relationships, TSM is an entirely intrapsychic model. It developed from the realization that before one could interface with others in the world in a healthy way, they needed to do their own personal work and reorganize their internal role atom (Hudgins & Toscani, 2013). The trauma survivor's inner role atom provides a template of 18 inner roles that contribute to stability, integration, and growth. The simplest way to describe the TSIRA is using a visual of a spiral with three strands—prescriptive roles, trauma-based roles, and transformative roles (Giacomucci, 2017). The first strand represents prescriptive roles which focus on developing the ability for nonjudgmental observation, containment, and strengths. The term prescriptive is used to reflect that these roles are directives from a professional and are necessary for the change to occur, just like a prescription from a medical doctor. The second spiral symbolizes the internalization of the trauma. And the transformation that emerges between the interaction of prescriptive and trauma-based roles is represented by the final strand of the spiral. The TSIRA provides a template with intervention steps that target the development of specific psychological functions necessary for healthy functioning after trauma (Hudgins, 2017, 2019).

7.8.1 Prescriptive Roles and Safety Structures

The clinical map includes eight prescriptive roles with the functions of observation, containment, and restoration/strength (see Table 7.1).

In addition to the prescriptive roles, the TSM model includes six experiential safety structures to establish connection, containment, and safety in any group (Giacomucci et al., 2018). Some of these safety structures pull from classical sociometry (including spectrograms, step-in sociometry, and hands-on-shoulders sociometry), one safety structure is an art project, and two of the safety structures are inherently new to TSM and concretize prescriptive roles. These will be covered in further detail in Chap. 11.

The TSM model also offers two new types of psychodrama doubles—the *containing double* and the *body double*, which are often combined into one role in clinical settings. While classical psychodrama doubling has evolved to often be employed as one sentence of doubling, the body double and containing double are roles assigned to group members which stay with the protagonist at all times throughout the entire group. This method of giving the double a stable and centralized role in a psychodrama, as opposed to only employing doubling statements, more closely resembles Zerka Moreno's teaching on doubling (Moreno, 1965/2006). The body double mirrors body movements/postures while making grounding statements to prevent dissociation and enhance somatic processing (Burden & Ciotola, 2001; Carnabucci & Ciotola, 2013). The body double reconnects the trauma survivor with awareness of their own body, thus strengthening vertical neural integration and providing grounding (Lawrence, 2011).

The containing double offers statements anchoring the protagonist in the present moment by expanding or containing feelings or thinking, depending on what is clinically appropriate. The containing double adapts based on the needs of each protagonist. For a protagonist with overwhelming feelings, the containing double would

Table 7.1 Prescriptive roles and functions	Function	Prescriptive roles
	A. Observation	1. Observing ego 2. Client role
	B. Containment	3. Containing double 4. Body double 5. Manager of defenses
	C. Restoration/strength	6. Intrapsychic strengths 7. Interpersonal strengths 8. Transpersonal strengths

Reprinted with Permission from Giacomucci, 2018, p. 117

contain the feelings while helping to label internal experience; but for a protagonist prone to intellectualizing or overthinking, the containing double would contain the thinking while helping him access his feelings and physical sensations. One might say that it serves as the corpus callosum, connecting the left and right hemispheres of the brain and providing a balance between cognition and emotion (Hug, 2013).

7.8.2   The Triangle of Trauma Roles

The second phase of TSM's clinical map is only used once the protagonist and the group have adequately accessed their prescriptive roles. The trauma triangle is an evolution of Karpman's (1968) interpersonal drama triangle of victim, perpetrator, and rescuer. In one's experience of trauma, however, there was no rescuer; otherwise, the trauma would not have occurred. So, TSM teaches that a trauma survivor unconsciously internalizes the roles of *victim, perpetrator*, and *abandoning authority* (Hudgins & Toscani 2013; Toscani & Hudgins, 1995). These three trauma-based roles are the TSM operational definition of PTSD symptomology in action (Giacomucci, 2018).

These three internal roles—victim, perpetrator, and abandoning authority—create a triangulation of role reciprocity. TSM theory conceptualizes the trauma as living within the survivor in terms of these roles, which can be thought of as the introjections of the spoken and unspoken messages from the perpetrator and abandoning authority at the time of the trauma. Although the actual trauma is over, it lives within the survivor and is reexperienced through the surplus reality of flashbacks, night terrors, negative cognitions and feeling states, avoidance, dissociation, and insecure attachments (American Psychiatric Association, 2013).

The interaction of the prescriptive roles with the trauma-based roles is exactly what creates the intrapsychic change according to TSM theory. TSM defines its prescriptive roles as the operational definition of spontaneity in action (Hudgins, 2017) which, when interacting with the trauma-based roles, allows the protagonist to respond in a new, adequate way instead of resorting to the repetitive trauma triangle patterns (Giacomucci & Stone, 2019). The alchemy of prescriptive roles interacting with trauma-based roles is precisely what creates transformative roles—the final stage of the TSIRA clinical map.

7.8.3   Transformative Roles of Post-traumatic Growth

Post-traumatic growth, which will be covered in depth in Sect. 9.2.2, refers to phenomenon of positive transformation that is often experienced after a traumatic life event (Calhoun & Tedeschi, 2014). The TSIRA's transformative roles are the operational definition of post-traumatic growth in action and embodied in the simplicity of role theory. The TSIRA's transformative roles include eight labeled roles organized on the three poles of transformative functions—autonomy, integration, and correction. These functions can be conceptualized of as the opposite sides of the trauma triangle roles constituting role transformations from abandonment to integration, victimhood to autonomy, and perpetration to correction (Giacomucci, 2018) (see Fig. 7.2).

One of the most important transformative roles on the TSIRA clinical map is the *appropriate authority*, which is necessary to help remove one's self from cycling around the internal trauma triangle (Hudgins & Toscani 2013). The appropriate authority is an internal role that intervenes in the repetition of continued abandonment, victimization, and perpetration of the self. TSM's other role of integration, the *ultimate authority*, is the integration of all eight of the transformative roles having been internalized, enacted in the protagonist's intrapsychic world, then their interpersonal world, and finally out in the world. This role is, in a spiritual sense, awakening to the fact that one is a co-creator and co-responsible for mankind (Moreno, 2012).

The *sleeping-awakening child* is another role unique to TSM. Many trauma survivors indicate that they feel as though they have lost their innocence, spontaneity, creativity, or inherent goodness. The sleeping-awakening child role reframes these beliefs and offers a new construct; this is the role that holds all of the innocence, goodness, uniqueness, creativity, and spontaneity. It was never lost or taken, it simply went to sleep at the time of the trauma and waits for the protagonist to make their life safe enough to be awoken (Hudgins, 2017). It is a truly beautiful moment in a TSM psychodrama to experience an auxiliary play the role of the sleeping child as the protagonist awakens this part of self, and in doing so, taps into a source of inner goodness.

Fig. 7.2 TSM Trauma Triangle Role Transformations. This figure depicts the TSM transformative triangle (heart-shaped) as an evolution of the TSM trauma triangle with the alignment of trauma-based roles and the corresponding TSM Transformative roles and functions

The transformative roles of corrective connection, which are *good-enough parents*, *good-enough significant other*, and *good-enough spirituality*, are significant in their ability to provide protagonists with corrective emotional experiences that have the power to repair the negative influence of prior experiences (Alexander & French, 1946; Cozolino, 2014). TSM psychodrama allows participants to embody the roles of transformation and post-traumatic growth in the safety of a psychodrama, effectively role training them to hold the roles in other arenas of their lives.

While the TSIRA provides a template for transforming trauma, these templated roles are sure to materialize differently in each psychodrama, and especially from culture to culture. TSM has been taught and practiced in over 40 countries with its clinical map consistently providing a framework for inner change (Hudgins, 2017). Some have come to believe that TSM is the most clinically sophisticated psychodrama model available and that its application extends beyond just utilization with trauma survivors (Hudgins & Toscani, 2013).

7.9 Relational Trauma Repair Model

The Relational Trauma Repair (RTR) model, developed by Tian Dayton, sometimes referred to as *NeuroPsychodrama*, is another clinically modified approach for using psychodrama and other action methods for work with trauma. RTR is also grounded in the interpersonal neurobiology research and attachment literature offering a variety of sociometric group processes ranging from experiential psychoeducation, action-based sociometry tools, and psychodramatic enactments (Dayton, 2015; Giacomucci & Marquit, 2020). A major strength of RTR is that it can be adapted for clinical use in shorter groups and offers a potent alternative to full psychodrama sessions while employing psychodrama interventions. A common RTR group includes a series of an action-based sociometry exercises followed by a small, but precise, psychodrama vignette. While a TSM or classical psychodrama would often include multiple roles and scenes, an RTR psychodrama most often only has two or three roles but still has the option of growing into a larger psychodrama.

The RTR model has two levels. Level 1 is present moment focused and helps to identify group themes, provide psychoeducation, cultivate interpersonal connection in the group, and warm-up participants for deeper work. RTR level 1 addresses trauma survivors' disconnection from self and others through group processes that encourage inner reflection and social communication which effectively treats both PTSD symptoms and the underlying trauma. Level 2 is more oriented on the past and involves experiential regression work through the surplus reality psychodrama in addition to role training for the future. RTR's first level is primarily psychoeducational and sociometric processes, while the second level involves both sociometry and psychodrama (Dayton, 2014).

7.9.1 Level 1: Sociometrics

The first level was designed to engage, educate, and enhance group cohesion and safety. It was originally developed by Tian Dayton for use in treatment with addictions, trauma, and grief-related issues but has been incorporated into a wide variety of group treatment settings in addition to one-to-one sessions. The facilitation of processes from RTR level 1 requires less psychodrama training than level 2 as it emphasizes educational exercises, sociometry processes, and psychodramatic journaling or letter writing. This phase of treatment includes sociometry processes such as the spectrogram, locograms, and floor checks, as well as writing exercises involving timelines, journaling, and psychodramatic letter writing. RTR's trauma timeline is a notable contribution to the field which helps contextualize, clarify, and provide coherence to trauma survivors' often fragmented narratives of the past (Dayton, 2014) (see Sect. 16.3 for more information). Advanced level one practice also includes some simple empty chair work using the letter writing to keep the process contained.

One of RTR's biggest contributions to the field is the *floor check* structure, which takes the traditional sociometric locogram and expands it into a more dynamic group tool (Dayton, 2014). This process will be covered extensively in Sect. 11.5. RTR developed with an emphasis on experiential processes "that could put healing in the hands of the process itself rather than exclusively in the hands of the therapists" (2015, p. 10). The RTR model uses mutual aid as its lynchpin by positioning group members as therapeutic agents for each other (Giacomucci, 2019, 2020b). These psychosocial processes are congruent with 12-step principles focused on sharing and identification and are widely employed into addictions treatment programs at both inpatient and outpatient levels of care (Dayton, 2014; Giacomucci, 2020a).

7.9.2 Level 2: Reconstructive Role Plays

The second level of RTR practice focuses on traumatic "role reconstructions" and "frozen moments," in addition to strengthening positive, resilient roles, which does require more psychodrama training.Dayton (2014) describes it as "surgical role reconstruction" which allows trauma survivors to renegotiate internalized trauma scenes for moments of repair. Various processes described in this phase include social atom exercises, family sculpting, creating moving sculptures of painful or healing moments, and short psychodrama vignettes.

RTR's therapist handbook (2014, revised edition) outlines various ways of creating a social atom including basing it on a point in the past, the present, or the future. Level two RTR work brings these pen-to-paper exercises to life using sculpting—an experiential process by which a group member uses other group members to stand-in as the roles depicted on the social atom. Sculpting is different from psychodrama in that it often only involves body posturing, short and prescribed movement, and/or short messages from the roles (see Sect. 13.1.9). Sculptures provide living scenes of past or internal experiences—they are simple and effective processes that can be moved into further action by a trained facilitator. The protagonist can talk to themself or others from outside the scene, role reverse with roles the scene, or offer doubling statements for roles. After exploring the scene, it can be recreated in a new way to provide corrective emotional experiences and role training—effectively making up for what was missing, lost, or craved-for in the original experience. In sculpting, the protagonist takes a more active role co-directing the scene and often observing it from a mirror position. Some action sculptures may only involve placing role players on the stage using proximity and posture without words or movement. Sculpting is versatile in that it can be used to concretize internal parts, the family system, the social atom, or other social situations in the past or future.

RTR's "frozen moment sculptures" describe the process of identifying a *frozen moment* for the protagonist—an experience in which a trauma occurred, and the protagonist feels stuck. These frozen moments might be instances from the past when one resorted to a freeze response due to the danger at hand or when one felt helpless or simply stuck and unable to take action. In describing the RTR process of sculpting, Dayton writes:

> We are helping clients to revisit moments from their past that block them from moving forward and to resolve them through a process of making their split-off emotions conscious and then translating them into words and processing them rather than defending against feeling them (2016, p. 49).

These specific moments are reconstructed using sculpting or role playing with the purpose of empowering the protagonist with an opportunity to alter the situation for closure or transformation. The same process can also be used as an integrative experience whereby positive memories or celebratory moments from time are sculpted (Dayton, 2014).

7.10 Conclusion

The increased awareness of the impact of trauma upon individuals, groups, and communities challenges professionals to create systems, organizations, groups, and interventions that are trauma-informed and directly address the impact of trauma. The evolution of the fields of social work, group therapy, sociometry, and psychodrama appears to increasingly be integrating new information and approaches related to trauma-informed and trauma-focused practice. The centrality of the role trauma as an underlying fueling factor of many psychological and social ailments demands that it is given attention and addressed in a truly therapeutic procedure.

Acknowledgements Content on pages 131-134 (Sect. 7.8) was initially published in Giacomucci, S. (2018). The Trauma Survivor's Inner Role Atom: A clinical map for post-traumatic growth. *Journal of Psychodrama, Sociometry, and Group Psychotherapy.* 66(1): 115–129. Reprinted with permission from the publisher (www.asgppjournal.org).

References

Abrams, J., & Shapiro, M. (2014). Teaching trauma theory and practice in MSW programs: A clinically focused, case-based method. *Clinical Social Work Journal, 42*(4), 408–418.

Alexander, F., & French, T. (1946). *Psychoanalytic therapy: Principles and Application.* New York, NY: Ronald Press.

American Psychiatric Association. (2013). *Diagnostic and statistical manual of mental disorders: DSM-5.* Washington, D.C: American Psychiatric Association.

Avinger, K. A., & Jones, R. A. (2007). Group treatment of sexually abused adolescent girls: A review of outcome studies. *The American Journal of Family Therapy, 35*(4), 315–326.

Banks, A. (2006). Relational therapy for trauma. *Journal of Trauma Practice, 5*(1), 25–47.

Bloom, S. (1997). *Creating sanctuary: Toward the evolution of sane societies.* London: Taylor & Francis.

Bloom, S. L. (2013). *Creating Sanctuary: Toward the Evolution of Sane Societies* (2nd ed.). New York, NY: Routledge.

Briere, J., & Scott, C. (2006). *Principles of trauma therapy: A guide to symptoms, evaluation and treatment.* Thousand Oaks, CA: Sage.

Buchanan, D. R., & Swink, D. F. (2017). Golden Age of Psychodrama at Saint Elizabeths Hospital (1939–2004). *The Journal of Psychodrama, Sociometry, and Group Psychotherapy, 65*(1), 9–32.

Burden, K., & Ciotola, L. (2001). *The body double: An advanced clinical action intervention module in the therapeutic spiral model to treat Trauma.* Retrieved from https://www.healing-bridges.com/psychodrama.html.

Bussey, M. C. (2008). Trauma response and recovery certificate program: Preparing students for effective practice. *Journal of Teaching in Social Work, 28*(1–2), 117–144.

Calhoun, L. G., & Tedeschi, R. G. (2014). *The Handbook of post-traumatic growth: Research and practice.* New York, NY: Psychology Press.

Carnabucci, K., & Ciotola, L. (2013). *Healing eating disorders with psychodrama and other action methods: Beyond the silence and the Fury.* London: Jessica Kingsley Publishers.

Christoforou, A., & Kipper, D. A. (2006). The spontaneity assessment inventory (SAI), anxiety, obsessive-compulsive tendency, and temporal orientation. *Journal of Group Psychotherapy, Psychodrama and Sociometry, 59*(1), 23.

Corey, M. S., Corey, G., & Corey, C. (2018). *Groups: Process and practice* (10th ed.). Boston, MA: Cengage Learning.

Council on Social Work Education [CSWE]. (2012). *Advanced social work practice in trauma.* Alexandria, VA: CSWE.

Courtois, C. A. (2002). Traumatic stress studies: The need for curricula inclusion. *Journal of Trauma Practice, 1,* 1.

Courtois, C. A. (2004). Complex trauma, complex reactions: Assessment and treatment. *Psychotherapy: Theory, Research, Practice, Training, 41*(4), 412–425.

Courtois, C. A., & Ford, J. D. (2016). *Treatment of complex trauma: A sequenced, relationship-based approach.* New York, NY: The Guildford Press.

Courtois, C. A., & Ford, J. D. (Eds.). (2009). *Treating complex traumatic stress disorders: An evidence-based guide.* New York: Guilford Press.

Courtois, C. A., & Gold, S. N. (2009). The Need for Inclusion of psychological trauma in the professional curriculum: A call to action. *Psychological Trauma: Theory, Research, Practice, and Policy, 1*(1), 3–23.

Covington, S. S. (2002). Helping women recover: Creating gender-responsive treatment. In S. Straussner & S. Brown (Eds.), *Handbook of women's addictions treatment* (pp. 52–72). San Francisco: Jossey-Bass.

Cozolino, L. J. (2014). *The neuroscience of human relationships* (2nd ed.). New York: W.W. Norton & Company.

Dass-Brailsford, P. (2007). *A practical approach to trauma: Empowering interventions.* Los Angeles: Sage Publications.

Davelaar, P. M., Araujo, F. S., & Kipper, D. A. (2008). The revised spontaneity assessment inventory (SAI-R): Relationship to goal orientation, motivation, perceived self-efficacy, and self-esteem. *The Arts in Psychotherapy, 35*(2), 117–128.

Davies, D. R., Burlingame, G. M., & Layne, C. M. (2006). Integrating small-group process principles into trauma-focused group psychotherapy: What should a group trauma therapist know? In L. A. Schein, H. I. Spitz, G. M. Burlingame, P. R. Muskin, & S. Vargo (Eds.), *Psychological effects of catastrophic disasters: Group approaches to treatment* (pp. 385–423). Binghampton, NY: Haworth Press.

Dayton, T. (2005). *The living stage: A step-by-step guide to psychodrama, sociometry, and experiential group therapy*. Deerfield, FL: Health Communications Inc.

Dayton, T. (2014). *Relational Trauma Repair (RTR) therapist's guide* (Revised). New York, NY: Innerlook Inc.

Dayton, T. (2015). *NeuroPsychodrama in the treatment of relational trauma: A strength-based, experiential model for healing PTSD*. Deerfield Beach, FL: Health Communications Inc.

Dayton, T. (2016). Neuropsychodrama in the treatment of relational trauma: Relational Trauma repair—An experiential model for treating posttraumatic stress disorder. *The Journal of Psychodrama, Sociometry, and Group Psychotherapy, 64*(1), 41–50.

Dong, M., Anda, R., Felitti, V., Dube, S., Williamson, D., Thompson, T., … Giles, W. (2004). The interrelatedness of multiple forms of childhood abuse, neglect, and household dysfunction. *Child Abuse and Neglect, 28*, 771–784.

Felitti, V. J., Anda, R. F., Nordenberg, D., Williamson, D. F., Spitz, A. M., Edwards, V., & Marks, J. S. (1998). Adverse childhood experiences. *American Journal of Preventive Medicine, 14*(4), 245–258.

Foa, E. B., Keane, T. M., Friedman, M. J., & Cohen, J. A. (Eds.). (2008). *Effective treatments for PTSD: Practice guidelines from the International Society for Traumatic Stress Studies*. New York: Guilford Press.

Gene-Cos, N., Fisher, J., Ogden, P., & Cantrell, A. (2016). Sensorimotor psychotherapy group therapy in the treatment of complex PTSD. *Annals of Psychiatry and Mental Health, 4*(6), 1080.

Giacomucci, S. (2017). The sociodrama of life or death: Young adults and addiction treatment. *Journal of Psychodrama, Sociometry, and Group Psychotherapy, 65*(1), 137–143. https://doi.org/10.12926/0731-1273-65.1.137

Giacomucci, S. (2018). The trauma survivor's inner role atom: A clinical map for post-traumatic growth. *Journal of Psychodrama, Sociometry, and Group Psychotherapy, 66*(1), 115–129.

Giacomucci, S. (2019). *Social group work in action: A Sociometry, psychodrama, and experiential trauma therapy curriculum*. Doctorate in Social Work (DSW) Dissertations (p. 124). https://repository.upenn.edu/cgi/viewcontent.cgi?article=1128&context=edissertations_sp2.

Giacomucci, S. (2020). Addiction, traumatic loss, and guilt: A case study resolving grief through psychodrama and sociometric connections. *The Arts in Psychotherapy, 67,* 101627. https://doi.org/10.1016/j.aip.2019.101627.

Giacomucci, S. (2020b). Experiential sociometry in group work: mutual aid for the group-as-a-whole. *Social Work with Groups.* Advanced online publication. https://doi.org/10.1080/01609513.2020.1747726.

Giacomucci, S., Gera, S., Briggs, D., & Bass, K. (2018). Experiential addiction treatment: Creating positive connection through sociometry and Therapeutic Spiral Model safety structures. *Journal of Addiction and Addictive Disorders, 5*, 17. https://doi.org/10.24966/AAD-7276/100017.

Giacomucci, S., & Marquit, J. (2020). The effectiveness of trauma-focused psychodrama in the treatment of PTSD in inpatient substance abuse treatment. *Frontiers in Psychology, 11*, 896. https://doi.org/10.3389/2Ffpsyg.2020.00896.

Giacomucci, S., & Stone, A. M. (2019). Being in two places at once: Renegotiating traumatic experience through the surplus reality of psychodrama. *Social Work with Groups, 42*(3), 184–196. https://doi.org/10.1080/01609513.2018.1533913.

Gitterman, A., & Knight, C. (2016). Promoting resilience through social work practice with groups: Implications for the practice and field curricula. *Journal of Social Work Education, 52*(4), 448–461.

Gross, S. (2018). The power of optimism. In T. Marks-Tarlow, M. Solomon, & D. J. Siegel (Eds.) *Play and creativity in psychotherapy.* New York: W.W. Norton & Company.

Harris, M., & Fallot, R. (2001). *Using trauma theory to design service systems.* San Francisco: Jossey-Bass.

Herman, J. L. (1992). *Trauma and recovery: The aftermath of violence—from domestic abuse to political terror.* New York: Basic Books.

Horowitz, M. J. (1997). *Stress response syndromes* (3rd ed.). Northvale, NJ: Jason Aronson.

Hudgins, M.K. (2017) PTSD Unites the World: Prevention, intervention and training in the therapeutic spiral model. In C.E. Stout, & G. Want (Eds.), *Why global health matters: Guidebook for innovation and inspiration.* Self-Published Online.

Hudgins, K. (2019). Psychodrama Revisited: through the lens of the internal role map of the therapeutic spiral model to promote post-traumatic growth. *Zeitschrift Für Psychodrama Und Soziometrie, 18*(1), 59–74.

Hudgins, M. K., & Toscani, F. (2013). *Healing World trauma with the therapeutic spiral model: Stories from the frontlines.* London: Jessica Kingsley Publishers.

Hug, E. (2013). A Neuroscience perspective on trauma and action methods. In K. Hudgins & F. Toscani (Eds.), *Healing world trauma with the therapeutic spiral model.* London: Jessica Kingsley Publishers.

Johnson, D. R., & Sajnani, N. (2014). The role of drama therapy in trauma treatment. *Trauma informed drama therapy: Transforming clinics, classrooms, and communities* (pp. 5–23). Springfield, IL: Charles C. Thomas Publishers.

Joseph, S., & Murphy, D. (2014). Trauma: A unifying concept for social workers. *British Journal of Social Work, 44*(5), 1094–1109.

Kabat Zinn, J. (1990). *Full catastrophe living: Using the wisdom of your body and mind to face stress, pain and illness.* New York: Delacorte.

Kabat Zinn, J. (2003). Mindfulness based intervention in context: Past, present, and future. *Clinical Psychology: Science and Practice, 10,* 144–156.

Kabat Zinn, J. (2005). *Coming to our senses.* New York: Hyperion.

Karpman, S. (1968). Fairy tales and script drama analysis. *Transactional Analysis Bulletin, 7*(26), 39–43.

Kellermann, P. F. (2000). The therapeutic effects of psychodrama with traumatized people. In P. F. Kellermann & K. Hudgins (Eds.), *Psychodrama with trauma survivors: Acting out your pain* (pp. 23–40). Philadelphia: Jessica Kingsley Publishing.

Kestly, T. (2018). A cross-cultural and cross-disciplinary perspective of play. In T. Marks-Tarlow, M. Solomon, & D. J. Siegel (Eds.) *Play and creativity in psychotherapy.* New York: W.W. Norton & Company.

Kipper, D. A., Green, D. J., & Prorak, A. (2010). The relationship among spontaneity, impulsivity, and creativity. *Journal of Creativity in Mental Health, 5*(1), 39–53.

Kipper, D. A., & Hundal, J. (2005). The Spontaneity Assessment Inventory: The relationship between spontaneity and nonspontaneity. *Journal of Group Psychotherapy, Psychodrama and Sociometry, 58*(3), 119.

Kipper, D. A., & Shemer, H. (2006). The revised spontaneity assessment inventory (SAI-R): Spontaneity, well-being, and stress. *Journal of Group Psychotherapy, Psychodrama and Sociometry, 59*(3), 127.

Klein, R. H., & Schermer, V. L. (Eds.). (2000). *Group psychotherapy for psychological trauma.* Guilford Press.

Knight, C. (2006). Groups for individuals with traumatic histories: Practice considerations for social workers. *Social Work, 51*(1), 20–30.

Krupnick, J. L. (2002). Brief psychodynamic theory and PTSD. *Journal of Clinical Psychology, 58*(8), 919–932.

Lawrence, C. (2011). *The architecture of mindfulness: Integrating the therapeutic spiral model and interpersonal neurobiology*. Retrieved from https://www.drkatehudgins.com.

Levine, P. A. (2010). *In an Unspoken Voice: How the body releases trauma and restores goodness*. Berkeley, CA: North Atlantic Books.

Levine, P. A. (2015). *Trauma and Memory: Brain and body in a search for the living past*. Berkeley, CA: North Atlantic Books.

Marks-Tarlow, T. (2018). Awakening clinical intuition: Creativity and play. In T. Marks-Tarlow, M. Solomon, & D. J. Siegel (Eds.) *Play and creativity in psychotherapy*. New York: W.W. Norton & Company.

McKenzie-Mohr, S. (2004). Creating space for radical trauma theory in generalist social work education. *Journal of Progressive Human Services, 15,* 45–55.

Mendelsohn, M., Zachary, R., & Harney, P. (2007). Group therapy as an ecological bridge to new community for trauma survivors. *Journal of Aggression, Maltreatment & Trauma, 14,* 227–243.

Moreno, J. L. (1946). *Psychodrama Volume 1*. Beacon, NY: Beacon House Press.

Moreno, J. L. (1953). *Who shall survive? Foundations of sociometry, group psychotherapy and sociodrama* (2nd ed.). Beacon, NY: Beacon House.

Moreno, J. L. (2019). *The autobiography of a genius*. In E. Schreiber, S. Kelley, & S. Giacomucci (Eds.), United Kingdom: North West Psychodrama Association.

Moreno, Z. T. (1965/2006). Psychodramatic rules, techniques, and adjunctive methods. In T. Horvatin & E. Schreiber (Eds.), *The Quintessential Zerka* (pp. 104–114). New York: Routledge.

Moreno, Z. T. (2012). *To dream again: A memoir*. New York: Mental Health Resources.

National Center for Trauma-Informed Care. (2012). Retrieved November 18, 2012, from www.men talhealth.samhsa.gov/nctic/trauma.asp.

Nieto, L. (2010). Look behind you: Using anti-oppression models to inform a protagonist's psychodrama. In E. Leveton (Ed.), *Healing collective trauma using sociodrama and drama therapy* (pp. 103–125). New York: Springer Publishing Company.

Nolte, J. (2014). *The philosophy, theory, and methods of J.L. Moreno: The man who tried to become God*. New York, NY: Routledge.

O'Halloran, M. S., & O'Halloran, T. (2001). Secondary traumatic stress in the classroom: Ameliorating stress in graduate students. *Teaching of Psychology, 28,* 92–97.

Ogden, P., Minton, K., & Pain, C. (2006). *Trauma and the body: A sensorimotor approach to psychotherapy (norton series on interpersonal neurobiology*. New York: W.W. Norton & Company.

Putnam, F. (2006). The impact of trauma on child development. *Journal of Juvenile and Family Court, 57,* 1–11.

Ringel, S., & Brandell, J. R. (Eds.). (2011). *Trauma: Contemporary directions in theory, practice, and research*. Sage.

Rivard, J. C., Bloom, S. L., Abramovitz, R., et al. (2003). Assessing the implementation and effects of a trauma-focused intervention for youths in residential treatment. *Psychiatric Quarterly, 74,* 137–154.

Rosenwald, M., & Baird, J. (2019). An integrated trauma-informed, mutual aid model of group work. *Social Work with Groups*. https://doi.org/10.1080/01609513.2019.1656145.

Schouten, K. A., de Niet, G. J., Knipscheer, J. W., Kleber, R. J., & Hutschemaekers, G. J. (2015). The effectiveness of art therapy in the treatment of traumatized adults: A systematic review on art therapy and trauma. *Trauma, Violence, & Abuse, 16*(2), 220–228.

Siegel, D. J. (2010). *Mindsight: The new science of personal transformation*. New York: Bantam.

Sloan, D. M., Bovin, M. J., & Schnurr, P. P. (2012). Review of group treatment for PTSD. *Journal of Rehabilitation Research & Development, 49*(5), 689–702.

Strand, V. C., Abramovitz, R., Layne, C. M., Robinson, H., & Way, I. (2014). Meeting the critical need for trauma education in social work: A problem-based learning approach. *Journal of Social Work Education, 50*(1), 120–135.

Substance Abuse and Mental Health Services Administration. (2014a). SAMHSA's concept of trauma and guidance for a trauma-informed approach. HHS Publication No. (SMA) 14-4884. Rockville, MD: Substance Abuse and Mental Health Services Administration.

Substance Abuse and Mental Health Services Administration. (2014b). Trauma-informed care in behavioral health services. Treatment Improvement Protocol (TIP) Series 57. HHS Publication No. (SMA) 13-4801. Rockville, MD: Substance Abuse and Mental Health Services Administration.

Tarashoeva, G., Marinova-Djambazova, P., & Kojuharov, H. (2017). Effectiveness of psychodrama therapy in patients with panic disorders: Final results. *International Journal of Psychotherapy, 21*(2), 55–66.

Testoni, I., Wieser, M., Armenti, A., Ronconi, L., Guglielmin, M. S., Cottone, P., & Zamperini, A. (2016). Spontaneity as predictive factor for well-being. In *Psychodrama: Empirical research and science* (pp. 11–23). Springer, Wiesbaden.

Toscani, M. F., & Hudgins, M. K. (1995). *The trauma survivor's intrapsychic role atom.* Workshop Handout. Madison, WI: The Center for Experiential Learning.

Trevarthen, C., & Panksepp, J. (2016). In tune with feeling. *Inclusion, Play and Empathy: Neuroaffective Development in Children's Groups*, 29

van de Kamp, M. M., Scheffers, M., Hatzmann, J., Emck, C., Cuijpers, P., & Beek, P. J. (2019). Body- and movement-oriented interventions for posttraumatic stress disorder: A Systematic review and meta-analysis. *Journal of Traumatic Stress.* https://doi.org/10.1002/jts.22465.

van der Kolk, B. A. (2005). Developmental trauma disorder: Toward a rational diagnosis for children with complex trauma histories. *Psychiatric Annals, 35*(5), 401–408.

Van der Kolk, B. A. (2014). *The body keeps the score: Brain, mind, and body in the healing of trauma.* New York: Viking Press.

von Ameln, F., & Becker-Ebel, J. (2020). *Fundamentals of psychodrama.* Singapore: Springer Nature.

Wilson, B., & Nochajski, T. H. (2016). Evaluating the impact of trauma informed care (TIC) perspective in social work curriculum. *Social Work Education, 35*(5), 589–602.

Wilson, C., Pence, D. M., & Conradi, L. (2013). Trauma-informed care. In *Encyclopedia of social work.* National Association of Social Work and Oxford Press. https://doi.org/10.1093/acrefore/9780199975839.013.1063.

Chapter 8
Interpersonal Neurobiology, Social Work, Sociometry, and Psychodrama

Abstract The rapidly emerging neuroscience research continues to validate the practice of social work, group therapy, and psychodrama. The centrality of human relationships is being supported by the field of interpersonal neurobiology. New technologies allow us to learn more about the brain and the ways it is impacted by adversity, healing, and action. The importance of safety, connection, integration, and a strength-s-based approach is supported in the neuroscience literature. The neurobiological mechanisms which promote change in psychodrama are becoming clearer. Furthermore, the words of contemporary neuroscientists appear to echo Moreno's writings of sociometry and psychodrama nearly a decade earlier.

Keywords Neuroscience · Interpersonal neurobiology · Group psychotherapy · Psychodrama · Social work · Trauma

8.1 Trauma and Neuroscience

The evolution of technology has stimulated an advancement in research in the field of neurobiology in the past few decades. Many refer to the 1990s as *The Decade of the Brain*, due to the significant findings that emerged in the field of neuroscience (Gabbard, 1992). The field of trauma and post-traumatic stress has been revolutionized in the past few decades with an influx of new information about how trauma impacts the body and the brain. Some core neurobiological processes to understand when it comes to trauma include the structure of the brain, attachment and affect regulation, poly-vagal theory, and trauma responses, HPA axis, memory and learning, and healing from trauma.

8.1.1 Brain Structure and Brain Systems

The brain is an incredibly complex organ, most of which we still do not fully understand due to its many complexities. Some foundational understandings of the structure of the brain include the conceptualization of the brain as a part of multiple larger

© The Author(s) 2021

S. Giacomucci, *Social Work, Sociometry, and Psychodrama*, Psychodrama in Counselling, Coaching and Education 1,
https://doi.org/10.1007/978-981-33-6342-7_8

systems including the nervous system, the body, the family system, and larger social systems. Neurons, or brain cells, develop neural networks through connections with each other. Neural connections are strengthened by repetition, resulting in the famous neuroscience rhymes "neurons that fire together, wire together," and "use it or lose it" (Hebb, 1949). The brain is most malleable and develops at its quickest rate in the early years of life. Following its evolutionary history, brain structures develop hierarchically from oldest to newest; beginning with the brain stem (sometimes called the reptilian brain) which regulates basic bodily functions such as heart rate, breathing, and temperature. Next, the limbic system (sometimes called the mammalian brain) develops which includes the thalamus, amygdala, hippocampus, and hypothalamus responsible for the facilitation of sensory information, emotions, relationships, and memory. The final part of the brain to develop is the cortex, which is responsible for more sophisticated aspects of human life including language, meaning making, ideas, processing information, and fine motor movement. The cortex is broken into two hemispheres, connected by the corpus collosum. Generally speaking, the right hemisphere specializes in emotions and sensory information while the left hemisphere specializes in detail related to language, meaning making, and fine motor movements (Shapiro & Applegate, 2018; Siegel, 2012).

8.1.2   Attachment and Brain Development

The brain develops along this trajectory in relationship to close attachment figures of the individual. Cozolino (2014) suggests that instead of the Darwin's idea of *survival of the fittest*, the neuroscience research suggests *survival of the nurtured* is more accurate. He writes that "there are no single human brains—brains only exist within networks of other brains" (2014, p. xvi). The infant's caregivers, through attuned presence and nurturing, contribute to optimal conditions for healthy brain development and the child's capacity for emotional self-regulation as an adult (Schore, 2015). The human child is dependent on others for their survival for a longer time than any other species—"they survive based on the abilities of their caretakers to detect the needs and intentions of those around them" (Cozolino, 2014, p. 6). Emotional and physical neglect or abuse have the potential to disrupt the brain's development and cause psychosocial problems throughout the lifespan (van der Kolk, 2014). Our need for connection and relationships is wired into us as humans and continues long after maturation. Even in adulthood, we continue to regulate our emotions through relationships and social engagement with others (Porges, 2017).

8.1.3   Polyvagal Theory and Danger Responses

Stephen Porges' Polyvagal Theory suggests that "in humans, three basic neural energy subsystems underpin the overall state of the nervous system and correlative behaviors and emotions" (Levine, 2010, p. 97). These three subsystems developed evolutionarily to facilitate our responses to external threats and to maintain homeostasis or a sense of safety (Porges, 2017). The most primitive of these systems is the unmyelinated dorsal vagal complex—the immobilization system (freeze response) that we have in common with almost all vertebrates. The next system to develop phylogenetically is the mammalian sympathetic nervous system that supports mobilization of fight and flight responses. And finally, the most recently developed stage of the hierarchy is the myelinated ventral vagal complex, a major component of the social engagement system. The more refined ventral vagal system, or "smart vagus," is linked to facial expression, orienting, listening, and vocalization which facilitate (verbal and non-verbal) social communication, relationships, and attachment (Porges, 2017). These three subsystems compose a map of human response strategies employed as physiological reactions to external threats—beginning with the social engagement system as a first utilized adaptive response, preceding the mobilization responses, and finally calling upon the immobilization response as a last effort to survive.

Both the immobilization and mobilization responses are necessary for healthy functioning and human survival. The responses to danger are meant to be short and quick responses; however, some traumatized individuals can experience chronic hyperarousal (fight/flight) or immobilization (freeze) because the nervous system does not discriminate between a perceived, current threat and a distress about an experience in the past (Levine, 2010).

8.1.4 Stress Regulation and the HPA Axis

The hypothalamic–pituitary–adrenal (HPA) axis regulates and controls the release of hormones to the body which produce stress and prepare the body for responses to threat or danger. The immediacy of this process is essential for short-term survival while the quick return to normalcy is essential for long-term survival (Cozolino, 2014). Chronic or prolonged stress from repeated trauma responses disrupts various processes in the body and can result in the breakdown of different systems including the musculoskeletal, cardiovascular, endocrine, respiratory, gastrointestinal, immune, reproductive, and nervous systems (Cozolino, 2014; Maté, 2011; McFarlane, 2010; van der Kolk, 2014).

8.1.5 Experience and Memory

The neurobiological underpinnings of experience, learning, and memory are highly relevant in the approach to trauma and PTSD. The finding that the brain maintains its neuroplasticity means that the brain, and thus the person, continues to be impacted and shaped by experiences throughout their lifespan (Cozolino, 2010; Siegel, 2012).

Experiences, especially relational experiences, result in meaningful learning due to the social nature of our brain circuitry (Cozolino, 2014). Trauma, adversity, and chronic stress have the potential to disrupt the brain's capacity for normal learning due to the resulting hyperarousal, overwhelming emotions, negative thoughts and beliefs, intrusive images, avoidance, and dissociation (Levine, 2010; Shapiro & Applegate, 2018).

There are various types of memory including explicit and implicit memory, both of which play a role in traumatic stress. Explicit memories are consciously remembered experiences while implicit memories are not conscious but affect our feelings, sensations, and actions in the here-and-now (Levine, 2010). Until the hippocampus is formed around 18 months old, the infant is operating without explicit memory and their learning is based entirely on experiences that result in implicit memories. Traumatic experiences result in both implicit and explicit memory—while the individual may or may not recall the traumatic event, the body continues to keep the score and responds to stimuli related to the trauma (van der Kolk, 2014).

Research by Rauch and colleagues (1996) indicates that when a traumatic memory is activated it appears to significantly impact the functioning of the speech and language centers of the brain (van der Kolk, 2014), which theoretically challenges the effectiveness of talk therapy. These findings also highlight a neurobiological understanding as to why trauma survivors may have difficulty talking about their experiences. Bessel van der Kolk explains that the "imprint of trauma doesn't sit in the verbal, understanding part of the brain…but in much deeper regions—amygdala, hippocampus, hypothalamus, brain stem—which are only marginally affected by thinking and cognition" (as cited in Wylie, 2004, pp. 30–41).

8.1.6   Dissociation, Fragmentation, and Integration

Trauma experts seem to agree that when someone experiences something as traumatic, it is because their capacity to process and integrate the experience was overwhelmed—often resulting in fragmentation, dissociation, avoidance, and/or re-experiencing of the traumatic material (Fisher, 2017; Herman, 1992; Levine, 2010; Shapiro, 2018; Siegel, 2012; van der Kolk, 2014). Trauma creates fragmentation and dissociation interpersonally, intrapsychically, and neurobiologically (Giacomucci, 2019). Neurobiologically, a trauma survivor's vertical and hemispherical integration is disrupted. Psychologically, their sense of self, narrative, cognition, and memories become fragmented. And interpersonally, their relationships are often characterized by reenactment, insecure attachment, and discord. In order to diminish these PTSD symptoms, the traumatic experience must be processed and integrated by the individual at the mind, body, and relational levels.

8.2 Social Work and Neuroscience

Social workers frequently are working with individuals, groups, or communities that have experienced trauma, neglect, or adversity. The influx of new neurobiology research has provided social workers with another layer of information and evidence on which to base our profession and our practice. Farmer (2009) even declares that neuroscience is a missing link for social workers. Neuroscience research has challenged previously held beliefs of the separateness of mind and body in favor of an integrated mind–body perspective (Johnson, 2008). Furthermore, interpersonal neurobiology endorses an integrated biopsychosocial viewpoint demonstrating the interconnectedness of mind, body, and relationships. In addition to suggesting new ways of practicing for clinical social workers, "findings from neurobiology help them appreciate the biopsychosocial substrate of relational dynamics that serve as a context for effectively applying techniques they already use" (Shapiro & Applegate, 2018, p. xxi).

Interpersonal neurobiology research supports many of the core theories that have become integrated within the foundation of the field of clinical social work. In *Neurobiology for Clinical Social Work*, Shapiro and Applegate (2018), highlight multiple facets of neurobiology which are relevant and important for social work practice including how neuroscience relates to memory, learning, stress, trauma, narrative, affect regulation, emotion, human behavior, attachment, human development, adult relationships, and psychotherapy. Neuroscience provides an increased understanding of the complexities of most personal and societal problems encounter on a regular basis by social workers (Farmer, 2009).

8.2.1 Foundation of Relationships

Social work philosophy emphasizes the value of relationships and specifically the importance of the therapeutic relationship between client and social worker. Research in the field of psychotherapy has validated social work philosophy by demonstrated the therapeutic relationship to be the most important aspect related to psychotherapy outcomes (Ardito & Rabellino, 2011; Horvath & Symonds, 1991). The field of interpersonal neurobiology uncovers the biopsychosocial factors that resulting in the significance of human relationships in psychotherapy and "why the humanity we share with our patients can be as powerful as any drug" (Cozolino, 2018, p. xii). Findings in epigenetics demonstrate how experiences impact the expression or inhibition of genetic potential. An individual's environment and their life experiences influence their genetic expression which supports social work's person-in-environment perspective (Shapiro & Applegate, 2018).

Many neuroscience experts agree that one of the most important neuroscience implications for psychotherapy is an understanding and movement toward neural integration. Siegel (2012) points to integration as the key to mental health, while

Cozolino (2010) emphasizes neural integration as the key to optimal outcomes in psychotherapy. He outlines key areas to include: (1) the safe and trusting holding environment of the therapeutic relationship; (2) new corrective experiences that lead to learning across neural networks; (3) integration of neural networks, especially those that have been fragmented or disconnected; and (4) practicing affect regulation and stress tolerance within the safety of the therapeutic alliance. These considerations for psychotherapy provide social workers with a neurobiology-informed approach to clinical work.

Through the framework of interpersonal neurobiology, relationships can be conceptualized as biological interventions (Cozolino, 2018). It seems that interpersonal neurobiology has fulfilled J. L. Moreno's vision a half-century earlier of a scientifically based interpersonal therapy. The increased value placement in relationships and their importance in human life seems to have emerged concurrently with the increased practice of group psychotherapy in the past few decades.

8.3   Group Psychotherapy and Neuroscience

Similar to social work practice, the practice of group psychotherapy is validated by new neuroscience findings (Flores, 2013). While much has been written about neuroscience as it relates to mental health and individual psychotherapy, the literature on group therapy and neuroscience is lacking. Considering relationships as one of the most important aspects of psychotherapy, it would make sense that a group setting may offer exponentially more opportunities for relational healing than individual work. Because of this, Gantt and Badenoch suggest that from a brain-based perspective, group therapy may be "a more powerful and logical choice" than individual therapy (2013, p. xx).

Badenoch and Cox (2013), in *Integrating Interpersonal Neurobiology with Group Psychotherapy*, suggest three primary focus points for group therapists to incorporate neuroscience into their work: (1) early brain development and memories (explicit, implicit, and autobiographical); (2) the group as an regulating holding environment for both group members' emotions and nervous systems; and (3) attention to the four domains of neural integration—consciousness, interpersonal, vertical, and bilateral integration.

8.3.1   Group Holding Environment

The aforementioned clinical recommendations for the integration of interpersonal neurobiology into group work echo the same suggestions provided by Cozolino (2010) for individual psychotherapy. The primary difference in the suggested areas is that in individual therapy the relationship between client and therapist is emphasized for its safety, regulation, and capacity for corrective experiences—while in group psychotherapy the group-as-a-whole is emphasized as possessing these same capacities. The holding environment shifts from being the relationship between client and therapist, to the matrix of relationships between all group members. Gantt and Agazarian (2013) articulate this in suggesting that:

> Maximising neuroplasticity requires that we create an experiential group environment that provides a secure relational context, with neural and emotional regulation within and between brains, where moderate levels of emotion can be experienced with the right-brain resonance and responsiveness that enables modulation, development, and greater implicit integration. (p. 82)

The brain's capacity for change throughout the lifespan is leveraged as a mechanism for therapeutic effect in group psychotherapy whereby individual participants come together creating a collective and are healed by the group-as-a-whole. One might argue that the value of group psychotherapy becomes especially realized when working with individuals who have experienced adverse or traumatic relationships in their life. The social nature of group psychotherapy activates the social engagement system in a way that "the group-as-a-whole can be supported in gradually becoming havens of safety and regulation for all members" (Badenoch & Cox, 2013, p. 10).

8.3.2 Early Childhood Experiences

Early childhood experiences become encoded in the brain and nervous system as implicit memories and attachment styles which impact our lives going forward (Cozolino, 2014; Siegel, 2012). In the first 12–18 months of an infant's life, these are the only type of memory created—"embodied, wordless, yet rich and foundational to our view of the world" (Badenoch & Cox, 2013, p. 4). The right-brain to right-brain communication and resonance between individuals of an attuned group provides a holding environment to regulate the activation of these implicit memory systems and offer an avenue toward neural integration (Siegel, 2013). Early childhood experiences, often encoded as implicit memories are difficult to work with in traditional psychotherapy settings however, the "group is a unique context that can trigger, amplify, contain, and provide resonance for a broad range of human experiences, creating robust conditions for changing the brain" (Gantt & Badenoch, 2013, p. xix).

8.3.3 Neural Integration Through Group Psychotherapy

The *integration of consciousness* is defined as the mind's ability to compassionately observe itself (Siegel, 2007). This capacity becomes enhanced through group psychotherapy's process of story-telling and compassionate witnessing between group members. When safety and cohesion is established within the group, *interpersonal integration* emerges and contributes to integration of consciousness for each individual group member. "Energy and information constantly flow not only within brains, but between brains" (Badenoch & Cox, 2013, p. 14). Coincidentally, both interpersonal integration and integration of consciousness work together to enhance vertical and bilateral integration. On the other hand, *bilateral integration* refers to the bridge between right hemisphere sensations and emotions with left hemisphere words and insight to develop a coherent narrative of an experience. Siegel, the developer of interpersonal neurobiology, writes that integration is at the heart of health and that humans who come together with a common history, identity, and purpose have an innate drive toward integration and wholeness (2013).

8.4 Sociometry, Psychodrama, and Neuroscience

The evolution of neuroscience research in the past two decades has provided psychodrama and experiential trauma therapies with a richer foundation for an evidence base. These neuroscience findings have led many to even claim that experiential therapies are the treatment of choice for specific mental health and trauma-related clinical issues (Dayton, 2015; Giacomucci, 2018; Hudgins, 2017; van der Kolk, 1996, 2014). Over 100 years ago, Moreno was actively developing the foundational philosophy for his sociometric and psychodramatic methods. His active attempts to associate his ideas with science are demonstrated in his choice of words for his new ideas, such as: social atom, cultural atom, role atom, sociometry, sociostasis, sociogram, sociogenetic law, the law of social gravity, and social microscopy among others. Yaniv writes that "his eagerness to relate sociometry to other traditional scientific domains, such as biology, physics, or mathematics, led him to some outstanding hypotheses and predictions that turned out to be empirically valid a century later" (2014, p. 108).

8.4.1 Action

The brain is an action-oriented organ, so it should not be surprising that its integrative potential is realized through action. Where words are inadequate or blocked from access to primary material, the brain is open to other avenues of expression. The psychological dynamics explored by psychodrama reflect fundamental operations within the brain/body in which emotional dynamics favor more subcortical layers and rational modes favor more neocortical layers of the brain (Hug, 2007, p. 227). J.L. Moreno's action theory and approach to psychotherapy is supported nearly 100 years later by the growing body of neuroscience research. As noted previously, psychodrama is one of the first body-oriented models of psychotherapy. Many treatment approaches focus entirely on thoughts, narrative, emotion, and talking, which are neglecting a major element of human experience. It is imperative that treatment include the whole individual—their cognitions, emotions, their body, their social context, and in many cases a spiritual component.

The field of "interpersonal neurobiology assumes that the brain is a social organ built via experience" (Cozolino, 2014, p. xvii). The brain develops in relationships with others through experience, which is facilitated, in part, by experience-dependent neuroplasticity. This phenomenon describes the interplay of nature and nurture whereby "our brains are structured and restructured by interactions with our social and natural environments" (Cozolino, 2014, pp. 77–78). In the early stages of a child's life, all communication is in action—gesturing, motioning, facial expression, and body language. It is not until later that one develops the capacity to communicate through words and language, and even then, a large portion of communication remains nonverbal. Psychodrama's emphasis on action, interaction, and enactment speaks to this facet of our nature as human beings of action.

8.4.2 Healing Trauma with Psychodrama

Many treatments for trauma focus heavily on the cognitive, emotional, social, and spiritual impacts of trauma but do not include intervention and sensitivity to the ways in which trauma effects an individual's central nervous system. Psychodrama includes the body and the central nervous system in its interventions which may be a large component of their efficacy. Neurobiology research suggests that experiential and body-centered treatments may be better suited for trauma treatment (Dayton, 2015; Levine, 2010; van der Kolk, 2014).

> Prone to action, and deficient in words, these patients (trauma survivors) can often express their internal states more articulately in physical movements or in pictures than in words. Utilizing drawings and psychodrama may help them develop a language that is essential for effective communication and for the symbolic transformation that can occur in psychotherapy. (van der Kolk, 1996, p. 195)

These findings have been used to suggest that experiential therapy and trauma-focused psychodrama is a treatment of choice when working with PTSD (Dayton, 2015; Giacomucci, 2018; Hudgins, 2017; Kellermann & Hudgins, 2000; Hug, 2013).

The brain changes through experience (Siegel, 2012). A psychodramatic experience has the power to change psychological and somatic imprints of trauma by activating traumatic neural networks while safely renegotiating the traumatic content and providing completion of the previously incomplete survival response of the nervous system (Giacomucci & Stone, 2019; Levine, 2010; Porges, 2017). While other trauma therapies seem to focus on desensitization or symptom control, psychodrama may offer an path for renegotiation, integration, and resolution of PTSD (Dayton, 2015; Giacomucci, 2018; Giacomucci & Marquit, 2020; Giacomucci & Stone, 2019; Hudgins, 2017; Hudgins & Toscani, 2013).

8.4.3 Integration as the Key to Wellness

The purpose of all types of psychotherapy, Cozolino (2010) writes, is to enhance the integration of neural networks. He suggests that bilateral hemispheric integration and vertical neural integration are most relevant to neuroscience and psychotherapy. Vertical integration refers to the "unification of body, emotion, and conscious awareness" and includes "the ability of the cortex to process, inhibit, and organize the reflexes, impulses, and emotions generated by the brainstem and limbic system (Alexander, DeLong, & Strick, 1986; Cummings, 1993; as cited in Cozolino, 2010, p. 27). At the same time, bilateral integration is necessary to put language to our inner experience. The right hemisphere is more connected with body sensations and emotions–the limbic system and brain stem. The left hemisphere is more identified with cortical functioning and language (Shapiro, 2018). Hug (2007) and Robbins (2018) posit that the action of psychodrama, which stimulates the body and levels of functioning beyond cortical, provides an opportunity for information from the limbic system to emerge and be integrated—including implicit memory such as attachment schemas, traumatic experiences, and affect regulation processes. He maintains that psychodrama has a unique potential to renegotiate not just explicit memory (hippocampus), but also affective memory (centered with the amygdala). "Psychodrama has to do with connective body and language through enactment and action…the body remembers what the conscious mind may confabulate or may not remember at all" (Hug, 2007, pp. 230–231).

The term interpersonal neurobiology was coined by Siegel, who defines integration as the key to mental health. He offers eight different domains of integration—consciousness, bilateral, vertical, memory, narrative, state, interpersonal, and temporal (2012). He states that "our task is to find the impediments to the eight domains of integration and liberate the mind's natural drive to heal—to integrate mind, brain, and relationships" (2010, p. 76). Strikingly, Siegel's statement mirrors the following statement by Zerka Moreno—"protagonists themselves do the healing. My task is to find and touch that autonomous healing center within, to assist and direct the protagonist to do the same" (2012, p. 504). Furthermore, Moreno's (1953) emphasis on catharsis of integration finds neuroscientific merit through the research of interpersonal neurobiology (Giacomucci, 2018). "Integration is the goal, not catharsis" (Hug, 2013, p. 129). Or, to express it in classical psychodrama terms, a catharsis of integration must follow a catharsis of abreaction (Hollander, 1969; Moreno, 1953). Beyond neurobiological and psychological integration, psychodrama group work also offers opportunities for social and spiritual integration.

8.4.4 Mirror Neurons—The Double, The Mirror, and Audience Catharsis

Returning to the psychodramatic technique of doubling, Hug (2007) offers a neuro-biological basis at the core of doubling—mirror neurons. Mirror neurons describe the phenomenon within the frontal lobes, or the "seat of empathy," during which one's brain activity will mirror the brain activity of another whom they are watching in action (Keysers & Gazzola, 2010). It is likely that mirror neurons are at the foundation of one's ability to double the protagonist. Mirror neurons were originally discovered by accident when researchers had connected electrodes to a monkey's brain to measure their premotor area as the monkey picked up a food object. At one point, as the monkey sat still and watched, the researcher picked up a food pellet—to everyone's surprise, the monkey's brain cells fired in the same exact way as if he himself had picked up the food (van der Kolk, 2014). In the same way, as group participants observe a psychodrama protagonist in action, it is likely that their brain is activated as if they were participating in the action too. This may provide a neurobiological understanding to clients' experience of psychodrama as having a "catching force" that emotionally engages even the audience members. Operationally, this may mean that each group member receives similar therapeutic effects as the protagonist of the psychodrama.

Schermer (2013) suggests that mirror neurons and their related systems "serve as a biological substrate for systemic group-as-a-whole relations" (p. 31). The two primary poles of functioning of mirror neurons are action and recognition, which together lead to the development of human connection and larger social units (Schermer, 2013). Klein writes that the observer or mirror position in psychodrama is mostly associated with neocortex activation while role-playing activates the brainstem and limbic system (2015). Considering this neurobiological understanding, the mirror position can be used by the psychodrama director to facilitate affect regulation and cognitive processing for the protagonist (Klein, 2015; von Ameln & Becker-Ebel, 2020). The mirror position helps a protagonist accurately see themselves in action from a place of safety and distance which may also promote multiple types of integration including vertical and bilateral.

8.4.5 Role-Playing and Role Reversal

When a protagonist volunteers, offers a trauma-related topic to the group, and states a goal for the work, they are tapping into both the memory of the trauma and the associated neural network. Beginning the drama with strengths-based roles helps to renegotiate the emotional context of the traumatic memory by activating different affective systems and providing a felt sense of safety after the memory has been stimulated. These strengths-based roles are most likely to initiate the PLAY, CARE, and SEEKING social–emotional systems, as described by Panksepp and Biven (2012), which in effect provide a renegotiation and recontextualization of the traumatic memory (Levine, 2015).

In role reversals with positive roles, a psychodramatist utilizes the role reciprocity between the protagonist and role to activate both the protagonist's creativity spontaneity and CARE system as they role train compassion and care for self (Giacomucci, 2018). Panksepp and Biven (2012) write that experiencing feelings of PANIC/GRIEF in others (even through a role-player!) is one of the most powerful triggers of the CARE system—thus highlighting one of the neurobiological mechanisms of role reciprocity in psychodrama. Furthermore, activating the protagonist's CARE system (in the role reversal) will inhibit their GRIEF system (p. 285), effectively strengthening the renegotiation of the memory's emotional context.

The fact that another human plays the role of these roles is neurobiologically significant. The interaction with a role (and thus the group member playing the role) activates the protagonist's ventral vagal nerve ("Smart Vagus") and social engagement system providing emotional regulation (Porges, 2017). On the other hand, the auxiliary roles' interactions with the protagonist throughout the drama provide an experience of consistent attunement which is also associated with emotional regulation and feelings of security, safety, self-esteem, confidence, and connection (Fishbane, 2007). Furthermore, because "the 'self' is largely a construction of the prefrontal cortex or the thinking mind" (Dayton, 2015, p. 111), which is often frozen when trauma becomes activated, the experience of role reversing into any other role allows the protagonist to concretize and physically see one's self—helping to keep the prefrontal cortex of the brain actively stimulated. The role reversal requires the protagonist to utilize internal representations of the other along with their spontaneity and creativity as they continue to engage in the psychodrama (Yaniv, 2011, 2012).

8.4.6   Neurospirituality of Spontaneity

Jacob Moreno's definition of spontaneity is an adequate response to novelty and a new response to an old situation (1953). Furthermore, Moreno believed spontaneity to be cosmic in nature and directly related to spirituality and the Godhead (Moreno, 2019). Martin and colleagues (1997) conducted research measuring neural activation when participants performed novel tasks, as compared to routine tasks. In novel situation, medial temporal structures of the right brain were particularly active along with left-brain structures, while routine tasks showed only left-brain activation. This research sheds light on psychodrama's ability, through the activation of spontaneity to awaken a bilateral integration within the brain (Goldberg, 2001; Hug, 2007, 2013). Interestingly, the right medial temporal lobe which was especially active in Martin's (1997) research is also involved in out-of-body experiences and religious experiences—thus neuroscience seems to support Moreno's (1921) notion that "God is spontaneity."

8.5 Sociometry and Interpersonal Neurobiology

J. L. Moreno's understanding of individuals existing within social networks and social atoms, as well as his statement that "an individual is tied to his social atom as closely as to his body" (1953, p. 703), seem to be echoed in Cozolino's description of the *social synapse*, "there are no single human brains – brains only exist within networks of other brains" (2014, p. xvi). An exploration of the social atom and tele, as they related to neuroscience was published by Yaniv (2014) in which he compares tele to neurophysiological experience of emotional valence. Moreno even wrote in 1953 that "it seems to us a valuable working hypothesis to assume *that back of all social and psychological interactions between individuals there must once have been and still are two or more reciprocating physiological organs which interact with each other*" (Moreno, 1953, p. 313, italics in origin).

Moreno even offered hypotheses on the evolution of mankind's social nature which reflect modern evolutionary neuropsychology findings (Yaniv, 2014). He writes of the evolution of society and the evolution of groups, from undifferentiated to more complex and highly differentiated parts which integrated together make up the larger whole (Moreno, 1953). This idea parallels the development of the individual brain, mind, and social atom which rapidly develop from less differentiated to highly differentiated parts and systems which support the wholeness of the brain, mind, and social atom. Moreno's *Who Shall Survive?* text indicates that:

> For this "affinity" we could not avoid considering the possibility of a "social" physiology…
> At a certain point man emancipated from the animal not only as a species but also as a society.
> *And it is within this society that the most important "social" organs of man developed*. The
> degree of attraction and repulsion of one person towards others suggests a point of view by
> means of which an interpretation of the evolution of the social organs can be given. (1953,
> p. 313)

Nearly a half-century before the emergence of Interpersonal Neurobiology and "The Social Brain" hypothesis, Moreno was writing of a "social physiology." Cozolino underlines a similar parallel process, that the communicative space between connected neurons, called a synapse, reflects the same relational space between humans–the social synapse (2014).

Moreno's role theory of personality also seems to reflect Cozolino's (2014) theory of self which is based on the social brain. Interpersonal neurobiology describes the *self* as developing from the infant's early relationships which reflects Moreno's theory of development in that Moreno highlights the developing self as a function of new roles emerging through role reciprocity and accurate doubling from caregivers. Cozolino writes:

> How does the self come to develop within the social brain? It is safe to assume that the self
> consists of many layers of neural processing that develop from the bottom up as we grow.
> The first systems of internal bodily sensations are joined by sensory-motor systems, added to
> by emotional and cognitive processing, and later topped off with abstract ideas and beliefs.
> All these systems are woven together in the context of our relationships. (2014, p. 422)

This description of the layers of self, from body and action, to emotions and cognitions, along with abstract ideas, all within a relational context seems to reflect Moreno's role theory and role categories of somatic roles, psychodramatic roles, and social roles (Moreno, 1972). Cozolino goes on to articulate that the *self* does not exist in one part of the brain but is an emergent function of multiple systems. Again, this reflects Moreno's statement that the self emerges from all the roles in one's life and expresses itself through roles. The complex web of role relationships between an individual and their social atom is called the cultural atom–which provides a depiction of the co-constructed self within its web of role relationships and role reciprocity.

Moreno introduced the term *sociostasis*, describing that "the emotional economy of the social atom is operating in accord with an unconscious postulate-to keep the social atoms in equilibrium" (1947, p. 81). Interestingly, Cozolino used the same term, sociostasis, as a chapter title in *The Neuroscienceof Human Relationships* (2014) to describe how our brains are regulated through the matrix of our relationships. He concludes the chapter by stating that "sociostatic processes … reflect the basic interconnectedness of our brains, minds, and bodies and point to the sometimes unseen reality that we are far more interdependent than our individualistic philosophies would lead us to believe" (p. 257). The interconnectedness between sociometry, the social atom, and interpersonal neurobiology has yet to be fully explored by psychodramatists and sociometrists.

8.6 Conclusion

Moreno's 1934 title, *Who Shall Survive?* was influenced by Darwin's theory of natural selection which indicates that the most adapted organisms survive and reproduce—*survival of the fittest*. Moreno writes that Darwin asked the question of who shall survive from the role of a biologist while Moreno reintroduces the question from the perspective of a sociologist or sociometrist—the "microscopic social laws which we have discovered may correlate with the gross evolutionary laws of the biologist" (Moreno, 1978, p. 7). He raised the question of how social forces and relationships impact the survival of individuals, groups, and society itself. What is the natural process of social selection? Why do some get large numbers of choices, selections, and social wealth while others are unselected, isolated, and deprived of connection or love? The interpersonal neurobiologists offer another answer to the question of who shall survive—*the survival of the nurtured*. As human beings, we survive because of our relationships—because of our sociometry.

The importance of relationships is central to the fields of interpersonal neurobiology, social work, and Moreno's methods. One might take the stance that the greatest overlap between social work, sociometry, and psychodrama is also the emphasis on the *social*. It is only paradoxical then that the continued study of the human brain, mind, and biology repeatedly brings us back to the importance of relationships and the social nature of man. Interpersonal neurobiology offers further scientific validation to the practices of social work, sociometry, psychodrama, and group psychotherapy.

References

Alexander, G. E., DeLong, M. R., & Strick, P. L. (1986). Parallel organization of functionally segregated circuits linking basal ganglia and cortex. *Annual Review of Neuroscience, 9,* 357–381.

Ardito, R. B., & Rabellino, D. (2011). Therapeutic alliance and outcome of psychotherapy: Historical excursus, measurements, and prospects for research. *Frontiers in Psychology, 2,* 270.

Badenach, B., & Cox, P. (2013). Integrating interpersonal neurobiology with group psychotherapy. In S. P. Gantt & B. Badenoch (Eds.), *The interpersonal neurobiology of group psychotherapy and group process.* London: Karnac Books, Ltd.

Cozolino, L. J. (2010). *The neuroscience of psychotherapy: Building and rebuilding the human brain* (2nd ed.). New York: W.W. Norton & Company.

Cozolino, L. J. (2014). *The neuroscience of human relationships* (2nd ed.). New York: W.W. Norton & Company.

Cozolino, L. (2018). Foreword. In J. R. Shapiro & J. S. (Eds.), Applegate, *Neurobiology for clinical social work: Theory and practice* (2nd ed., pp. xi–xii) [Foreword]. New York, NY: W.W. Norton & Company.

Cummings, J. L. (1993). Frontal-subcortical circuits and human behavior. *Archives of Neurology, 50,* 873–880.

Dayton, T. (2015). *NeuroPsychodrama in the treatment of relational trauma: A strength-based, experiential model for healing PTSD.* Deerfield Beach, FL: Health Communications Inc.

Farmer, R. L. (2009). *Neuroscience and social work practice: The missing link.* Los Angeles, California: Sage Publications Inc.

Fishbane, M. D. (2007). Wired to connect: Neuroscience, relationships, and therapy. *Family Process, 46,* 395–412.

Fisher, J. (2017). *Healing the fragmented selves of trauma survivors: Overcoming internal self-alienation.* New York: Routledge.

Flores, P. J. (2013). Group psychotherapy and neuro-plasticity: an attachment theory perspective. In S. P. Gantt & B. Badenoch (Eds.), *The interpersonal neurobiology of group psychotherapy and group process.* London: Karnac Books, Ltd.

Gabbard, G. O. (1992). Psychodynamic psychiatry in the "decade of the brain." . *The American Journal of Psychiatry, 149*(8), 991–998.

Gantt, S. P., & Agazarian, Y. M. (2013). Developing the group mind through functional subgrouping: linking systems-centered training (SCT) and interpersonal neurobiology. In S. P. Gantt & B. Badenoch (Eds.), *The Interpersonal neurobiology of group psychotherapy and group process.* London: Karnac Books, Ltd.

Gantt, S. P., & Badenoch, B. (2013). *The interpersonal neurobiology of group psychotherapy and group process.* London: Karnac Books Ltd.

Giacomucci, S. (2018). The trauma survivor's inner role atom: A clinical map for post-traumatic growth. *Journal of Psychodrama, Sociometry, and Group Psychotherapy, 66*(1), 115–129.

Giacomucci, S. (2019). Bio-psycho-social-spiritual integration through experiential trauma therapies. In *Beykent 1st International Health Sciences Research Days Congress,* Istanbul, Turkey. Retrieved from https://earsiv.beykent.edu.tr:8080/xmlui/bitstream/handle/123456789/1120/1.Beykent%20IHSRDC%20Abstract%20Book_31.07.19.pdf?sequence=1.

Giacomucci, S., & Marquit, J. (2020). The effectiveness of trauma-focused psychodrama in the treatment of PTSD in inpatient substance abuse treatment. *Frontiers in Psychology, 11,* 896. https://doi.org/10.3389/2Ffpsyg.2020.00896.

Giacomucci, S., & Stone, A. M. (2019). Being in two places at once: Renegotiating traumatic experience through the surplus reality of psychodrama. *Social Work with Groups, 42*(3), 184–196. https://doi.org/10.1080/01609513.2018.1533913.

Goldberg, E. (2001). *The executive brain: Frontal lobes and the civilized mind*. New York: Oxford University Press.

Hebb, D. (1949). *The organisation of behaviour*. New York, NY: Wiley.

Herman, J. L. (1992). *Trauma and recovery: The aftermath of violence—from domestic abuse to political terror*. New York: Basic Books.

Hollander, C. E. (1969). *A process for psychodrama training: The Hollander psychodrama curve*. Denver, CO: Snow Lion Press.

Horvath, A. O., & Symonds, B. D. (1991). Relation between working alliance and outcome in psychotherapy: A meta-analysis. *Journal of Counseling Psychology, 38*(2), 139–149.

Hudgins, M. K. (2017) PTSD Unites the World: Prevention, intervention and training in the therapeutic spiral model. In C. E. Stout & G. Want (Eds.), *Why global health matters: Guidebook for innovation and inspiration*. Self-Published Online.

Hudgins, M. K., & Toscani, F. (2013). *Healing world trauma with the therapeutic spiral model: Stories from the frontlines*. London: Jessica Kingsley Publishers.

Hug, E. (2007). A Neuroscience perspective on psychodrama. In C. Baim, J. Burmeister, & M. Maciel (Eds.), *Psychodrama: Advances in theory and practice*. London: Routledge.

Hug, E. (2013). A Neuroscience perspective on trauma and action methods. In K. Hudgins & F. Toscani (Eds.), *Healing world trauma with the therapeutic spiral model*. London: Jessica Kingsley Publishers.

Johnson, H. C. (2008). Neuroscience in social work practice and education. *Journal of Social Work Practice in the Addictions, 1*(3), 81–102.

Kellermann, P. K., & Hudgins, M. K. (Eds.). (2000). *Psychodrama with trauma survivors: Acting out your pain*. London: Jessica Kingsley Publishers.

Keysers, C., & Gazzola, V. (2010). Social neuroscience: Mirror neurons recorded in humans. *Current Biology, 20*(8), R353-354.

Klein, U. (2015). Zur Neurophysiologie des psychodramatischen Spiegelns. *Zeitschrift Für Psychodrama Und Soziometrie, 14*(2), 201–211.

Levine, P. A. (2010). *In an unspoken voice: How the body releases trauma and restores goodness*. Berkeley, CA: North Atlantic Books.

Levine, P. A. (2015). *Trauma and memory: Brain and body in a search for the living past*. Berkeley, CA: North Atlantic Books.

Martin, A., Wiggs, C., & Weisberg, J. (1997). Modulation of human medial temporal lobe activity by form, meaning, and experience. *Hippocampus, 7*(6), 587–593.

Maté, G. (2011). *When the body says no: The cost of hidden stress*. New Jersey: Wiley.

McFarlane, A. C. (2010). The long-term costs of traumatic stress: Intertwined physical and psychological consequences. *World Psychiatry, 9*(1), 3–10.

Moreno, J. L. (1921). *Das Testament Des Vaters*. Vienna, Austria: Gustav Kiepenheuer Verlag.

Moreno, J. L. (1947). The social atom and death. *Sociometry, 10*(1), 80–84.

Moreno, J. L. (1953). *Who shall survive? Foundations of sociometry, group psychotherapy and sociodrama* (2nd ed.). Beacon, NY: Beacon House.

Moreno, J. L. (1972). *Psychodrama Volume 1* (4th ed.). New York: Beacon House.

Moreno, J. L. (1978). *Who shall survive? Foundations of sociometry, group psychotherapy and psychodrama* (3rd ed.). Beacon, NY: Beacon House.

Moreno, J. L. (2019). *The autobiography of a genius*. In E. Schreiber, S. Kelley, & S. Giacomucci (Eds.). United Kingdom: North West Psychodrama Association.

Moreno, Z. T. (2012). *To dream again: A memoir*. New York: Mental Health Resources.

Panksepp, J., & Biven, L. (2012). *The archaeology of mind: Neuroevolutionary origins of human emotions*. New York, NY: W.W. Norton & Company Inc.

Porges, S. W. (2017). *The Pocket guide to the polyvagal theory: The transformative power of feeling safe*. New York, NY: W.W. Norton & Company.

Rauch, S. L., van der Kolk, B. A., Fisler, R. E., et al. (1996). A symptom provocation study of posttraumatic stress disorder using positron emission tomography and script-driven imagery. *Archives of General Psychiatry, 53*(5), 380–387.

Robins, K. (2018). *The effectiveness of group and psychodrama therapies with female survivors of sexual trauma* (Order No. 10746439). Available from ProQuest Dissertations & Theses Global. (2019695071). Retrieved from https://proxy.library.upenn.edu/login?url=https://proxy.library.upenn.edu:2072/docview/2019695071?accountid=14707.

Schermer, V. L. (2013). Mirror neurons: Their implication for group psychotherapy. In S. P. Gantt & B. Badenoch (Eds.), *The interpersonal neurobiology of group psychotherapy and group process.* London: Karnac Books, Ltd.

Schore, A. N. (2015). *Affect regulation and the origin of the self: The neurobiology of emotional development.* New York: Routledge.

Shapiro, F. (2018). *Eye-movement desensitization and reprocessing (EMDR) therapy* (3rd ed.). New York: Guilford Press.

Shapiro, J. R., & Applegate, J. S. (2018). *Neurobiology for clinical social work: Theory and practice* (2nd ed.). New York, NY: W.W. Norton & Company.

Siegel, D. J. (2007). *The mindful brain: Reflection and attunement in the cultivation of well-being.* New York: W.W. Norton & Company.

Siegel, D. J. (2010). *Mindsight: The new science of personal transformation.* New York: Bantam.

Siegel, D. J. (2012). *Developing mind: How relationships and the brain interact to shape who we are.* New York: Guilford Press.

Siegel, D. J. (2013). Reflections on mind, brain, and relationships in group psychotherapy. In S. P. Gantt & B. Badenoch (Eds.), *The interpersonal neurobiology of group psychotherapy and group process.* London: Karnac Books, Ltd.

Van der Kolk, B.A. (1996). The body keeps the score: Approaches to the psychobiology of posttraumatic stress disorder. In B. A. van der Kolk, A.C. McFarlane, & L. Weisaeth (Eds.), *Traumatic stress: The effects of overwhelming experiences on mind, body, and society.* New York: Guilford Press.

Van der Kolk, B. A. (2014). *The body keeps the score: Brain, mind, and body in the healing of trauma.* New York: Viking Press.

von Ameln, F., & Becker-Ebel, J. (2020). *Fundamentals of psychodrama.* Singapore: Springer Nature.

Wylie, M. S. (2004). The limits of talk: Bessel van der Kolk wants to transform the treatment of trauma. *Psychotherapy Networker, 28,* 30–41.

Yaniv, D. (2011). Revisiting Morenian psychodramatic encounter in light of contemporary neuroscience: Relationship between empathy and creativity. *The Arts in Psychotherapy, 38*(1), 52–58.

Yaniv, D. (2012). Dynamics of creativity and empathy in role reversal: Contributions from neuroscience. *Review of General Psychology, 16*(1), 70–77.

Yaniv, D. (2014). Tele and the social atom. *Zeitschrift Für Psychodrama Und Soziometrie, 13*(1), 107–120.

Chapter 9
Strengths-Based and Mutual Aid Approaches in Social Work and Psychodrama

Abstract Social work and psychodrama are both inherently strengths-based approaches with person-centered philosophies that affirm the inherent goodness of individuals. The chapter outlines social work's strengths-based perspective while connecting it to mutual aid, positive psychology, humanistic psychology, and Morenean philosophy. Social group work's emphasis on mutual aid and group-as-a-whole processes is outlined with similarities to the theory and practice of psychodrama. The importance of a strengths-based approach in trauma work is affirmed and depicted through resilience theory and post-traumatic growth. Modern adaptations of classical psychodrama which emphasize strengths work are depicted, including positive psychodrama, the Therapeutic Spiral Model, and Souldrama.

Keywords Strengths-based social work · Mutual aid · Strengths-based approach · Positive psychology · Strengths perspective

9.1 Strengths-Based Social Work Practice

The social work field has incorporated a strengths-based approach as a core aspect of its identity. The social work profession and strengths-based approach appear to have a harmonious fit considering the core values of treating everyone with dignity and worth, emphasizing relationships, and steadfastly holding hope for personal and societal change (Witkin, 2017). Instead of solely focusing on pathology, suffering, trauma, injustice, and problems, social workers uphold the belief that each individual has unique strengths and should be treated with dignity and respect. "One thing is certain … Once a client is engaged in building up the strengths within and without, a desire to do more and to be more absorbed in daily life and drawn by future possibilities breaks out" (Saleebey, 2012, p. 111).

The emphasis on strengths is nothing new to society; history has a wealth of examples of spiritual leaders, gurus, archetypes, gods, doctors, advocates, politicians, philosophers, and writers that "sought to find the best in human capacity and desire, both individually and collectively" (Rapp, Saleebey, & Sullivan, 2006, p. 80). The flavor of the strengths-based perspective was present from the start of the social work profession, especially in the settlement movement, the emergence of social group

© The Author(s) 2021
S. Giacomucci, *Social Work, Sociometry, and Psychodrama*, Psychodrama in Counselling, Coaching and Education 1,
https://doi.org/10.1007/978-981-33-6342-7_9

work, and macro-social work's emphasis on democratic ideals and empowerment within society.

The application of a strengths-based approach finds itself useful in multiple facets of social work including strengths-based casework (Rapp & Chaimberlain, 1985), strengths-based assessment (Epstein & Sharma, 1998), the use of clients strengths in clinical social work and psychotherapy (Cohen, 1999; Rapp et al., 2006; Rashid, 2015; Saleebey, 1996; Smith, 2006), a relational emphasis of social worker and client's strengths (Rapp, 1998; Rapp et al., 2006; Witkin, 2017), group work's use of mutual aid (Gitterman & Shulman, 2005; Northen & Kurland, 2001; Shulman, 2015; Steinberg, 2010), community work focused on strengths or assets (Kretzmann & McKnight, 1993; Saleebey, 1996), supervision (Alschuler, Silver, & McArdle, 2015; Cohen, 1999; Wade & Jones, 2014), education (Probst, 2010), and an overall paradigm shift from pathology-oriented perspectives to a health-oriented philosophy (Kim & Bolton, 2013; Rapp, Saleebey, & Sullivan, 2006; Saleebey, 2012).

Dennis Saleebey, in *The Strengths Perspective in Social Work Practice* (2012), outlines six core principles underlying the strengths-based perspective:

1. **Every Individual, Group, Family, and Community Has Strengths.** This foundational belief assumes that the client always has strengths and positive resources that can be used to help with the presenting problem. Regardless of the presenting problems, there are also presenting strengths that exist within the client and the environment. The strengths-based perspective allows us to see the whole picture when it comes to working with individuals, groups, families, and communities.

2. **Trauma and Abuse, Illness and Struggle May Be Injurious, but They May also Be Sources of Challenge and Opportunity.** This principle challenges the viewpoint that trauma and injury only create victims. Instead, the possibility of growth and new opportunities after trauma or hardship is acknowledged. This principle will be discussed at length in Sect. 9.2.2 on post-traumatic growth. Instead of strengthening a narrative of victimization after trauma, newfound strengths, post-traumatic growth, and "survivor's pride" are celebrated (Wolins, 1993).

3. **Assume That You Do Not Know the Upper Limits of the Capacity to Grow and Change and Take Individual, Group, and Community Aspirations Seriously.** This principle asserts that strengths-based social workers maintain high expectations and hope for clients regardless of their history or diagnosis. When a social worker perceives that growth is not possible or restricted due to deficits or diagnoses, it has a limiting impact on the client (van Breda, 2018). The strengths-based worker takes clients visions and dreams seriously while believing in the capacity for self-healing for all clients, groups, families, and communities.

4. **We Best Serve Clients by Collaborating with Them.** Rather than operating as the *expert* and recreating an imbalance of power dynamics within the therapeutic relationship, strengths-based workers approach clients as collaborators. This principle challenges us to *work with clients* rather than to *treat their disorder* or *work on them.*

5. **Every Environment is Full of Resources.** Regardless of place or environment, the strengths-based social worker recognizes that strengths, ideas, and possibilities exist within the environment. Even when a community is plagued with poverty, violence, and collective trauma, there are still strengths, wisdom, and important resources within the community that can be tapped for transformation.
6. **Caring, Caretaking, and Context.** This principle emphasizes the centrality of caring relationships in the human experience and the praxis of social work. Social caretaking is recognized as core to both the social work profession and the strengths-based perspective. The therapeutic relationship itself is a strength (Witkins, 2017), and the relationships within the client's life are celebrated as strengths.

These six principles outline the basis of the strengths-based approach, which Saleebey acknowledges is fluid and subject to changing as the strengths-based approach continues to evolve.

Working from a strengths-based approach does not mean that one avoids addressing social or psychological issues. Problems are addressed, but they are addressed from the starting point of strengths. Strengths-based social workers would argue that neglecting to acknowledge clients' problems is just as faulty as neglecting to acknowledge their strengths (Saleebey, 2012). The strengths-based approach attempts to restore "balance to the understanding of the human condition—as social workers we recognize and respect the strengths and capacities of people as well as their afflictions and agonies" (Saleebey, 2012, p. 279).

9.1.1 Positive Psychology and Strengths-Based Social Work

While the strengths-based social work approach emerged about a decade earlier (Weick, Rapp, Sullivan, & Kisthardt, 1989; Saleebey, 1996) than positive psychology (Seligman, 1998), early evidence of this way of thinking in the helping professions can be traced back to William James and Abraham Maslow (Froh, 2004; Maslow, 1954). Many social workers experience positive psychology as the new face of the strengths-based approach (Witkin, 2017). The movement of positive psychology appears to have professionalized in a way that strengths-based social work hasn't, which has led to a large body of research, a graduate degree in positive psychology, and a surge of positive psychology awareness in the larger culture. Witkins (2017) critiques positive psychology for its adherence to individualism, neoliberalism, neglect of cultural subjectivity, and the lack of recognition positive psychologists give to the strengths-based social work approach which preceded it. He suggests that the strengths-based approach, like the social work field as a whole, offers positive psychologists a more relationally grounded, context-aware, and anti-oppression framework rooted in narratives of disenfranchised, marginalized, and colonized communities. While positive psychology aims for objectivity and universalism to complement its research-driven agenda, the strengths-based social work approach "does not claim nor seek to claim a universal template of virtues to which all should aspire, but that simply re-directs people to identify and utilize whatever resources and assets make sense within their social and cultural contexts" (Witkins, 2017, p. 122).

Saleebey (2012) differentiates the social work strengths-based approach from positive psychology in that the strengths-based approach: (1) recognizes that almost anything can be a strength or asset, depending on context; (2) strengths and resources exist within all relationships, groups, communities, and environments; (3) practice with clients involves helping them utilize both their internal resources/strengths and their external/environmental resources to enhance their lived experience.

9.2 Strengths-Based Approach with Trauma

The field of trauma therapy has evolved to integrate the use of strengths-based approaches at its core. These approaches are evidenced in the first phase of nearly every clinical map for trauma therapy which focus on strengths, safety, connection, skills building, and containment (Chesner, 2020; Courtois & Ford, 2016; Herman, 1997; Hudgins & Toscani, 2013; Najavits, 2002; Shapiro, 2018). The emphasis on clients' strengths in the post-traumatic context provides an avenue for (re)establishing safety on multiple layers including inner safety for the client, safety within the therapeutic relationship, and safety in the environment. Strengths are the building blocks to cultivating safety. Trauma is, at its root, a violation of safety or perceived safety. Najavitis (2002) states that "just as violations of safety are life-destroying, the means of establishing safety are life-enhancing" (pp. 5–6).

9.2.1 Resilience

The strengths-based approach is also present in the social worker's emphasis and celebration of clients' resilience. This emphasis on resilience has increased within the social work field in the past few decades (Gitterman & Knight, 2016; van Breda, 2018). Norman even suggests that "resiliency enhancement is probably the most reasonable way that social worker can put the strengths perspective into practice" (2000, p. 3). Resilience is defined as the ability to bounce back from hardship or adversity, to survive, and to adapt. Resilience is strikingly similar to Moreno's definition of spontaneity in terms of the act of adaptive response (Cossa, 2020). Resiliency is at the intersection of adversity and strengths (Norman, 2000). Three types of resilience are presented by Fraser and colleagues (2004): recovery after trauma, overcoming adversity, and maintaining competence while under stress. Various factors are outlined in the literature related to resilience protective factors including intelligence, interpersonal skills, temperament, life outlook, self-esteem, self-efficacy, humor, adaptability, hardiness, and spirituality (Baruth & Carroll, 2002; Gilligan, 2004; Gitterman & Knight, 2016).

Canda (2012) proposes a new framing of resilience through a spiritual lens which he calls *transilience*. Transilience is defined as "a whole person process of moving forward, backward, upward, downward, sideways, or back-around in a life committed to well-being and well-becoming" which validates the nonlinear spiritual experience of resilience "and transcends the moment-to-moment details of living and dying" (p. 94). Social work with group experts also proposes a nonlinear conceptualization of resilience rooted in the relational framework of group participants helping each other—mutual aid (Gitterman & Knight, 2016). Mutual aid, social group work's strengths-based core principle, will be explored in detail in the coming sections. "Group [membership] counteracts the isolating effects of [adversity] and enables survivors to connect with sources of resilience within themselves and others" (Mendelsohn, Zachary, & Harney, 2007, p. 227). Mutual aid and group work move us from an individual-based conceptual of resilience to a relationally grounded, group-based understanding of resilience in social contexts and communities.

While resilience is often described as a response to adversity or the ability to bounce back from trauma, some are suggesting that it goes beyond bouncing back, but includes bouncing forward into new growth and thriving. Walsh suggests that "resiliency is promoted when hardship, tragedy, failure, or disappointment can also be instructive and serve as an impetus for change and growth" (2006, p. 79). This statement frames resilience as a type of growth after trauma, or what has been more recently termed *post-traumatic growth*.

9.2.2 Post-Traumatic Growth

Post-traumatic growth refers to phenomenon of frequently experienced following a trauma or adverse experience (Calhoun & Tedeschi, 2014). While the term *post-traumatic growth* was initially used by Richard Tedeschi and Lawrence Calhoun in the mid-1990s, the phenomenon of transformation after trauma has existed for all of human history (1995, 1996, 2014). Experiences of post-traumatic growth are organized into five domains (see Fig. 9.1):

1. **New Possibilities in Life**—trauma, by its nature, overwhelms and challenges an individual in ways that may have not been imagined previously. As a result, many survivors begin to see new possibilities in life and the opening of new doors of opportunity.
2. **Increased Awareness of Personal Strengths**—Surviving trauma and asking for help to cope with its aftermath requires incredible strength. Trauma survivors demonstrate extraordinary courage, resilience, trust, hope, and compassion, among other strengths. When an overwhelming event forces one to utilize all the strengths available (and often develop new ones), they become much more

Fig. 9.1 Five domains of post-traumatic growth

aware of these strengths going forward. Many trauma survivors remark that "if I survived that trauma, I could survive anything".

3. **Enhanced Relationships with Others**—The process of coping with trauma requires relationships—friends, family, therapists, support groups, etc. As humans, we are neurobiologically wired to regulate our emotions through relationships. The experience of utilizing support after trauma deepens these connections and reaffirms their importance. Having experienced trauma or loss also increases one's ability to feel compassion and empathy for others in similar situations (Bauwens & Tosone, 2010).

4. **Stronger Appreciation of Life**—Trauma, by its nature, threatens safety, security, and often one's life. Trauma and loss remind us how precious life is and how fragile it can be. Trauma has the ability to challenge us to see the world in a new way and to reconsider our priorities in life.

5. **Spiritual or Religious Change**—Trauma is so often experienced through relationships and involving other human beings, as a result, many trauma survivors turn to spirituality or religion for strength, hope, and inspiration. Trauma is an existential crisis that challenges us to make sense of it, often through spiritual, religious, or existential belief systems.

These five domains are further simplified into three conceptual categories: an enhanced sense of self, enhanced sense of relationships with others, and enhanced philosophy of life (Calhoun & Tedeschi, 2012; Tedeschi & Calhoun, 1996). Post-traumatic growth is the realization of a transformation that begins with a catalyst for change—the trauma. One might even argue that all of our personal strengths are a result of surviving and finding our way through difficulties, struggles, and hardships.

Calhoun and Tedeschi (2014) estimate that between 30–90% of people report at least some element of growth when dealing with major difficulty life events. A later systematic review and meta-analysis of the research concluded that nearly half of participants reported moderate-to-high post-traumatic growth after a traumatic experience (Wu et al., 2019). Compared to less than a 25% of developing PTSD after a traumatic event (Breslau, Davis, Andreski, & Peterson, 1991; Kessler et al, 1995; Santiago et al, 2013), these statistics of post-traumatic growth are very hopeful. It is also important to state that post-traumatic growth and post-traumatic stress disorder can also be experienced simultaneously—multiple research studies have highlighted this with various populations (Alisic, Van der Schoot, van Ginkel, & Kleber 2008; Bluvstein, Moravchick, Sheps, Schreiber, & Bloch, 2013; Jia, Ying, Zhou, Wu, & Lin, 2015; Parikh et al., 2015; Ssenyonga, Owens, & Olema, 2013). At the same time, the literature shows that higher levels of post-traumatic growth are related to lower levels of PTSD symptomology (Frazier, Conlon, & Glaser, 2001; Frazier et al., 2009; McMillen, Smith, & Fisher, 1997; Park, Cohen, & Murch, 1996; Ssenyonga et al., 2013). A trauma survivor is significantly more likely to report post-traumatic growth after a traumatic event then they are to develop post-traumatic stress disorder!

Multiple studies have highlighted the prevalence of vicarious post-traumatic growth for therapists and advocates working with trauma (Arnold, Calhoun, Tedeschi, & Cann, 2005; Cohen & Collins, 2013; Cosden, Sanford, Koch, & Lepore, 2016; Hyatt-Burkhart, 2014; Manning, de Terte, & Stephens, 2015). The experience of being a part of trauma therapy appears to potentially be stimulating of post-traumatic growth. Considering that this is validated for professionals, there is likely also a vicarious post-traumatic growth effect on client participants within group work. Group work positions individuals within the group to help each other cultivate post-traumatic growth through the recognition of each other strengths, the sharing of new perspectives and belief systems, and the enhancement of positive relationships.

9.3 Mutual Aid as a Strengths-Based Group-As-A-Whole Approach

Mutual aid is the foundation of social work with groups (Gitterman & Shulman, 2005; Glassman & Kates, 1990; Northern & Kurland, 2001; Skolnik-Basulto, 2016; Steinberg, 2010). Through the mutual aid process, group members contribute to supporting and healing each other. The job of the group worker is to help facilitate the mutual aid process within groups (Kurland & Salmon, 2006). Schwartz (1961) captures this dynamic: "This need to use each other, to create not one but many helping relationships, is a vital ingredient of the group process and constituted a common need over and above the specific task for which the group was formed" (p. 158). While the term "mutual aid" wasn't introduced to social workers until

1961 (Schwartz), others wrote about this unique group phenomenon decades earlier (Dewey, 1916; Kropotkin, 1922; Mead, 1934; Moreno, 1947, 1955). One such mutual aid writer was Jacob L. Moreno. Moreno's experiential sociometric processes offer group workers with action-based tools to activate mutual aid within a group while working with the group-as-a-whole (Giacomucci, 2019; Skolnik, 2018).

Yalom and Leszcz (2005), in their seminal text on group psychotherapy, describe mutual aid within the framing of the therapeutic factor of *altruism*. They offer the poignant story of a rabbi having a conversation with God about heaven and hell in which he is shown two groups representing each. The first, symbolizing hell—a group of starving and desperate people sitting around a huge pot of delicious stew but unable to feed themselves because the only spoons available were too long-handled to reach one's own mouth. Nobody ate and everyone suffered. Heaven was represented by a second group also sitting around the same large pot of stew with the same long-handled spoons, but everyone was well nourished, healthy, and joyful because they had learned to feed each other. The altruistic nature of the second group, particularly their experience of mutually nourishing each other, is symbolic of not only heaven, but also a successful group psychotherapy session.

9.3.1 Mutual Aid in Social Work

William Schwartz introduced the term "mutual aid" to social workers in his 1961 article "The social worker in the group." Mutual aid refers to the process by which group members support and help each other. Steinberg (2003) posits that "catalyzing mutual aid is the heart and soul of social work practice with groups" (p. 36). A mutual aid group worker believes essentially that each group has the inherent capacity to heal itself through mutual aid. Each member of a group possesses unique strengths, insights, and experiences, in addition to a shared group intention, which can be leveraged to empower the group-as-a-whole. Shulman (2015) describes mutual aid as allowing group members to "use the group to integrate their inner and outer selves and to find more adaptive mechanisms to cope with oppression, including personal and social action" (p. 548). Various evidence sources highlight the capacity of the mutual aid process to enhance self-esteem and problem-solving skills while decreasing shame and isolation (Gitterman & Shulman, 2005; Knight, 2006; Steinberg, 2010).

In group work, Kurland and Salmon (2006) exclaim, "the worker's role is to set in motion a process of mutual aid in the group" (p. 131). Mutual aid is a strengths-based, holistic, and anti-oppressive approach to group work, which inherently integrates the psychological, social, and experiential (Steinberg, 2010). Mutual aid group work encourages both inclusion of every group member and a sense of group autonomy (Steinberg, 2003). The interconnectedness of mutual aid and a group-as-a-whole approach is highlighted in Steinberg's description of mutual aid practice as seeking "to establish a relationship not only between the worker and group members in the name of professional help but also among members in the name of creating exponential sources of help" (2003, pp. 36–37). The experience of empowering and supporting another group member, or engaging in the mutual aid process, increases one's sense of self-efficacy and empowerment (Knight & Gitterman, 2014). The shared goals and experiences of group members promotes an "all-in-the-same-boat phenomenon" (Shulman, 2015) and a sense of universality (Yalom & Leszcz, 2005).

9.3.2 Group-As-A-Whole

In order to access the power of mutual aid within the group, the group must be treated as a group-as-a-whole rather than just one individual at a time—"the quality of the mutual aid process that occurs in a group is what differentiates group work from casework in a group." (Kurland & Salmon, 2006, p. 130). At the same time, mutual aid and the group-as-a-whole phenomenon cannot take place until safety has been established (Kleinmuntz, 2011). When individuals come together to form a group, a unique phenomenon occurs and the group has the potential of solidifying into its own unique organism. The group-as-a-whole experience takes place through the process of group cohesion.

Group cohesion is emphasized by the International Association of Social Work with Groups Standards of Practice as an important beginning task of the social worker. The standards state that the group worker "aids the group members in establishing relationships with one another so as to promote group cohesion" (IASWG, 2015, p. 11). Research demonstrates that increasing group cohesion is related to increasing the influence of the group upon its members (Northen & Kurland, 2001). Group cohesion's significance in group work has been compared to the importance of the therapeutic relationship in individual therapy (Yalom & Lesczc, 2005). Group cohesion, the group-as-a-whole experience, group safety, and mutual aid emerge as an interdependent system in the group process.

Many social group work experts have criticized social workers for doing individual therapy or casework in a group setting instead of treating the group-as-a-whole (Bitel, 2014; Gitterman, 2004; Knight, 2017; Kurland & Salmon, 2006). "The worker who sets in motion the process of mutual aid takes into account the entire group as an entity rather than just one individual at a time" (Kurland & Salmon, 2006, p. 131). Unfortunately, the lack of group work education and training in social work education seems to be contributing to social workers' limited ability to work with the group-as-a-whole. Most group sessions today are unengaging, boring, and seem to be alternating segments of individual therapy with a group audience (Konopka, 1990). Jacob L. Moreno, the founder of sociometry and psychodrama, also criticized group workers for doing the same (1947).

> Moreno's idea of group psychotherapy meant treating the group; other group therapists remained focused on the individual, and their methods could often be better described as treating individuals in a group setting. Individual psychotherapy, Moreno pointed out, is based on the psychodynamics of the individual. The treatment of a group is based on socio-dynamics that involve the interrelationships and interactions of the members of the group, not just the collection of individuals and their personal dynamics. (Nolte, 2014, p. 122)

The action-based tools that Moreno developed are inherently group-as-a-whole processes that treat the collective group as the identified client.

9.3.3 Moreno's Sociometry as a Group-As-A-Whole Mutual Aid Process

Jacob L. Moreno coined the terms "group therapy" and "group psychotherapy" in 1931 (Moreno, 1945; Moreno & Whitin, 1932). However, he is an often forgotten pioneer of mutual aid and group-as-a-whole process. Very little has been written about the connection between Moreno's methods and social work with groups. Some view Moreno as a social worker due to his emphasis on working with society's oppressed and underserved communities with a focus on person-in-environment expressed by his sociometric system (Giacomucci, 2018a, 2018b, 2019; Giacomucci & Stone, 2019; Skolnik, 2018; Stimmer, 2004; Wang & Liu, 2020).

Moreno's mutual aid ideas began in 1913 through his experience of organizing a group of sex workers in Vienna—"we began to see then that one individual could become a therapeutic agent of the other and the potentialities of a group psychotherapy on the reality level crystallized in our mind" (1955, p. 22). Moreno attempted to dismantle the power dynamics between doctor and patient by pronouncing each group member as a therapeutic agent (Nolte, 2014). He argued that in group work, especially sociometry and psychodrama, participants experience healing through action and interaction between each other and the roles they play for each other—not from the psychodrama director or group facilitator (Moreno, 2000). He writes "the underlying principle is that each individual—not just the physician himself—may act as a therapeutic agent for every other individual, and each group as a therapeutic agent for another group" (1963, p. 149).

J. L. Moreno's existential theory of human nature posits that each individual possesses an "autonomous healing center"—the innate capacity to heal one's self (Moreno, 2012, 2019b). He believed that spontaneity is the key to the autonomous healing center and the curative agent in therapy (1953). In psychodrama's theory of change, spontaneity–creativity theory, spontaneity is defined as the ability to respond to new situations adequately and the capacity to respond in new ways to old, reoccurring (external or internal) circumstances (Moreno, 1964). In the contemporary social work with groups literature, Kleinmuntz argues that "mutual aid requires spontaneity" (2011, p. 222). In a group experience, the act of engaging in mutual aid and support for fellow group members is an adequate response to the group issues.

Zerka Moreno, the co-founder of psychodrama and wife of Jacob Moreno, writes in her memoir that "awakening the autonomous healing center, the power to heal oneself, is how I see the value of psychodrama and all forms of therapy" (2012, p. 504). Just as each individual has an autonomous healing center within and the capacity to heal one's self—so does each group (Giacomucci, 2019; Schreiber, 2018). The group process taps into the autonomous healing center once the group is properly warmed-up, connections are formed, safety is established, and the topic is representative of the group-as-a-whole. The group-as-a-whole is the protagonist accessing its autonomous healing center to heal itself. Mutual aid is the mechanism through which the group heals itself. J. L. Moreno not only believed in the healing potential of an individual and a group, but he also believed in society's potential to heal itself. This is evidenced by one of his most well-known quotes, "a truly therapeutic procedure must have no less objective than the whole of mankind" (Moreno, 1953, p. 1).

Moreno's sociometric and psychodramatic systems are intrinsically group-as-a-whole, mutual aid processes (Giacomucci, 2019; Skolnik, 2018). Mutual aid "is inherently *psycho* and *social* in concept and in action" (Glassman & Kates, 1990; Roberts & Northen, 1976; Steinberg, 2004; as cited in Steinberg, 2010, p. 57). This quote from Steinberg describing mutual aid is also an accurate description of Moreno's experiential system of sociometry, psychodrama, and group psychotherapy. In his 1947 *Open Letter to Group Psychotherapists*, 14 years before Schwartz introduced mutual aid to social work, Moreno writes that "one patient can be a therapeutic agent to the other, let us invent devices by which they can help each other, in contrast to the older idea that all the therapeutic power rests with the physician" (p. 23).

9.4 Strengths-Based Psychodrama

The practice of psychodrama focused on mutual aid and strengths is still developing, as is its literature base—especially within the social work field (Giacomucci, 2019; Konopik & Cheung, 2013). While psychodrama philosophy inherently emphasizes the strengths and positive healing power of individuals and groups, the intentional use of strengths within psychodrama practice is relatively new. It appears that there are four major forces that have led to the infusion of strengths-based approaches within the practice of psychodrama—Moreno's core philosophy of human nature, positive psychology, the Therapeutic Spiral Model, and Souldrama.

Saleebey's six core principles of the strengths-based approach (2012) are highly complementary and intrinsic to sociometry and psychodrama practice. The Morenean approach acknowledges the strengths of each individual, group, and community while also assuming that every environment is full of resources and mutual aid. Psychodrama employs surplus reality which transcends the limits of the environment and accesses resources from beyond reality. Psychodramatists empower protagonists and groups through collaboration, mutual aid, and co-creation toward the goals and aspirations of the group. The psychodramatic approach inspires clients, within the compassionate relational framework of the group, to revisit past trauma and injury with opportunities for correction, repair, and post-traumatic growth in action.

The three categories of post-traumatic growth—enhanced sense of self, relationships, and life philosophy (Calhoun & Tedeschi, 2012)—strongly related to the body of work of Jacob Moreno. In his *Sociometry and the Cultural Order* (1943), Moreno writes that he developed three core ideas—his spiritual/existential philosophy, psychodrama, and sociometry. "The first idea initiates a cannon of the universe, the second a cannon of the individual, the third a cannon of human society" (Moreno, 1943, p. 299). These three cannons parallel the three categories of post-traumatic growth. Psychodrama offers an avenue for improved sense of self; sociometry provides an increased sense of relationships; and Moreno's spiritual philosophy offers an optimistic framework for understanding life, the universe, and the boundlessness of possibilities.

9.4.1 Morenean Philosophy as Strengths-Based Humanistic Approach

The existential and spiritual philosophy from which psychodrama emerged is fundamentally a strengths-based humanistic approach. Moreno exclaims that "psychodrama is based on the premise that every man is a genius" (2019b, p. 12). Moreno's framework challenges the medical model and its pathologizing nature while conceptualizing human beings as genius, godlike, and active agents within the world (Moreno, 2019b). In his autobiography, he explicitly declares all human beings as potential geniuses. He puts forth three hypotheses in the introduction to his *Autobiography of a Genius* stating: (1) spontaneity-creativity is the propelling force of human progress; (2) love and mutual sharing are of the most important principles of group life, and we should have faith in the intentions of others; (3) a super-dynamic society can be built upon these principles in which all humans are empowered as co-creators and co-responsible. For Moreno, Fox writes, "what characterizes human nature is an unlimited capacity for spontaneous and creative action. Moreno believed this and as such his outlook is an optimistic one" (1987, p. 39).

Zerka Moreno states in her memoir that her husband believed that instead of focusing on man's failings, we should emphasize man's genius (2012). Jonathan, Jacob Moreno's son, echoes this stance and stating:

> His confidence in the healing power of the group was founded upon his faith that, in principle, altruistic human love is an infinite resource. In those days the prevailing psychoanalytic temper in America reduced human nature to its basest components, an attitude Moreno found one-dimensional and destructive. (Moreno, 2019a, p. 108)

Taking this into consideration, Moreno seems to have been one of the first to promote a humanistic strengths-based approach in psychiatry and psychotherapy. Bustos (1994), credits Moreno to have "offered a new way of looking at human suffering which was more sympathetic and based on health rather than on pathology" (p. 50). It is only fitting then that his tombstone reads "the man who brought laughter into psychiatry" (Orkibi, 2019).

Moreno's vision of the goodness and potential within human nature is quite similar to Maslow's writings on self-actualization and "Being psychology" or "positive psychology" (Maslow, 1962, 1964). There are also many comparisons that could be drawn between Moreno's approach with the humanistic theories and person-centered approach proposed by Carl Rogers (Rogers, 1951, 1966; Moreno, 2014; von Ameln &

Becker-Ebel, 2020). Perhaps the biggest difference is that client-centered approaches were primarily employed with individual psychotherapy clients. Considering the group as the client, Moreno's group approaches are inherently group-centered or client-centered. Moreno's philosophy of human nature and his approach to clients appear largely congruent with the humanistic psychologists.

Moreno's group therapy movement and the humanistic psychology movement had much in common philosophically. Both were rooted in existential philosophy. They both emerged in opposition to psychoanalysis and behaviorism promoting a more positive view of human nature. Coincidentally, leaders of both group therapy and the humanistic psychology fields have declared their own respective movements as the third wave or third revolution in psychology (Moreno, 2014).

9.4.2 Positive Psychology and Positive Psychodrama

The relationship between strengths-based social work and positive psychology seems to reflect the relationship between psychodrama and positive psychology in that psychodrama preceded positive psychology by nearly a century but failed to professionalize in and be accepted in the larger culture in the way positive psychology did. Positive psychology emphasizes the importance of a psychology of health and the exploration of character strengths, well-being, and happiness. Moreno's challenge to psychoanalysis and the medical model reflected a similar shift in perspective. The rise of positive psychology in the late 1990s and early 2000s brought with it new language and increased momentum for consciously integrating positive psychology principles into the field of psychodrama. Tomasulo (2018) notes that there are overlapping elements within the pre-history of positive psychology and psychodrama. The Human Potential Movement of the 1960s embraced psychodrama, along with other approaches, and concretized a foundation for contemporary positive psychology (Atkinson & Kirsner, 2019; Moreno, 2014). Tomasulo highlights that Csikszentmihalyi, co-founder of positive psychology, was influenced by Moreno's philosophy of spontaneity. Csikszentmihalyi even had help from prominent psychodramatist, David Kipper, in preparing his groundbreaking publication *Flow: The Psychology of Optimal Experience* (1976/1990) which reflects many similarities to Moreno's concept of spontaneity. Tomasulo describes psychodrama, positive psychology, and positive psychotherapy as "three strands of a braided vine... woven together since their beginnings" (2018, p. 49).

Goldberg (2009) offers one of the first articles integrating positive psychology and psychodrama into a new model she described as Positive Psychodrama. She writes that Positive Psychodrama's goal "is to access strengths and virtues, the genius within, as well as to conceptualize how to use these strengths in life" (Goldberg, 2009, p. 367). Atkinson and Kirsner (2019) outline their use of the Values In Action Character Strengths integrated with experiential sociometry and psychodrama interventions—effectively synthesizing the content of positive psychology and strengths-based approach with the process of sociometry and psychodrama. Tomasulo has also written various pieces on the topic (2011, 2014, 2018, 2019)—maybe best known for the Virtual Gratitude Visit which uses psychodrama role-playing techniques to enhance a popular positive psychology intervention involving writing and delivering a letter of gratitude (Tomasulo, 2019). Tomasulo also notes that many psychodramatists have integrated the assessment of character strengths into their work which he originally did through a modified social atom assessment called a *strengths atom* (2018). Orkibi (2019) offers a structured framework for integrating positive psychology and psychodrama into what he also calls *Positive Psychodrama.* Orkibi's (2019) article presents the intersections between positive psychology and psychodrama through the five following psychodrama concepts: (1) spontaneity, creativity, and adaptation; (2) sociatry and positive relationships; (3) co-creation and mutual responsibility; (4) roles repertoire and character strengths; and (5) act hunger, flow, and engagement. Orkibi writes that Positive Psychodrama "therefore highlights the inherently positive theoretical underpinning of Moreno's theory and philosophy" (2019, p. 6). Atkinson & Kirsner (2019) echo these theoretical similarities and declare that "positive psychology and action methods fit together like hand and glove"—sharing a humanistic, existential view of mankind while emphasizing connection, authenticity, well-being, creativity, spontaneity, flow, choice, the here-and-now, and the use of future projection of possible selves (p. 316).

9.4.3   Therapeutic Spiral Model

The Therapeutic Spiral Model (TSM) was developed in the early 1990s as a response to classical psychodrama's potential for retraumatizing participants with trauma histories. TSM is a clinically modified approach with emphasis on strengths, safety, and containment (Giacomucci & Marquit, 2020). As noted in Sect. 7.8, TSM offers multiple strengths-based contributions to the field including the *Circle of Strengths* warm-up exercise as a clinical map *prescribing* roles of strength before addressing trauma psychodramatically (Hudgins & Toscani, 2013). TSM proposes three categories of strengths required for healthy personality functioning after trauma—intrapsychic strengths, interpersonal strengths, and transpersonal strengths (Hudgins, 2019). TSM's clinical map, the Trauma Survivors Intrapsychic Role Atom (TSIRA) outlines nine strengths-based roles in the first phase of the clinical map (Giacomucci, 2018c). TSM psychodrama in practice often includes what are called prescriptive role psychodramas which are psychodrama focused entirely on strengths-based roles without any antagonist, trauma-based, or negative roles in the scene (Hudgins, 2002).

The second phase of the TSM clinical map orients itself upon trauma content and trauma-based roles, while the third phase proposes transformative role templates (Giacomucci, 2017). The third phase of transformative roles have been described as roles of post-traumatic growth and compared to the categories of post-traumatic growth (Giacomucci, 2018c). TSM's clinical map guides facilitators to start with roles of strength and to end with roles of post-traumatic growth which provides increased safety and a *cushioning* from the trauma. The use of strengths as roles in TSM psychodrama enactments is foundational and utilized in every TSM psychodrama. This implementation of strengths as psychodrama roles seems to have become integrated throughout the larger psychodrama community in part because of TSM's contribution.

9.4.4 Souldrama

Souldrama is a modified psychodrama approach, developed by Miller (2000, 2004) with a focus on spirituality and the 12-steps from *Alcoholics Anonymous*. Souldrama emphasizes Moreno's concept of the divinity of each human being (Ozcan, 2019) and is primarily used with populations interested in religion, spirituality, and/or struggling with addiction or codependency. Miller (2008) writes:

> A goal of the Souldrama experience is to help individuals identify their authentic meaning and purpose in life. This is a formidable goal, as our purpose reflects what we naturally do best in life and helps us best use our gifts, talents, and skills. (p. 139)

Interestingly, Miller (2008) even references Csikszentmihalyi's concept of flow as it relates to Souldrama's focus on spirituality and well-being. Miller describes seven stages or *doors* to spiritual transformation including faith, truth, compassion, love, humility, gratitude, and inspiration (2008). These seven stages encompass the development of rational, emotional, and spiritual intelligence. Miller describes Souldrama as a "transpersonal psycho-spiritual action technique" that "combines mind, body, and spirit to create therapeutic energy within a group process" (2019, p. 289). The entire framework of Souldrama appears to be one based in strengths, virtues, and spirituality. Like TSM, Souldrama's strengths-based approach has taken root around the world with regular training groups and now trained practitioners practicing in multiple countries and continents.

9.5   Conclusion

Classical psychodrama, along with the aforementioned modified psychodrama models, are experiential group processes that both explicitly and implicitly employ a strengths-based approach. Implicit within the philosophy and theory of sociometry and psychodrama is an emphasis on the strengths, goodness, and even the godlikeness of each individual, group, and society. Psychodrama explicitly acknowledges and interfaces with strengths through the psychodramatic process. The core concepts of strengths-based psychodrama and of post-traumatic growth are parallel to Moreno's philosophy and methods. Mutual aid, the foundation of social group work, is also central in sociometric and psychodramatic approaches (Giacomucci, 2020). As the practice of psychodrama evolved with new psychodrama models (positive psychodrama, the Therapeutic Spiral Model, Souldrama, and others), it continues to move more toward a strengths-based orientation. While mutual aid and a strengths-based approach are core to the social work profession and especially social work with groups, Moreno's work seems to have outlined a strengths-based mutual aid model decades prior to their emergence in the social work field.

Acknowledgements Content on pages 166–169 (Sect. 9.3) is republished from Giacomucci, S. (2020). Experiential sociometry in group work: Mutual aid for the group-as-a-whole. *Social Work with Groups*, Advanced Online Publication: https://www.tandfonline.com/doi/abs/10.1080/01609513.2020.1747726. Reprinted by permission of the publisher (Taylor and Francis Ltd., https://www.tandfonline.com).

References

Alisic, E., Van der Schoot, T. A., van Ginkel, J. R., & Kleber, R. J. (2008). Looking beyond posttraumatic stress disorder in children: Posttraumatic stress reactions, posttraumatic growth, and quality of life in a general population sample. *Journal of Clinical Psychiatry, 69*(9), 1455–1461.

Alschuler, M., Silver, T., & McArdle, L. (2015). Strengths-based group supervision with social work students. *Groupwork, 25*(1), 34–57.

Arnold, D., Calhoun, L. G., Tedeschi, R., & Cann, A. (2005). Vicarious posttraumatic growth in psychotherapy. *Journal of Humanistic Psychology, 45*(2), 239–263.

Atkinson, P., & Kirsner, N. (2019). Positive psychology and psychodrama. In A. Blatner (Ed.), *Action explorations: Using psychodramatic methods in non-therapeutic settings* (pp. 315–332). Seattle, WA: Parallax Publications.

Baruth, K., & Carroll, J. (2002). A formal assessment inventory of resilience: The Baruth protective factors inventory. *Journal of Individual Psychology, 58,* 235–244.

Bauwens, J., & Tosone, C. (2010). Professional posttraumatic growth after a shared traumatic experience: Manhattan clinicians' perspectives on post-9/11 practice. *Journal of Loss and Trauma, 15*(6), 498–517.

Bitel, M. (2014). Flipping the equation: The need for context-focused group work education. *Social Work with Groups, 37,* 48–60.

Bluvstein, I., Moravchick, L., Sheps, D., Schreiber, S., & Bloch, M. (2013). Posttraumatic growth, posttraumatic stress symptoms and mental health among coronary heart disease survivors. *Journal of Clinical Psychology in Medical Settings, 20*(2), 164–172.

Breslau, N., Davis, G. C., Andreski, P., & Peterson, E. (1991). Traumatic events and posttraumatic stress disorder in an urban population of young adults. *Archives of General Psychiatry, 48*(3), 216–222.

Bustos, D. M. (1994). Locus, matrix, status nascendi and the concept of clusters. In P. Holmes, M. Karp, & M. Watson (Eds.), *Psychodrama since Moreno: Innovations in theory and practice* (pp. 45–55). New York: Routledge.

Calhoun, L. G., & Tedeschi, R. G. (2012). *Posttraumatic growth in clinical practice.* New York: Routledge.

Calhoun, L. G., & Tedeschi, R. G. (Eds.). (2014). *Handbook of posttraumatic growth: Research and practice.* Routledge.

Canda, E. R. (2012). Chronic illness and spiritual transformation. In D. Saleebey (Ed.), *The strengths perspective in social work practice* (6th ed., pp. 79–96). Boston: Pearson Education.

Chesner, A. (2020). Psychodrama and healing the traumatic wound. In A. Chesner & S. Lykou (Eds.), *Trauma in the creative and embodied therapies: When words are not enough* (pp. 69–80). London: Routledge.

Cohen, B. Z. (1999). Intervention and supervision in strengths-based social work practice. *Families in Society, 80*(5), 460–466.

Cohen, K., & Collens, P. (2013). The impact of trauma work on trauma workers: A metasynthesis on vicarious trauma and vicarious posttraumatic growth. *Psychological Trauma: Theory, Research, Practice, and Policy, 5*(6), 570–580.

Cossa, M. (2020). Building resilience in youth with Therapeutic Spiral Model™(TSM) psychodrama. *Zeitschrift Für Psychodrama Und Soziometrie, 19*(1), 51–62.

Courtois, C. A., & Ford, J. D. (2016). *Treatment of complex trauma: A sequenced, relationship-based approach.* New York, NY: The Guildford Press.

Cosden, M., Sanford, A., Koch, L. M., & Lepore, C. E. (2016). Vicarious trauma and vicarious posttraumatic growth among substance abuse treatment providers. *Substance Abuse, 37*(4), 619–624.

Csikszentmihalyi, M. (1976/1990). *Flow: The psychology of optimal experience: Steps toward enhancing the quality of life.* New York, NY: Harper Collins.

Dewey, J. (1916). *Democracy and education: An introduction to the philosophy of education.* New York: The Free Press.

Epstein, M. H., & Sharma, J. M. (1998). *Behavioral and emotional rating scale: A strength-based approach to assessment.* Austin, TX: PRO-ED.

Fox, J. (Ed.). (1987). *The essential Moreno: Writings on psychodrama, group method, and spontaneity by J. L. Moreno, M.D.* New York: Springer.

Fraser, M. W., Kirby, L. D., & Smokowski, P. R. (2004). Risk and resilience in childhood. *Risk and Resilience in Childhood: An Ecological Perspective, 2,* 13–66.

Frazier, P., Conlon, A., & Glaser, T. (2001). Positive and negative life changes following sexual assault. *Journal of Consulting and Clinical Psychology, 69,* 1048–1055.

Frazier, P., Tennen, H., Gavian, M., Park, C., Tomich, P., & Tashiro, T. (2009). Does self-reported posttraumatic growth reflect genuine positive change? *Psychological Science, 20,* 912–919.

Froh, J. J. (2004). The history of positive psychology: Truth be told. *NYS Psychologist, 16*(3), 18–20.

Giacomucci, S. (2017). The sociodrama of life or death: Young adults and addiction treatment. *Journal of Psychodrama, Sociometry, and Group Psychotherapy, 65*(1), 137–143. https://doi.org/10.12926/0731-1273-65.1.137.

Giacomucci, S. (2018). Social work and sociometry: An integration of theory and clinical practice. *The Pennsylvania Social Worker, 39*(1), 14–16.

Giacomucci, S. (2018b). Social work and sociometry: Integrating history, theory, and practice. In *Clinical Voice* (pp. 15–16). Richboro, PA: Pennsylvania Society for Clinical Social Work.

Giacomucci, S. (2018). The trauma survivor's inner role atom: A clinical map for post-traumatic growth. *Journal of Psychodrama, Sociometry, and Group Psychotherapy., 66*(1), 115–129.

Giacomucci, S. (2019). *Social group work in action: A sociometry, psychodrama, and experiential trauma therapy curriculum.* Doctorate in Social Work (DSW) Dissertations, pp. 124. https://repository.upenn.edu/cgi/viewcontent.cgi?article=1128&context=edissertations_sp2.

Giacomucci, S. (2020). Experiential sociometry in group work: Mutual aid for the group-as-a-whole. *Social Work with Groups.* https://doi.org/10.1080/01609513.2020.1747726.

Giacomucci, S., & Marquit, J. (2020). The effectiveness of trauma-focused psychodrama in the treatment of PTSD in inpatient substance abuse treatment. *Frontiers in Psychology, 11,* 896. https://doi.org/10.3389/2Ffpsyg.2020.00896.

Giacomucci, S., & Stone, A. M. (2019). Being in two places at once: Renegotiating traumatic experience through the surplus reality of psychodrama. *Social Work with Groups, 42*(3), 184–196. https://doi.org/10.1080/01609513.2018.1533913.

Gilligan, R. (2004). Promoting resilience in child and family social work: Issues for social work practice, education, and policy. *Social Work Education, 23,* 93–104.

Gitterman, A. (2004). Interactive andragogy: Principles, methods, and skills. *Journal of Teaching in Social Work, 24*(3/4), 95–112.

Gitterman, A., & Knight, C. (2016). Promoting resilience through social work practice with groups: Implications for the practice and field curricula. *Journal of Social Work Education, 52*(4), 448–461.

Gitterman, A., & Shulman, L. (2005). *Mutual aid groups, vulnerable and resilient populations, and the life cycle* (3rd ed.). New York, NY: Columbia University Press.

Glassman, U., & Kates, L. (1990). *Group work: A humanistic approach.* Newbury Park, CA: Sage.

Goldberg, M. C. (2009). Positive psychodrama and the early works of JL Moreno. *Group, 359–372.*

Herman, J. L. (1997). *Trauma and recovery: The aftermath of violence—from domestic abuse to political terror.* New York: Basic Books.

Hudgins, M. K. (2002). *Experiential treatment for PTSD: The therapeutic spiral model.* New York: Springer Publishing Company.

Hudgins, K. (2019). Psychodrama revisited: Through the lens of the internal role map of the therapeutic spiral model to promote post-traumatic growth. *Zeitschrift Für Psychodrama Und Soziometrie, 18*(1), 59–74.

Hudgins, M. K., & Toscani, F. (2013). *Healing world trauma with the therapeutic spiral model: stories from the frontlines.* London: Jessica Kingsley Publishers.

Hyatt-Burkhart, D. (2014). The experience of vicarious posttraumatic growth in mental health workers. *Journal of Loss and Trauma, 19*(5), 452–461.

International Association of Social Work with Groups. (2015). *Standards for Social Work Practice with Groups* (2nd ed.). Retrieved from: https://www.iaswg.org/assets/docs/Resources/2015_I ASWG_STANDARDS_FOR_SOCIAL_WORK_PRACTICE_WITH_GROUPS.pdf.

Jia, X., Ying, L., Zhou, X., Wu, X., & Lin, C. (2015). The effects of extraversion, social support on the posttraumatic stress disorder and posttraumatic growth of adolescent survivors of the Wenchuan earthquake. *PLoS One, 10*(3).

Kessler, R. C., Sonnega, A., Bromet, E., Hughes, M., & Nelson, C. B. (1995). Posttraumatic stress disorder in the national comorbidity survey. *Archives of General Psychiatry, 52*(12), 1048–1060.

Kim, J. S., & Bolton, K. W. (2013). Strengths perspective. In *Encyclopedia of Social Work.* Retrieved February 29, 2020, from https://oxfordre.com/socialwork/view/https://doi.org/10.1093/acrefore/9780199975839.001.0001/acrefore-9780199975839-e-382.

Kleinmuntz, J. (2011). On becoming a group worker. *Social Work with Groups, 34*(3–4), 219–232.

Knight, C. (2006). Groups for individuals with traumatic histories: Practice considerations for social workers. *Social Work, 51*(1), 20–30.

Knight, C. (2017). Social work students' experiences with group work in the field practicum. *Journal of Teaching in Social Work, 37*(2), 138–155.

Knight, C., & Gitterman, A. (2014). Group work with bereaved individuals: The power of mutual aid. *Social Work, 59*(1), 5–12.

Konopik, D. A., & Cheung, M. (2013). Psychodrama as a social work modality. *Journal of Social Work, 58*(1), 9–20.

Konopka, G. (1990). Past/present issues in group work with the emotionally disabled: Part II, thirty-five years of group work in psychiatric settings. *Social Work with Groups, 13*(1).

Kretzmann, J. P., & McKnight, J. (1993). *Building communities from the inside out* (pp. 2–10). Evanston, IL: Center for Urban Affairs and Policy Research, Neighborhood Innovations Network.

Kropotkin, P. A. (1922). *Mutual aid: A factor of evolution.* New York, NY: Knopf.

Kurland, R., & Salmon, R. (2006). Group work vs. casework in a group: Principles and implications for teaching and practice. *Social Work with Groups, 28*(3–4), 121–132.

Maslow, A. H. (1954). *Motivation and personality.* New York: Harper & Row, Publishers.

Maslow, A. H. (1962). *Toward a psychology of being.* New York: Wiley.

Maslow, A. H. (1964). *Religions, values, and peak-experiences.* Columbus: Ohio State University Press.

Manning, S. F., de Terte, I., & Stephens, C. (2015). Vicarious posttraumatic growth: A systematic literature review. *International Journal of Wellbeing, 5*(2).

McMillen, C., Smith, E. M., & Fisher, R. H. (1997). Perceived benefit and mental health after three types of disaster. *Journal of Consulting and Clinical Psychology, 65,* 733–739.

Mead, G. H. (1934). *Mind, self and society* (Vol. 111). Chicago, IL: University of Chicago Press.

Mendelsohn, M., Zachary, R., & Harney, P. (2007). Group therapy as an ecological bridge to new community for trauma survivors. *Journal of Aggression, Maltreatment and Trauma, 14*, 227–243.

Miller, C. (2000). The technique of Souldrama and its applications. *Journal of Group Psychotherapy, Psychodrama and Sociometry, 52*(4), 173–186.

Miller, C. (2004). *Souldrama: A journey into the heart of God.* NJ: Self-published.

Miller, C. (2008). Souldrama®: Spirituality in action. *Journal of Creativity in Mental Health, 3*(2), 139–156.

Miller, C. (2019). Souldrama. In A. Blatner (Ed.), *Action explorations: Using psychodramatic methods in non-therapeutic settings* (pp. 287–298). Seattle, WA: Parallax Publications.

Moreno, J. L. (1943). Sociometry and the cultural order. *Sociometry, 6*(3), 299–344.

Moreno, J. L. (1945). *Group psychotherapy: A symposium.* Beacon, NY: Beacon House Press.

Moreno, J. L. (1947). Open letter to group psychotherapists. *Psychodrama Monograms*, No. 23. Beacon, NY: Beacon House.

Moreno, J. L. (1953). *Who shall survive? Foundations of sociometry, group psychotherapy and sociodrama* (2nd ed.). Beacon, NY: Beacon House.

Moreno, J. L. (1955). *Preludes to my autobiography.* Beacon, NY: Beacon House.

Moreno, J. L. (1963). Reflections on my method of group psychotherapy and psychodrama. *Ciba Symposium, 11*(4), 148–157.

Moreno, J. L. (1964). *Psychodrama, first volume* (3rd ed.). Beacon, NY: Beacon House Press.

Moreno, J. D. (2014). *Impromptu man: JL Moreno and the origins of psychodrama, encounter culture, and the social network.* Bellevue Literary Press.

Moreno, J. D. (2019a). Introduction. In J. L. Moreno (Ed.), *The autobiography of a genius* (pp. 107–115). United Kingdom: North West Psychodrama Association.

Moreno, J. L. (2019b). *The autobiography of a genius.* In: E. Schreiber, S. Kelley, & S. Giacomucci (Eds.). United Kingdom: North West Psychodrama Association.

Moreno, J. L., & Whitin, E. S. (1932). *Application of the group method to classification.* New York: National Committee on Prisons and Prison Labor.

Moreno, Z.T. (2000). Interview with Leif Dag Blomkvist regarding Surplus Reality. In Z. T. Moreno, L. D. Blomkvist, & T. Rutzel (Eds.), *Psychodrama, surplus reality and the art of healing* (Chap. 4, pp. 17–23). London, UK: Routledge.

Moreno, Z. T. (2012). *To dream again: A memoir.* New York: Mental Health Resources.

Najavits, L. (2002). *Seeking safety: A treatment manual for PTSD and substance abuse.* Guilford Publications.

Nolte, J. (2014). *The philosophy, theory, and methods of J. L. Moreno: The man who tried to become god.* New York, NY: Routledge.

Norman, E. (Ed.). (2000). *Resiliency enhancement: Putting the strength perspective into social work practice.* New York: Columbia University Press.

Northen, H., & Kurland, R. (2001). *Social work with groups.* New York: Columbia University Press.

Orkibi, H. (2019). Positive psychodrama: A framework for practice and research. *Arts in Psychotherapy, 66*, 1–8. https://doi.org/10.1016/j.aip.2019.101603.

Özcan, G. (2019). Psychodrama and spirituality: A practice-friendly review. *Spiritual Psychology and Counseling, 4*(1), 39–55.

Parikh, D., De Ieso, P., Garvey, G., Thachil, T., Ramamoorthi, R., Penniment, M., & Jayaraj, R. (2015). Post-traumatic stress disorder and post-traumatic growth in breast cancer patients-a systematic review. *Asian Pacific Journal of Cancer Prevention, 16*(2), 641–646.

Park, C. L., Cohen, L. H., & Murch, R. L. (1996). Assessment and prediction of stress-related growth. *Journal of Personality, 64*, 71–105.

Probst, B. (2010). Implicit and explicit use of the strengths perspective in social work education. *Journal of Teaching in Social Work, 30*(4), 468–484.

Rapp, C. A. (1998). *The strengths model: Case management with people suffering from severe and persistent mental illness.* New York: Oxford University Press.

Rapp, C. A., & Chamberlain, R. (1985). Case management services for the chronically mentally ill. *Social Work, 30*(5), 417–422.

Rapp, C. A., Saleebey, D., & Sullivan, W. P. (2006). The future of strengths-based social work. *Advances in Social Work: Special Issue on the Futures of Social Work, 6*(1), 79–90.

Rashid, T. (2015). Positive psychotherapy: A strength-based approach. *The Journal of Positive Psychology, 10*(1), 25–40.

Roberts, R., & Northen, H. (1976). *Theories of social work with groups*. New York: Columbia University Press.

Rogers, C. (1951). *Client-centered therapy: Its current practice, implications and theory*. London: Constable.

Rogers, C. R. (1966). *Client-centered therapy*. Washington, DC: American Psychological Association.

Saleebey, D. (1996). The strengths perspective in social work practice: Extensions and cautions. *Social Work, 41*(3), 296–305.

Saleebey, D. (2012). *The strengths perspective in social work practice* (6th ed.). Boston: Pearson Education.

Santiago, P. N., Ursano, R. J., Gray, C. L., Pynoos, R. S., Spiegel, D., Lewis-Fernandez, R., … & Fullerton, C. S. (2013). A systematic review of PTSD prevalence and trajectories in DSM-5 defined trauma exposed populations: intentional and non-intentional traumatic events. *PloS one, 8*(4).

Schreiber, E. (2018). Sociatry Part 2: Moreno's Mysticism. In *Psychodrama network news* (Winter 2018, pp. 24–25). American Society of Group Psychotherapy and Psychodrama.

Schwartz, W. (1961). The social worker in the group. In *New perspectives on services to groups: Theory, organization, and practice* (pp. 7–34).

Seligman, M. E. P. (1998). Building human strengths: psychology's forgotten mission. *APA Monitor*, January 2.

Shapiro, F. (2018). *Eye-movement desensitization and reprocessing (EMDR) therapy* (3rd ed.). New York: Guilford Press.

Shulman, L. (2015). *The skills of helping individuals, families, groups, and communities* (8th ed.). Boston, MA: Cengage Learning.

Skolnik-Basulto, S. (2016). *Coming together: A study of factors that influence social workers' connection to group work practice* (Order No. 10758221). Available from ProQuest Dissertations & Theses Global. (1988269052). Retrieved from https://proxy.library.upenn.edu/login?url=https://proxy.library.upenn.edu:2072/docview/1988269052?accountid=14707.

Skolnik, S. (2018). A synergistic union: Group work meets psychodrama. *Social Work with Groups, 41*(1–2), 60–73.

Smith, E. J. (2006). The strength-based counseling model. *The Counseling Psychologist, 34*(1), 13–79.

Ssenyonga, J., Owens, V., & Olema, D. K. (2013). Posttraumatic growth, resilience, and posttraumatic stress disorder (PTSD) among refugees. *Procedia-Social and Behavioral Sciences, 82*, 144–148.

Steinberg, D. M. (2003). The magic of mutual aid. *Social Work with Groups, 25*(1–2), 31–38.

Steinberg, D. M. (2004). *The mutual-aid approach to working with groups* (2nd ed.). Binghamton, NY: Haworth Press.

Steinberg, D. M. (2010). Mutual aid: A contribution to best-practice social work. *Social Work with Groups, 33*(1), 53–68.

Stimmer, F. (2004). Psychodrama – Soziale Arbeit – Netzwerke. *Zeitschrift Für Psychodrama Und Soziometrie, 3*(1), 17–27.

Tedeschi, R. G., & Calhoun, L. G. (1996). The Posttraumatic growth inventory: Measuring the positive legacy of trauma. *Journal of Traumatic Stress, 9*(3), 455–471.

Tomasulo, D. (2011). *The virtual gratitude visit (VGV): Psychodrama in action*. Retrieved from PsychologyToday.com.

Tomasulo, D. J. (2014). Positive group psychotherapy modified for adults with intellectual disabilities. *Journal of Intellectual Disabilities, 18*(4), 337–350.

Tomasulo, D. (2018). Beautiful thinking in action: Positive psychology, psychodrama, and positive psychotherapy. *The Journal of Psychodrama, Sociometry, and Group Psychotherapy, 66*(1), 49–67.

Tomasulo D. J. (2019). The virtual gratitude visit (VGV): Using psychodrama and role-playing as a positive intervention. In L. Van Zyl & S. Rothmann (Eds.), *Positive psychological intervention design and protocols for multi-cultural contexts*. Cham: Springer.

van Breda, A. D. (2018). A critical review of resilience theory and its relevance for social work. *Social Work, 54*(1), 1–18. https://doi.org/10.15270/54-1-611.

von Ameln, F., & Becker-Ebel, J. (2020). *Fundamentals of psychodrama*. Singapore: Springer Nature.

Wade, J. C., & Jones, J. E. (2014). *Strength-based clinical supervision: A positive psychology approach to clinical training*. Springer Publishing Company.

Walsh, F. (2006). *Strengthening family resilience* (2nd ed.). New York: The Guilford Press.

Wang, X. H., & Liu, A. Q. (2020). Psychodrama: A professional method for social work. *Social Work and Management, 20*(2), 65–70.

Weick, A., Rapp, C., Sullivan, W. P., & Kisthardt, W. (1989). A strengths perspective for social work practice. *Social Work, 34*(4), 350–354.

Witkin, S. (2017). *Transforming social work: Social constructionist reflections on contemporary and enduring issues*. London: Palgrave.

Wolin, S., & Wolin, S. J. (1993). *The resilient self: How survivors of troubled families rise above adversity*. New York: Villard.

Wu, X., Kaminga, A. C., Dai, W., Deng, J., Wang, Z., Pan, X., & Liu, A. (2019). The prevalence of moderate-to-high posttraumatic growth: A systematic review and meta-analysis. *Journal of Affective Disorders, 243*, 408–415.

Yalom, I., & Leszcz, M. (2005). *The theory and practice of group psychotherapy*. New York: Basic Books.

Chapter 10
Creating an Evidence Base for Social Work, Group Work, and Psychodrama

Abstract This chapter is devoted to outlining the research literature of psychodrama and group therapy. Evidence-based practice trends and their impact on practice in the field of social work are described. Psychodrama is also framed within the research bases of the humanistic-experiential psychotherapies, creative arts therapies, and body- and movement-oriented therapies. While the quality and quantity of research available on the effectiveness of psychodrama are limited, current findings support its use to as a treatment for various mental health conditions. Shortcomings and critiques of research in psychodrama are included while indicating a need for higher quality psychodrama research studies. The research history of psychodrama's founder, Jacob Moreno, is also described to provide insight on psychodrama's historical relationship to research.

Keywords Evidence-based social work · Psychodrama research · Group psychotherapy research · Experiential psychotherapy · Effectiveness

10.1 Social Work and Evidence-Based Practice

The social work's struggle to establish itself as a professionalized field traces back to the beginnings of social work. Okpych and Yu (2014) highlight three major shifts in social work's practice paradigm—first a paradigm based on morality and charity, then a paradigm based on tradition and authority of the psychoanalytic approach, and now a paradigm grounded in empirical research.

This shift toward empirical clinical practice (ECP) seems to have begun in the late 1960s and shifted the paradigm from practicing based on appeal, tradition, or consensus to a clinical practice rooted in evidence and effectiveness (Okpych & Yu, 2014; Witkin, 2017). This new ECP paradigm challenged social workers to routinely assess and evaluate the effectiveness of their work while also urging social work researchers to systematically evaluate the effectiveness of various approaches on a large scale. In part, the ECP movement was stimulated by a series of research studies concluding that certain social work approaches were not effective or even

© The Author(s) 2021

S. Giacomucci, *Social Work, Sociometry, and Psychodrama*, Psychodrama in Counselling, Coaching and Education 1,

https://doi.org/10.1007/978-981-33-6342-7_10

causing harm (Briar, 1967; Fischer, 1973, 1978; Okpych & Yu, 2014). Simultaneously, computer technology had advanced to the point of making complex data analysis and research publication significantly more effective (Bronson & Blythe, 1987; Glass, 1976; Glisson, 1982). The influence of the ECP movement in social work at that time is evidenced by the 1984 Council on Social Work Education (CSWE) change in curriculum standards requiring social workers to "evaluate their own practice systematically" (1988, 127). Still, in 1991, the Task Force on Social Work Research exclaimed that the social work field was too detached from research (Okpych & Yu, 2014).

Empirical clinical practice created controversy within the social work field and was criticized by some (Witkin, 2017). Witkin (1991, 2017) argued that the ECP model placed too much focus on objectivity and disregarded the social, cultural, and political influences in clinical social work—in effect, ignoring the relational and social aspects of person-in-environment. Okpych and Yu further highlight this conflict in the following passage:

> In particular, critics drew attention to logical positivist assumptions that undergirded ECP: that social phenomena were absolute entities and that researchers could impartially and objectively observe these phenomena through preconstructed, standardized measurement. Alternatively, some argued that social phenomena emerge in structures of power, systems of language, and webs of meaning, and that methodologies should be adopted that explore rather than delimit phenomena, reveal rather than control extraneous factors, and acknowledge rather than disavow the researcher's interpretive frame. (Okpych and Yu 2014, p. 19)

The ECP movement in social work had begun to lose traction in the 1990s, until it was revitalized by the evidence-based medicine (EBM) movement which had engulfed the fields of medicine and psychology (2017). As systematic reviews and meta-analyses began to emerge in exponential numbers, policy makers, government agencies, nonprofit funders, and insurance companies began requiring evidence-based practice (EBP) implementation for funded programs. Multiple registries and organizations emerged to systematically review the evidence base of different programs and interventions including the Cochrane Review, the Campbell Collaborative, the Substance Abuse and Mental Health Service Administration's Registry of Evidence-Based Programs and Practices, and the list of EBPs evaluated by Division 12 of the American Psychological Association.

The contemporary EBP model outlined by Haynes et al. (2002) includes the integration and intersection of four parts:

1. The clinical presentation and circumstances of the client
2. The literature base of related research
3. The values and preferences of the client
4. The skill, expertise, and area of competence of the clinician.

Evidence-based practice has been defined as "a process that incorporates current research evidence with clinical expertise and client expectations and values" (Sackett et al., 1996, as cited by Wike et al., 2014, p. 161). The movement toward EBP is fueled by the virtuous goal of preventing harm and providing the absolute best practices for clients. In some ways, social work's adoption of EBP was an attempt to move the profession toward a scientific base for clinical practice and away from the intuition-based clinical practice that much of the field continues to operate from.

When it comes to different types of evidence or research, EBP subscribes to a hierarchy of evidence that places low value in qualitative studies and high value in controlled, randomized quantitative research and meta-analysis. McNeece and Thyer (2004) outline this hierarchy of evidence below:

1. Systematic reviews/meta-analyses
2. Randomized controlled trials
3. Quasi-experimental studies
4. Case–control and cohort studies
5. Pre-experimental group studies
6. Surveys
7. Qualitative studies.

Though not highly regarded in the hierarchy of evidence, some social work research experts have promoted qualitative methods as most complimentary to the social work practice values because of their overlap in making sense of client narratives, conducting qualitative interviews, understanding social phenomenon, exploring complexities of direct experience, meeting the client where they are at, and attention to person-in-environment (Fortune et al., 2013; Gray et al., 2009; Gilgun, 1994; Padgett, 1998; Shaw & Holland, 2014). Cheetham (1992) suggests that studying outcomes and efficacy in social work has little value unless we also use qualitative methods to understand the process of change.

10.2 Limitations and Critiques of Evidence-Based Practice

By the mid-2000s, the term evidence-based practice had become increasingly popular and was frequently used without attention to its precise meaning or the quality and rigor of evidence that a practice was effective (Shlonsky & Gibbs, 2004). Treatment approaches that made their way onto one of the evidence-based practice registries based on research for treating one specific mental health disorder are often misleadingly promoted as an evidence-based practice for any condition. Critics of EBP have argued that it is too medicalized and attempts to separate the individual from their biopsychosocial reality while prescribing rigid interventions that do not honor client diversity, client preferences, the therapeutic relationship, or the practice wisdom of the social worker (Adams et al., 2009; Berger, 2010; Borntrager et al., 2009; Drisko & Grady, 2015; Goldstein et al., 2009; Magill, 2006; Manuel et al., 2009; Witkin, 2017). Others criticize the use of treatment manuals, citing the growing literature base supporting the effectiveness of the therapeutic relationship (Norcross & Lampbert, 2011). Wike et al. (2014) underscore that while EBP has become popular in the field of social work, "effective approaches for translating research evidence into social work practice remain elusive" (p. 161). Witkin (2017) argues that EBP focuses more on *cognitive knowing* than on the *practical doing* of clinical work. Many social workers report that they do not fully understand the statistics and research methods in the literature and cannot differentiate between useful and misleading results (Bledsoe-Mansori et al., 2013; Wike et al., 2014). Researchers organize information based on units of measurement, while therapists organize information into a meaningful psychosocial narrative (Witkin, 2017).

While the EBP movement has its limitations and faults, it is also important to acknowledge the ethical responsibilities of social workers to utilize approaches that are effective and do not cause harm to clients. There is no disagreement with this ethical principle and the overall goal of EBP. Many argue that when it comes to generalizing best practices of creating evidence, evaluating evidence, prioritizing different types of evidence, generalizing research, and integrating knowledge of best practices from controlled research environments into real-world clinical practice, important distinctions are not taking into consideration which suggest that EBPs lead to the disintegration of core social work values in clinical practice, namely the importance of relationships (Goldstein et al., 2009; Okpych & Yu, 2014; Witkin, 2017). Shulman (2016) highlights how EBP used in the social work field is often created by nonsocial workers and does not reflect the core values of the social work profession. EBP has the potential of reenacting and upholding systems of oppression and the imbalance of power dynamics within clinical social work (Witkin, 2017). Even the National Institutes of Health have acknowledged the problems with using EBPs in social work agencies (Shulman, 2016). Reamer (1992) eloquently states that:

> Empiricism can be taken too far.... While [it] can certainly inform and guide intervention, we must be sure that it does not strip interventions of its essential ingredients – a keen sense of humanity, compassion, and justice and the ability to engage and work with people.... Truly enlightened practice integrates the systematic method of empiricism with the valuable knowledge that social workers have once regarded as .... Practice wisdom and professional intuition. (p. 258, as cited in Goldstein et al., 2009, p. 17)

In the search for best practices for our clients, we must not forget to continue to meet clients where they are. A rigid adherence to EBP seems to negate a client-centered approach in favor of a therapist-centered or, more precisely, an intervention-centered approach.

While the EBP approach has become central to the social work field, some advocate the *Common Factors Perspective* as an alternative narrative to evaluating efficacy research (Witkin, 2017). Various research studies have demonstrated that the specifics of treatment interventions are less important than certain common factors when it comes to their efficacy in psychotherapy—especially the therapeutic relationship (Laska et al., 2014; Messer & Wampold, 2002; Wampold, 2005; Witkin, 2017). These common factors are outlined by Laska et al. (2014) to include:

1. The therapeutic relationship between client and therapist
2. A safe and healing setting within which sessions take place
3. A therapist offering a culturally appropriate psychological understanding of suffering
4. An adaptive framework for change that the client understands and believes

5. A process/ritual enacted by therapist and client that provides something useful.

These common factors have been simplified by Wampold (2012) into a humanistic framework focused on "(a) making sense of the world, (b) influencing through social means, and (c) connectedness, expectation, and mastery" (p. 445). The common factor approach seems to orient itself on the *overall process of psychotherapy* as evidence-based practice rather than emphasizing *specific manualized content in psychotherapy.* Witkin (2017) suggests that this focus on process of common factors offers a fitting alternative to EBP for the social work profession.

One of the most respected group therapists of the century, Irving Yalom, reminds us that when it comes to EBP, *non-validated* therapies are not *invalidated* therapies (2002). He writes that EBP and the nature of controlled scientific research favor interventions that are brief, replicable, and manualized—which gives cognitive behavioral therapy (CBT) and other cognitive or behavioral approaches an advantage. Other approaches that orient themselves on genuine therapeutic relationship, the here-and-now experience, and spontaneity are inherently disadvantaged. Yalom finishes his chapter on empirically validated therapy (EVT) by proposing the following "mischievous point." "I have a strong hunch (substantiated only anecdotally) that EVT practitioners requiring personal psychotherapeutic help do not seek brief cognitive-behavioral therapy but instead turn to highly trained, experienced, dynamic, manualless therapists" (Yalom, 2002, p. 224). Perhaps clinicians early in their career may be more inclined to rely on manualized treatments, while seasoned therapists may be less likely to.

10.3 Group Psychotherapy Research

Most of the evidence-based practice movement seems to be focused on individual psychotherapy rather than group therapy. Individual therapy outcomes may not be generalizable to group work settings as "there are in fact different factors reflecting different processes that occur in group and individual treatment" (Holmes & Kivlighan, 2000, p. 482). Nevertheless, a wealth of research on the efficacy of group psychotherapy has emerged in the past few decades elevating it to at least the same level of effectiveness as individual psychotherapy (Burlingame & Krogel, 2005; McRoberts et al., 1998). While individual psychotherapy often underlines the therapeutic relationship as the most important factor, group psychotherapy elevates group cohesion as the most important factor (Burlingame et al., 2002; Yalom & Lesczc, 2005). Research has demonstrated a strong relationship between group cohesion and positive outcomes in group psychotherapy across various theoretical orientations (Burlingame et al., 2018).

Burlingame and Jensen (2017) write that "many disorders now have good or excellent evidence supporting group treatment's ability to lead to improved outcomes (panic, social phobia, OCD, eating disorders, substance abuse, trauma-related disorders, breast cancer, schizophrenia, and personality disorders)" (p. S200). More specifically, the group psychotherapy research has produced systematic reviews and meta-analyses outlining its efficacy in the treatment of panic disorder (Schwartze et al., 2017), anxiety (Barkowski et al., 2016), obsessive–compulsive disorder (Schwartze et al., 2016), depression (Huntley et al., 2012; Krishna et al., 2015; McDermut et al., 2001; Pearson & Burlingame, 2013), bipolar disorder (Pearson & Burlingame, 2013), post-traumatic stress disorder (Bisson et al., 2013; Schwartze et al., 2019; Sloan et al., 2013), and alcoholism/addiction (Coco et al., 2019). An evidence base has emerged to show no difference between the effectiveness of individual and group therapy approaches for mood disorders (Burlingame et al., 2004; Roselló et al., 2008), panic disorders (Sharp et al., 2004), personality disorders (Arnevik et al., 2009), schizophrenia (Lockwood et al., 2004), obsessive compulsive disorder (O'Leary et al., 2009), substance abuse (Burlingame et al., 2013; Panas et al., 2003), and eating disorders (Nevonen & Broberg, 2006; Renjilian et al., 2001).

The group psychotherapy research has established its efficacy as compared to a waitlist, compared to alternative treatments, and through pre- to post-treatment tests (Burlingame et al., 2003). Group psychotherapy's effectiveness has been demonstrated across the treatment continuum from inpatient, residential, and outpatient contexts including university-based and prison counseling settings (Burlingame et al., 2003; Kosters et al., 2006). Burlingame and Jenson note that in the past 25 years, cognitive behavioral group therapy has dominated the research base in terms of quantity of publications with a five-to-one ratio compared to all other theoretical orientations (Burlingame & Jensen, 2017).

10.4   Humanistic-Experiential Psychotherapy Research

Experiential psychotherapy contains multiple action-based approaches including psychodrama, gestalt therapy, existential therapy, humanistic therapy, and emotion-focused therapy. Experiential psychotherapy's efficacy has been demonstrated through multiple research studies which suggest it is at least equally efficacious as CBT, psychodynamic psychotherapy, and other talk therapy or behavioral approaches (Elliott, 1996, 2001; Elliott & Freire, 2008; Elliott et al., 2004; Greenberg, 2013; Greenberg et al., 1994; Greenberg & Malcolm, 2002; Greenberg & Paivio, 1998; Greenberg et al., 1998; Mullings, 2017; Smith et al., 1980). A meta-analysis examining 86 studies, published Elliott et al. (2004), concluded that experiential therapies are statistically equal in effectiveness to talk therapies. They write in 2004 that "is now more than sufficient to warrant a positive valuation of experiential conclusion in four important areas: depression, anxiety disorders, trauma, and marital problems" (p. 423). Greenberg's (2013) chapter in *Healing World Trauma with the Therapeutic Spiral Model* positions the Therapeutic Spiral Model of psychodrama within this larger literature base of experiential psychotherapy research indicating that "there is now solid evidence for the efficacy and effectiveness of experiential therapies" (2013, p. 144).

Elliott et al. (2013) conducted a major meta-analysis in which they found that humanistic-experiential psychotherapies (HEP) were equally as efficacious as CBT for the treatment of depression and for coping with medical conditions, and superior to CBT in effectiveness for the treatment of interpersonal difficulties and unresolved relationship issues. In contrast, the meta-analysis found that HEPs were somewhat less effective than CBT in treating anxiety disorders, though still probably efficacious. Their meta-analysis also analyzed HEPs implementation with specific categories of mental health disorders based on Chambless and Hollon's criteria for efficacy (Chambless & Hollon, 1998). Their outcomes suggest HEPs are *specific and efficacious* (the highest standard) in the treatment of depression and unresolved relationship issues while also *probably efficacious* in the treatment of anxiety and psychosis (Elliott et al., 2013; Mullings, 2017).

10.5   Research on Drama Therapy, Creative Arts Therapies, and Body- and Movement-Oriented Therapies

Similar to its relationship to humanistic-experiential psychotherapy, psychodrama is often categorized within the larger umbrellas of the creative arts therapies and the body- and movement-oriented intervention (BMOI). Many meta-analyses and systematic reviews categorize psychodrama and drama therapy in the same category as well. Feniger-Schaal and Orkibi (2020) published the first integrative systematic review on drama therapy interventions concluding that the evidence base is small but shows promising results, especially with populations with developmental disabilities, cognitive difficulties, and difficulties in verbal expression. Bourne et al. (2018) published a systematic analysis on drama therapy group work for adults with mental illness which concluded that drama therapy offers important social benefits, emotional support, self-awareness, creativity, and self-esteem. A 2013 literature review on the effectiveness of expressive arts therapies concluded that "overall, despite many inconclusive studies, the effectiveness of creative arts therapies for a range of conditions in indicated" (Dunphy et al., 2013).

One area that creative arts therapies and BMOI may be uniquely situated is in the treatment of PTSD and trauma-related issues. Baker et al. (2018), in their systematic review on PTSD and creative arts therapies, report that decreased PTSD symptoms may be related to symbolic and nonverbal expression of painful experiences through the creative arts therapies. Neuroscience research has demonstrated that PTSD symptoms are related to right hemisphere and limbic system brain structures only marginally impacted by cognition and verbal expression (Rauch et al., 1996; van der Kolk, 2014). Malchiodi (2014) writes that creative arts therapies may be effective for PTSD due to their nature of being right brain dominant. The creative arts allow clients to renegotiate trauma with containment, empowerment, control, and the playfulness of art-making (Baker et al., 2018). A recent systematic review and meta-analysis on treatment of PTSD with body-oriented and movement-oriented intervention (BMOI) concluded that BMOI as an adjunct treatment or stand-alone treatment may result in decreased PTSD symptoms (van de Kamp et al., 2019). The same study concluded that body-oriented therapies had smaller dropout rates than other PTSD treatments and other positive health outcomes. BMOI engages the traumatized limbic system and nervous system of the client using a *bottom-up* approach, while cognitive, verbal, and other *top-down* approaches primarily engage the prefrontal cortex (Levine, 2010; Ogden et al., 2006; van der Kolk, 2014).

10.6 Psychodrama's Evidence Base

The evidence base for psychodrama as a psychotherapy approach is limited, though continuously evolving and growing. Orkibi and Feniger-Schaal (2019), in their recent systematic review of the evidence base of psychodrama, state that "psychodrama intervention research in the last decade suggests there are promising results" (p. 1). Wieser's (2007) meta-analysis on psychodrama's efficacy as a psychotherapy approach indicated that although more rigorous and higher-quality research is needed, there is evidence of positive effects for various different mental health disorders. Wieser concludes that "neurotic, stress-related and somatoform disorders are the best validated area for psychodrama therapy" (2007, p. 278). A meta-analysis by Kipper and Ritchie concluded that psychodrama psychotherapy groups show an overall effect size "similar to, or better than that commonly reported for group psychotherapy in general" (2003, p. 1). They also stated that "although the initial empirical research on the effectiveness of psychodrama revealed some encouraging results, the data were insufficient" (Kipper & Ritchie, 2003, p. 14). Similarly, Rawlinson's literature review (2000) determined "there is some research evidence to support the use of psychodrama" and that it may be best utilized "as a tool for helping people to develop self-esteem, to change elements of their behavior and to develop empathy and social relationships" (p. 93). Kellermann's review of psychodrama's evidence base noted its limitations while also stating "psychodrama was a very valid alternative to other therapeutic approaches, primarily in promoting behavior change with adjustment, antisocial, and related disorders" (1987, p. 467). Other studies include exploring sociometry and psychodrama's effectiveness in supervision (Daniel, 2016; Tabib, 2017) and educational settings (Azoulay & Orkibi, 2018; Schnabel & Reif, 2016; Veiga et al., 2015) while calling for increased research in these areas.

In the context of psychotherapy, the current evidence base of psychodrama as a treatment approach supports its effectiveness in treating depressive disorders (Avinger & Jones, 2007; Carbonell & Parteleno-Barehmi, 1999; Costa et al., 2006; Erbay et al., 2018; Hall, 1977; Rezaeian et al., 1997; Sharma, 2017; Smokowsky & Bacallao, 2009; Souilm & Ali, 2017; Wang et al., 2020; Wieser, 2007), anxiety and panic disorders (Avinger & Jones, 2007; Carbonell & Parteleno-Barehmi, 1999;

Erbay et al., 2018; Hall, 1977; Park & Lim, 2002; Schramski et al., 1984; Sharma, 2017; Smokowsky & Bacallao, 2009; Tarashoeva et al., 2017; Wang et al., 2020), PTSD and trauma-related disorders (Bannister, 1990, 1991, 1997; Baumgartner, 1986; Burge, 1996; Clarke, 1993; Hudgins & Drucker, 1998; Giacomucci & Marquit, 2020; Hudgins et al., 2000; Lind et al., 2006; Paivio & Greenberg, 1995), and schizophrenia, schizotypal, and delusional disorders (Harrow, 1952; Jones & Peters, 1952; Parrish, 1959).

Psychodrama has also been found to have some effectiveness with various other psychosocial conditions including improving emotional or psychological stability (Carpenter & Sandberg, 1985; Choi, 2003; Kang & Son, 2004; Schmidt, 1978; White et al., 1982; Wood et al., 1979), interpersonal relationships (Bendel, 2017; Gow et al., 2011; Gow & McVea, 2006; Petzold, 1979; Shim, 2002), improving conflict resolution skills (Karatas, 2011), increased self-esteem (Gow et al., 2011; Carbonell & Parteleno-Barehmi, 1999), increasing empathy and self-awareness (Dogan, 2018),

In terms of populations, the psychodrama research base includes studies with various age groups, ethnicities, and social groups. A large majority of the research in the past decade (43%) has focused on students and youth and demonstrates positive improvements in multiple areas (Daemi & Rahimparvar, 2018; Orkibi & Feniger-Schaal, 2019). Other research has included promising results with prison inmates (Harkins et al., 2011; Schramski et al., 1984; Testoni et al., 2020) and adults coping with various medical conditions (Alby et al., 2017; Dehnavi et al., 2016; Karabilgin et al., 2012; Menichetti et al., 2016; Sproesser et al., 2010; Terzioglu & Özkan, 2017). Smokowsky and Bacallao (2009) found a significant difference in effect between an action-based intervention program and a talk-based support groups for Latino families, and this effect favored the experiential groups in terms of decreasing anxiety, depression, and interpersonal conflict.

Multiple studies in the field of addictions have pointed to psychodrama's effectiveness in increasing quality of life (Dehnavi et al., 2016), enhancing motivation (Testoni et al., 2018), reducing depression (Dehnavi et al., 2015; Testoni et al., 2020), reducing aggression (Nooripour et al., 2016), and for relapse prevention (Somov, 2008). A recent study by Testoni et al. (2020) pointed to psychodrama's effectiveness for treating addiction in prison; they found it helped access emotions, increased social and emotional functioning, and decreased depressive, anxiety, and traumatic symptoms. Giacomucci and Marquit (2020) offer support for trauma-focused psychodrama's effectiveness in treating PTSD in inpatient addiction settings. Though the utilization of psychodrama by addiction professionals gradually becomes more common (Dayton, 2005, 2015; Giacomucci, 2017, 2018, 2019, 2020; Giacomucci et al., 2018; Giacomucci & Stone, 2019), few research studies have explored its effectiveness.

Kipper and Ritchie (2003) offer one of the only explorations of the effect of specific psychodrama interventions as compared to others. In their meta-analysis, they suggest that while the intervention of role-playing showed barely any improvement effect, "role reversal and doubling showed means suggesting large improvement effect size" (p. 19). Future research is needed to explore the effect of various psychodrama interventions used to varying degrees within psychodrama practice.

Although the American community does not recognize psychodrama as an evidence-based practice, it has been accredited by other governments or insurance systems including in Austria (Ottomeyer et al., 1996), Hungary (Pinter, 2001), and the European Association of Psychotherapy (Cruz et al., 2018). Psychodrama was born in Austria but later developed as a psychotherapy approach in the USA after Jacob Moreno immigrated. Coincidentally, the USA lags behind other countries when it comes to producing and evaluating psychodrama research. It appears that the EBP movement of the 1990s led European psychodramatists to pursue psychodrama's validation as an evidence-based practice while as the same time it seems that psychodrama was never submitted for review as an evidence-based practice in the USA.

Orkibi and Feniger-Schaal (2019) note that in the past decade, 39% of psychodrama research studies were from Turkey, 13% from Italy, 10% from Israel, and 10% from the USA. They also discovered that "psychodrama intervention research in the last decade has followed an upward trajectory" as the frequency of studies has increased from only one published in 2008 to eight in 2017 (Orkibi & Feniger-Schaal, 2019, p. 21).

When it comes to quantitative psychodrama research, Kirk (2016) notes that psychodrama practitioners often struggle because of "the predominance of positivist quantitative research that seems apparently at odds with the philosophy and tenets of psychodrama" (p. 323). The psychodrama literature base is primarily composed of theoretical, philosophical, and practice-oriented publications—many of which include descriptions of client experiences and case studies. The literature focuses more on meaning than on measurements (Kirk, 2016). Some psychodrama researchers are suggesting qualitative research, the ideal research methodology for psychodrama because it would be able to "meet the spontaneous and creative approach of psychodrama" (Hintermeier, 2011). Dima and Bucuta (2016) suggest that the process-oriented nature of psychodrama is complimented by the process-oriented nature of qualitative research methods. They also note that the majority of qualitative psychodrama studies are descriptive in nature and the field would benefit from deeper, interpretive qualitative psychodrama research.

When it comes to the embracing of qualitative research methods due to their complimentary nature to the values of the profession, social work and psychodrama share common ground. Both highlight the importance of making sense of the subjective experience of participants, exploring social context, and investigating the process—all of which seem to favor a qualitative research methodology.

10.6.1 Psychodrama Research Limitations

Many others have cited the need for future psychodrama research to be of higher quality and scientific rigor (Kellermann, 1987; Kipper & Ritchie, 2003; Orkibi & Feniger-Schaal, 2019; Wieser, 2007). Kellermann notes that "practitioners of psychodrama traditionally rely more on clinical experience than on experimental research data when advocating the effectiveness of this method. As a consequence, psychodrama literature mostly includes descriptive rather than empirical studies" (1987, p. 459).

At the same time, there are some inherent limitations to conducting research on psychodrama (Kellermann, 1992; Kipper & Ritchie, 2003; Ridge, 2010). Psychodrama is process-oriented and based on spontaneity and creativity which means that psychodrama sessions are never identical (Giacomucci, 2019). A psychodrama session involves a variety of clinical interventions including role-playing, role reversal, doubling (various types outlined in the literature), and mirroring. These interventions are utilized based on the facilitator's judgment throughout the process and sometimes spontaneously used by other participants as well. These factors make it quite difficult to manualize the psychodramatic approach which is often a prerequisite for evidence-based reviews.

Orkibi and Feniger-Schaal (2019) note that almost all psychodrama training takes place at private institutes focused on clinical applications rather than in research-focused university settings. Psychodrama's disconnection from academia makes it difficult for psychodramatists to have access to academic journals, Internal Review Boards (IRB), research support, and research funding. It appears that most psychodramatists are much more interested in practice than research and simply do not have the research training to design and conduct research studies. Buchanan and Taylor's (1986) study using the Myers–Briggs personality inventory with 170 certified psychodramatists (72.65% of ABE certified psychodramatists at the time) indicated that they are 87% innovative vs conservative, 87% intuitive over sensing, 72% feeling-oriented over thinking-oriented, and 65% extraverted vs introverted. The innovative, intuitive, feeling-oriented, and extroverted personality types may be less likely to engage in research, which is inherently more sensing, thinking-oriented, and conservative. When questioned about psychodrama group psychotherapy research in 1957, Moreno comments on the differentiation between producers of art and analysts of art—suggesting that demonstrating or experiencing the method is superior to systematic analysis or theoretical publications of the method. He promotes direct experience, or existential validation, as greater in influence to scientific validation:

> The combination of the professional skill of practicing group psychotherapy and the skill of scientific analysis is rare… It is very difficult to duplicate in written form the group experiences which take place in actual sessions. This is the meaning of my distinction between existential and scientific validation. (p 136)

It seems that the combined lack of research training, lack of access to university resources, and the personality types of most psychodramatists largely contribute to the absence of psychodrama research.

Orkibi and Feniger-Schaal (2019) also comment on the issue of psychodrama credentialing and training in the research. Though many are teaching, learning, and practicing psychodrama without certification, the American Board of Examiners in Sociometry, Psychodrama, and Group Psychotherapy note that they have certified over 400 professionals (not all of which are therapists), which is a small fraction of the total number of certified practitioners in other modalities. Multiple CBT credentialing boards in the USA indicate that they have certified several thousand CBT therapists and that over a thousand scientific studies of CBT have been published. In comparison, the small number of certified psychodramatists only contributes to the limitations of conducting research studies on psychodrama. In an attempt to bridge the gap between psychodrama and CBT, Treadwell has developed a Cognitive Experiential Group Therapy (CEGT) model which unites CBT content with psychodrama processes (2020).

10.7   Moreno the Researcher

While some have critiqued Moreno for his lack of attention to research, a simple review of his early professional career demonstrates his experience as a researcher in various roles beginning in medical school where he was a research assistant in an Austrian psychiatric clinic (Moreno, 2019). In his autobiography, he later writes of this experience stating that "I have always been appalled at the idea of experimenting on helpless mental patients" (2019, p. 185). Upon completion of his medical degree, Moreno turned his research focus to the theater where he explored measurements of time, space, and interaction between his actors at the *Theater of Spontaneity*. After immigrating to the USA, he was appointed to the role of Director of Social Research of the New York State Department of Welfare where he primarily worked at Sing Sing Prison and New York State Training School for Girls. The presentation of his Sing Sing Prison research resulted in the *First Book on Group Psychotherapy* (1932/1957), and his research from the New York Training School for Girls became foundational to his sociometric method and his book *Who Shall Survive?* (1934).

Since Moreno's research in *Who Shall Survive?* (1934) was published, sociometry and psychodrama appear to have been considered for their potential as research methodologies. By 1940, other writers were commenting on the potential utility of sociometry and psychodrama as research instruments—"The research value of sociometry is not doubted. The sociometric tests and re-tests have given us reliable data in the form of. psychological networks, social atoms, isolates, and leadership structures in groups. In a different way, psychodrama offers to give us information about processes going on within the social atom" (Franz, 1940, p. 59). Moreno (1947) highlights the contributions of sociometry to sociology research with groups, intergroup relations, and social networks, while later in 1950, Borgatta highlights the potential of psychodrama and sociodrama in social psychology research. Moreno posits sociometry as a theory of human relations and "a central research technology for the social sciences" (1954, p. 185). It also appears that in the 1990s with the re-emergence of EBP and new computer technologies the utility of sociometry as research instruments was reconsidered (Treadwell et al., 1997). Various sociometric tools appear to have been integrated as research tools in the fields of education (Avramidis et al., 2017; Ferrandiz-Vindel & Jimenez, 2011), counseling (Koehly & Shivy, 1998), psychology (Terry, 2000), sociology (Tubaro et al., 2016), social network analysis (Grunspan et al., 2014; Hare, 1991; Jones, 2006; Treadwell et al., 1992), and business (Adams et al., 1994; Lucius & Kuhnert, 1997; Waber et al., 2007).

Moreno argues that the previous methodologies used for research in psychology, biology, and medicine were insufficient for human groups and that the scientific laboratory could not recreate real conditions for adequately researching interpersonal relations. Instead, he suggests the theater as a research vehicle—one that has already been used for centuries for "acting out of the problems of society of the human society in miniature within a setting removed from reality" (Moreno, 1954, p. 182). He also promotes sociometry as a research method that mitigates this problem of research in the social sciences:

> Until recently we had only two alternatives, the clinical method, maintaining the contact with social reality, however primitive the analysis of the scientific data might have been, or the laboratory method, overly scientific but sterile. But now we have a way out, a third alternative between these two extremes, the inhumanity of the experimental laboratory and the overhumanity and magic of the medical office; this way out is the sociometric revision of the experimental method. (Moreno, 1978, p. 679)

He writes that his new theory of research using sociometry and psychodrama offered two major shifts: "(1) Change the status of the research subjects and turn them into research partners and social investigators and (2) change the status of the social investigator and turn him into a research subject and participant actor" (1954, p. 182). Moreno's research philosophy mirrors his approach to group psychotherapy, elevating all participants to the same status as the facilitator.

Moreno's writings about research seem to reflect the method of Participatory Action Research (PAR), an inclusive approach to research that emphasizes community engagement in the research process while empowering participants as co-researchers and agents of social change (Kemmis et al., 2013). Most publications on the history of PAR attribute Kurt Lewin with its development in the 1940s; others have noted the influence Moreno had upon Lewin through his 1934 sociometry research in *Who Shall Survive?* and their multiple meetings in New York in 1935 (Greenwood, 2015; Gunz, 1996; Kemmis et al., 2013; Moreno, 1953, 2019; Renouvier, 1958). While some criticize Moreno for his lack of scientific rigor and his defiance of academic norms, in *The Sage Handbook of Action Research*, Greenwood (2015) acknowledges Moreno's often-forgotten contribution stating, "he did not abandon science but desired to create a humane social science" (p. 430).

It seems that when it came to the topic of research, Moreno primarily wrote of the *process* of using sociometry and psychodrama as research instruments rather than assessing the effectiveness of sociometry or psychodrama as psychotherapy approaches. Had he lived another decade and been influenced by the emerging empirical clinical practice movement of the late 1960s, we might speculate that he may have turned his attention to researching the effectiveness of his methods in psychotherapy. Others may argue against this citing his emphasis on psychodrama as much more than just an approach to psychotherapy, but a way of life. Nevertheless, social work's shift away from the psychoanalytic perspective toward an empirically validated approach in the 1960s was a missed opportunity for psychodrama to become embedded within the social work field—as outlined previously, social workers would have found psychodrama's philosophy and theory complimentary. Instead, social work turned to the empirically supported behavioral and later cognitive behavioral therapies as a new source of authority and a vehicle for professionalizing. Similar to social work's adoption of psychoanalytic theory in the 1930s as an attempt to establish itself as a recognized profession, this push to professionalize in the 1960s also further separated the fields of social work and psychodrama (Schwinger, 2014). As the wave of influence from the evidence-based practice movement in the 1990s and 2000s expanded, psychodrama in the USA simultaneously lost its popularity and momentum.

10.8 Conclusion

The evidence-based practice movement emerged with the goal of critically evaluating the effectiveness of practice to enhance the field and protect society from harmful practices. EBP challenges social work and psychodrama practitioners to reflect on the effectiveness of their approaches while considering how the growing bodies of research literature might guide practice. Social work's ongoing attempts to professionalize and obtain legitimacy within the larger field influenced its adoption of EBP and cognitive behavioral therapies which have, in some ways, threatened its core values. The prevalence of cognitive behavioral therapies in social work seems to have further marginalized psychodrama and sociometry while have failed to adequately respond to the demands of EBP in the USA. At the same time, it seems that social work and psychodrama find common ground in the complimentary nature of qualitative methods. Though Jacob Moreno's early career was research-oriented, he seemed entirely focused on using his methods as research processes rather than researching the effectiveness of them. His position that existential validation is superior to scientific validation seems to be replicated by the generations of psychodramatists that have come after him. Nevertheless, the past decade has seen an increase in quantitative psychodrama research, primarily in Asia and Europe, which has the potential of enhancing the scientific validity of psychodrama around the world. More psychodrama research is needed with higher-quality research designs to establish psychodrama as an evidence-based practice.

References

Adams, G. A., Elacqua, T. C., & Colarelli, S. M. (1994). The employment interview as a sociometric selection technique. *Journal of Group Psychotherapy, Psychodrama & Sociometry, 47*(3), 99–113.

Adams, K. B., Matto, H. C., & LeCroy, C. W. (2009). Limitations of evidence based practice for social work education: Unpacking the complexity. *Journal of Social Work Education, 45*(2), 165–186.

Alby, F., Angelici, G., Picinotti, S., & Zucchermaglio, C. (2017). A pilot study on an analytic psychodrama group for cancer patients and family members. *Rassegna di Psicologia, 34*(1), 67–77.

Arnevik, E., Wilberg, T., Urnes, Ø., Johansen, M., Monsen, J. T., & Karterud, S. (2009). Psychotherapy for personality disorders: Short-term day hospital psychotherapy versus outpatient individual therapy—A randomized controlled study. *European Psychiatry, 24,* 71–78.

Avinger, K., & Jones, R. (2007). Group treatment of sexually abused adolescent girls: A review of outcome studies. *American Journal of Family Therapy, 35,* 315–326.

Avramidis, E., Strogilos, V., Aroni, K., & Kantaraki, C. T. (2017). Using sociometric techniques to assess the social impacts of inclusion: Some methodological considerations. *Educational Research Review, 20,* 68–80.

Azoulay, B., & Orkibi, H. (2018). Helpful and hindering factors in psychodrama field training: A longitudinal mixed methods study of student development. *Frontiers in Psychology, 9,* 196.

Baker, F. A., Metcalf, O., Varker, T., & O'Donnell, M. (2018). A systematic review of the efficacy of creative arts therapies in the treatment of adults with PTSD. *Psychological Trauma: Theory, Research, Practice, and Policy, 10*(6), 643.

Bannister, A. (1990). *From hearing to healing: Working with the aftermath of childhood sexual abuse.* Chichester: Wiley.

Bannister, A. (1991). Learning to live again: Psychodramatic techniques with sexually abused young people. In P. Holmes & M. Karp (Eds.), *Psychodrama: Inspiration and technique.* London: Tavistock/Routledge.

Bannister, A. (1997). *The healing drama: Psychodrama and dramatherapy with abused children.* London: Free Association Books.

Barkowski, S., Schwartze, D., Strauss, B., Burlingame, G. M., Barth, J., & Rosendahl, J. (2016). Efficacy of group psychotherapy for social anxiety disorder: A meta-analysis of randomized-controlled trials. *Journal of Anxiety Disorders, 39,* 44–64.

Baumgartner, D. (1986). Sociodrama and the Vietnam combat veteran: A therapeutic release for a wartime experience. *Journal of Group Psychotherapy and Sociometry, 38,* 31–39.

Bendel, K. E. (2017). Social work and Moreno: A systematic review of psychodrama methods and implications. *ProQuest Dissertations and Theses.* Retrieved from https://proxy.library.upenn.edu:7450/docview/1920065271?accountid=14707.

Berger, R. (2010). EBP: Practitioners in search of evidence. *Journal of Social Work, 10*(2), 175–191.

Bisson, J. I., Roberts, N. P., Andrew, M., Cooper, R., & Lewis, C. (2013). Psychological therapies for chronic post-traumatic stress disorder (PTSD) in adults. *Cochrane Database of Systematic Reviews,* Issue 12. Art. No.: CD003388.

Bledsoe-Mansori, S. E., Manuel, J. I., Bellamy, J. L., Fang, L., Dinata, E., & Mullen, E. J. (2013). Implementing evidence-based practice: Practitioner assessment of an agency-based training program. *Journal of Evidence-Based Social Work, 10,* 73–90.

Borgatta, E. (1950). The use of psychodrama, sociodrama and related techniques in social psychological research. *Sociometry, 13*(3), 244–258.

Borntrager, C. F., Chorpita, B. F., Higa-McMillan, C., & Weisz, J. R. (2009). Provider attitudes toward evidence-based practices: Are the concerns with the evidence or with the manuals? *Psychiatric Services, 60*(5), 677–681.

Bourne, J., Andersen-Warren, M., & Hackett, S. (2018). A systematic review to investigate dramatherapy group work with working age adults who have a mental health problem. *The Arts in Psychotherapy, 61,* 1–9.

Briar, S. (1967). The current crisis in social casework. In A. M. Pins & the Editorial Committee of the National Conference on Social Welfare (Eds.), *Social Work Practice.* (pp. 19–33). New York: Columbia University Press.

Bronson, D. E., & Blythe, B. J. (1987). Computer support for single-case evaluation of practice. *Social Work Research and Abstracts, 23*(3), 10–13.

Buchanan, D., & Taylor, J. (1986). Jungian typology of professional psychodramatists: Myers-briggs type indicator analysis of certified psychodramatists. *Psychological Reports, 58*(2), 391–400.

Burge, M. (1996). The Vietnam veteran and the family 'both victims of post traumatic stress' – a psychodramatic perspective. *The Australian and Aotearoa New Zealand Psychodrama Association, 5*, 25–36.

Burlingame, G., Fuhriman, A., & Johnson, J. (2002). Cohesion in group psychotherapy. In J. C. Norcross (Ed.), *Psychotherapy relationships that work* (pp. 71–87). New York, NY: Oxford University Press.

Burlingame, G., Fuhriman, A., & Mosier, J. (2003). The differential effectiveness of group psychotherapy: A meta-analytic perspective. *Group Dynamics: Theory, Research, and Practice, 7*(1), 3–12.

Burlingame, G. M., & Jensen, J. L. (2017). Small group process and outcome research highlights: A 25-year perspective. *International Journal of Group Psychotherapy, 67*(1), S194–S218.

Burlingame, G., & Krogel, J. (2005). Relative efficacy of individual versus group psychotherapy. *International Journal of Group Psychotherapy, 55*(4), 607–611.

Burlingame, G., MacKenzie, K. R., & Strauss, B. (2004). Small group treatment: Evidence for effectiveness and mechanisms of change. *Handbook of Psychotherapy and Behavior Change* (pp. 647–696).

Burlingame, G. M., McClendon, D. T., & Yang, C. (2018). Cohesion in group therapy: A meta-analysis. *Psychotherapy, 55*(4), 384.

Burlingame, G., Strauss, B., & Joyce, A. (2013). Change mechanisms and effectiveness of small group treatments. In M. J. Lambert (Ed.), *Bergin and Garfield's handbook of psychotherapy and behavior change* (6th ed., pp. 640–689). New York, NY: Wiley.

Carbonell, D. M., & Parteleno-Barehmi, C. (1999). Psychodrama groups for girls coping with trauma. *The International Journal of Group Psychotherapy, 49*(3), 285–306.

Carpenter, P., & Sandberg, S. (1985). Further psychodrama with delinquent adolescents. *Adolescence, 20*, 599–604.

Chambless, D. L., & Hollon, S. D. (1998). Defining empirically supported therapies. *Journal of Consulting and Clinical Psychology, 66*(1), 7–18.

Cheetham, J. (1992). Evaluating social work effectiveness. *Research on Social Work Practice, 2*(3), 265–287.

Choi, H. J. (2003). *Psychodrama: Theory and practice.* Hakjisa: Seoul, Republic of Korea.

Clarke, K. M. (1993). Creation of meaning in incest survivors. *Journal of Cognitive Psychotherapy, 7*, 195–203.

Coco, G. L., Melchiori, F., Oieni, V., Infurna, M. R., Strauss, B., Schwartze, D., … & Gullo, S. (2019). Group treatment for substance use disorder in adults: A systematic review and meta-analysis of randomized-controlled trials. *Journal of Substance Abuse Treatment, 99*, 104–116.

Costa, E., Antonio, R., Soares, M., & Moreno, R. (2006). Psychodramatic psychotherapy combined with pharmacotherapy in major depressive disorder: an open and naturalistic study. *Revista Brasileira de Psiquiatria, 28*(1), 40–43.

Council on Social Work Education, Commission on Accreditation. (1988). *Handbook of accreditation standards and procedures.* Washington, D.C.: Council on Social Work Education.

Cruz, A., Sales, C., Alves, P., & Moita, G. (2018). The core techniques of Morenian psychodrama: A systematic review of literature. *Frontiers in Psychology, 9*, 1263. https://doi.org/10.3389/fpsyg.2018.01263.

Daemi, F., & Vasegh Rahimparvar, S. F. (2018). The Effects of Psychodrama on the Health of Adolescent Girls: A Systematic Review. *Journal of Client-Centered Nursing Care, 4*(1), 13–20.

Daniel, S. (2016). The usefulness of role reversal in one-to-one supervision: a qualitative research project using heuristic enquiry. In *Psychodrama. Empirical Research and Science 2* (pp. 235–253). Wiesbaden: Springer.

Dayton, T. (2005). *The Living Stage: A step-by-step guide to psychodrama, sociometry, and experiential group therapy.* Deerfield, FL: Health Communications Inc.

Dayton, T. (2015). *Neuro-psychodrama in the treatment of relational trauma: A strength-based, experiential model for healing PTSD.* Deerfield Beach, FL: Health Communications Inc.

Dehnavi, S., Ayazi, N. M., & Bajelan, M. (2015). The effectiveness of psychodrama in relapse prevention and reducing depression among opiate-dependent men. *Journal of Addiction Studies, 9*(34), 111–121.

Dehnavi, S., Hashemi, S. F., & Zadeh-Mohammadi, A. (2016). The effectiveness of psychodrama on reducing depression among multiple sclerosis patients. *International Journal of Behavioral Sciences, 9*(4), 32–35.

Dima, G., & Bucuță, M. D. (2016). The method of interpretative phenomenological analysis in psychodrama research. *Zeitschrift für Psychodrama und Soziometrie, 15*(1), 69–81.

Dogan, T. (2018). The effects of the psychodrama in instilling empathy and self-awareness: A pilot study. *PsyCh Journal.* https://doi.org/10.1002/pchj.228.

Drisko, J. W., & Grady, M. D. (2015). Evidence-based practice in social work: A contemporary perspective. *Clinical Social Work Journal, 43*(3), 274–282.

Dunphy, K., Mullane, S., & Jacobsson, M. (2013). *The effectiveness of expressive arts therapies: A review of the literature.* Melbourne: PACFA.

Elliott, R. (1996). Are client-centered/experiential therapies effective? A meta-analysis of outcome research. In U. Esser, H. Pabst, & G-W. Speierer (Eds.), *The power of the person-centered approach: New challenges-perspectives-answers* (pp. 125–138). Koln, Germany: GwG Verlag.

Elliott, R. (2001). Research on the effectiveness of humanistic therapies: A meta-analysis. In D. J. Cain & J. Seeman (Eds.), *Humanistic psychotherapies: Handbook of research and practice* (pp. 57–81). Washington, DC: American Psychological Association.

Elliott, R., & Freire, E. (2008). Person-centered/experiential therapies are highly effective: Summary of the 2008 meta-analysis. *Person-Centered Quarterly,* November 1–3.

Elliott, R., Greensberg, L., & Lietaer, G. (2004). Research on experiential psychotherapy. In M. Lambert, A. Bergin, & S. Garfield (Eds.), *Handbook of psychotherapy and behavior change.* New York, NY: Wiley.

Elliott, R., Watson, J., Greenberg, L. S., Timulak, L., & Freire, E. (2013). Research on humanistic-experiential psychotherapies. In M. J. Lambert (Ed.), *Bergin & Garfield's Handbook of psychotherapy and behavior change* (6th ed., pp. 495–538). New York: Wiley.

Erbay, L. G., Reyhani, İ., Ünal, S., Özcan, C., Özgöçer, T., Uçar, C., et al. (2018). Does psychodrama affect perceived stress, anxiety-depression scores and saliva cortisol in patients with depression? *Psychiatry Investigation, 15*(10), 970–975.

Feniger-Schaal, R., & Orkibi, H. (2020). Integrative systematic review of drama therapy intervention research. *Psychology of Aesthetics, Creativity, and the Arts, 14*(1), 68–80.

Ferrandiz-Vindel, I.-M., & Jimenez, B. C. (2011). The sociogram: The analysis of interpersonal relationships in higher education. *Journal of International Education Research (JIER), 7*(5), 9–14.

Fischer, J. (1973). Is casework effective? A Review. *Social Work, 18*(1), 5–20.

Fishcer, J. (1978). Does anything work? *Journal of Social Service Research, 1*(3), 215–243.

Fortune, A. E., Reid, W. J., & Miller, R. L., Jr. (2013). *Qualitative research in social work.* New York: Columbia University Press.

Franz, J. (1940). The place of the psychodrama in research. *Sociometry, 3*(1), 49–61.

Giacomucci, S. (2017). The sociodrama of life and death: Young adults and addiction treatment. *The Journal of Psychodrama, Sociometry, and Group Psychotherapy, 65*(1), 137–143. https://doi.org/10.12926/0731-1273-65.1.137.

Giacomucci, S. (2018). The trauma survivor's inner role atom: A clinical map for post-traumatic growth. *Journal of Psychodrama, Sociometry, and Group Psychotherapy, 66*(1), 115–129.

Giacomucci, S. (2019). *Social group work in action: A sociometry, psychodrama, and experiential trauma therapy curriculum.* Doctorate in Social Work (DSW) Dissertations. 124. https://repository.upenn.edu/cgi/viewcontent.cgi?article=1128&context=edissertations_sp2.

Giacomucci, S. (2020). Addiction, traumatic loss, and guilt: A case study resolving grief through psychodrama and sociometric connections. *The Arts in Psychotherapy, 67,* 101627. https://doi.org/10.1016/j.aip.2019.101627.

Giacomucci, S., Gera, S., Briggs, D., & Bass, K. (2018). Experiential addiction treatment: Creating positive connection through sociometry and Therapeutic Spiral Model safety structures. *Journal of Addiction and Addictive Disorders, 5,* 17. http://doi.org/10.24966/AAD-7276/100017.

Giacomucci, S., & Marquit, J. (2020). The effectiveness of trauma-focused psychodrama in the treatment of PTSD in inpatient substance abuse treatment. *Frontiers in Psychology, 11,* 896. https://dx.doi.org/10.3389%2Ffpsyg.2020.00896.

Giacomucci, S., & Stone, A. M. (2019). Being in two places at once: Renegotiating traumatic experience through the surplus reality of psychodrama. *Social Work with Groups, 42*(3), 184–196. https://doi.org/10.1080/01609513.2018.1533913.

Gilgun, J. (1994). Hand into glove. The grounded theory approach and social work practice research. In E. Sherman & W. J. Reid (Eds.), *Qualitative research in social work* (pp. 115–125). New York: Columbia University Press.

Glass, G. V. (1976). Primary, secondary, and meta-analysis of research. *Educational Researcher, 5*(10), 3–8.

Glisson, C. A. (1982). Notes on advanced social work education: Research teaching in social work doctoral programs. *Social Service Review, 56*(4), 629–639.

Goldstein, E. G., Miehls, D., & Ringel, S. (2009). *Advanced clinical social work practice: Relational principles and techniques.* New York, NY: Columbia University Press.

Gow, K., Lowe, R., & McVea, C. S. (2011). Corrective interpersonal experience in psychodrama group therapy: A comprehensive process analysis of significant therapeutic events. *Psychotherapy Research, 21*(4), 416–429.

Gow, K., & McVea, C. (2006). Healing a Mother's emotional pain: Protagonist and director recall of a therapeutic spiral model (TSM) session. *Journal of Group Psychotherapy, Psychodrama & Sociometry, 59*(1), 3–22.

Gray, M., Plath, D., & Webb, S. (2009). *Evidence-based social work: A critical stance.* New York: Routledge.

Greenberg, L. S. (2013). Anchoring the therapeutic spiral model into research on experiential psychotherapies. In K. Hudgins & F. Toscani (Eds.), *Healing world trauma with the therapeutic spiral model. Psychodramatic stories from the frontlines* (pp. 132–148). Philadelphia: Jessica Kingsley Publishing.

Greenberg, L. S., & Malcolm, W. (2002). Resolving unfinished business: Relating process to outcome. *Journal of Consulting and Clinical Psychology, 70,* 406–416.

Greenberg, L. S., Elliott, R., & Lietaer, G. (1994). Research on humanistic and experiential psychotherapies. In A. E. Bergin & S. L. Garfield (Eds.), *Handbook of psychotherapy and behavior change* (4th ed., pp. 509–539). New York: Wiley.

Greenberg, L. S., & Paivio, S. C. (1998). Allowing and accepting painful emotional experiences. *Journal of Group Psychotherapy, Psychodrama and Sociometry, 51*(2), 47.

Greenberg, L. S., Watson, J., & Lietaer, G. (1998). *Handbook of experiential psychotherapy.* New York: Guilford Press.

Greenwood, D. J. (2015). Evolutionary systems thinking: What Gregory Bateson, Kurt Lewin, and Jacob Moreno offered to action research that still remains to be learned. In H. Bradbury (Ed.), *Handbook of action research* (3rd ed., pp. 425–433). London: Sage Publications.

Grunspan, D. Z., Wiggins, B. L., & Goodreau, S. M. (2014). Understanding classrooms through social network analysis: A primer for social network analysis in education research. *CBE—Life Sciences Education, 13*(2), 167–178.

Gunz, J. (1996). Jacob L. Moreno and the origins of action research. *Educational Action Research, 4*(1), 145–148.

Hall, I. (1977). *The effects of an intensive weekend psychodrama vs. spaced psychodrama sessions on anxiety, distress and attitude toward group interaction in nursing students.* Unpublished doctoral dissertation, University of New Mexico.

Hare, A. P. (1991). Sociometry and small group research: A footnote to history. *Journal of Group Psychotherapy, Psychodrama & Sociometry, 44*(2), 87–91.

Harkins, L., Pritchard, C., Haskayne, D., Watson, A., & Beech, A. R. (2011). Evaluation of geese theatre's re-connect program: Addressing resettlement issues in prison. *International Journal of Offender Therapy and Comparative Criminology, 55*(4), 546–566.

Harrow, G. (1952). Psychodrama group therapy: Its effect upon the role behavior of schizophrenic patients. *Group Psychotherapy, 5,* 120–172.

Haynes, R., Devereaux, P., & Guyatt, G. (2002). Clinical expertise in the era of evidence based-medicine and patient choice. *Evidence-Based Medicine, 7,* 36–38.

Hintermeier, S. (2011). Qualitative psychodramaforschung. *Zeitschrift für Psychodrama und Soziometrie, 10*(1), 89–107.

Holmes, S. E., & Kivlighan, D. M., Jr. (2000). Comparison of therapeutic factors in group and individual treatment processes. *Journal of Counseling Psychology, 47*(4), 478–484. https://doi.org/10.1037/0022-0167.47.4.478.

Hudgins, M. K., & Drucker, K. (1998). The containing double as part of the therapeutic spiral model for treating trauma survivors. *The International Journal of Action Methods, 51*(2), 63–74.

Hudgins, M. K., Drucker, K., & Metcalf, K. (2000). The containing double: A clinically effective psychodrama intervention for PTSD. *The British Journal of Psychodrama and Sociodrama, 15*(1), 58–77.

Huntley, A. L., Araya, R., & Salisbury, C. (2012). Group psychological therapies for depression in the community: Systematic review and meta-analysis. *The British Journal of Psychiatry, 200*(3), 184–190.

Jones, D. (2006). Sociometry and social network analysis: Applications and implications. *Australian and Aotearoa New Zealand Psychodrama Association Journal, 15,* 76.

Jones, F. D., & Peters, H. N. (1952). An experimental evaluation of group psychotherapy. *Journal of Abnormal and Social Psychology, 47,* 345–353.

Kang, S. H., & Son, C. N. (2004). The effect of psychodrama on the alexithymia, somatization and quality of life of college students. *Korean Journal of Health Psychology, 9*(2), 243–263.

Karabilgin, O. S., Gokengin, G. B., Doğaner, İ., & Gokengin, D. (2012). The effect of psychodrama on people living with HIV/AIDS. *European Journal of Psychotherapy & Counselling, 14*(4), 317–333.

Karatas, Z. (2011). Investigating the effects of group practice performed using psychodrama techniques on adolescents' conflict resolution skills. *Educational Sciences: Theory and Practice, 11*(2), 609–614.

Karatas, Z., & Gokcakan, Z. (2009). A comparative investigation of the effects of cognitive-behavioral group practices and psychodrama on adolescent aggression. *Educational Sciences: Theory and Practice, 9*(3), 1441–1452.

Kellermann, P. F. (1987). Outcome research in classical psychodrama. *Small Group Research, 18*(4), 459–469.

Kellermann, P. F. (1992). *Focus on psychodrama: The therapeutic aspects of psychodrama.* London, UK: Jessica Kingsley.

Kemmis, S., McTaggart, R., & Nixon, R. (2013). *The action research planner: Doing critical participatory action research.* Chicago, IL: Springer.

Kipper, D., & Ritchie, T. (2003). The effectiveness of psychodramatic techniques: A meta-analysis. *Group Dynamics: Theory, Research and Practice, 7*(1), 13–25.

Kirk, K. (2016). Grasping the tail of a comet: Researching and writing about psychodrama in the 21st century. In *Psychodrama. Empirical Research and Science 2* (pp. 323–325). Wiesbaden: Springer.

Koehly, L. M., & Shivy, V. A. (1998). Social network analysis: A new methodology for counseling research. *Journal of Counseling Psychology, 45*(1), 3–17.

Kosters, M., Burlingame, G., Nachtigall, C., & Strauss, B. (2006). A meta-analytic review of the effectiveness of inpatient group psychotherapy. *Group Dynamics-Theory Research and Practice, 10*(2), 146–163.

Krishna, M., Lepping, P., Jones, S., & Lane, S. (2015). Systematic review and meta-analysis of group cognitive behavioural psychotherapy treatment for sub-clinical depression. *Asian Journal of Psychiatry, 16*, 7–16.

Laska, K. M., Gurman, A. S., & Wampold, B. E. (2014). Expanding the lens of evidence-based practice in psychotherapy: A common factors perspective. *Psychotherapy, 51*(4), 467.

Levine, P. A. (2010). *In an unspoken voice: How the body releases trauma and restores goodness.* Berkeley, CA: North Atlantic Books.

Lind, M., Renner, W., & Ottomeyer, K. (2006). Die Wirksamkeit psychodramatischer Gruppenther-apie bei traumatisierten MigrantInnen-eine Pilotstudie [How effective is psychodramatic group therapy with traumatized migrants? A pilot study]. *Zeitschrift für Psychotraumatologie und Psychologische Medizin, 4,* 75–91.

Lockwood, C., Page, T., & Conroy-Hiller, T. (2004). Effectiveness of individual therapy and group therapy in the treatment of schizophrenia. *JBI Reports, 2,* 309–338.

Lucius, R. H., & Kuhnert, K. W. (1997). Using sociometry to predict team performance in the work place. *The Journal of Psychology, 131*(1), 21–32.

Magill, M. (2006). The future of evidence in evidence-based practice: Who will answer the call for clinical relevance? *Journal of Social Work, 6*(2), 101–115.

Malchiodi, C. A. (2014). Neurobiology creative interventions, and childhood trauma. In C. A. Malchiodi (Ed.), *Creative interventions with traumatized children* (pp. 3–23). New York, NY: Guilford Press.

Manuel, J. I., Mullen, E. J., Fang, L., Bellamy, J. L., & Bledsoe, S. E. (2009). Preparing social work practitioners to use evidence-based practice. *Research on Social Work Practice, 19*(5), 613–627.

McDermut, W., Miller, I. W., & Brown, R. A. (2001). The efficacy of group psychotherapy for depression: A meta-analysis and review of the empirical research. *Clinical Psychology: Science and Practice, 8*(1), 98–116.

McNeece, C. A., & Thyer, B. A. (2004). Evidence-based practice and social work. *Journal of Evidence-Based Social Work, 1*(1), 7–25.

McRoberts, C., Burlingame, G., & Hoag, M. (1998). Comparative efficacy of individual and group psychotherapy: A meta-analytic perspective. *Group Dynamics: Theory, Research, and Practice, 2*(2), 101–117.

Menichetti, J., Giusti, L., Fossati, I., & Vegni, E. (2016). Adjustment to cancer: Exploring patients' experiences of participating in a psychodramatic group intervention. *European Journal of Cancer Care, 25*(5), 903–915.

Messer, S. B., & Wampold, B. E. (2002). Let's face facts: Common factors are more potent than specific therapy ingredients. *Clinical Psychology: Science and Practice, 9*(1), 21–25.

Moreno, J. L. (1934). *Who shall survive? A new approach to the problems of human interrelations.* Washington, D.C.: Nervous and Mental Disease Publishing Co.

Moreno, J. (1947). Contributions of sociometry to research methodology in sociology. *American Sociological Review, 12,* 287–292.

Moreno, J. (1953). How Kurt Lewin's "research center for group dynamics" started. *Sociometry, 16*(1), 101–104.

Moreno, J. (1954). Old and new trends in sociometry: Turning points in small group research. *Sociometry, 71*(2), 179–193.

Moreno, J. L. (1957). *The first book on group psychotherapy* (3rd ed.). Beacon, NY: Beacon House.

Moreno, J. L. (1978). *Who shall survive?: Foundations of sociometry, group psychotherapy and psychodrama* (3rd ed.). Beacon, NY: Beacon House.

Moreno, J. L. (2019). In E. Schreiber, S. Kelley, & S. Giacomucci (Eds.), *The autobiography of a genius.* United Kingdom: North West Psychodrama Association.

Mullings, B. (2017). *A literature review of the evidence for the effectiveness of experiential psychotherapies.* Melbourne: PACFA.

Nevonen, L., & Broberg, A. G. (2006). A comparison of sequenced individual and group psychotherapy for patients with bulimia nervosa. *International Journal of Eating Disorders, 39,* 117–127.

Nooripour, R., Rahmani, S., Tavalaei, S. A., Alikhani, M., & Hosseinian, S. (2016). Effectiveness of psychodrama on aggression of female addicts with bipolar personality. *J Addiction Prevention, 4*(1), 4.

Norcross, J. C., & Lampbert, M. J. (2011). Evidence-based therapy relationships. In J. C. Norcross (Ed.), *Psychological relationships that work: Evidence-based responsiveness* (2nd ed., pp. 3–21). New York: Oxford University Press.

O'Leary, E. M. M., Barrett, P., & Fjermestad, K. W. (2009). Cognitive-behavioral family treatment for childhood obsessive-compulsive disorder: A 7-year follow-up study. *Journal of Anxiety Disorders, 23,* 973–978.

Ogden, P., Pain, C., & Fisher, J. (2006). A sensorimotor approach to the treatment of trauma and dissociation. *Psychiatric Clinics of North America, 29*(1), 263–279.

Okpych, N. J., & Yu, J. L. (2014). A historical analysis of evidence-based practice in social work: The unfinished journey toward an empirically grounded profession. *Social Service Review, 88*(1), 3–58.

Orkibi, H., & Feniger-Schaal, R. (2019). Integrative systematic review of psychodrama psychotherapy research: Trends and methodological implications. *PLoS ONE, 14*(2), e0212575. https://doi.org/10.1371/journal.pone.0212575.

Ottomeyer, K., Wieser, M., mit einem Beitrag von Jorda, C. & unter Mitwirkung der AusbildungsleiterInnen für Psychodrama im ÖAGG. (1996). Dokumentation – Informationspapier über die metho¬denspezifische Ausrichtung des Psychodramas, Rollenspiels und der Soziometrie. Einleitung A. Schigutt. Psychodrama. *Zeitschrift für Theorie und Praxis, 9,* 185–222.

Padgett, D. K. (1998). Does the glove really fit? Qualitative research and clinical social work practice. *Social Work, 43*(4), 373–381.

Panas, L., Caspi, Y., Fournier, E., & McCarty, D. (2003). Performance measures for outpatient substance abuse services. *Journal of Substance Abuse Treatment, 25,* 271–278.

Paivio, S. C., & Greenberg, L. (1995). Resolving "unfinished business": Efficacy of experiential therapy using empty-chair dialogue. *Journal of Consulting and Clinical Psychology, 63,* 419–425.

Park, H. S., Lim S. J. (2002). The effects of psychodrama on depression level, social support, self-esteem, and stress in depressed college students. *Korean Journal of Psychodrama, 5*(1), 93–115.

Parrish, M. M. (1959). The effect of short-term psychodrama on chronic schizophrenic patients. *Group Psychotherapy, 12,* 15–26.

Pearson, M., & Burlingame, G. (2013). Cognitive approaches to group therapy: Prevention of relapse in major depressive and bipolar disorders. *International Journal of Group Psychotherapy, 63*(2), 303–309.

Petzold, H. (1979). *Psychodrama-therapie: Theorie, Methoden, Anwendung in der Arbeit mit alten Menschen.* Paderborn: Junfermann.

Pinter, G. (2001). Psychodrama training: A way to become a psychotherapist in Hungary. In P. Fontaine (Ed.), *Psychodrama training: A European view* (2nd ed.). Leuven: FEPTO Publications.

Rauch, S. L., van der Kolk, B. A., Fisler, R. E., et al. (1996). A symptom provocation study of posttraumatic stress disorder using positron emission tomography and script-driven imagery. *Archives of General Psychiatry, 53*(5), 380–387.

Rawlinson, J. W. (2000). Does psychodrama work? A review of the literature. *British Journal of Psychodrama and Sociometry, 15,* 67–101.

Reamer, F. J. (1992). The place of empiricism in social work. *Journal of Social Work Education, 28,* 260–269.

Renjilian, D. A., Perri, M. G., Nezu, A. M., McKelvey, W. F., Shermer, R. L., & Anton, S. D. (2001). Individual versus group therapy for obesity. *Journal of Consulting and Clinical Psychology, 69,* 717–721.

Renouvier, P. (1958). *The group psychotherapy movement: J.L. Moreno, its pioneer and founder.* Psychodrama and Group Psychotherapy Monographs, No. 33. Beacon, NY: Beacon House.

Rezaeian, M. P., Mazumdar, D. P., & Sen, A. K. (1997). The effectiveness of psychodrama in changing the attitudes among depressed patients. *Journal of Personality and Clinical Studies.*

Roselló, J., Bernal, G., & Rivera-Medina, C. (2008). Individual and group CBT and IPT for Puerto Rican adolescents with depressive symptoms. *Cultural Diversity and Ethnic Minority Psychology, 14,* 234–245.

Ridge, R. M. (2010). A literature review of psychodrama. *Journal of Group Psychotherapy, Psychodrama, and Sociometry.* Originally published in Ridge, R. M. (2007). *The body alchemy of psychodrama: A phenomenologically-based qualitative evaluation of a training manual for trainers and practitioners of psychodrama and group psychotherapy.* Union Institute and University, ProQuest Dissertations Publishing. Retrieved from: http://asgpp.org/pdf/Ridge%20Journal.pdf.

Sackett, D. L., Rosenberg, W. M. C., Gray, J. A. M., Haynes, R. B., & Richardson, W. S. (1996). Evidence-based medicine: What it is and what it isn't. *British Medical Journal, 312*(7023), 71–72.

Schmidt, B. (1978). *Selbsterfahrung im Psychodrama als methode der Sozialtherapie fur studenten.* Unpublished doctoral dissertation, University of Wurzburg.

Schnabel, K., & Reif, J. (2016). Ways to evaluate psychodramatic training. In C. Stadler, M. Wieser, & K. Kirk (Eds.), *Psychodrama: Empirical research and science* (Vol. 2, pp. 289–296). Wiesbaden: Springer.

Schramski, T. G., Feldman, C. A., Harvey, D. R., & Holiman, M. A. (1984). A comparative evaluation of group treatment in an adult correctional facility. *Journal of Group Psychotherapy, Psychodrama, & Sociometry, 36,* 133–147.

Shulman, L. (2016). Shifting the social work practice paradigm: The contribution of the Interactional Model. *Journal of Social Work Education, 52*(sup1), S16–S27.

Schwartze, D., Barkowski, S., Burlingame, G. M., Strauss, B., & Rosendahl, J. (2016). Efficacy of group psychotherapy for obsessive-compulsive disorder: A meta-analysis of randomized controlled trials. *Journal of Obsessive-Compulsive and Related Disorders, 10,* 49–61.

Schwartze, D., Barkowski, S., Strauss, B., Burlingame, G. M., Barth, J., & Rosendahl, J. (2017). Efficacy of group psychotherapy for panic disorder: Meta-analysis of randomized, controlled trials. *Group Dynamics: Theory, Research, and Practice, 21*(2), 77.

Schwartze, D., Barkowski, S., Strauss, B., Knaevelsrud, C., & Rosendahl, J. (2019). Efficacy of group psychotherapy for posttraumatic stress disorder: Systematic review and meta-analysis of randomized controlled trials. *Psychotherapy Research, 29*(4), 415–431.

Schwinger, T. (2014). Die Rolle des Psychodramas in der Sozialarbeit. *Zeitschrift für Psychodrama und Soziometrie, 13*(1), 257–273.

Sharma, N. (2017). Effect of psychodrama therapy on depression and anxiety of Juvenile Delinquents. *International Journal of Indian Psychology, 5*(1), 38–47.

Sharp, D. M., Power, K. G., & Swanson, V. (2004). A comparison of the efficacy and acceptability of group versus individual cognitive behaviour therapy in the treatment of panic disorder and agoraphobia in primary care. *Clinical Psychology and Psychotherapy, 11,* 73–82.

Shaw, I. G. R., & Holland, S. (2014). *Doing qualitative research in social work.* London: Sage.

Shim, J. S. (2002). *Psychodrama in improving the effects of interpersonal factors and treatment (Unpublished master's thesis).* Seoul, Republic of Korea: Korea University.

Shlonsky, A., & Gibbs, L. (2004). Will the real evidence-based practice please stand up? Teaching the process of evidence-based practice to the helping professions. *Brief Treatment and Crisis Intervention, 4*(2), 137–153.

Sloan, D. M., Feinstein, B., Gallagher, M. W., Beck, J. G., & Keane, T. M. (2013). Efficacy of group treatment for posttraumatic stress disorder: A meta-analysis. *Psychological Trauma: Theory, Research, Practice, and Policy, 5,* 176–183.

Smith, M. L., Glass, G. V., & Miller, T. I. (1980). *The benefits of psychotherapy.* Baltimore, MD: John Hopkins University Press.

Smokowsky, P., & Bacallao, M. (2009). Entre Dos Mundos/between two worlds youth violence prevention: Comparing psychodramatic and support group delivery formats. *Small Group Research, 40*(1), 3–27.

Somov, P. G. (2008). A psychodrama group for substance use relapse prevention training. *The Arts in Psychotherapy, 35*(2), 151–161.

Sproesser, E., Viana, M. A., Quagliato, E., & de Souza, E. (2010). The effect of psychotherapy in patients with PD: A controlled study. *Parkinsonism & Related Disorders, 16*(4), 298–300.

Souilm, N. M., & Ali, S. A. (2017). Effect of psychodrama on the severity of symptoms in depressed patients. *American Journal of Nursing Research, 5*(5), 158–164.

Tabib, S. L. (2017). *Effective psychodrama supervision a grounded theory study on senior supervisors' perspectives* (Doctoral dissertation, Lesley University). Expressive Therapies Dissertations. 4. https://digitalcommons.lesley.edu/expressive_dissertations/4.

Tarashoeva, G., Marinova-Djambazova, P., & Kojuharov, H. (2017). Effectiveness of psychodrama therapy in patients with panic disorders—Final results. *International Journal of Psychotherapy, 21,* 55–66.

Terry, R. (2000). Recent advances in measurement theory and the use of sociometric techniques. *New Directions for Child and Adolescent Development, 88,* 27–53.

Testoni, I., Bonelli, B., Biancalani, G., Zuliani, L., & Nava, F. A. (2020). *Psychodrama in attenuated custody prison-based treatment of substance dependence: The promotion of changes in wellbeing* (p. 101650). Spontaneity: Perceived Self-Efficacy, and Alexithymia. The Arts in Psychotherapy.

Testoni, I., Cecchini, C., Zulian, M., Guglielmin, M. S., Ronconi, L., Kirk, K., et al. (2018). Psychodrama in therapeutic communities for drug addiction: A study of four cases investigated using idiographic change process analysis. *The Arts in Psychotherapy, 61,* 10–20.

Terzioğlu, C., & Özkan, B. (2017). Psychodrama and the emotional state of women dealing with infertility. *Sex Disability, 36,* 87–99.

Treadwell, T. (2020). *Integrating CBT with experiential theory and practice: A group therapy workbook.* New York: Taylor & Francis.

Treadwell, T., Collins, L., & Stein, S. (1992). The Moreno social atom test—Revised (MSAT—R): A sociometric instrument measuring interpersonal networks. *Journal of Group Psychotherapy, Psychodrama & Sociometry, 45*(3), 122–124.

Treadwell, T., Kumar, V., Stein, S., & Prosnick, K. (1997). Sociometry: Tools for research and practice. *The Journal for Specialists in Group Work, 22*(1), 52–65.

Tubaro, P., Ryan, L., & D'angelo, A. (2016). The visual sociogram in qualitative and mixed-methods research. *Sociological Research Online, 21*(2), 180–197.

van de Kamp, M. M., Scheffers, M., Hatzmann, J., Emck, C., Cuijpers, P., & Beek, P. J. (2019). Body- and movement-oriented interventions for posttraumatic stress disorder: A systematic review and meta-analysis. *Journal of Traumatic Stress, 32*(6), 967–976.

van der Kolk, B. A. (2014). *The body keeps the score: Brain, mind, and body in the healing of trauma.* New York: Viking Press.

Veiga, S., Bertão, A., & Franco, V. (2015). Sociodrama in the training of social educators: An exploratory research. *The Journal of Psychodrama, Sociometry, and Group Psychotherapy, 63*(1), 47–64.

Waber, B. N., Olguin, D., Kim, T., Mohan, A., Ara, K., & Pentland, A. (2007). Organizational engineering using sociometric badges. *Social Science Research Network,* 1073342.

Wampold, B. E. (2005). Establishing specificity in psychotherapy scientifically: Design and evidence issues. *Clinical Psychology: Science and Practice, 12*(2), 194–197.

Wampold, B. E. (2012). Humanism as a common factor in psychotherapy. *Psychotherapy, 49*(4), 445.

Wang, Q., Ding, F., Chen, D., Zhang, X., Shen, K., Fan, Y., & Li, L. (2020). Intervention effect of psychodrama on depression and anxiety: A meta-analysis based on Chinese samples. *The Arts in Psychotherapy,* 101661.

White, E. W., Rosenblatt, E., Love, A., & Little, D. (1982). *Psychodrama and life skills: A treatment alternative in child abuse.* Unpublished manuscript, Toronto Center for Psychodrama and Sociometry.

Wieser, M. (2007). Studies on treatment effects of psychodrama psychotherapy. In C. Baim, Clark, J. Burmeister, & M. Maciel (Eds.), *Psychodrama: Advances in theory and practice* (pp. 271–292). New York: Routledge/Taylor & Francis Group.

Wike, T. L., Bledsoe, S. E., Manuel, J. I., Despard, M., Johnson, L. V., Bellamy, J. L., et al. (2014). Evidence-based practice in social work: Challenges and opportunities for clinicians and organizations. *Clinical Social Work Journal, 42*(2), 161–170.

Witkin, S. L. (1991). Empirical clinical practice: A critical analysis. *Social Work, 36*(2), 158–163.

Witkin, S. (2017). *Transforming social work: Social constructionist reflections on contemporary and enduring issues.* London: Palgrave.

Wood, D., Del Nuovo, A., Bucky, S. F., Schein, S., & Michalik, M. (1979). Psychodrama with an alcohol abuser population. *Group Psychotherapy, Psychodrama, & Sociometry, 32,* 75–88.

Yalom, I. D. (2002). *The gift of therapy: An open letter to a new generation of therapists and their patients.* New York: HarperCollins Publishers.

Yalom, I. D., & Leszcz, M. (2005). *The theory and practice of group psychotherapy* (5th ed.). New York, NY: Basic Books.

Part IV
Sociometry and Psychodrama in Social Group Work

Part IV devotes itself to the practice of sociometry and psychodrama in clinical social work with groups. The previous parts (Parts II and III) focused on philosophy, theory, and research of sociometry and psychodrama while the following collection of chapters will focus on practice. The chapters to come will describe various elements, interventions, and experiential processes with groups while also offering depictions of how these processes are used in social work practice. Examples from the author's social work practice experience will be offered to demonstrate the utilization of these experiential tools in action. With each experiential process, we will also explore its therapeutic benefits and limitations while offering practical suggestions and guidelines for social work practitioners to consider when employing sociometry and psychodrama into their practice.

Before we begin, it is important to acknowledge that experiential tools, especially psychodrama, can be unexpectedly powerful and impactful. They have the potential to promote great healing—and also the potential for inflicting serious harm for clients. This section on the practice of sociometry and psychodrama is meant to provide an introduction to these methods in social work practice but will not prepare readers to competently facilitate a full psychodrama process. Many students note that after reading about the various experiential sociometry processes and seeing them in action, they are able to implement them safely into their own groups. At the same time, it is not recommended that any practitioner attempt to facilitate a psychodrama until they have received sufficient training and supervision by a qualified psychodramatist.

There are multiple ways to find a certified psychodrama trainer near you; the simplest is to access the directory of your regional psychodrama credentialing body. Following is a list of some of the larger psychodrama credentialing bodies and professional societies along with their websites (although websites are not available for each association, many have active Facebook pages)—training institutes and individual trainers have not been included. There also appears to be no formal psychodrama society or association in any country in Africa, though psychodrama training groups meet regularly in Egypt and South Africa:

Trans-continental
• Ibero-American Forum of Psychodrama—www.iberopsicodramauy.com

- International Association of Group Psychotherapy and Group Processes, Psychodrama Section—www.iagp.com
- Federation of European Psychodrama Training Organizations—www.fepto.com

North America

- American Board of Examiners in Sociometry, Psychodrama and Group Psychotherapy—www.psychodramacertification.org
- American Society of Group Psychotherapy and Psychodrama—www.asgpp.org
- Association of Psychodrama, Sociometry, and Spontaneous Theater of Costa Rica—www.asistecostarica.jimdo.com
- Mexican School of Psychodrama and Sociometry—www.psicodrama.wixsite.com/emps/inicio

South America

- Argentine Psychodrama Society (SAP)
- Association of Psychodrama and Sociometry of Ecuadorian (APSE)
- Brazilian Association of Psychodrama and Sociodrama—www.abps.org.br
- Brazilian Federation of Psychodrama—www.febrap.org.br
- Paraguayan Association of Psychodrama and Group Psychotherapy
- Venezuelan School of Psychodrama (EVP)

Europe

- Psychodrama Association for Europe E.V.—www.psychodrama-for-europe.eu/
- Albanian Association for Psychodrama
- Association for Psychodrama in the Netherlands and Belgium—www.psychodrama.nu
- Association of Group Psychodrama and Psychotherapy (Spain)—www.assg.org
- Austrian Psychodrama Section—https://www.psychodrama-austria.at/
- Balkan Association in Psychodrama, Sociometry, and Group Psychotherapy—www.balkanpsychodramaedu.com
- British Psychodrama Association—www.psychodrama.org.uk
- Bulgarian Society for Psychodrama and Group Therapy—www.psychodrama-bg.org
- Danish Society of Psychodrama and Action Therapy—www.dp.dk/decentrale-enheder/dansk-psykodrama-selskab/
- Estonian Psychodrama Association—www.fepto.com/estonia
- German Psychodrama Association—www.psychodrama-deutschland.de
- Hungarian Psychodrama Association—www.pszichodrama.hu
- Italian Association of Morenian Psychodramatists—www.aipsim.it
- Nordic Board of Examiners in Psychodrama, Sociometry and Group Psychotherapy—www.nbbe.eu
- Polish Psychodrama Association—www.psychodrama.pl
- Portuguese Psychodrama Association—www.sociedadeportuguesapsicodrama.com
- Psychodrama Helvetia (Association of Interest of Swiss Psychodramatists)—www.pdh.ch/de/
- Psychodrama Society in Norway—www.psykodramaforeningen.no/
- Romanian Association of Classical Psychodrama—www.psihodramaclasica.ro

- (Romanian) Psychodrama Society "Jacob Moreno"—www.old.psihodrama.ro
- Russian Academy of Psychodrama and Spontaneous Training—www.academy-psychodrama.ru
- (Russia) Southern Regional Association of Psychodramatherapists—https://psycho drama-srpa.ru
- Spanish Association of Psychodrama—www.aepsicodrama.es
- Swedish Psychodrama Association—www.psykodrama.nu
- (Switzerland) Psychodrama Helvetia PDH—https://www.pdh.ch/de/

    Africa
- Egypt—though there is no national psychodrama association, there is an active psychodrama section of the Egyptian Association for Group Therapies and Processes (EAGT)—www.eagt.net

    Asia
- Chinese Psychodrama Association
- Hong Kong Psychodrama Association
- Israeli Association for Psychodrama—www.iafp.org.il
- Japan Psychodrama Association—www.psychodrama.jp
- Korean Association for Psychodrama and Sociodrama—www.kpsychodrama.com
- Taiwan Association of Psychodrama—www.taptaiwan.com.tw/
- Union of Turkish Psychodrama Institutes

    Australia
- Australian and Aotearoa New Zealand Psychodrama Association—www.aan zpa.org

Chapter 11
Experiential Sociometry Practice and Safety Structures with Groups

Abstract This chapter is devoted to the description and depiction of action sociometry processes and safety structures in group settings, especially in group therapy. Each of these is presented with considerations to theory, safety, and multiple examples of structured prompts for their application in diverse social work group settings. Experiential sociometry processes outlined include the use of small groups, spectrograms, locograms, floor checks, step-in sociometry, hand-on-shoulder soicograms, and the circle of strength safety structure. These action-based processes can be modified for use in any group setting to enliven the group experience.

Keywords Experiential sociometry · Spectrogram · Locogram · Floor check · Sociogram · Circle of strengths

A previous chapter explored sociometry as a theoretical system and a research methodology for exploring and understanding small groups, social networks, and society (see Chap. 5). This chapter is entirely devoted to the clinical practice of sociometry within group work and group therapy. In addition to five commonly used experiential sociometric processes (small groups, spectrograms, step-in sociometry, hands-on-shoulder sociometry, and locograms), this chapter will also present the circle of strength safety structure from the Therapeutic Spiral Model and the sociometric floor check instrument from the Relational Trauma Repair Model. While the emphasis of this chapter will be on in-person groups, content on adapting these methods for teletherapy will also be introduced throughout the text.

11.1 Clinical Applications of Sociometry

The clinical applications of sociometry include a variety of pen-to-paper activities that explore an individual's social atom or social network, or experiential action structures that explore the series of attractions, repulsions, similarities, and differences within the group (Hale, 1981, 2009). In the context of this discussion of

© The Author(s) 2021   215
S. Giacomucci, *Social Work, Sociometry, and Psychodrama*, Psychodrama in Counselling, Coaching and Education 1,
https://doi.org/10.1007/978-981-33-6342-7_11

group psychotherapy, clinical applications for groups will be primarily emphasized—though sociometric tools are also used in individual settings (see Chap. 16), community work (see Chap. 18), and education (see Chap. 20).

There are numerous other commonly used experiential sociometric group processes that are employed in clinical settings including dyadic or triadic sharing, spectrograms, locograms, floor checks, step-in sociometry, and hands-on-shoulder sociometry (Dayton, 2005, 2014, 2015; Giacomucci, 2017, 2018a, 2019, 2020b; Giacomucci et al., 2018; Hale, 1981, 2009; Hudgins & Toscani, 2013). Each of these processes can be modified with content appropriate for any population or chosen topic. In terms of clinical uses of sociometry, these sociometric tools often stand on their own as multidimensional action-based group processes that provide the group with an avenue to discover and enrich their connections with each other. Sociometry can also be employed with an objective of recognizing shared identity between group members including membership to privileged or oppressed groups (Nieto, 2010). These same sociometric action structures frequently serve as a group warm-up exercise before conducting a psychodrama but can be used in the beginning, middle, or ending stages of a group. Each of these experiential sociometry structures can be used for group assessment, exploration, intervention, and evaluation.

Regardless of which sociometry tool is being utilized, it is useful for both the group and the facilitator if a clinical map is employed. To cultivate an experience of safety, vulnerability, containment, and warming-up, it can help to select criteria for prompts while adhering to the three clinical maps for trauma (Chesner, 2020; Courtois & Ford, 2016; Herman, 1997; Giacomucci, 2018b; Hudgins & Toscani, 2013). Initial prompts would be simple and strengths-based with the goal of facilitating connection. The next prompt(s) invite the group to share deeper with a focus on difficult emotions, defense mechanisms, trauma, loss, addiction, or mental illness. And to finish, making an offer of prompt(s) that facilitate or engage with meaning-making, integration, future projection, and post-traumatic growth. Essentially, this clinical map starts with *positive* prompts, moves into *negative* prompts, and ends with *positive* prompts again. This process reflects the process of slowly moving in and out of difficult emotional content—called pendulation and titration described by trauma experts (Courtois & Ford, 2016; Herman, 1997; Levine, 2010; Shapiro, 2018; van der Kolk, 2014). While providing containment, direction, and safety for the larger group process, this practice may also help clients internalize a sense of containment, self-efficacy, and safety related to their trauma (Giacomucci & Marquit, 2020).

11.2 Dyads, Triads, and Small Groups

Moreno often wrote of the importance of dyadic connection within groups and suggested that group cohesion was a function of the number of reciprocated mutual choices within the group (Hale, 2009; Moreno, 1934). Consequently, the use of dyadic sharing and breaking the larger group into smaller pairs can help facilitate interpersonal connection, mutual aid, and overall group cohesion (Giacomucci, 2020b).

Using dyads, triads, or small breakout groups seems to be especially useful at the early stages of groups and when working with larger groups. Many clients do not feel comfortable sharing in front of large groups—using smaller groups allows for participants to feel safer as they are invited to share with one or two others. This process also mitigates the chances of one participant monopolizing the group discussion and preventing the more reluctant or introverted group members from actively engaging (Olesen et al., 2017). The process of a traditional talk-based group only permits one discussion to take place at a time, but using dyads or small groups allows for multiple discussions to take place concurrently. The nature of small group discussions, especially dyads, invokes a role demand for each participant to respond, attend to, support, and share with their partner—thus engaging in mutual aid. The process of utilizing small group discussion frees up the facilitator to move around the room and listen to or check in with each group. This allows the facilitator to take a less active role and indirectly reveals the facilitator's confidence, trust, and faith in each participant's ability to serve as a therapeutic agent for each other.

The method of choosing configurations of small groups or dyads can be modified depending on the facilitator's intention or the nature of the group. Partners or small groups can be assigned randomly, intentionally chosen by the facilitator, self-selected by participants, or chosen based on prompts. When inviting participants to self-select a partner or break into triads, participants are likely to choose the person(s) physically closest to them. Often, they are already sitting next to the group members that they feel most connected to so this may lead to already cohesive small groups and few new connections. Prompting participants to "partner with someone you do not know well" is a simple way to facilitate dyads ripe with new opportunities to connect.

In terms of the content of the discussion within the small groups, it helps to offer directed prompts related to the nature of the group or the therapeutic goals of the session guided by the aforementioned three-stage clinical map. Generally, 3–5 prompts seem to be sufficient for small group discussions in terms of adequately warming up the group without losing the interest of participants. Below are some examples of prompts following the aforementioned clinical map based on different topics for clinical groups:

Topic: Relationships

1. Share about one of your favorite relationships.
2. Share about a person who has helped you in some way recently.
3. Share about a relationship that you have difficulty or conflict in.
4. Share how you would a difficult relationship to be different in the future.
5. Share about one way you would like to change your behavior in relationships.

Topic: Emotions

1. Share a memory that gives you a positive feeling.
2. Share about the emotion that you have most difficulty with.
3. Share about ways you could respond to difficult emotions different in the future.

Topic: Mental Illness

1. Share about tools you have to cope with symptoms of mental illness.
2. Share about one role model for living with mental illness (personal, societal, archetypal, historical, religious, or even a fantasy character).
3. Share about how your mental illness impacts you.
4. Share about what you image your life would look like in the future without mental illness.

Topic: Trauma

1. Share about one strength you have that can help you work through your trauma.
2. Share about one step you have already taken toward healing from trauma.
3. Share about one way your trauma has negatively impacted you.
4. Share about one way you would like to grow from your trauma.
5. Share about one step you plan to take in the future toward healing from trauma.

Another method for facilitating dyadic connections within groups is to place cards, objects, or images in the center of the group space and ask participants to choose one based on a guiding prompt. Some prompts might include inviting participants to choose a card that can represent "your strength," "the next step on your journey of healing," "defense mechanism," "your spirituality," "your goal for today," or "your ideal self in the future." Once chosen, group members are instructed to share in dyads about their choice of cards and the symbolic representation. Sharing can be extended with new prompts and/or new partners to facilitate increased connection. This process can be done with any set of cards and used as a warm-up to any topic with various prompts.

The Therapeutic Spiral Model (TSM) utilizes this process of choosing cards to represent the role of the *observing ego*—sometimes called the *compassionate witness* or *caring observer* (Hudgins & Toscani, 2013; Lawrence, 2015). The observing ego is a concept, borrowed from Freud (1932), which in this context refers to the part of self that can accurately observe self and others without shame, blame, or judgment (Giacomucci, 2018b). In TSM groups, the cards are then placed on the walls of the group room to provide a conscious reminder of this role and its importance. The use of cards to concretize the observing ego, a strength, or any other positive role provides an anchor of safety for the group experience going forward (Giacomucci et al., 2018). The presence of the cards on the walls behind the group offers a sense of being contained as well as an already defined strengths-based role for the psychodrama director to utilize during the group if extra grounding is needed. TSM practitioners primarily use this process to concretize a psychodramatic role, but it is important to note here for the sociometric aspect of using cards or objects to cultivate dyadic sharing at the beginning of a group process. The experience of using small groups or dyads offers participants the opportunity to create new connections, deepen relationships, enhance their sense of belonging, warm up to a topic, and increase overall group cohesion.

11.3 Spectrograms

The spectrogram is essentially a group-as-a-whole assessment tool that allows the facilitator to efficiently gather information about the group while providing participants with the chance to see where they fit in within the group and to connect with each other. A spectrogram is an action-based self-assessment along a spectrum within the room. Facilitation of a spectrogram is done by designating two different objects or two opposite walls of the room to represent the beginning and end of the spectrum. Generally, one side is designated as a 0/10 or 0% and the opposite side as a 10/10 or 100% while emphasizing that the imaginary line between the poles includes every possibility between 0 to 10 and 0% to 100%. Participants are invited to physically place themselves on the imaginary line based on where they believe they belong when considering the prompt(s).

"box[Spectrogram Video] starts"
    The following video depicts the use of spectrograms with a live group.

http://www.phoenixtraumacenter.com/spectrograms/

"box[Spectrogram Video] ends"
    Some examples of spectrogram prompts following the aforementioned clinical map are depicted below:

Topic: Connection and Loss

1. How many supportive relationships do you have in your life today?
2. How much loss have you experienced in your life?
3. How well do you think you handle grief?
4. How resilient do you judge yourself to be?

Topic: Addiction and Recovery

1. How many resources (supports, coping skills, tools, etc.) do you have to help in your recovery?
2. How motivated are you today for your recovery?
3. How much has addiction impacted your life?
4. How hopeful are you for your future in recovery?

Topic: Inpatient Treatment Experiences

1. How many days have you been in inpatient treatment?
2. How connected do you feel to the inpatient community of clients?
3. How difficult has it been for you to remain in treatment?
4. How much progress do you feel you have made since the day of your entered treatment?

Topic: Stress and Self-care

1. How many tools for self-care do you have?

2. How often do you find yourself stressed out?
3. How much tolerance for stress do you judge yourself to have?
4. How many new strategies for coping with stress have you learned from the group?

Topic: Psychoeducation of Trauma

1. How curious are you to learn more about trauma?
2. How familiar are you with the common ways that trauma impacts people?

    a. How aware are you of how trauma has impacted you or your loved ones?

3. How knowledgeable are you in the different treatments and approaches to healing from trauma?

With each new prompt, it is helpful to change the axis of the spectrogram, using different areas in the room. This facilitates more physical movement and prevents participants from staying in the same physical place. Each prompt results in a new configuration of participants along the spectrogram. There are multiple ways to facilitate sharing. The simplest form of sharing is to have the group sharing in groups of 2–3 based on whoever is physically closest to them on the spectrogram. The use of dyadic sharing allows for everyone to share about why they are standing on the spectrogram at the point they are at without taking up too much time. Similarly, participants could be invited to share in clusters of larger groups about where they have chosen to stand on the spectrum. Another option is to ask for group members to share aloud to the group about their placement on the spectrogram. Other nonverbal ways to facilitate spectrogram sharing include with body posture, movement and gestures, or sound.

It is important to consider that the spectrogram is a self-assessment and how that may impact one's choices in the process (Giacomucci et al., 2018). There are spectrogram prompts where it would be advantageous to change the spectrum to a 1–10, or even a 5–10 spectrum. For example, when using the prompt "how resilient do you judge yourself to be?" with a group of trauma survivors, it may be empowering to limit the spectrogram to a 5–10 while indicating the belief that everyone in the room is at least of 5/10 in resilience whether they believe it or not. Most of the clients that social workers work with are struggling with trauma, loss, addiction, oppression, mental illness, or other forms of suffering and may have distorted judgments about themselves which will impact their self-assessment in the spectrogram process. When the facilitator notices this happening with a group member, it can be helpful to gently challenge the individual to reconsider or to reflect back to the group member where the facilitator would assess them to be on the spectrum. Another option would be to ask the group to share with the individual about where on the spectrogram they would assess that person to be based on the prompt—thus creating an opportunity for mutual aid.

A spectrogram prompt results in a distribution of group members along a continuum, sometimes with participants spread out, sometimes with clusters of participants in different places, and occasionally with isolates on the high or low end of the spectrum. When a prompt results in an obvious isolate on the spectrogram, it can be helpful to explore that person's experience at the group level. If they are an outlier on the higher end of a strengths-based prompt, they likely have important information that they could share to help the rest of the group. If they are an outlier on the lower end of a positive prompt, they might have questions about how to gain more understanding or competence related to the criteria. It can also be helpful to invite group members to raise their hands if they can remember a time in the past when they were at that point on the spectrogram and offer suggestions or identification with the person who is currently an outlier. A psychodramatist might also direct role reversals between group members on the spectrogram to have them explore what it is like to be at various spots. When participants have mobility limitations, the process can be modified by using an object to represent participants on the spectrogram or by having participants raise their hands to varying degrees (10/10 is as high as you can raise your hand; 0/10 is placing your hand on your lap) (Simmons, 2017). Spectrograms can also be easily modified for use during teletherapy or online teaching sessions by using the top and bottom of each participant's video feed as the top and bottom of the spectrum. Participants are simply instructed to place their hand along the vertical spectrum of their camera window to indicate where on the spectrogram they are.

Spectrograms allow the facilitator to meet the group where they are at in terms of their warm-up to a specific topic or their understanding of the topic. They are especially useful in psychoeducational sessions, training workshops, classrooms, and supervision groups to assess the knowledge level of participants at the start of the session. This gives the facilitator the chance to change the content of the session to meet the learning needs of the group (Giacomucci, 2018a). Spectrograms are also useful for evaluation in that the same spectrogram prompt could be asked at the beginning and end of a session or program or pen-to-paper assessments can be modified into experiential spectrograms (Giacomucci, 2020a).

11.4 Locograms

The locogram is a sociometry tool that offers a quick visual group assessment or democratic group vote in an experiential format based on different options or categories. As suggested by the prefix of the term *locogram*, this process is an exploration of choices using places in the room. While the spectrogram orients itself upon a spectrum, the locogram is oriented based on designated locations in the room. One of the simplest ways to facilitate a locogram is using the four corners of the room to each representing a different choice and asking participants to physically indicate their preference by standing at the corresponding location (Giacomucci, 2020a). Other styles of directing a locogram involve using objects or chairs to represent the various choices. Most locograms offer at least 3 options which usually include an option for "other"—this invites other suggestions from the group. Locograms are useful for quick assessments or group choices in action. They can be used for many purposes including choosing a topic, discerning when to take a break, making a group decision, assessing group preference, uncovering similarities, and exploring a group's warm-up.

"box[Floor Check Video] starts"

The following video depicts the use of floor check with a live group.

http://www.phoenixtraumacenter.com/floor-check/

"box[Floor Check Video] ends"

Here are some examples with the bullet points representing the different locations in the room (represented by the corners of the room or objects):

Purpose: Choosing a Topic in an Outpatient Group

- Anxiety
- Depression
- Trauma
- Other.

Purpose: Discerning What the Group is Warmed up for Next

- Discussion
- More sociometry
- Psychodrama
- Writing activity
- Other.

Purpose: Outpatient Group Decision About Holiday Scheduling Conflict

- Schedule the session on the holiday
- Cancel the session on the holiday
- Meet a different day that week
- Meet twice as long the following session
- Other.

Purpose: Uncovering Shared Experiences in School

- I hated school
- I loved school
- I had mixed feelings about school
- Other.

Purpose: Exploring Religious/Spiritual Beliefs

- Christianity
- Islam
- Judaism
- Buddhism

- Hinduism
- Non-religious spirituality
- Non-believer
- Shamanic
- Other.

The locogram can be used for a quick group-as-a-whole assessment and group choice, or for an exploration of shared perspective, experience, or identity. When facilitating a locogram, it helps to limit or expand the number of options based on the size of the group. For example, in the final example about religious/spiritual belief systems, the nine offered choices in the locogram would be useful in a large group setting as it would facilitate connection, but in a small group it could lead to multiple participants standing alone. In a smaller group, the choices might be modified to religious, spiritual, agnostic/atheist, and other. The facilitation of a locogram may or may not include sharing. If the goal is to make a quick group choice, then sharing is likely unnecessary. But if the goal is to facilitate connection and explore shared experience, then sharing is likely to be helpful.

A locogram can also be used in teletherapy groups and online teaching sessions. This could be done in a variety of ways including using a poll feature, instructing participants to write their choice/preference in the chat box, or assigning numbers to each locogram choice and instructing participants to indicate their choice/preference by showing the number of fingers that corresponds with their choice. If the technology platform utilized allows for breakout rooms, the facilitator can initiate breakout rooms which will allow for participants to talk about their shared preference/choice. This method of adapting the locogram for teletherapy or online sessions is identical to how the floor check is modified for online groups. The floor check, a similar sociometry tool that evolved from the locogram, is outlined in the next section.

11.5 Floor Checks

The floor check is an experiential psychosocial process in the Relational Trauma Repair Model (RTR) created by Dayton (2014, 2015). It was inspired by the locogram process of using various places in the room for different options—the primary difference is that with the floor check the facilitator utilizes printed pieces of paper to label the options and offers a series of prompts each involving sharing. The floor check expands choice-making potential with increased options that transcend here-and-now prompts into past or future-oriented questions. The floor check expands the process with continual groupings and clustering which offer exponentially more chances for individual reflection, choice-making, group connection, education, and healing. The floor check was developed, based on evolving research on trauma, grief, mental health, addiction, and post-traumatic growth, to meet the pressing needs within addiction treatment centers which were faced with shorter group times, larger group sizes, varying degrees of client vulnerability, and therapists with different levels of psychodrama training. When employing the floor check process, it is advantageous to construct prompts or floor check options with research-based content. This can be done by simply choosing floor check options that correspond to the recognized symptomatology of a diagnosis or evidence-based research findings, theories, or practices (as described by Dayton, 2014, 2015). Thus, the floor check offers a psychoeducational and therapeutic healing avenue for addressing symptomatology in an engaging and dynamic process involving intrapsychic and interpersonal explorations. The multiple, focused prompts in a floor check sociometrically align participants based on the content while providing a progression of spontaneous connection and healing.

With each prompt, participants physically place themselves at the paper that corresponds to their preference or response. A floor check prompt results in group members clustering in small groups based on shared experience for verbal sharing about their choice. The process, similar to the locogram, provides a group-as-a-whole assessment but also cultivates a deepening of sharing and connection between group members in small groups. Floor checks "put healing in the hands of the process itself rather than exclusively in the hands of the therapists" (2015, p. 10) while empowering participants to become therapeutic agents for each other and quickly activating the mutual aid within a group (Giacomucci, 2019, 2020a, 2020b).

Once a floor check is put into action and group members have physically indicated their choices, they are invited to share with whoever is standing with them. When participants are standing alone at a choice, the facilitator simply directs them to join others nearby for sharing about their choice. This process creates sociometrically configured small groups, opening up opportunities for social–emotional learning and healing. Similar to the use of dyads or small groups, it allows the director to take a passive role in the process and move around the room listening or checking in on each cluster of clients. Floor checks are versatile and can be used in any group context with nearly any topic.

"box[Floor Check Video] starts"

The following video depicts the use of floor check with a live group.

http://www.phoenixtraumacenter.com/floor-check/

"box[Floor Check Video] ends"

Some useful clinical examples are listed below (more detailed prompts available in Dayton, 2014) including prompts following the previously described clinical map:

Feeling Floor Check—Anger; Sadness; Fear; Guilt/Shame; Happiness; Other

1. Which feeling best describes your experience today?
2. Which feeling most characterized your experience last week?
3. Which feeling do you most try to avoid?
4. Which feeling is hardest for you to tolerate in others?
5. Which feeling have you gotten better with?

Relationships Floor Check—Family; Friends; Self; Groups/Communities; God/Higher Power; Other

1. Which relationship do you feel most supported by today?
2. Which relationship has the most conflict in it for you?
3. Which relationship has improved the most since you started therapy?
4. Which relationship would you like/need to work on today?

Defense Mechanisms Floor Check—Humor; Denial or Minimization; Rationalization or Intellectualization; Acting Out; Passive Aggression; Dissociation; Fight; Flight; Freeze; Other

1. Which defense do you feel you are most aware of using in your life today?
2. Which defense do you feel you have used the most in this group?
3. Which defense is most difficult for you to tolerate when someone else uses it?
4. Which defense do you no longer use as much as you used to?

Post-traumatic Stress Disorder Symptom Cluster Floor Check—Avoidance; Hyperarousal; Re-experiencing and Intrusions; Negative Mood and Cognitions

1. Which would you like to learn more about?
2. Which best describes how trauma has impacted you?
3. Which describes symptoms you previously experienced but now have effective coping skills for?

Domains of Post-traumatic Growth Floor Check—Personal Strength; Appreciation of Life; Relationships; Spiritual/Religious Growth; New Possibilities

1. Which domain do you feel you have grown in most?
2. Which domain do you feel you struggle with the most?
3. Which domain do you feel you could help someone in this group with?

The floor check can be modified for any group topic or theme that can be sectioned down into categories or choices. Other useful examples include the stages of change, the stages of grief, the tasks of resilience in ambiguous loss, mental health diagnoses, treatment themes, and strengths. This process is also valuable in educational spaces and can be used as an experiential teaching tool promoting reflection and the integration of concepts into personal experience (Giacomucci & Skolnik, in-press). In social work education, it can be used with the social work core values, social work practice areas, or content from other theories (Giacomucci, 2019). The floor check is a holistic instrument that effectively warms people up physically, emotionally, socially, and to the chosen topic. It can be utilized alone as a group process or as a warm-up to another group process such as a psychodrama, art therapy piece, or writing process.

11.6   Step-in Sociometry

The next sociometry process that we will explore is *step-in sociometry*—sometimes called *circle of similarities*. This experiential process is effective at quickly identifying shared experience or similarities in the group-as-a-whole (Archer, 2016). Buchanan (2016) notes that step-in sociometry is a newer addition to the sociometry toolbox in the 1970s from the New Games Movement (Fluegelman, 1976). Step-in sociometry is facilitated with the group stand in a circle. Prompts are offered with the instruction to step into the circle if you identify with the prompt. Prompts can be offered spontaneously, or the facilitator can ask participants to offer step-in prompts one at a time by going around the entire circle. It is helpful to encourage group members to make their statements broad and general rather than specific as it creates a more inclusive experience and prevents individuals from making statements so specific that they end up stepping in alone. If a prompt does result in one person alone in the circle, it is helpful to reframe the prompt in a more general way—for example, the prompt "I enjoy water color painting" could be generalized to "I enjoy creating art" which would result in more participants stepping in.

Either the facilitator offers prompts asking participants to physically step in if they identify, or group members take turns stepping in while making statements about themselves while others who identify also step in. Buchanan (2016) describes the latter as the *democratic approach* and the former as the *totalitarian approach* to step-in sociometry. This writer has discovered that the democratic approach is favorable in nearly all contexts. One exception where the totalitarian approach may be useful is when offering trauma-related prompts in a group where it could be harmful if the process goes too far into the trauma. The totalitarian approach would allow the facilitator to intentionally choose very broad trauma-related prompts that ensure the largest number of participants identify. In this context, the facilitator providing all of the prompts would contribute to group safety and containment. Another facilitation consideration is the facilitator's decision to participate in the process or not. The choice to participate or not, or participate in some rounds but not others, would come back to the facilitator's style, the goals for the group, the group population, and the group context. In some groups and with some prompts, it may be advantageous for the facilitator to participate which allows the group to connect with them while in other groups and with other prompts, it may be best for the director not to participate (Buchanan, 2016; Giacomucci, 2017).

In facilitating this process, it is also important to inform participants that they can choose whether they want to self-disclose or not on any given criteria as there may be prompts offered that some participants are willing to self-disclose while others may not be ready to do so (Buchanan, 2016). When a group member offers a prompt and other participants step in, it allows the group to visually see others who have a shared experience. Step-in sociometry makes the invisible connections and similarities within the group visible and conscious—thus increasing overall group connection and cohesion (Giacomucci et al., 2018). Once participants have stepped in, concretizing their connection to the prompt, the facilitator invites them to quietly acknowledge others who have stepped in then step back into the larger circle. This process seems to be appealing to introverted clients and young adults who find it to be an opportunity for peer identification without much verbal sharing (Giacomucci, 2017). Alternative ways of facilitating include inviting participants who have stepped into briefly share why they stepped in or to use sound or movement to express their connection to the prompt.

Step-in sociometry can be facilitated with multiple rounds, each with a larger theme, or as a single open-ended process without a theme. Both options have benefits. An open-ended step-in sociometry experience allows the group to choose any prompts which is likely to be revealing of the group's overall warm-up and allows the group to control the process (Archer, 2016). The method of using multiple rounds of step-in sociometry, each with themes, allows the facilitator to create a more directed and intentional group warm-up which may be most useful in clinical settings. When using multiple rounds of step-in sociometry, it is useful to follow the clinical map referenced previously.

"box[Step-in Sociometry Video] starts"

The following video depicts the use of step-in sociometry with a live group.

http://www.phoenixtraumacenter.com/step-in-sociometry/

"box[Step-in Sociometry Video] ends"

Below are some examples of different themes for step-in rounds:

Group: Inpatient Addiction Treatment

1. Step in and name something you like to do that is not related to your addiction.
2. Step in and name a consequence of your addiction (medical, emotional, social, legal, etc.).
3. Step in and share a hope or goal for your future in recovery from addiction.

Group: Immigrant Families

1. Step in and name something that is important to you about your family or culture.
2. Step in and label something that has been difficult for you related to immigration.
3. Step in and share a hope you have for you family going forward.

Group: Grief and Loss Group for Parents

1. Step in and share one thing that has helped you in your grief and loss.
2. Step in and share one difficult aspect related to your grief and loss.
3. Step in and share one goal for yourself and your family going forward in the grief process.

Group: Hospital-Based Cancer Support Group

1. Step in and share something about yourself beyond your medical condition.
2. Step in and share one difficult aspect of your cancer diagnosis.
3. Step in and name one goal for yourself going forward.

Group: High School Group

1. Step in and share something about yourself.
2. Step in and share one thing you find difficult about high school.
3. Step in and share something you would like to accomplish by the end of high school.

Group: New Social Work Graduate Students

1. Step in and share one thing that influenced your decision to get a graduate degree in social work.
2. Step in and name one fear you have about the graduate program.
3. Step in and name a professional role that you would like to have in the future.

Step-in sociometry cultivates curiosity, connection, and inclusion with the group experience and can be adapted for any topic or group setting (Buchanan, 2016; Giacomucci, 2020a). Archer (2016) provides an in-depth exploration of various ways to adapt step-in sociometry with groups that consist of participants with physical limitations including group members who are visually impaired, wheelchair bound, or on crutches. In larger groups, or group spaces where creating a circle is not possible, the step-in sociometry process is often modified to utilize standing up or raising hands instead (Archer, 2016).

Similar to the previously described experiential sociometry processes, step-in sociometry can be used as a warm-up or as a group process on its own. Furthermore, the utilization of step-in sociometry for closure, processing, and integration after a psychodrama enactment or other group process has been described (Giacomucci, 2017). This may be most useful in the context of large groups or when time is limited and a quick, efficient method for sharing is called for.

11.7 Hands-on-Shoulder Sociograms

Section 5.5 of this book covered the theoretical aspects of the sociogram which was one of the first sociometry instruments that Moreno developed (Moreno, 1934). A sociogram shows the number of times group members choose each other based on specific criteria. Using pen-to-paper sociometric tests, Moreno collected the written choices of participants and drew complex sociograms to depict the distribution of choices within the group. The hands-on-shoulder sociogram, sometimes called an action sociogram, moves this process from paper into the room as an experiential process. The action sociogram makes the unseen choices within a group conscious, revealing the invisible web of attractions, and repulsions within a group (Korshak & Shapiro, 2013). Hale (1981) refers to this as enhancing the sociometric consciousness of the group. While the previously described sociometry processes are all based on self-assessment, the sociogram is oriented on the assessment of others and the group's overall assessment of itself (Giacomucci, 2018a).

The experiential sociogram process prompts participants to put their hand on the shoulder of one other group member based on a specific prompt, simultaneously revealing the distribution of choices and preference within the group. This process uses physical touch, so it is important to check in with the group about their comfort level with physical touch and obtain their consent—especially when working with trauma survivors. Sometimes, the aforementioned sociometry processes are used to explore comfort with physical touch such as a spectrogram, locogram, or step-in sociometry. If participants are not comfortable with others putting their hand on their shoulder, the process can be amended by having participants indicate their choices by touching their shoe to the shoe of another, standing next to another, pointing at their choices, or holding a scarf or string to indicate their choice (Hudgins & Toscani, 2013; Olesen et al., 2017; Simmons, 2017). While some may find the experience of physical touch as uncomfortable or intolerable, others may find it soothing and comforting (Giacomucci et al., 2018). Moreno wrote of the power of physical touch and highlighted the practice wisdom from the field of nursing in this area (McIntosh, 2010; Moreno, 1972).

The sociogram often helps participants become aware of their own tendencies around choosing, waiting to be chosen, and prioritizing their first choice. When one has difficulty with making a choice, they are encouraged to choose with their intuition or to trust their tele. Once each participant has indicated their choice by putting their hand on the shoulder of one person in the room, the facilitator may offer a brief interpretation of the sociometric constellation—for example, noting prevalence of mutual choices, the equal distribution of choices, or the choices being highly concentrated with social stars and social isolates. The sociogram quickly depicts the distribution of criteria-specific social wealth within the group, thus highlighting the presence of tele and the sociodynamic effect. Then, participants are invited to share briefly with the person they chose about their reasoning for choosing them. This effectively increases interpersonal relationships within the group while enhancing overall group cohesion. Below are some examples of prompts tailored to different groups using the prescribed stages of the clinical map:

Group: Veterans Support Group

1. Place your hand on the shoulder of someone who you experienced take a significant step in their growth last month.
2. Place your hand on the shoulder of someone who has said something related to your identity as a veteran which was meaningful to you.
3. Place your hand on the shoulder of someone whose experience you would like to know more about.
4. Place your hand on the shoulder of someone who you could see yourself connecting with outside of group.

Group: Substance Use Relapse Prevention Group

1. Place your hand on the shoulder of someone who inspires you.
2. Place your hand on the shoulder of someone who has said something that worries you.

3. Place your hand on the shoulder of someone who you could call if you had a craving to use drugs.
4. Place your hand on the shoulder of someone who you could call for relationship advice.

Each of the given examples demonstrates the use of hands-on-shoulder sociogram criteria that is reality-based and sociometric-based. Another option is to offer prompts that are surplus reality and psychodramatically oriented. The difference between reality-based sociometric prompts and surplus reality-based psychodrama prompts is depicted below:

Sociometric Reality-Based Prompts:

A. Place your hand on the shoulder of someone who you experience as courageous.
B. Place your hand on the shoulder of someone who you look up to as a role model.
C. Place your hand on the shoulder of someone who reminds you of yourself.
D. Place your hand on the shoulder of someone who you would call for spiritual guidance.
E. Place your hand on the shoulder of someone who you experience as motherly.

Psychodramatic Surplus Reality-Based Prompts:

A. Place your hand on the shoulder of someone who you would choose to play the role of your courage.
B. Place your hand on the shoulder of someone who you would choose to play the role of one of your role models.
C. Place your hand on the shoulder of someone who you would choose to play the role of yourself.
D. Place your hand on the shoulder of someone who you would choose to play the role of God.
E. Place your hand on the shoulder of someone who you would choose to play the role of your mother.

Some find that psychodramatic prompts provide more distance and thus more safety for group members when choosing and being chosen. Psychodramatic prompts also have the benefit of getting participants warmed up to choosing roles in a psychodrama. Many practitioners employ both sociometric and psychodramatic prompts in their use of sociograms in groups. Below are some examples of mixed prompts:

Group: Depression Support

1. Place your hand on the shoulder of someone who you would has helped you feel comfortable in the group.
2. Place your hand on the shoulder of someone who you would choose to play the role of your resilience.
3. Place your hand on the shoulder of someone who has helped you understand depression better.

4. Place your hand on the shoulder of someone who you could call if your depression increased.
5. Place your hand on the shoulder of someone who you would choose to play the role of yourself in the future no longer experiencing depression.

Group: Healthy Relationships for Couples

1. Place your hand on the shoulder of someone whose sharing has helped you understand yourself better.
2. Place your hand on the shoulder of someone who you would choose to play the role of your willingness to work on your relationship.
3. Place your hand on the shoulder of someone whose love for their partner has inspired you.
4. Place your hand on the shoulder of someone who you would choose to play the role of your honesty or vulnerability.
5. Place your hand on the shoulder of someone who you would call if you needed support in the future.

While these are examples of prompts that could be offered in groups, it is important for the facilitator to remain attentive to the group process and to offer new prompts when needed to create a more inclusive experience. For example, if a facilitator notices that a participant repeatedly is unchosen, it would be important to spontaneously offer a new prompt that makes this person highly chosen. Group facilitators have a responsibility to be aware of the sociodynamic effect and to reverse its impact within the group to create an inclusive experience. While one may be unchosen in this group based on this criterion, they are almost certainly a social star when it comes to other criteria and in other groups. Korshak and Shapiro (2013) note that reversing the sharing in a sociogram is another method of reversing the sociodynamic effect. Rather than having participants *share their reason for choosing* another, the person chosen *shares their experience of being chosen* with the person choosing them. Moreno (2006) writes that the "essential reason for doing sociometric investigations is not just to make relationships visible and available for interpretation, but to reconstruct groups to maximize sociostasis and find some resolution to the problem of the unchosen and rejected" (p. 296).

At this point, it is important to note that of all of the experiential processes described in this chapter, the action sociogram has the most risk. Unless conducted attentively, spontaneously, and skillfully, the group may have a negative response to the hands-on-shoulder sociogram. This process is best utilized in higher functioning groups where participants are familiar with each other and have demonstrated a capacity for tolerating vulnerability and discomfort.

11.8   Circle of Strengths

The circle of strengths is a safety structure that originates from the Therapeutic Spiral Model (TSM) (Hudgins & Toscani, 2013). It is an experiential process of concretizing the collective strengths of the group and strongly compliments social work's strengths-based approach (Saleebey, 2012). Generally, this exercise begins with a large pile of scarves or other fabric in the center of the group room (though it can also be done with objects in the room or with pen/paper). As group members enter the room, the scarves spark their curiosity, playfulness, and creativity. One simple way of facilitating the circle of strengths is to have the group break up into dyads; if there are an odd number, the facilitator can join—this method of using dyads prevents anyone from being chosen last (Giacomucci et al., 2018). Participants are provided with psychoeducation on the importance of strengths and various types of strengths (intrapsychic, interpersonal, and transpersonal strengths). Participants are then asked to choose a scarf to represent a strength that they see in their partner and to present the strength to their partner one at a time while reminding their partner of examples of how they have demonstrated the strength. This provides a ritual for group members to practice healthy risks and vulnerability with each other based on positive criteria. The rest of the group witnesses the individual exchanges of strengths. As each strength is concretized (with scarves), they are placed on the floor of the group room, creating a large circle of strengths. This process can be repeated in new dyads or spontaneously between group members. The facilitator may choose to do one round in dyads, then a round where everyone identifies one of their own strengths, and finally a round where everyone concretizes a strength they experience in the group-as-a-whole.

The resulting circle of strengths on the floor serves as a conscious reminder of the individual and collective strengths within the group. They can be utilized by the facilitator later in the process if a group member becomes overwhelmed and might benefit from a reminder of their strengths. Symbolically, the circle is representative of the unity of the group and the ability of the collective group strengths to contain any participant's stories, experiences, trauma, or feelings. Logistically, the circle of strengths can serve as a stage for a future psychodrama in the group (Hudgins & Toscani, 2013).

The exercise was initially developed through the process of having group members choose scarves to symbolize their own personal strengths that they bring to the group. As TSM became utilized around the world, especially in Asia, this process evolved to become more culturally sensitive and new methods developed including having group members choose scarves to concretize the strengths they see in each other (Hudgins & Toscani, 2013). Novel methods for creating the circle of strengths continue to be developed including using short enactments of strengths, inviting group members to ask for reminders of specific strengths, and concretizing strengths of an organization or program. The experience of engaging in this process seems to significantly increase connections in the group, cultivate mutual aid, renegotiate one's sense of self, enhance group cohesion, and establish an "all in the same boat" mentality (Giacomucci, 2019, 2020b; Giacomucci et al., 2018; Shulman, 2010).

"box[Circle of Strengths Video] starts"
    The following video depicts the use of circle of strengths with a live group.

http://www.phoenixtraumacenter.com/circle-of-strengths/

"box[Circle of Strengths Video] ends"
    Some examples of statements from clients engaging in this process are provided below.

Interpersonal Recognitions of Strengths

- "I chose this for your courage because it is a strong and bold scarf. I have seen you demonstrate courage in the times you are vulnerable with us and in the stories you have shared about your childhood."
- "I chose this scarf to represent the compassion and kindness that I experience from you each time we are together. You always are friendly and are quick to offer support whenever anyone needs it—I know I can count on your support."
- "I picked this scarf to be your spirituality and the sense of purpose it gives you. It is clear that your spirituality is important to you and gives meaning to your life in the way you help others and maintain faith through uncertainty."

Acknowledging Personal Strengths

- "I chose this one to symbolize my resilience. Even though I have experienced hardship, I keep bouncing back and I survive no matter what."
- "This represents my relationship to my family. I believe family is the most important thing in life and they are always there to support me."
- "I chose this scarf for my ability to ground myself. I have learned breathing techniques and meditation which allow me to center myself internally even when things get chaotic."

Strengths in the Group-as-a-Whole

- "I chose this to represent our willingness to change. Everyone here demonstrates this strength each time you show up to group. Regardless of our failures or successes, we continue to be willing to change and grow."
- "I chose this colorful scarf to symbolize the diversity in this group. We all come from different walks of life and various backgrounds which gives us each a unique perspective that we bring to the group. I always learn new ways of looking at things because of you all."
- "I picked this scarf to represent the safety of this group. I usually don't trust people, but I know that this is a safe place and this group of people are worthy of my trust."

The circle of strength process can be quite powerful for participants and has the potential of tapping into strong emotions for some. As social workers, we often are working with traumatized, oppressed, and disenfranchised populations. The process of taking the time to recognize strengths can be incredibly restorative, especially for those that have been marginalized within society, dehumanized in their interpersonal relationships, or stuck in self-loathing. This process could be employed as a warm-up for a psychodrama or as its own group process. The circle of strengths can also be facilitated in online groups by having participants choose objects in their own room to concretize the strengths of others and themselves. It can also be adapted for use in community groups, supervision groups, student groups, and organizational settings to increase confidence and cohesion in a meaningful and strengths-based process.

11.9 Conclusion

The seven experiential sociometric processes outlined in this chapter provide social workers with essential strengths-based group tools that actively engage the group-as-a-whole. Each of these sociometric processes has their strengths and limitations, and is better equipped to meet different group work goals. For example, dyads, small groups, spectrograms, step-in sociometry, locograms, and floor checks are better equipped for early phases of a group to help initiate connection and sharing while the circle of strengths and hands-on-shoulder sociograms are best used once participants have already become more familiar with each other. Sociograms are superior compared to the other processes when it comes to uncovering the sociodynamic effect. Group choices are better decided with spectrograms, step-in sociometry, or locograms. Identifying where the group is at on the continuum of understanding or interest in a topic would best be done with spectrograms or locograms. Floor checks seem best equipped for psychoeducation and experiential teaching.

Each of these processes can be adapted for use with any topic, any population, any social work context, any type of group, any group size, and any phase of the group process. These experiential sociometry processes offer instruments for accessing the mutual aid that exists within all groups. Social workers are increasingly expected to facilitate group sessions in practice, while the provision of group work training has significantly decreased in graduate social work programs (Giacomucci, 2019; Skolnik-Basulto, 2016). These sociometry tools, with their countless applications, offer social workers with increased competencies to facilitate groups that keep participants engaged and active (Giacomucci & Stone, 2019). The utilization of sociometry in clinical settings offers the social worker a system that is complimentary to both the unique philosophies of social work and social group work. The integration of sociometry into the repertoire of social work with groups gives social group work the backing to further differentiate itself from group psychology, group counseling, and sociology.

References

Archer, M. (2016). Who, like me, loves to use the step-in circle? *The Journal of Psychodrama, Sociometry, and Group Psychotherapy, 64*(1), 79–82.

Buchanan, D. R. (2016). Practical applications of step-in sociometry: Increas-ing sociometric intelligence via self-disclosure and connection. *Journal of Psychodrama, Sociometry, and Group Psychotherapy, 64*, 71–78.

Chesner, A. (2020). Psychodrama and healing the traumatic wound. In A. Chesner & S. Lykou (Eds.), *Trauma in the creative and embodied therapies: When words are not enough* (pp. 69–80). London: Routledge.

Courtois, C. A., & Ford, J. D. (2016). *Treatment of complex trauma: A sequenced, relationship-based approach.* New York, NY: The Guildford Press.

Dayton, T. (2005). *The Living Stage: A step-by-step guide to psychodrama, sociometry, and experiential group therapy.* Deerfield, FL: Health Communications Inc.

Dayton, T. (2014). *Relational Trauma Repair (RTR) Therapist's Guide* (Revised ed.). New York, NY: Innerlook Inc.

Dayton, T. (2015). *Neuro-psychodrama in the treatment of relational trauma: A strength-based, experiential model for healing PTSD.* Deerfield Beach, FL: Health Communications Inc.

Fluegelman, A. (1976). *The new games book.* San Francisco, CA: New Games Foundation.

Freud, S. (1932). *The dissection of the psychical personality. Standard edition* (Vol. 22, pp. 67–80). London: Hogarth Press.

Giacomucci, S. (2017). The sociodrama of life or death: Young adults and addiction treatment. *Journal of Psychodrama, Sociometry, and Group Psychotherapy, 65*(1), 137–143. https://doi.org/10.12926/0731-1273-65.1.137.

Giacomucci, S. (2018a). Social work and sociometry: An integration of theory and clinical practice. *The Pennsylvania Social Worker, 39*(1), 14–16.

Giacomucci, S. (2018b). The trauma survivor's inner role atom: A clinical map for post-traumatic growth. *Journal of Psychodrama, Sociometry, and Group Psychotherapy, 66*(1), 115–129.

Giacomucci, S. (2019). *Social group work in action: A sociometry, psychodrama, and experiential trauma therapy curriculum.* Doctorate in Social Work (DSW) Dissertations. 124. https://repository.upenn.edu/cgi/viewcontent.cgi?article=1128&context=edissertations_sp2.

Giacomucci, S. (2020a). Addiction, traumatic loss, and guilt: A case study resolving grief through psychodrama and sociometric connections. *The Arts in Psychotherapy, 67*, 101627. https://doi.org/10.1016/j.aip.2019.101627.

Giacomucci, S. (2020b). Experiential sociometry in group work: Mutual aid for the group-as-a-whole. *Social Work with Groups, Advanced Online Publication.* https://doi.org/10.1080/01609513.2020.1747726.

Giacomucci, S., Gera, S., Briggs, D., & Bass, K. (2018). Experiential Addiction Treatment: Creating Positive Connection through Sociometry and Therapeutic Spiral Model Safety Structures. *Journal of Addiction and Addictive Disorders, 5*, 17. http://doi.org/10.24966/AAD-7276/100017.

Giacomucci, S., & Marquit, J. (2020). The effectiveness of trauma-focused psychodrama in the treatment of PTSD in inpatient substance abuse treatment. *Frontiers in Psychology, 11*, 896. https://dx.doi.org/10.3389%2Ffpsyg.2020.00896.

Giacomucci, S., & Skolnik, S. (in-press). The experiential social work educator: Integrating sociometry into the classroom environment. *Journal of Teaching Social Work.*

Giacomucci, S., & Stone, A. M. (2019). Being in two places at once: Renegotiating traumatic experience through the surplus reality of psychodrama. *Social Work with Groups, 42*(3), 184–196. https://doi.org/10.1080/01609513.2018.1533913.

Hale, A. E. (1981). *Conducting clinical sociometric explorations: A manual for psychodramatists and sociometrists.* Roanoke, VA: Royal Publishing Company.

Hale, A. E. (2009). Moreno's sociometry: Exploring interpersonal connection. *Group, 33*(4), 347–358.

Herman, J. L. (1997). *Trauma and recovery: The aftermath of violence—From domestic abuse to political terror*. New York: Basic Books.

Hudgins, M. K., & Toscani, F. (2013). *Healing world trauma with the therapeutic spiral model: Stories from the frontlines*. London: Jessica Kingsley Publishers.

Korshak, S. J., & Shapiro, M. (2013). Choosing the unchosen: counteracting the sociodynamic effect using complementary sharing. *The Journal of Psychodrama, Sociometry, and Group Psychotherapy, 61*(1), 7–15.

Lawrence, C. (2015). The caring observer: Creating self-compassion through psychodrama. *The Journal of Psychodrama, Sociometry, and Group Psychotherapy, 63*(1), 65–72.

Levine, P. A. (2010). *In an unspoken voice: How the body releases trauma and restores goodness*. Berkeley, CA: North Atlantic Books.

McIntosh, W. (2010). Walking with Moreno: A historical journey of psychodrama and nursing. *Australian and Aotearoa New Zealand Psychodrama Association Journal, 19,* 30.

Moreno, J. L. (1934). *Who shall survive? A new approach to the problems of human interrelations.* Washington, D.C.: Nervous and Mental Disease Publishing Co.

Moreno, J. L. (1972). *Psychodrama Volume 1* (4th ed.). New York: Beacon House.

Moreno, Z. (2006). The function of "tele" in human relations. In T. Horvatin & E. Shreiber (Eds.), *The quintessential Zerka: Writings by Zerka Toeman moreno on psychodrama, sociometry and group psychotherapy* (pp. 289–301). New York, NY: Routledge.

Nieto, L. (2010). Look behind you: Using anti-oppression models to inform a protagonist's psychodrama. In E. Leveton (Ed.), *Healing collective trauma using sociodrama and drama therapy* (pp. 103–125). New York: Springer Publishing Company.

Olesen, J., Campbell, J., & Gross, M. (2017). Using action methods to counter social isolation and shame among gay men. *Journal of Gay & Lesbian Social Services, 29*(2), 91–108.

Saleebey, D. (2012). *The strengths perspective in social work practice* (6th ed.). Boston: Pearson Education.

Shulman, L. (2010). *Dynamics and skills of group counseling*. Belmont, CA: Cengage Learning.

Simmons, D. (2017). Implementing sociometry in a long-term care institutional setting for the elderly: Exploring social relationships and choices. *The Journal of Psychodrama, Sociometry, and Group Psychotherapy, 65*(1), 85–98.

Shapiro, F. (2018). *Eye-movement desensitization and reprocessing (EMDR) therapy* (3rd ed.). New York: Guilford Press.

Skolnik-Basulto, S. (2016). *Coming together: A study of factors that influence social workers' connection to group work practice* (Order No. 10758221). Available from ProQuest Dissertations & Theses Global. (1988269052). Retrieved from https://proxy.library.upenn.edu/login?url=https://proxy.library.upenn.edu:2072/docview/1988269052?accountid=14707.

van der Kolk, B. A. (2014). *The body keeps the score: Brain, mind, and body in the healing of trauma*. New York: Viking Press.

Chapter 12
Warming-up, Sociometric Selection, and Therapeutic Factors

Abstract The content of this chapter is focused on the importance of the warming-up process, the sociometric selection of a group topic and protagonist, and Yalom's therapeutic factors as they relate to psychodrama groups. The warming-up process, often overlooked, is presented as integral to the success of any experiential structure. The role of the psychodrama director is described while presenting four sub-roles—therapist, analyst, group leader/sociometrist, and producer. The importance of contracting and the initial interview at the start of a psychodrama enactment are emphasized. Each of Yalom's therapeutic factors is introduced while identifying their significance in psychodrama practice.

Keywords Warming-up process · Sociometric selection · Therapeutic factors · Roles of director · Psychodrama warm-up

The content of this chapter explores the importance of the warm-up as it relates to both sociometry and psychodrama processes and specifically the choosing of a topic and protagonist of a psychodrama. The warming-up process will also be explored considering the psychodrama director, their role, and function in the group. The importance of a clinical contract will be touched upon as it relates to setting up a psychodrama enactment. The therapeutic factors of group psychotherapy (Yalom & Leszcz, 2005) will be outlined with their connection to Moreno's methods in the hopes of offering a bridge between these two group psychotherapy philosophies.

12.1 The Warming-up Process

Warming-up describes the process of preparing one's self for action. We cannot be in action if we have not first warmed up to it (Moreno, 1940). Moreno's concept of warming-up was borrowed from his theater work and implanted into his therapeutic work. The warming-up process for each act and for each person looks different and is experienced differently, even when resulting in the same action. Moreno defines the warming-up process as "the *operational* expression of spontaneity" (1953, p. 42). His Canon of Creativity, outlined in Sect. 4.4, depicts the warming-up process as a

© The Author(s) 2021

S. Giacomucci, *Social Work, Sociometry, and Psychodrama*, Psychodrama in Counselling, Coaching and Education 1,
https://doi.org/10.1007/978-981-33-6342-7_12

movement toward spontaneity and creativity. This warming-up process takes place on the individual level, the group level, and the societal level. While a warm-up may start with body movement, with thinking, or socializing, it inevitably comes to encompass the somatic, the psychological, and the social. The warm-up is a holistic biopsychosocial experience preparing one for intentional and spontaneous action.

The warm-up is the first phase of a psychodrama group, followed by the actual enactment. Moreno's emphasis on the warm-up is important to note—he often suggested that there was no such thing as a bad psychodrama, only poorly conducted warm-ups to it. Attempting a psychodrama without any warm-up is doomed to failure. Warm-ups can be unstructured or structured and vary from setting to setting. In clinical or educational spaces, the contract of the group may already be established by a set curriculum and the director may facilitate a structured warm-up toward the already established topic or goal. In an open-ended outpatient group or community event, the director may take an unstructured warm-up approach and assess the spontaneous warm-up of the group.

The warm-up used in a psychodrama group is most often some sort of sociometric process (Giacomucci, 2017; Giacomucci et al., 2018) (see examples from Chap. 11). Other warm-ups may include revisiting group norms, introductions, an educational lecture, verbal discussion, art, music, or drama/improv games involving movement. Contemporary psychodrama warm-up processes often employ the use of improv techniques, theater games, or drama therapy warm-ups based on spontaneity and playfulness (Blatner, 2013). The warming-up process helps to increase connections with group members while decreasing anxiety so spontaneity can emerge. In the warming-up process, the group often accesses a sense of playfulness, safety, cohesiveness, and a shared purpose for the session often emerges (Giacomucci, 2017, 2020b). Yablonsky (1952) describes the warming-up process as follows:

> An adequate "warming-up" process is the foundation of a successful group experiment of this type. An attempt is made to actively: (1) Create a "warm" feeling between all interacting members of the group. (2) Interest and involve the group into the experimental situation. (3) Have the experiment contribute something of personal value for all members of the group. (Yablonsky, 1952, p. 177)

It is also important to note that while the group-as-a-whole has its own collective warming-up process, so too does each individual within the group. Initially, group members likely arrive to the session with warm-ups to different topics or themes—making the group warm-up a fundamental precursor to a successful group therapy session. When clients are experienced as *resistant*, a psychodramatist understands them as *warmed-up to something else*.

12.2 Warming-up as Director

When it comes to warming-up, the warm-up of the director must be foremost. A director that is not warmed up will have difficulty providing an adequate warm-up for the group or properly assessing the group's direction of warm-up. Moreno writes that the psychodrama director must be the most spontaneous person in the group (1969). The director needs to be aware of the group's warm-up, the warm-up of each individual group member, and their own warm-up. Some psychodrama directors have their own rituals of warming-up, others warm up through preparation of the room and some through checking in with a co-facilitator, and others feed off of the group's warm-up. In many cases, the group warm-up is a parallel process of for the larger themes active within society or the community. Many psychodramatists use a collection of scarves to serve as props (used to concretize objects or roles) which may serve as transitional objects—memories of past successful psychodramas.

Kellermann (1992) describes four essential roles of the psychodrama director (see Fig. 12.1) which include:

1. **Therapist**—the agent of change providing influence through the use of self and the therapeutic relationship.
2. **Analyst** provides interpretation, assessment, and understanding; an integration of theory and clinical wisdom into practice.
3. **Group leader/sociometrist** maintains awareness of the group-as-a-whole and interpersonal relationships within the group, and holds leadership of the group managing boundaries, norms, and conflicts.
4. **Producer** attends to the aesthetics of the drama, staging, props, and the group space, and creatively uses props, the room, and roles as needed within the spontaneity of the psychodrama.

Fig. 12.1 The four roles of director

Therapist

Analyst

Producer

Sociometrist/
Group Leader

These four sub-roles collectively integrate to form the basis of a grounded and balanced psychodrama director. An imbalance between therapist and analyst can lead to a director that is too cognitive or practicing without theoretical guidance. A lack of group leadership and attention to sociometry results in fragmentation within the group and mistuned choices about the direction of the group warm-up. The absence of the producer role leads to limited creativity and the underutilization of surplus reality. Each of these four roles of director is essential. Most directors are well developed in some of these roles and less developed in others. In warming yourself up as a director, it may be helpful to reflect on which of the roles of director are you strongest and which might you need more warming-up for.

A unique aspect of the psychodrama training process is that the trainee learns by doing—thus by the time one is certified as a psychodramatist, they have experienced hundreds of psychodramas, done significant personal work as protagonist, and come to trust the power of the model. An experienced psychodramatist simply has faith in the process based on witnessing it work hundreds of times prior—"the director must trust the psychodrama method as the final arbiter and guide in the therapeutic process" (Moreno, 1965/2006, p. 110). This trust and faith in the psychodramatic approach reduce anxiety, thus enhancing spontaneity. Furthermore, the fact that a director has done multiple major pieces of their own personal work prior to directing other people's psychodramas is likely to decrease chances of countertransference influencing the process. Instead of countertransference, the director has more access to the tele within the group and is better able to facilitate the psychodrama. Zerka Moreno writes that when a director is able to trust the process and engage with spontaneity, "the psychodrama method becomes a flexible, all-embracing medium leading systematically to the heart of the patient's suffering, enabling the director, the protagonist, the auxiliary egos and the group members to become a cohesive force, welded into maximizing emotional learning" (1965/2006, p. 110).

12.3   Sociometric Selection of Topic and Protagonist

Once a group is adequately warmed up and is ready to move onto the enactment phase of the process, a topic and a protagonist must be chosen. There are four methods for choosing a protagonist: The protagonist self-selects, the director chooses, protagonists are scheduled in a uniform way, and the protagonist is sociometrically selected by the group (Dayton, 2005). The first three methods of choosing a protagonist risk having a protagonist that is not warmed up to be in the role or a protagonist whose topic is not aligned with the group's warm-up. In shorter group sessions, it may be necessary to use one of these methods for protagonist selection, but when possible, it is almost always best to sociometrically choose a protagonist and topic.

The protagonist selection process begins with a director describing the psychodrama process and highlighting the various role options for participants during the enactment—protagonist role, auxiliary role, or audience member role. Volunteers for protagonist are invited to step forward and briefly name their topic and goal for the psychodrama. Once each volunteer protagonist states their topic and goal, a locogram is facilitated by asking each group member to place their hand on the shoulder of (or stand next to) the volunteer protagonist whose topic would most help them today. In this process, it is important to clarify for participants that they choose solely on the content of the proposed topics and not on their relationships to the group members volunteering. Group members (especially those with codependent tendencies) tend to also choose based on who they feel *needs* to be protagonist, or who *deserves* to be protagonist. It is important that everyone makes the choice of topic that would most help them in the here-and-now. This ensures that the topic chosen best represents the group-as-a-whole and cultivates a sense of universality in the process for others. In this way, the protagonist becomes a representative of the group and through the psychodrama process the group can see themselves in the protagonist (Giacomucci & Stone, 2019). The sociometric protagonist selection largely contributes to the group-as-a-whole approach rather than doing individual therapy with a group audience (Giacomucci, 2019, 2020a). This method of choosing a topic and protagonist also promotes spontaneity and co-creation, empowers the group, enhances engagement, honors autonomy, and promotes a sense of co-responsibility of the group process. The democratic process of a sociometric protagonist selection in the here-and-now is meeting the group-as-a-whole where they are at.

After participants identify their choice for the psychodrama topic, they are usually invited to share in smaller groups why they chose the topic they chose—similar to the traditional locogram process. This provides each volunteer protagonist with a sense of connection to others who related to their topic. If a volunteer protagonist's topic was not chosen by anyone in the group, it can be helpful to simply ask the group to raise their hand if they can also relate to the unchosen topic which will initiate connection and inclusion for the unchosen protagonist volunteer. Then, they can be invited to indicate which of the other topics they could identify with and join that group for sharing. An experienced director at this point may take note of the unchosen topics and the group members who volunteered each with the intention of weaving these topics and group members into the psychodrama using clinical role assignments—this will be described in detail in Sect. 14.4.

12.4 Contracting and Initial Interview

Once a protagonist and a topic have been identified by the group through sociometric selection, it is time to set the parameters of the process and move into the psychodrama enactment. It can be helpful here to remind the protagonist that they have full control over the process and can choose to modify the pace or direction of the psychodrama if needed. The initial interview and contracting can be done through a short and simple verbal discussion where the director and protagonist become fully clear on the scope and purpose of the enactment to follow. The protagonist may be invited by the director to walk in a circle around the perimeter of the stage area while providing more information on their topic during the contracting and initial interview. This is often called a *walk and talk*. The contracting and initial interview serves multiple functions. It allows the director and the protagonist to connect, warm up to the topic, and warm up to each other while physically engaging together in movement (if walking and talking). At the same time, group members listening are able to warm up to the protagonist's topic and prepare themselves to support the process. In the initial interview, the director helps the protagonist define a clear contract for the goal of the enactment which will provide both containment and direction for the psychodrama. At this time, the director may also provide the protagonist and/or the group with information about their style of directing or what to expect in the psychodrama process (von Ameln & Becker-Ebel, 2020).

In the initial interview and contracting, it can be helpful to use the simple sociometry of asking group members to raise their hand when they hear the protagonist say anything that they identify with. This keeps the rest of the group actively engaged, further warms them up to hold future roles in the psychodrama, and demonstrates to the protagonist that the group can support them. The initial interview also is an opportunity for the director to interview the protagonist, assess the problem, ask important questions about the topic, and begin to warm up to the initial scene setting. This is the point where the group moves from reality into the surplus reality of the psychodrama.

12.5   Warming-up to Therapeutic Factors

The discussion of warming-up and directing a psychodrama group can be enhanced through consideration of the factors that promote change in group psychotherapy. Yalom and Leszcz (2005) outline these therapeutic factors of group psychotherapy in their seminal text *The Theory and Practice of Group Psychotherapy*:

1. Instillation of hope
2. Universality
3. Imparting information
4. Altruism
5. The corrective recapitulation of the primary family group
6. Development of socializing techniques
7. Imitative behavior
8. Interpersonal learning
9. Group cohesiveness
10. Catharsis
11. Existential factors.

At this point in the psychodrama group, as the group process shifts from sociometric warm-up, identifying a common theme, and contracting for the psychodrama enactment, multiple therapeutic factors have already been set in motion. The warming-up process in the psychodrama group often cultivates hope, universality, socializing techniques, group cohesion, and addresses existential factors related to the collective problems or goals of the group. The sociometric protagonist selection overtly enhances universality, altruism, and group cohesiveness. Fundamental goals of the psychodrama enactment will include imparting information, altruism, corrective recapitulation of the primary family group, imitative behavior, interpersonal learning, catharsis, and grappling with existential factors. The psychodramatic interventions of role-playing, doubling, and role reversal specifically boost the imparting of information, altruism, socializing techniques, imitative behavior, and interpersonal learning. And the final phase of the group, the sharing, prioritizes the instillation of hope moving forward, universality, imparting information, interpersonal learning, and existential factors. Awareness of these therapeutic factors in the psychodrama directing process can help the director consciously assess the needs of the group and guide the process in a way that these therapeutic factors materialize.

12.6 Therapeutic Factors in Group Therapy

The therapeutic factors outlined by Yalom and Leszcz have been largely adopted by the greater group psychotherapy world but rarely mentioned in psychodrama circles. The list of therapeutic factors above seems to have changed slightly in terms of terminology and the inclusion of new therapeutic factors over the past 30 years since Yalom's (1975) introduction of the therapeutic factors. Some psychodramatists have written about these therapeutic factors and their relationship to sociometry and psychodrama (Blatner, 2000; Holmes, 2015; Kellermann, 1985, 1987, 1992; Kim, 2002; Ron, 2018; Tomasulo, 2014; Yoon et al., 1998, 1999).

Some research has been conducted to explore participants' experience of these therapeutic factors in psychodrama. Kellermann's 1985 and 1987 studies both indicate that psychodrama participants and verbal group therapy participants perceive the same therapeutic factors to be helpful—*insight*, *catharsis*, and *interpersonal learning*. Yoon et al. (1998) explored experience of therapeutic factors with psychotic patients in a Korean partial hospitalization program. They found that all protagonists placed high value on *catharsis* and *the corrective recapitulation of the primary family group* as therapeutic factors, whereas the audience members placed high value on *universality* of the process. Additionally, they found that higher functioning patients valued *interpersonal learning* more, while lower functioning patients valued the therapeutic factor of *development of socializing techniques*. Yoon et al. (1999) conducted another study focused on large psychodrama sessions in inpatient psychiatry and explored differences in experiences of therapeutic factors based on roles—therapists, protagonists, auxiliary egos, participants in sharing, and audience. In their results, they found commonality across roles in the emphasis on *existential factors* and *the corrective recapitulation of the primary family group*. Differences were found in that participants stressed *the development of socializing techniques*, active participants (protagonists and auxiliary egos) valued *catharsis*, and audience members prioritized *identification* and *universality* as therapeutic factors.

Placing psychodrama within the larger field of group psychotherapy offers advantages, including new perspectives and language to understand what creates change in psychodrama. The therapeutic factors are one of the popular ways of conceptualizing group psychotherapy's mechanisms of change and thus may be useful to provide common language when discussing psychodrama as a group psychotherapy. Below are the eleven therapeutic factors (Yalom & Leszcz, 2005) with brief reflections on their infusion within the psychodrama group therapy experience.

12.6.1 Instillation of Hope

Hope is essential in the process of therapy and often a contributing factor that leads to clients reaching out for therapy or help. The instillation of hope can come in many forms including the client's faith in the therapist, in the group, in themselves, and even in the treatment methodology (Yalom & Leszcz, 2005). Group psychotherapy is unique in its ability to cultivate hope through the positive changes, observable growth, and the sharing of experience between group members with a similar problem. Psychodrama is unique in its ability to concretize hoped-for experiences or situations—or even hope itself, in the surplus reality of the psychodrama stage. In psychodrama group work, rather than the instillation of hope being an implicit and quiet process, it can be made explicit and put into action directly through an enactment of a psychodrama utilizing hope or other hopeful roles in the scene.

12.6.2 Universality

Many clients struggle with the feeling of isolation or aloneness in their painful experiences. This therapeutic factor refers to the acknowledgment of shared experience between group members. Universality provides a sense or normalization and validation that "there is no human deed or thought that lies fully outside the experience of other people" (Yalom & Leszcz, 2005, p. 6). Group psychotherapy is better equipped than individual therapy to instill a sense of universality—and perhaps experiential sociometry tools have a unique potential of cultivating the therapeutic factor of universality within groups. Through the use of step-in sociometry, spectrograms, floor checks, and small group discussions, a sense of universality emerges from the uncovering of sociometric connections. As noted above, the process of sociometric protagonist selection ensures a greater sense of universality regarding the psychodrama enactment as the protagonist represents the group-as-a-whole. Holmes (2015) also notes that the third phase of a psychodrama group, the sharing, helps with the discovery and integration of universality between participants.

12.6.3 Imparting Information

Within this category, Yalom and Leszcz (2005) include both didactic instruction from the facilitator and advice giving from participants. Didactic instruction provides participants with understanding, clarity, universality, and meaning making when it comes to conceptualizing their own experiences. While psychodramatists may be less likely to utilize didactic teaching in their groups, they may find that their action-based techniques can be easily modified into effective experiential teaching methods (Giacomucci, 2019). While the imparting of information is explicitly done through verbal methods in traditional group therapy, in psychodrama it is conveyed explicitly in words and action. Through each psychodrama enactment, information is imparted about role dynamics, the nature of psychosocial problems, and potential remedies. Each doubling statement is an attempt to offer the protagonist new information, insight, and enhanced expression into the situation. And through the experience of role reversal and role play, new information is imparted to participants through engagement with different roles. While other group therapy approaches often encourage advice giving between participants, many psychodramatists discourage it in favor of the sharing of personal experience.

12.6.4 Altruism

Altruism refers to the philosophy and action of selflessness and helping others. Social work with groups and psychodrama emphasize the centrality of altruistic mutual aid in the group process. Tomasulo (2014) writes that altruism often emerges spontaneously in groups through the reciprocity of helping one another. This process of helping another person in a group often has a positive effect on the helper—it is especially transformative for clients who previously believed they were worthless and had no value to offer others (Yalom & Leszcz, 2005). In a psychodrama group, altruism extends into the action of the psychodrama and is demonstrated by participants through their willingness to play roles, double, and offer sharing at the end of the process. Altruism and mutual aid between group members contribute to positive relationships, enhance universality, offer corrective relational experiences, highlight universality, and give hopes, information, and social learning. Most of the other therapeutic factors seem to intersect with altruism which validates the centrality of mutual aid in the approach to social group work and psychodrama.

12.6.5   The Corrective Recapitulation of the Primary Family Group

Yalom and Leszcz write that nearly all patients "have a background of a highly unsatisfactory experience in their first and most important group: the primary family" (2005, p. 15). The process of engaging in group therapy unconsciously simulates the family experience resulting in unconscious role enactments and relational reenactments with opportunities for corrective emotional experiences. Tomasulo (2014) suggests that there is no more important therapeutic factor than this as it allows participants to heal from the past and explore new ways of being in relationship. While these reenactments are often unconscious in group psychotherapy, psychodrama makes them conscious and explicit while providing corrective emotional experiences (Blatner, 2000; Giacomucci & Stone, 2019). Many psychodramas even involve directly enacting scenes from one's family life which offers opportunity to renegotiate their relationships with family members on the psychodrama stage.

12.6.6   Development of Socializing Techniques

The learning of techniques for socializing is another process that happens implicitly in group psychotherapy which can be made more explicit through psychodramatic techniques—especially role play, role reversal, doubling, and role training (Blatner, 2000; Holmes, 2015; Yalom & Leszcz, 2005). The inherently social aspect of group work helps participants consciously and unconsciously evaluate their social skills and develop new ones that can be practiced in the group process. Yalom notes that many participants have maladaptive social skills which contribute to their isolation and rejection by others. The group provides everyone with a plethora of opportunities to socialize in new and more adaptive ways. The significance of this therapeutic factor may vary from group to group—inpatient groups may place more emphasis on this while higher functioning outpatient groups may attend to this less.

12.6.7   Imitative Behavior

Human nature is such that we learn by seeing and imitating others—this is described as the role taking phase of role development in Morenean philosophy. Mirror neurons seem to play a role in this mechanism of learning through role models. Participants may imitate the behavior and communication styles of the therapist or others in the group. Yalom notes that group members may "try on" different ways of being or doing demonstrated by others in the process. In psychodrama, this process becomes explicit through the mechanisms of the double, the mirror, and the role reversal. Doubling essentially uses the imitation of behavior in novel and adaptive ways based on the situation in the enactment. Audience members in the psychodrama process may also benefit from the psychodrama through imitating the behavior of others from the surplus reality scene in their real life.

12.6.8 Interpersonal Learning

Yalom and Leszcz (2005) describe three aspects of interpersonal learning including the importance of relationships, the corrective emotional experience, and the group as its own social microcosm. Here, we find much overlap in these three aspects with the value systems of social work and sociometry. The importance of human relationships is highlighted through the group process where past relational abandonments or traumas can be corrected with new positive relational experiences. The concept of the group as its own social microcosm describes the phenomenon of group members inevitably reenacting the relational patterns from their life in the group itself. Yalom writes "There is no need for them to describe or give a detailed history of their pathology: they will sooner or later enact it before the other group members' eyes" (2005, p. 32). They go on to write that the more spontaneous the group is, the more likely their core issues will be evoked and addressed in an authentic manner. The acknowledgment of the group as a social microcosm for each individual's social interactions—a parallel process between their way of relating to others—creates ripe possibilities for interpersonal learning and change. In this way, transference is used as a tool for change in the group.

In relation to this therapeutic factor, sociometry provides group facilitators with a toolbox of experiential processes that allow for here-and-now assessment of the nature of interpersonal relationships within the group and interventions to enhance them. Psychodrama is unique in its ability to offer embodied corrective experiences in surplus reality where even the impossible becomes can be experienced (Giacomucci, 2018; Giacomucci & Stone, 2019). Yalom's concept of the social microcosm seems to relate to the way Moreno writes of the social atom as being replicated by individuals throughout their life. Perhaps Moreno's contribution of the concept of tele and its relationship to transference could offer a deepened understanding of the social microcosm and the social phenomenon that contribute to its development.

12.6.9 Group Cohesiveness

This factor is evidenced by a sense of collective belonging, connection, and an "all in the same boat" experience between group members. Yalom and Leszcz indicate its importance in the statement that "cohesiveness is the group therapy analogue to the relationship in individual therapy" (2005, p. 53). Group cohesiveness reflects the degree of influence that the group exerts upon its members. Yalom (1985) notes that cohesion in the group lends itself to healthy risk taking, self-disclosure, expression, and increased self-esteem. Group cohesion, trust, and safety are intimately connected in the group-as-a-whole experience. Sociometry offers group workers with unique tools for assessing the sociodynamics and cohesiveness of the group while promoting enhanced connection. The sociometric selection of a psychodrama topic and protagonist seems to have a role in not only establishing universality within the group, but also instituting group cohesion.

12.6.10   Catharsis

Yalom and Leszcz (2005) echo Moreno's descriptions of catharsis as being essential in the change process, but by itself inadequate. Lieberman et al. (1973) found in a group therapy study that catharsis was valued by participants but only effectively created change when linked with cognitive learning. Catharsis as it relates to psychodrama has been extensively covered in Sect. 6.2 with the differentiations between catharsis of abreaction, catharsis of integration, actor catharsis, and audience catharsis. Psychodrama seems to offer an enhanced form of catharsis due to its experiential, somatic, and action-based methodology (Moreno & Enneis, 1950; Nolte, 2014). Moreno reminds us that catharsis is related to spontaneity and the social experience of the group members in connection with each other (1940, 1972). Since Breuer and Freud's seminal work on catharsis (1895/1957), Moreno may have contributed more than anyone to our understanding of catharsis in group therapy (Moreno, 1971).

12.6.11   Existential Factors

Yalom completes his list with existential factors which describes the encounter with human experience and basic philosophical elements of existence—including death, suffering, responsibility, freedom, consequences, isolation, purpose, and meaning. Tomasulo (2014) suggests including spirituality into the discussion of these existential factors. Yalom reports that every research study on his therapeutic factors resulted in participants ranking existential factors in the upper 50% in terms of value (Yalom & Leszcz, 2005). Holmes (2015) notes that both Yalom and Moreno's philosophies emerged from the same foundations of existentialist philosophy. In his autobiography, Moreno (2019) describes his founding of the *Religion of the Encounter* and the *Daimon* journal as part of the existentialist movement in Vienna. Most clients that seek psychotherapy are grappling with existential issues related to suffering, mortality, responsibility, spirituality, isolation, meaning, or purpose. Group psychotherapy may offer a unique experience in sharing and normalizing existential conflict. Psychodrama may be unique in its ability to offer participants with direct encounters with death, purpose, God, and other existential roles on the psychodrama stage.

12.7   Conclusion

The warming-up process is essential to any successful group, especially a psychodrama enactment. Psychodrama directors must develop effective warm-up methods for their groups and for themselves. In a psychodrama group, the warming-up process culminates with a protagonist selection—usually through sociometric means. A sociometrically selected topic and protagonist ensures that the topic represents the group-as-a-whole and provides an optimal sense of relatability, identification, and universality. Attention to the warming-up process and the uses of sociometrically selected topics are two foundational psychodrama skills that social workers would profit from adopting into their practice.

Yalom's eleven therapeutic factors of group psychotherapy have been largely integrated into group psychotherapy practice but have not been absorbed by psychodrama practitioners or social group workers. These therapeutic factors may even present more explicitly in groups based on sociometry and psychodrama. The therapeutic factors provide psychodramatists and social workers with a common language when conversing with other group therapists. Moreno seems to have developed dozens of his own terms related to group therapy which may limit communication between psychodramatists and other group workers. These therapeutic factors offer a bridge in understanding, language, and conceptualization. A search of the *Social Work with Groups Journal* article titles from 1978 to 2020 (issue 2) only results in two articles that have the term "therapeutic factors" or "curative factors" in their titles. The same search resulted in zero titles in the Journal of Psychodrama, Sociometry, and Group Psychotherapy. In conclusion, both psychodramatists and social group workers may benefit from the adoption of Yalom's therapeutic factors into their conceptual framework.

References

Blatner, A. (2000). *Foundations of psychodrama: History, theory, and practice* (4th ed.). New York City: Springer Publishing Company.

Blatner, A. (2013). Warming-up, action methods, and related processes. *The Journal of Psychodrama, Sociometry, and Group Psychotherapy, 61*(1), 43–50.

Breuer, J. & Freud, S. (1895/1957). *Studies on hysteria.* New York: Basic Books.

Dayton, T. (2005). *The Living Stage: A step-by-step guide to psychodrama, sociometry, and experiential group therapy.* Deerfield, FL: Health Communications Inc.

Giacomucci, S. (2017). The sociodrama of life or death: Young adults and addiction treatment. *Journal of Psychodrama, Sociometry, and Group Psychotherapy, 65*(1), 137–143. https://doi.org/10.12926/0731-1273-65.1.137.

Giacomucci, S. (2018). The trauma survivor's inner role atom: A clinical map for post-traumatic growth. *Journal of Psychodrama, Sociometry, and Group Psychotherapy, 66*(1), 115–129.

Giacomucci, S. (2019). *Social group work in action: A sociometry, psychodrama, and experiential trauma therapy curriculum.* Doctorate in Social Work (DSW) Dissertations. 124. https://repository.upenn.edu/cgi/viewcontent.cgi?article=1128&context=edissertations_sp2.

Giacomucci, S. (2020a). Addiction, traumatic loss, and guilt: A case study resolving grief through psychodrama and sociometric connections. *The Arts in Psychotherapy, 67,* 101627. https://doi.org/10.1016/j.aip.2019.101627.

Giacomucci, S. (2020b). Experiential sociometry in group work: Mutual aid for the group-as-a-whole. *Social Work with Groups, Advanced online publication.* https://doi.org/10.1080/01609513.2020.1747726.

Giacomucci, S., Gera, S., Briggs, D., & Bass, K. (2018). Experiential addiction treatment: Creating positive connection through sociometry and therapeutic spiral model safety structures. *Journal of Addiction and Addictive Disorders,* 5, 17. http://doi.org/10.24966/AAD-7276/100017.

Giacomucci, S., & Stone, A. M. (2019). Being in two places at once: Renegotiating traumatic experience through the surplus reality of psychodrama. *Social Work with Groups, 42*(3), 184–196. https://doi.org/10.1080/01609513.2018.1533913.

Holmes, P. (2015). *The inner world outside: Object relations theory and psychodrama.* Routledge.

Kellermann, P. F. (1985). Participants' perception of therapeutic factors in psychodrama. *Journal of Group Psychotherapy, Psychodrama and Sociometry, 38*(3), 123–132.

Kellermann, P. F. (1987). Psychodrama participants' perception of therapeutic factors. *Small Group Behavior, 18*(3), 408–419.

Kellermann, P. F. (1992). *Focus on psychodrama: The therapeutic aspects of psychodrama.* Philadelphia: Jessica Kingsley Publishers.

Kim, K. W. (2002). The effects of being the protagonist in psychodrama. *Journal of Group Psychotherapy, Psychodrama, & Sociometry, 55*(4), 115–127.

Lieberman, M. A., Yalom, I. D., & Miles, M. (1973). *Encounter groups: First facts.* New York: Basic Books.

Moreno, J. L. (1940). Mental catharsis and the psychodrama. *Sociometry, 3,* 209–244.

Moreno, J. L. (1972). *Psychodrama Volume 1* (4th ed.). New York: Beacon House.

Moreno, J. L. (2019). In E. Schreiber, S. Kelley, & S. Giacomucci (Eds.), *The autobiography of a genius.* United Kingdom: North West Psychodrama Association.

Moreno, J. L., & Enneis, J. M. (1950). *Hypnodrama and psychodrama.* New York: Beacon House.

Moreno, Z. T. (1965/2006). Psychodramatic rules, techniques, and adjunctive methods. In T. Horvatin & E. Schreiber (Eds.), *The Quintessential Zerka* (pp. 104–114). New York: Routledge.

Moreno, Z. T. (1969). Practical aspects of psychodrama. *Group Psychotherapy, 22*(3–4), 213–219.

Moreno, Z. T. (1971). Beyond Aristotle, Breuer and Freud Moreno's contribution to the concept of catharsis. *Group Psychotherapy & Psychodrama, 24,* 34–43.

Nolte, J. (2014). *The philosophy, theory, and methods of J.L. Moreno: The man who tried to become god.* New York, NY: Routledge.

Ron, Y. (2018). Psychodrama's role in alleviating acute distress: A case study of an open therapy group in a psychiatric inpatient ward. *Frontiers in Psychology, 9,* 2075.

Tomasulo, D. J. (2014). *Action methods in group psychotherapy: Practical aspects.* New York: Routledge.

von Ameln, F., & Becker-Ebel, J. (2020). *Fundamentals of psychodrama.* Singapore: Springer Nature.

Yablonsky, L. (1952). A sociometric investigation into the development of an experimental model for small group analysis. *Sociometry, 15*(3/4), 175–205.

Yalom, I. D. (1975). *The theory and practice of group psychotherapy* (2nd rev. ed.). New York: Basic Books.

Yalom, I. D. (1985). *The theory and practice of group psychotherapy* (3rd ed.). New York, NY: Basic Books.

Yalom, I. D., & Leszcz, M. (2005). *The theory and practice of group psychotherapy* (5th ed.). New York, NY: Basic Books.

Yoon, S. C., Lee, H. K., Jung, I. K., Lee, K. H., Hahm, W., & Cha, J. H. (1998). A comparative study on the therapeutic factors of group psychotherapy and psychodrama applied to psychotic patients. *Journal of Korean Neuropsychiatric Association, 37*(3), 437–452.

Yoon, S. C., Lee, H. K., Kim, S. J., Lee, K. H., Hahm, W., & Hong, H. H. (1999). Therapeutic factors of large group psychodrama for psychiatric inpatients. *Journal of Korean Neuropsychiatric Association, 38*(2), 306–316.

Chapter 13
Essentials of Psychodrama Practice

Abstract The essentials of psychodrama practice are covered in depth within this chapter. Fourteen core psychodrama interventions or techniques are described with corresponding depictions of their use within psychodrama group sessions. The psychodrama techniques of doubling, mirroring, and role reversal are presented with their relationship to Moreno's developmental theory. Considerations for the application of psychodrama interventions on teletherapy is also provided. Various types of psychodrama scenes are described with reference to the Psychodramatic Spiral and the Hollander Curve. The processes of closure, de-roling, and sharing at the end of a psychodrama enactment are outlined.

Keywords Psychodrama · Doubling · Mirroring · Role reversal · Empty chair

Psychodrama is an experiential approach that moves the group process beyond words and into action. A psychodrama is only as good as its warm-up. While many are interested in facilitating or experiencing psychodrama, it would be a mistake to attempt an enactment without any warm-up. After adequate warm-up, the director facilitates the protagonist and topic selection before moving into the psychodrama enactment. The protagonist is interviewed, a scene is set on the stage, roles are identified, and group members are chosen by the protagonist to play the roles needed. The director skillfully facilitates the psychodrama using role reversal, doubling, mirroring, and other interventions as needed to move toward the clinical contract or goal of the psychodrama. Once achieved, a final scene or action is initiated for closure of the drama, followed by each role player de-roling, and returning to their chair in the circle. The final phase of a psychodrama is sharing—where participants are invited to share how they are connected with the roles and themes from the psychodrama by sharing their own feelings, thoughts, and experiences. This chapter will outline the basic techniques and interventions of psychodrama, different types of psychodrama scenes, the importance of closure and de-roling, and the sharing phase of the group process. In this chapter, considerations for utilizing psychodrama interventions through teletherapy will also be presented.

S. Giacomucci, *Social Work, Sociometry, and Psychodrama*, Psychodrama in Counselling, Coaching and Education 1,
https://doi.org/10.1007/978-981-33-6342-7_13

13.1 Psychodramatic Techniques and Interventions

Within any psychodrama, there are numerous techniques available for the use of the director. In 1958, Moreno reported that a colleague had counted 350 unique techniques within psychodrama (as cited in Nolte, 2020). New techniques and psychodramatic interventions are being developed by modern psychodramatists on a regular basis. Eleven core psychodrama techniques emerged from a recent systematic review of the psychodrama literature (Cruz et al, 2018). Though their initial list included 56 techniques, these eleven were considered "core techniques of Morenean Psychodrama": doubling, mirroring, role reversal, soliloquy, sculpture, resistance interpolation, games, social atom, sociometry, intermediate objects, and role training. Other significant techniques noted in the review included symbolic representation, amplification, concretization, and the empty chair. Nolte's (2020) book on the practice of psychodrama includes additional psychodramatic techniques such as the initial interview, self-presentation, scene setting, and spontaneous improvisation.

This section will introduce psychodrama's core techniques beginning with the double, the mirror, and role reversal. These three techniques represent Moreno's developmental theory (see Sect. 4.8)—the stage of identity (doubling), the stage of recognizing the self (mirroring), and the stage of recognizing others (role reversal) (Moreno, 1952). Moreno writes that the inherent tragedy of our interpersonal world is the lack of transparency of our psyche and our inability to fully and accurately communicate our experience, thoughts, and feelings with others. "The full psychodrama of our interrelations does not emerge; it is buried in and between us. Psychodramatics has had to develop a number of techniques to bring deeper levels of our inter-personal world to expression" (1972, p. 190).

13.1.1 Doubling

The *double* speaks (or attempts to speak) the inner world of the protagonist, giving voice to their inner reality. Zerka Moreno (1946b, p. 180) described the function of the double as "to reach deeper layers of expression by peeling off the outer, socially visible 'I' of the subject and by reaching for those experiences and imageries which a person would reveal in talking to herself, alone, in the privacy of her own room." Operationally, this is done simply by standing next to the protagonist, mimicking their body posture, and speaking in the first person as if one is the protagonist. If the protagonist experiences the doubling as inaccurate, they correct it—if it is accurate, the protagonist repeats it and owns it as their own. A double can be assigned by the director to stay with the protagonist throughout the enactment. The Morenos both generally used a single auxiliary to play the double role—Zerka frequently held the double role when Jacob Moreno's was directing. Doubling is also a technique that can be performed by anyone in the group, including the director or therapist. As psychodrama practice has evolved, doubling has become more spontaneous to the point that many directors invite "hit and run" doubling statements. In this more modern approach to doubling, anyone who is warmed up from the group can offer a single doubling sentence when invited or requested.

> Jodi is in the midst of a psychodramatic dialogue between herself and her courage. In the role reversal with her courage she becomes stuck and seemingly cannot find the words to engage with herself from this strength-based role. The director invites other group members to double for Jodi (in the role of courage) one at a time, offering statements from courage to Jodi. If the statement is accurate, Jodi is asked to repeat it from her role of courage to herself; if the statement is not accurate, Jodi is asked to simply change it. The first group member states, "I am your courage and although you don't always feel me, I am always with you". Jodi repeats it with some hesitance. The next group member doubles, "You and me, we go way back - I've been with you your entire life. You use me every time you have overcome difficulty and every success you have had." Jodi again repeats it with some hesitancy, but this time with a more relaxed body. The director offers a doubling statement, "Jodi you have the courage to grow—you have done it before". Jodi looks to the director with appreciation and repeats the statement, letting down her defenses. A third group member doubles, "Jodi, you have so much courage—way more than you could ever realize. You are using me now and your courage inspires others in the group!" Jodi looks to other group members nodding in agreement and repeats the statement with compassion towards herself. Jodi continues in the role of courage speaking to herself spontaneously without prompting. "Jodi, you can do this. You are a courageous woman and the world needs your courage more than ever. You have the courage to be vulnerable in your relationships and to trust the group here who cares about you…".

In the example above, Jodi seems to get stuck in the role and loses her spontaneity. The doubling from the group helped her to stabilize in the role of courage and to establish herself within the surplus reality of the psychodrama scene. The doubling statement from the director offers Jodi a reminder of the therapeutic relationship with her therapist. Each doubling statement from the group implicitly includes an affirmation of empathy, support, and reassurance of the interpersonal connection and identification. The group members, who doubled, each offered Jodi a small window into their perception of her which allowed her to begin to renegotiate her sense of self. While the doubling in this case was primarily to help Jodi access spontaneity in the role, it also served to keep group members involved and emotionally engaged to the topic. Tian Dayton remarks that:

> a good double can be very effective in helping the protagonist to feel seen and understood, in acting as a therapeutic ally while confronting painful emotional material and in moving the protagonist's action to a deeper level by giving voice to that level. (2005, p. 37).

Doubling becomes especially important when working with traumatic material because it helps the protagonist to integrate emotions and cognitions that have been previously split out of consciousness due to the overwhelming nature of the traumatic experience (Hudgins & Toscani, 2013). The Therapeutic Spiral Model offers modified doubles including the body double and the containing double, which are frequently combined into one role in practice (Hudgins & Toscani, 2013). This role is generally the first to be incorporated into the psychodrama to provide increased safety, stability, and connection for the protagonist in trauma-focused psychodrama (Giacomucci, 2018). The body double and the containing double are roles that stay with the protagonist throughout the entire process mirroring all movement and body posturing of the protagonist while incorporating doubling statements regularly. This TSM double has the function of helping a protagonist ground in the present moment and the body, express difficult feelings, and contain overwhelming feelings (Giacomucci, 2018). This double maintains attunement with the protagonist and adapts statements based on what is clinically needed to balance emotional and cognitive experience. It also provides the protagonist with an opportunity to renegotiate and reframe the experience with more mature perspective of the situation by seeing it through two sets of eyes—the eyes of herself in the past and the eyes of herself today (Dayton, 2005).

13.1.2   Mirroring

The *mirror* technique allows the protagonist to observe from a distance and to "see herself as others see her" (J.L. Moreno, 1946a, p. 182). In a psychodrama enactment, the director may instruct the protagonist to take a seat in the audience while another group member, an auxiliary ego, reenacts the scene for the protagonist to see himself in action—as if he is looking at himself in the mirror (Moreno, 1965/2006). This is especially useful when a protagonist appears stuck in a role, acting out defenses, or simply unaware of how their responses are experienced by others. The mirror intervention can be helpful to continue a scene when the protagonist is unwilling or unable to do so—it allows them to experience the action from a distance while they warm up to returning to the role of self in the action (Yablonsky, 1976). The mirror position provides emotional distance from the scene, offers the protagonist an opportunity to view the situation from outside in order to develop greater perspective, and sees self with more clarity and compassion (Dayton, 2005). The mirror technique, in a sense, is the protagonist role reversing with an audience member and becoming a spectator of self (Cruz, Sales, Alves, & Moita, 2018).

> James is in the midst of a psychodrama scene exploring his relationships to his defense mechanisms. In his interactions with other roles he presented as engaged with some difficulty accepting their positive messaging. When interacting with his defenses, he appeared much more engaged and non-verbally in agreement with its messages. As his strengths-based roles spoke, he listened—but when his defenses spoke he listened attentively and nodded his head up and down in agreement. The director was struck by James' inability to see how enmeshed he was with his defenses and invites him to step into the mirror position, choosing someone else to play his role. James watches the group replay his interactions with his strengths-based roles and his defenses while demonstrating his non-verbal communication. From the mirror position, James was able to fully see his enmeshment with his defenses and was able to expand his perception. The director invites him to speak to himself from this place, offering suggestions on how to change his relationship to his defenses. Then he is role reversed back into the role of himself to put these suggestions into action.

While the mirror intervention is useful to help a protagonist see their maladaptive relational patterns, it is also useful as a tool for integration of positive scenes. Another use of the mirror intervention is at the end of a transformative psychodrama. Inviting a protagonist to move into the mirror position to fully see the change they have created in the scene and take it all in can be very integrative.

13.1.3 Role Reversal

In a psychodramatic enactment, a role reversal allows one the experience of trading places with another person, stepping out of one's own identity and into the identity of another to see through their eyes. J.L. Moreno outlines the philosophy of role reversal in his 1914 *Invitation to an Encounter* poem:

> A meeting of two: eye to eye, face to face. And when you are near I will tear your eyes out and place them instead of mine and you will tear my eyes out and place them instead of yours then I will look at you with your eyes and you will look at me with mine. (J.L. Moreno, 1914).

Zerka Moreno refers to role reversal as the *sine qua non* of psychodrama—without it there is no true psychodrama (Dayton, 2005). Many psychodramatists consider it to be the most effective psychodrama technique (Kellermann, 1994). In a psychodrama enactment, a husband and wife could role reverse to develop a better sense of each other's perspective; one could reverse roles with a historical figure or a role model; the protagonist could reverse roles with one of their intrapsychic roles (such as courage, their inner hero, or their inner critic); or even reverse roles with God! Role reverse could be used with two individuals in the group, or between the protagonist and one who is only psychodramatically present through surplus reality. There are many different shapes that the role reversal can take, ranging from intrapsychic, intrapersonal, and transpersonal roles. The following depicts a psychodrama role reversal with the role of God.

> George is a protagonist in inpatient addictions treatment and has expressed his sense of guilt and shame around his addiction and how it has impacted others in his life. His goal in the psychodrama is to move towards self-forgiveness and more spiritual connection. In the psychodramatic dialogue with God, he begins to express his feelings of self-hatred, remorse, and shame. He shares about feeling like the things he has done to his family are unforgiveable and irreversible. The director invites him to role reverse with God. Another group member begins to play the role of George repeating his sharing of self-hatred, guilt, and shame to God (now played by George). In the role of God, George looks at himself full of remorse and pain. He begins to speak to himself, "George, please stop beating yourself up for things you did in your past. You have a disease called addiction which caused you to do things you wouldn't have done otherwise. You are really a good man; I know because I created you. I want you to know that I forgive you for those things you did and the people you hurt. I need you to go out into the world and make amends to them and work at loving yourself. You have the gifts to help countless others suffering with addiction now. Make this your purpose." George is then instructed to role reverse back into the role of himself and another group member becomes God, repeating the same messages. George savors the messages from God as the weight of his guilt and shame begin to dissipate.

In the example above, George appears stuck in his own feelings of shame and guilt, unable to expand his perception of the situation or any positive that could come from his experience of addiction. The role reversal with God allowed him to see himself from God's eyes and to see his life from a larger perspective. As God, he was able to offer direction, affirmation, and even suggest meaning and purpose from the experience of pain and suffering. The role reversal allows for new integration and action insights which lead to an expansion of the self. It is a technique with the functions of building ego strength, spontaneity, sensitivity, empathy, awareness, and self-integration while facilitating socialization and an exploration of interpersonal relations (Dayton, 2005; Hudgins & Toscani, 2013; Kellermann, 1994; J.L. Moreno, 1959). There are of course guidelines and clinical considerations to take into account when using the role reversal technique, especially when working with trauma, these will be outlined in Sect. 14.5.

> And so we may say that the double, the mirror, and the reversal are like three stages in the development of the infant which have their counterpart in the therapeutic techniques which we can use in the treatment of all human relations problems. (J.L. Moreno, 1952, p. 275).

13.1.4 Soliloquy

The soliloquy is a technique from classical drama, however when used in psychodrama its focus is to give the participant the opportunity for expression and catharsis that might not be otherwise possible (Moreno, 1972). Moreno describes the soliloquy as an enlargement of the self as it intertwines the self of the role player with the role being played in the psychodrama. However, Moreno cautions directors that having auxiliaries or protagonists provide soliloquys too often disrupts the intensity of continuity of the role and the spontaneous act (1972).

The use of soliloquy allows the protagonist or auxiliary egos to give voice to the unspoken thoughts or feelings related to the psychodrama scene. This technique is often used when the protagonist is in the role reversed position as it challenges them to develop a deepened understanding of the role they are playing (Nolte, 2020). A soliloquy is also helpful when a protagonist has become stuck or appears resistant (Moreno, 1965/2006). Inviting them to pause the psychodrama scene and offer a soliloquy, or internal dialog as if nobody was in the room, can be illuminating for both the director and the protagonist about where the scene needs to go next (Rojas-Bermúdez, 1997). Yablonsky (1976) describes the soliloquy as most similar to psychoanalytic process of free association. For example:

> In a psychodrama scene, Lori has begun a dialogue with God with the goal of gaining insight into her life purpose. Her interactions with the other roles in the psychodrama have been spontaneous and engaged. After beginning to talk to God, she quickly becomes guarded and avoidant. Noticing the significant change in the protagonist's presentation, the director invites her to offer a brief soliloquy, freezing the scene. She begins to speak freely – "It is harder to talk to God than I realized. I thought that I only had positive feelings towards God but when I started to talk, I realized that I also feel intense anger towards God. I have tried to live a good life, but he keeps allowing trauma and loss to enter my life. I feel shameful for being angry at God and afraid of what might happen if I tap into my anger." This short soliloquy provides the director with essential information about the protagonist's experience and offers clues of how to help Lori get unstuck.

13.1.5 Initial Interview

After the selection of the protagonist, the initial interview takes place between the director and the protagonist. This serves many purposes including:

- To continue the warm-up of the protagonist
- To continue the warm-up of the group based on the topic of the psychodrama
- To warm up the director to the forthcoming enactment
- For the protagonist and the director to further develop trust, connection, and understanding
- For the protagonist and director to create a contract for the goal of the psychodrama
- For the director to gather important information about the presenting topic

Moreno suggested that the initial interview should be kept short as to avoid talking about the issue instead of putting it into action (Nolte, 2020). Many psychodrama directors conduct the initial interview while walking in a circle on the stage with the protagonist to create physical movement which is outlined in more detail in Sect. 12.4.

13.1.6 Scene Setting

Scene setting is employed almost immediately after the initial interview. This technique is significant in that it marks the initial plunge from reality into surplus reality. The director encourages the protagonist to choose a setting for the psychodrama enactment and to begin to use objects or role players to set up the scene. This is done through creative symbolism and concretization. The process of physically setting up the scene moves the protagonist into action and warms up their body, their imagination, and their emotions while also warming up the group to the protagonist and the forthcoming enactment. For these reasons, it is often helpful to allow the protagonist to set up the scene by themselves. Rather than talking about the scene, the protagonist is instructed to show us the scene on the stage. In cases of psychodramas related to past experiences, the act of setting up the scene helps the protagonist further access the memory related to the scene which seems to be better accessed through the body, movement, and action than by solely talking (Nolte, 2020).

13.1.7 Self-Presentation

This technique facilitates the protagonist to accurately show how they and/or others act in a given situation. Self-presentation is often used as an early scene in a psychodrama for assessment, establishing the starting point, and to warm up the protagonist and enter surplus reality. Moreno writes that it is especially useful as an early intervention to help reduce anxiety, increase spontaneity, and establish tele between the protagonist and facilitator (1946). Moreno describes it as the simplest psychodramatic technique (1937). Self-presentation allows the protagonist to externalize their own subjective reality, perspective, and experience which is used as the basis for moving forward in the psychodrama enactment. This technique is used for past, present, or future situations.

13.1.8   Spontaneous Improvisation

This technique brings the director to facilitate the protagonist in enacting fictitious or imagined roles or responses in the scene, as opposed to acting out their actual responses. In some ways, spontaneous improvisation is the opposite of the intervention of self-presentation—one being the acting out of reality while the other being fictitious. The task is to challenge the protagonist to leave their own role and take on the role of a fictitious character—to access spontaneity from a role other than their self. The use of spontaneous improvisation allows the director to put a strong role demand on the protagonist while giving them aesthetic distance from the intensity of the initial psychodrama topic.

The following is a clinical use of spontaneous improvisation. In John's psychodrama, he faces his addiction but becomes stuck in the encounter and cannot find the words or spontaneity to talk back to his addiction. The director pauses the scene, enrolling John into the role of a father protecting his family from a seagull coming to eat their dinner. In this role, John is able to access the spontaneity to confront the seagull without hesitation. Though the content of this scene is very different, the process and role demands are similar. After which, the original scene can be revisited as John has been role trained through spontaneous improvisation.

> The technique of improvisation is the royal route of spontaneity training as it throws the patient into roles, situations, and worlds in which he has never lived before and in which he has instantly to produce a new role to meet the novel environment. More than therapy is provided. It is training and development of a new personality which may differ greatly from the one which was brought for treatment (Moreno, 1972, pp. 210–211).

This technique also provides diagnostic information to the director about the protagonist's ability to access spontaneity and alternative roles (Nolte, 2020). It is both useful as a spontaneity warm-up, an intervention within a psychodrama enactment, and a grounding exercise after the intensity of a psychodrama.

13.1.9   Sculpting

Sculpting describes the process of using auxiliaries to concretize the perceived relationships within a family, social atom, sociogram, memory of an experience, or even internal parts of self (Blatner, 2000). Other group members are chosen to step in as auxiliaries needed for the scene and are directed by the protagonist in terms of location, distance from the other roles, posture, movement, messages, and/or expression. Doubling and role reversal interventions are also utilized in action sculpting. This process provides an externalized, workable expression of a system's structure (Cruz et al., 2018). An action sculpture is much more contained, slower, and prescribed than a psychodrama process. It also employs the mirror intervention much more regularly than a psychodrama enactment would. For these reasons, it is useful for time limited groups, less warmed up group, less experienced participants, and demonstrations. The use of sculpting has become popular beyond psychodrama, especially in family therapy (Blatner, 2000).

13.1.10 Resistance Interpolation

This intervention describes the process of testing the protagonist's spontaneity, in terms of responding to new situations, by modifying the psychodrama scene. The protagonist presents the situation, and it is enacted with a scripted outcome, then the director modifies the scene in a way to change major elements and put new role demands upon the protagonist in the scene (Cruz et al., 2018; Moreno, 1972). For example:

> Adam has just engaged in a self-presentation of a recurrent relational dynamic in his marriage. He demonstrates how he and his partner frequently find themselves in a back and forth argument where neither of them can connect with the other because they both become defensive and guarded. Adam describes getting to a place where he feels he is unable to admit that his partner is right about anything and becomes increasingly combative. The director instructs Adam and the auxiliaries to replay the scene, waiting for Adam's combativeness to become activated. Once Adam and his partner are engaged in the back and forth rejection of each statement the other makes, the director instructs the auxiliary in the role of Adam's partner to begin including statements related to the content of their disagreement that are undeniably true such as "we have been married for 4 years now" or "we have been fighting for five minutes". The factual statements throw Adam off as he can't deny that they are true—he is challenged to respond in a new way rather than continuing to reject each statement. He begins to contemplate each statement from his partner for its merit and truth before responding.

This intervention attempts to uncover new behavioral responses and aspects of personality from the protagonist (Rojas-Bermudez, 1997). The use of resistance interpolation can be used to help a protagonist access new spontaneity that can later be integrated into the reality of an interpersonal situation.

13.1.11 Games

Group games are frequently involved in psychodrama groups in the warming up process or cooling down process. Simple and playful games are implemented with the goals of increasing spontaneity, trust, cohesion, and movement—or in the context of cooling down after an intense group, with the goals of reconnecting the group with a sense of playfulness, grounding, and spontaneity in the here-and-now. Most of the games employed in psychodrama groups have been borrowed from other fields such as the theater games, improv, drama therapy, the New Games Movement, and pop culture (Blatner, 2000, 2013). Collections of these games have been published by others, such as *Drama Games* (1990) by Tian Dayton, *Improvisation for the Theater* (1999) by Viola Spolin, *101 Improv Games for Children and Adults* (2004) by Bob Bedore, and *275 Acting Games Connected* (2010) by Gavin Levy.

The use of games can also be traced back to social work with groups practice, specifically in the non-deliberative approach (Lang, 2010). Group games and activities serve "to engage the members and advance them interactionally toward achievement of groupness, mobilizing and enhancing the natural interactional capabilities of participants" (Lang, 2010, p. 169). Group activities offer opportunities for participants to feel a sense of belonging and developing "connection between the self and the external world and experiencing themselves as effective in the world" (Lang, 2010, p. 173). The action and experiential nature of games creates a playful space for increasing self-efficacy, self-confidence, and social skills.

13.1.12 Intermediate Objects

The use of objects in psychodrama has been described previously in the context of concretization and surplus reality. Although objects are not used in every psychodrama, many facilitators do employ them for their utility in enhancing the production. The use of scarves has already been mentioned, other commonly used objects include chairs, masks, cards, puppets, dolls, and small figures (Blatner, 1996). The functions of using objects include warming up to spontaneity/creativity, concretizing roles, and providing aesthetic distance for clients. While Moreno often used objects in his psychodrama directing, the theory of *intermediate objects* is traced back to Jaime Rojas-Bermudez (Cruz et al., 2018; Rojas-Bermudez, 1997). Rojas-Bermudez's (1997) specific use of intermediate objects relates to the use of an object to symbolize the therapist when a client cannot tolerate the vulnerability of direct human interaction. Instead of the dialog taking place between therapist–client, it takes place between object–client to reduce intensity and decrease activation or alarm. The intermediate object is then removed once the client is able to tolerate face-to-face engagement.

13.1.13 Role Training

Role training is an intervention process used to help a protagonist practice and rehearse new roles or responses related to future interpersonal situations (Blatner, 2000). Role training can be used as a warm-up structure for groups, as the primary psychodrama enactment, or as a closing scene in a psychodrama. Role training allows the protagonist and the group to replay a scene multiple times with modified responses to explore optimal actions and develop competence in a given situation. A role training process can also involve using role reversals or the mirror position to best evaluate the impact of different responses. Role training is used in psychotherapy with varying goals including the practice of difficult conversations, boundary setting, anger management, anger expression, vulnerability in relationships, job interviews, and other social skills. It can also be used to the role train for intrapsychic situations such as responding in new ways to thoughts of self-harm, addiction cravings, defense mechanism, feelings of inadequacy, depression, anxiety, and any other internal experience. Role training is utilized beyond psychotherapy and is commonly used in sociodrama, role-plays, and other simulations within the contexts of professional training, education, supervision, activism, community organizing, personal development, conflict resolution, business, coaching, and acting (see Sect. 19.3).

13.1.14 The Empty Chair and Multiple Empty Chairs

The empty chair seems to have become popularized by Fritz Perls' gestalt therapy which was influenced by Moreno's psychodrama. The major difference in the use of the empty chair is that gestalt uses it primarily for the client to talk to another, while psychodrama also utilizes the role reversal and doubling in the empty chair process (Knittel, 2010). This will be explored further in Sect. 15.5.4. The empty chair is another intervention used by psychodramatists in replacement of an auxiliary. Moreno used to refer to the empty chair as a four-legged auxiliary (Nolte, 2020). In a psychodrama, an empty chair may be superior to group members playing auxiliary roles when a protagonist has limited ego strength, significant trauma, anxiety, or when working with a perpetrator role. Using the empty chair to concretize a role limits the influence of that role in the psychodrama, whereas when another human being plays the role, it increases the role demands and role reciprocity on the protagonist.

The empty chair can be used in a variety of contexts including as a warm-up for a psychodrama, in groups or individual sessions, psychodramatically or sociodramatically, and with a single empty chair or multiple empty chairs. The differences between psychodrama and sociodrama will be explored in a Sect. 15.1, as is the use of psychodrama methods in individual therapy (see Chaps. 16 and 17). The utilization of multiple empty chairs is lesser known but an effective process for helping a client or group to express messages or feelings to others in their life while also having the opportunity to role reverse, speaking to themselves from the role of others.

An example of employing a multiple empty chair structure comes from this writer's clinical experience in inpatient addictions groups at Mirmont Treatment Center. After a sociometric warm-up on the topic of relationships, five empty chairs are pulled into the center of the circle, each labeled with a different type of relationship—family, friends, self, groups/communities/society, and God/spiritual roles. Group members are invited spontaneously to sit in one of the five empty chairs and verbalize positive or negative messages that they have received (verbally or non-verbally) from others in their life. Multiple rounds of this multiempty chair process can be facilitated with varied instructions including:

- Role reverse with one of these types of relationships and verbalize a negative message you have received from others about your addiction
- Role reverse with one of these types of relationships and verbalize a positive message you have received from others about your addiction
- Role reverse with one of these types of relationships and verbalize a message you wish you could have heard in the past
- Stand in front of one or more of these empty chairs and articulate a message you need to express to one of these relationships
- It is now 5 years in the future; stand in front of one or more of these empty chairs and articulate a message you hope to express to one of these relationships in the future
- It is now 5 years in the future; role reverse with one of these types of relationships and verbalize a message you crave to hear in the future

Through this process, step-in sociometry or simply raising hands is used to indicate shared experience related to each message offered. After the process moves toward closure, the group advances into the sharing phase.

13.2   Psychodrama Interventions Adapted for Teletherapy

Though psychodrama practice online is relatively new, unique advantages to psychodramatic teletherapy are being discovered. Teletherapy and the use of technology seem to produce both limitations and benefits for psychodrama practitioners and trainers. While it creates a more accessible group experience for participants who are not geographically nearby, it also limits the ways in which participants can connect with each other due to the absence of physical proximity and lost non-verbal communication.

One unique aspect of using psychodrama online is the access to a nearly unlimited collection of images on the Internet and an avenue to easily share an image or video for all participants to see. This feature can be used to enhance many psychodramatic warm-ups or enactments and raises the question of how psychodrama's surplus reality and virtual reality might be complimentary to each other. In teletherapy or online teaching sessions, images could be used to help with scene setting, defining roles, psychodramatic dialogs, or doubling practice. An image of an empty chair can even be shared on the screen for group members to engage in an empty chair process.

In commonly employed teletherapy or online teaching platforms, each person in the group can also see a live video feed of themselves during the session. This unique aspect of online work is similar to psychodrama's mirror position and can be leveraged to help enhance the therapeutic nature of the session for clients. Because a client can literally see themselves on the computer screen, it is easier to facilitate a psychodramatic dialog of the client speaking to themselves or a part of self. This feature can also make role reversals in individual teletherapy easier because the client can see themselves on the screen even when they have psychologically role reversed into another role.

Another one of the unique benefits to teletherapy includes the use of objects in a client's living space as props for concretizing strengths-based roles. These objects can be strategically used by the psychodramatist to serve as transitional objects or physical reminders for the client of their strengths or the work they are doing. Rather than relying on objects in the therapist's office, teletherapy makes it easy to use objects in the client's space too.

Furthermore, many trauma survivors report feeling safer doing teletherapy from the comfort of their homes (assuming that home is a safe place for them). While this is not true for everyone, some clients benefit from increased safety and comfort of their home environment and increased emotional regulation strategies available to them at home (pets, loved ones, personal objects, walking outside, etc.). When engaging in trauma teletherapy, this writer has also found the mute feature and the option to turn off one's camera feed as opportunities for clinical interventions. For example, if a client is unsure if they are ready to share details of a traumatic event, they could be offered the option to turn off their camera and/or their audio and see if it feels more tolerable to speak the details aloud knowing they cannot be seen and/or heard when doing so. This may help warm a client up to sharing the same difficult details with the therapist directly or in a future session.

The use of the chat feature on most teletherapy platforms can be employed for clinical or educational groups online. This feature can also be used as another avenue that clients can share personal details beyond verbally articulating them. Some clients will feel more comfortable expressing or sharing themselves through text rather than verbally. In large educational groups or multilingual groups, the chat box is particularly useful as it facilitates participant engagement and expression in a contained way. Participants' responses in the chat box can be read aloud by the facilitator, translator, or another group member to avoid the issue of too many people talking at the same time.

While teletherapy and online teaching methods are relatively new in the psychodrama field, they offer multiple new creative ways of engaging groups and utilizing sociometric or psychodramatic interventions. As teletherapy and online teaching methods become more common and continue to evolve with increased technological sophistication, it is expected that they will be more prevalent for psychodrama practitioners and trainers (Giacomucci, 2020b).

13.3   Psychodrama Scenes

The psychodrama stage offers unlimited potential and infinite possibilities in terms of scenes that could be enacted (Giacomucci & Stone, 2019). Psychodrama scenes may be entirely interpersonal scenes with roles being exclusively other people, scenes might be intrapsychic and only employ roles that represent parts of self, or the scene could include a mix of intrapsychic and interpersonal roles. It seems that Moreno's early directing was primarily interpersonal but as the practice of psychodrama evolved, it came to include much more intrapsychic roles. Some psychodramas include fantasy characters or archetypes, while others are composed of roles based on reality. The exploration of dreams using psychodrama is another area of psychodrama practice (Scategni, 2005). While psychodrama is a useful modality for conflict resolution and often involves antagonist roles, some psychodramas only employ strengths-based and supportive roles. It is important to note that an antagonist role is not always necessary in a psychodrama scene and scenes including only strengths-based roles can be equally cathartic and transformative.

A psychodrama is enacted as if it were happening in the here-and-now. Nevertheless, psychodramas can be scenes from the past, present, or future. Time and space are transcended on the psychodrama stage (Giacomucci, 2017, 2020). As noted previously, some psychodramas are focused specifically on role training for future situations. Other psychodramas are based on reenactments of the past or wished for experience in the past. This becomes especially prominent in psychodramatic work with trauma (Giacomucci & Marquit, 2020). Many psychodramas include multiple scenes, each at different points in time, while some psychodrama enactments only have one or two scenes. Important contributions to this discussion come from The Psychodramatic Spiral (Goldman & Morrison, 1984) and The Hollander Curve (Hollander, 1978) which will be described with additions from the author in the next subsections.

13.3.1   The Psychodramatic Spiral

Goldman and Morrison (1984) offer the conceptualization of The Psychodramatic Spiral as a guide for the psychodrama directing process (see Fig. 13.1). The Psychodramatic Spiral depicts the levels of present, recent-past, and deeper past scenes related to a classical psychodrama enactment. The developers note that the Psychodramatic Spiral also visually resembles Moreno's original psychodrama stage design. This symbol shows how the psychodrama process moves from the periphery to the core and returns full circle to the presenting problem with new spontaneity, creativity, and roles (Goldman & Morrison, 1984). It is interesting to note that the process of following the Psychodrama Spiral seems to be almost identical to the approach to treatment in eye movement desensitization and reprocessing (EMDR). Both start with a presenting problem, move through a memory network of similar

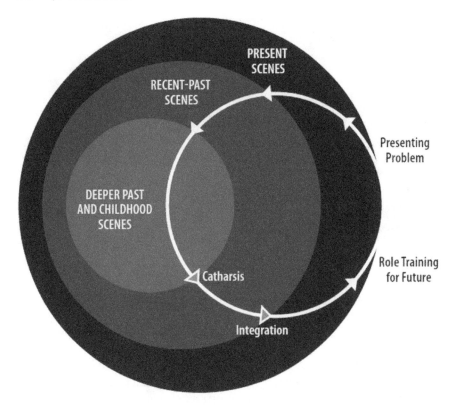

Fig. 13.1 The Psychodramatic Spiral based on Goldman and Morrison, (1984)

scenes to a touchstone memory with the goals of catharsis, cognitive integration, and finally practicing future templates related to the presenting problem. While some psychodramas will include scenes in the present, recent past, childhood, and future, other psychodramas might only involve one or two scenes. Regardless of the number of scenes, the movement is from the periphery to the core and moves full circle to the clinical contract and presenting problem. As scenes progress, they spiral further into the surplus reality of the past until a climax is achieved. With the climactic catharsis, the process begins to spiral back toward the presenting problem with a concretization of insight and integration and finally role training for the future (Santos & Conceição, 2014).

13.3.2 Hollander Curve

The Hollander Curve (1978) depicts the three phases of a psychodrama group, labeled with the terminology of Moreno's triadic system—sociometry, psychodrama, and group psychotherapy (see Fig. 13.2).

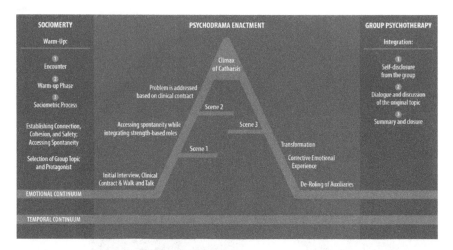

Fig. 13.2 The Hollander Curve. Based on Hollander, (1978)

The sociometry phase involves the initial encounter between group members, the warming up process, and a sociometric exploration to discern a group topic and protagonist. In this first phase of the group, connection is increased, group cohesion and safety are established, and spontaneity begins to emerge. Once chosen, the protagonist and director engage in a walk and talk while solidifying and clarifying a clinical contract around the topic and a goal for the psychodrama. The first scene is set up—traditionally, this would involve a self-presentation of the problem at hand from the subjective reality of the protagonist. Strengths-based psychodrama processes, especially the Therapeutic Spiral Model, would integrate a variety of positive roles into the first scene to help the protagonist access spontaneity and cultivate safety before moving toward a climax of catharsis (see Sect. 14.4.2). This first scene is very diagnostic for the director and provides important information about the content of the protagonist's situation and an experiential assessment of the protagonist's ego strength, stability, insight, and personality. The second scene moves the protagonist and the group toward catharsis of abreaction and often involves working through past scenes (or traumas) related to the presenting problem. An example of this multiscene process is depicted in the example below:

> Roy is chosen by the group as protagonist to explore the topic of his fear of asking his employer for a raise. In the first scene, Roy sets up the stage based on a recent experience of attempting to advocate for himself and ask for a raise in a meeting with his boss. He describes feeling frozen and intimidated by his boss and the situation and can't bring himself to ask. When probed, he indicates that his boss reminds him of his father who was demanding and violent at times. The second scene brings Roy to a dialogue with his father where he integrates strengths-based roles needed to confront his father and express his fear, sadness, and anger. This is where the climax of catharsis takes place for Roy and for the group. A positive ending could be incorporated between Roy and his father to offer a corrective emotional experience. After this scene, a final scene is enacted for closure, integration, and role training. The third scene brings Roy back to the office with his boss (and the strengths from the previous scenes) to practice advocating for himself with the support of the group.

Now that he has addressed issues related to his father, the transference he had with his boss has dissipated and he feels more confident advocating for himself with success (see Sect. 19.3.3 for more on role training self-advocacy skills).

In many ways, the Hollander Curve brings the group from the here-and-now (warm-up) to the near past (scene 1) to the past (scene 2), flings the group forward to the near future (scene 3), and lands in the here-and-now for group sharing and closure. Similarly, but on an intrapsychic level, TSM's different types of psychodramas (Giacomucci, 2018; Hudgins, 2002) seem to reflect the three types of scenes in the Hollander Curve:

(1) Prescriptive Role Psychodramas—focused on building up the strengths and safety needed to face trauma
(2) Re-Experiencing with Developmental Repair Psychodramas—revisiting the trauma and related internalized roles with newfound strength, support, and adaptive information to renegotiate the internalized trauma while psychodramatically experiencing a corrective experience
(3) Transformative Psychodramas—exploring post-traumatic growth and the transformation of trauma-based roles into transformative roles.

Regardless of the nature of the scenes in a psychodrama, after closure is accomplished the auxiliary egos de-role and return to the group. The third phase of the group begins with group members sharing from their own experience how they are related to the psychodrama scenes that were enacted. Self-disclosure in this phase provides the protagonist with reintegration into the group and provides other participants with the opportunity to share how they saw themselves in the psychodrama. Here the group-as-a-whole nature of the topic is re-emphasized as each person indicates how they identified with the psychodrama before the group ends. One might suggest that traditional group psychotherapy employs phases one and three without the psychodramatic enactment. It uses a talk-based version of the warm-up, encounter, and discerning a group topic then moves directly to phase three with self-disclosure from group members about their connection to the topic and group dialog.

13.4 Closure, De-roling, and Striking the Set

Without adequate closure, the psychodrama may feel incomplete or unfinished for the protagonist and the group. The closure of the psychodrama ends the process "on a high note or some other positive possibility" (Goldman & Morrison, 1984, p. 31). It also is helpful to connect the chosen method of closure with the clinical contract or goal from the start of the psychodrama (Kellermann, 1992). Closure is one aspect of the psychodrama process that little has been written about. There are various ways of facilitating completion of a psychodrama enactment. Closure to the psychodrama scene may be performed with a final statement, action, or commitment forming the protagonist or the group. In many psychodramas, after the climax and catharsis, the scene organically moves itself toward closure and a good ending. There are multiple layers of closure in the process including an aesthetically pleasing closure to the scene, emotional closure for the protagonist, closure for the role players, closure for the group, and closure for the psychodrama director and any other team members.

A simple way of engaging in closure to the psychodrama scene is to ask the protagonist what they would need to happen as a good way of closing the scene. Other closure actions might involve asking the protagonist to summarize the primary cognitive insights or memorable moments from the scene (Weiner & Sacks, 1969). Others emphasize the role training aspect of a final psychodrama scene to be essential for integration and closure—often revisiting the presenting problem and first psychodrama scene (Goldman & Morrison, 1984; Hollander, 1978; Schramski, 1979). Kipper (1986) and Kellermann (1992) offer multiple different purposes for closure in the psychodrama process including: restoring emotional stability, cultivating hope for the future and future plans, provide a sense of symbolic or real satisfaction, move from surplus reality back to reality, encourage cognitive restructuring of the psychodrama problem, role training and behavior learning, and to integrate the learning back into the lives of group members going forward. Furthermore, Kellermann (1992) lists 29 different types of commonly used actions for closure to a psychodrama enactment.

Part of the closure process includes the de-roling of each role in the psychodrama. De-roling provides a ritual of returning from the psychodramatic trance of surplus reality back to one's self and the here-and-now. It is an explicit action of consciously letting go of the role one played in the enactment. There are also frequently times when role players feel the need to hold onto aspects of the role while they de-role—such as a group member who played the role of self-love who also wants to integrate this role into their own repertoire (Blatner, 2000). Most often the de-roling process is as simple as each role player physically wiping off or shaking off the role while stating to the protagonist, "I am no longer your mother, I am a group member named Scott". If the role players used scarves (or other props) to represent the roles, then these objects are also symbolically removed to help facilitate de-roling. This simple process takes only a few seconds while encompassing physical, verbal, and symbolic elements of de-roling.

Just as the process of scene setting is used to help assist a protagonist and a group to move into surplus reality, the process of striking the set helps the protagonist and the group to move out of surplus reality. Scene setting facilitates the warming up process while striking the scene facilitates a cooling down process. One might think of striking the set as de-roling the objects used in the scene and finalizing the movement from the surplus reality of the psychodrama stage back to the reality of the group room.

13.5   Sharing in Psychodrama

Upon de-roling and striking the set, participants return to their seats and final sharing phase of the group begins. In this last part of a group, participants are provided with the opportunity to share with each other about how they could identify with the psychodrama enactment. This allows for the protagonist to be integrated back into the group while offering other group members with the chance to express how they saw themselves in the protagonist on stage (Giacomucci, 2019). Sharing from participants sometimes also involves sharing insights into the role they played then sharing from themselves to help role players fully de-role (Holmes, 1991; Wilkins, 1999). Sharing from the role is called role feedback and can provide a broader perspective of the scene for the protagonist (von Ameln & Becker-Ebel, 2020). The sharing from group members at the end of a psychodrama generally does not involve feedback or advice giving—instead, it is focused on self-disclosure. Zerka writes that in the sharing phase, "group members should speak about themselves, not the protagonist; here we share our common humanity" (1987/2006, p. 234).

When a protagonist's topic is chosen sociometrically, the psychodrama represents the group-as-a-whole—as such, the rest of the group will have much to share upon completion of the enactment. The role dynamics, the scene, the messages, and actions of the group topic will almost certainly provoke feelings, insights, and act hungers from the group. The sharing after the psychodrama allows other group members to express, articulate, and name their own difficult experiences as it relates to the enactment (Dayton, 2005). In many cases, participants who played other roles will have their own catharses and insights because of the role they played. Dayton (2005) writes that the protagonist's psychodrama acts as a tunnel into the group's experience or a mirror for each individual group member. The protagonist reveals himself during the psychodrama enactment, and the group reveals itself during the sharing phase (Nolte, 2014).

The sharing process can be as simple as each person sharing, in order of seating arrangement. It could be done spontaneously with the option to share or not. When there is limited time remaining in the group, the director might invite a few participants to share or invite the protagonist to choose a few group members that they would like to hear share. Another option for quick and efficient sharing is to employ dyads, small groups, step-in sociometry, or spectrograms to facilitate this process. In the phase of sharing after a psychodrama, it is not uncommon for a psychodrama director to also share their personal connection to the topic. Traditionally, psychodramatists seem to use much more self-disclosure than other therapists. It is recommended that each director uses discretion and discernment around professional boundaries and personal disclosure in the sharing phase.

The sharing phase of the group instills a sense of universality in the group and hope for the future (Kellermann, 1992; Wilkins, 1999). Upon the completion of the psychodrama, just like the completion of any other involved action, group members will likely feel a sense of relief, satisfaction, and relaxation as they de-role, and the group moves closer to closure. It seems that in the sharing portion of the group, the group sharing often touches upon a discussion of wonder and awe related to the power of the psychodrama process, the synchronicity of roles chosen (tele), and the surprise of how real the surplus reality scene felt. When a group is properly warmed up, the group-as-a-whole becomes invested in the psychodrama enactment and collectively acts as-if. The telic connections from the sociometric warm-up carry over into the psychodrama, especially evidenced in the protagonist's (conscious or unconscious) choosing of role players. Frequently in the process of choosing role players, the person chosen happens to have an unresolved relationship to the role they are asked to play. The act of playing the role offers the auxiliaries with opportunity catharses, action insights, and role training. At the end of a psychodrama group, participants often report feeling tired or exhausted emotionally. It is important that the sharing assists the group to cultivate new cognitive insights, connections, and integrations.

Historically, it is interesting to note the evolution of the sharing phase. Initially, this phase involved the director (Moreno) offering comments and interpretation of the protagonist's performance in the psychodrama while other group members offered their own observations. This changed after an experience Moreno had with a group that involved a young woman protagonist with multiple other psychiatrists in the audience. When it came to the sharing phase of the group, the psychiatrists gave their interpretations and analyses without consideration to the feelings of the protagonist who felt neglected, confused, and hurt by their comments. Moreno became frustrated and confronted the group—"Do you have children? What is your relationship to your daughter? Here we share with our hearts, not our brains" (Z. T. Moreno, 1945/2006, p. 22). After this experience, psychodrama sharing excluded professional interpretation and advice giving and become centered on personal disclosure (Nolte, 2014). Furthermore, Moreno disliked the term *feedback*, often reminding others that it is also used to describe the annoying sounds that two electronic machines make when in discord with each other. Zerka writes that instead of feedback, he suggested we think of sharing as "love-back". When a protagonist offers a psychodrama, it can only be conceptualized as an act of love and vulnerability—which can only be repaid with love (Moreno, 2000/2006).

13.6   Conclusions

The essential practice of components of psychodrama has been outlined in this chapter including the foundational interventions of psychodrama. A mixture of the aforementioned psychodrama interventions are employed in each psychodrama varying due to the presentation of the protagonist/group, the goals of the session, and the style of the director. Attention was given to the varying types of psychodrama scenes including the use of the Psychodramatic Spiral and the Hollander Curve to guide the direction of scenes from present-day to past scenes, ending with role training for future situations. The significance of closure and de-roling in psychodrama has been presented including the importance of the sharing phase in a psychodrama group.

References

Bedore, B. (2004). *101 Improv Games for Children and Adults: Fun and Creativity with Improvisation and Acting.* Hunter House.

Blatner, A. (2000). *Foundations of psychodrama: History, theory, and practice* (4th ed.). New York City: Springer Publishing Company.

Blatner, A. (2013). Warming-up, action methods, and related processes. *The Journal of Psychodrama, Sociometry, and Group Psychotherapy, 61*(1), 43–50.

Blatner, A. (1996). *Acting-in: Practical applications of psychodramatic methods.* New York: Springer Publishing Company.

Cruz, A., Sales, C. M. D., Alves, P., & Moita, G. (2018). The core techniques of morenian psychodrama: A systematic review of literature. *Frontiers in Psychology, 9*(1263), 1–11. https://doi.org/10.3389/fpsyg.2018.01263.

Dayton, T. (1990). *Drama games XE "games" : Techniques for self-development.* Deerfield Beach, FL: Health Communications Inc.

Dayton, T. (2005). *The Living Stage: A step-by-step guide to psychodrama, sociometry, and experiential group therapy XE "group therapy" .* Deerfield, FL: Health Communications Inc.

Giacomucci, S. (2017). The sociodrama of life or death: Young adults and addiction treatment. *Journal of Psychodrama, Sociometry, and Group Psychotherapy 65*(1): 137–143. https://doi.org/10.12926/0731-1273-65.1.137

Giacomucci, S. (2018). The trauma survivor's inner role atom XE "role atom" : A clinical map XE "clinical map" for post-traumatic growth XE "post-traumatic growth" . *Journal of Psychodrama, Sociometry, and Group Psychotherapy., 66*(1), 115–129.

Giacomucci, S. (2019). *Social Group Work in Action: A Sociometry, Psychodrama, and Experiential Trauma Therapy Curriculum.* Doctorate in Social Work (DSW) Dissertations. 124. https://repository.upenn.edu/cgi/viewcontent.cgi?article=1128&context=edissertations_sp2

Giacomucci, S. (2020). Addiction, traumatic loss, and guilt: A case study resolving grief XE "grief" through psychodrama and sociometric connections. *the Arts in Psychotherapy, 67,* 101627. https://doi.org/10.1016/j.aip.2019.101627.

Giacomucci, S. (2020b). The Sociodrama of Coronavirus and Humanity through TeleTherapy. *The Group Psychologist*, 31(2).

Giacomucci, S., & Marquit, J. (2020). The Effectiveness of Trauma-Focused Psychodrama in the Treatment of PTSD in Inpatient Substance Abuse Treatment. *Frontiers in Psychology, 11*, 896. https://dx.doi.org/https://doi.org/10.3389%2Ffpsyg.2020.00896

Giacomucci, S., & Stone, A. M. (2019). Being in two places at once: Renegotiating traumatic experience through the surplus reality XE "surplus reality" of psychodrama. *Social Work with Groups., 42*(3), 184–196. https://doi.org/10.1080/01609513.2018.1533913.

Goldman, E. E., & Morrison, D. S. (1984). *Psychodrama: Experience and process.* Dubuque, IA: Kendall.

Hollander, C. E. (1978). *A process for psychodrama training XE "psychodrama training" : The Hollander psychodrama curve.* Incorporated: Snow Lion Press.

Holmes, P. (1991). Classical psychodrama: An overview. In P. Holmes & M. Karp (Eds.), *Psychodrama: Inspiration and technique* (pp. 7–14). New York: Routledge.

Hudgins, M. K. (2002). *Experiential Treatment of PTSD XE "Post-traumatic stress disorder" : The Therapeutic Spiral Model XE "Therapeutic Spiral Model" .* New York, NY: Springer Publishing.

Hudgins, M. K., & Toscani, F. (2013). *Healing World Trauma with The Therapeutic Spiral Model XE "Therapeutic Spiral Model" : Stories from the Frontlines.* London: Jessica Kingsley Publishers.

Kellermann, P. F. (1992). *Focus on psychodrama: The therapeutic aspects of psychodrama.* Philadelphia: Jessica Kingsley Publishers.

Kellermann, P. F. (1994). Role reversal in psychodrama. In P. Holmes, M. Karp, & M. Watson (Eds.), *Psychodrama since Moreno* (pp. 263–279). London: Routledge.

Kipper, D. A. (1986). *Psychotherapy through clinical role-playing XE "Role theory:Role-playing" .* New York: Brunner/Mazel.

Knittel, M. G. (2010). Empty chair grief XE "grief" work from psychodrama perspective. *Counseling Today, 52*(10), 50–51.

Lang, N. C. (2010). *Group work practice to advance social competence: A specialized methodology for social work.* New York: Columbia University Press.

Levy, G. (2010). *275 Acting Games: Connected: A Comprehensive Workbook of Theatre Games for Developing Acting Skills.* Limited: Meriwether Pub.

Moreno, J. L. (1914). *Einladung zu einer Begegnung.* Vienna: Anzengruber Verlag.

Moreno, J. L. (1937). Inter-personal therapy and the psychopathology of inter-personal relations. *Sociometry*, pp. 9–76.

Moreno, J. L. (1946a). *Psychodrama* Vol. 1. Beacon, NY: Beacon House Press.

Moreno, J. L. (1952). Psychodramatic production techniques. *Group Psychotherapy, Psychodrama, and Sociometry, 4,* 273–303.

Moreno, J.L. (in collaboration with Z.T. Moreno) (1959). *Psychodrama second volume, foundations of psychotherapy.* Beacon, NY: Beacon House.

Moreno, Z. T. (1965/2006). Psychodramatic Rules, Techniques, and Adjunctive Methods. In T. Horvatin and E. Schreiber (Eds.), *The Quintessential Zerka* (pp. 104–114). New York: Routledge.

Moreno, J. L. (1972). *Psychodrama* Vol. 1, 4th edn. New York: Beacon House.

Moreno, Z. T. (1946b). Clinical Psychodrama: Auxiliary ego, double, and mirror techniques. *Sociometry: A Journal of Inter-Personal Relations,* 9(2–3): 178–183

Moreno, Z. T. (1945/2006). A sociodramatic audience test. In T. Horvatin and E. Schreiber (Eds.), *The Quintessential Zerka (pp. 22–31).* New York: Routledge.

Moreno, Z. T. (1987/2006). Psychodrama, role theory and the concept of the social atom. In T. Horvatin and E. Schreiber (Eds.), *The Quintessential Zerka (pp. 222–242).* New York: Routledge.

Moreno, Z. T. (2000/2006). In the Spirit of Two Thousand. In T. Horvatin and E. Schreiber (Eds.), *The Quintessential Zerka (pp. 275–288).* New York: Routledge.

Nolte, J. (2014). *The Philosophy, Theory, and Methods of J.L. Moreno: The Man Who Tried to Become God.* New York, NY: Routledge.

Nolte, J. (2020). *J.L. Moreno and the Psychodramatic Method: On the Practice of Psychodrama.* New York: Routledge.

Rojas-Bermúdez, J. (1997). *Teoria e Técnica Psicodramáticas.* Barcelona: Paidós.

Santos, A. J. D., & Conceição, M. I. G. (2014). Espiral psicodramático: Ciência e arte do aquecimento. *Revista Brasileira De Psicodrama, 22*(1), 54–64.

Scategni, W. (2005). *Psychodrama, group processes and dreams: Archetypal images of individuation.* New York: Routledge.

Schramski, T. G. (1979). A systematic model of psychodrama. *Group Psychotherapy, Psychodrama, & Sociometry, 32,* 20–30.

Spolin, V., (1999). *Improvisation for the theater: A handbook of teaching and directing techniques.* Northwestern University Press.

von Ameln, F., & Becker-, J. (2020). *Fundamentals of Psychodrama.* Singapore: Springer Nature.

Weiner, H. B., & Sacks, J. M. (1969). Warm-up and sum-up. *Group. Psychotherapy, 22*(1–2), 85–102.

Wilkins, P. (1999). *Psychodrama.* London: Sage Publications.

Yablonsky, L. (1976). *Psychodrama: Resolving emotional problems through role-playing XE "Role theory:Role-playing" .* New York: Basic Books.

Chapter 14
Advanced Psychodrama Directing

Abstract Advanced psychodrama directing techniques are presented in this chapter. These advanced interventions offer a depiction of the level of clinical sophistication demonstrated by expert psychodrama directors. The awareness of group sociometry within the psychodrama enactment is described while portraying the multiple layers of object relations activated for participants in a psychodrama session. Advanced techniques for involving audience group members and deepening the emotional involvement of auxiliary role players are discussed. Also included in this chapter are an overview of clinical role assignments, facilitating moments of multiple protagonists, and constructively using projective identification in the group process. Content from the Therapeutic Spiral Model is offered, specifically the practice of prescribing strengths-based roles and considerations for safely facilitating scenes with trauma-based roles. Multiple strategies are offered for de-roling when more emotionally charged roles are played by group members.

Keyword Psychodrama directing · Trauma-focused psychodrama · Psychodrama de-roling · Clinical role assignment · Projective identification

In this chapter, we will move beyond the basics of psychodrama directing and explore some advanced concepts for experienced psychodrama directors. Each subsection of this chapter will offer different methods for engaging the group-as-a-whole during the protagonist's psychodrama. The following advanced directing skills prevent the psychodrama process from becoming an individual therapy session within a group setting. The use of active sociometry within the psychodrama process will be outlined to keep the audience or group actively engaged and identified with the protagonist. The skillful weaving of group members' stories will be depicted through the use of surplus reality and clinical role assignments at the director's discretion. The use of clinical role assignments for both strengths-based roles and other roles will be explored. Psychological safety will be emphasized extracting elements of the Therapeutic Spiral Model's clinical map—the Trauma Survivor's Intrapsychic Role Atom (TSIRA) (see Sect. 7.8). Complexities related to the multiple layers of object relations, role relations, and interpersonal relationships in a psychodrama group experience will be depicted. This section will also portray the use of projective identification

S. Giacomucci, *Social Work, Sociometry, and Psychodrama*, Psychodrama in Counselling, Coaching and Education 1,
https://doi.org/10.1007/978-981-33-6342-7_14

in the psychodrama process in service of the protagonist, the scene, and the group-as-a-whole. Brief interventions that explicitly expand the role of protagonist from the individual to the group will also be demonstrated.

14.1   Sociometry Within a Psychodrama

Sociometry and psychodrama are different parts of Moreno's triadic system, albeit they have an intimate relationship to each other. As a director, it is important to maintain sociometric awareness throughout the psychodrama process (Gershoni, 2016). Each participant exists at the intersection of multiple systems, including their nervous system and other somatic systems, psychological systems, family systems, the group system, social systems, political system, cultural systems, and economic systems (Holmes, 2015). A psychodrama enactment and the roles within it interface with multiple systems and can only be fully understood through the lens of each of these systems. In social work, we describe this as person-in-environment or the biopsychosocial approach. This perspective of various systems intersecting offers insight into the overlapping systems of sociometry and psychodrama within a group psychotherapy session.

The sociometric warm-up is the first phase of a psychodrama group. Nevertheless, the sociometry of the group is useful to both be aware of and to actively utilize throughout the psychodrama enactment (Moreno, 1972). Although participants are being asked to play various psychodramatic roles in the scene, the interpersonal relationships between group members are inevitably still present during the process (Giacomucci, 2018; McVea, 2013). Knowing the nature of relationships between the group members may shed light on the nature of the role relationships in the scene. This often cultivates positive role relationships as the protagonist is likely to choose role players that they have positive relationships to. But the sociometry in the group can also be counterproductive to the psychodrama at times. For example, in the middle of a psychodrama, the protagonist might be asked to choose a group member to play the role of their younger self. If there is only one remaining audience member available for roles, they will not have a choice. If that remaining group member is someone who the protagonist has a negative relationship with, it could impact their ability to engage with the role of their younger self in a compassionate manner. The image below depicts the complexities of interpersonal relationships between group members, the role relationships between the psychodramatic roles they are playing in the scene, and each individual group members' relationships from their social atom that may be activated during the psychodrama process due to the role dynamics and role reciprocity of the scene.

In the following image, the rectangles represent the roles within John's psychodrama scene with his father, grandmother, and grandfather. Lines are used to connect each of the rectangles to the other rectangles indicating their role relationships to each other. The adjacent circles represent the actual group member who is playing that role with lines again used to depict the interpersonal relationships between each group member. Furthermore, each auxiliary role has another connective dotted line that leads to a portrayal of that group members' relationships to others in their social atom that may be activate due to the role they are playing and the role dynamics within the psychodrama scene. The larger square with dotted lines shows the boundary between the psychodrama being enacted by group members and the related roles from each group members' social atoms that may (consciously or unconsciously) influence their experience in the role they are playing (see Fig. 14.1).

Many psychodrama groups involve many more than four roles, so the depiction above is simple compared to most real psychodramas. Furthermore, the image above only portrays the web of relationships without depicting the positive, negative, and neutral relationships within each layer of sociometry. This image is a good depiction of the multiple layers of sociometry or object relations that are engaged in any psychodrama enactment. An advanced director attempts to maintain awareness of these various layers of sociometry and use psychodrama interventions to skillfully weave in and out of these layers to provide optimal therapeutic effect for each group member—not just the protagonist.

In the role dynamics depicted above, a director might be aware of Jane's own conflictual relationship with her grandson and emphasize conflict resolution in the psychodrama role dynamics. Or the director might be aware that Anthony struggles with his marriage and could underscore the healthy marriage between John's grandparents in the process. Or the director might know that Tim's father died recently, so the directing of Tim as an auxiliary in the role of a father could be accentuated. In this way, the director carefully weaves the layers of sociometry together in a way that offers role training, catharsis, insight, and corrective experiences for each group member. A skillful director can facilitate a psychodrama for the protagonist where the other role players are also protagonists doing their own work.

14.2 Advanced Directing of the Audience

The simplest use of sociometry interventions with the audience in a psychodrama is to invite group members to raise their hand if they identify with specific elements of the scene. Offering this simple sociometric intervention at various points in the psychodrama reminds the protagonist of the connection and peer support in the room while also encouraging continued engagement from audience members. It enhances the sense of shared experience, universality, and group-as-a-whole experience while the protagonist's scene is enacted. Another simple sociometry intervention during the psychodrama process is to invite audience members to repeat significant statements from various roles when they relate to them (Blatner, 1996). This creates an echo of important message and a sociometric connection through sound. Through this intervention, the protagonist becomes the double of the audience who are repeating messages that they connect with from the protagonist's psychodrama.

Another use of the sociometry is to invite audience members to stand behind or put their hand on the shoulder of the role that they feel most identified with—or a

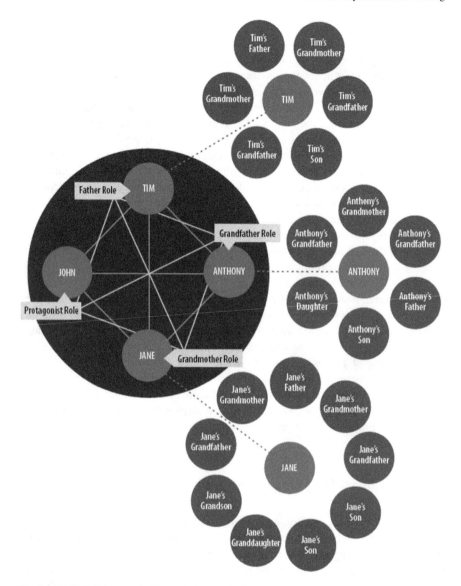

Fig. 14.1 Multiple layers of object relations and role relations within a psychodrama enactment

role that they feel they need to speak to. Essentially, this is a locogram or hands-on-shoulder sociogram using the roles of the psychodrama as the options for choices. This can be used to cluster participants into a role—having multiple people play one role for more impact, to warm up to psychodrama sub-scenes with the various roles, and/or to promote sharing. This process can be used in a simple, contained manner by inviting participants who identify with the protagonist's experience to stand behind the protagonist for support during the climax of the drama.

14.3   Moments of Multiple Protagonists

Traditionally, a psychodrama has one protagonist and other group members play auxiliary roles needed for the scene enacted by the protagonist. An advanced psychodrama director begins to weave together the story lines of group members with both implicit and explicit interventions. One explicit intervention that accomplishes this is to direct moments where role players briefly step out of their psychodrama role and interact as themselves with another role in the psychodrama. Everyone is invited to become the protagonist for a moment and speak to whoever or what-ever the roles represent for them in their life. This needs to be done in a way that is quick, contained, and does not interfere with the protagonist's scene or warm-up process. When done well, it can enhance the protagonist's experience by highlighting and enhancing group members' investment and identification with the psychodrama scene's roles, dynamics, and themes.

> Using the psychodrama scene from the image above as an example, let's say the that John is revisiting a difficult, but meaningful moment with her grandparents sharing with him about their immigration story characterized by trauma, loss, and resilience. John's father was with him during the conversation for support. In the original, real-life scene John was overwhelmed hearing his grandparents' story for the first time and didn't know how to respond. Instead, he froze and shut down emotionally, unable to express his pain, sadness, shock, gratitude, love, and admiration for his grandparents after hearing the details of their experience. His goal in this psychodrama was to revisit this moment in time, get unstuck, and be able to express the complex feelings that emerged for him. With the help of the group, he was able to do so in the psychodrama and had powerful catharsis letting out his sorrow for the trauma his grandparents experience and his anger towards those who discriminated against his ancestors. After releasing his anger and sadness, he was able to articulate his newfound appreciation, respect, and love directly to his grandparents. After John has thoroughly expressed his feelings, the director invites audience members to stand behind John, stepping briefly into the protagonist role and to state a sentence or two to the grandparent roles as if they were their grandparents (or whoever else they might represent for another group member). One at time, group members step forward next to John and offer statements of gratitude to their own grandparents or other grandparent-like figures from their own lives. As each group member takes their turn, John and the rest of the group drop into a deeper appreciation for each other and the shared experience of the psychodrama.

This moment of multiple protagonists provides John and the rest of the group with a concretization of the universality of the psychodrama topic and the role dynamics within. It reminds John that he has been a representative of the group while reminding participants of their own work related to the topic. This intervention allows the director to explicitly work with the group-as-a-whole and operationalizes the perspective of the group as the protagonist. In this way, group members not only see themselves in the protagonist, but also get to step into the protagonist role briefly. Audience involvement is maximized providing avenues for catharsis and integration to satisfy act hungers. In the example above, the intervention of a moment of multiple protagonists also served to cool down the protagonist after the scene climax and to move toward closure of the scene. This intervention can also be used in other phases of the psychodrama when deemed appropriate.

14.4   Clinical Role Assignments and Advanced Auxiliary Directing

While the protagonist usually is empowered to choose who they would like to play each role, there are times where the director might make use of clinical role assignments to enhance the experience for the group (Giacomucci, 2019). The practice of clinically assigning roles to participants based on the director's understanding of their personal/therapeutic goals or needs can be traced back to Moreno's original work around actor catharsis with the Theater of Spontaneity and Impromptu Theater (Garcia, 2010; Moreno, 2019). Clinical role assignments are most applicable when working with ongoing therapy groups where the director is familiar with each participants' stories. Although a director might be working with a group that they are not familiar with participants' back stories, information offered through the warm-up process and the protagonist selection can also be used to guide clinical role assignments. A simple way of using this is by incorporating the other group members who had volunteered as protagonist into the psychodrama in a role that allows them to do their own work in service of the protagonist's psychodrama. This is not always possible, but in most cases, it can be done without taking away from the protagonist's experience. An example of this is depicted below:

> Four group members volunteer as protagonist offering the following topics: worthlessness and self-worth by Lindsey; letting down defensesto trust others by Frank; hope for the future by Steven; and guilt, shame, and self-forgiveness offered by Jake. Jake's topic is sociometrically chosen by the group. As the psychodrama begins to unfold, Jake agrees when the director inquires if the role of a positive inner voice might be helpful for the scene. The director suggests Lindsey could play the role based on her proposed topic of self-worth. Through playing the role of Jake's inner supportive voice, Lindsey is able to achieve her own goals that she had hoped for as protagonist. Not only does she benefit from it, but because she is substantially invested in the role for her own gain, Jake benefits from having her as a strong auxiliary. Next in the psychodrama scene, Jake begins to share about his uncertainty about ever being able to forgive himself. Jake describes his negative beliefs about himself and his habit of pushing others away because he feels ashamed. At this point, the director suggests that Frank enter the role of the negative beliefs and behaviors that block Jake from self-forgiveness and connection. Frank is able to play the role without any role training based on his own warm-up to his topic. When role reversed with Jake, Frank (as Jake) gets to work on his topic through the interaction with Jake's negative beliefs/behaviors. As Jake renegotiates his relationship to these negative beliefs, he begins to warm-up to the potential of a future with self-forgiveness. Noticing the connection with Steven's topic of hope for the future, the director clinically assigns the role of future self to Steven after checking it out with Jake first. Steven steps into the role of Jake in the future having attained self-forgiveness and a positive relationship with himself. In the back and forth dialogue and role reversal between Jake and his future self, the director facilitates Steven's work at the same time.

Through the use of clinical role assignments related to the other volunteers for protagonist, the director is able to provide a group-as-a-whole experience for participants while meeting the therapeutic goals and needs for the maximum number of group members (Buchanan & Dubbs-Siroka, 1980). While the role relationships in the protagonist's psychodrama are always given priority, each participant is seen as a protagonist just below the surface of the psychodrama roles. The director often reminds role players that as they are speaking to Jake, they are also speaking their messages to themselves—as they are playing the role for Jake, they are also playing the role for themselves (Giacomucci & Stone, 2019). In this process, it is also important to consider the sociometric relationships between the protagonist and the other group members before making a decision to assign a role. If Jake had a negative relationship with Steven playing the role of himself in the future, it could have jeopardized the success of his psychodrama. However, at the same time, a negative relationship between Jake and Frank playing the role of his negative beliefs and behaviors may have actually been helpful and even transformative for their interpersonal relationships as it would have provided an opportunity for conflict, catharsis, anger, rejection, and change with the aesthetic distance of the roles. The skillful use of clinical role assignments makes for a more engaged, vulnerable, and fruitful psychodrama for everyone involved.

In a basic psychodrama enactment, the auxiliaries are simply playing roles for the protagonist's scene based on direction from the protagonist and/or director. An advanced director can encourage auxiliaries to bring themselves to the role they are playing using emotional content from their own connection to the topic or role dynamics (Blatner, 1996; McVea, 2013; Moreno, 1946). Drawing upon the awareness of the auxiliary role player's own social atom, the director can direct them to warm up to the role they are playing by accessing emotions related to how their own lived experience of this role. This type of directing for auxiliaries can be used at any time and is especially relevant for auxiliaries that have been enrolled through clinical role assignments. It is also important to note that while clinical role assignments are one way to enhance the connection of participants to the psychodrama, the same group members are likely to be chosen for the roles based on the active tele between the protagonist and their peers (McVea, 2013).

14.4.1 Projective Identification

The here-and-now experience of group members is another source of information that can guide clinical role assignments. Using the same psychodrama example above, let us say that Tiffany is an audience member observing the psychodrama process with tears in her eyes, feeling vulnerable. Jake had referenced a desire to practice more vulnerability and be open with his emotions rather than defensive. With Jake's permission, Tiffany is integrated into the scene in the role of vulnerability where she is encouraged to use the emotions she is experiencing in service of the psychodrama scene while representing the strength of vulnerability for Jake.

The example of Tiffany used above is conceptualized in the Therapeutic Spiral Model as the use of projective identification in the group process (Hogenboom, 2020; Hudgins & Toscani, 2013). TSM teaches that the protagonist is projecting parts of self or emotions out upon group members who will at times identify with a projection and start to play out that role or emotion unconsciously. It is the role of the director and/or team members to be aware of the potential presence of projective identification and incorporate audience members who have identified with projections into the psychodrama scene so the protagonist can reintegrate the split off part. The first instinct of a therapist might be to ignore Tiffany or allow her to leave the room to contain herself, but it is worth considering if her emotional experience might be one of the projective identification and useful in the psychodrama scene. This process of projective identification in group therapy has also been described as it relates to group roles in traditional group work (Moxnes, 1999) and classical psychodrama groups (Holmes, 2015). The Therapeutic Spiral Model uses projective identification in service of this group-as-a-whole experience. Although we start with one protagonist, everyone becomes a protagonist. Although we start with one narrative, everyone's narrative joins into a collective narrative. And although on the surface, we are concerned with the protagonist's inner role atom; each individual group members' role atoms begin to emerge in alignment with the drama. The layers of object relations form a symmetrical union—Moreno termed this as this *the organic unity of mankind* (Moreno, 1953). The group mind emerges and accesses the autonomous healing center within (Giacomucci, 2019).

Holmes (2015) also describes the influence of projective identification on role players within classical psychodrama. He writes that the protagonist, in their interaction with a role on the psychodrama stage, is projecting that role and their experience of that role upon the role player who often identifies with the projections. It could be argued that projection and projective identification are the parallel mechanisms underlying the experience of role reciprocity. Projective identification may also be underlying the process of doubling of the protagonist from other group members. In both cases, the projections from the protagonist are able to be held, articulated, and reintegrated by the protagonist in action.

14.4.2 Prescribing Roles

Another use of role assignment comes from the director's clinical judgment of roles that are missing in the psychodrama scene itself. A common use of this type of role assignment comes in the form of prescribing strengths-based roles or supportive roles when working with trauma or addiction (Dayton, 2005; Hudgins, 2002). The Therapeutic Spiral Model (TSM) offers a comprehensive clinical map that includes eight different prescriptive roles (see Sect. 7.8.1) with the functions of containment, strength/restoration, and accurate observation (Giacomucci, 2018). When working with trauma, these roles are prescribed by the psychodrama director into the scene to ensure safety. Some different examples might include prescribing the role of a *body double* to a protagonist struggling with body image; *interpersonal support* for a protagonist struggling to ask others for help; *courage* or *willingness* for a protagonist intimidated by the process; *self-love* for a protagonist struggling with self-hatred; *boundaries* for a protagonist struggling with healthy boundaries; a *manager of defenses* for a client struggling with maladaptive defense mechanisms; or a *compassionate witness* for a protagonist struggling with accurate labeling or self-judgment. As noted previously, the prescriptive roles enhance the sense of safety and spontaneity in the psychodrama scene, especially when working with traumatic material and trauma survivors. In many cases, without the presence of strengths-based roles, a protagonist risks repeating or reenacting maladaptive behavior patterns or trauma in the actual psychodrama scene. If nothing changes, nothing changes. Regardless of the psychodrama enactment, it is also important to balance the use of clinical role assignments and prescribed roles with the protagonist's own choice of roles and role players. It can be helpful to think of the psychodrama process as a co-created scene between the protagonist, the director, and the group.

14.5 Trauma-Based Role Considerations for Safety

As noted in Chap. 7, psychodrama can be potentially re-traumatizing with trauma survivors which has both impacted its reputation in negative ways and led to the development of different trauma-focused psychodrama models (Dayton, 2015; Giacomucci & Marquit, 2020; Hudgins & Toscani, 2013). Essential for any psychodrama director is a basic understanding of role considerations related to safety for trauma survivors. When facilitating trauma-related scenes, the director is ultimately responsible for the safety of the process and preventing any harm from being experienced by participants. The previous subsection outlines the use of prescribing strengths-based roles with attention to safety which offers an alternative to reenacting one's trauma scene.

When working directly with trauma-based roles such as perpetrators or victim roles, there are some clinical factors that the director should consider (Giacomucci, 2018; Hudgins & Toscani, 2013; Nolte, 2020; Toscani & Hudgins, 2013). One such consideration is that of the individual ego strength of the protagonist, each participant, and the group-as-a-whole. It is not uncommon for group members to have varying levels of ego strength and different windows of tolerance. Consistency in this area is best cultivated through thorough assessment prior to group sessions. In some cases, the protagonist may have the ego strength to encounter a trauma-based role in the psychodrama, but the rest of the group might be unable to tolerate the level of intensity that comes by observing the scene. Or the group may have chosen a topic that involves a trauma-based role only to find that the protagonist who volunteered the topic does not seem to have the stability to go there. When there is concern about lack of ego strength and stability to encounter trauma-based roles, it would be wise for the director to either focus the scene on building up strengths, internalized trauma roles, and/or using metaphorical roles. Another option is to utilize an empty chair to hold the trauma-based role instead of another role player which will limit the power of the role.

When facilitating psychodramas focused on trauma, another foundational understanding for the director is around common defense mechanisms and trauma responses (Giacomucci, 2018). A director working with trauma needs to be able to identify and intervene when a group member is experiencing dissociation, common trauma responses (fight, flight, and freeze), flashbacks, hyperarousal, difficulty with physical touch, body memories, regression, and symptoms related to dissociative identity disorder. Many of these defenses or symptoms can appear to be resistance, defiance, disinterest, unrelated to trauma, or even a form of role playing to the untrained eye when in fact they are often related to traumatic symptoms or defenses. An understanding of defenses and trauma responses becomes necessary to adequately respond with spontaneity to a protagonist or group members (Toscani & Hudgins, 2013). Recognizing the importance of defenses and their role as a psychological attempt to establish safety or reduce threat/anxiety allows the director to honor them and help a protagonist honor them when they involuntarily emerge in the drama.

In classical psychodrama, a protagonist often is immediately role reversed with a role to provide role training for the auxiliary before interacting with the role as one's self. When working with the victim or perpetrator roles, it is advisable to have the protagonist first demonstrate their ability to interact with these roles from their adult ego state prior to directing them to role reverse into the trauma role (Toscani & Hudgins, 2013). This provides the director with an assessment of the protagonists spontaneity and ego strength, while also evaluating their ability to differentiate themselves from the trauma-based role, to access adaptive information in the trauma-based role dynamic, to nurture or validate the victim role, and to confront the perpetrator role in appropriate ways. Only once a protagonist has sufficiently demonstrated their capacity to appropriately nurture the traumatized parts of self would it be safe to role reverse them into that role. Otherwise there is a risk of the protagonist being unable to role reverse or de-role back to their original role due to the vortex of the trauma and regression. Similarly, with the perpetrator role it is important to have the protagonist first demonstrate their ability to encounter the role before the role reversal. If this is not done, we risk overidentification with the perpetrator or the role training of violence. The practice of immediately role reversing protagonists into new roles seems to be a newer pattern in psychodrama directing as the Morenos did not immediately use role reversal and sometimes directed scenes without any role reversals.

A reminder that the role reversal is the final stage of development in Moreno's theory can be useful here. Using the developmental theory as a guide, a director would start with the interventions of the double and the mirror before role reversing. Encountering a trauma role in a psychodrama with adequate doubling provides the protagonist with stability, support, expression, and the labeling of non-verbal traumatic content. Instructing the protagonist to first experience the trauma-based role interaction from the mirror position would provide distance, safety, and the ability to accurately label the experience while warming up to necessary changes in the scene (Yablonsky, 1976). Once the functions of doubling (stabilization, expression, and labeling inner experience) and mirroring (differentiation and accurate sense of self) have been achieved, then it is safe to role reverse the protagonist into a trauma role. The role reversal with a trauma-based role, when used safely, provides further differentiation, understanding, catharsis, integration, and empowerment (Nolte, 2020; Roine, 2000; Toscani & Hudgins, 2013).

After a scene involving trauma-based roles, it is important that the director gives special attention to the integration process, closure, and de-roling. The director needs to remember that catharsis alone does not create change. It must be followed with integration, transformation, meaning making, growth, and/or future role training. In trauma-focused psychodramas, an enactment involving catharsis but no integration is simply a trauma reenactment and may only serve to increase the imprint of the trauma. Trauma scenes in psychodrama are often followed up with scenes for corrective emotional experiences, developmental repair, and/or unmet needs being fulfilled (Giacomucci, 2018, 2020; Giacomucci & Stone, 2019; Hudgins, 2002).

14.6 De-Roling Difficult Roles

There are times when de-roling can become difficult for auxiliaries and group members, especially related to trauma-based roles (Burmeister, 2000). It seems that the experience of playing a role for someone else that relates to a role that one has unresolved business with, especially trauma, increases the likelihood of an auxiliary getting stuck in the role and having difficult de-roling. There are multiple layers to the de-roling process which are important to consider, especially when working with antagonist and trauma-based roles. The de-roling needs to occur for the role player de-roling self in addition to the group, the protagonist, and the director seeing the role player as de-roled. While a role player might privately de-role, the rest of the group could continue to project the role upon them. This has the potential to lead to transferences between group members and even countertransference from the director.

When it comes to audience members, it can also be beneficial to invite them to de-role from the audience at the end of the psychodrama. This promotes action and engagement from audience members as the rest of the group de-roles and integrates back into the here-and-now group. It is certainly possible for audience members to get stuck in the role of audience even after the enactment is complete. When this happens, they are less likely to share in the next phase of the group and might feel disconnected and distant from the process.

It is also possible for the protagonist to role reverse with a difficult role and have trouble reversing out of that role again. This becomes especially evident when working with trauma-based roles and needs to be considered. As outlined previously, a good rule of thumb is to make sure protagonists can interact appropriately and spontaneously with the trauma-based role as themselves before directing them to role reverse (Hudgins & Toscani, 2013).

When encountering a group member who needs extra attention to de-roling, there are multiple avenues to further the de-roling process. The auxiliary could be asked to use additional body movement to shake off the role with spontaneity or be asked to make statements about how they are different than the role they played in front of the group. For example, a group member after playing the role of an angry demanding mother might further de-role by stating, "I am not the angry demanding mother because: I don't have any children; I am loving and forgiving; and I am patient and understanding with others". Another playful way of de-roling is to use surplus reality to set up a *de-roling station* where role players are washed from their roles, unzipped from their roles, or transformed back into themselves with other creative and imaginary processes. One further method of de-roling difficult roles is through the use of a mini empty chair dialog between the role player and the role in front of the group. The role player is asked to separate themselves from the role by putting it into the empty chair. Then, they are directed to speak to the role with a focus on differentiation. This provides the role player and the group with a visual, emotional, and cognitive experience of separating the group member from the role they played in the scene. When de-roling in this way from an antagonist or trauma-based role, this also provides the role player with a chance to demonstrate safe, compassionate, insightful, and grounded statements or action in front of the group after playing a role that may have been angry, dismissive, or antagonistic.

The aforementioned de-roling interventions can also be useful in any therapeutic process when it is identified that one participant is projecting upon another or in the midst of transference with another. The same de-roling methods can be used to help participants explore transference and projections to better relate to each other in the here-and-now. In this way, de-roling provides an avenue to transcend transference to engage with tele.

14.7 Conclusion

This chapter outlines various advanced psychodrama directing competencies and interventions focused on providing a group-as-a-whole therapeutic experience through the skillful interweaving of client stories and sociometric layers. The outlined interventions in this chapter are often too complex for one facilitator to track while also holding the other roles of director. It can be advantageous to work on a team of trained psychodrama professionals to share the responsibilities and directing functions (Cho, 2013; McVea, 2013). Outlined considerations for trauma-based roles and integrating strengths-based roles ensure the presence and maintenance of a sense of safety for the group. The use of active sociometry, clinical role assignments, and moments of multiple protagonists provide maximum emotional involvement for the audience and auxiliaries during the psychodrama process.

References

Blatner, A. (1996). *Acting-in: Practical applications of psychodramatic methods*. New York: Springer Publishing Company.

Buchanan, D. R., & Dubbs-Siroka, J. (1980). Psychodramatic treatment for psychiatric patients. *Journal of the National Association of Private Psychiatric Hospitals, 11*(2), 27–31.

Cho, W. C. (2013). Learning to Be on the Action Healing Team in the Therapeutic Spiral Model XE "Therapeutic Spiral Model". In M. K. Hudgins & F. Toscani (Eds.), *Healing World Trauma with the Therapeutic Spiral Model: Stories from the Frontlines* (pp. 149–167). Philadelphia: Jessica Kingsley Publishers.

Burmeister, J. (2000). Psychodrama with Survivors of Traffic Accidents. In P. F. Kellermann & M. K. Hudgins (Eds.), *Psychodrama with Trauma Survivors: Acting out your pain* (pp. 198–228). Philadelphia: Jessica Kingsley Publishers.

Dayton, T. (2015). *NeuroPsychodrama in the Treatment of Relational Trauma: A Strength-based, Experiential Model for Healing PTSD XE "Post-traumatic stress disorder"*. Deerfield Beach, FL: Health Communications Inc.

Garcia, A. (2010). Healing with action methods on the world stage. In E. Leveton (Ed.), *Healing collective trauma using sociodrama XE "sociodrama" and drama therapy XE "drama therapy"* (pp. 3–24). New York: Springer.

Gershoni, J. (2016). Highlighting Sociometry in the Psychodramatic Process. *Zeitschrift Für Psychodrama Und Soziometrie, 15,* 353–357.

Giacomucci, S. (2018). The trauma survivor's inner role atom XE "role atom" : A clinical map XE "clinical map" for post-traumatic growth XE "post-traumatic growth". *Journal of Psychodrama, Sociometry, and Group Psychotherapy., 66*(1), 115–129.

Giacomucci, S. (2019). *Social Group Work in Action: A Sociometry, Psychodrama, and Experiential Trauma Therapy Curriculum*. Doctorate in Social Work (DSW) Dissertations. 124. https://repository.upenn.edu/cgi/viewcontent.cgi?article=1128&context=edissertations_sp2

Giacomucci, S. (2020). Addiction, traumatic loss, and guilt: A case study resolving grief XE "grief" through psychodrama and sociometric connections. *the Arts in Psychotherapy, 67,* 101627. 10.1016/j.aip.2019.101627

Giacomucci, S., & Marquit, J. (2020). The Effectiveness of Trauma-Focused Psychodrama in the Treatment of PTSD in Inpatient Substance Abuse Treatment. *Frontiers in Psychology, 11,* 896. 10.3389%2Ffpsyg.2020.00896

Giacomucci, S., & Stone, A. M. (2019). Being in two places at once: Renegotiating traumatic experience through the surplus reality XE "surplus reality" of psychodrama. *Social Work with Groups., 42*(3), 184–196. https://doi.org/10.1080/01609513.2018.1533913.

Hogenboom, I. (2020, April 9). Working with projective identification in the Therapeutic Spiral Model (TSM). Retrieved from https://therapeuticspiralmodel.com/blog/working-with-projective-identification-in-the-therapeutic-spiral-model-tsm/

Holmes, P. (2015). *The inner world outside: Object relations theory and psychodrama*. London: Routledge.

Hudgins, M. K. (2002). *Experiential Treatment of PTSD XE "Post-traumatic stress disorder" : The Therapeutic Spiral Model XE "Therapeutic Spiral Model"*. New York, NY: Springer Publishing.

Hudgins, M. K., & Toscani, F. (2013). *Healing World Trauma with The Therapeutic Spiral Model XE "Therapeutic Spiral Model" : Stories from the Frontlines*. London: Jessica Kingsley Publishers.

McVea, C. (2013). The Therapeutic Alliance Between the Protagonist and Auxiliaries. In M. K. Hudgins & F. Toscani (Eds.), *Healing World Trauma with the Therapeutic Spiral Model XE "Therapeutic Spiral Model" : Stories from the Frontlines* (pp. 168–180). Philadelphia: Jessica Kingsley Publishers.

Moreno, J. L. (1946). *Psychodrama Volume 1*. New York: Beacon House

Moreno, J. L. (1953). *Who shall survive? Foundations of sociometry, group psychotherapy and sociodrama (2nd edition)*. Beacon, NY: Beacon House.

Moreno, J. L. (1972). *Psychodrama Volume 1 (4ᵗʰ edition)*. New York: Beacon House

Moreno, J.L. (2019). *The Autobiography of a Genius* (E. Schreiber, S. Kelley, & S. Giacomucci, Eds.). United Kingdom: North West Psychodrama Association

Moxnes, P. (1999). Understanding roles: A psychodynamic XE "psychodynamic" model for role differentiation in groups. *Group Dynamics: Theory, Research, and Practice, 3*(2), 99–113.

Nolte, J. (2020). *J.L. Moreno and the Psychodramatic Method: On the Practice of Psychodrama.* New York: Routledge.

Roine, E. (2000). The Use of Psychodrama with Trauma Victims. In P. F. Kellermann & M. K. Hudgins (Eds.), *Psychodrama with Trauma Survivors: Acting out your pain* (pp. 83–96). Philadelphia: Jessica Kingsley Publishers.

Toscani, F., & Hudgins, M. K. (2013). The Evolution of the Therapeutic Spiral Model XE "Therapeutic Spiral Model" . In M. K. Hudgins & F. Toscani (Eds.), *Healing World Trauma with the Therapeutic Spiral Model: Stories from the Frontlines* (pp. 75–110). Philadelphia: Jessica Kingsley Publishers.

Chapter 15
Other Experiential Approaches Similar to Psychodrama

Abstract This chapter will briefly introduce further methods that Moreno created related to psychodrama, as well as other approaches similar to psychodrama but developed by others. Social microscopy and sociodrama will be outlined pertaining to Moreno's additional dramatic approaches. Axiodrama, monodrama, autodrama, ethnodrama, bibliodrama, and teledrama each will be introduced as other dramatic approaches based on psychodrama. Drama therapy, gestalt therapy, Playback Theater, Theater of the Oppressed, Internal Family Systems Therapy, Pesso Boyden System Psychomotor Therapy, and family/systemic constellations will each be briefly presented with their similarities and differences to psychodrama.

Keywords Sociodrama · Sociatry · Drama therapy · Gestalt therapy · Experiential approaches · Teledrama

Moreno is most recognized for his contributions to the field through his development of sociometry and psychodrama. Nevertheless, he also developed multiple other experiential approaches similar to psychodrama which are outlined below. Furthermore, other pioneers since Moreno have created experiential approaches have core elements in common with Moreno's methods. Some of these other methods were directly or indirectly influenced by Moreno's work while others emerged independently from his influence.

15.1 Sociodrama

Sociodrama seems to be particularly complimentary to social work in its focus on social issues and versatility as an approach in clinical, educational, and community settings. Browne defines sociodrama as "a learning method that creates deep understanding of the social systems and social forces that shape us individually and collectively" (2011, p. 12). While a psychodrama enacts the topic or concerns of an individual group member, a sociodrama enacts a collective group concern (Giacomucci, 2017; Minkin, 2016). Moreno states that "the true subject of a sociodrama is the group" (1943, p. 437). In sociodrama, there is an element of aesthetic distance

© The Author(s) 2021
S. Giacomucci, *Social Work, Sociometry, and Psychodrama*, Psychodrama in Counselling, Coaching and Education 1,
https://doi.org/10.1007/978-981-33-6342-7_15

that helps maintain a sense of safety as the sociodrama is not an individual's story; it is the story of the group. In a sociodrama, the group-as-a-whole is explicitly identified as the protagonist. The sociodramatic enactment "unlocks the common threads of human experience for everyone" (Sternberg & Garcia, 2000, p. xvii). Rather than sitting and talking about a social issue, group members take roles and enact scenes and themes related to the social issue. In doing so, group members are able to see the issue from the roles of others, clarify their values, and express their thoughts and feelings in a spontaneous manner. The goals of a sociodrama include catharsis and expression, insight and new perception, and role training or behavioral practice (Sternberg & Garcia, 2000).

A sociodrama session follows the same three phases of a psychodrama group—warm-up, enactment, and sharing. However, in a sociodrama, the enactment is not scripted in anyway and does not revolve around one person's experience. Instead, the sociodrama scene is spontaneously put into action through co-creation between participants. Sociodramas tend to be more playful than psychodramas because of this and the aesthetic distance they provide. Sociodrama roles are focused on collective elements of the roles while psychodrama orients on the protagonist's private elements of the role (Sternberg & Garcia, 2000). For example, in a group focused on parenting, a psychodrama would enact a protagonist's parent–child relationship while a sociodrama would enact a hypothetical parent–child relationship. The role difference is—*your* child versus *a* child.

> After a group warm-up identifying a central concern of dealing with a defiant child, the enactment phase of the sociodrama commences. The director invites two group members to take on the roles of a parent and a child while the audience is prompted to spontaneously define each of the roles in terms of age, gender, relationship, and other pertinent details. The group collectively defines the enactment which is put into action be the role-players. Once the originally identified concern of the group is embodied through the action, the facilitator pauses the action to ask for observations from audience members which allows them to reflect on the nature of the social interaction. Then the director invites doubling statements from participants for either the role of the parent or the child. Through doubling, the group begins to give voice to the internal experiences of both the parent and the child caught in this relational conflict characterized by the child's defiance. New understandings emerge in this process that point to new ways of responding to a child's defiance. The child's defiance is re-enacted while participants take turns in the parent role offering new ways of responding. Once the director senses that the role training has been adequate, they move the scene to closure, de-roling, and finally sharing from the group.

The example above demonstrates a fundamental difference between psychodrama and sociodrama in that the scene is not scripted based on the protagonist's experience—instead, it is spontaneously created by the group. In sociodrama, the themes, issues, roles, and scene can be defined by the group, the director, or a mix of the group and the director. In many cases, a sociodramatist is asked to facilitate a session with an already established contract or theme. A sociodrama can be person-centered or group-centered, but the roles remain collective instead of private roles (Garcia, 2011).

Because of its non-threatening but collective group focus, sociodrama is especially fit for education, professional training, community groups, conflict resolution, education, and social activism. Moreno described sociodrama as "a new approach to the problem of inter-cultural relations" in one of his earliest writings about it (1943, p. 434). He argues that social problems cannot be solved in the seclusion of individual therapy, but instead must be solved in a forum accessible to the entire community such as a sociodrama (1943). Sociodrama is frequently used in non-clinical settings and educational settings but can also be used in clinical groups (Giacomucci, 2017; Kellermann, 2007; Sternberg & Garcia, 2000). Sociodrama examples will be depicted in future chapters (especially Chap. 19) related to community work, social activism, and education.

15.2 Social Microscopy and Sociatry

Moreno believed that "a truly therapeutic procedure must have no less objective than the whole of mankind" (1953, p. 1). All of his methods fall under the umbrella of his vision of *Sociatry*—healing for society (Moreno, 2006). He writes that "Psychiatry is the branch in medicine that relates to mental disease and its treatment; it treats the individual psyche and soma. Sociatry treats the diseases of inter-related individuals and of inter-related groups" (Moreno, 1947, p. 11). Sociatry, in practice, orients itself with Moreno's mystical tradition and focuses on the larger societal picture and social justice (Giacomucci, 2018; Schreiber, 2018a).

The *social microscope* is a group, or societal, technique that Moreno developed to explore the invisible social forces that impact groups and society. Moreno comments that:

> most sociodynamic phenomena disclosed by sociometry and sociatry "are" unconscious. But not unconscious in the sense of psychoanalysis, as repressed aggressive tendencies for instance, but unconscious almost in the sense in which the arrangements of the astronomic world were unconscious to man before he was able to study the stellar movements by means of scientific instruments. There are millions of atomic items buried in the group structures of human society which no human genius could divine and which no psychoanalysis of an individual mind lasting a thousand years could disclose. (1947, p. 22)

He wrote that these unseen forces "operate first in groups on the micro-sociological level then spread into the macro-sociological, leading to ever-larger ones" (Moreno, 2006, p. 514). Moreno created the social microscope in 1935 to explore how smaller groups are impacted by various psychosocial dynamics, believing that it could provide us with insight into how the larger society is impacted by the same dynamics. The social microscope makes visible the parallel process between group and society (Giacomucci, 2019). As Edward Schreiber says, "the group becomes a social microscope to the world sociometry" (2018a, p. 24). Moreno believed that we cannot prescribe a treatment for society, or for a group, if we do not understand the sociodynamics and organization of the group (Moreno, 1953). "Human society has an atomic structure which corresponds to the atomic structure of matter. Its existence can be brought to an empirical test by means of social microscopy" (1953, p. 697).

The social microscope is an experiential "instrument designed to illuminate sociatry" (Schreiber, 2018b, 18). This process uses a specific prescription of sociometric tests guided by Moreno's developmental theory (Schreiber, 2017). Participants are warmed up to Moreno's mysticism and engage in a hands-on-shoulder sociogram for each phase of the developmental theory—double, mirror, and role reversal—reflecting the phases of human development. With each new constellation of choices, the distribution of choices and connections is interpreted with emphasis on the sociocultural roles and identities of participants within the context of the current sociopolitical climate in society and the world. The following example comes from the ASGPP conference workshop.

> After a series of warm-ups related to Moreno's concept of the godhead, the encounter symbol, and the autonomous healing center within, the facilitator offers a prompt to participants, "put your hand on the shoulder of the person in the room who you experience as giving voice and expression to something that is already within you". Participants move to make their choice creating a distribution of choices. The constellation results in the youngest group members chosen by the group as social stars and the older group members isolated with less choices. The facilitator describes this occurrence and suggests its connection to the importance of youth in society today giving voice to the injustices in society and how they need to be taken more seriously. At the same time he suggests that the elders being unchosen in the group may also reflect society's lost sense of respect for elders. Then the facilitator moves to the next prompt, "put your hand on the shoulder of the person in the group who you experience as a mirror, reflecting back to you something important to know and grow into". Participants make their choices, resulting in the majority of choices going to the women and transgender participants in the group with the men on the outsides of the constellations without many choices. The director acknowledges this to the group, commenting on the importance of reflecting on the significant role of women and trans folks in society today and going forward. That perhaps it is time for men to move to the periphery while dismantling patriarchal systems and create space for women and trans folks to be at the center of society and politics. The group becomes mystified by the truths emerging from the social microscope as the final criteria is given—"put your hand on the shoulder of the group member who, if you were to role reverse and experience the world through their role, your understanding and view of the world would expand". Again, participants indicate their choices, this time resulting in the people of color being highly chosen while white group members were unchosen. The facilitator reflects to participants the distribution of choices as it relates to the continued racial inequalities and white supremacy in American culture. The need for role reversal, inclusion, and social justice is emphasized while relating back to Moreno's concept of the organic unity of mankind. Group members reported feeling a sense of wonder and awe with a newfound understanding and motivation to work towards a socially just society. The director stresses the significance of the revelations from the social microscope as the emergence of the Godhead within the group.

The social microscope highlights both the social atoms and the cultural atoms impacting the group dynamics or its "the socio-atomic organization" within the sociometric matrix of group members (Moreno, 1953). It is designed to uncover both the sociodynamic effect and the organic unity of mankind (covered in detail in Chap. 5). The sociometric constellations of the process offer an opportunity for co-creation between the group and the Godhead—pointing to the organic unity of mankind and shattering the illusion of separateness between humans and groups. This instrument provides the group with insight into the sociocultural forces that threaten the unity of society while also helping the group to access its own autonomous healing center—the capacity to heal itself. "Sociatry's task is to awaken us to the autonomous healing center in a group and organization, and to plant that awakening within the sociometric fabric of society" (Schreiber, 2018a, p. 24).

15.3 Other Morenean or Psychodrama Approaches

In addition to sociometry, psychodrama, and group psychotherapy, Moreno also developed other action methods. His psychodrama textbooks introduce ethnodrama, axiodrama, monodrama, autodrama, and the use of psychodrama with dance, music, radio, and cinema (Moreno, 1946). A number of other action methods later developed drawing from or integrating psychodrama as a foundation, including bibliodrama, Souldrama, Therapeutic Spiral Model, Relational Trauma Repair Model, teledrama, and other culturally specific psychodrama approaches such as Sambadrama (Brazil) and Vedadrama (India). The etymology of terms becomes especially relevant here as Moreno created multiple new terms to label his ideas or methods.

Psycho—having to do with the mental, psychological, or soul.

Socio—related to society and the social.

Axio—meaning worth, truth, or value.

Mono—indicating a single aspect or the number one.

Auto—referring to self.

Ethno—related to ethnicity, race, or culture

Biblio—referring to books or the Bible.

Tele—meaning "at a distance" or "from afar," communication over distances.

15.3.1 Axiodrama

Moreno writes that axiodrama was the first of his dramatic methods to develop in 1918, later followed by sociodrama (1921), and psychodrama in the 1930 (Moreno, 2019a). He describes axiodrama by using spontaneous drama for dealing with issues related to values—cultural, religious, spiritual, and ethical. Axiodrama is most similar to sociodrama. Moreno's personal life and attraction to existential and religious philosophies played a major role in his development of dramatic methods. Marineau (2013) writes that psychodrama, sociodrama, and axiodrama are intimately linked through their enactments of individual life (psychodrama), community life (socio-drama), and existential or religious life (axiodrama). Most psychodrama and socio-dramatic enactments have roles or aspects that are axiodramatic in nature such as personal values, spiritual roles, social ideals, and death. "Ideally, Moreno's followers should all be axiodramatists, psychodramatists and sociodramatists" (Marineau, 2013, p. 24). Some have suggested that axiodrama is a natural fit for religious communities (Blatner, 1996) and organizations (Souza & Drummond, 2017).

15.3.2   Monodrama

In a monodrama, the protagonist plays all of the roles of the drama without any auxiliaries. There is only one role player. This approach is often used in individual therapy due to the absence of other participants (Blatner, 2000). Most often in a monodrama, other roles are indicated through the use of empty chairs. Monodrama is a core technique in gestalt therapy (Blatner, 1996). Monodrama is also referred to as *bipersonal psychodrama* or *psychodrama a deux*—meaning it involves two people, the director and the protagonist in one-on-one sessions (Cukier, 2008; Knittel, 2009).

15.3.3   Autodrama

The terms monodrama and autodrama are often confused and used interchangeably though they have a subtle difference. A monodrama has only one role player, the protagonist—but it is facilitated by another person, the director. In autodrama, the protagonist *is* the director. Simply put, an autodrama is a self-directed enactment. When a drama is self-directed and involving only one person, then it is both an auto-drama and a monodrama. Autodramas are often useful for experienced psychodrama participants or practitioners seeking to engage in their own personal work in an efficient manner.

15.3.4   Ethnodrama

The integration of a psychodrama or sociodramatic process with the content of ethnic or racial conflicts is referred to as an ethnodrama (Malaquias, Nonoya, Cesarino, & Nery, 2016). Moreno initially describes sociodrama as an effective method for inter-cultural relations (1943), later using the term ethnodrama (1953). While Moreno is one of the earliest writers to use the term ethnodrama, he appears to have written very little about it. Ethnodrama seems to have become much more popular in theater, anthropology, drama therapy, and research (Mienczakowski, 2001; Saldaña, 2005). Snow and Herbison (2012) introduced *Ethnodramatherapy* as primarily an integra-tion of ethnodrama with drama therapy, but also borrows techniques from sociom-etry, psychodrama, and Playback Theater. Snow and Herbison base their approach on Mienczakowski's definition of ethnodrama:

ethnodrama is explicitly concerned with decoding and rendering accessible the culturally specific signs, symbols, aesthetics, behaviours, language and experience of health informants using accepted theatrical practices. It seeks to perform research findings in a language and code accessible to its wide audiences. (Mienczakowski, 2001, p. 468)

Ethnodramatherapy work has been used in psychotherapy contexts, diversity training, public performance, research, and educational groups (Snow et al, 2017).

15.3.5   Bibliodrama

While similar to axiodrama or sociodrama, bibliodrama is uniquely different in that it focuses on using role playing to bring to life stories and characters from religious texts (Pitzele, 1998). Bibliodrama is often used in religious communities or educational settings—it is also applicable as a process for exploring meaning of other mythical or archetypal stories and legends (Blatner, 2000).

A bibliodrama may be based around a protagonist or not—but follows the same group phases as a psychodrama or sociodrama and integrates the same interventions (Pitzele, 1998). While bibliodrama primarily enacts the written scripture, it is also used to explore the unspoken or unwritten parts of religious texts. It provides participants with an experiential understanding of the relational dynamics and existential dilemmas outlined in religious history. Bibliodrama provides an avenue for participants to deepen their connection to characters from scripture.

15.4   Teledrama and Telemedicine

With the increased accessibility, reliance, and sophistication with technology, a new way of using Moreno's methods has emerged (Fleury, 2020). Teletherapy is simply the provision of therapy services through the Internet or phone. Teledrama describes a method for using action methods for psychotherapy, training, and coaching in an online video format (Simmons, 2018). The term teledrama was coined by Daniela Simmons, albeit many other psychodramatists have been using action methods online for several years (Farnsworth, 2017; Hudgins, 2017; Pamplona da Costa, 2005). She writes on teledrama's Web site that "teledrama is a very important part of the future of action methods and it is a bridge between countries and cultures". Perhaps teledrama and telemedicine in general are the fulfillment of Moreno's vision of using technology to create a therapeutic experience for larger groups within society (Moreno, 1946; Pamplona da Costa, 2005).

Two major recent events are likely to contribute to a significant increase in the use of Moreno's methods online for teletherapy and distance learning. The first major change was a 2019 change in the American Board of Examiners in Sociometry, Psychodrama, and Group Psychotherapy regulations for distance learning which now permit a portion of training hours to be accrued through distance learning. The second major event was the 2020 CoVid-19 pandemic which proved to be a spontaneity test and catalyst for many in the international psychodrama community to begin offering online therapy and training events using Moreno's methods (Giacomucci, 2020; Mindoljević & Radman, 2020; Vidal & Castro, 2020).

In the larger culture of the psychotherapy field, it seems that teletherapy is likely to become more utilized, in addition to online education, supervision, and training. Moreno (2019a) describes three revolutions in psychiatry: (1) Philippe Pinel's humane treatment instead of punishment for the mentally ill in the eighteenth century; (2) Freud's re-conceptualization of mental illness as psychological instead of neurological at the beginning of the twentieth century; (3) Moreno's introduction of group psychotherapy in the 1930. Perhaps the movement to teletherapy and online professional development is the fourth major revolution in the field of psychiatry.

Nearly 100 years ago, Moreno had introduced ideas of using radio, film, and technology to create healing experiences for large groups of people—he used audio recordings in his 1930 Sing Prison work and video recordings from his work in Hudson New York at the girls training school. Around 80 years ago, Moreno founded a company called Therapeutic Motion Pictures with the hopes of providing healing and role training to larger audiences (Moreno, 2014). Jonathan Moreno, in his book recounting his father's history, quotes from an unpublished Moreno paper in the 1940 which states:

> The day will come when the engineer will provide us with a 'two-way' television system... every tele spectator will be able to televise himself back and so establish a communication between the therapist and himself multiplying the potentialities of a visual telephone by millions (Moreno, 2014, p. 257).

It seems that Moreno had envisioned the live video calls used for teletherapy today. I expect that he would have been excited at the evolution of teletherapy and online education as methods that meet people where they are and offer potentialities of large-scale therapeutic experiences. It is likely that Moreno would have also been pleased by the name "teletherapy" or "telemedicine" as it is related to his concept of "tele" (see Sect. 5.5.2). The psychodramatic concept of tele is defined as an accurate and reciprocated knowing or experiencing of between two people. Tele is seen as an interpersonal phenomenon necessary for the success of all relationships, including the working relationship between client and therapist (Z. T. Moreno, 2000). In a Morenean sense, one might argue that all therapy is "teletherapy."

15.5   Other Approaches Similar to Psychodrama

Beyond Moreno's methods and modified psychodrama approaches are multiple other methods that developed with considerable overlap to psychodrama. Some explicitly trace their history back to Moreno while others use methods Moreno developed without much or any reference to him.

15.5.1 Drama Therapy

While the term drama therapy is sometimes used interchangeably with psychodrama in the literature, it is its own unique field and approach separate from psychodrama with its own professional society, journal, degree programs, and credentialing board. Nevertheless, many drama therapists consider Jacob Moreno to be the first drama therapist (Bailey, 2006). There may be far more similarities than differences when it comes to psychodrama and drama therapy. Both are used as approaches in psychotherapy, education, and community work integrating role theory, drama, improv games, role playing, symbolism, spontaneity, creativity, and a biopsychosocial perspective.

In terms of differences, psychodrama focuses on enacting one individual's story or topic while drama therapy enacts stories or topics related to the group-as-a-whole (similar to sociodrama). Psychodrama is more structured while drama therapy is more fluid. While psychodrama uses imagination and reality, drama therapy is more focused on symbolic or surplus reality. Psychodrama can be traced back *solely* to Moreno's theoretical and philosophical foundation in the early 1900. On the other hand, drama therapy emerged with multiple different theoretical and practical approaches developed by different pioneers several decades after Moreno (Johnson & Emunah, 2009; Landy, 2017). Kadem-Tahar and Kellermann (1996) offer an eloquently stated differentiation below:

> we have found that there is a fundamental difference between psychodrama and drama therapy. It seems that whereas in psychodrama the "soul" (psyche) is the aim and the "action" (drama) is the means, the opposite is true for drama therapy in which drama itself (as pure art) is the aim and the psyche is the means (of expression) (Kedem-Tahar & Kellermann, 1996, p. 29).

Drama therapy is more connected to theater and sometimes moves from a therapeutic process to a focus on creating a theater production (Landy, 2017). While some psychodramatists are also theater professionals, most are not. Interestingly, the field of drama therapy seems to have professionalized and integrated within academia, research, and higher education in the USA far more than psychodrama has. Multiple graduate degrees are offered in drama therapy in the USA while there is not a single graduate program in psychodrama.

Learning psychodrama is a required part of drama therapy education, as such, psychodrama interventions become a part of every drama therapist's toolbox in an explicit way. Alternatively, psychodramatists do not all learn drama therapy interventions, though many psychodramatists are also drama therapists and some drama therapy techniques, especially warm-up games, have become integrated into the psychodrama culture.

15.5.2   Playback Theater

Playback Theater emerged in the early 1970, developed by Jonathan Fox who was experienced in psychodrama (Blatner, 2000; Fox, Fox, Salas, & Sparrow, 2000). Fox explicitly credits psychodrama for the foundation of Playback Theater and even notes how Playback Theater was largely developed on the original Moreno psychodrama stage in New Paltz, NY (2018). Playback Theater utilizes a small group of trained actors to spontaneously enact personal stories from the audience (Fox, 1994). Jonathan Fox writes that he sees Playback Theater as more connected to Moreno's Theater of Spontaneity than it is connected to psychodrama (Fox, 2004). Playback Theater seems to be more closely related to sociodrama and drama therapy than psychodrama in that it uses metaphor and symbolism with a focus on the drama more so than the individual's story. Playback Theater is more concerned with the process of putting stories into action than using drama or theater as a means to uncovering solutions for personal or collective problems (Fox, 2004). In Playback Theater, the storyteller remains an audience member while in psychodrama or drama therapy they become an active role player. It is important to note that Playback Theater is not a psychotherapy, though sometimes used within therapy and often providing a therapeutic experience for audiences.

Playback Theater is often integrated into psychodrama work and often is used in major events at the national psychodrama conferences. Playback Theater and Theater of the Oppressed are sometimes confused with each other though they also have fundamental differences. Playback emerged from Fox's experience in theater and psychodrama while Theater of the Oppressed developed from Augusto Boal's socio-political experience in Latin America.

15.5.3   Theater of the Oppressed

While Playback Theater is focused on personal changes or revolution, Theater of the Oppressed uses the individual's story as a catalyst for social revolution and collective change (Weinblatt, 2015). Theater of the Oppressed focuses on developing solutions to social issues while Playback Theater is less solution focused (Fox, 2004). Theater of the Oppressed and Playback Theater are similar in their use of an individual's story as the script for the enactment, which differs from sociodrama's spontaneously emerging storyline. Augusto Boal developed Theater of the Oppressed in the 1970 in South America which evolved to include multiple theater modalities including forum theater, image theater, invisible theater, and the rainbow of desire (Boal, 2000, 2013; Feldhendler, 1993; Oliveira & Araujo, 2012). Perhaps one of the simplest ways of differentiating Moreno and Boal is to remember the paradigms from which they developed their ideas. Moreno was an existential psychiatrist while Boal was a Marxist playwright (Oliveira & Araujo, 2012). Feldhendler (1993) notes that Boal's

Newspaper Theater and Moreno's Living Newspaper are nearly identical. Boal participated psychodrama groups in the 1960 but denies that psychodrama or Moreno had
influence on his developing of Theater of the Oppressed. Later in 1994, Boal dedicates
his Rainbow of Desire book focused on using theater in therapy to Zerka Moreno
(Boal, 2013). Similar to Moreno's trajectory, Boal's work was initially based on
social justice issues in society but later he developed an approach for psychotherapy
(Boal, 2013; Feldhendler, 1993).

In Theater of the Oppressed, a scene is played out for the storyteller until the point
of the central conflict, at which point audience members are invited to step onto the
stage and offer experiential demonstrations of solutions or responses to the situation.
This method is quite similar to psychodramatic doubling. As the name suggests,
Theater of the Oppressed concerns itself primarily with issues of social justice and
oppression. Later, when living in France, Boal developed methods for working with
European bourgeoisie by conceptualizing mild neurosis as internal forms of oppression (Blatner, 2000). The experience of a Theater of Oppressed session provides
audience members with new ways of confronting moments of oppression and injustice through the co-created process. Theater of the Oppressed, Playback Theater,
drama therapy, and Moreno's methods have much in common and are often integrated
together by psychodrama practitioners.

15.5.4   Gestalt Therapy

Gestalt therapy is an existential therapy focusing on the whole person while incorporating here-and-now awareness, relational emphasis, and experiential techniques
(Perls, 1969a). Fritz and Laura Perls created gestalt therapy in the 1940 and put it
forth in their 1951 book *Gestalt Therapy* (Perls, Hefferline, & Goodman, 1951).
Similarly, to psychodrama, gestalt emerged from the rejection of aspects of psycho-
analysis, with emphasis on relationships, and use of the empty chair with role playing.
Gestalt therapy seems to have outdone psychodrama in terms of popularity in the
USA and offers a modality framed as both an individual and a group approach.
Gestalt therapy's focus on individual therapy, while psychodrama is much more
group focused, may be one of the reasons it has achieved and maintained popularity.
At the same time, some group workers critique gestalt therapists for simply doing
individual therapy in a group setting and being unable to engage the group-as-a-
whole. From a psychodrama perspective, gestalt therapy is considered a monodrama
where the client works one-on-one with the therapist without auxiliary egos—even
in group settings (Yablonsky, 1976). The audience in gestalt therapy has very little
involvement compared to psychodrama. Psychodrama seems to be much more action-
based using an open stage while gestalt puts the client into the *hot seat* and uses more
introspection.

Who created the empty chair technique? Gestalt therapists often claim it for their
founder, Fritz Perls while psychodramatists insist that Moreno created it. There is
much misunderstanding about this, and it seems Perls is frequently credited with the

development of the empty chair because he made it popular and brought it into mainstream culture with his public demonstrations at Esalen Institute. Nevertheless, historical analysis reveals that Perls was a frequent attendee of psychodrama sessions in New York and later writes in his memoir, *In and Out of the Garbage Pail*, that Moreno and psychodrama had considerable influence on him (Berne, 1970; Blatner, 1996, 2000; Moreno, 2019b; Perls, 1969b; Yablonsky, 1976). Walter Truett Anderson, journalist and encounter group leader, recalls an encounter between Moreno and Fritz Perls in 1969 at a psychology convention where they presented on the same panel— Moreno publicly confronts Perls, "I don't mind you stealing my stuff, but you should have stolen all of it". Perls responded, "Ah, Jacob, Jacob, when will you just accept your greatness?" (Moreno, 2014, p. 218).

15.5.5   Internal Family Systems

Internal Family Systems Therapy (IFS) conceptualizes the psyche as having multiple parts with a centralized self—the core essence of an individual (Schwartz, 1994). This perspective is quite similar to Moreno's role theory, with the self having parallels to the Morenean concept of the autonomous healing center within (Longer & Giacomucci, 2020). Like gestalt and psychodrama, IFS uses a non-pathologizing person-centered approach with a primary goal of promoting further integration within the self and in the external environment. In IFS, parts are categorized as either *exiled* parts or *protective* parts. Furthermore, there are two types of protective parts—proactive *managers* or reactive *firefighters*. IFS places considerable emphasis on defense mechanisms and asking permission from parts before engaging with interventions.

Internal Family Systems Therapy (IFS) was developed by Richard Schwartz in the 1980–1990 integrating a mix of family therapy, systems theory, and parts work. In the development of IFS, Schwartz was influenced by Fritz Perls empty chair work and by his work with Virginia Satir, who had integrated Moreno's methods into the family therapy field (Schwartz & Sweezy, 2019). IFS seems to be utilized primarily in individual work, but also adapted to group work. IFS and gestalt are similar in this way, and in that they both emphasize parts of self while exploring inner parts with mindfulness and interoception. IFS group work is much more similar to psychodrama than IFS individual work as parts are *externalized* in the group with role players, but in individual therapy parts are interfaced *within* the individual. Very little has been published about the connection between IFS and psychodrama, albeit many practitioners and trainers integrate both into their work. Rachel Longer and I published a recent short article outlining their similarities and how both IFS practitioners and psychodramatists could benefit from adapting aspects of the other's approaches (2020).

15.5.6 *Pesso Boyden System Psychomotor Therapy*

The Pesso Boyden System Psychomotor (PBSP) Therapy, sometimes called *psychomotor therapy* for short, was created by dance teachers Albert Pesso and Diane Boyden-Pesso in the 1960 in New York. PBSP is focused on providing experiential corrective experiences with idealized roles to reverse the impact of unmet needs from childhood (Winnette & Baylin, 2017). A PBSP session or *structure* appears to be quite similar to a psychodrama enactment as they both use role playing within a group to recreate scenes from the past and wished for scenes (Blatner, 2000). Similar to the psychodrama process, the PBSP approach follows the lead of the protagonist, constructs a dramatic scene, facilitates de-roling of role players, and finishes by sharing from participants in the group. PBSP's *witness* role has many similarities to the mirror position in psychodrama or the observing ego role in the Therapeutic Spiral Model.

Psychomotor therapy has a similar process as psychodrama but also has its own terminology, theory, and training process (Pesso, 1969; Pesso & Crandall, 1991). It also is more explicitly trauma-focused and body-oriented than classical psychodrama. A psychomotor therapist uses *microtracking* to follow the subtle nonverbal communication from the protagonist (van der Kolk, 2014). The facilitation of psychomotor structures is more contained, scripted, and intentional than a spontaneous psychodrama enactment. Although the Pesso Boyden therapeutic approach seems to have limited research and publications, it has received an increased spotlight due to Bessel van der Kolk's 2014 chapter on it in his best-selling book *The Body Keeps the Score* and his newly offered *experiential psychodramatic workshops* based on his training with Albert Pesso.

15.5.7 *Family Constellations and Systemic Constellations*

Family constellations and systemic constellations therapy were developed by Bert Hellinger in the 1970s with a focus on the family ancestral system or other system such as an organization (Hellinger, 2003). The constellations therapy process revolves around one client, usually in a group setting, who chooses group members to hold the places of different family members, ancestors, or members of the system (Carnabucci & Anderson, 2012). Instead of being referred to as roles or auxiliary egos like in psychodrama, they are referred to as *representatives*. The place where the experience emerges is called the *field*, akin to the psychodrama stage. The client physically places representatives in the field and returns to their seat to observe. A constellations session is much less action-based or dramatic as psychodrama and focuses on information that emerges for the client or representatives through intuition, thoughts, impulses, body sensations, or energy. Rather than acting, doubling, or role reversal, the representatives are instructed to attune themselves to the field. The facilitator checks in with the representatives asking them to report what they are experiencing in the field and encouraging brief movements or statements. The process involves very subtle movement, periods of silence, and significant time spent with each representative attuned to their inner experience. Once an issue is concretized in the field between members of the system, the facilitator will instruct them to make simple gestures or statements to each other in attempts to move toward resolution while the client observes (Carnabucci, 2018). Constellations work can get to systemic issues in a streamlined manner but misses nuances of experience due to minimal verbal involvement (von Ameln & Becker-Ebel, 2020).

Family constellation sessions are based on three *orders of love* outlined by Hellinger—(1) every member has the right to belong to the family, (2) wrongs in previous generations will be redressed in future generations, and (3) people have rank according to who entered the system first (Hellinger, Weber, & Beaumont, 1998). Carnabucci (2018) comments on Hellinger's work as being related to Moreno's concept of tele and making it the central mechanism of change in an explicit way. Carnabucci and Anderson (2012) write four major differences between the two approaches: (1) psychodrama focuses on conscious reality while constellations work focuses on the unconscious and ancestral; (2) psychodrama auxiliaries are role trained by information from the protagonist while constellation representatives learn information about their character from their inner experience; (3) in constellation work, *resonating statements* are used in a way similar to doubling statements in psychodrama but much less frequent and usually provided by the facilitator; (4) the psychodrama enactment places the protagonist within the drama which explores elements of their life while the family constellation session is takes places within the field of one's ancestry. Psychodrama enactments generally have a clearly defined scene while constellation work takes places without concrete context (Carnabucci, 2018). While clear differences exist between the two approaches, they also have much in common, including being experiential group methods focused on the person within their social environment and larger systems. Both approaches are based in comprehensive existential philosophical systems with emphasis on spirituality that include applications in psychotherapy and beyond (Carnabucci & Anderson, 2012).

15.6   Conclusion

While Moreno's triadic system of sociometry, psychodrama, and group psychotherapy offers a comprehensive approach for work with individuals, groups, and communities, much value is also added to the social worker's repertoire from Moreno's other methods and approaches similar to psychodrama which developed later. A brief introduction to the aforementioned methods, most of which seem to be influenced by psychodrama, demonstrates the richness of methods involving role playing in the larger field while providing a greater appreciation for Moreno's influence. The approaches above are outlined in a way differentiating each from the other, however in practice these approaches are often blended together by practitioners. A thorough investigation of each of these models is beyond the scope of this publication but has been presented elsewhere in the literature.

References

Bailey, S. (2006). Ancient and modern roots of drama therapy XE "drama therapy" . In S. L. Brooke (Ed.), *Creative arts therapies manual: A guide to the history, theoretical approaches, assessment, and work with special populations of art, play XE "play", dance, music, drama, and poetry therapies* (pp. 214–222). Springfield, IL: Charles C. Thomas Publisher.

Berne, E. (1970). A review of gestalt therapy XE "Gestalt Therapy" verbatim. *American Journal of Psychiatry, 126*(10), 164.

Blatner, A. (1996). *Acting-in: Practical applications of psychodramatic methods.* New York: Springer Publishing Company.

Blatner, A. (2000). *Foundations of Psychodrama: History, Theory, and Practice* (4th ed.). New York City: Springer Publishing Company.

Boal, A. (2000). *Theater of the Oppressed XE "Theater of the Oppressed" .* London: Pluto press.

Boal, A. (2013). *The rainbow of desire: The Boal method of theatre and therapy.* New York: Routledge.

Browne, R. (2011). Sociodrama with a marketing team. In R. Wiener, D. Adderley, & K. Kirk (Eds.), *Sociodrama in a Changing World* (pp. 11–29). United Kingdom: Author.

Carnabucci, K. (2018). The challenge and promise for psychodrama and family and systemic constellations. *The Journal of Psychodrama, Sociometry, and Group Psychotherapy, 66*(1), 81–91.

Carnabucci, K., & Anderson, R. (2012). *Integrating psychodrama and systemic constellation work: New directions for action methods, mind-body therapies and energy healing.* Philadelphia: Jessica Kingsley Publishers.

Cukier, R. (2008). *Bipersonal Psychodrama: Its techniques, therapists, and clients.* São Paulo, Brazil: Author.

Farnsworth, J. (2017). Online Sociometry and Creative Therapies. In S. L. Brooke (Ed.), *Combining the Creative Therapies with Technology: Using Social Media and Online Counseling to Treat Clients* (pp. 137–168). Springfield, IL: Charles C. Thomas Publishers.

Feldhendler, D. (2002). Augusto Boal and Jacob L. Moreno: theatre and therapy. In J. Cohen-Cruz & M. Schutzman (Eds.), *Playing Boal: Theater, Therapy, Activism* (pp. 97–119). London: Routledge.

Fleury, H. J. (2020). Psicodrama e as especificidades da psicoterapia on-line. *Revista Brasileira De Psicodrama, 28*(1), 1–4.

Fox, H., Fox, H., Salas, J., & Sparrow, J. (2000). *The Beginnings: Reflecting on 25 years of Playback Theater XE "Playback Theater" .* New Paltz, NY: Center for Playback Theater.

Fox, J. (1994). *Acts of service: Spontaneity, commitment, tradition in the nonscripted theatre.* New Paltz, NY: Tusitala Publishers.

Fox, J. (2004). *Playback Theatre compared to psychodrama and Theatre of the Oppressed.* New Paltz, NY: Centre for Playback Theatre.

Fox, J. (2018). Playback theatre's debt to Moreno. *The Journal of Psychodrama, Sociometry, and Group Psychotherapy, 66*(1), 31–35.

Garcia, N. (2011). Exploring the Boundaries between Psychodrama and Sociodrama. In R. Wiener, D. Adderley, & K. Kirk (Eds.), *Sociodrama in a Changing World* (pp. 33–44). United Kingdom: Author.

Giacomucci, S. (2017). The Sociodrama of Life or Death: Young Adults and Addiction Treatment. *Journal of Psychodrama, Sociometry, and Group Psychotherapy* 65(1): 137–143 https://doi.org/https://doi.org/10.12926/0731-1273-65.1.137

Giacomucci, S. (2018). Traveling as Spontaneity Training: If you want to become a psychodramatist, travel the world! *International Group Psychotherapies and Psychodrama Journal., 4*(1), 34–41.

Giacomucci, S. (2019). *Social Group Work in Action: A Sociometry, Psychodrama, and Experiential Trauma Therapy Curriculum.* Doctorate in Social Work (DSW) Dissertations. 124. https://reposi tory.upenn.edu/cgi/viewcontent.cgi?article=1128&context=edissertations_sp2

Giacomucci, S. (2020). The Sociodrama of Coronavirus and Humanity through TeleTherapy. *The Group Psychologist*, 31(2).

Hellinger, B. (2003). *Peace Begins in the Soul: Family Constellations in the Service of Reconcilia-tions.* Heidelberg, Germany: Carl-Auer-Systeme-Verlag.

Hellinger, B., Weber, G., & Beaumont, H. (1998). *Love's hidden symmetry: What makes love work in relationships.* Phoenix, AZ: Zeig Tucker & Theisen Publishers.

Hudgins, M. K. (2017). Action Across the Distance with Telemedicine: The Therapeutic Spiral Model XE "Therapeutic Spiral Model" to -Treat Trauma - Online. In S. L. Brooke (Ed.), *Combining the Creative Therapies with Technology: Using Social Media and Online Counseling to Treat Clients* (pp. 137–168). Springfield, IL: Charles C. Thomas Publishers.

Johnson, D. R., & Emunah, R. (2009). *Current approaches in drama therapy XE "drama therapy"* . Springfield, IL: Charles C. Thomas Publishers.

Kedem-Tahar, E., & Felix-Kellermann, P. (1996). Psychodrama and drama therapy XE "drama therapy" : A comparison. *the Arts in Psychotherapy, 23*(1), 27–36.

Kellermann, P. F. (2007). *Sociodrama and Collective Trauma.* London: Jessica Kingsley Publishers.

Knittel, M. G. (2009). *Counseling and drama: Psychodrama a deux.* Tuscan, AZ: Author.

Landy, R. J. (2017). The Love and Marriage of Psychodrama and Drama Therapy. *the Journal of Psychodrama, Sociometry, and Group Psychotherapy, 65*(1), 33–40.

Longer, R. & Giacomucci, S. (2020). Parts, Roles, and the Spark of Creation: An Early Look at the Integration of Internal Family Systems Therapy and Psychodrama. *Psychodrama Network News.* Winter Issue, p. 7. Princeton, NJ: American Society of Group Psychotherapy & Psychodrama.

Malaquias, M. C., Nonoya, D. S., Cesarino, A. C. M., & Nery, M. D. P. (2016). Psychodrama and race relations. *Revista Brasileira De Psicodrama, 24*(2), 91–100.

Marineau, R. F. (2013). The foundations of sociodrama XE "sociodrama" : Reflecting on our past and looking at the future. *Journal of Psychodrama, Sociometry, and Group Psychotherapy, 61*(1), 17–27.

Mienczakowski, J. (2001). Ethnodrama: Performed Research – Limitations and Potential. In P. Atkinson, A. Coffey, S. Delamont, J. Lofland, & L. Lofland (Eds.), *Handbook of Ethnography* (pp. 468–476). London: Sage.

Mindoljević Drakulić, A., & Radman, V. (2020). Crisis psychodrama in the era of Covid-19. *Psychiatria Danubina, 32*(1), 22–24.

Minkin, R. (2016). *Sociodrama for Our Time: A Sociodrama Manual* (3rd ed.). Philadelphia, PA: East West Center for Psychodrama and Sociodrama.

Moreno, J.D. (2014). *Impromptu Man: J.L. Moreno and the Origins of Psychodrama, Encounter Culture, and the Social Network.* New York, NY: Bellevue Literary Press.

Moreno, J.D. (2019a). Introduction. In J.L. Moreno, *The Autobiography of a Genius.* (E. Schreiber, S. Kelley, & S. Giacomucci, Eds.). United Kingdom: North West Psychodrama Association.

Moreno, J. L. (1943). The Concept of Sociodrama. *Sociometry, 6*(4), 434–449.

Moreno, J. L. (1946). *Psychodrama Volume 1.* Beacon, NY: Beacon House Press.

Moreno, J. L. (1947). *Open Letter to Group Psychotherapists.* Psychodrama Monograms, No. 23. *Beacon, NY: Beacon House*

Moreno, J. L. (1953). *Who shall survive? Foundations of sociometry, group psychotherapy and sociodrama (2nd edition).* Beacon, NY: Beacon House.

Moreno, J. L. (2019b). *The Autobiography of a Genius* (E. Schreiber, S. Kelley, & S. Giacomucci, Eds.). United Kingdom: North West Psychodrama Association.

Moreno, Z.T. (2000). The Function of 'Tele' in Human Relations. In J. Zeig (ed) *The Evolution of Psychotherapy: A Meeting of the Minds.* Phoenix, AZ: Erickson Foundation Press.

Moreno, Z.T. (2006). *The Quintessential Zerka*. Horvatin, T. & Schreiber, E. (Eds.). New York, NY: Routledge.

Oliveira, E. C. S., & Araújo, M. F. (2012). Aproximações do teatro do oprimido com a Psicologia e o Psicodrama. *Psicologia: Ciencia e Profissao*, 32(2), 340–355.

Pamplona da Costa, R. (2005). Video-psychodrama and tele XE "tele" -psychodrama: The research of a morenian dream. In Z. Figusch (Ed.), *Sambadrama – The arena of Brazilian psychodrama* (pp. 250–267). London: Jessica Kingsley.

Peris, F., Hefferline, R. F., Goodman, P. (1951/1994). *Gestalt therapy: Excitement and growth in the human personality*. Gouldsboro, ME: Gestalt Journal Press

Perls, F. (1969). *Gestalt therapy verbatim*. Lafayette, CA: Real People Press.

Perls, F. (1969). *In and out the garbage pail*. Lafayette, CA: Real People Press.

Pesso, A. (1969). *Movement in Psychotherapy*. New York: New York University Press.

Pesso, A., & Crandall, J. (Eds.). (1991). *Moving Psychotherapy*. Cambridge, MA: Brookline.

Pitzele, P. (1998). *Scripture windows: Towards a practice of bibliodrama XE "Bibliodrama"* . Los Angeles: Torah Aura Productions.

Saldaña, J. (Ed.). (2005). *Ethnodrama: An anthology of reality theatre*. Walnut Creek: Rowman Altamira.

Schreiber, E. (2017). Sociatry – Healing of Society: Tools for Social Justice Transformation. *Psychodrama Network News*. Fall 2017, pp. 16–17. American Society of Group Psychotherapy and Psychodrama.

Schreiber, E. (2018a). Sociatry Part 2: Moreno's Mysticism. *Psychodrama Network News*. Winter 2018, pp. 24–25. American Society of Group Psychotherapy and Psychodrama.

Schreiber, E. (2018b). Sociatry Part 3: Sociatry and the Social Microscope. *Psychodrama Network News*. Summer 2018. American Society of Group Psychotherapy and Psychodrama.

Schwartz, R. C. (1994). *The Internal Family Systems XE "Internal Family Systems" Model*. New York: Guilford Press.

Schwartz, R. C., & Sweezy, M. (2019). *Internal family systems therapy* (2nd ed.). New York: Guilford Publications.

Simmons, D. (2018). Teledrama. Retrieved from www.teledrama.org

Snow, S., D'Amico, M., Mongerson, E., Anthony, E., Rozenberg, M., Opolko, C., & Anandampillai, S. (2017). Ethnodramatherapy applied in a project focusing on relationships in the lives of adults with developmental disabilities, especially romance, intimacy and sexuality. *Drama Therapy Review, 3*(2), 241–260.

Snow, S., & Herbison, P. (2012). *Ethnodramatherapy: A New Methodology as Applied to Diversity Training Outreach*. Montreal, Quebec: Concordia University.

Sternberg, P., & Garcia, A. (2000). *Sociodrama: Who's in Your Shoes?* (2nd ed.). Westport, CT: Praeger Publishers.

Souza, A. C., & Drummond, J. R. (2017). Axiodrama nas organizações. *Revista Brasileira De Psicodrama, 25*(1), 87–93.

van der Kolk, B. A. (2014). *The body keeps the score: Brain, mind, and body in the healing of trauma*. New York: Viking Press.

Vidal, G. P., & Castro, A. (2020). Online clinical psychodrama: A possible connection. *Revista Brasileira De Psicodrama, 28*(1), 54–64.

von Ameln, F., & Becker-Ebel, J. (2020). *Fundamentals of Psychodrama*. Singapore: Springer Nature.

Weinblatt, M. (2015). Combining Theatre of the Oppressed and Playback Theatre: A Powerful and Delicate Marriage. Retrieved from www.mandalaforchange.com.

Winnette, P., & Baylin, J. (2017). *Working with Traumatic Memories to Heal Adults with Unresolved Childhood Trauma: Neuroscience XE "neuroscience", Attachment Theory and Pesso Boyden XE "Pesso Boyden" System Psychomotor Psychotherapy*. Philadelphia: Jessica Kingsley Publishers.

Yablonsky, L. (1976). *Psychodrama: Resolving emotional problems through role-playing XE "Role theory:Role-playing"* . New York: Basic Books.

Part V
Sociometry and Psychodrama in Individual Social Work Practice

Social work practice, from its inception, placed considerable emphasis on individual casework. In the United States, it seems that clinical social workers have emerged as the largest group of mental health practitioners and regularly provide individual psychotherapy. While sociometry and psychodrama are primarily used in group settings, they are also applicable in a variety of individual social work settings. The field of sociometry offers various assessment tools which provide a more complete picture of the individual within their environment. The creative use of psychodramatic interventions initiates a dynamic experience in individual psychotherapy sessions. This section will outline the use of common interventions in individual settings, including the social atom, the role atom, timelines, psychodramatic letter writing, concretization, doubling, and psychodrama vignettes. It is important to note that while these interventions will be described in this chapter as they relate to individual sessions, they are each also applicable for group settings.

Historically, it is interesting to note that Jacob Moreno's first clinical use of psychodrama and role-playing was actually in individual work with a suicidal nobleman. One of Moreno's first professional roles after finishing medical school was as a doctor of a small Austrian town called Bad Voslau. Moreno himself writes that the first psychodrama took place in 1921 at the Komedius Hall in Vienna, however in his autobiography he describes in detail a case from around the same time period in which he worked psychodramatically with a wealthy man who wanted help committing suicide. He depicts the various ways that he helped this man act out his suicidal fantasies over several weeks' time which eventually led to his commitment to life again (Moreno, 2019). Moreno also describes other patients that he used psychodrama with in individual settings, both with and without trained auxiliaries, including frequently with married couples in his early work (Figusch, 2009, 2019). Perhaps his most famous psychodrama in individual work was with at his psychiatric hospital with a patient who believed he was Adolf Hitler during World War II. With a team of auxiliaries, Moreno worked with the patient and helped him to act out his delusion of being Hitler. Through the psychodrama process and the sharing afterwards Moreno reports that the patient overcame his compulsion (Moreno, 1959).

Sociometry and psychodrama are almost always categorized as a group approach, but these cases reminds us psychodrama's historical roots in individual work as well.

Moreno rarely wrote about the use of psychodrama in individual settings. In the few times that he does mention it, he usually comments on its limitations and suggests the use of trained auxiliary egos within individual sessions (Figusch, 2009, 2019; Moreno, 1959, 1972). Figusch (2009, 2019) writes, "despite of Moreno's opposition towards and lack of interest for one-to-one psychodrama, this working modality has quietly found its way into the everyday practice of psychodrama therapists around the world" (p. 11). Today, practitioners are using psychodrama, mostly without auxiliary egos, in individual sessions regularly. Because Moreno considered the dyad to be the smallest group, some have suggested that one-to-one psychodrama is simply another modality with Moreno's group psychotherapy (Brito, 2019). This approach has been described with many names including monodrama, bipersonal psychodrama, one-to-one psychodrama, psychodrama a deux, and individual psychodrama. The next two chapters will provide a brief introduction to the use of Moreno's methods in individual work. This topic has been covered in depth by other contemporary authors including Fonseca (2004), Cukier (2008), Knittel (2009), Figusch (2009/2019), and Chesner (2019).

References

Brito, V. C. A. (2019). One-to-one psychodrama: Reflections on the theory and practice of psychodrama with an individual patient. In Z. Figusch (Ed.). *From one-to-one psychodrama to large group socio-psychodrama* (2nd ed.) (pp. 15–28). United Kingdom: lulu.com.

Chesner, A. (Ed.). (2019). *One-to-one Psychodrama Psychotherapy: Applications and Technique.* New York: Routledge.

Cukier, R. (2008). *Bipersonal Psychodrama: Its techniques, therapists, and clients.* São Paulo, Brazil: Author.

Figusch, Z. (2019). *From one-to-one psychodrama to large group socio-psychodrama: More writings from the arena of Brazilian psychodrama.* United Kingdom: lulu.com.

Fonseca, J. (2004). *Contemporary psychodrama: New approaches to theory and technique.* New York: Routledge.

Knittel, M. G. (2009). *Counseling and drama: Psychodrama a deux.* Tuscan, AZ: Author.

Moreno, J.L. (in collaboration with Z.T. Moreno) (1959). Psychodrama second volume, foundations of psychotherapy. , NY: Beacon House.

Moreno, J. L. (1972) *Psychodrama Volume 1* (4th ed.). Beacon, NY: Beacon House Press.

Moreno, J. L. (2019). In E. Schreiber, S. Kelley, & S. Giacomucci, (Eds.), *The autobiography of a genius.* United Kingdom: North West Psychodrama Association.

Chapter 16
Sociometric Assessment and Written Psychodramatic Interventions in Individual Social Work Practice

Abstract The application of sociometry assessments and written psychodrama interventions within one-to-one social work settings is the focus of this chapter. Interventions covered include the social atom, the role atom, modified role atoms, clinical timelines, psychodramatic journaling, and psychodramatic letter writing. Step-by-step instructions are provided for clinicians new to these techniques. Practice examples and clinical processing are offered with depictions of the social atom and role atoms. These tools are presented individually with supporting theory but are often employed together or as a warm-up for a psychodrama enactment. Novice psychodramatists or those less experienced in action methods will find these approaches as a good starting point for beginning to integration sociometry and psychodramatic interventions into their clinical practice with individuals. Though these tools will be presented for individual work, they are also applicable tools for group work and community settings.

Keywords Sociometric assessment · Individual social work practice · Social atom · Role atom · Psychodrama timeline · Psychodramatic letter writing

An extensive overview of sociometry has already been presented in previous chapters (see Chaps. 5 and 11). This section will focus on the practical applications of written sociometric and psychodramatic interventions in individual social work and psychotherapy contexts. Clinical social workers are increasingly tasked by providing individual psychotherapy services for clients. The provision of one-to-one clinical social work, infused with basic sociometric and psychodramatic interventions, would provide an avenue for social work's core values to be more fully embodied in a way that differentiates clinical social work from counseling and clinical psychology. As proposed previously, Moreno's methods engage with social group work in a synergistic union (Skolnik, 2018). This chapter proposes a similar synergistic union between clinical social work practice with individuals and the use of Moreno's methods in individual contexts.

An overview of the social atom will be presented as an inherently person-in-environment assessment and intervention tool predating the genogram and ecomap. The role atom will be presented with its utility as a brief personality assessment rooted in role theory. The use of timelines for assessment and interventions will be

© The Author(s) 2021
S. Giacomucci, *Social Work, Sociometry, and Psychodrama*, Psychodrama in Counselling, Coaching and Education 1,
https://doi.org/10.1007/978-981-33-6342-7_16

briefly described as it relates to client assessment and warm-up for psychodrama. Also included in this discussion will be the utility of psychodramatic letter writing and journaling processes for contained psychodramatic work in sessions or as homework in-between sessions. The blend of the social atom, role atom, timeline, and psychodramatic letter writing provides a social worker with assessment tools that explore a client's intrapsychic role atom and social relationships within the past, present, and future timeline of their life.

16.1   The Social Atom

The social atom, a fundamental instrument of sociometry, is one of the most useful assessment tools for individual work. The social atom provides a depiction of the individual within their social environment (Giacomucci, 2019). Using the social atom as an early assessment in clinical work or case work offers the social worker an efficient and revealing overview of the social life of the individual client through their eyes (Buchanan, 1984). In some cases, the social atom is able to provide more information about the state of a client's social life than several months of interviewing them. This pen-to-paper assessment also provides the client with an opportunity for self-reflection regarding the status of their social life.

Simple instructions for creating a social atom are described below:

1. Using circles to represent females, triangles for males, stars for non-gender conforming persons, and squares for non-human entities or objects—draw yourself at the center of the page and your relationships to others around you.

   a. An alternative is to invite participants to use whichever shapes, symbols, or images they would like to in representing each person in their social atom. This is much less prescriptive in terms of gender and may be preferable, especially with groups focusing on LGBTQ issues.

2. Taking into consideration size and proximity, draw shapes to represent the significant people in your life on the page based on their closeness to you in the center and the amount of social space they take up in your life.
3. Shapes with dotted lines can be used to represent people or things that are meaningful but no longer alive or present.
4. Use different types of lines to resemble the connection between self and the other people or things on the social atom—solid line is good connection, bold line is very strong connection, dotted line is a lost connection, and a wavy line is a conflictual connection.

The social atom exercise can be used solely as an assessment tool in individual work, or as a reference point for future sessions. J.L. and Zerka Moreno suggested that each person draws their social atom monthly to assess the changes within their interpersonal relationships (Moreno, 1953; , 2014). It is also used as a validated research instrument to graph the changes in one's social life from pretest to post-test

(Treadwell, Collins, & Stein, 1992). In group work, the social atom is frequently used as a pen-to-paper warm-up exercise that moves into psychodramatic action.

In the following social atom example (see Fig. 16.1), a social worker is working individually with a seventy-year-old woman named Mary whose primary treatment concerns are depression, anxiety, and social isolation. She presents as dissociative and depressed in most sessions and sometimes has difficulty communicating. After multiple sessions, the clinician feels that they still do not have thorough information regarding the client's social landscape. The social worker explains the social atom process and invites Mary to draw herself within the center of her social relationships, resulting in the following depiction:

From this social atom drawing, one might get curious about Mary's sense of self considering how small she drew herself in the center compared to the others depicted. While she had not verbally disclosed that many friends had died, it became clear from her social atom that she has experienced considerable losses and ambiguous losses. The largest aspects of her social atom are her deceased mother, her husband, and her depression/anxiety, suggesting that these relationships take up the most internal space for Mary. She frequently had referred to her husband as her biggest support and had hinted that her mother may have been abusive. It is also interesting to see her placement of depression and anxiety between herself and her church friends. After more discussion, she disclosed that she felt shameful for having a mental health diagnosis and did not want her friends at church to know. Also notable on her social atom are the multiple friends that she drew as close to her but had not mentioned in

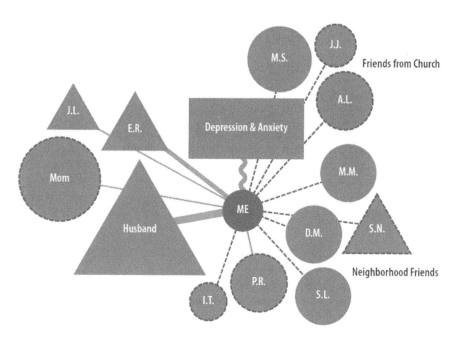

Fig. 16.1 Mary's social atom

previous sessions either. As a result of this assessment, the social worker was able to help Mary reach out to her existing friends for more support and explore her multiple experiences of loss in later sessions. While Mary had not verbally articulated the nature of her relationships with her multiple friends, both those alive and deceased, the simple drawing of her social atom opened the door for new clinical work (see Sect. 17.3 for a continuation of psychodramatic work with Mary).

The social atom can be adapted in creative ways to serve various functions. While one's social atom is usually drawn by themselves, another possible intervention is to invite loved ones to draw each other's social atoms as they perceive them. This process would be revealing for each participant, as well as the therapist to discover how participants experience each other's social lives. The drawing of a perceived social atom could be a useful source of information for a client who is unwilling or unable to give an accurate depiction of their relationships due to minimization, denial, memory loss, a distorted sense of self or others, psychosis, or language barriers.

The social atom, once created on paper, can be externalized through the use of objects, empty chairs, or auxiliaries to create a social atom sculpture in a group. Once a social atom is externalized, the client can be instructed to explore the multiple social atom roles and relationships through the interventions of doubling, the mirror position, role reversals, and soliloquy. In moving the social atom from a written assessment into an experiential intervention, one can get unstuck from their current situations in the surplus reality of the psychodramatic process. Messages that were not, or could not, be expressed in person can be articulated in the social atom sculpture. This promotes opportunities for closure, catharsis, renegotiating relationships, insight, and integration. The next chapter will depict a series of one-to-one psychodrama sessions based on Mary and her social atom assessment.

16.2   The Role Atom

Moreno's personality theory suggests that the self is composed of all of the roles one plays in their life and that a healthy personality has a wide role repertoire (1953). A detailed description of Moreno's role theory is outlined in Sect. 4.7 of this book. This conceptualization of personality is congruent with social work's non-pathologizing stance and easily understood by most clients. The role atom, sometimes called a role diagram, is a simple depiction of all the major roles that one holds in their life. It is drawn in the similar way that the social atom is constructed:

1. Using circles, draw yourself at the center of the page and other circles to represent roles that you play in your life
2. Taking into consideration size and proximity, draw circles to represent the significant roles in your life based on the space they take up in your life.
3. Shapes with dotted lines can be used to represent roles that are meaningful but no longer alive or present.

4. Use different types of lines to resemble the connection between self and the roles your role atom—solid line is good connection, bold line is very strong connection, dotted line is a lost connection, and a wavy line is a conflictual connection.

There are many different ways to create a role atom, the simplest being the here-and-now assessment of one's roles. This process helps client see themselves reflected back to them through their assessment of self in the language of roles. Different modifications of the role atom include drawing role atoms from the past or future. Similar to the social atom, the role atom can be created at different points on a client's timeline or as a treatment planning tool. A simple role atom is depicted below by a client named Andrew (see Fig. 16.2).

The role atom can be modified in many ways based on clinical goals or clinical contexts. A social justice variant is to use the role atom to depict all of one's layers of personal identity and their perceived relationships to each identity—gender, sexuality, race, ethnicity, language, class, religion, ancestry, age, etc. The proximity and size of identities in this modified identity role atom could be drawn based on importance to the individual, relevance to a specific experience, or even their perception of how others in society experience each identity.

The role atom process can also go a step further and be used to depict sub-roles within one role (Dayton, 2005). This modified role atom can be helpful for creating

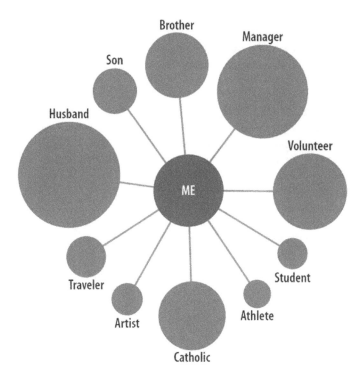

Fig. 16.2 Andrew's role atom

Fig. 16.3 Sub-roles within Andrew's role of husband

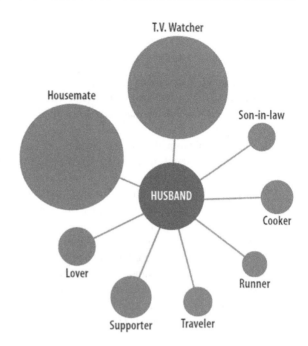

a vision that depicts the current or ideal nature of a particular role. For example, after drawing a role atom, Andrew warms up to a more in-depth exploration of their experience in the role of *husband*. Using the same process outlined above, the client can depict the sub-roles of their experience in the role of husband (see Fig. 16.3).

After drawing a role atom to depict the sub-roles of husband, Andrew became increasingly aware of how he and his partner currently spend the majority of their time together watching television or attending to their home when they used to spend much more time traveling, running together, or creating art. The remaining time of the session is used to explore his feelings about the changes in his marriage over time and what he would like to change going forward. The same role atom process can be used to create a vision of a future role atom based on the sub-roles of husband for Andrew.

Another adaptation of the role atom process is using adjectives to describe the nature of how one holds the role—or in the case of a future projection, how a client would like to play the role. These adjectives can be depicted as another extension of sub-roles or sub-characteristics of a specific role. The role atom is useful to get to know a new client or to help a client better see when one role has consumed most of their life. This is especially useful for clients who might be in denial about the extent of their excessive working, exercising, video game use, television use, or other compulsive behavior.

The role atom also has utility for the professional development of the social worker. Social workers are regularly called to hold various sub-roles within their professional role repertoire which can be assessed and explored through a role atom.

This could be useful in multiple contexts including to depict the sub-roles of a job opening, to explore one's relationships to the sub-roles of their social work internship position or student role, to assess and/or grade one's performance in the sub-roles of their job, or as a future projection tool for visioning one's ideal work life. Social workers are increasingly working in private practice or hold contracts at multiple agencies which allows them to diversify their work. The future projection role atom allows a social worker to create a vision of their ideal balance between the sub-roles of social worker—for example: psychotherapist, supervisor, trainer, writer, administrator, advocate, learner, and volunteer (see Sect. 20.3.2 for a depiction of this).

Similarly to the social atom, the role atom can be concretized through the use of objects, empty chairs, or role players. This process creates an action sculpture of one's role atom which offers opportunities for deeper exploration and transformation. In this process, a client can engage directly with their various roles, dialog with lost roles for closure, reposition roles in new ways, and practice integrating new roles. This externalization of roles also allows one to investigate role conflicts between roles while accessing spontaneity for new solutions in the future.

16.3   Timeline Assessments

It is interesting to note that Moreno created life event timelines, which also included sociocultural roles, in his 1932 publication about the psychosocial assessment of prison inmates (Moreno & Whitin, 1932). The use of timelines in social work and psychotherapy is not new, nor it is a process that originated from the field of psychodrama. Nevertheless, the use of timelines has become integrated within psychodrama practice, often as a warm-up for a psychodramatic enactment or within the drama itself (Carnabucci & Ciotola, 2013; Dayton, 2005, 2014, 2015a,2015b; Giacomucci, 2017; Mak, 2019; Wells, 2018). Timeline exercises can be adapted for a variety of clinical themes to offer specific diagnostic information for both the clinician and client. Some common uses of the pen-to-paper timeline exercise are to depict the progression of one's addiction(s), mental illness, medical concerns, recovery, resiliency, relationships, specific personal strengths, professional develop-ment, a general life timeline, or nearly any other topic. In many cases, multiple themes are integrated into the same timeline to explore and reflect on the intersections of various themes. For example, in inpatient addictions treatment, asking participants to create a timeline including the progression of their drug addiction, co-occurring mental health issues, traumas, and losses can help illuminate the underlying nature of trauma and loss (Dayton, 2015a). In this example, instructions would be:

1. Draw a horizontal line on your paper; mark the left end as "0" and the right as your age today
2. Using one colored marker, indicate major milestones on your timeline for the progression of your addiction —such as the ages you were the first time you used

a drug, when your use increased significantly, when you believe you became physically addicted, etc.

3. Using another colored marker, indicate any major milestones on your timeline for the progression of any co-occurring disorders you experience, such as depression, anxiety, PTSD, bipolar, ADHD, etc.

4. Use a third color to depict any experiences of trauma, loss, abandonment, or periods of neglect.

5. Take a look at the collective timeline you have created and get curious about any connections between trauma, addiction, and co-occurring disorders. What do you notice?

This process is especially helpful for clients that have experienced trauma and addiction as it helps to integrate fragmented memories, experiences, and histories (Dayton, 2015a). As an assessment tool, the timeline helps the social worker to obtain clarity on the client's history. Once a timeline is created by the client, there are various psychodramatic tools that can be used to put the timeline into action. The social worker could use the length of the room to represent the timeline and invite the client to walk their timeline while giving voice to their experiences at various points in their personal history. Another option is to use objects or empty chairs to concretize the client at various significant points in time and to invite them to speak to their past selves. Doubling, mirroring, role reversal, soliloquy, psychodramatic journaling, psychodramatic letter writing, the social atom, and the role atom can be used to further explore any point on the timeline and promote healing. Sometimes it can be helpful to ask a client to even use images of themselves from the past to enhance their timeline.

Though only the past or present can be definitively put on one's timeline, clients can also use the timeline to depict hoped-for future experiences. This can be a simple way of setting short-term or long-term goals related to the content of the timeline. The inclusion of future positive experiences on the trauma timeline can be an important aspect as it helps keep the process balanced with positive elements and promotes hope for clients.

Beyond its utility in individual sessions, the timeline assessment can be used as a group process that is initially created individually by participants. Then, the timeline can be put into action as a spectrogram with prompts such as "stand at the age on this timeline representing how old you were the first time you used a drug," "stand on this timeline at an age in your life that you experienced something difficult that still feels unresolved for you," or "stand at a future age on the timeline where you would like to explore about a vision for yourself in recovery from trauma and addiction". With each of these prompts, participants can be instructed to share with each other about their choices, to role reverse with themselves at that age, or to speak to themselves at that age (Dayton, 2015a).

16.4 Psychodramatic Letter Writing and Journaling

Psychodramatic letter writing and journaling offer contained alternatives to full psychodramas and can be employed as either warm-up or closure to an experiential psychodrama in individual or group settings (Blatner, 2000; Dayton, 2005, 2015b; Giacomucci, 2020; Sacks, 1974). In this process, rather than using an auxiliary, empty chair, or object to externalize another person or entity, the client is simply asked to write a letter to someone or something in their life. A client could be invited to write a letter to a deceased loved one, to an abuser, to a role model, to themselves in the past or future, to their addiction, to their body, to the part of self that feels hopeless, to society, or even to God. It is stressed that this letter will not actually be sent to the recipient, instead the purpose of the letter writing process is for expression, catharsis, and insight. Letter writing is adaptable for nearly any topic, and the recipient of psychodramatic letters can be people who are real, imagined, or deceased, as well as entities, objects, or groups. Some common uses of psychodramatic letter writing are for expressing anger, processing grief, warming up to making amends, articulating hurt, verbalizing gratitude, and offering inspiration.

Clients can also be instructed to engage in psychodramatic letter writing through role reversal. Some common examples of this might include writing a letter to yourself from a deceased loved one for closure, a letter to yourself from someone you hurt offering forgiveness, a letter to yourself from a role model offering inspiration, or a letter to yourself today from yourself in the future. When facilitating psychodramatic letter writing with clients, it can be helpful to conceptualize the letter writing from self as having the goal of catharsis of abreaction while the letter writing in the role reversed position has the goal of catharsis of integration.

Another similar process is psychodramatic journaling which is fundamentally the psychodramatic intervention of soliloquy or a monolog in written form (Dayton, 2015b). The client is asked to role reverse with someone, something, or a part of themselves in the past, present, or future and articulate the thoughts and feelings of that role in the form of journaling. Another option is to invite the client to role reverse with a witness or "a fly on the wall" to explore their experience of a situation (Dayton, 2005). This is essentially using the psychodramatic intervention of the mirror position through psychodramatic journaling. Psychodramatic journaling can be helpful in promoting cathartic abreaction or integration. While psychodramatic letter writing is inherently directing a message between two roles or people, psychodramatic journaling is exploring the inner experience of one role or person.

Both psychodramatic letter writing and journaling are used as interventions, but they also provide the social worker with diagnostic information about the client's experience of self and others. A more modern adaptation of these processes is through the use of vlogging or video recording instead of writing. The younger generation seems to have developed a culture where the recording and sending of short videos have become normalized (YouTube, Facebook, Snapchat, Instagram, TikTok, etc.). A clinician could invite a client to record a psychodramatic video message that they wish they could send to someone or to reverse roles with someone and record a soliloquy or message from the role of the other. This can even be utilized by clients in-between sessions as a means for expressing thoughts or feelings through recorded soliloquys that they will share with their therapist in session.

The letter writing and journaling processes can be integrated with the social atom, role atom, and timeline exercises as a way of facilitating a psychodramatic experience entirely on paper. After drawing their social atom or role atom, a client could be invited to write psychodramatic letters to and/or from the most significant people or roles on their social atom or role atom. In a similar way, the client could be invited to engage in psychodramatic journaling from the perspective of one of the people or roles on their social or role atom. When the timeline is brought into this mix of interventions, it offers an exponential increase in the number of social atoms, role atoms, psychodramatic letters, and journal entries that could be facilitated in the past, present, or future.

The psychodramatic letter writing and journaling processes help clients articulate and make sense of difficult experiences. This may be, in part, because of the left brain-oriented nature of writing and language. When traumatic memories are activated, brain scans indicate a lack of left brain activity; psychodramatic letter writing and journaling help to promote hemispherical integration in the brain (Dayton, 2005). Multiple research studies have provided evidence that various forms of therapeutic writing or journaling offer psychological, emotional, and other health benefits (Baikie & Wilhelm, 2005; Pennebaker, 1997; van der Kolk, 2014). The contained and slower-paced nature of psychodramatic letter writing and journaling make them great interventions for professionals new to psychodrama. An in-depth exploration of these written interventions can be found in Tian Dayton's *The Living Stage* (2005) or *NeuroPsychodrama* (2015a,2015b) books.

16.5   Conclusion

Social work casework and individual assessments can be enhanced through the integration of various sociometric assessment tools including the social atom and the role atom. The social atom offers clients an avenue for depicting their meaningful relationships with others, objects, and institutions while the role atom offers a process for portraying their relationship to significant roles and sub-roles as they relate to the construction of personality. The combined use of the role atom and social atom offers a holistic framework for exploring both internal parts and social environments of clients. The integration of timeline assessments in the diagnostic process offers numerous layers of exploration into clients' histories and futures. Each of these tools is adaptable as a written assessment or experiential process when working with individual clients or in group settings. Psychodramatic letter writing and journaling offer further interventions for contained psychodramatic processes within the social atom, role atom, or timeline. These pen-to-paper tools provide new psychodrama students or less warmed up clients with a contained mechanism for beginning to integrate sociometry and psychodrama into their work.

References

Baikie, K. A., & Wilhelm, K. (2005). Emotional and physical health benefits of expressive writing. *Advances in Psychiatric Treatment, 11*(5), 338–346.

Blatner, A. (2000). *Foundations of psychodrama: History, theory, and practice* (4th ed.). New York City: Springer.

Buchanan, D. R. (1984). Moreno's social atom: A diagnostic and treatment tool for exploring interpersonal relationships. *The Arts in Psychotherapy, 11*(3), 155–164.

Campbell, J. (2011). The use of art with social atoms in substance abuse treatment planning. *Journal of Psychodrama, Sociometry, and Group Psychotherapy, 60*(1), 37–48.

Carnabucci, K., & Ciotola, L. (2013). *Healing eating disorders with psychodrama and other action methods: Beyond the silence and the fury*. Philadelphia: Jessica Kingsley Publishers.

Dayton, T. (2005). *The Living Stage: A step-by-step guide to psychodrama, sociometry, and experiential group therapy*. Deerfield, FL: Health Communications Inc.

Dayton, T. (2014). *Relational trauma repair (RTR) therapist's guide, Revised edition*. New York, USA: Innerlook Inc.

Dayton, T. (2015a). The trauma time line. *The Journal of Psychodrama, Sociometry, and Group Psychotherapy, 63*(1), 83–86.

Dayton, T. (2015b). *NeuroPsychodrama in the treatment of relational trauma: A strength-based, experiential model for healing PTSD*. Deerfield Beach, FL: Health Communications Inc.

Giacomucci, S. (2017). The sociodrama of life or death: Young adults and addiction treatment. *Journal of Psychodrama, Sociometry, and Group Psychotherapy, 65*(1), 137–143. https://doi.org/10.12926/0731-1273-65.1.137.

Giacomucci, S. (2019). *Social group work in action: A sociometry, psychodrama, and experiential trauma therapy curriculum* (Doctorate in Social Work (DSW) Dissertations) (p. 124). https://repository.upenn.edu/cgi/viewcontent.cgi?article=1128&context=edissertations_sp2.

Giacomucci, S. (2020). Addiction, traumatic loss, and guilt: A case study resolving grief through psychodrama and sociometric connections. *The Arts in Psychotherapy, 67*, 101627. https://doi.org/10.1016/j.aip.2019.101627.

Mak, L. (2019). Working with grief and loss. In A. Chesner (Ed.), *One-to-one psychodrama psychotherapy: Applications and technique* (pp. 119–129). New York: Routledge.

Moreno, J. L. (1953). *Who shall survive? Foundations of sociometry, group psychotherapy and sociodrama* (2nd ed.). Beacon, NY: Beacon House.

Moreno, J. L., & Whitin, E. S. (1932). *Application of the group method to classification*. New York, USA: National Committee on Prisons and Prison Labor.

Moreno, Z. T. (2014). Drawing the personal perceptual socio-cultural atom: An exercise in sharpening and stretching tele function. *The Journal of Psychodrama, Sociometry, and Group Psychotherapy, 62*(1), 29–34.

Pennebaker, J. W. (1997). Writing about emotional experiences as a therapeutic process. *Psychological Science, 8*(3), 162–166.

Sacks, J. M. (1974). The letter. *Group Psychotherapy and Psychodrama, 27*(3–4), 184–190.

Skolnik, S. (2018). A synergistic union: Group work meets psychodrama. *Social Work with Groups, 41*(1–2), 60–73.

Treadwell, T., Collins, L., & Stein, S. (1992). The Moreno Social Atom Test—Revised (MSAT—R): A sociometric instrument measuring interpersonal networks. *Journal of Group Psychotherapy, Psychodrama & Sociometry, 45*(3), 122–124.

Van der Kolk, B. A. (2014). *The body keeps the score: Brain, mind, and body in the healing of trauma*. New York: Viking Press.

Wells, J. (2018). Psychodramatic resiliency timeline. *The Journal of Psychodrama, Sociometry, and Group Psychotherapy, 66*(1), 131–140.

Chapter 17
Psychodrama Practice in Clinical Social Work with Individuals

Abstract This chapter is devoted to the clinical practice of psychodrama in individual sessions. Fundamental differences between psychodrama in groups and one-to-one contexts are discussed including the use of auxiliary roles, the therapeutic relationship, and modifications for basic psychodrama interventions. An overview of the use of the empty chair, objects, and/or the therapist as an auxiliary ego is included. The limitations and strengths of using psychodrama in individual sessions are discussed. Multiple psychodrama scenes (strengths-based, intrapsychic, and interpersonal) are depicted from a social work practice example with clinical processing.

Keywords Individual psychodrama · One-to-one psychodrama · Empty chair · Psychodrama a deux · Bi-personal psychodrama · Monodrama

This chapter will outline the use of psychodrama in individual psychotherapy and clinical social work settings. The processes described below will be focused on psychotherapy, but are also applicable in individual supervision, coaching, and consulting sessions. Psychodrama with individuals, sometimes called bi-personal psychodrama, monodrama, one-to-one psychodrama, or psychodrama a deux, has both its limitations and its benefits when compared group psychodrama in groups. Some find Moreno's methods to be more easily integrated by practitioners in individual settings than group settings. There are uniquely different clinical concerns with the process of psychodrama work with individuals as opposed to group work. Considerations for individual psychodrama work, including the therapeutic relationship, doubling, mirroring, role reversal, and auxiliary roles will be explored. And finally, a psychodrama case will be presented with multiple psychodrama sessions to depict the unique aspects of psychodrama in individual sessions.

17.1 Providing Context for Psychodrama in Individual Sessions

The use psychodrama in individual sessions is based on the same foundational philosophy and interventions outlined throughout this book. Nearly all of Moreno's

© The Author(s) 2021   323
S. Giacomucci, *Social Work, Sociometry, and Psychodrama*, Psychodrama in Counselling, Coaching and Education 1,
https://doi.org/10.1007/978-981-33-6342-7_17

psychodramatic theories are applicable and easily adaptable for conceptualizing psychodrama work with individuals (von Ameln & Becker-Ebel, 2020). The process remains mostly the same in terms of the phases of warming up, enactment, and processing; however, there are no role players. The primary difference between individual sessions and group sessions is the context. In the one-to-one psychodrama context, each of the five primary instruments of a classical psychodrama (see Sect. 6.5) are modified—the director, the protagonist, the stage, the auxiliaries, and the audience (Aguiar, 2019; Hirschfeld & McVea, 1998).

Group sessions take place with a group and usually are scheduled as longer sessions than individual appointments. While a psychodrama group generally employs a psychodramatic enactment in every session, this is not the case with individual work. Individual psychodrama practitioners usually integrate psychodrama enactments, written sociometric/psychodramatic processes, traditional talk therapy, and often other structured therapeutic approaches (such as art therapy, cognitive behavioral therapy, and eye-movement desensitization and reprocessing) into their sessions. Though Moreno's group psychotherapy and psychodrama model emerged from his opposition of psychoanalysis, practitioners employing psychodrama in individual sessions seem much more likely to also integrate psychanalytic and psychodynamic theories into their work. Another logistical concern is the physical space in the individual therapy room, which is generally much more restrictive than the space of a group room. The stage for the one-to-one psychodrama may need to be reconsidered in creative ways making use of the space available (Aguiar, 2019).

Group psychodrama sessions seem to be held across the treatment continuum, from inpatient and residential treatment centers, partial programs, intensive outpatients, private practices, and multiday workshop intensives. On the contrary, one-to-one psychodrama sessions seem to primarily be utilized in outpatient private practice settings. Though the 50–60 min session length seems to be the norm in outpatient work, it may be advantageous to schedule longer sessions when a psychodrama is expected (Chesner, 2019a; Fonseca, 2019). Chesner (2019a) notes that while group psychodramas focus on one topic following a Psychodramatic Spiral to closure with the session, individual psychodramatic work often follows a longer arc as one topic can extend through several sessions with psychodrama scenes dispersed among sessions. She compares a group session to an immersive two hour movie and individual work to a television series with weekly episodes—"while a group session is like a feast with many courses, which requires time to digest, the one-to-one frame offers regular bite-sized therapeutic nourishment" (Chesner, 2019a, p. 12).

17.1.1 The Therapeutic Relationship

Perhaps one of the larger differences between group work and individual work is that in group work the group is the client while in individual work, the individual is the client (Moreno, 1947). Yalom and Leszcz (2005) write that group cohesion in group work is analogous to the therapeutic relationship between clinician and client in individual work. In individual work, there is no group—thus no group cohesion exerting its healing influences upon the individual. Instead, the working relationship between client and clinician is elevated in importance. The primary role of the social worker in a group is to help participants access the healing power of mutual aid between participants, but this is not applicable in individual work—instead, the social worker must take a much more active role as a participant in the therapeutic dyad. The use of self, direct suggestions or advice giving, feedback, and analysis from the therapist play a more centralized role in individual work because the group is not present to fulfill some of these functions. Aguiar (2019) writes that "one of psychodrama's most revolutionary proposals was attributing the therapist role to all of the group members" becomes null in the therapist–client dyad where roles are clearly defined with rank.

Antonio (2019) and Kim (2019) highlight the increased relevance of the encounter, tele, transference, and countertransference within the therapeutic relationship in one-to-one psychodrama contrasted to group work. Moreno's encounter philosophy suggests that the self only exists in relationship to others. The *client* role only exists through the role reciprocity of *client–therapist*. In one-to-one psychodrama, the multiple layers of role relationships between client and therapist become more conscious, while in group work, the role relationships between participants are more in focus. Moreno (1959) conceptualizes transference as a function of role relationships; Bustos (1979) adds that transference is characterized by a loss of spontaneity and increased anxiety within the dyad. In the process of individual work, the presence of transference and countertransference between client and therapist are much more explicit, expected, and significant to the therapeutic process. The blend of playfulness and intensity that the client experiences in a psychodrama may lead to an increased chance of transference emerging, especially when the therapist is interviewing the client playing a different role (Bustos, 2019). Similarly, the intensity of the psychodramatic process and the role demands of being a therapist may activate a therapist's countertransference which would interrupt tele (Kim, 2019). Moreno writes that underneath transference exists a telic relationship as an accurate two-way connection between individuals which is essential to a successful therapeutic relationship (1959,1972). Tele is conceptualized as a fundamental ingredient in any healthy interpersonal relationship characterized by spontaneity, especially between client and therapist. Ongoing assessment and awareness of tele, transference, and countertransference in the therapeutic dyad provide a balanced attunement to both the psychodynamics of the client and therapist, as well as the sociodynamics of the relational space.

17.1.2 Limitations to Individual Psychodrama Work

There are various limitations to using psychodrama in individual settings. One of the largest limitations is the lack of a group and auxiliaries to play the roles needed for psychodrama enactments. While the other psychodrama roles can be concretized with objects or empty chairs, there is an interactional element lost when the role is not being played by another human being. The absence of an audience means that the only person that can offer doubling statements is the therapist. In group psychodrama, physical touch is often an important element between group members—most often through a hand on the shoulder when choosing a topic, doubling, or offering support, a supportive hug when needed, or other physical contact between roles in the scene (Giacomucci, Gera, Briggs, & Bass, 2018). Therapists are much more restricted in their physical touch with a client than group members are which significantly limits opportunities for the client in individual psychodrama sessions to experience safe and supportive touch (Chesner, 2019a).

The intensity of role reciprocity, tele, and spontaneity is decreased between roles due to the absence of human role players. The multiplicity of human relationships in the group is also relied upon by the psychodrama director in the process of co-creating the psychodrama enactment. Brito (2019) describes the implications of this in the following passage:

> As opposed to what usually happens in larger groups, in one-to-one psychodrama the subjec-tivity of the therapist is more directly involved in the establishment of the protagonic climate. In larger groups this originality is diluted in the complexity of relational possibilities of the other therapeutic agents. Restricted to the role of the director, the therapist relies on the other members of the group as auxiliary egos to facilitate the development of the dramatic project. (p. 23).

The one-to-one psychodrama enactment is void of the additional therapeutic agents present in a group psychodrama enactment. Because of this fundamental difference, the therapist must become more involved as a therapeutic agent and place more reliance on the concretized roles as agents in the therapeutic process.

The absence of a group also decreases the sense of universality and the ability for mutual aid between participants. The group member's process of using their own experience to help another group member is empowering, healing, and therapeutic—this possibility is mostly lost within the therapeutic dyad. The social dynamics of a group often lead to what Yalom calls *the corrective recapitulation of the primary family group*, which is still present in individual work, but not with the same number of possibilities. Other therapeutic factors remain present, but become diminished in individual work including social learning, instillation of hope, imparting of informa-tion, altruism, socializing techniques, imitative behavior, interpersonal learning, and group cohesion. Each of these factors in group work emerge in the constellation of sociodynamics between multiple group members but lose some of their effect in the dyad. In the group, there are a multiplicity of relationships from which these factors materialize, but in the therapeutic dyad, they can only exist between therapist and client.

Individual work also does not offer the possibility for the client to be in the role of an audience member or auxiliary role for someone else's psychodrama. Both of these roles in group psychodrama provide unique learning perspectives for clients and role relief from being the center of attention. Moreno (1972) highlights that catharsis has an interpersonal nature, which loses its potential in individual work as well. There are unique cathartic and integrative phenomena that a participant only experiences through the role of an audience member or auxiliary role. The individual client is always the center of attention in individual work. Every psychodrama that takes place through individual psychotherapy places the client as the protagonist. This aspect may be considered both a limitation and a benefit of one-to-one psychodrama work. Another limitation that exists in one-to-one psychodrama work is the lack of group sharing after an enactment which often leads to new insights and integrations.

A larger limitation to the practice of psychodrama in individual work is the lack of formalized training offered in this specific context (Brito, 2019). Most formal psychodrama training programs orient themselves on Moreno's triadic system of sociometry, psychodrama, and group psychotherapy. As such, psychodrama is almost always categorized within the larger group work field without much attention given to its utility in individual sessions. The psychodrama field would benefit from increased attention to the needs of individual practitioners learning one-to-one psychodrama.

17.1.3 Strengths of Individual Psychodrama Work

Beyond the aforementioned limitations, there are also multiple strengths inherent to the one-to-one psychodrama process. The therapist does not need to maintain awareness of multiple group members which means that the individual psychotherapy client will experience much more attention from the therapist. The therapist's attunement to the client is uninterrupted by the needs of other group members or the group-as-a-whole. This attunement to the client also translates to a warming up process and topic selection that is client-centered rather than group-centered. The risk of an individual client's topic not being chosen or individual clients being at varying levels of warm-up to a topic is eradicated in the individual psychodrama process. As mentioned previously, the client in individual therapy is always the protagonist in the psychodrama which has its benefits. Every psychodrama in individual therapy is relevant to the protagonist and meets them where they are at in terms of warm-up, clinical issues, ego strength, and willingness.

The ongoing nature of individual work with clients makes it easier to build upon previous sessions and resume psychodramatic work on clinical issues from previous sessions. This becomes more complicated in a group as the facilitator must balance the wants and needs of every client in a fair manner. While group psychodrama sessions often have topics that vary from session to session, individual psychodrama sessions can afford more continuity and follow-up on topics. The psychodramatist can more readily meet the individual client where they are at in each session modifying the pace, topics, and processes in attunement with the client. For all of these reasons, individual therapy may feel less threatening and safer for clients to engage in than group work. In the one-to-one psychodrama context, both the therapist and client have significantly more control of the process than they would in a group setting.

17.2 The Double, Mirror, and Role Reversal in Individual Psychodrama

The interventions of doubling, mirroring, and role reversal were developed specifically in the group psychodrama context and each is modified for individual psychodrama work. In the group setting, other group members often step into the double role and/or offer doubling statements which contribute to the protagonist's expression of emotion, support from the group, and sense of identification with the participants. In the one-to-one psychodrama situation, the only person available to double is the therapist. In some ways, the double position is the best place for the therapist due to their insight and understanding of the client's clinical issues. The utilization of doubling by the therapist both relies on the therapeutic relationship and enhances it through the client's sense of being understood by their therapist. It is suggested that the therapist reflects on the use of doubling in their individual work as to avoid overusing it and potentially being experienced as controlling by the client (Chesner, 2019b).

The mirror position is also useful in one-to-one psychodrama but relies more on the imagination and surplus reality as there are no role players to re-enact the scene while the client watches from the mirror position. Instead, the client is instructed to move into the mirror position, and using objects to concretize roles from the scene, the client is invited to imagine the enactment from this place of observation and distance. The mirror position can be helpful for discerning choices, enhancing clarity, containing emotion, accessing cognition, and cultivating integration for the client. It can also be useful in difficult moments between the client and therapist as it provides the distance to obtain clarity and intervene on transferential dynamics or misunderstandings. If the therapist notices that the client is in the mists of transference with the therapist, from the mirror position they could use concretization to differentiate therapist and the person or role being projected upon them. Transferences can be worked out psychodramatically in this way.

The role reversal in one-to-one psychodrama is fundamentally the same as it is in group work, but without a role player in the other role. If trained auxiliaries are available, they can be helpful for conducting psychodramas in individual sessions as the role reversals and role-playing are more embodied. Though in most cases, it becomes financially unreasonable to work with trained auxiliaries. Without role players in psychodrama, the client is asked to role reverse and speak to objects or empty chairs that have been designated to concretize the other roles. When returning to the role of self, they can be invited to imagining that they are hearing and receiving the message from the role of the other. This process of role reversal keeps the psychodrama more contained, which is advantageous in some situations but a limitation in other situations.

17.2.1 Therapist as Auxiliary Roles?

There is ongoing debate about the appropriateness of the therapist taking on auxiliary roles in psychodramas with individual clients (Aguiar, 2019; Antonio, 2019; Brito, 2019; Cukier, 2008; Figusch, 2019; Fonseca, 2019; Knittel, 2009). A major crux of the dilemma is based upon the tradition of therapists upholding power dynamics between the roles of therapist and client by avoiding personal involvement. A therapist playing auxiliary roles needed in the client's psychodrama scene has a very active involvement in their work. Brito (2019) frames it as, "the dilemma of how to co-act, co-create and co-experience without 'mixing' with the patient" (p. 26). There are, of course, professional boundaries that a social worker upholds in the therapeutic dyad. And, at the same time, it seems that social workers in general might be more willing than other professionals to mix with their client in co-acting, co-creating, and co-experiencing. Theoretically, the dilemma touches upon the question of whether or not the psychodrama session is treated as a group of two people (therapist and client) or as an individual therapist and individual client (Brito, 2019). It seems therefore that those who approach one-to-one psychodrama as a group of two will be likely to play auxiliary roles. On the contrary, those who maintain the traditional view of the session being two individuals would be more likely not to play auxiliary roles and to maintain their individual role of therapist/director. There are, of course, benefits and limitations to each approach.

The biggest benefit to the therapist playing auxiliary roles is an enhanced psychodrama enactment with more interaction and production between roles and between the therapist and client. The role reversal experiences become especially more real when another person is playing the roles. The therapist becomes a more active participant in the process rather than a facilitator outside of the scene. The playing of roles by the therapist could contribute to a client's sense of being joined in the drama. The enactment between client and therapist in new roles offers opportunities for a deepening of the therapeutic dyad. A skillful and experienced psychodramatist can facilitate the enactment by shifting between the director role and an auxiliary role and even passively directing the scene from the auxiliary role. By playing a role in the client's psychodrama, the therapist is likely to gain increased insight into the nature of the client's relationships. It is also likely that the therapist will experience therapeutic benefits and personal growth of their own through the engagement as an auxiliary ego. When choosing to play roles, the therapist would be wise to specify which types of auxiliary roles would be therapeutic for them to play and which would not be. For instance, they might choose to engage as an auxiliary in strengths-based and supportive roles, but decline playing antagonistic or perpetrator roles from the client's life.

There are also limitations to the therapist choosing to play auxiliary roles in the client's psychodrama. The directing of the psychodrama becomes more difficult and complicated when the therapist is playing a role and trying to be both an auxiliary and a director. In doing so, they may lose their objectivity and thus their ability to direct the scene with minimal bias. The therapist's ability to offer doubling statements is also compromised if they are playing an auxiliary role in a scene. There is an increased potential of losing role clarity when the therapist is shifting between the roles of director, auxiliary, and double (Chesner, 2019b). Auxiliary role-playing by the therapist also increases the possibility of the therapist's use of self being overused through the auxiliary role or their own emotional material and countertransference becoming activate in the psychodrama. The likelihood of client transference and projections upon the therapist increases especially if the therapist plays an emotionally charged role in the client's psychodrama and the client is unable to fully de-role them (Hirschfeld & McVea, 1998). Being that the therapist is the recipient of the client's transference and projection from the role they played, they will have more difficult shifting back into a director role and de-roling. Chesner (2019b) suggests that the here-and-now space of the client–therapist dialogue should be physically different than the surplus reality space of the psychodrama enactment to increase role clarity and de-roling abilities.

The question of therapists playing auxiliary roles is one that each therapist will need to respond to when facilitating one-to-one psychodrama sessions. It may be a question that permits different answers based on the varying needs, ego strengths, and relationships with each client. It is suggested that the therapist engages in a reflective process and discerns which approach may be best for their clients. The following vignette will depict one-to-one psychodrama with a therapist choosing not to play auxiliary roles.

17.3   A One-To-One Psychodrama Scenes Throughout the Treatment Process

The following subsections will depict different one-to-one psychodrama vignettes with Mary, whose social atom was included in Sect. 16.1. The development of her social atom helped warm her up to new work around grief and loss, as well as childhood trauma. The social worker slowly began to introduce psychodramatic interventions into their individual therapy sessions. Short psychodrama vignettes with strengths-based roles were introduced to set the foundation for later scenes. The first vignette below depicts a strengths-based scene, the second vignette describes an intrapsychic psychodrama scene, and the third vignette offers a portrayal of an interpersonal one-to-one psychodrama. The exploration of a single case over time shows the utility of individual psychodrama work and its unique potential to build upon past psychodramas in a linear manner.

17.3.1 Strengths-Based Scenes

The social worker first ensures Mary's consent, permission, and warm-up to engage in a psychodrama vignette. When asked which strengths she would need to heal from her trauma, loss, and work through her anxiety and depression, Mary indicated that she would need more courage. The social worker invites Mary to choose an object in the room to represent courage, and she chooses the painting on the wall. The therapist invites her to role reverse with courage—becoming courage. Mary steps into the role of courage, standing in front of the painting and begins speaking to herself as if she were still sitting on the couch.

MARY AS COURAGE: Hi Mary, remember me? You used to use me so much in your life, but we have not been so close lately.

THERAPIST: Courage, can you remind Mary of some of the times she did use you throughout her life? remind her of the times that you were close.

MARY AS COURAGE: Well... Mary, I know it is difficult for you to talk about things in your life so I help you do that... (Mary appears stuck).

THERAPIST: Courage, is it okay if I offer a doubling statement for you? If it is accurate you can repeat it to Mary, if it does not fit, you can simply change it to make it fit for you.

MARY AS COURAGE: Okay.

THERAPIST AS DOUBLE: Mary, you have a lot more courage than you realize. You use me (courage) every time you come to therapy.

MARY AS COURAGE: (a soft smile emerges as her body loosens up) Mary, you have way more courage than you can see right now. Every time you come to therapy, you use me.

THERAPIST: (steps out of double role) Yes. That is right, every time Mary comes to the office here, she brings you. Seems like you are a pretty important part of Mary. Tell her more about you and how she can connect with you.

MARY AS COURAGE: When you feel scared to do something, I am what helps you push through and do it anyway Mary. I have helped you have meaningful relationships, a successful marriage, to ask for help, to thrive as a woman in your career, to survive your childhood, and to live a good life. You might not realize it, but I am an important part of you. I'm especially important now because I can help you walk through your anxiety and depression. When you feel scared or stuck, just tap into me.

THERAPIST: Can you tell Mary how she can tap into you?

MARY AS COURAGE: You can tap into me by standing up proudly, taking a few deep breathes, and remembering the many other times you have been courageous in your long life.

THERAPIST: Great job courage. Go ahead and reverse roles.

(Mary moves back to her place sitting on the couch).

THERAPIST: Okay, Mary, just take a minute to look over here at courage (pointing to the painting on the wall) and take in all those messages and reminders of your courage—especially the advice on how to tap into courage. When you are ready, lets practice implementing the advice from courage about standing proudly, taking deep breathes, and remembering past experiences of courage.

Mary stands up, takes a few deep breathes and closes her eyes. As she recalls previous moments of courage, her posture and facial expression begin to depict confidence and courage. She begins to smile gently, opens her eyes, and comments on how surprised she is about her current sense of courage. Following the enactment, Mary and the therapist organically shift into a reflective discussion about the scene.

In the sharing phase of the one-to-one psychodrama, the therapist shares more of themselves, while maintaining their professional boundaries (von Ameln & Becker-Ebel, 2020). This is a time for the Mary to cool down from her psychodrama experience and to integrate the learning from the enactment. In the ongoing individual psychotherapy context, this is the time for the therapist and Mary to also discuss a concrete plan for how she will implement their new learning in between sessions. Mary agrees to take time each day to practice standing proudly and taking deep breathes while remembering memories of courage.

Having completed this strengths-based psychodrama above, every time Mary returns to the office, she sees the painting on the wall and is reminded of her courage. This may happen unconsciously or consciously—and the therapist now has another strengths-based tool to weave into future sessions. In subsequent sessions, Mary completes similar strengths-based psychodrama vignettes using the office plant to symbolize *compassion for self*, the lamp to represent her *hope,* the clock to play the role of her *future self* no longer stuck in depression or anxiety, and the pillow to represent *God*. With each journey into surplus reality, Mary increases her level of connection to the therapist, her trust and familiarity with the psychodramatic method, and her psychological stability or ego strength. The office becomes inherently resourcing after a few psychodrama sessions as Mary experiences the positive projections with the previously chosen objects in each session. Every time she walks back into the space of the office, she is greeted by her strengths and reminders of previous therapeutic successes through psychodrama.

17.3.2 Intrapsychic Scene

Having spent time resourcing her with strengths-based roles and enhancing the therapeutic relationship, Mary becomes more willing to share and be vulnerable with the therapist over time. She begins to talk about feeling stuck in anxiety and depression and that there is a part of her that just wants to stay stuck and be taken care of by others. She describes it as an old feeling that resembled her experience as a child with a depressed father and an abusive mother that were not always able to adequately fulfill her developmental needs. Mary and her therapist schedule a longer session with the intent of doing a more intensive internal psychodrama scene exploring her relationship with a wounded/younger self role. The psychodrama scene begins with an integration of the strengths from previous enactments with a focus on their utility for today's topic. Mary is instructed to reverse roles and offer a statement to herself from each of the roles of courage, self-compassion, hope, future self, and God.

MARY AS COURAGE: You have the courage to explore your past and heal from it. You can do it!

MARY AS SELF-COMPASSION: I am so proud of you for the work you are doing to better yourself. You are a good, kind woman.

MARY AS HOPE: Mary, although your depression, anxiety, loss, and trauma may seem overwhelming at times, none of it has to define you today. You can heal from it and work though all of it, one step at a time.

MARY AS FUTURE SELF: Though you are unsure about today's psychodrama, trust me when I say that it will be worth it.

MARY AS GOD: I am with you always. You are perfectly imperfect—I created you in this way so you could walk this unique path that I have laid out for you. This is the next step today.

After giving voice to supporting message from each of these strengths-based roles, Mary returns to her own chair and is encouraged by the therapist to take a moment to ground herself in the support and presence of all of her strengths-based roles. Then, the therapist pulls out an empty chair and instructs Mary to imagine that her wounded self is in the empty chair. When working with trauma-based roles in individual work, it is often best to avoid concretizing them with objects in the room as it could encourage negative projections in future sessions when the client sees the same object.

THERAPIST: Mary, here is the part of yourself that did not get her needs met as a child and was hurt and neglected by her parents at times. Perhaps this is the same part of yourself that today feels paralyzed with depression and anxiety. What is it you need to say to this part of yourself?

MARY: I know how hard it was for you growing up and that at times it felt like nobody cared about you. I know you felt stuck and afraid—that you think you are trapped forever in this situation. It is okay. You did the best that you could and I am so happy you survived and got out of that family. I know you still exist within me because I can feel your pain and your anxiety all the time. I just want to find a way so you don't have to hurt so much.

THERAPIST: Great job Mary. You are really using that strength of self-compassion here. I am wondering if there are other strength roles that have anything to say this hurt part of you?

MARY: Yes, I think wounded Mary needs to talk to hope.

THERAPIST: Okay, reverse roles with hope. What do you have to say to wounded Mary?

MARY AS HOPE: (speaking to wounded Mary) Hi Mary, I know you feel hopeless sometimes but I am here to remind you that thinks will get better. There is always hope. Don't give up on yourself. This is all just temporary, and you have a good life ahead of you.

THERAPIST: Go ahead and role reverse with wounded Mary. From this role, can you articulate the feelings and thoughts you experience?

MARY AS WOUNDED SELF: I just feel so trapped and stuck all the time. I don't feel like trying sometimes— would rather someone else take care of things for me. It is so unfair that I have to deal with all this loss, depression, and anxiety. My life has been hard enough. I feel so shameful for having these problems. I am afraid that things won't get better and instead they will just get worse until I die.

THERAPIST: Is there more that you need to say? It sounds like you have been neglected for a long time and have accumulated a lot of hurt over the years… What haven't you been able to say about your parents?

MARY AS WOUNDED SELF: Well, yeah. I am so angry at my mom for how she treated me and upset that my dad never gave me attention and love when I wanted it. I was just a kid and they were supposed to love me. I had to grow up so early and figure out how to take care of myself. (Mary begins to cry) I still hear the voice of my mom shaming my dad for being depressed. She always told him to stop being selfish and to suck it up. She thought depression wasn't real, and so did I. I can imagine my mom saying the same things to me today because of my depression. I feel worthless when I think about it.

THERAPIST: You have waited a long time to express these feelings Mary, just let them out here. What else is there?

MARY AS WOUNDED SELF: (Mary continues tearfully) I just feel so upset with myself. How did I end up so stuck and depressed? I feel like I've wasted so much of my life and I hate myself for it.

THERAPIST: Sounds like you are really hurting here. I'm wondering what Mary's relationship with you has been like?

MARY AS WOUNDED SELF: She ignores me and pretends that I don't exist, or she shames me for the feelings I have.

THERAPIST: Can you tell her what it is that you need from her?

MARY AS WOUNDED SELF: Mary, I need you to pay attention to me. Stop ignoring me or shaming me for how I feel. You are doing the same thing that Mom did to Dad. I need your help or we both are going to be stuck. Will you help me?

THERAPIST: Reverse roles. Mary, you've heard everything this wounded part of yourself has to say, she is asking you to help her, pay attention to her, and stop shaming her. How do you want to respond?

MARY: (begins to cry) Mary, I'm so sorry that I've treated you like this for so long. You have already been through so much and you deserve better…

THERAPIST: Don't forget that all of your strengths are here to help you with this too Mary.

MARY: (looks around the room remembering her strengths. Then she stands up, takes a few breathes and steps closer to the empty chair containing her wounded self) Mary, I'm sorry for shaming you for your feelings. I'm sorry for ignoring you. I see how much you are hurting, and I am going to take care of you from now on. I can see why you felt so stuck and hopeless. I was afraid of your feelings and afraid of accepting you. I'm going to give you the love you deserve. You are a precious part of me, and I am going to treat you like that going forward.

THERAPIST: As we move towards closure Mary, I wonder if there is a commitment you can make to yourself about something concrete you can do to put this love into action?

MARY: I am going to commit to you that I will take time to journal about you at least twice this week. If it is helpful, then I will make it a regular habit to write about you.

THERAPIST: I think that is a great commitment and a good plan for implementing this work into your life going forward. You can use the psychodramatic letter writing and psychodramatic journaling tools that I've shown you previously.

From here, the therapist and Mary de-role the empty chair and transition to the sharing phase of the psychodrama process. Mary expresses her experience as the protagonist while remembering the different roles and dialogues she just engaged in. She comments on how helpful it was to have the strength roles present and that she does not know that she would have been able to have the discussion she had if it were not for her courage, hope, and self-compassion. The therapist frames this inner scene between her, her strengths, and her wounded self as an ongoing dialogue that will continue within her beyond this session. The therapist celebrates Mary's work today while also reminding her that it will take practice and consistency to change the internalized messages that she has been carrying with her for several decades.

In psychodramatic terms, Mary has accessed the spontaneity to change her intrapsychic relationship with this part of herself. She responded to in a new and adequate way while creating a new cultural conserve for a more accepting in loving relationship with herself. Now that she has engaged in the strengths-based work and internal work, she is more prepared for the interpersonal psychodrama that is to come.

17.3.3 Interpersonal Scene

Based on Mary's ongoing clinical work, it became clear that she had unresolved issues with her mother. This was apparent in her social atom depiction (see Sect. 16.1), within which her deceased mother was nearly the same size as her husband and her depression/anxiety. The previous, intrapsychic psychodrama enactment revealed the internalized shame that Mary carries about having depression and anxiety because of her mother's comments to her depressed father. She describes a common situation to involve her father watching television on the couch, while her mother yells at him for being lazy, depressed, and a poor husband. Mary describes how as a child, she would hide in her room during these instances and wait for it to be over, wishing that her father would stand up for himself. Mary and her therapist set an intention to engage in a psychodrama enactment to work through some of the unfinished business with her mom.

When Mary arrives to the session, the therapist instructs her to connect with her strengths by role reversing with each and offering herself a message of support. The messaging from her strengths and supportive roles fortifies her and affirms her commitment to moving forward with the clinical contract. Mary is invited to recreate the scene described above using pillows or chairs in the office to represent her mother, father, and herself as a child. From the mirror position, she is asked to describe the scene, including the messages and actions of each person. The therapist, having assessed her as emotionally capable of re-experiencing the scene, directs her to step into the role of her mother.

THERAPIST: Mom, what is it that you feel about your husband here, tell him.

MARY AS MOM: You are pathetic. You barely can hold a job because you call out all the time and stay home watching television. I can't believe you. This depression is all in your head. You need to snap out of it and act like a man before I leave you.

THERAPIST: Sounds like you are pretty angry that he can't just be normal?

MARY AS MOM: Yeah, I'm furious at him. I have to work twice as hard around the house and at my job in order to pick up the slack.

THERAPIST: Are you afraid that he will lose his job? Sounds like his depression has created additional burdens for you. Can you give us an internal soliloquy of mom?

Mary AS MOM (soliloquy): Of course. I'm afraid he will lose his job and how it will impact our family. I feel like I am the only adult in the home, and I have to take care of him too. It's not fair. I'm upset that my husband isn't able to be fully present with me. I feel stuck in this situation too.

THERAPIST: Okay. Mary—reverse roles with your father. Now, show us how you respond to your wife.

MARY AS FATHER: (lays on couch with detached expression—says nothing).

THERAPIST: You have nothing to say huh?

MARY AS FATHER: What's the point. Nothing I say or do will be good enough.

THERAPIST: I see. So, you are pretty stuck in the depression and this unhealthy dynamic. Do you know your daughter is in the other room hiding and wishes you would stand up for yourself?

MARY AS FATHER: (affect changes and eyes become tearful) I know. I don't know how to change this. I feel stuck and I'm afraid of how my depression and my wife's anger will impact Mary.

THERAPIST: What do you want to say to Mary that you never had the chance to?

MARY AS FATHER: Mary, I'm so sorry about all of this. This wasn't the type of house I wanted you to grow up in. I wish I could have been there for you more and I wish I could have provided a safer home.

THERAPIST: Dad, do you know Mary grew up to struggle with depression just like you? What do you want to tell her about depression?

MARY AS FATHER: Mary, it's okay to be depressed. It's not your fault that you have depression—it runs in the family. There is no shame in having a mental health issue. But now you have an opportunity to change this generational pattern and take care of yourself.

THERAPIST: Can you tell Mary what you think about all the work she has been doing to take care of herself lately?

MARY AS FATHER: I'm so proud of you Mary. You are handling your depression in a way that I couldn't.

THERAPIST: Reverse roles. Mary what do you want to say to dad in response?

MARY: (tearful) Thank you dad. I always wanted to hear you say you are proud of me. I can see how much you suffered because of your depression and because of mom. I wish you were more available to me growing up, but I understand what it's like to be stuck in depression. I am going to get better for both of us.

THERAPIST: Reverse roles. Mary, as your father, can you show us how you wish he would have stood up to mom?

MARY AS FATHER: Okay. (turns to role of mom) I'm sorry how my depression impacts you. Regardless, I am not going to allow you to talk to me like that anymore. You are scaring Mary. And just because I am depressed, doesn't make me any less of a man. I have a mental illness and there is no shame in that. Your yelling at me and shaming me doesn't help at all—it only makes things worse. And you clearly have some of your own issues to work out.

THERAPIST: Okay, Mary. Reverse roles with yourself today. What is it that you'd like to say to mom?

MARY: (presents as emotional and unsure about what to say to mom).

THERAPIST: Mary, take a look around at all of your strengths in the room (pointing to the plant, the painting on the wall, the lamp, the clock, and the pillow—representing compassion, courage, hope, herself in the future, and God).

(As Mary looks around remembering her strengths, she stabilizes emotionally).

THERAPIST: I'm going to offer a doubling statement for you Mary, if it fits you can repeat it. If not, simply change it…

THERAPIST AS DOUBLE: I've never stood up to you before mom, but I'm going to do it today with the support of my strengths.

MARY: Mom, I've never done this before, but today I'm going to stand up to you because I have all these new strengths and supports.

THERAPIST AS DOUBLE: I am so damn angry and upset!

MARY: I am so damn angry and upset at you Mom. You were so mean and abusive to dad and I. Half a century later I am still impacted by your behavior. You were so hard on dad and it wasn't fair. You clearly didn't understand depression or mental illness. Do you think he wanted to be depressed? I grew up believing that it was shameful to have a mental illness because of you. This belief has made it so difficult to ask for help or to tell my friends that I am depressed.

THERAPIST: Mary, choose one of these scarves to represent this belief that it is shameful to have a mental illness.

(she chooses a gray scarf from the therapists' collection of scarves).

THERAPIST: Now, tell mom how this has impacted you and when you are ready, I want you to give it back to her. It sounds like you've been carrying around this belief that you inherited from Mom which hasn't been so helpful.

MARY: See this mom? This is yours, not mine. I'm sick of carrying this around. It has done nothing but make me judge other people, hate myself, and stay stuck. Because of this belief, I've isolated myself from my friends. This is yours—not mine.

(Mary physically places the scarf on the chair representing her mom).

THERAPIST: Mary, take a moment to notice what it feels like to no longer carry this belief around.

MARY: I feel much lighter. That belief has weighed me down for so long. I feel like I don't have to be shameful for my mental illness, or for needing help to work through it.

THERAPIST: Tell your mom how things will be different now that you won't carry this belief any longer.

MARY: Mom, I not going to shame myself for needing help. It's your burden for not understanding mental illness, not mine. You should have educated yourself. I'm not going to carry that burden for your ignorance—or anyone else's. This is a part of who I am and if you or someone else can't accept that then I don't want them to be in my life anyways. I wish you would understand.

THERAPIST: Reverse roles. Okay mom, I know you didn't understand mental illness when you were alive, and you were pretty hurtful to Mary and her father. Now that you've died, where are you? What has God said to you about your life?

MARY AS MOM: Well, I am dead and have moved onto the afterlife. I spent some time in purgatory being punished for my sins, but God has forgiven me and I am in heaven now.

THERAPIST: Okay, sounds like you have changed. Now that you have shed the imperfections of character and are in heaven, what would you like to say to Mary?

MARY AS MOM: (tearful) Mary I made many mistakes in my life. Now I can see how hurtful and selfish I was with you and your father. I was really just scared and in a lot of my own pain that I didn't know how to deal with. I hope you can forgive me for not being the best mother and for how I hurt you in my life.

THERAPIST: Reverse Roles. What do you want to say to Mom?

MARY: Mom, you were so angry and abusive to me. I just wanted a loving mom. (Begins to cry) Honestly, I felt relieved when you died because I thought I would be free from the trauma and negativity, but I wasn't. I've been so angry at you and I'm ready to let that go so I can move on and be free (continues to cry). This is the first time I've really felt sad about your death. I wish we could have had a better relationship while you were alive. I still think about you regularly. There were times that you were loving and fun to be around and I cherish those memories. Although you were hurtful, there were also important things you taught me about life which have been helpful. I was so focused on the negative experiences with you that I forgot about the other positive parts of you. I think I can see all of you now.

THERAPIST: Good Mary. As we move towards closure, is there a final statement to say to mom?

MARY: Mom, thank you for the positive things you've taught me. I am going to let go of the negative parts of our relationships so I can move on and be free going forward.

After this final statement, Mary de-roles the scene and the session moves into sharing and processing the experience. Mary shares that she feels exhausted but also much lighter and accomplished. She reports that she was surprised at being able to remember positive memories with mom after expressing her anger and equally surprised at being able to access her sadness at mom's death. She shares about her newfound commitment to taking care of herself and her mental illness after connecting it to the larger generational history and her father. She says that the negative memories of her family dysfunction are still present but that they do not have the same emotional charge that they used to have for her. Mary describes her plan to stop hiding her struggles with mental illness from her friends that she had been avoiding and that she plans to trust that they will understand. Finally, she describes her new insight of how her depression and anxiety may have impacted others in her life and that she will use this as increased motivation to take care of herself.

In the case at hand, it is also important to highlight how cultural factors may have impacted the process. The closure with Mom was accessed by conceptualizing a scene based on Mary's spiritual/religious beliefs. When directing a psychodrama, it is essential to enter the reality of the protagonist rather than to instruct the protagonist to enact a scene that is incongruent with their religious or cultural belief system. Similarly, some cultural belief systems might inhibit an individual from psychodramatically expressing anger toward a parent or saying anything that might be seen as disrespectful. There are other creative ways of navigating this such as splitting Mom into two parts—a "good mom" and "bad mom" or seeing if the mother role might offer permission to the protagonist about expressing anger. When directing a protagonist, it is important to consider interventions or suggested actions/scenes that reflect the cultural realities for the protagonist. The trajectory of Mary's psychodrama would look very different depending on her religious/spiritual beliefs as well as her cultural values around family, anger, and parental role relationships.

17.4 Conclusion

The sequence of one-to-one psychodrama session with Mary described above shed light on the unique strengths of using psychodrama in individual settings. Although there were no role players, the surplus reality of the psychodrama still offered potentiality for corrective emotional experiences and the renegotiation of both trauma and loss (Giacomucci, 2018, 2020; Giacomucci & Marquit, 2020; Giacomucci & Stone, 2019). The continuity of work with Mary would have been much more difficult to achieve in a group setting as the therapist would have also been responsible for the needs of the rest of the group. Though the one-to-one psychodrama process is absent of auxiliary role players, there is still value in engaging in the dramatization. In some cases, the client may be too anxious or concerned with the judgment of others to participate in this level of work within a group setting. Because it was a one-to-one setting, the therapist can meet the client where they are at in each session and tailor the psychodrama to their here-and-now warm-up. The movement from sociometric assessment to strengths-based work, intrapsychic work, and finally interpersonal work portrays a useful route of pacing with a client to create both inner and interpersonal change using Moreno's methods in a safe way. This process moved from the peripheral to the center and back to the peripheral—from the social to the internal and back to the social. The client was treated as a person within their social environment.

Sociometry and psychodrama interventions can be seamlessly integrated into a social worker's clinical repertoire, especially in the one-to-one context. These depictions of psychodramatic work in individual contexts suggest a natural fit for clinical social work practice with individuals encompassing elements of casework, assessment, and intervention. The same one-to-one interventions can be employed in individual teletherapy sessions with clients (see Sect. 13.2). Sociometric and psychodramatic interventions allow the social worker to meet the client where they are while honoring their subjective experience. With these tools, the client is conceptualized within their social atom while exploring both psychodynamics and sociodynamics (Giacomucci, 2019). The importance of relationships is central to both the process and the content of sociometry and psychodrama in one-to-one contexts. The relationship between client and therapist is particularly essential in the one-to-one psychodrama situation.

References

Aguiar, M. (2019). Spontaneous theater and one-to-one psychodrama. In Z. Figusch (Ed.), *From one-to-one psychodrama to large group socio-psychodrama* (2nd ed., pp. 124–146). Morrisville, UK: lulu.com.

Antonio, R. (2019). Dramatic action and inter-subjectivity: One-to-one psychodrama with a depressed patient. In Z. Figusch (Ed.), *From one-to-one psychodrama to large group socio-psychodrama* (2nd ed., pp. 43–70). Morrisville, UK: lulu.com.

Brito, V. C. A. (2019). One-to-one psychodrama: Reflections on the theory and practice of psychodrama with an individual patient. In Z. Figusch (Ed.). *From One-to-One Psychodrama to Large Group Socio-psychodrama* (2nd ed.) (pp. 15–28). United Kingdom: lulu.com.

Bustos, D.M. (2019). One-to-one psychodrama psychotherapy. In Z. Figusch (Ed.), *From one-to-one psychodrama to large group socio-psychodrama* (2nd ed., pp. 29–42). Morrisville, UK: lulu.com.

Bustos, D. M. (1979). *Psicoterapia psicodramática (Psychodrama psychotherapy)*. São Paulo: Brasiliense.

Chesner, A. (2019a). Framing creativity. In A. Chesner (Ed.), *One-to-one psychodrama psychotherapy: applications and technique* (pp. 7–18). New York, USA: Routledge.

Chesner, A. (2019b). Working with role. In A. Chesner (Ed.), *one-to-one psychodrama psychotherapy: applications and technique* (pp. 51–67). New York, USA: Routledge.

Cukier, R. (2008). *Bipersonal Psychodrama: Its techniques, therapists, and clients.* São Paulo, Brazil: Author.

Figusch, Z. (2019). *From one-to-one psychodrama to large group socio-psychodrama: More writings from the arena of Brazilian psychodrama.* United Kingdom: lulu.com

Fonseca, J. (2019). Relationship psychotherapy: A minimalist psychodrama. In Z. Figusch (Ed.), *From one-to-one psychodrama to large group socio-psychodrama* (2nd ed., pp. 87–111). Morrisville, UK: lulu.com.

Giacomucci, S. (2018). The trauma survivor's inner role atom: A clinical map for post-traumatic growth. *Journal of Psychodrama, Sociometry, and Group Psychotherapy., 66*(1), 115–129.

Giacomucci, S. (2019). *Social group work in action: A sociometry, psychodrama, and experiential trauma therapy curriculum* (Doctorate in Social Work (DSW) Dissertations) (p. 124). https://repository.upenn.edu/cgi/viewcontent.cgi?article=1128&context=edissertations_sp2.

Giacomucci, S. (2020). Addiction, traumatic loss, and guilt: A case study resolving grief through psychodrama and sociometric connections. *The Arts in Psychotherapy, 67,* 101627. https://doi.org/10.1016/j.aip.2019.101627.

Giacomucci, S., Gera, S., Briggs, D., & Bass, K. (2018). Experiential addiction treatment: Creating positive connection through sociometry and therapeutic spiral model safety structures. *Journal of Addiction and Addictive Disorders, 5,* 17. https://doi.org/10.24966/AAD-7276/100017.

Giacomucci, S., & Marquit, J. (2020). The effectiveness of trauma-focused psychodrama in the treatment of PTSD in inpatient substance abuse treatment. *Frontiers in Psychology, 11*, 896. 10.3389%2Ffpsyg.2020.00896.

Giacomucci, S., & Stone, A. M. (2019). Being in two places at once: Renegotiating traumatic experience through the surplus reality of psychodrama. *Social Work with Groups., 42*(3), 184–196. https://doi.org/10.1080/01609513.2018.1533913.

Hirschfeld, B., & McVea, C. (1998). A Cast of Thousands' working with the five instruments of psychodrama in the therapeutic relationship. *Australian and Aotearoa New Zealand Psychodrama Association Journal, 7,* 51.

Kim, L. M. V. (2019). Tele and transference in psychodrama psychotherapy. In Z. Figusch (Ed.), *From one-to-one psychodrama to large group socio-psychodrama* (2nd ed., pp. 82–95). Morrisville, UK: lulu.com.

Knittel, M. G. (2009). *Counseling and drama: Psychodrama a deux.* Tuscan, AZ: Author.

Moreno, J. L. (1947). *Open letter to group psychotherapists.* Psychodrama monographs, No. 23. Beacon, NY: Beacon House.

Moreno, J. L., Moreno, Z. T. (1959) *Psychodrama second volume, foundations of psychotherapy.* Beacon, NY: Beacon House.

Moreno, J. L. (1972) *Psychodrama* (Vol. 1, 4th ed.). New York: Beacon House.

von Ameln, F., & Becker-Ebel, J. (2020). *Fundamentals of psychodrama.* Singapore: Springer.

Yalom, I. D., & Leszcz, M. (2005). *The theory and practice of group psychotherapy* (5th ed.). New York, NY: Basic Books.

Part VI
Sociometry and Psychodrama in Community, Organizational, and Educational Work

Community practice in social work has been defined as the use of "practice skills to alter the behavioral patterns of community groups, organizations, and institutions or people's relationships and interactions with the community structures" (Hardcastle, Powers, & Wenocur, 2011, p. 1). The social work profession's inclusion of community work and its core value of social justice arguably are what most differentiate social work from the other mental health fields. In the past few decades, the decline of group work concentrations in social work education have led to increased focus on one-to-one clinical social work and community practice. Nevertheless, social work practice includes the integration of work with individuals, groups, and communities. Similarly, the implementation of Moreno's methods around the world has been executed with attention to work with individuals, groups, and communities.

The use of Moreno's methods in community work can be traced back to the beginning of psychodrama's history. Prior to applications in psychotherapy, Moreno's methods and his work were primarily with communities. The field of sociometry emerged from Moreno's work with at a community of refugees—sociometry began as community work. Similarly, the event Moreno recognizes as the birth of psychodrama and sociodrama was also clearly community work. In Austria, he worked with groups of children in the parks of Vienna, with sex workers in Vienna, with immigrants and refugees in the city and in Mittendorf refugee camp, and with public audiences through his Theater of Spontaneity. Even after his migration to New York, his initial work was also all community based—with prison communities, a residential community in Hudson at the New York Training School for Girls, and with public audiences at Carnegie Hall through his Impromptu Theater. Even Moreno's clinical roles could be framed through the lens of community work as he was working with a psychiatric inpatient community and creating a professional communities oriented around sociometry, psychodrama, and group psychotherapy.

Moreno's vision of Sociatry, or healing for society, portrays his larger emphasis on community work (Moreno, 2019). Considering the nature of his first *group psychotherapy* projects in the 1930s, one might argue that Moreno's original conceptualization of group psychotherapy was really a community approach. These initial group therapy initiatives were focused on large groups or communities, primarily with underserved and oppressed populations (Giacomucci, 2019). Although he is most recognized as a psychodramatist and as a pioneer in group therapy, historical analysis suggests he initially was engaged in community work. A simple review of the titles and contents of his book publications reveal that he wrote comprehensively about society and communities. For example, these books are heavily focused on societal and community issues:

Moreno, J. L. (1934). *Who Shall Survive? A new approach to the problems of human interrelations.* Washington, DC: Nervous and Mental Disease Publishing Co.

Moreno, J. L. (1951). *Sociometry, experimental method and the science of society: An Approach to a New Political Orientation.* Beacon, NY: Beacon House

Moreno, J. L. (1956). *Sociometry and the Science of Man.* Beacon, NY: Beacon House.

In addition to these publications, he also released multiple monographs and journal articles focused entirely on theories of society, community, culture, and the future of mankind. This section will highlight Moreno's focus on communities and society while depicting the usefulness of sociometry and sociodrama in community and organizational settings.

References

Giacomucci, S. (2019). *Social group work in action: A sociometry, psychodrama, and experiential trauma therapy curriculum.* Doctorate in Social Work (DSW) Dissertations. 124. https://reposi tory.upenn.edu/cgi/viewcontent.cgi?article=1128&context=edissertations_sp2.

Hardcastle, D. A., Powers, P. R., & Wencour, S. (2011). *Community practice: theories and skills for social workers* (3rd ed.). New York: Oxford University Press.

Moreno, J. L. (2019). In E. Schreiber, S. Kelley, & S. Giacomucci (Eds.). *The autobiography of a genius.* London, UK: North West Psychodrama Association.

Chapter 18
Sociometric Social Work with Communities

Abstract This chapter uncovers Moreno's often overlooked contributions to community practice through his sociometric approaches. His early work with communities is presented including in refugee camps, prisons, a reform school, and his psychiatric hospital. Brief introductions to social work with communities, therapeutic communities, and the Sanctuary Model are included. Multiple action-based sociometry processes are described with their utility for use in diverse community settings and example prompts. Sociometry processes depicted include spectrograms, locograms, floor checks, step-in sociometry, hands-on-shoulder sociograms, and the circle of strength safety structure.

Keywords Social work community practice · Therapeutic communities · The sanctuary model · Experiential sociometry · Experiential community work · Community organizing

Social work community practice can be enhanced thought the application of sociometric tools, especially in the process of community assessment, engagement, intervention, and evaluation. Moreno's methods offer opportunities for experiential empowerment and mutual aid in communities or organizations, just as in group work. Traditionally, social workers engage in community assessments through written surveys, data analysis, verbal discussions, case studies, and community observations. Experiential sociometry processes offer another avenue for community assessment using more embodied, here-and-now, and participatory approach. Sociometry provides social workers with instruments for group-as-a-whole engagement within community or organizational meetings. These devices offer additional methods for social workers to avoid the pitfalls of doing individual work in a community setting. Some of the same sociometry tools previously outlined in Chap. 11 on group work will be presented with their utility in community work .

© The Author(s) 2021
S. Giacomucci, *Social Work, Sociometry, and Psychodrama*, Psychodrama in Counselling, Coaching and Education 1,
https://doi.org/10.1007/978-981-33-6342-7_18

18.1   Moreno's Historical Use of Sociometry with Communities

Sociometry emerged from Moreno's work as a medical doctor in Mittendorf refugee camp during World War I in Austria (see Fig. 18.1). Moreno describes the camp as more of a German "prison camp" consisting of over ten thousand Italian women, children, and elders who were interned in this newly formed community (Moreno, 2019). Within the camp, social structures organically developed and the sociodynamic effect impacted the distribution of food, clothes, lodgings, and other supplies. In his autobiography, Moreno describes the conditions of the camp as giving "rise to the most tremendous corruption I have ever witnessed" (2019, p. 192). He writes that his study of the camp's community life highlighted different psychological currents (ethnicity, nationality, politics, class, sex, identity, etc.) which he understood as the underlying factors of the major problems in the community. From this new conceptualization of psychosocial elements in the community, Moreno wrote the following letter to the Austro-Hungarian Minister of the Interior in 1916 (later included in *Who Shall Survive?* publication):

> The positive and negative feelings that emerge from every house, between houses, from every factory, and every national and political group in the community can be explored by means of sociometric analysis. A new order, by means of sociometric methods, is herewith recommended. (Translated from German by Moreno from the frontpiece of *Who Shall Survive? 2nd Edition*) (Moreno, 2019, p. 193).

This is Moreno's first use of the term "sociometry." Using his professional connections within the refugee camp, he describes his attempts to put his sociometric ideas into action, suggesting the movement of families based on their mutual connections, preferences, and shared identities. He noticed that the camp administration paid no attention to the placement of families within the camp and that when families were grouped in the camp with other families that held shared values, preferences, and identities, the preexisting social problems were replaced with mutual aid within the community (Moreno, 2019). He used the same approach to propose a reorganization of factory workers within the camp. The first sociograms were created in Mittendorf which seems to have had a lasting impact on Moreno's sociometric work (Moreno, 2019).

After his immigration to the USA, Moreno was appointed Director of Social Research of the New York State Department of Welfare where he worked in Sing Sing Prison and the New York State Training School for Girls in Hudson. Moreno's sociometric work with these two communities produced two of his most important early contributions to the field—*The First Book on Group Psychotherapy* (Moreno & Whitin, 1932) and *Who Shall Survive?* (1934). His work from Sing Sing Prison approached issues in the prison community with the hopes of creating a therapeutic social environment through psychosocial assessment and reorganization of inmates. Moreno describes it below:

> It was our goal to turn the prison into a therapeutic society where the men were organized into groups on the basis of the needs and strengths of each of the men in the group. I knew,

Fig. 18.1 Jacob Moreno
around 1920 in Austria.
Reprinted with permission
from Figusch (2014)

from previous experience, that the mere assignment of people to groups in which each one
could function positively would go a long way towards improving their mental health and
have positive consequences for their social interactions. (Moreno, 2019, p. 263).

He interviewed inmates and prison staff and strategically assigned them to units,
groups, or roles based on shared aspects of identity or preference. Through psychosocial analysis and his assessments of the attractions and repulsions between each
inmate, he appointed inmates with positive attitudes and positive sociometric wealth
as leaders of groups of inmates. When describing one such inmate appointed to
a leadership role he writes, "There are in every prison a considerable number of
inmates like M.1 [man 1] who can be transformed into active therapeutic agents,
forces which are otherwise not made use of" (Moreno, 1957, p. 60).

Previously, prisons had only been using *individual* and *psychological* assessment
of inmates. Moreno's focus was on *community* assessment of both *psychological*
and *social* factors. "Individual classification alone is insufficient. Man lives within
groups and is in his actions to a great extent regulated by them" (Moreno, 1957,
p. 21). In his report, Moreno writes of the reenactment of power dynamics through

the common approach to individual psychiatry with inmates. He argues instead that through group psychotherapy and his sociometrically constructed therapeutic community , "the groups function for themselves and the therapeutic process streams through their mutual inter-relationships. Every man has equal rank" (1957, p. 61). The results of Moreno's sociometric work at Sing Sing Prison were presented at the 1931 and 1932 American Psychiatric Association meetings in Toronto and Philadelphia marking the first times the terms *group psychotherapy* or *group therapy* were used. At the end of the APA roundtable discussion, Moreno notes that the methods necessary for qualitative and quantitative analysis of groups, a scientific foundation for a group psychotherapy, were actively being developed and tested in his work at the New York State Training School for Girls at Hudson. He writes of the importance of "a sociometrized community" and suggests that "genuine foundations of group psychotherapy cannot be established otherwise" (1953, p. lxiv).

The sociometric community work implanted at the Hudson school for girls became the foundation for one of Moreno's most important books—*Who Shall Survive?* . In this book, Moreno describes his threefold position for creating a therapeutic community—(1) spontaneity–creativity propel human progress; (2) love, mutual sharing, and faith in each other are essential principles in groups; and (3) a superdynamic community or society based on these principles can be actualized through new techniques (1953). During his time at Hudson, Moreno studied various informal and formal groupings and psychosocial networks within the residential community of 500 girls. He refined his sociometric tests, sociograms , spontaneity tests, role diagrams, social atoms , role training , sociodrama , psychodrama, and his theories for a therapeutic community and group psychotherapy. Much of his sociometry oriented around the restructuring of the 16 cottages that the 500 + girls was housed in. Moreno successfully confronted the task of reducing the number of runaway girls from the school through sociometric analysis and reconstruction of social groups within the school (Moreno, 1953). He conducted sociometric test collecting and visually depicting the data of which cottages, cottage leaders, and cottage-mates each girl preferred to live with. In some reprints of *Who Shall Survive?*, this community sociogram was included in a foldout diagram taking up nearly 10 pages (Moreno, 2014). Moreno and his colleagues implemented a new intake process for new members of the community that involved sociometric and role testing between new members and staff who were cottage leaders with openings for new members (Nolte, 2014). In this way, the staff were included within the sociometric analysis as part of the community.

Moreno's early work on social networks emerged from his sociometric discoveries at the Hudson school. In exploring the invisible social connections between runaway girls in the community, he began to utilize his sociograms to depict unseen psychosocial networks within the larger community overlapping multiple cottages. He tested his social network theories by spreading rumors in the girls' community and tracking how long it took to reach certain individuals or cottages within the larger community (1953). He writes that "there are certain structural processes observable in groups studied which are best explained if it is assumed that networks exist" (1953, p. 640). His work at Hudson attracted the attention of the media and even President Roosevelt—Moreno emerged as one of the most famous social scientists in the 1930s for his ideas on community and social networks (Moreno, 2014). Though he worked sociometrically with other communities including schools, classrooms, farm workers, factories, organizations, businesses, the military , and other small groups, his work at Hudson, Sing Sing, and Mittendorf seems to be most foundational in his approach.

18.2 Community Social Work Contexts

Moreno's approach to community work finds seamless congruence with Hardcastle, Powers, and Wencour (2011) description of social work—"social work practice is about using the community and using naturally occurring and socially constructed networks within the social environment to provide social support" (p. 3). Moreno's early work with immigrants, refugees, sex workers, inmates, and the underlying philosophy of his methods of sociometry, psychodrama, and group psychotherapy pivots on the foundational concept of using the resources within the group or community to provide support. He described each community or group member as a therapeutic agent and worked to restructure the group or community process to cultivate mutual aid between members.

Macrosocial work practice has evolved to include three primary domains—the community, organizational management, and policy (Austin, Anthony, Knee, & Mathias, 2016). It has been proposed that the primary goal of community social workers is to utilize social networks within communities to connect community members to organizational or community resources (Rodriguez & Ferreira, 2018). An argument could be made that all community work is based on the engagement, assessment, intervention, and evaluation of social networks within the community. Social workers intervene on the individual level by connecting individuals or families to social networks or agencies within the community who can meet their needs or enhance their living conditions. De Robertis (2003) notes that one of the most essential tasks of community social workers is to (re)establish connections of people to the community or society, and to (re)establish connections of the community to society. Community organizing has been described as a process by which a community discerns its goals or needs, prioritizes them, commits to working toward them, accesses related internal or external resources, takes action, and in doing so cultivates collaboration and mutuality within a community (Ross & Lappin, 1967).

Social workers utilize individual (micro), group (mezzo), and community (macro) interventions in clinical practice. It is worth noting that every individual and group intervention take place within the context of community (often multiple overlapping communities). *Person-in-environment* means that the client must be conceptualized within their social and community contexts. Even casework interventions and referrals have an element of community practice as a referral is essentially the facilitated connection between a client and a community resource (Hardcastle et al., 2011).

Many agencies actually contain multiple (formal or informally recognized) communities or social networks within the organizational structure (a community of staff, a community of patients, a community of alumni, a community of volunteers, etc.).

A community is simply defined as a unified group of people, usually with a shared history, identity, goal, or interest. Communities are often categorized into five different types, based on either interest, location, action, practice, or circumstance. There are, of course, many different types of specific communities including neighborhoods, national communities, ethnic communities, religious communities, political communities, professional communities, educational communities, organizational communities, treatment communities, and recreational communities, among others. Social workers engage with all of these types of communities to bring about change. In some cases, the entire community is actively engaged at once, but in most cases the social worker is engaging with a subgroup of a community. For example, it may be logistically impossible the convene a group of the entire Pennsylvania medical community, but a subgroup of the community may respond to a call to meet and information, decisions, and calls to action can be distributed back to the entire community.

While clinical and group work are connected to community work , social work with communities is a uniquely different arena of practice (Austin et al., 2016). The goals of community work, though sometimes similar, differ in nature from the goals of clinical or group work. Though the goals in each social work arena may overlap, the means (interventions, practice skills, tools, etc.) used to work toward these goals have much more differentiation between clinical social work, social group work , and social community work. Perhaps the most obvious difference between these three levels of social work practice is the size of the client. In individual work, the client is an individual; in group work, the client is a group; in community work, the client is the community or organization. Another major factor distinguishing community work from group work and clinical work is that it is not typically framed as therapy. Though it is not psychotherapy or treatment, community work is often therapeutic and healing. The specific use of community as therapy, such as the therapeutic community , will be discussed shortly. Regardless of the community context, it can be helpful to revisit Yalom's therapeutic factors of group psychotherapy in the framework of community.

Yalom and Leszcz (2005) propose these eleven factors for a therapeutic group experience—instillation of hope , universality , imparting information, altruism , the corrective recapitulation of the primary family group, development of socializing techniques, imitative behavior, interpersonal learning, group cohesiveness , catharsis , and existential factors. When the community-as-a-whole is approached as its own group, each of these eleven elements can be considered. In a similar fashion, these therapeutic factors also become relevant to the development of a therapeutic society . The synthesis of these curative factors provides a sense of connection, purpose, meaning, healing of past wounds, and future orientation for groups, communities, and society.

18.2.1 Therapeutic Communities

The concept of therapeutic communities (TCs) has emerged in various points in time, mostly connected to religious/spiritual sects, educational groups, or mental health advocates (De Leon, 2000). The most common types of contemporary therapeutic communities are specifically for psychiatric patients or folks recovering from addiction . Therapeutic communities for psychiatric patients were organized by psychiatrists while the TCs for addiction developed in opposition to psychiatry and medicine (Ayyagari, 2014). Main (1946) and Jones (1953) are generally considered as the founders and pioneers of the modern therapeutic community , originating from their work in the UK in the mid-twentieth century. In the therapeutic community perspective, treatment is not located in the provision of therapy by staff, but instead, in the therapeutic effects of involvement in healthy community life (Jones, 1953). The community itself is seen as the doctor (Rapoport, 2013). Main, in his 1946 manuscript first utilizing the term *therapeutic community* , states that, "the fact must be faced that radical individual psychotherapy is not a practicable proposition for the huge numbers of patients confronting the psychiatric world today" (p.67). The therapeutic communities were major advocates of group therapy due to its congruence with the TC philosophy (Bloom, 2013).Therapeutic communities were based on the following assumptions: Patients should be co-responsible for their own treatment; patients have the ability to help each other; the community should be led democratically; treatment should be voluntary (as often as possible); physical restraint should be avoided whenever possible; psychological therapies were preferred to physical treatments (Almond, 1974; Bloom, 2013; Cumming & Cumming, 1962; Wilmer, 1981). Maxwell Jones' therapeutic community in England included the use of theater and drama by 1943, later integrating psychodrama when Jones became aware of Moreno's work around 1949 (Bloom, 2013; Casson, 2000; Jones, 1949, 1953).

Moreno's Beacon Hill Sanitarium , later renamed Moreno Sanitarium , was founded in 1936 in Beacon, New York, and resembled the structure of a therapeutic community in terms of the democratic and equal nature of role relationships between participants (Moreno, 2014). Robert Landy describes it to have "represented Moreno's notion of an integrated community, an early exemplar of a therapeutic milieu, where all staff and patients, family and visitors were encouraged to engage with one another openly and equitably" (2008, p. 53). Another connection between Moreno and the emergence of the therapeutic community model in psychiatry comes from Bierer (1960), who was a close friend of Moreno and pioneer of the TC movement (Moreno, 2014). Like other fields, scholars of the therapeutic community movement rarely make mention of Moreno's work, even though it predated Main and Jones by a decade or two. It is likely that Moreno's resistance to operating within mainstream psychiatry also contributed to the absence of reference to his ideas.

The addiction -focused therapeutic community movement emerged in 1958 with the founding of *Synanon* by Charles Dederich in Santa Monica, California. One of the primary supporters of Synanon and the therapeutic community model, who served as their director of research, was Lewis Yablonsky —a prominent psychodrama-tist, sociology   professor, and close colleague of Jacob Moreno   (Yablonsky, 1962,1965,1976,2002). Yablonsky notes that Dederich was an admirer of Moreno's work and that psychodrama techniques become an embedded part of nearly every Synanon group (Moreno, 2014). Synanon experienced early success and integrated philosophies and approaches from Alcoholics Anonymous , the Human Potential Movement , encounter groups and psychodrama (Janzen, 2000; Yablonsky, 1989, 2002). In 1963, *Daytop Village* was founded in New York, its leaders motivated by Synanon's model. Daytop and Synanon were the most influential and well-known therapeutic communities in the addiction industry. The addiction-focused thera-peutic community structure draws inspiration from Alcoholics Anonymous in that they elevate ex-addicts to the status of co-therapists or peer supports with a large emphasis on mutual aid (Yablonsky, 1989). While the TCs created by the social psychiatrists used pharmaceutical interventions and maintained equal status between all community members, the addiction TCs rejected pharmaceutical treatments and developed hierarchies within the community structure. Synanon and Daytop Village communities were recreated around the world and helped tens of thousands of former criminals or addicts. Yablonsky writes that the Synanon project "facilitates the real-ization of a true total therapeutic community , a live demonstration of Moreno's concept of the total therapeutic community , where everyone is a therapist (and at the same time a patient) to everyone else" (1976, pp. 151–152). In its later years, Synanon and its members became associated with intense catharsis , violence, abuse, coer-cion, cults, and crime—including putting a rattlesnake into the mailbox of a lawyer (Janzen, 2000).

Therapeutic communities became widely implemented and have demonstrated successful outcomes (De Leon, 2010; Vanderplasschen et al., 2013). At the same time, many TCs, particularly in the addiction field, developed poor reputations for their use of confrontation, humiliation, shaming members, and the intense emotional nature of community meetings. The philosophy of "tough love" and "break them down to build them back up" became guiding forces as TCs began implementing what they called "attack therapy" and excessive confrontation (Ayyagari, 2014; Polcin, 2003; White & Miller, 2007; Yablonsky, 1976). Lieberman, Yalom, and Miles (1973) major research study on encounter groups , which included 17 encounter groups with different leadership styles and approaches, found the Synanon groups to have the biggest dropout rates (38%). Many became concerned with the ways in which these TCs were harming and re-traumatizing community members more than helping them (Ayyagari, 2014; White & Miller, 2007). Cadiz and colleagues (2011) write that "many of the basic philosophies of a traditional therapeutic community conflict with philosophies about how to treat trauma and what a survivor needs to recover" (p. 133). The high rates of trauma underlying addictive disorders make some practices of the therapeutic community especially inappropriate or even unethical (Ayyagari, 2014; IDHS, 2005). As the field of trauma therapy quickly evolved in the past few decades, *The Sanctuary Model* for trauma-informed therapeutic communities and systems developed.

18.2.2   The Sanctuary Model as Trauma-Informed Therapeutic Community

The Sanctuary Model emerged from Sandra Bloom and colleagues' work between 1985 and 1991 in a suburban Philadelphia inpatient psychiatric hospital (Bloom, 2013). The Sanctuary Model is essentially a trauma-informed and democratic therapeutic community approach developed with attention to the importance of attachment, neurobiology of trauma, and community life (Bloom, 1997, 2008). After years of refinement and implementation around the world, it has become well respected as a trauma-informed philosophy for treatment centers, organizations, systems, cities, and society (Bloom, 2012, 2013). The sanctuary approach is centered around seven commitments: (1) nonviolence; (2) emotional intelligence; (3) social learning; (4) open communication; (5) democracy ; (6) social responsibility; and (7) growth and change (Bloom & Farragher, 2013). Each of these seven commitments is regarded as essential and interconnected elements of a system's operating framework which guide the formal and informal relationships between staff, patients, and administration.

The Sanctuary Model offers "a compass for recovery" called "S.E.L.F." which is an acronym for Safety, Emotions, Loss, and Future (Bloom, 2013). These four simple concepts represent major areas in one's life that can be disrupted by trauma and adversity, as well as the four domains in which sanctuary programs base their treatment plans, organizational changes, community dialogues, and decision-making process (Bloom & Farragher, 2013). The S.E.L.F. compass is operationalized through the regular use of safety plans, treatment planning, psychoeducational groups, structured team meetings, and community meetings (Bloom, 2008). Bloom writes that, "ultimately in the Sanctuary Model, the purpose of our shared assumptions, goals, practice, and vision is to create what Maxwell Jones, a half-century ago, described as a 'living-learning environment' within which healing, growth, and creative expression can occur" (Jones, 1968; as cited by Bloom, 2008, p. 16). In addition to her inspiration from Jones' early therapeutic community philosophy, it is interesting to note Bloom's positive regard for psychodrama evidenced in regular references to how helpful it had been in her psychiatric treatment programs (Bloom, 2000, 2013; Bloom & Farragher, 2013)—she even wrote the foreword for a textbook focused on the clinical uses of drama in therapy with children (Weber & Haen, 2005). Similar to Moreno, Bloom's writing transcended clinical contexts and also considered the objective of a healthy society.

18.3   Toward a Sane, Therapeutic, and Democratic Society

Bloom (2013) comments on how the problems, issues, and dialogues within society often reflect the same problems and issues within the therapeutic community or treatment community—"after all, the problems that confront us as individuals, as small groups, and as an entire society reflect the same basic human themes" (p. 221).

Moreno writes of a similar idea and intervention structure called *the social micro-scope* , outlined in Sect. 15.2 (Moreno, 1953). Trauma, loss, anger, suffering, abusive authority, neglect, abandonment, avoidance, addictions, and injustice—these issues addressed in psychotherapy or an inpatient psychiatric community are the same pressing issues within society (Bloom, 2013). Bloom and Norton write:

> the goal of the TC is not to maintain an unhappy status quo but to create the 'heat' that generates change. This change is generated largely through the democratically informed interactions between staff and clients and clients with each other. And today, the institution-ally based practice of this 'deep democracy ' is itself a subversive notion in that it seeks to subvert the militaristic, hierarchical, and frequently punitive retributive control structures that typically characterize most of our social systems and replace them with an environment offering different styles of relating that seek to avoid the repeating of past traumas. (2004, pp. 230–231).

This passage highlights the parallel process between change within the therapeutic community and within a democratic society. Moreno's philosophies of sociatry , group psychotherapy, and community work —elevating every participant to equal status with therapeutic agency and power, demonstrate the essential quality of an active democratic process. Sociometry has even been described as a science by, for, and of the people (Moreno, 2014).

Who Shall Survive? (1934) was published in between world wars and addressed the problems of society and the question of its survival (Moreno, 2012). In it, Jacob Moreno writes that "a truly therapeutic procedure cannot have less an objective than the whole of mankind" (Moreno, 1953, p. 119) and that "sociometry can well be considered the cornerstone of a still underdeveloped science of democracy " (Moreno, 1953, p. 113). Moreno's description of an action-based and democratic sociometry is congruent with Bloom's statement that "democracy is better understood as a verb than a noun. It is a creative process that must be created and recreated constantly if it is to survive" (2013, p. 260). Moreno and Bloom seem to echo John Dewey 's ideas of democracy, in that he describes it as a mode of connected living and a commitment to inclusion and active participation (Dewey, 1916; Kristoffersen, 2018). For Moreno, this concept can be traced throughout the evolution of his writings back to his early mysticism and his 1920 *Words of the Father* publication. He writes of his inspiration for the *Words of the Father* coming from the realization that "we are all bound to one another by responsibility for all things. There is no limited, partial responsible. And our responsibility makes us, automatically co-creators of the world" (Moreno, 2019, p. 253). Later, in his monograph titled *The Future of Man's World* (1945), he conveys this same philosophy while urging society to consider a system where all humans, without exception, can engage spontaneously as initiators and co-creators. He attempted to put this into action through the founding of *The Sociometric Institute* in 1942 with the intention of training sociometrists to help bring about a new democracy. Its introductory statement indicated:

> a truly living democracy cannot be attained unless it is based upon the science of the actually operating interpersonal and intergroup relations which exist and function below the surface... The true, full meaning of sociometry will be unrealized unless it considers a worldwide scope. Its task cannot be accomplished in an isolated laboratory, remote from

the living web of the social present... The total fabric of human relations represented by the nation at large must be faced as one single objective. (Moreno, 2019, p. 317).

While writing his autobiography at the end of his life, he comments on his inability to accomplish this therapeutic society in his lifetime. Forty years later, Bloom continues the dialogue, also indicating that we have a long way to go before a truly democratic and sane society is realized (2013).

Moreno's overarching vision of sociatry is the framework within which all of his work was contained (Giacomucci, 2019). This vision of healing society was best operationalized through Moreno's development of sociometry, sociodrama , public psychodrama sessions, his work in various communities, and his founding of multiple organizations. Group psychotherapy extended beyond the limited reach of individual psychiatry or psychotherapy, while community work allows one to effect change on a significantly larger scale. Just as one individual can provide healing for another, so too can one group contribute to the healing of another group. The attainment of a truly democratic and therapeutic society may require the involvement of communities contributing to the healing of other communities and an enhancement of the cohesive social fabric or organic unity that binds us together as a human species. A realization of the organic unity of humankind has yet to be actualized and operationalized at the societal level. Perhaps the future generations of society, more closely connected through technology and social networking, will have the tools to actualize a sane and therapeutic society.

18.4 Experiential Sociometric Assessment of Communities

This section will orient on the use of experiential sociometry tools for large groups, communities, and organizations, including public community sessions, treatment communities, and professional communities. Other, non-experiential sociometry tools are also applicable for community work , especially sociograms and social networks , but are beyond the scope of this chapter. New technology has emerged that facilitates the efficient and easy depiction of sociograms and social networks, similar to Moreno's community work using the sociometric test to hand draw sociograms and social networks (Nolte, 2014). Many of the experiential group processes described in Chap. 11 can be utilized in community settings for sociometric assessment and intervention. Sociometry tools are uniquely adept for addressing issues of privilege, inclusion, and oppression in groups or communities (Nieto, 2010). Perhaps the most useful action-based sociometry tools for community work are spectrograms , locograms, floor checks, step-in sociometry , hands-on-shoulder sociograms , and circle of strengths .

Similar to the implementation of these experiential processes in group work (see Chap. 11), it is helpful to follow a basic three-stage clinical map when choosing criteria for sociometry prompts in community work as well. While community work is usually not psychotherapy, there are clinical tools that a community worker can integrate into their interventions to keep the process safe. Many community issues are related to collective trauma or loss, especially community activism and social justice events. Perhaps every social injustice is also collective trauma. The facilitation of a community event with attention to the three stages of a trauma-informed clinical map can help keep the community safe and prevent re-traumatization. As noted in previous chapters, three-stage clinical maps for trauma work are similar between multiple models (Chesner, 2020; Courtois & Ford, 2016; Giacomucci, 2018; Herman, 1997; Hudgins & Toscani, 2013; Shapiro, 2018). The first stage begins with establishing safety , strengths, and containment . The second stage orients on the trauma, adversity, or difficulties. And the final stage is focused on transformation, integration, growth, and future planning. These three stages can be used, along with the three phases of a psychodrama group process—warm-up, action, and sharing. Using these two three-stage models, a community worker can ensure safety while considering a community's warm-up to action and cooling down from it.

18.5   Spectrograms

The spectrogram (see Sect. 11.3 for more detail and a video link) offers a quick process for revealing important information about a community. Many community organizers already utilize this process, calling it the *thermometer, temperature check,* or *spectrum line*, but little has been published in about it by community organizers (Hunter & Lakey, 2004; Seeds for Change, 2019). A spectrogram assessment with a community can be thought of as similar to a questionnaire item using a Likert scale experientially (Giacomucci, 2020a). The community worker designates different ends of the spectrum within the space, often using the walls of the room to represent the two extremes of 0 and 10% or 0 and 100%. Participants are provided with a prompt and invited to physically place themselves on the spectrum based on their response. This process allows the facilitator to quickly assess the community based on their self-report on various topics. The experience of participating in the spectrogram allows community members to see where they fit in within the community based on different qualifiers and to connect with others who are similar to them in this way. Furthermore, it reveals to both the community and the facilitator which community members have self-assessed themselves to be the highest and lowest on the spectrum. Depending on the criteria, this provides important information about who might have experience to help others in the community or who may need help in order to more fully integrate into the community. Here are some examples of spectrogram prompts in various community settings:

Open Community Dialogue on Racism for Students on a University Campus

1.   How many resources do you have to help you confront racism ?
2.   How comfortable do you feel talking about racism ?
3.   How frequently do you experience racism on this campus?

4. How willing/able are you to volunteer your time to support anti-racism initiatives on campus?

Townhall Meeting for Local Residents Exploring Feelings About a Pipeline Building Plans

1. How aware are you of the plans to install a major gas pipeline through this neighborhood?
2. How knowledgeable are you in terms of the risks of this type of gas pipeline?
3. How much do you support the building of this pipeline?
4. How interested are you in participating in a protest of the pipeline next month?

Addiction Recovery House Community

1. How connected do you feel within the community?
2. How helpful has this community been for your continued recovery?
3. How satisfied are you with the quantity and quality of services offered at the recovery house?
4. How satisfied are you with the leadership of this recovery community?
5. How strongly do you feel about changing a specific aspect of this recovery program?

Membership Meeting of Professional Society of Social Workers at Annual Conference

1. How satisfying has this conference been for you thus far?
2. How long have you been a member of this professional community?
3. How pleased are you with your member benefits?
4. How interested are you in getting involved in the future with committees in this organization?

Psychiatric Hospital Staff Meeting to Discuss Concerns of Patient Violence/Aggression

1. How safe do you feel coming to work on a typical day?
2. How supported do you feel by your peers if there was a violent incident on the unit?
3. How happy are you with the current hospital policies around handling violent or aggressive patients?
4. How interested are you in receiving further training in dealing with violent or aggressive patients?
5. How interested are you in participating in a peer support group to process feelings related to past experiences of patient violence or aggression?

The use of spectrograms , as depicted in staff meeting example above, allows the organizational community to assess their needs or wants while initiating connections and proposing future plans to address concerns. This staff meeting could have been facilitated only through discussion, but it would have significantly limited the number of employees who could have participated in the discussion. It is likely that there would be multiple employees who would be unwilling to verbally share in front of the entire community, and thus their preferences would have gone unheard. The spectrogram engages the entire community, each individual at the same time, and reveals the collective feelings or preferences of a community. It offers co-workers a chance to see who feels similar to them on various prompts which facilitates more meaningful connection. At the same time, organization leaders can assess the favorability of various proposed solutions before implementing them—in the example above, the following potential solutions were considered and assessed for the community's interest in them: policy changes, trainings, and support groups.

Spectrograms with community members can be modified for communities that include members who might have physical limitations. An object could be placed on the spectrogram to represent a member who cannot physically move onto the spectrum. Or, participants could be instructed to indicate their place on a spectrum by raising their hands higher or lower—hand on your lap to represent 0 on the spectrum, hand as high as you can reach to represent a 10/10 on the spectrum (Simmons, 2017). Similarly, the spectrogram can be used during online meetings by asking participants to imagine the top and bottom boundary of their camera feed to be the high and low end of the spectrum and to physically position their hand within that spectrum based on their response to the prompt.

18.6   Locograms

The locogram process offers a quick evaluation of the community's preference or experience based on a given prompt. It offers opportunities for quick democratic voting processes when a community decision needs to be made. Designating different areas of the space to represent different choices or qualifiers, participants are asked to physically place themselves at the option that best represents their preference or experience. A locogram can be useful as a warm-up, voting process, evaluation, or movement for future planning.

Purpose: Prioritizing Issues in a Neighborhood

- Economic and financial issues
- Violence and crime
- Addiction and mental health services
- Sports and recreation opportunities
- Other

Purpose: Community Hospital Assessment of What Customers Believe as Most Important for the Hospital to Improve

- Aesthetics of the campus and building
- Quality of treatment
- Customer service from hospital staff
- Financial accessibility
- Other

Purpose: Community Organizing Event to Involve Members in Initiatives

- Fund-raising
- Participating in marches or demonstrations
- Organizing community recreational events
- Advocating to politicians or community leaders
- Other

Purpose: Professional Conference Workshop Selection

- Workshop 1
- Workshop 2
- Workshop 3
- Workshop 4
- Workshop 5
- Workshop 6
- Other.

*This structure is utilized at the annual American Society of Group Psychotherapy and Psychodrama Conference for a here-and-now sociometric selection of workshop attendance by participants rather than all workshop attendance being based on preregistration.

Purpose: Assessing Common Co-occurring Disorders in Addiction Therapeutic Community

- Anxiety
- Depression
- PTSD
- ADHD/ADD
- Bipolar disorder
- Other.

The example above of an addiction therapeutic community using a locogram to explore community members' shared experiences of co-occurring disorders provides a meaningful path for connection and normalization of mental health issues which are very prevalent for folks in addiction recovery. This process allows participants to identify with each other about their shared experiences with specific mental health issues beyond their addictions and to identify allies for future mutual aid when struggling with their co-occurring disorder. A locogram with these qualifiers would also provide community leaders with a community-as-a-whole assessment of which co-occurring disorder(s) their members most struggle with. This information could be used to develop future educational events, clinical service offerings, or basic resources to community members related to specific mental health issues.

One modified locogram that is used often in immigrant community organizing spaces or at international psychodrama conferences is a world map locogram that allows participants to connect with others who live or migrated from the same countries or continents (Seeds of Change, 2019).

Purpose: Facilitating Connections Between Community Members Based on Country of Origin (or Ancestors' Country of Origin)

- North America
- South America
- Europe
- Africa
- Asia
- Australia.

This world map locogram is implemented by the author and co-facilitator Maria Jose Sotomayor-Giacomucci in community workshops focused on exploring family immigration histories of participants and retracing one's family or ancestral immigration journeys. Once the world map is designated on the floor of the workshop space, multiple prompts can be offered, facilitating the movement of participants with each new prompt. Some examples include "where do you live currently?," "where have you lived in the past?," "where did you, your family, or your ancestors immigrate from?," "where is one place you love to travel to?," or "where would you like to travel to in the future?". With each prompt, participants can be invited to share in smaller groups with those who are standing near them on the world map. This process of using multiple prompts on a locogram is usually called a floor check , which is another sociometry tool.

18.7   Floor Checks

The floor check (see Sect. 11.5 for more detail and a video link) is a psychosocial intervention tool from the Relational Trauma Repair Model (RTR) by Tian Dayton, which is primarily used in clinical or educational settings but can also be adapted for use in communities or large groups. It seems that many community leaders intuitively use processes similar to the floor check that result in similar outcomes of breaking up the larger group into small groups based on shared experience or intention (Hunter & Lakey, 2004). The floor check is especially useful in community groups due to its ability to access mutual aid within the community and position community members as therapeutic or educational agents for each other. There is also an element of community assessment that the floor check puts into action as it reveals specific experiences of community members. When facilitating a floor check, the social worker prints paper indicating different options based on a specific theme or topic and places them throughout the space. Usually, they are simply placed on the floor, but they can also be taped to the walls so they are easier to read. Then, a prompt is offered, and each participant is asked to go stand at the option that best answers the prompt for themselves. With each prompt, participants are invited to share with those standing with them about why they put themselves there. When facilitating this process, depending on the goals, it can help to consider the size of the group when discerning how many options to offer. If there is a group of 100 people and we want to facilitate as much dialogue as possible, it might help to offer 10–20 floor check options to spread participants out into smaller groups. However, if the goal is to help community members see similarities and not feel alone, then it might make more sense to offer less options. With 100 people and 5 floor check options, the resulting small groups are likely to be much larger. Here are some examples of floor check topics, options, and prompts in different community settings:

High School Student Community Meeting—Exploring Social Issues in the School

- Options: Bullying; Discrimination; Academic Pressures; Alcohol/Drug Use; In-groups & Out-groups; Home Life; Sports, Clubs, & School Activities; Other
- Which do you think you handle best?
- Which do you think is most difficult for others in high school?
- Which has been most difficult for you to handle in high school?
- Which do you feel that you have gotten better at handling since you started school?

Group of Local Business Leaders—Identifying Strengths and Limitations

• Options: Financial Resources; Community or Customer Relationships; Staffing; Leadership; Community Partners; Other

1. Which do you feel your business is most secure in?
2. Which do you feel your company is most lacking in?
3. Which do you feel you could help another business with?
4. Which would you like support on developing in the future?

Outpatient Psychotherapy Clinic Staff Meeting—Professional Growth Strengths and Needs

- Options: Trauma Therapy; Substance Abuse; Ethics and Legal Concerns; Assessment and Evaluation; Group Therapy; Family Therapy; Casework and Referrals; Other

1. Which area do you feel most competent in?

2. Which area would you like more training in?
3. Which is an area you would like more focus on during supervision?
4. Which is an area you feel that you could present a workshop on for the team?

Professional Conference Community Meeting—Exploring Membership Wants/Needs

- Options: Professional Development; Networking; Journal and Newsletter Publications; Committees; Regional Chapters; Presenting at Events; Advertising and Promotions; Organizational Leadership; Other

1. Which membership benefit do you utilize most?
2. Which membership benefit do you wish to use more going forward?
3. Which membership benefit least interests you?
4. Which membership benefit might you be willing to volunteer to support?

The final example offered above for a conference event offers the leadership and membership of a professional society an opportunity to reflect on the benefits of membership. Using the prompts above, one would be able to assess which member benefits are most utilized by members and which least interest members. This would be important information for the organization to consider as it discerns which member benefits it might increase or decrease its organizational investment in. The inclusion of an option for "other" also would give members an avenue for offering new ideas for member benefits. And, the final prompt "which member benefit might you be willing to volunteer to support?" would provide an opportunity to efficiently get members connected with leaders of each initiative for future involvement. This same process could be used as a floor check for each organizational committee to evaluate the interest levels for each committee.

18.8   Step-In Sociometry

Another useful experiential sociometric process for community work is step-in sociometry (see Sect. 11.6 for more detail and a video link), which allows for the quick and efficient identifying of similarities between community members. This exercise is best conducted by having community members create a large standing circle. Participants can take turns making statements and moving into the center of the circle, while others who identify with their statement also step into the circle. This process can be useful for a facilitator as an assessment or evaluation tool, or as an intervention for helping the community increase its cohesion and connectedness (Giacomucci, 2017). The step-in process can easily be modified in large groups, instead using hand raising or standing up as a motion for indicating identification. Step-in sociometry is already used regularly in community organizing spaces (Hunter & Lakey, 2004), and many facilitators use a simple form of it when asking participants to raise their hand if they agree or identify with a point. Here are some examples of its application in community contexts using broad prompts (multiple statements would be made within each prompt by community members) that follow the three-stage clinical map:

Religious Community Meeting

1. Step in and name something that is important to you about your religion.
2. Step in and share something that you find difficult about your religious practice.
3. Step in and label a goal you have for yourself going forward about increasing your religious practice.

Prison Community Meeting

1. Step in and name something that helps you get by in prison.
2. Step in and share something that is difficult or frustrating for you about being in prison.
3. Step in and share a hope you have for yourself going forward in life.

Neighborhood Anti-violence Coalition Community Meeting

1. Step in and name something you love about this community.
2. Step in and share one way that violence has impacted you in the community.
3. Step in and share a vision you have for community change in the future.

International Social Work Conference

1. Step in and share one area of social work that you work within.
2. Step in and name one part of being a social worker that is difficult for you.
3. Step in and label a hope you have for your conference experience.

University Faculty Meeting

1. Step in and share one of your favorite things about the university or your role here.
2. Step in and label something difficult about your work at the university.
3. Step in and name one way you would like to help the university improve.

LGBTQ Community Center Opening Celebration

1. Step in and share what you hoped for in attending our opening event.
2. Step in and name an issue you see in the community.
3. Step in and share something you think this center could offer to be helpful to the community.

In the final example of an opening event for a new LGBTQ community center, the use of step-in sociometry provides an opportunity for assessing community issues, needs, wants, and expectations while also facilitating connection between community members. The first prompt explores what attendees hoped for in terms of attending the event which would provide the center's leadership with a sense of what could be helpful for the rest of the event while also keeping this information in mind for future events. The second prompt helps with the assessment of issues in the community and how many people think each issue is relevant. The level of energy for any given statement within this second round could provide the center with information about which issues may need to be prioritized. And the prompt of the final round gives community members a chance to give voice to what they would like from the community center. Rather than opening a center with at top-down issued list of initiatives, services, or goals, this type of sociometric community assessment allows the community center to take the pulse of the community they are serving and tailor their services to the real needs of the community. This process of assessment inherently recognizes the community as the expert in their own issues and needs.

18.9   Hands-On-Shoulder Sociograms

The use of hands-on-shoulder sociograms is also applicable in community work , especially useful for organizational meetings. Moreno's use of sociograms in community work seems to have been focused on written sociometric test which was compiled to create intricate sociograms of entire communities. Nevertheless, the similar assessments can be conducted in action with the experiential sociogram by offering prompts and inviting participants to put their hand on the shoulder of one person in the room to answer the prompt. One advantage of the written sociogram is that participants could list and rank multiple choices or preference while the hands-on-shoulder process only really works with one choice. As noted in Sect. 11.7, a limitation of this exercise is its reliance on physical touch , it is important to first assess the community's preferences and level of safety around physical touch. This becomes especially important when working with communities that have religious or cultural beliefs related to physical touch, especially between different genders. The hands-on-shoulder process can be modified without physical touch to use a scarf of piece of fabric as a connector instead of physical touch. The use of experiential sociograms with communities also makes it more difficult for the facilitator to track which group members have not been chosen between prompts. It is suggested that this exercise be reserved for small community or organizational groups unless a facil-itator has a team of co-facilitators or significant experience with sociometry in large groups. In a large group, it can be useful to invite a smaller group of participants to engage in this exercise with others observing or to break the community into smaller more manageable groups with their own facilitators to concurrently participate in the hands-on-shoulder sociogram process with the same prompts. Below are some examples of how hands-on-shoulder sociograms could be useful in community settings.

Community: Long-Term Residential Treatment Program

1.   Place your hand on the shoulder of someone who you have connected with in a meaningful way recently.
2.   Place your hand on the shoulder of someone who has inspired you during your time here.
3.   Place your hand on the shoulder of someone who you think you could learn something important from.
4.   Place your hand on the shoulder of someone who you would like to get to know better.

Community: Spiritual Fellowship

1.   Place your hand on the shoulder of the person you have known the longest in this community.
2.   Place your hand on the shoulder of someone who's spiritual dedication you admire.
3.   Place your hand on the shoulder of someone who you could call if you needed to talk about a spiritual problem.
4.   Place your hand on the shoulder of one person that you think is an unrecognized leader in this community.

Community: Conference for Social Activism

1.   Place your hand on the shoulder of someone whose work you would like to get to know better.
2.   Place your hand on the shoulder of someone whose passion you are inspired by.
3.   Place your hand on the shoulder of someone who you would like to collaborate with in the future.

Community: Agency Meeting of Caseworkers

1.   Place your hand on the shoulder of one person who you think demonstrates exceptional advocacy skills.
2.   Place your hand on the shoulder of one person you would ask for help regarding resources within the community.
3.   Place your hand on the shoulder of someone who you could talk to if you needed to process emotions related to the job.
4.   Place your hand on the shoulder of one person that you think could be a leader in the organization in the future.

In the last example, of an agency meeting of caseworkers at an organization, the sociodynamics within the team are revealed by the experiential sociogram process. Each prompt highlights how the community members experience different employees of the organization. This information is quite useful for organization leaders. Knowing who the team thinks is the best advocate or the most knowledge-able about community resources would allow agency leaders to strategically put those employees in formal or informal roles based on their perceived skills and strengths. Essentially, this sociogram process is an organization-as-a-whole evalua-tion of how employees experience each other based on different criteria. This infor-mation could prove very valuable when considering promotions within the company as well. Consideration of the perceptions between staff members could facilitate more insight into who the team is already experiencing as informal leaders in the commu-nity and thus would be more willing to work with in formal leadership roles. Moreno used sociograms in his research with groups in the military and choosing leaders based primarily on sociometric connection. In doing so, he found that soldiers were more willing to follow leaders that they had chosen over leaders that were appointed by others outside of their small group. This has implications for every organization and suggests a more democratic approach to promotions within organizations might be ideal.

18.10   Circle of Strengths

The circle of strengths (see Sect. 11.8 for more detail and a video link) is a safety structure for experiential trauma therapy from the Therapeutic Spiral Model (TSM) which focuses on intrapsychic, interpersonal, and transpersonal strengths (Giaco-mucci, 2020b; Hudgins & Toscani, 2013). This process uses the concretization of strengths to create safety, containment , and conscious acknowledgment of strengths within the group. It can be facilitated in many different ways including having partic-ipants identify their own strengths, another group member's strengths, or strengths of the group-as-a-whole (Giacomucci, Gera, Briggs, & Bass, 2018). As strengths are identified and concretized, they are placed in a large circle in the group space to symbolically represent unity, strength, and containment of the group. This process appears to be especially useful for developing group cohesion which can be advanta-geous in both community and organizational contexts. The circle of strength prompts can be modified to focus on specific community topics such as:

Inpatient Psychiatric Hospital Client Community Session

1. Choose a scarf to represent a strength you have that can help you with mental health.
2. Choose a scarf to represent a strength you experience in the person to your left in the circle that can help them in their mental health.
3. Choose a scarf to represent a strength you experience in this entire inpatient community that can help with mental health.

Refugee Community Support Group

1. Choose a scarf to represent a strength that helps you cope with the difficulty of being a refugee.
2. (Break out into dyads) Choose a scarf to represent a strength you see in your partner that can help them cope with the difficulties of being a refugee.
3. Choose a scarf to represent a strength you experience in this entire community of refugees.

Community Support Session After a Natural Disaster

1. Choose a scarf to represent a strength you can help you recover from the disaster.
2. Choose a scarf to represent a strength you experience in someone else in the group that has helped them recover from the disaster.
3. Choose a scarf to represent a strength you experience in this community that can help with recovery after the disaster.

Organizational Board of Directors' Meeting

1. Choose a scarf to represent a strength you bring to the board.
2. Choose a scarf to represent a strength you experience in someone else on the board.
3. Choose a scarf to represent a strength you experience in the organization-as-a-whole.

Trauma Treatment Center Team Meeting on Vicarious Trauma

1. Choose a scarf to represent a strength you have that can help you prevent vicarious trauma.
2. (Break out into dyads) Choose a scarf to represent a strength you experience your partner that you think can help them prevent or cope with vicarious trauma.
3. Choose a scarf to represent a strength you experience in this entire treatment team that can help with vicarious trauma.

In the example above of a trauma treatment center team engaging in the circle of strength process, participants have an opportunity to connect with each other on an emotional level with positive criteria. Team members have a chance to reflect on their own self-care process as it relates to vicarious trauma while also acknowledging strengths they see in each other and the team-as-a-whole. Regardless of topic, nearly every treatment team that has participated in the circle of strength process with this author has commented on how it has helped to enhance connection between team members and overall cohesion within the team.

18.11   Conclusion

Any of the above sociometric exploration could be conducted through digital or paper assessments of individual community members, but in doing so would lose the inherently social and relational element of the experiential sociometric process. These sociometric explorations allow participants to see in real time where and how their responses fit into the larger community-as-a-whole response and to initiate dialogue with others about their choice. This type of community-as-a-whole assessment facilitates connection, normalization, and dialogue in ways that would not be possible through digital or paper assessments of individuals within a community. Sociometric group tools help social workers work with the group-as-a-whole instead of falling into the trap of individual work within a group setting. In the same way, these sociometric tools offer social workers community-as-a-whole processes that avoid the risk of doing individual work within community settings.

A social worker equipped with these simple sociometric tools can create an infinite number of experiential processes with community groups that assess, engage with, and evaluate dynamics within the community while providing participants with a sense of connection, cohesion, belonging, and empowerment. Each of these individual sociometry tools can be used as the primary part of a community session with sharing afterward or as a warm-up for another activity. Multiple of the aforementioned tools could be used in a single session, or they all could be adapted into a curriculum for ongoing community groups or a multiday event. These sociometric processes are often used as warm-ups for sociodrama enactments in community settings which will be outlined in Chap. 19.

References

Almond, R. (1974). *The healing community: Dynamics of the therapeutic Milieu.* New York: Jason Aronson.

Austin, M. J., Anthony, E. K., Knee, R. T., & Mathias, J. (2016). Revisiting the relationship between micro and macro social work practice. *Families in Society, 97*(4), 270–277.

Ayyagari, A. (2014). Exploring the dynamics of high-challenge encounters in residential substance abuse treatment settings. *Doctorate in Social Work (DSW) Dissertations*, 52. https://repository.upenn.edu/edissertations_sp2/52.

Bierer, J. (1960). The therapeutic community hostel. *International Journal of Social Psychiatry, 7*(1), 5–10.

Bloom, S. L. (1997). *Creating sanctuary: Toward the evolution of sane societies.* New York: Routledge.

Bloom, S. L. (2000). Creating Sanctuary: Healing from systematic abuses of power. *Therapeutic Communities: The International Journal for Therapeutic and Supportive Organizations, 21*(2), 67–91.

Bloom, S. L. (2008). The sanctuary model of trauma-informed organizational change. *Reclaiming Children and Youth, 17*(3), 48–53.

Bloom, S. L. (2012). Trauma-organized systems. In C. R. Figley (Ed.), *Encyclopedia of Trauma* (pp. 741–743). Thousand Oaks, CA: Sage.

Bloom, S. L. (2013). *Creating sanctuary: Toward the evolution of sane societies* (Revised). New York: Routledge.

Bloom, S. L., & Farragher, B. (2013). *Restoring sanctuary: A new operating system for trauma-informed systems of care*. New York: Oxford University Press.

Bloom, S. L., & Norton, K. (2004). Introduction to the special section: The therapeutic community in the 21st century. *Psychiatric Quarterly, 75*(3), 229–231.

Cadiz, S., Savage, A., Bonavota, D., Hollywood, J., Butters, E., Neary, M., & Quiros, L. (2011). The portal project: A layered approach to integrating trauma into alcohol and other drug treatment for women. In B. Veysey & C. Clark (Eds.), *Responding to physical and sexual abuse in women with alcohol and other drug and mental disorders* (pp. 129–148). New York: Routledge.

Casson, J. (2000). Maxwell Jones: Dramatherapy and psychodrama, 1942–9. *Dramatherapy, 22*(2), 18–21.

Chesner, A. (2020). Psychodrama and healing the traumatic wound. In A. Chesner & S. Lykou (Eds.), *Trauma in the creative and embodied therapies: When words are not enough* (pp. 69–80). London: Routledge.

Courtois, C. A., & Ford, J. D. (2016). *Treatment of complex trauma: A sequenced, relationship-based approach*. New York, USA: The Guildford Press.

Cumming, J., & Cumming, E. (1962). *Ego & Milieu: Theory and practice of environmental therapy*. New York: Aldine Publishing Company.

De Leon, G. (2000). *The therapeutic community: Theory, model, and method*. New York: Springer.

De Leon, G. (2010). Is the therapeutic community an evidence-based treatment? *What the Evidence Says. Therapeutic Communities, 31*(2), 104.

De Robertis, C. (2003). *Fundamentos del trabajo social. Ética y metodología*. Valencia: Universidad de Valencia.

Dewey, J. (1916). *Education and democracy*. New York: Macmillan.

Figusch, Z. (2014). *The JL Moreno memorial photo album*. London: lulu.com.

Giacomucci, S. (2017). The sociodrama of life or death: Young adults and addiction treatment. *Journal of Psychodrama, Sociometry, and Group Psychotherapy, 65*(1), 137–143. https://doi.org/10.12926/0731-1273-65.1.137.

Giacomucci, S. (2018). The trauma survivor's inner role atom: A clinical map for post-traumatic growth. *Journal of Psychodrama, Sociometry, and Group Psychotherapy., 66*(1), 115–129.

Giacomucci, S. (2019). *Social group work in action: A sociometry, psychodrama, and experiential trauma therapy curriculum* (Doctorate in Social Work (DSW) Dissertations) (p. 124). https://repository.upenn.edu/cgi/viewcontent.cgi?article=1128&context=edissertations_sp2

Giacomucci, S. (2020a). Addiction, traumatic loss, and guilt: A case study resolving grief through psychodrama and sociometric connections. *The Arts in Psychotherapy, 67,* 101627. https://doi.org/10.1016/j.aip.2019.101627.

Giacomucci, S. (2020b). Experiential sociometry in group work: Mutual aid for the group-as-a-whole. In *Social work with groups*. Advanced Online Publication. https://doi.org/10.1080/01609513.2020.1747726

Giacomucci, S., Gera, S., Briggs, D., & Bass, K. (2018). Experiential addiction treatment: Creating positive connection through sociometry and therapeutic spiral model safety structures. *Journal of Addiction and Addictive Disorders, 5,* 17. https://doi.org/10.24966/AAD-7276/100017.

Hardcastle, D. A., Powers, P. R., & Wencour, S. (2011). *Community practice: theories and skills for social workers* (3rd ed.). New York: Oxford University Press.

Herman, J. L. (1997). *Trauma and recovery: The aftermath of violence—from domestic abuse to political terror*. New York: Basic Books.

Hudgins, M. K., & Toscani, F. (2013). *Healing world trauma with the therapeutic spiral model: Stories from the frontlines*. London: Jessica Kingsley Publishers.

Hunter, D., & Lakey, G. (2004). *Opening space for democracy. training manual for third-party nonviolent intervention*. Philadelphia: Training for Change.

Illinois Department of Human Services, Domestic Violence/Substance Abuse 112 Interdisciplinary Task Force. (2005). *Safety and sobriety: Best practices in domestic violence and substance abuse.*

Springfield, IL: Illinois Department of Human Services. Retrieved from https://www.dhs.state.il.us/onenetlibrary/27897/documents/chp/dsvp/safetysobrietymanual.pdf

Janzen, R. (2000). *The rise and fall of Synanon*. Baltimore: Johns Hopkins University Press.

Jones, M. (1949). Acting as an aid to therapy in a Neurosis Centre. *British Medical Journal, 1*(4608), 756–758.

Jones, M. (1953). *The therapeutic community: A new treatment method in psychiatry*. New York: Basic Books.

Jones, M. (1968). *Beyond the therapeutic community: Social learning and social psychiatry*. Yale University Press.

Kristoffersen, B. (2018). Sociometry in democracy. *Zeitschrift Für Psychodrama Und Soziometrie, 17*(1), 109–120.

Landy, R. J. (2008). *The couch and the stage: Integrating words and action in psychotherapy*. Lanham, MD: Jason Aronson.

Lieberman, M. A., Yalom, I. D., & Miles, M. (1973). *Encounter Groups: First Facts*. New York: Basic Books.

Main, T. F. (1946). The hospital as a therapeutic institution. *Bulletin of the Menninger Clinic, 10*(3), 66.

Moreno, J. L. (1920). *Das Testament des Vaters*. Genossenschafts-Verlag.

Moreno, J. L. (1934). *Who shall survive? A new approach to the problems of human interrelations*. Washington, DC: Nervous and Mental Disease Publishing Co.

Moreno, J. L. (1945). The future of man's world. *Sociometry, 8*(3/4), 297–304.

Moreno, J. L. (1953). *Who shall survive? Foundations of sociometry, group psychotherapy and sociodrama* (2nd ed.). Beacon, NY: Beacon House.

Moreno, J. L. (1957). *The first book on group psychotherapy* (3rd ed.). Beacon, NY: Beacon House.

Moreno, Z. T. (2012). *To dream again: A memoir*. New York, USA: Mental Health Resources.

Moreno, J. D. (2014). *Impromptu Man: J.L. Moreno and the Origins of Psychodrama, Encounter Culture, and the Social Network*. New York, NY: Bellevue Literary Press.

Moreno, J. L. (2019). In E. Schreiber, S. Kelley, & S. Giacomucci (Eds.). *The autobiography of a genius*. London, UK: North West Psychodrama Association.

Moreno, J. L., & Whitin, E. S. (1932). *Application of the group method to classification*. New York, USA: National Committee on Prisons and Prison Labor.

Nieto, L. (2010). Look Behind You: Using Anti-Oppression Models to Inform a Protagonist's Psychodrama. In E. Leveton (Ed.), *Healing collective trauma using sociodrama and drama therapy* (pp. 103–125). New York, USA: Springer.

Nolte, J. (2014). *The philosophy, theory, and methods of J.L. Moreno: The man who tried to become God*. New York, USA: Routledge.

Polcin, D. L. (2003). Rethinking confrontation in alcohol and drug treatment: Consideration of the clinical context. *Substance Use & Misuse, 38*(2), 165–184.

Rapoport, R. N. (2013). *Community as doctor: New perspectives on a therapeutic community*. London, UK: Routledge.

Rodríguez, M. D., & Ferreira, J. (2018). The contribution of the intervention in social networks and community social work at the local level to social and human development. *European Journal of Social Work, 21*(6), 863–875.

Ross M., & Lappin, B. W. (1967). Community organization: Theory, principles, and practice. New York, USA: Harper & Row

Seeds for Change. (2019). *Facilitation tools for meetings and workshops* (2nd ed.). UK: Seeds for Change.

Shapiro, F. (2018). *Eye-movement desensitization and reprocessing (EMDR) therapy* (3rd ed.). New York: Guilford Press.

Simmons, D. (2017). Implementing sociometry in a long-term care institutional setting for the elderly: Exploring social relationships and choices. *Journal of Psychodrama, Sociometry, and Group Psychotherapy, 65*(1), 85–98.

Vanderplasschen, W., Colpaert, K., Autrique, M., Rapp, R. C., Pearce, S., Broekaert, E., & Vande-velde, S. (2013). *Therapeutic communities for addictions: A review of their effectiveness from a recovery-oriented perspective* (p. 427817). Article ID: Scientific World Journal.

Weber, A. M., & Haen, C. (Eds.). (2005). *Clinical applications of drama therapy in child and adolescent treatment*. New York, USA: Psychology Press.

White, W., & Miller, W. R. (2007). Confrontation in addiction treatment: History, science and time for change. *Counselor, 8*(4), 12–30.

Wilmer, H. A. (1981). Defining and understanding the therapeutic community. *Hospital and Community Psychiatry., 32*(2), 95–99.

Yablonsky, L. (1962). The Anticriminal Society: Synanon. *Federal Probation, 26,* 50.

Yablonsky, L. (1965). *The tunnel back: Synanon*. New York: Macmillan.

Yablonsky, L. (1976). *Psychodrama: Resolving emotional problems through role-playing*. New York, USA: Basic Books.

Yablonsky, L. (1989). *The therapeutic community: A successful approach for treating substance abusers*. New York: Gardner Press.

Yablonsky, L. (2002). Whatever happened to Synanon? The birth of the anticriminal therapeutic community methodology. *Criminal Justice Policy Review, 13*(4), 329–336.

Yalom, I. D., & Leszcz, M. (2005). *The theory and practice of group psychotherapy* (5th ed.). New York, USA: Basic Books.

Chapter 19
Sociodrama, Activism, and Role Training to Empower Communities

Abstract This chapter will highlight the use of role-playing, especially sociodrama and role training in community empowerment and social activist movements. Historical context will be provided for the traditions of using drama, theater, and role-play in social work and social activism including Jacob Moreno's vision of the theater as a modality for societal change. The sociodramatic approach will be outlined with focus on its utility in community settings as an experiential and communal experience of social action. Multiple examples of sociodrama or role training in communities are depicted with an emphasis on its adaptability for different settings and its effectiveness at empowering people. Examples include its application with youth, law enforcement, intergenerational dialogues, domestic violence response teams, undocumented immigrant communities, social work students, and to empower advocacy with employers, insurance providers, funders, or policy makers.

Keywords Sociodrama · Social activism · Role training · Community empowerment · Social justice

The use of art is foundational in nearly every social movement. As such, sociodrama, a spontaneous and creative arts approach, is a fitting modality for community work related to social movements. The etymology of the word *psychodrama* conveys the meaning of "psyche in action", on the other hand, the term *sociodrama* suggests a meaning of "social in action" or "social action". Considering an etymological lens, the terms *social movement, social activism*, and *social action* all suggest a fundamental emphasis on creating action or movement within, or of, society or social groups as an end goal. It is more than fitting then that the goal of social action be achieved through the means of sociodrama and action-based group approaches. In this way, the means and the ends, as well as the process and content of community sessions, are synergistically related.

© The Author(s) 2021
S. Giacomucci, *Social Work, Sociometry, and Psychodrama*, Psychodrama in Counselling, Coaching and Education 1,
https://doi.org/10.1007/978-981-33-6342-7_19

19.1 Theater as a Modality for Social Activism

Drama and the theater have traditionally played a significant role in community life tracing its histories across cultures and continents, with some of the oldest written histories coming from Ancient Egypt and Ancient Greece (Freedley & Reeves, 1964; Leahy, 2008; McCammon, 2007; Moreno, 1972). Drama and theater existed with connections to community entertainment, religion, politics, education, psychotherapy, and social action. The use of theater in community social work can be traced back to Jane Addam's Hull House in Chicago which had a very popular theater program as early as the 1890s (Hecht, 1982). Hull House's use of theater was based on its potential of inspiring and empowering the community with an emphasis on highlighting social and political ills. "Theatre and politics are intrinsically connected. The art of politics is extremely theatrical and the art of theatre has always been infused with political relationships" (Leahy, 2008, p. 1). Many activists employ drama within their activism as a means of cultivating social change with theater; and many actors employ social or political content in their shows to produce theater with social change. Considerable overlap exists between these two worlds, nevertheless, debate remains active between actors and activists about the boundary and overlap of their domains (Schlossman, 2002).

Leahy (2008) argues that theater and politics share much in common including both fundamentally being tools of persuasion with the goals of convincing audiences to adhere to specific conclusions. Social activism, advocacy, and social movements appear to operate with similar approaches to influence the opinions of individuals, groups, or society. While traditional politics and theater both seem to adhere to their own respective scripts to persuade audiences, Moreno's Theater of Spontaneity and other therapeutic uses of theater or drama replace the script with spontaneity. Instead, they focus less on an end goal of persuasion and more on the therapeutic experience of engaging in the dramatic process. The emphasis shifts from the *content* or final theater *production* to the *process* of drama.

The dramatic process has the power to create change for both actors and spectators (Moreno, 1972). Aristotle wrote of the Ancient Greek theater creating catharsis within audience members as an important social function of purification (Aristotle, 1951). Moreno later noted the cathartic experience of drama for both the audience and the actors (Moreno, 1940). Moreno's original vision of his theater work (Theater of Spontaneity of Vienna in 1920s and Impromptu Theater of New York in the 1930s) was as a vehicle for creating large-scale social change and a creative revolution— "I foresaw an enormous task, to change the public. It would have required a total revolution in our culture, a creative revolution. That was my goal in life" (2019, p. 213). Public psychodrama sessions were held in New York, open to anyone in the community, six nights a week between the late 1940s until the early 70s (Moreno, 2014). Though these were public community sessions, it appears that the content was mostly psychodramatic rather than sociodramatic.

In the 1960–1970s, many theater groups emerged connected to various social movements with the objective of cultivating social change (Shank, 1982). These included both *Playback Theater* in the United States and *Theater of the Oppressed* in South America. Perhaps Augusto Boal's Theater of the Oppressed is the most popular and most successful use of theater for social change around the world. Both Moreno and Boal's use of theater started with a vision of social change and later included models specific for psychotherapy. Nevertheless, it seems Moreno's work became much more integrated into psychotherapy (particularly in the United States) while Boal's remained focused on social change. Perhaps this differentiation can be explained by their backgrounds as Moreno was a European/American psychiatrist and pioneer of group psychotherapy while Boal was a Marxist playwright from Brazil (Oliveira & Araujo, 2012). Theater of the Oppressed maintained a goal of social and political change, while psychodrama became focused on creating psychological change or change in small groups. Interestingly, however, the utilization of psychodrama in Brazil (which has the largest psychodrama community in the world) appears to be much less individualistic with more community focused practice addressing social and political issues. In 2001, the city of São Paulo in Brazil even held a special psychodrama day at the request of the mayor, which involved over 10,000 citizens at 158 public locations throughout the city with the topic of "ethics and citizenship" (Greeb, 2019).

19.2 Sociodrama and Social Activism

Psychodrama's potential for powerful catharsis is, in part, what makes it a formidable tool in psychotherapy but also limits its safe use in community groups. While psychodrama is focused on the externalization of individual issues, sociodrama dramatizes social issues. The fundamental nature of roles in psychodrama focuses on private elements of roles, while sociodrama focuses on collective elements of roles (Sternberg & Garcia, 2000). Moreno (1943) writes that social issues cannot be adequately addressed within the confines of individual psychotherapy, instead, social issues must be addressed within community forums, preferably with sociodrama. Most would agree that psychodrama is a better approach for personal growth, while sociodrama is better designed for social change. As such, sociodrama is used much more frequently than psychodrama within social activism or public spaces.

The goals of a sociodrama enactment include expression, catharsis, insight, learning, and role training (Sternberg & Garcia, 2000). A sociodrama does not enact any one person's story, but instead puts into action a co-created story that contains elements of the entire group's experience without using the specific details of their narratives. This creates a sense of aesthetic distance similar to the experience of watching a movie or theater play containing social themes that resemble one's personal life experience. The major difference between a sociodrama and a movie or theater performance is that the sociodrama has no script or predefined characters, and it is spontaneously improvised and co-created by the group. Here, we also touch upon a fundamental difference between sociodrama, Playback Theater, Theater of the Oppressed, and traditional theater. In the traditional theater, the script is written by a playwriter; Playback Theater and Theater of the Oppressed utilize an audience member's narrative as the script; and the sociodramatic script emerges from the collective conscious of the group. In some sociodramas, the theme or issue might be predetermined, but the actual script is spontaneously generated.

Sociodramatic role-plays are being used regularly in therapy, community organizing, and social activism spaces, though most often simply referred to as "role-plays" or "simulations" (Hunter & Lakey, 2004; Jemal, Urmey, & Caliste, 2020). Activists and sociodramatists bring community issues to life using role-plays as an educational tool which provides participants with action insights, catharsis, new perspective, and role training. Below are multiple examples of both sociodramas and sociodramatic role-plays in community settings focused on social activism, beginning with a description of the first sociodrama by Moreno. It is important to note that the experiential sociometry tools from Sects. 18.5–18.10 are especially useful to warm up community groups before moving into any type of role-play or action sociodrama.

19.2.1   Moreno's Search for a Leader of the New World Order

The first sociodrama session took place on April 1, 1921, in Vienna, facilitated by Jacob Moreno. This session took place at the Vienna Comedian House just a few years after the end of World War I and the collapse of the Austria-Hungarian Empire. "Postwar Vienna was seething with revolt. There was no stable government, no emperor, no king, no leader…And, like the other nations of the earth, Austria was restless, in search of a new soul" (Moreno, 2019, p. 206). Moreno describes the audience as consisting of around one thousand people including politicians, foreign dignitaries, religious leaders, and cultural leaders of Vienna. Moreno appeared on stage with no script, no actors, and with only a chair resembling a throne and a gilded crown. In his autobiography, he describes this experience in his own words:

> I was entirely unprepared… But, psychodramatically speaking, I had a cast and I had a play. The audience was my cast. The people in the audience were like a thousand unconscious playwrights. The play was the situation into which they were thrown by historical events in which each of them had a real part to play. It was my aim, as we would say today, to tap sociodrama in *statu nascendi* and to analyze the production which emerged. If I could only succeed in turning the audience into actors, actors in their own collective drama, the collective drama of social conflict in which they were actually involved every day of their lives, then my boldness would be redeemed and the session would have accomplished something. (2019, p. 206)

He invited audience members to ascend from the crowd to the throne and offer a new philosophy of leadership for the new world order. "No one was prepared ahead of time. Unprepared characters acted in an unprepared play before an unprepared audience. The audience played the role of the jury" (Moreno, 2019, p. 206). Nobody won the approval of the audience—including Moreno and his spontaneous experiment. This first sociodrama resulted in newspapers harshly criticizing him, friends leaving him, harm to his reputation in Vienna, and a newfound commitment to spontaneous theater by Moreno and his theater group.

Though the session was described as a failure, it led to the production of the Impromptu Theater, sociodrama, and psychodrama. Most trained psychodramatists, who have the benefit of the 100 years of practice wisdom since this event, would comment on the lack of audience warm-up and the value of using doubling, mirroring, and role reversal that Moreno had not yet conceived of at that time. Consideration of the contract with the group is also significant in analyzing Moreno's failed session. The audience attended under the assumption that they would sit quietly in the role of audience, as is the informal contract they agree to in every other theater session. Moreno changed the contract and asked audience member to become not only an actor, but the protagonist of the show without proper warm-up. Perhaps Moreno was to be the most influential leader in the building that night and the session would have benefitted from him sitting on the throne. Or, maybe the crowd's inability to produce a leader was the perfect conclusion of the sociodrama as it symbolically represented Austria's governmental shift from that of a monarchy to a republic.

19.2.2 Youth and Police in Philadelphia

The use of role-playing techniques, psychodrama, sociodrama, and drama therapy seems to be well received by young people and has been covered by various other authors (Cahill, 2015; Cossa, 2006; Giacomucci, 2017; Jennings, 2014; Maier, 2002; Weber & Haen, 2005). The elements of play, spontaneity, creativity, and social connection seem to highly compliment the developmental tasks of young people (Giacomucci, 2017). Cossa (2006) highlights specifically how sociodrama and psychodrama create opportunities for youth to explore new roles, practice social skills, express emotions, meet developmental needs, and experiment with new emerging aspects of identity.

My first personal experience of sociodramatic role-play in a community setting was as an observer at a community event in North Philadelphia. The event was focused on mitigating conflict and enhancing relationships between youth and police officers in the community. Many of the youth in the community felt as though they were being unfairly harassed by police officers or discriminated against due to their race or ethnicity while the police officers felt as though they were unfairly disrespected by the youth. The warming up process included a moderated discussion between the two groups and the voicing of difficult encounters between both groups. From there, the session moved into action enacting several of the described encounters. One of the most memorable was a described experience of youth feeling harassed by the police for hanging out on the sidewalk with friends.

The moderator invited three police officers from the group to play the roles of three youth hanging out together on the sidewalk. Then, one of the adolescents from the community volunteered and was enrolled into the police officer role. The situation was that the officer had been told to respond to a noise complaint in the neighborhood. As he approached the three kids, he respectfully asked them to be quiet, they responded telling him to stop harassing them and that they were not doing anything wrong. The police officer tried again to redirect them, this time with more firmness, asking them to go home. The kids protested louder with more energy and frustration at the officer. After multiple failed attempts, the teen playing the role of the police officer became visibly frustrated with the kids. The audience shared his frustration with outbursts of laughter which turned to nervous laughter when the kid role-playing as the police officer jokingly pretended to pull out a gun and threaten the three kids. Here, the moderator paused the scene and took the opportunity to de-role the auxiliaries and move into a discussion about the experience as it relates to the realities of the community.

The youth commented on their newfound insight into how they might unknowingly make police officers' jobs more difficult—especially how their reactions to law enforcement might increase the likelihood of violence. The discussion shifted to the reasons why teens might spend time on the street together which included acknowledging the high rates of household violence, drug abuse, and poverty in the community. The teenagers shared about their avoidance of going home because of these issues which provided the police with a more complete picture of the lives of the youth. Naturally, this increased understanding led to enhanced compassion and a softening of the police officers' attitudes toward the kids. The sociodramatic enactments had successfully allowed each group to role reverse with the other and enhance their understanding of the other group's experience. Though many issues persist between police and the community, this encounter depicts sociodrama's ability to improve intergroup relationships. Perhaps an indicator of the intervention's success was the friendly, but competitive basketball game between the youth and police that took place in the park after the community session.

A similar program is outlined in the Center for Court Innovation toolkit for police–youth dialogues (2015) which emphasizes the role-playing component of the program:

> Role-plays—especially reverse role-plays where young people act as officers and vice versa—can help participants address challenging street interactions while having some fun. When playing officers, young people learn how difficult it can be to make quick decisions in fraught situations, while police playing young people get a taste of how intrusive questioning can feel. (p. 21)

In this publication, role-playing between police and youth was highlighted by researchers and observers as the favorite aspect of the program by both police and youth participants.

19.2.3 Sociodramatic Dialogue Between Generations in Baltimore City Barbershops

Another use of sociodrama to explore and enhance intergroup relationships comes from the work of Joshua Lee, MSW, CP, a social worker and psychodramatist in Baltimore City who has created multiple innovative experiential approaches to community social work including *ShopTalk: Share. Heal. Grow. ShopTalk* is a project Joshua developed using Moreno's methods in urban barbershops with the African-American community after the 2015 Baltimore uprisings responding to police brutality (Lee, 2018). In his 2018 article about his approach, Lee writes that his experiential work in barbershops has explored various topics pertinent to the community including violence, addiction, relationships, trauma, and loss. He outlines a sociodramatic empty chair dialogue that emerged between the older and younger generations due to a comment from an older man that "those young people are lost these days". Seizing the opportunity for dialogue, Joshua pulls out an empty chair to represent young people and begins spontaneously facilitating the drama. From the role of the younger generation, someone exclaims "you all failed us!" As it emerges, the dialogue draws in participants within the barbershop as they become curious and warmed up, speaking from the various roles until the encounter moves to closure. Another enactment from the barbershop group centered on a man who wanted to psychodramatically speak to God in the other empty chair. He began to thank God for saving him from childhood trauma, addiction, incarceration, and violence as the rest of the group witnessed with reverence. Observers in the barbershop responded with a standing ovation, followed by general sharing of similarities and a sense of relief and gratitude for the chance to share their stories.

When a psychodrama or sociodrama really represents the issues in the group, it catches everyone's attention and pulls them into engagement with excitement, interest, and anticipation. Lee writes that "action methods in barbershops seemed to pull people into the conversation quickly, thereby causing deeper connections and heartfelt-experiences with 'strangers' to develop" (Lee, 2018, p. 146). Joshua highlights the importance of trusting the community to support each other and find their own answers within the sociodrama structure (J. Lee, personal communication, May 18th, 2020). Joshua notes that ShopTalk sessions have, at times, broken out into spontaneous dance and music—and that attendees often attend future community-based psychodrama events. Joshua's work within the community strongly resembles the original methods of both the social work profession and the Morenean approach of meeting people where they are at. This involves going out into the community to where people live to be of service, rather than meeting individual clients in neatly organized professional offices. The use of Moreno's methods through *ShopTalk* incorporates a range of interventions focused on both social and emotional issues of individual protagonists, groups, and the larger community.

19.2.4   Crisis Intervention Training for Law Enforcement on Domestic Violence, Mental Health, and Addiction

The use of sociodrama and role-play techniques has been used in training programs and events with law enforcement to both challenge biases about mental illness and domestic violence while also providing role training on more sensitive ways to respond (Buchanan & Hankins, 1987; Buchanan & Swink, 2017; Moreno, 2014). This use of Moreno's methods in training law enforcement was spearheaded by the St. Elizabeths Hospital prestigious psychodrama program which developed a collaboration with the Washington DC. Police Department in the 1970s. An objective was set to provide training for all Washington DC. police officers on family crisis intervention (Buchanan & Swink, 2017). The popularity of this type of training program is evidenced by its promotion in many major national newspapers and its adaptation into training programs for other government agencies including the Federal Bureau of Investigation hostage negotiation team, Social Security Administration, the State Department, U.S. Army, U.S. Secret Service, Dulles Airport security, and the U.S. Capital Police.

Advocating for a new approach to domestic violence. The most successful training program of this nature was the Family Crisis Intervention Program, a collaboration between psychodramatists at St. Elizabeths Hospital and the Metropolitan Police Department of Washington DC. It was also the most extensive training program in the United States at that time (Hankins & Buchanan, 1987). This program curriculum is outlined in the publication *The Badge and the Battered*, edited by Buchanan and Hankins (1987). This program emerged due to the problem of family violence, police officers' high rates of assault or death while responding to domestic violence calls, and critiques at nature of police officers' interventions (or lack of) (Callahan, 1987; Hankins, 1987). The program implemented sociodramatic role-play enactments so participants could experientially explore common family disturbance situations, potential family dynamics that lead to family conflict, and practice responding to these situations in different ways while also exploring their personal biases related to sexuality, gender, religion, family status, substance abuse, and mental illness (Chasnoff, 1987). The role-plays included consideration to non-verbal behavior and adhered to a five-phase intervention model—safety, diffusion, communication, resolution, and referral. Afterward, participants engaged in a discussion about which interventions seemed most effective and their own action insights during the process. Multiple studies were conducted evaluating the impact of the program which concluded that (1) there was a significant reduction of assaults on police who were trained by the program (Buchanan & Hankins, 1983), (2) significant changes in police attitudes about domestic violence and their ability to respond to it (Buchanan & Perry, 1985), (3) an increased ability to defuse conflictual situations (Bandy, Buchanan, & Pinto, 1986), and (4) an overall improvement in communication skills, role repertoire, and spontaneity in responses (Hankins & Buchanan, 1987). In describing the program, the Chief of Police commented that "I am convinced that our officers are providing more sensitive intervention; and as a result, are more capable in handling family disturbances. The significant reduction in assaults on police officers is a direct result of this new competence" (Buchanan & Hankins, 1987, n.p.). The utility of sociodrama and role training to improve behavioral responses is highlighted by this project which created lasting change in the law enforcement community and the communities in which they serve.

Challenging perceptions on mental illness and addiction. The success of the Family Crisis Intervention Program described above resulted in many later programs including the training of police in Pennsylvania using sociodramatic methods to challenge perspectives on mental illness. This project advocated for less criminalization and more human police treatment of those suffering from addiction and mental health issues. After didactic presentations are offered by facilitators on common mental health disorders, a sociodramatic role-play ensues. One such example comes from the work of David Moran, LCSW, CADC, TEP with a behavioral health crisis intervention unit of police officers in the Philadelphia suburbs.

The group is exploring their response as police officers to an escalated situation which involves an individual with schizophrenia. Police participants in the group are cast in the various roles including the responding officers, the victim, the aggressive person suffering from schizophrenia, and the multiple schizophrenia-related voices that this individual is experiencing. The impact of the schizophrenic voices on the individual become apparent when externalized through the role-play as the participant in the role of this person attempts to communicate with others in the scene while also hearing internal voices. In the role-play, law enforcement agents have an opportunity to practice different methods of responding to the individual with severe mental illness to determine the most effective approach. This process allows the responding officers to develop an experiential understanding of the internal reality of someone with schizophrenia so that they can respond on the job with more empathy and understanding.

The training program also uses a similar sociodramatic training vignette focused on persons with addictive disorders where a similar scene is enacted but with auxiliaries playing the roles of "the voice of addiction," "alcohol," "drugs," or "drug cravings". While many have biases against people with addictions, the role-play also helps participants develop a better understanding and sense of empathy for the suffering of those inflicted with addictions. In this module, the high rates of alcohol and substance abuse within law enforcement communities are also acknowledged as a way of helping trainees cultivate empathy and prevent an "us versus them" mentality. Overall, the program helps to mitigate the tendency to stigmatize or dehumanize persons with severe mental illness or addictions, enhance understanding and empathy, and increase practical communication skills for officers when communicating with persons with addictions and severe mental illness.

Research on a similar police training program demonstrated a significant increase in recognition of mental health issues, improved efficiency dealing with mental illness, and decreased physical altercations and weapon-involved interactions with mentally ill individuals (Krameddine, DeMarco, Hassel, & Silverstone, 2013). The outcomes of this study suggested that a one-day training for police costed about

$120 per officer but resulted in more than $80,000 in savings over the next 6 months because of the improved interpersonal skills of officers interacting with mentally ill individuals in the community. Other studies focused on using role-playing simulations to improve police interactions with mentally ill individuals have also produced positive results (Bonfine, Ritter, & Munetz, 2014; Krameddine & Silverstone, 2015; Reuland & Schwarzfeld, 2008; Silverstone, Krameddine, DeMarco, & Hassel, 2013; Watson, Morabito, Draine, & Ottati, 2008).

19.3   Role Training for Community Empowerment

The use of role-playing to practice for future situations or refining interactive skills is described as role training (Blatner, 2000). The utilization of role training has many applications in community work as it emphasizes learning and experiential skills practice while generally being less cathartic than other psychodrama scenes. Role training is future-oriented toward hoped-for outcomes, so it is also much less anxiety producing than other types of role-play scenes. Role training is already being used regularly in community settings though it is usually simple referred to as "role-playing" or "simulations". The next set of examples will focus specifically on using role training simulations to empower community members to advocate for themselves, others, and their community.

19.3.1   Know Your Rights Role Training for Undocumented Immigrant Communities

As noted previously, role-play and role training are frequently used by community organizers, especially with immigrant communities. Know your rights sessions for immigrant communities have been offered by community leaders and organizations around the country for quite some time (Tipler & Gates, 2019) but became especially important after the presidential election of Donald Trump and the increased threat experienced by undocumented communities in the United States. These sessions generally are facilitated by community organizers collaborating with attorneys specializing in immigration law and interpreters/translators to provide accurate and accessible information related to the legal rights of undocumented immigrants. The sociodramatic role-plays begin after a didactic information session focused specifically on the legal rights of undocumented persons when encountering Immigration and Custom Enforcement (ICE) authorities.

This specific example comes from the work of Maria Sotomayor-Giacomucci and the Pennsylvania Immigration and Citizenship Coalition (PICC) (see their online toolbox for more info—(www.paimmigrant.org/toolbox/know-your-rights). A common know your rights simulation that is employed is that of an ICE agent appearing at the home of an immigrant family requesting that they open the door and provide information to authorities. After being informed of their legal obligations in this situations, and possible responses, the role-play simulations begin with the purpose of role training community members on how to respond. Community members are taught that they do not need to open the door unless presented with a signed judicial warrant. The differences between judicial warrants and ICE administrative warrants are explained, and community members are instructed to inspect the warrant for the listed address, name, and a signature by a judge. If a judicial warrant with correct information is not presented, community members are informed that they are within their rights not to open the door and instead to call a lawyer and/or a local immigrant rights organization. If a judicial warrant is presented by ICE agents, then community members are instructed to comply but only for the names of the people on the warrant—that they should leave the home and lock the door as not to give ICE the chance to question others in the home who were not listed on the warrant. After the information has been conveyed, then the role training phase of the session begins, and community members practice role-playing the situation of an ICE agent knocking on someone's door while participants practice their newly learned responses. After the role training practice, participants de-role and engage in a debriefing phase before the session ends.

Participants often report a sense of relief at learning that they do have rights as undocumented people in the country. Many undocumented countries have migrated from countries with governments that are much more authoritarian than those in the United States, and they simply are not aware of their rights or were never informed of them. While they continue to have concerns and fears related to the uncertainties created by their status, they feel relief at knowing they do not have to open the door for ICE except in specific circumstances. Community members report feeling empowered to protect themselves, their families, and communities—that they now feel like they have the ability and permission to resist. Tipler & Gates' (2019) study of the impact of know your rights trainings with undocumented communities validates that participation: (1) reduced fear and increased a sense of power or control, (2) reduced stigma/isolation and increased social support, and (3) increased a sense of dignity and empowerment. This role training piece demonstrates the operationalization of the provided know your rights information which effectively empowers community members and helps reduce anxieties or uncertainties. Perhaps the visual component of the demonstration also helps transcend possible language barriers for community members who speak different languages. Instead of only transmitting information through verbal or spoken words, the information is embodied in the scene.

19.3.2   MSW Students Responding to Racism and Microaggressions

The utilization of role training simulations can help participants develop competency and skill responding to racism and microaggressions in everyday life while enhancing cultural competencies (Colvin, Saleh, Ricks, & Rosa-Davila, 2020; Lee, Blythe, & Goforth, 2009; Pope, Pangelinan, & Angela, 2011; Schreiber & Minarik, 2018). The following example comes from a guest lecture by this author at the University of Pennsylvania School of Social Policy & Practice's MSW course on racism. After a series of sociometric warm-ups based on the tenants of critical race theory (Delgado & Stefancic, 2017), participants were invited to create concentric circles to participate in a role-playing process called "The Role Wheel". In this exercise, one member from the inner circle and the outer circle are paired together, each assigned with a role by the facilitator. The facilitator may also provide context related to the scene or the goal of the enactment before participants simultaneously initiate a spontaneous interaction with their partners. Each enactment is kept short, to a minute or two at most with participants being instructed to de-role, say good-bye to their partner, and greet their new partner as the outer circle participants are directed to move one space to their left. Then, another set of roles are provided for each group, and a new spontaneously improvised scene enacted. As noted in previous sections, it helps to begin with simple, fun, and positive prompts/roles before moving into more difficult prompts, and ending with positive, future-oriented content. The following roles were offered to participants:

First Scene

Role 1: Someone considering social work school.
Role 2: MSW student offering insight into benefits/difficulties of being an MSW student.

Second Scene

Role 1: Social worker taking the position that race has more impact on one's life than class.
Role 2: Social worker taking the position that class has more impact on one's life than race.

Third Scene

Role 1: MSW student advocating for new anti-racist policies on campus.
Role 2: Dean of a social work school.

Fourth Scene

Role 1: Group therapy client who unknowingly said something offensive regarding race.
Role 2: Social worker leading the group addressing the accidental microaggression.

Fifth Scene

Role 1: MSW student with newfound commitment to address racism in everyday life.
Role 2: Student's intoxicated uncle at a family party making a racist comment.

Sixth Scene

Role 1: African-American client who feels hurt or frustrated by something insensitive their therapist said in previous session.
Role 2: Clinical social worker making amends and being accountable for their microaggression in previous session.

Seventh Scene

Role 1: NASW award recipient for anti-racist work congratulating another award winner.
Role 2: NASW award recipient for anti-racist work congratulating another award winner.

The scenes started with roles that each student would be familiar with to help with the warming up process and establish a sense of connection, playfulness, and safety with the role-playing exercise. Then, we moved into an intellectually based role-play arguing an opinion related to the content of the racism class. Next, students engaged in a series of role-plays focused on responding to microaggressions or advocating for anti-racist policies in situations related to their experience as students beginning to work in the field. In addition to rotating partners with each scene, it is important to note that the nature of the roles was intentionally switched with each emotionally charged prompt. For example, in scene three, group one played the role of a student advocating for anti-racism policies, while group two played the role of the social work school's dean. In the following scene, the roles were reversed in a sense as group two then played the role of a social worker addressing a microaggression, while group one played the role of a client. The final scene offers a chance for participants to end on a positive note and through the roles, recognize each other for their willingness to engage in the difficult and often uncomfortable process of learning to address racism in everyday life.

While it helps to prepare a list of roles and scenes prior to facilitating this process, it is also important for the facilitator to maintain awareness and attunement of how the group is experiencing the scenes and their level of spontaneity. A less warmed up and less spontaneous group might need more prompts that are simple and easy before offering more emotionally difficult prompts. If presented with this situation, the facilitator could offer another prompt that is less emotionally charged, or roles that are more fantasy-based. For example, if the group depicted above was lacking in their warm-up, the following roles could have been proposed to cultivate more playfulness and aesthetic distance:

Role 1: Draco Malfoy from the Harry Potter series arguing that only "pure bloods" should be admitted to Hogwarts School for Witchcraft & Wizardry.
Role 2: Harry Potter advocating that the admissions process should be open to all regardless of their ancestry.

This scene would have moved the process into fantasy roles that many students would be familiar with while keeping the content of the dialogue and role dynamics congruent with the topic of student advocates addressing racism. Because the roles are fantasy-based, it would have reduced anxiety for students while increasing spontaneity and playfulness.

After the session, participants de-role, return to their seats, and the sharing phase of the group begins. Students are prompted to share what it was like for them to participate in the series of role-plays, including what was difficult and what was helpful. Multiple students in this session commented on how some of the role-plays were uncomfortable but challenged them to grow personally and professionally. Some commented that they found the regular discussion about racism limiting compared to the sociodramatic role-plays which helped them to operationalize their intellectual learning into practical real-world situations. This is a simple experiential teaching structure could be integrated into anti-racism social work courses to enhance the learning experience of students.

19.3.3 Empowering Community Members to Advocate to Funders, Politicians, and Employers

Advocacy, empowerment, and social work are intricately linked (Mackay, 2007). Advocacy is a form of both structural and psychological empowerment that challenges the current distribution of power or resources (Thompson, 2002). "Both the intent and outcome of such advocacy should be to increase the individual's sense of power; help them feel more confident, to become more assertive and gain increased choices" (Brandon, 1995, p. 1). Role training simulations offer participants empowerment through increased sense of personal agency and the ability to advocate for themselves, others, and their communities. The use of role-play simulations to teach advocacy skills has been highlighted in multiple contexts and with multiple populations (Burns, 1995; Gillespie, Brown, Grubb, Shay, & Montoya, 2015; Lopez, 2016; Ruyters, Douglas, Law, & Siew, 2011; Sievert, Cuvo, & Davis, 1988). Following are three examples of role training advocacy skills in community social work contexts.

Advocating for policy change to benefit communities. Role training exercises are used regularly by community organizers and social workers to provide role training experiences for participants warming up to advocate for funding or policy change from those with financial or political power. The previous subsection describing MSW students responding to microaggressions included a depiction of this in scene three which positions participants in the roles of a university dean and a student advocating for anti-racist policy changes. This same structure can be used to create opportunities for participants to practice advocating to funders, legislators, school board members, or any other person in power. The structure can simply be modified to fit the issues and political actors related to the community at hand. Participation in role training for advocacy to funders or politicians offers individuals a chance to practice their scripts, learn by observing other's enactments, and develop confidence with their advocacy skills.

Advocating to insurance companies. With the rise of managed care, social workers find themselves regularly advocating for clients to insurance companies to cover medical and mental health services. While the previous role training descriptions did not depict the use of role reversal, the development of advocacy skills with insurance companies can be enhanced through role reversal. The following vignette comes from an ongoing educational group of social workers working in inpatient addiction treatment.

One social worker begins to express their frustration and anger toward insurance companies for unjustly refusing to authorize more days in treatment for his clients. The other participants begin to empathize and share their own irritation at insurance providers. Noticing the group's organic warm-up, the facilitator seizes the opportunity to move the group into a role training enactment with the goals of expressing frustrations, increasing insight, and improving advocacy skills. The facilitator invites the social worker who raised the topic to openly express his anger and frustration to an empty chair representing the insurance company. Already warmed up, he begins to angrily speak to the insurance company in the empty chair. Other participants are invited to offer doubling statements, while channeling their own frustrations. After the anger catharses began to subside, the facilitator instructs the protagonist to role reverse with a case manager from the insurance company. The director then begins to interview the insurance case manager inquiring about their ability to authorize more time for treatment. In the process, it becomes apparent that the case manager of the insurance company desires to authorize time in treatment for patients but can only do so when medical necessity has been demonstrated through adequate documentation by the social worker. The facilitator moves the session toward closure and de-roling, after which a dialogue emerges between participants about best practices for documenting and articulating medical criteria to insurance providers. At the completion of the session, the social work participants expressed their newfound insights into how to advocate to their clients' insurance companies with increased knowledge, sophistication, and confidence. A new paradigm emerges—instead of feeling like they are working against the case manager from the insurance company, they see an opportunity to work together with the case manager to help the mutual client.

Learning to advocate for self. While social workers develop professional skills for advocating for others, we sometimes have trouble advocating for ourselves. Social workers are underpaid compared to their counterparts with the same educational level in other helping professions (Hughes, Kim, & Twill, 2018; Wright, 2010). Numerous researchers have written about social workers lack of self-advocacy when it comes to their own salary negotiations (Schweitzer, Chianello, & Kothari, 2013; Wermeling & Smith, 2009). A large disparity ($11,000 difference between median salaries) exists between salaries of men and women social workers (NASW, 2010), though studies have also uncovered that men are four times more likely to ask for salary increases than women (Babcock & Laschever, 2009). Role training for salary negotiations and increased financial compensation offers an avenue for empowering social workers to advocate for themselves.

Similar to the previous example, this vignette describes the use of role reversal in a role training enactment to cultivate action insights. The role reversal allows participants to step into the shoes of the other and expand their sense of the other person's needs, wants, or goals in the encounter. The situation describes the use of role-playing techniques to help social workers practice advocating for self at a contract or salary negotiation. Participants are invited to choose a real or imagined situation to practice advocating for themselves. After choosing another group member to play the role of their supervisor, they are invited to begin the dialogue. Participants are instructed to role reverse into the role of their supervisor, hearing their argument replayed through the eyes of the other. After considering the supervisor's organizational limitations and needs, a response is provided, and the dialogue continues with back and forth role reversals. This action vignette offers social workers the chance to step into the shoes of their supervisor to consider the perspective of the other and to develop insight into what the organization may need to hear in order to initiate a salary increase. While participants appeared more focused on conveying the value they offer to their clients initially, the action insights of the role-play helped them consider and articulate the value they offer the organization, especially in terms of the financial bottom line. This example comes from the author's personal experience working with social work supervisor and psychodramatist, David Moran, LCSW, CADC, TEP.

19.4   Conclusion

The aforementioned examples demonstrate the implementation of sociodrama role-plays focused on intergroup relations and role training for community empowerment. Drama and theater offer community social workers useful tools for sessions focused on social activism and social change. Through simulated role-plays, a social worker facilitating community sessions can offer engaging structures with proven effectiveness at teaching skills for communication, behavioral rehearsals, social skills, and advocacy. The use of drama and theater in community life can be traced back to the origins of the social work field and various ancient cultures. The application of Moreno's methods in community work positions community members as therapeutic and educational agents for each other while bringing the content of the session to life in an embodied process. This is congruent with Moreno's early visions of Sociatry, the Theater of Spontaneity, a therapeutic society, and group psychotherapy. This author joins others who advocate for sociodrama as the most appropriate Morenean method for community work due to its educational power.

References

Aristotle. (1951). *Poetics* (S. H. Butcher, Trans.). Mineola, NY: Dover Publications.

Babcock, L., & Laschever, S. (2009). *Women don't ask: Negotiation and the gender divide.* Princeton University Press.

Bandy, C., Buchanan, D. R., & Pinto, C. (1986). Police performance in resolving family disputes: Evaluating the effectiveness of a training program. *Psychological Reports, 58,* 743–756.

Blatner, A. (2000). *Foundations of psychodrama: History, theory, and practice* (4th ed.). New York City: Springer Publishing Company.

Bonfine, N., Ritter, C., & Munetz, M. R. (2014). Police officer perceptions of the impact of crisis intervention team (CIT) programs. *International Journal of Law and Psychiatry, 37*(4), 341–350.

Brandon, D. (1995). Peer support and advocacy: International comparisons and developments. In R. Jack (Ed.), *Empowerment in community care* (pp. 108–133). Boston: Springer.

Buchanan, D. R., & Hankins, J. M. (1983). Family disturbance intervention program. *FBI Law Enforcement Bulletin, 52,* 10.

Buchanan, D. R., & Hankins, J. (1987). Introduction. In D. R. Buchanan & J. Hankins (Eds.), *The badge and the battered: A family crisis intervention training manual for law enforcement agencies.* Washington, DC: Government of the District of Colombia.

Buchanan, D. R., & Perry, P. A. (1985). Attitudes of police recruits towards domestic disturbances: An evaluation of amily crisis intervention training. *Journal of Criminal Justice, 13,* 561–572.

Buchanan, D. R., & Swink, D. F. (2017). Golden age of psychodrama at Saint Elizabeths hospital (1939–2004). *The Journal of Psychodrama, Sociometry, and Group Psychotherapy, 65*(1), 9–32.

Burns, R. P. (1995). Teaching the basic ethics class through simulation: The Northwestern program in advocacy and professionalism. *Law and Contemporary Problems, 58*(3/4), 37–50.

Cahill, H. (2015). Rethinking role-play for health and wellbeing: Creating a pedagogy of possibility. In K. Wright & J. McLeod (Eds.), *Rethinking youth wellbeing* (pp. 127–142). Singapore: Springer.

Callahan, M. L. (1987). The evolution of a program: The DC metropolitan police family crisis intervention training project. In D. R. Buchanan & J. Hankins (Eds.), *The badge and the battered: A family crisis intervention training manual for law enforcement agencies* (pp. 3–10). Washington, DC: Government of the District of Colombia.

Center for Court Innovation. (2015). *Guide for improving relationships and public safety through engagement and conversation: Police-youth dialogues toolkit.* Washington, DC: Office of Community Oriented Policing Services.

Chasnoff, P. (1987). Curriculum. In D. R. Buchanan & J. Hankins (Eds.), *The badge and the battered: A family crisis intervention training manual for law enforcement agencies* (pp. 19–46). Washington, DC: Government of the District of Colombia.

Colvin, A. D., Saleh, M., Ricks, N., & Rosa-Davila, E. (2020). Using simulated instruction to prepare students to engage in culturally competent practice. *Journal of Social Work in the Global Community, 5*(1), 1.

Cossa, M. (2006). *Rebels with a cause: Working with adolescents using action techniques.* Jessica Kingsley Publishers.

Delgado, R., & Stefancic, J. (2017). *Critical race theory: An introduction* (Vol. 20). New York: NYU Press.

Freedley, G., & Reeves, J. A. (1964). *A history of the theatre*. New York, NY: Crown Publishers Inc.

Giacomucci, S. (2017). The sociodrama of life or death: Young adults and addiction treatment. *Journal of Psychodrama, Sociometry, and Group Psychotherapy, 65*(1), 137–143. https://doi.org/10.12926/0731-1273-65.1.137.

Gillespie, G. L., Brown, K., Grubb, P., Shay, A., & Montoya, K. (2015). Qualitative evaluation of a role-play bullying simulation. *Journal of Nursing Education and Practice, 5*(7), 73.

Greeb, M. N. (2019). The psychodrama of São Paulo City. In Z. Figusch (Ed.), *From one-to-one psychodrama to large group socio-psychodrama*, (2nd ed., pp. 223–231). UK: lulu.com.

Hankins, J. (1987). Police response to family violence. In D. R. Buchanan & J. Hankins (Eds.), *The badge and the battered: A family crisis intervention training manual for law enforcement agencies* (pp. 1–2). Washington, DC: Government of the District of Colombia.

Hankins, J., & Buchanan, D. R. (1987). Results and conclusions. In D. R. Buchanan & J. Hankins (Eds.), *The badge and the battered: A family crisis intervention training manual for law enforcement agencies* (pp. 51–52). Washington, DC: Governemnt of the District of Colombia.

Hecht, S. (1982). Social and artistic integration: The emergence of hull-house theatre. *Theatre Journal, 34*(2), 172–182.

Hughes, J. C., Kim, H., & Twill, S. E. (2018). Social work educational debt and salary survey: A snapshot from Ohio. *Social Work, 63*(2), 105–114.

Hunter, D., & Lakey, G. (2004). *Opening space for democracy. Training manual for third-party nonviolent intervention*. Philadelphia: Training for Change.

Jemal, A., Urmey, L. S., & Caliste, S. (2020). From sculpting an intervention to healing in action. *Social Work with Groups*. https://doi.org/10.1080/01609513.2020.1757923.

Jennings, S. (Ed.). (2014). *Dramatherapy with children and adolescents*. London: Routledge.

Krameddine, Y., DeMarco, D., Hassel, R., & Silverstone, P. H. (2013). A novel training program for police officers that improves interactions with mentally ill individuals and is cost-effective. *Frontiers in Psychiatry, 4*, 9.

Krameddine, Y. I., & Silverstone, P. H. (2015). How to improve interactions between police and the mentally ill. *Frontiers in Psychiatry, 5*, 186.

Leahy, R. A. (2008). *The theatre as an examination of power: Combining political theory and theatre history* (Honors theses, 1576). Retrieved May 7th, 2020 from https://digitalworks.union.edu/theses/1576.

Lee, E. K. O., Blythe, B., & Goforth, K. (2009). Teaching note: Can you call it racism? An educational case study and role-play approach. *Journal of Social Work Education, 45*(1), 123–130.

Lee, J. S. (2018). The use of psychodrama and sociodrama in barbershops. *The Journal of Psychodrama, Sociometry, and Group Psychotherapy, 66*(1), 141–146.

Lopez, N. J. (2016). *Effects of a self-advocacy intervention on the ability of high school students with high incidence disabilities to advocate for academic accommodations* (Theses and dissertations, 582). Retrieved from https://ir.library.illinoisstate.edu/cgi/viewcontent.cgi?article=1582&context=etd

Mackay, R. (2007). Empowerment and advocacy. In J. Lishman (Ed.), *Handbook for practice learning in social work and social care* (2nd ed., pp. 269–284). London: Jessica Kingsley Publishers.

Maier, H. W. (2002). Role-playing: Structures and educational objectives. *The International Child and Youth Care Network*, 36.

McCammon, L. A. (2007). Research on drama and theater for social change. In L. Bresler (Ed.), *International handbook of research in arts education* (pp. 945–964). Rotterdam: Springer.

Moreno, J. D. (2014). *Impromptu Man: J. L. Moreno and the origins of psychodrama, encounter culture, and the social network*. New York, NY: Bellevue Literary Press.

Moreno, J. L. (1940). Mental catharsis and the psychodrama. *Sociometry, 3*, 209–244.

Moreno, J. L. (1943). The concept of sociodrama. *Sociometry, 6*(4), 434–449.

Moreno, J. L. (1972). *Psychodrama* (Vol. 1, 4th ed.). New York: Beacon House.

Moreno, J. L. (2019). In E. Schreiber, S. Kelley, & S. Giacomucci, (Eds.), *The autobiography of a genius*. United Kingdom: North West Psychodrama Association.

National Association of Social Workers. (2010). *2009 compensation and benefits study: Summary of key compensation findings*. Washington, DC: NASW.

Oliveira, E. C. S., & Araújo, M. F. (2012). Aproximações do teatro do oprimido com a Psicologia e o Psicodrama. *Psicologia: Ciencia e Profissao, 32*(2), 340–355.

Pope, M., Pangelinan, J. S., & Coker, A. D. (Eds.). (2011). *Experiential activities for teaching multicultural competence in counseling*. Alexandria, VA: American Counseling Association.

Reuland, M. M., & Schwarzfeld, M. (2008). *Improving responses to people with mental illnesses: Strategies for effective law enforcement training*. Justice Center, the Council of State Governments.

Ruyters, M., Douglas, K., & Law, S. F. (2011). Blended learning using role-plays, wikis and blogs. *Journal of Learning Design, 4*(4), 45–55.

Schreiber, J. C., & Minarik, J. D. (2018). Simulated clients in a group practice course: Engaging facilitation and embodying diversity. *Journal of Social Work Education, 54*(2), 310–323.

Schweitzer, D., Chianello, T., & Kothari, B. (2013). Compensation in social work: Critical for satisfaction and a sustainable profession. *Administration in Social Work, 37*(2), 147–157.

Schlossman, D. A. (2002). *Actors and activists: Politics, performance, and exchange among social worlds*. Psychology Press.

Shank, T. (1982). Theatre of social change. In T. Shank (Ed.), *American alternative theatre* (pp. 50–90). London: Macmillan Modern Dramatists. Palgrave.

Sievert, A. L., Cuvo, A. J., & Davis, P. K. (1988). Training self-advocacy skills to adults with mild handicaps. *Journal of Applied Behavior Analysis, 21*(3), 299–309.

Silverstone, P. H., Krameddine, Y. I., DeMarco, D., & Hassel, R. (2013). A novel approach to training police officers to interact with individuals who may have a psychiatric disorder. *Journal of the American Academy of Psychiatry and the Law Online, 41*(3), 344–355.

Sternberg, P., & Garcia, A. (2000). *Sociodrama: Who's in your shoes?* (2nd ed.). Westport, CT: Praeger Publishers.

Thompson, N. (2002). Social work with adults. In R. Adams, L. Dominelli, & M. Payne (Eds.), *Social work: Themes, issues, and critical debates* (2nd ed., pp. 287–307). Basingstoke: Palgrave Macmillan.

Tipler, K., & Gates, A. B. (2019). Rights education without rights? Rights workshops and undocumented immigrants in the US. *Journal of Ethnic and Migration Studies*, 1–17.

Watson, A. C., Morabito, M. S., Draine, J., & Ottati, V. (2008). Improving police response to persons with mental illness: A multi-level conceptualization of CIT. *International Journal of Law and Psychiatry, 31*(4), 359–368.

Weber, A. M., & Haen, C. (Eds.). (2005). *Clinical applications of drama therapy in child and adolescent treatment*. New York: Brunner-Routledge.

Wermeling, L., & Smith, J. (2009). Retention is not an abstract notion: The effect of wages and caretaking. *Journal of Social Service Research, 35*(4), 380–388.

Wright, G. (2010). *NASW's new study provides better information on social work salaries*. Retrieved from https://www.socialworkers.org/News/News-Releases/ID/356/NASWs-New-Study-Provides-Better-Information-on-Social-Work-Salaries.

Chapter 20
Sociometry, Psychodrama, and Experiential Teaching in Social Work Education and Supervision

Abstract This chapter is devoted to the use of Moreno's methods within education and supervision contexts to prepare the next generation of competent social work practitioners. The history and current state of Moreno's methods in US and international academia is outlined, along with limitations to embedding psychodrama within university settings. Social work education's history of experiential education is described with its relevance to sociometry and psychodrama as experiential teaching tools. Research on the effectiveness of experiential teaching and role-play in the classroom is offered and the importance of supervision in social work and psychodrama is highlighted. Examples and structured prompts are provided with a focus on using experiential sociometry processes (spectrograms, locograms, floor checks, step-in sociometry, hands-on-shoulder sociograms, and the circle of strengths) to enhance the learning experience of social work students, interns, and supervisees in various settings. Vignettes are also included which depict the use of written sociometric processes and psychodramatic role-plays within supervision or mentorship contexts.

Keywords Social work education · Social work supervision · Experiential teaching · Experiential education · Teaching psychodrama

The use of Moreno's methods in education and supervision offers facilitators opportunities to contribute in unique ways to the emergence of the next generation of social workers. Little has been written about the use of Moreno's methods in social work education or supervision as either content or process. This chapter will introduce the state of psychodrama in academia while focusing primarily on the use of sociometry, psychodrama, and sociodrama as teaching and supervisory *processes* within social work education and supervision. The text below includes examples of using Moreno's methods with social workers in educational contexts and supervision groups. The application of Moreno's experiential methods within various social work contexts offers engaging opportunities to nurture the next generation of social workers.

S. Giacomucci, *Social Work, Sociometry, and Psychodrama*, Psychodrama in Counselling, Coaching and Education 1,
https://doi.org/10.1007/978-981-33-6342-7_20

20.1 Moreno's Methods in US and International Academic Contexts

J. L. Moreno introduced psychodrama courses into the US higher education system beginning in 1937 at Columbia University and the New School for Social Research (Moreno, 1955). He later became an adjunct professor in the department of sociology at NYU from 1952 to 1966 (Marineau, 2014). "It was in the year 1923 when I set forth the dictum: 'Spontaneity training is to be the main subject in the school of the future'" (1946, p. 130). Moreno even proposed a "Spontaneity Theory of Learning" in the 1949 book titled *Psychodrama and Sociodrama in American Education.* His learning theory challenged the education focus on content learning by proposing "act learning." He writes that we learn developmentally through spontaneous action, and that we should train students to act with spontaneity and creativity (responding adequately/creatively) rather than to memorize content or mimic role behaviors (1949). These ideas are also reflected in Paulo Freire's 1974 *Education for Critical Consciousness*—"Acquiring literacy does not involve memorizing sentences, words, or syllables—lifeless objects unconnected to an existential universe—but rather an attitude of creation and re-creation, a self-transformation producing a stance of intervention in one's context" (2013, p. 45). Just as Moreno's theory of group psychotherapy elevated patients to the status of therapeutic agent, his theory of education elevates students to the role of learner–teacher (Giacomucci, 2019b).

At the time of this writing, this author was unable to locate a single active psychodrama degree program or concentration in the USA. Zerka Moreno's (2012b, p. 5) statement in the *Psychodrama Network News* rings true today: "there are master's tracks in a number of universities abroad. Why not in our country?" While sociometry, psychodrama, and experiential group therapies have very limited influence within academia in the USA, they are widespread in international institutes of higher education (Propper, 2003). There are multiple graduate degree programs around the world that not only include an elective on sociometry, psychodrama, and group psychotherapy—but award an entire master's degree in it. Nevertheless, there are a handful of graduate programs (psychology, counseling, education, or drama therapy) that offer an elective course on psychodrama, including Bryn Mawr College, Yeshiva University, West Chester University, Lesley University, New York University, Lewis and Clark College, Russell Sage College, Kansas State University, Antioch University, California Institute for Integral Studies (CIIS), among others. Though psychodrama is rarely taught in US universities, it is noted by Blatner and Blatner (1997), that "a derivative of Moreno's psychodrama, role-playing is widely used in education from preschool to professional graduate programs" (p. 124).

In an attempt to promote the integration of psychodrama into university programs, this author published a call to action in the Fall 2019 issue of the ASGPP Psychodrama Newsletter that advocated for increasing psychodrama's presence in academia while listing some of the reasons for the absence of Moreno's methods in academia as being related to the emergence of evidence-based practice, psychodrama's limited research base, the decline in group work education in degree programs, individualism, the dominance of the medical model, and a demonstrated lack of professionalism from psychodrama trainers beginning with Moreno himself (Giacomucci, 2019a).

20.1.1 Psychodrama and Drama Therapy in Academia

Although psychodrama has been unsuccessful thus far in securely establishing itself within US academic institutions, there are currently five accredited drama therapy programs in North America—all with licensure paths in their respective states. These include New York University, Lesley University, Concordia University (Canada), Antioch University, and California Institute of Integral Studies (CIIS). Many drama therapists refer to J. L. Moreno as "the first drama therapist" due to his use of the theater as a therapeutic modality (Brooke, 2006, p. 218). Johnson and Emunah's historical presentation of drama therapy suggests that the field emerged to fill the gap left by psychodrama's movement away from theater, toward clinical mental health practice (2009). The process of founding the North American Drama Therapy Association (NADTA) in 1979 included multiple psychodramatists, among others from education, psychology, and theater. Within two years of its foundation, there were two established drama therapy master's programs—one in California and one in New York. Johnson and Emunah comment that "the future of the field was dependent upon these two programs, and others to be established" (2009, p. 9).

Landy (2017) highlights that while psychodrama developed from Moreno's critique of psychoanalysis and traditional theater, drama therapy recognizes psychoanalysis and traditional theater as two of its major roots. Moreno may have marginalized his method by challenging the already established fields of theater and psychoanalysis which had been accepted within academia (Gershoni, 2009; Moreno, 2011, 2012a; Nicholas, 2017). This may be a significant lesson available to psychodramatists in the history of drama therapy's path toward recognition as a profession and establishment in university settings.

20.1.2 Limitations to Psychodrama in the Classroom

There are, of course, limitations to teaching psychodrama in the context of a university classroom setting (Giacomucci, 2019b). A major limitation to providing psychodrama in the classroom is that there are only about 200 certified Trainer, Educator, Practitioners (TEP)s through the American Board of Examiners and less than 400 certified practitioners (including the TEPs) in the USA. Considering the limited number of certified psychodramatists, it may be difficult for universities to find professors knowledgeable and experienced enough to teach a full psychodrama course.

The nature of psychodrama training is that it is almost entirely experiential; it is taught and learned in action. This emphasis on experiential learning defies the cultural conserve in US education, though some programs are increasingly utilizing experiential learning. Psychodrama is a powerful tool, which can create opportunity for incredible healing but also has a potential to harm. Adequate training in psychodrama requires experience working at levels of emotional depth that could be uncomfortable to many academics and students in a university setting, while also placing higher emotional demands on students than their other courses. Furthermore, asking students to access these depths of vulnerability in a classroom is nontraditional and may impact their ability to be present in other classes throughout the day. These limitations suggest that a course teaching sociometry and psychodrama would be insufficient in itself in terms of preparing students to competently practice psychodrama.

The balance between left-brain cognitive learning and right-brain emotional learning requires delicacy and containment in both teaching preparation and implementation. This dual focus challenges students to bring both their professional selves and their personal selves to the classroom. This experience can be utilized by the professor as an opportunity to teach appropriate boundaries and personal disclosures for social workers. It is important that the class session not become a therapy group, but that the focus remains on teaching. One creative way of maneuvering this process might be to orient the experiential processes toward emotional work needed to become a competent social worker. A common theme in most social work courses is students' insecurities when sharing about their field placement. A psychodrama course could provide students with an opportunity to work out their field placement insecurities through psychodrama while also learning the psychodramatic process.

A best practices document for teaching psychodrama in academic contexts has been developed by this author and ASGPP's Professional Liaison Committee which outlines the further limitations and recommendations for adapting psychodrama for university settings (Giacomucci, 2020b). A psychodrama course can provide students with a comprehensive theoretical understanding of J. L. Moreno's philosophical system, an experiential understanding of sociometry, an introduction to psychodramatic techniques, and training in experiential group therapy. After completion of a course, students would be able to competently use multiple pen-to-paper and experiential sociometric tools, psychodramatic techniques, multiple experiential sociometry processes, and a variety of group warm-up exercises. Nevertheless, after completing a single semester course, students would not be prepared to direct a full psychodrama.

The ABE psychodrama certification process of 780 h is more classroom hours than the entirety of most graduate degrees. The completion of a course or program concentration in psychodrama would propel a student toward ABE certification in that they had obtained a wealth of hours in their educational program (for more info, visit www.psychodramacertification.org). The 45 h of classroom instruction from a 3 credit course could be credited toward the 90 h required for certification as an experiential therapist (CET) through the International Society of Experiential Professionals (ISEP), which puts students halfway to certification (for more info, visit www.ExperientialProfessionals.com).

20.2 Experiential Teaching, Moreno's Methods, and Social Work Education

J. L. Moreno states that in discerning between immigrating from Vienna to either the USA or Russia, he chose "the land of Dewey" and was attracted to Dewey's theory of constructivism—"knowing by doing" (Oudijk, 2007) and advocating for reforms in the educational system (Drakulić, 2014). John Dewey, regarded by many as the father of experiential education, in 1916 states, "give the pupils something to do, not something to learn; and the doing is of such a nature as to demand thinking; learning naturally results" (p. 191). Psychodrama offers a potent form of experiential learning that has been used in social work education only minimally. As early as 1944, a social worker, Mary Bosworth Treudley, had advocated for the use of psychodramatic role-plays in social work education and supervision to create opportunities for students to directly observe case scenarios. Around the same time, St. Elizabeths Hospital was using psychodrama to train social work, psychology, and nursing interns on communication skills with psychiatric patients (Buchanan & Swink, 2017). The *Journal of Teaching in Social Work* offers numerous articles that demonstrate that the experiential teaching process has a positive effect on learning outcomes (Banach, Foden, & Carter, 2018; Dalton & Kuhn, 1998; Fleischer, 2018; Foels & Bethel, 2018; Kaye & Fortune, 2001; Kramer & Wrenn, 1994; McKinney, O'Connor, & Pruitt, 2018; Powell & Causby, 1994; Quinn, Jacobsen, & LaBarber, 1992; Whebi, 2011; Whiteman & Nielson, 1990). While others have noted over the past 50 years that group work courses in social work education have gradually shifted away from strictly didactic teaching methods, toward experiential teaching (Euster, 1979; Gutman & Shennar-Golan, 2012; Stozier, 1997; Warkentin, 2017; Zastrow, 2001).

Many social work educators argue that social work education should focus more on the process of teaching than the content of teaching (Fox, 2013; Gitterman, 2004; Kolb, 2014; Rogers, 1961; Schön, 1987; Shulman, 1987). In social work education, the curriculum *content* traditionally has been overemphasized with much less attention given to the *process* of how students learn (Gitterman, 2004). In a practice profession such as social work, "the process of teaching and the content of the subject matter should go hand in hand" (Fox, 2013, p. xi). Kolb, a strong advocate of experiential learning, states that "the experiential learning model pursues a framework for examining and strengthening the critical linkages among education, work, and personal development" (1984, p. 4). While Keeton and Tate emphasize experiential learning in that:

> …the learning is directly in touch with the realities being studied…. It involves direct encounter with the phenomenon being studied rather than merely thinking about the encounter or only considering the possibility of doing something with it. (1978, p. 2)

Rogers (1961) highlights two types of learning—cognitive learning and experiential learning. He advocates for experiential learning by highlighting how it is more meaningful and relevant to the learner because it completely involves the student and integrates the instructional process with the course objectives. The experiential learning process includes the cycle of moving an abstract concept to concrete experience, personal reflection, and student experimentation (Georgiou, Zahn, & Meira, 2008; Koob & Funk, 2002; McCarthy, 2010). Wehbi offers her reflections on the mechanisms of experiential teaching:

> experiential teaching methods within the classroom may provide students with the opportunity to experience specific ways of being and doing, to model to one another skills and attitudes they could carry into practice, and to extend classroom activities outside the class setting. (Wehbi, 2011, p. 502)

Considering that the classroom is at its foundation a group (Shulman, 1987), and that the dynamics within the group experience are present and acted out (it would be impossible for it to be otherwise), it is fitting to teach group work in a group setting using experiential teaching (Fleischer, 2018). Kolb and Kolb highlight that "the magic of experiential learning lies in the unique relationship that is created between teacher, learner, and the subject matter under study" (2017, p. xxiv). The application of experiential teaching in the instruction of group work introduces students to the magic of these processes.

20.2.1 Experiential Learning and Role-Play in the Classroom

Research has demonstrated the efficacy of simulated sessions (Bogo, Rawlings, Katz, & Logie, 2014; Lu et al., 2011; Mooradian, 2007, 2008; Rawlings, 2012) and role-plays (Macgowan & Vakharia, 2012; McGovern & Harmsworth, 2010; Shera, Muskat, Delay, Quinn, & Tufford, 2013) for clinical skills training. Williams (1995) highlights that educational simulations often are designed by the facilitator to arrive at an already known learning objective while psychodramatic or sociodramatic role-plays are spontaneous enactments. Experiential learning is widely regarded as effective for teaching students in multiculturalism courses (Arthur & Achenbach, 2002) and for increasing competencies around diversity and working with oppressed groups (Schreiber & Minarik, 2018). Additionally, many studies have demonstrated that experiential learning is essential for students to translate theory into practice and understand group dynamics (Furman et al., 2009; Ieva et al., 2009; Macgowan & Vakharia, 2012; Swiller, 2011; Yalom & Leszcz, 2005).

A 1994 meta-analysis on the retention of knowledge demonstrated no difference in student's forgetfulness of the content, except in comparison to experiential teaching (Semb & Ellis, 1994). Specht and Sandlin's (1991) comparison study on the retention of course content between learning by lecture versus experiential role-plays had similar findings. At the six week follow-up, students who learned the content through lecture were showing a decline in problem solving by 54% and an 18% drop in concept recognition while the students who learned through experiential role-plays showed only a 13% drop in problem solving and did not demonstrate any decline in concept recognition (Specht & Sandlin, 1991).

Through the use of role-play in the classroom, the learning experience moves beyond a cognitive exercise to include skill development (Carey, 2016; Konopik & Cheung, 2013; Warkentin, 2017). This offers the student "an integrative approach to learning that balances feeling, thinking, acting and reflecting" (Kolb & Kolb, 2005, p. 200). Dennison (2005), Macgowan & Vakharia (2012), and Shera et al. (2013) found that students' participation in role-plays in the classroom contributed more than anything else to their development of knowledge and skill in group work. Warkentin describes the use of using role-playing to simulate a treatment group in the social group work classroom, indicating it as "one of the more significant learning activities for students" (2017, p. 237). The role-play is teaching technique that can be adapted for use with nearly any topic, skills training, or profession. Providing educators with a basic understanding of Moreno's phases of an enactment (warm-up, enactment, sharing) would greatly increase the efficacy of role-plays in the classroom. It is arguable that most role-plays in the classroom do not bear fruit because there was not an adequate warm-up to the enactment.

A Brazilian author proposes the use of "educational psychodrama" and highlights is frequent use in Brazil for training medical students through role-playing techniques (Gomes et al. 2006; Liberali & Grosseman, 2015). A team of Spanish researchers positively assessed educational psychodrama as a teaching strategy in university settings (Maya & Maraver, 2020). Sociodrama and psychodrama have been used in higher education to teach social educators (Haas, 1949; Jacobs, 1950; ter Avest, 2017; Veiga, Bertao, & Franco, 2015), lawyers (Cole, 2001), business professionals (Bidart-Novaes, Brunstein, Gil, & Drummond, 2014; Wiener, 1988), medical professionals (Baile & Blatner, 2014; Moreno & Moreno, 1959; Walters & Baile, 2014), nurses (McLaughlin, Freed, & Tadych, 2006; Moreno & Moreno, 1959), and other students (Blatner, 2006; Blatner & Blatner, 1997; Haworth & Vasiljevic, 2012; Michaels & Hatcher, 1972).

In a Sect. 15.1, I suggested sociodrama to be superior to psychodrama as a teaching method in classroom settings. Sternberg and Garcia even describe sociodrama as "a kinesthetic, intuitive, affective, and cognitive educational technique" (2000, p. 4). Brazilian authors Nery and Gisler (2019) describe sociodrama as an experiential education method par excellence. Role-playing can also be useful in the classroom to develop a richer understanding of various content including history, myth, religion, or literature (Haworth & Vasiljevic, 2012; Nolte, 2018).Others have highlighted sociodrama's utility as a therapeutic approach in high school settings (Landis, 2020). Propper (2003) describes using an empty chair process to provide students with an opportunity to psychodramatically encounter figures from history, myth, literature, and religion. This could give new social work students not just an intellectual relationship to major figures in social work history, but also an emotional connection. Imagine first year MSW students engaging in a psychodramatic dialogue with Jane Addams, Mary Richmond, Sigmund Freud, or even Jacob Moreno! Nolte (2018) describes using role-playing in the classroom as follows:

> It is one thing to read about a character's thoughts, words, and actions in a novel; it is different to enact and experience being that character in that character's situation through role-playing. Answering questions from classmates and justifying the character's actions

deepens the experience. Action learning is more natural, and more like everyday learning
from life events, than traditional methods. It is more interesting than being talked to or
engaging in questions and answers. Role-playing results in a more integrated, experienced,
felt understanding of the material. (p. 192)

Beyond teaching sociometry as content, the utilization of sociometry in the education
process offers educators meaningful opportunities to enhance the learning environment. Much has also been written about the utility of sociometry within the classroom as a tool for psychosocial safety, group cohesion, learning needs assessment,
assessment of preference, and training in interpersonal relations (Evans, 1962; Giacomucci, 2018, 2019b; Giacomucci & Skolnik, in-press; Guldner & Stone-Winestock,
1995; Haas, 1949; Haworth & Vasiljevic, 2012; Propper, 2003). Guldner and Stone-Winestock articulate that "the sociometric connections between people, the sociometric structure of groups, and the sociometric status of individuals are significantly
related to learning" (1995, p. 184). An instructor with a basic understanding of
sociometry can create an educational environment more conducive to learning by
conceptualizing learning as a social function (Cozolino, 2014; Jones, 1968; Siegel,
2012).

20.3 Moreno's Methods in Social Work Supervision

The centrality of supervision within the social work field has been established
since the early years of the profession and has been formalized through multiple
avenues including: CSWE standards for accreditation related to field placement
supervision, agency policies, and license requirements (Kadushin & Harkness,
2014; Shulman, 2010b). Supervision in clinical social work has multiple functions including mentoring, education, oversight, management, preventing negative
outcomes, and improving positive outcomes (Kadushin & Karness, 2014; Mor Barak
et al., 2009; Munson, 2012; Shulman, 2010b). Social work supervision, like the social
work profession, emphasizes the importance and centrality of relationships. Parallels
between the social worker–client relationship and the supervisor–supervisee relationship are often highlighted. In social work supervision, the relationship between
supervisor and supervisee is the vehicle for change (Shulman, 2010b). While supervision is a core component of the social work field, the prospect of using psychodrama
for clinical social work supervision has been underutilized and rarely written about
(Ramsauer, 2007).

Pugh remarks that "a central element to social work education is experiential
learning, most exemplified in the signature pedagogy of the field placement" (2014,
pp. 17–18; Kolb, 2014; Raschick, Maypole, & Day, 1998; Sachdev, 1997). From
the perspective of a role theory, the supervised student's field placement is a role-play. The MSW student is receiving supervision, education, and training to competently hold the role of *social worker* (medical, clinical, community, drug & alcohol,
etc.). The role training begins through dynamic doubling and mirroring between
student, educator, and supervisor until the student begins to develop competencies

and confidence in the role. At this point, they have shifted from the role training into role-playing phase of role-development.

Cheung, Alzate, and Nguyen (2012) offer a case study highlighting the role training of an MSW student completing a psychodrama internship resulting in an increase in student confidence and clinical skills. According to a study by Yalom and his colleagues, therapists facilitating group therapy without supervision and training were actually found to be less skilled at a six month assessment—presumably because "original errors may be reinforced by simple repetition" (Ebersole, Leiderman, & Yalom, 1969; Yalom & Leszcz, 2005, p. 549).

The 1969 CSWE curriculum change toward a more generalist practice approach significantly impacted the number of group work courses and concentrations for the previous generation of social work students, who are now the current generation of clinical social work educators, field instructors, and field placement supervisors (Carey, 2016). Lack of qualified social work field placement supervisors who have group work training is a serious concern (Carey, 2016; Goodman & Munoz, 2004; Knight, 2017; LaRocque, 2017; Tully, 2015). How can field instructors without group therapy training provide students with group therapy training? Furthermore, the number of clinical social workers and field educators with psychodrama training is significantly lower. In 2011, 11% of ABE certified psychodramatists held social work credentials (ABESPGP, 2011, as cited in Konopik & Cheung, 2013). As of 2020, the American Board of Examiners in Sociometry, Psychodrama, and Group Psychotherapy website includes 113 certified practitioners who also have social work degrees which is just under 30% of all ABE certified psychodramatists. This is a significant increase in social workers obtaining psychodrama certification in the past decade. The Bureau of Labor Statistic's estimates that in 2016, there were a total of 682,100 social workers in the USA (BLS, 2018). Considering these figures, the percentage of social workers that are also ABE psychodrama certified is as low as 0.017%. The richness of sociometry and psychodrama has only been utilized minimally by social workers, nevertheless it offers powerful group tools for social work facilitators.

When discussing the role of supervisor, is also helpful to consider the sub-roles within the role of supervisor. Using role theory to dissect the functions of the supervisor role is congruent with psychodrama's role theory and parallels Kellermann's model of the roles of psychodrama director (1992). Various conceptualizations of the sub-roles of supervisor exist in the literature (Bernard, 1979; Center for Substance Abuse Treatment, 2009; Daniel, 2012; Hawkins & Shohet, 2012; Williams, 1995); however, this writer finds the following to be simplest:

Educator—addresses learning needs of supervisee, identifies clinical competencies while offering suggestions for increasing effectiveness, provides resources, and focuses on skills training and continuing education.

Supporter—provides validation, inspiration, and offers emotional support to the supervisee related to job stress, countertransference, self-exploration, and personal issues as they impact professional work.

Fig. 20.1 Three roles of supervisor

Manager—assesses supervisee's performance, productivity, and functioning within code of ethics and organizational policies while supporting proper completion of documentation and professional responsibilities.

A competent supervisor integrates these three sub-roles (see Fig. 20.1) into their relationship with supervisees, effectively providing interpersonal support, education for increased competencies, and logistical management to help supervisees operate within organizational systems and professional code of ethics. This conceptualization of the sub-roles of supervisor can be useful for the training of new supervisors and assessing the balance of the supervisory relationship.

20.3.1 Importance of Psychodrama Supervision

One of the primary purposes of supervision could be described as helping the supervisee develop new response to old situations and adequate responses to novel situations in their work (Chesner, 2008). This is precisely Moreno's definition of spontaneity—which highlights the philosophical importance of spontaneity and supervision in psychodrama. The emphasis on spontaneity in psychodrama supervision is useful for helping supervisees get unstuck and develop new creative ways of working with their clients. The centrality of supervision in psychodrama is also evidenced in the stringent supervision requirements in both the psychodrama practitioner and trainer certifications in the USA and internationally (Krall, Fürst, & Fontaine, 2012). Psychodrama's practitioner certification (CP) requires at least a year-long supervised practicum while the trainer credential (TEP) requires a minimum of three years of supervised training while receiving regular supervision. As noted at various points in this book, psychodrama is a powerful tool that can create much harm when used inappropriately—because of this, supervision is especially important for competent and ethical practice.

Though supervision is a core component of the psychodrama training process, little has been written about it and almost no research is available on it (Krall, 2012; Tabib, 2017). Daniel (2012) notes that psychodrama training is focused on content, theory, philosophy, concepts, and techniques, while psychodrama supervision is more oriented on developing professional identity and competence in practice. Dudler and Weiß (2012) highlight the essential role of psychodrama supervision in helping the psychodramatist integrate their new professional identity while also adapting their psychodrama learning to fit their unique practice environment. Many have suggested that skills and knowledge related to clinical work are also applicable skills and knowledge for the supervisor's practice—especially emphasis on the relationship (in this case between supervisee and supervisor) and attention to the phases of a session (Krall & Fürst, 2012).

Though traditional case presentations in supervision are done verbally, psychodrama allows for the case presentation process to become experiential through role-playing. Using psychodramatic role-playing or sculpting to re-enact supervisee's experiences with clients creates "an environment similar to the one-way mirror setting, except we are in the room with the supervisee—observing, interacting, and co-creating" (Ochs & Webster, 2017, p. 112). Psychodrama role-plays in supervision allow for the exploration of a supervisee–client relationship embodied in action rather than through the recounting of memories from the supervisee (Ochs & Webster, 2017). In this process of re-enacting the supervisee's experience with their client, there are opportunities for reflection, processing, and experiential practice of new interventions (Apter, 2012). In psychodrama supervision, the process and content of supervision are integrated (Tabib, 2017). In a similar way, psychodrama processes can be used within the social work supervision context (Ochs, 2020). Furthermore, Gimenez Hinkle (2008) and Williams (1988, 1995) highlight the utility of using psychodrama in supervision to work through parallel processes and countertransference issues which will be depicted in a later vignette (see Sect. 20.5).

20.3.2 Written Sociometric and Psychodramatic Tools in Individual Social Work Supervision

The quality of individual social work supervision can be enhanced with an integration of simple written sociometric and psychodramatic tools that promote self-reflection, future goal setting, and action insight. Some of these written tools include the role atom, social atom, sociogram, psychodramatic timelines, psychodramatic journaling, and psychodramatic letter writing—for an in-depth presentation of these tools, see Chap. 16. While these instruments are primarily used with clients in clinical settings, they can also be modified to explore the professional self and professional development. For example, the social atom could be used as a relational assessment to depict the nature of a supervisee's professional relationships. Or a supervisee could use a sociogram to depict their perception of the sociodynamics within their agency team including coworkers, managers, and leadership. A timeline can be useful in assisting a supervisee in appreciating the development of their professional self or career. This writer has found timelines to be useful with retiring professionals to celebrate their achievements and with new professionals to create a future projection of where they what they would like their career to look like. Psychodramatic journaling and letter writing are useful as an adjunct to the timeline as they facilitate a supervisee role reversing with their past or future professional selves along their timeline of professional development. Psychodramatic journaling and letter writing can also be useful for working their emotional blocks related to professional life or exploring new professional possibilities. Perhaps the role atom is one of the most useful written Morenean tools for professional development as it orients itself as an assessment of the self—in this case, the professional self. This writer has developed a practice of using the role atom as a future visioning tool for navigating the time and space each professional role encompasses within my professional identity (see Fig. 20.2). I strive to annually draw my current professional role atom and my ideal professional role atom one year in the future which helps me to concretize and visualize which professional roles I want to increase or decrease going forward. This book is a manifestation of the effects of annually drawing my professional role atom as it helped me articulate and commit to reducing my clinical and administrative professional roles to make space for the writer role.

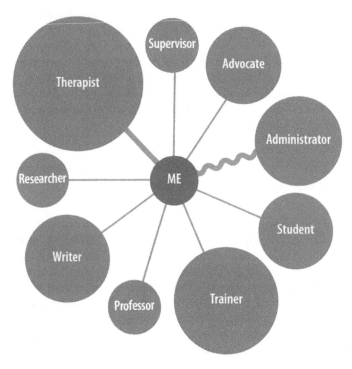

Fig. 20.2 Professional role atom

20.4   Experiential Sociometry in Social Work Education and Supervision Groups

Any content from social work courses can be presented to students or groups of supervisees through experiential teaching methods that utilize sociometry and/or role-playing techniques. Moreno's methods allow a social work educator or supervisor to bring the mentoring experience to life and move from lecture or discussion into action. Below are some simple examples of sociometry tools that can be implemented for various social work teaching structures for classroom sessions, post-graduate trainings, or supervision groups. Similar to clinical (see Chap. 11) and community sociometry prompts (see Chap. 18), it is helpful to use the three phase clinical map to discern the order of prompts in a way that warms up the group and keeps the process safe.

20.4.1   Spectrograms

As outlined in previously (see Sect. 11.3 for more detail and a video link), the spectrogram is a group-as-a-whole assessment that provides a facilitator with a quick and efficient assessment of the group's experience or understanding of a specific topic (Giacomucci, Gera, Briggs, & Bass, 2018). Using the room as a sliding scale from 0 to 10, participants are asked to physically place themselves on the spectrum based on their self-assessment of the prompt. Each spectrogram prompt provides opportunities for students to self-reflect, see where they fit within the group, and to access mutual aid by sharing with each other (Giacomucci, 2020a). As depicted in the examples below, spectrograms can be useful for social work educators and supervisors to explore students' relationships to the course content and their experience of the learning process.

Topic: Social Policy

1. How interested are you in social policy?
2. How much experience do you have in policy work?
3. How applicable is your learning of social policy to your current field placement?
4. How much do your agency policies effect your clients?

Topic: Research Methods

1. How much research experience do you have?
2. How motivated are you to learn research methods?

    a. How interested are you in quantitative methods?
    b. How interested are you in qualitative methods?

3. How competent do you feel interpreting the results of research studies?

4. How important do you think research is for the social work field?

Topic: Social Work with Groups

1. How much experience do you have participating in groups of any kind?
2. How often are you expected to facilitate groups in your field placement?
3. How confident do you feel as a group facilitator?

Topic: Social Justice

1. How much experience do you have participating in social justice movements?
2. How often do your field placement client sessions involve discussions of social justice?
3. How well do you think your field placement site does in advocating for social justice?
4. How confident do you feel as an advocate for social justice?

The use of spectrograms in the classroom actively engages students to consider their relationship to the content while discussing their experiences and beliefs with their peers. In a traditional classroom, the level of participation often varies significantly from student to student with some students offering input regularly while others rarely speak. The spectrogram is a tool that creates an inclusive experience where everyone can participate and share in smaller groups or dyads. Spectrograms are also useful for evaluations mid-semester or at the end of the semester. They provide an action-based alternative to written evaluations. In supervision groups, the spectrogram can be a cultivating agent for mutual aid between supervisees.

20.4.2   Floor Check

The floor check (see Sect. 11.5 for more detail and a video link) allows students or supervisees to interface with a topic and subtopics through a reflective mutual aid process. A floor check is facilitated by simply printing out pieces of paper labeled with various subtopic criteria and offering a series of prompts where participants stand at the criteria that best answers the prompt from them. With each prompt, a new configuration of smaller groups emerges based on similar experience and participants share briefly with those standing with them about their choice (Giacomucci, 2020c). It is helpful to offer an option for "other" with most topics and to also maintain a 3–5 person ratio between the size of the group and the number of options offered. Below are a series of floor check examples for social work educational and supervisory settings.

Social Work Core Values Floor Check—integrity; competence; services; social justice; importance of relationships; dignity/worth of each person.

1. Which value do you feel most represents the social work field?

2. Which value do you feel that you best embody in your work?
3. Which value do you feel your field placement agency best embodies?
4. Which value do you feel is most overlooked by social workers?
5. Which value would you like to more fully integrate into your work going forward?

Mental Health Diagnoses Floor Check—mood disorders (depression, bi-polar, etc.), anxiety disorders, personality disorders, substance abuse or eating disorders, dissociative disorders, psychotic disorders; other.

1. Which do you feel most comfortable working with?
2. Which do you feel is least understood in the field?
3. Which do you feel least competent to work with?
4. Which do you feel you have improved your knowledge of in the past year?

Social Work Practice Areas Floor Check—clinical social work; casework; social group work; macrosocial work; social work academia; other.

1. Which area do you feel most prepared to work in?
2. Which area do you feel most intimidated to work in?
3. Which area could contribute to improving the quality of your current field placement?
4. Which area have you become more interested in since starting your MSW program?

Social Work Practice Sites Floor Check—schools; prisons; treatment centers; universities; non-profit agencies; government agencies; hospitals; other.

1. Which practice site is your current field placement?
2. Which practice site do you have the most experience of in the past?
3. Which practice site do you think would be most difficult for you to work in?
4. Which practice site would you most want to work in?

The floor check process positions students or supervisees as mutual aid agents for each other as they share, support, and educate one another through throughout each floor check prompt. The floor check leverages relationships between participants to create a social learning experience while creating movement in the classroom. Each floor check prompt is inherently diagnostic as it reveals the preferences, experiences, or views of the group as they related to the content of the prompt. Having assessed a group of students with a floor check, the instructor can adapt the content of future sessions to follow the warm-up or meet the needs of students.

20.4.3   Step-In Sociometry

Step-in sociometry (see Sect. 11.6 for more detail and a video link), or circle of similarities, is a useful group tool for highlighting similarities and shared experiences between participants (Giacomucci, 2017). It is particularly useful for beginning stages of groups as it helps to uncover similarities while normalizing difficult experiences. Participants begin in a standing circle and take turns making statements about themselves while physically stepping into the circle. When a statement is offered, other participants also step into the circle to indicate their sense of connection to the statement. The process can be facilitated without any verbal sharing which is more time efficient and sometimes feels safer for participants as they can self-disclose without talking about details. Or brief sharing can take place related to the various step-in statements. Below are some examples of using step-in sociometry with students or supervisees:

Group: Inpatient Addictions Treatment Center Cohort of New Interns

1. Step in and name something you like to do that is not related to your career
2. Step in and identify something that attracted you to this field placement
3. Step in and name something you find difficult as a student or intern
4. Step in and share a hope or goal for your future career.

Group: Trauma-Informed Supervision Group

1. Step in and name something you do to practice in a trauma-informed way
2. Step in and identify a trauma-related issue that your clients struggle with
3. Step in and share one way you would like to grow as a trauma-informed social worker.

Group: MSW Students About to Graduate

1. Step in and share one thing that has helped you throughout your MSW program
2. Step in and share one thing that you found difficult throughout your MSW program
3. Step in and share one way you intend to use your MSW degree going forward.

Group: Social Work with Children Course

1. Step in and state one reason why you are interested in working with children
2. Step in and share one thing related to work with children that you would like to learn.

Group: Social Work License Exam Prep

1. Step in and share one aspect of the license exam you feel confident about

2. Step in and name one aspect of the exam you feel insecure about
3. Step in and share one way you plan to celebrate passing your exam.

Whether with social work supervisees or students, the step-in sociometry process reveals the invisible connections and similarities between participants which helps to increase group cohesion. Participants often come away from the exercise with an enhanced sense of universality and what Shulman (2010a) describes as the "all in the same boat" phenomenon.

20.4.4 Hands-on-Shoulder Sociograms

Another sociometry tool that offers utility for social work supervisors and educators is hands-on-shoulder sociograms. Much has been published about using sociograms in educational settings, especially with children and adolescents (Evans, 1962; Ferrá-Vindel & Jimenez, 2011; Jennings, 1948; Sobieski & Dell'Angelo, 2016). The sociogram reveals the underlying sociodynamics within the classroom or supervisory group. As outlined in previous chapters, the sociogram can be created through a pen-to-paper sociometric test or in action. Section 5.5 includes an example of a sociogram created within an MSW classroom using a sociometric test where students indicated their top three preferences for co-facilitators from the student group. The resulting sociogram was created using a computer program that efficiently generated the image while also making the data anonymous. An examination of the sociogram provides both students and the professor with an enhanced understanding of the distribution of choices within the group based on the criteria of the prompt. In this case, the sociometric test was used to teach sociograms while also choosing co-facilitators for a future assignment. Information from a sociogram can help participants and facilitators assess the social forces within the group, make group decisions based on the outcome, and intervene to develop a more inclusive group experience.

Sociograms can also be facilitated in action by providing a specific prompt and instructing participants to put their hand on the shoulder of the person who best answers the given criteria. The experiential sociogram, or hands-on-shoulder sociogram, allows participants to see in the here-and-now who is choosing them. Once participants have indicated their choice by putting their hand on the shoulder of one other group member, they can be invited to share briefly with that person their reasons for making their choice which can significantly enhance interpersonal relationships. In this process, it is important to obtain consent for physical touch and to be attentive to the possibility of specific students or supervisees being unchosen in multiple prompts. When this happens, the facilitator can create a new prompt with new criteria that makes the previously unchosen participants highly chosen. Hands-on-shoulder sociograms reveal to the group and individuals within it how individuals are experienced by other participants which can be useful information when making group decisions or warming-up to new collaborations. Below are some examples of hand-on-shoulder sociogram prompts in social work educational or supervisory settings:

Group: MSW Class on Community Social Work

1. Place your hand on the shoulder of someone who you feel has similar professional interests as you
2. Place your hand on the shoulder of someone who has said something that challenged you to look at an issue in a new way
3. Place your hand on the shoulder of someone who you would like to get to know better
4. Place your hand on the shoulder of someone who you could see yourself writing a paper with
5. Place your hand on the shoulder of someone who you would want to advocate on your behalf for something important to you.

Group: Social Work Doctoral Students After Presenting Dissertation Proposals

1. Place your hand on the shoulder of someone whose work relates to your own
2. Place your hand on the shoulder of someone whose dissertation topic is one that you do not know much about but would like to understand better
3. Place your hand on the shoulder of someone who you feel you could ask for support from if you felt stuck with your dissertation writing
4. Place your hand on the shoulder of someone who impressed you with their presentation skills.

Group: Clinical Social Work Interns

1. Place your hand on the shoulder of someone whose field placement site interests you
2. Place your hand on the shoulder of someone who has helped you understand your clients better
3. Place your hand on the shoulder of someone who you feel you could learn from to become a better social worker
4. Place your hand on the shoulder of someone who reminds you of one of your social work role models
5. Place your hand on the shoulder of someone whose work you would like to hear more about.

20.4.5   Circle of Strengths

The circle of strengths(see Sect. 11.8 for more detail and a video link) can also be adopted for supervisory and educational settings. This process uses concretization to externalize strengths of participants, the group-as-a-whole, or other entities (Giaco-mucci, 2020c). Generally, scarves are used as props to represent strengths, but any objects can be used instead. The circle of strengths can be useful in social work classrooms and supervision groups to help establish safety, connection, and cohe-sion between participants prior to emotionally charged or difficult discussions. The strengths-based process and attention to safety facilitate a more conductive learning environment for everyone involved. Here are a few different ways to modify prompts based on different settings or topics:

Group: MSW Racism Class

1. Choose a scarf to represent a strength that can help you have conversations about racism
2. Choose a scarf to represent a strength you see in your partner that can help them have discussions about racism
3. Choose a scarf to represent a strength you see in the social work field that can help combat racism.

Group: Social Work Students at the Start of their Field Placement

1. Choose a scarf to represent one of your strengths that can help you be successful at your field placement
2. Choose a scarf to represent a strength you see in your partner that can help them at their field placement
3. Choose a scarf to represent a strength you see in this group that can help support positive field placement experiences.

Group: Social Work with Groups Course

1. Choose a scarf to represent one of your strengths that can help you as a group facilitator
2. Choose a scarf to represent a strength you see in your partner that can help them as a group facilitator
3. Choose a scarf to represent a strength you experience as unique to the group work. approach

With each prompt, participants can identify their strengths and rational for their choice in front of the entire group, in smaller groups, or in dyads. After the strength has been concretized with a scarf or other object, it can be placed on the floor to create a large circle of strengths. The presence of the circle of strengths is a conscious reminder of each individual's strengths and the collective strength of the group which can help participants lean into difficult conversations later in the session. The process of creating the circle and identifying strengths, especially in others, culti-vates an atmosphere of vulnerability, appreciation, and positive connection between participants which can serve as a holding environment for difficult emotions later in the session.

20.5 Role-Play in Social Work Education and Supervision

The educational and supervisory process becomes moves beyond words and cognition through the use of experiential sociometry and role-play. The social work educational literature includes various examples of using role-play as an educational tool. Nevertheless, many students and professors are anxious about participating in or facilitating role-plays in the classroom. At this point, it is helpful to remember Moreno's hypothesis of the inverse correlation between anxiety and spontaneity (1953). If anxiety is high, the role-play will lack spontaneity. My own experience of social work educators using role-play is that they regularly neglect the warming-up process and instruct students to move directly into the enactment. It is this writer's belief that the failure of educational role-plays is largely related to the lack of attention given to the warm-up. The warming-up process will be different for each role-play, nevertheless, the sociometric processes described in Sect. 20.4 offer multiple experiential warm-ups for educators interested in improving the outcomes of role-plays in the classroom.

There are a plethora of ways that role-playing could be used in social work classrooms and supervisory settings. Chapter 19 depicts the use of role-playing in social work settings to role train responses to racism and microaggressions as well as teaching advocacy skills for social workers advocating to insurance companies, policy makers, and employers. A popular application is the use of role-playing in social work education is to re-enact students' interactions with clients from their field placement. This is a simple way to use the students' process recordings as a script allowing them to revisit clinical choices with the input of their peers and critically consider alternative interventions. The student can also be role reversed with their client to cultivate greater understanding and insight into their client's experience. This method removes much of the action demands on role players as they can rely on the process recording script for their role enactment. One way to enhance this process and infuse it with spontaneity would be to invite other students (and the professor/supervisor) to offer doubling statements or short role reversals that demonstrate different interventions or responses to the situation at hand. This method is particularly useful in supervision groups and offers an experience of mutual aid and role training for participants. This writer has employed the method at hand in a large supervision group for addictions counselors which included each therapist demonstrating their own unique way of responding to a difficult client situation. Throughout the process, participants were able to witness over 20 different styles of responding to the same situation which varied due to each individual therapists' personality, background, and clinical training.

Another useful implementation of role-playing in clinical social work settings is within license preparation courses or classes focused on assessment and diagnosis. Participants can be assigned, or sociometrically choose, a specific mental health diagnosis. Each participant reviews the diagnostic criteria for their diagnosis and uses role-playing techniques to embody a client with that diagnosis and self-present themselves to the group who then has an opportunity to practice their assessment and diagnosis skills. Through this role-playing process, participants would have an opportunity to embody and experientially assess symptoms of various mental health diagnoses rather than simply read about or talk about differential diagnosis.

Sociodrama can also be employed as an educational tool to help explore professional issues or social issues in a spontaneous forum. A depiction of this comes from this author's psychodrama MSW course. Mid-way through the semester, students were asked to articulate some of their specific fears related to group facilitation. Responses included "not knowing what to say to a client," "having to stop group members who are arguing with each other," "being told I am too young or inexperienced," "accidentally saying something offensive," "not being able to contain someone's emotions," and "group members being unsatisfied with me as a group leader." These responses were written down, then put into action in a playful and spontaneous manner with the class so they could practice responding to each situation in the here-and-now. The class spontaneously transitioned into a clinical group with each student taking on a fictitious client role within the group therapy session. The director instructed the role players on the issues to enact while strategically role reversing students into the group leader role to practice responding to the difficult group experiences. With each difficult scenario, multiple students were role reversed into the group leader role to demonstrated different strategies of responding. In this way, students had a chance to practice responding to feared moments as group facilitators while learning from each other in a playful and safe context. A similar sociodramatic process is described by Khouri, Sampaio, and Albuquerque (2014) in their work with organizational leaders using sociodrama to enact feared situations and developing leadership competencies.

In a social work education or a supervision group that has already established cohesion, connection, safety, and an atmosphere of personal disclosure, issues of countertransference can be explored using role-playing. This process is formalized through the Therapeutic Spiral Model's advanced clinical training module on transference and countertransference. In this process, a clinician engages in a role-play to re-enact a difficult moment with a client where their own countertransference has been activated. The facilitator then instructs the clinician to identify who it is that they are have projected upon their client and to choose someone in the group to play the role of that person from the therapist's own life. Often, it is a parent, friend, partner, child, or former client of the therapist. Once this person has been identified and enrolled, a psychodrama ensues focusing on working out the therapist's unresolved personal issues with the person they are projecting upon their client. Once the scene moves to closure and resolution, the client–therapist relationship is revisited to integrate a new experience of being fully present with the client without the influence of countertransference. In this process, it is also common to explore the client's transference with the therapist and to consider who the client may be projecting upon the therapist. This knowledge offers the therapist greater objectivity and insight into how they can better serve their client in the future and work through both transference and countertransference issues in future sessions.

A final use of role-playing in social work supervision and education is the use of strengths-based psychodrama to help emerging social workers affirm their strengths and future social work goals. This can be done in a group setting with auxiliaries or in individual supervision settings using empty chairs or objects to represent roles. Many social work or psychodrama students express feeling inadequate, fearful, uncertain, or under-appreciated at their field placement sites. These feelings are frequently expressed during supervision sessions or during class sessions. Using strengths-based psychodramas, one can be reminded of their inner strengths and interpersonal supports as it relates to their field placement experience. This writer has also found strengths-based psychodrama vignettes helpful for social work interns who express anxieties or insecurities related to facilitating groups. Below is a short excerpt from an individual supervision session where Cindy, the intern, expressed wanting to feel more confident facilitating a group for her first time:

INTERN:	I know I have all the education and knowledge to facilitate the group, but I feel a bit anxious. I wish I were more confident.
SUPERVISOR:	Would you like to do a short psychodrama to connect with confidence before your group?
INTERN:	Sure, maybe that will help.
SUPERVISOR:	Okay, go ahead and choose an object to represent your confidence.
INTERN:	(chooses small, framed painting in the office) This can represent my confidence.
SUPERVISOR:	Reverse Roles. From the role of confidence, speak to Cindy.
INTERN AS CONFIDENCE:	I am your confidence Cindy. You can connect with me more and remember the things we have accomplished together in the past. I am growing with each day in your internship. You don't have the run the best group ever, it just has to be good enough. And it is okay if you make mistakes. You are a student intern and the purpose of your internship is to practice, grow, and learn.
SUPERVISOR:	Great job. Confidence, can you also tell Cindy how she can tap into you if she feels anxious?
INTERN AS CONFIDENCE:	Cindy, remember to breathe. When you feel insecure, you can take a deep breathe, straighten up your stance, and feel me in your body. If that doesn't help you discern how to respond, then you can simply be authentic with the group and say that you don't know what to do or say. Trust that the group knows what they need. You don't have all the answers, so don't pretend that you do—all you need to do is help the group find their own answers.
SUPERVISOR:	Right! Well said confidence. Go ahead and role reverse back. Cindy, take a moment to take in

	and integrate those messages from your confidence (pointing to the small, framed painting concretizing confidence).
INTERN:	(quietly takes a few deep breathes while looking at the painting, then closes her eyes and shifts into a more confident posture).
SUPERVISOR:	Is this a good place to end?
INTERN:	Yeah, I feel much more confident—and much more relaxed at the same time. I think I was feeling like I had to be an expert, but this helped me remember my role as a facilitator helping the group find their own answers.
SUPERVISOR:	Here, why don't you take this with you and put it in the group room where it can remind you of your confidence (hands Cindy the small, framed painting).

This psychodrama vignette with Cindy was no more than ten minutes but helped to shift both her perception and her emotional experience related to facilitating her first group as an intern. The concretization of her confidence allowed her to integrate the psychodramatic learning into her experience as a group facilitator and throughout her internship as she was reminded of it each time she entered the supervisor's office and saw the small framed quote. Short strengths-based psychodrama vignettes like this can help support interns and students to tap into their strengths prior to facilitating groups, giving presentations, or even taking their license exams. A similar role reversal process is presented in a case study by Daniel (2016) resulting in a measured decrease in supervisee anxiety and an increase in supervisee confidence, spontaneity, and consciousness. Furthermore, Kayir (2012) offers a chapter devoted to using supervision to help psychodrama supervisees work through their anxiety of facilitation.

Through the use of role-playing techniques, including psychodrama, sociodrama, and other scripted role-plays, social work supervisors and educators can support students and supervisees as they emerge into professional social workers. Role-playing offers opportunities for strengths-based intrapsychic growth and interpersonal role training of clinical skills within both individual or group settings. The integration of simple psychodrama philosophy, theory, and interventions can enhance the effectiveness of role-play within social work classrooms and supervisory contexts.

20.6 Conclusion

Social work education and supervision sessions, when infused with sociometry and role-playing techniques, offer engaging and embodied learning experiences for emerging social workers. Moreno's methods, in the hands of social work educators and supervisors, provide experiential teaching processes that cultivate mutual aid, spontaneity, and creativity. These processes are inherently strengths-based and can be used in trauma-informed ways to promote social justice and optimal social learning environments in individual or group contexts. Moreno's methods can be employed in social work classrooms, organizations, and private practice contexts to promote professional development and personal growth. Through sociometry, psychodrama, and sociodrama, next generation of social workers can be role trained to play the role of social worker with competence, self-reflection, and excellence.

References

Apter, N. (2012). Humanistic processing: The supervisor's role through reverse enactment. In H. Krall, J. Fürst, & P. Fontaine (Eds.), *Supervision in psychodrama* (pp. 19–36). Wiesbaden: Springer.

Arthur, N., & Achenbach, K. (2002). Developing multicultural counseling competencies through experiential learning. *Counselor Education and Supervision, 42*(1), 2–14.

Baile, W. F., & Blatner, A. (2014). Teaching communication skills: Using action methods to enhance role-play in problem-based learning. *Simulation in Health Care, 9*(4), 220–227.

Banach, M., Foden, E. & Carter, V. B. (2018). Educating undergraduate group workers: Increasing confidence through experiential learning. Social Work with Groups.

Bernard, J. (1979). Supervisor training: A discrimination model. *Counselor Education and Supervision, 19,* 60–68.

Bidart-Novaes, M., Brunstein, J., Gil, A. C., & Drummond, J. (2014). Sociodrama as a creative learning strategy in business administration. *Creative Education, 5,* 1322–1333.

Blatner, A. (2006). Enacting the new academy: Sociodrama as a powerful tool in higher education. *Revision: A Journal of Consciousness & Transformation, 29,* 30–35.

Blatner, A., & Blatner, A. (1997). *The art of play: Helping adults reclaim imagination and spontaneity* (rev ed.). New York: Bruner/Mazel.

Bogo, M., Rawlings, M., Katz, E., & Logie, C. (2014). *Using simulation in assessment and teaching: OSCE adapted for social work*. Alexandria, VA: Council on Social Work Education.

Brooks, S. L. (2006). *Creative arts therapies manual: A guide to the history, theoretical approaches, assessment, and work with special populations of art, play, dance, music, drama, and poetry therapies* (1st ed.). Springfield, IL: Charles C. Thomas Publisher Ltd.

Buchanan, D. R., & Swink, D. F. (2017). Golden age of psychodrama at Saint Elizabeths hospital (1939–2004). *Journal of Psychodrama, Sociometry, and Group Psychotherapy, 65*(1), 9–32.

Bureau of Labor Statistics. (2018). Social workers. In *Occupational outlook handbook*. Retrieved from https://www.bls.gov/ooh/community-and-social-service/social-workers.htm.

Carey, L. A. (2016). Group work education: A call for renewed commitment. *Social Work with Groups, 39*(1), 48–61.

Center for Substance Abuse Treatment. (2009). *Clinical supervision and professional development of the substance abuse counselor*. Rockville, MD: U.S. Department of Health and Human Services.

Chesner, A. (2008). Psychodrama: A passion for action and non-action in supervision. In R. Shohet (Ed.), *Passionate supervision* (pp. 132–149). London: Jessica Kingsley Publishers.

Cheung, M., Alzate, K., & Nguyen, P. V. (2012). Psychodrama preparation for internship. *Field Educator: Practice Digest, 2*(2), 1–13.

Cole, D. K. (2001). Psychodrama and the training of trial lawyers: Finding the story. *Northern Illinois University Law Review, 21*(1), 1–35.

Cozolino, L. J. (2014). *Attachment-based teaching: creating a tribal classroom*. New York: W.W. Norton & Company.

Dalton, B., & Kuhn, A. C. (1998). Researching teaching methodologies in the classroom. *Journal of Teaching in Social Work, 17*(1/2), 169–184.

Daniel, S. (2012). The supervisory relationship in psychodrama training: More than a process. In H. Krall, J. Fürst, & P. Fontaine (Eds.), *Supervision in psychodrama* (pp. 111–128). Wiesbaden: Springer.

Daniel, S. (2016). The usefulness of role reversal in one-to-one supervision: a qualitative research project using heuristic enquiry. In *Psychodrama. Empirical research and science* (Vol. 2, pp. 235–253). Wiesbaden: Springer.

Dennison, S. (2005). Enhancing the integration of group theory with practice: A five-part teaching strategy. *Journal of Baccalaureate Social Work, 10*(2), 53–68.

Dewey, J. (1916). *Democracy and education: An introduction to the philosophy of education*. New York: The Free Press.

Drakulić, A. M. (2014). Critical reflections for understanding the complexity of psychodramatic theory. *Psychiatria Danubina, 26*(1), 12–19.

Dudler, A., & Weiß, K. (2012). Interlocking gear wheels—From training to practice in various professional fields. In H. Krall, J. Fürst, & P. Fontaine (Eds.), *Supervision in psychodrama* (pp. 57–72). Wiesbaden: Springer.

Ebersole, G., Leiderman, P., & Yalom, I. (1969). Training the nonprofessional group therapist. *Journal of Nervous and Mental Disorders, 149*, 294–302.

Euster, G. L. (1979). Trends in education for social work practice with groups. *Journal of Education for Social Work, 15*, 94–99.

Evans, K. M. (1962). *Sociometry and education*. London: Routledge and Kegan Paul.

Ferrándiz-Vindel, I. M., & Jimenez, B. C. (2011). The sociogram: The analysis of interpersonal relationships in higher education. *Journal of International Education Research (JIER), 7*(5), 9–14.

Fleischer, L. (2018). "Her anger frightens me!" using group-work practice principles and feature films in teaching clinical practice in mental health. *Social Work with Groups, 41*(3), 244–258.

Foels, L. E., & Bethel, J. C. (2018). Revitalizing social work education using the arts. *Social Work with Groups, 41*(1–2), 74–88.

Fox, R. (2013). *The call to teach: Philosophy, process, and pragmatics of social work education*. Alexandria, VA: Council on Social Work Education.

Freire, P. (2013). *Education for critical consciousness*. London: Bloomsbury.

Furman, R., Rowan, D., & Bender, K. (2009). *An experiential approach to group work*. Chicago, IL: Lyceum Books.

Georgiou, I., Zahn, C., & Meira, B. (2008). A systematic framework for case-based classroom experiential learning. *Systems Research and Behavioral Science, 25*(6), 807–819.

Gershoni, J. (2009). Bringing psychodrama to the main stage in group psychotherapy. *Group, 33*(4), 297–308.

Giacomucci, S. (2017). The sociodrama of life or death: Young adults and addiction treatment. *Journal of Psychodrama, Sociometry, and Group Psychotherapy, 65*(1), 137–143. https://doi.org/10.12926/0731-1273-65.1.137.

Giacomucci, S. (2018). Social work and sociometry: Integrating history, theory, and practice. The clinical voice. Richboro, PA: Pennsylvania Society for Clinical Social Work.

Giacomucci, S. (2019a). Moreno's methods in academia (or the lack of): A call to action. In *Psychodrama network news* (p. 20). American Society of Group Psychotherapy and Psychodrama, Fall 2019.

Giacomucci, S. (2019b). *Social group work in action: A sociometry, psychodrama, and experiential trauma therapy curriculum* (Doctorate in Social Work (DSW) Dissertations. 124. ProQuest Dissertations and Theses). https://repository.upenn.edu/cgi/viewcontent.cgi?article=1128&context=edissertations_sp2.

Giacomucci, S. (2020a). Addiction, traumatic loss, and guilt: A case study resolving grief through psychodrama and sociometric connections. *The Arts in Psychotherapy, 67,* 101627. https://doi.org/10.1016/j.aip.2019.101627.

Giacomucci, S. (2020b). *Best practices for psychodrama in academia: The role transition from trainer to professor.* American Society of Group Psychotherapy & Psychodrama Professional Liaison Committee. Retrieved from https://asgpp.org/wp-content/uploads/2020/08/Best-Practices-Psychodrama-in-Academia.pdf.

Giacomucci, S. (2020c). Experiential sociometry in group work: Mutual aid for the group-as-a-whole. *Social Work with Groups, Advanced Online Publication.* https://doi.org/10.1080/01609513.2020.1747726.

Giacomucci, S., Gera, S., Briggs, D., & Bass, K. (2018). Experiential addiction treatment: Creating positive connection through sociometry and therapeutic spiral model safety structures. *Journal of Addiction and Addictive Disorders, 5,* 17. https://doi.org/10.24966/AAD-7276/100017.

Giacomucci, S., & Skolnik, S. (in-press). The experiential social work educator: Integrating sociometry into the classroom environment. *Journal of Teaching Social Work.*

Gimenez Hinkle, M. (2008). Psychodrama: A creative approach for addressing parallel process in group supervision. *Journal of Creativity in Mental Health, 3*(4), 401–415.

Gitterman, A. (2004). Interactive andragogy: Principles, methods, and skills. *Journal of Teaching in Social Work, 24*(3/4), 95–112.

Gomes, A. M. A., Albuquerque, C. M., Moura, E. R. F., & Vieira, L. J. E. S. (2006). Aplicação do psicodrama pedagógico na compreensão do Sistema Único de Saúde: Relato de experiência. *Psicologia para America Latina, 6.*

Goodman, H., & Munoz, M. (2004). Developing social group work skills for contemporary agency practice. *Social Work with Groups, 27*(1), 17–33.

Guldner, C. A., & Stone-Winestock, P. (1995). The use of sociometry in teaching at the university level. *Journal of Group Psychotherapy, Psychodrama, and Sociometry, 47*(4), 177–186.

Gutman, C., & Shennar-Golan, V. (2012). Instilling the soul of group work in social work education. *Social Work with Groups, 35*(2), 138–149.

Haas, R. B. (1949). *Psychodrama and sociodrama in American education.* Beacon, NY: Beacon Press.

Hawkins, P., & Shohet, R. (2012). *Supervision in the helping professions* (4th ed.). United Kingdom: McGraw-Hill Education.

Haworth, P., & Vasiljevic, L. (2012). Psychodrama and action methods in education. *Andragoške Studije, 1,* 113–127.

Ieva, K. P., Ohrt, J. H., Swank, J. M., & Young, T. (2009). The impact of experiential groups on master students' counselor and personal development: A qualitative investigation. *The Journal for Specialists in Group Work, 34*(4), 351–368.

Jacobs, A. J. (1950). Sociodrama and teacher education. *Journal of Teacher Education, 1*(3), 192–198.

Jennings, H. H. (1948). *Sociometry in group relations: A work guide for teachers.* Washington, DC: American Council on Education.

Johnson, D. R., & Emunah, R. (2009). *Current approaches in drama therapy* (2nd ed.). Springfield, IL: Charles C. Thomas Publisher.

Jones, M. (1968). *Beyond the therapeutic community.* New Haven, CT: Yale University Press.

Kadushin, A., & Harkness, D. (2014). *Supervision in social work.* New York: Columbia University Press.

Kaye, L., & Fortune, A. (2001). Coping skills and learning in social work field education. *The Clinical Supervisor, 20*(2), 31–42.

Kayır, A. (2012). Trainee's anxiety to direct: Supervision as a journey from anxiety to curiosity. In H. Krall, J. Fürst, & P. Fontaine (Eds.), *Supervision in psychodrama* (pp. 151–160). Wiesbaden: Springer.

Keeton, M. T., & Tate, P. J. (Eds.). (1978). *Learning by experience—What, why, how: New directions for experiential learning.* San Francisco: Jossey-Bass Publishing.

Kellermann, P. F. (1992). *Focus on psychodrama: The therapeutic aspects of psychodrama.* London, UK: Jessica Kingsley.

Khouri, G. S., Sampaio, M., & Albuquerque, C. F. L. D. (2014). Dialogue with the leadership through the sociodrama: From feared scenes to the development of competencies. *Revista Brasileira de Psicodrama, 22*(1), 22–31.

Knight, C. (2017) Social work students' experiences with group work in the field practicum. *Journal of Teaching in Social Work, 37*(2), 138-155.

Kolb, D. A. (1984). *Experiential learning: Experience as the source of learning and development.* Englewood Cliffs, NJ: Prentice Hall.

Kolk, D. A. (2014). *Experiential learning: Experience as the source of learning and development* (2nd ed.). New Jersey: Pearson Education Inc.

Kolb, D. A., & Kolb, A. Y. (2005). Learning styles and learning spaces: Enhancing experiential learning in higher education. *Academy of Management Learning & Education, 4*(2), 193–212.

Kolb, D. A., & Kolb, A. Y. (2017). *The experiential educator: Principles and practices of experiential learning.* Kaunakakai, HI: Experienced Based Learning Systems Press.

Konopik, D. A., & Cheung, M. (2013). Psychodrama as a social work modality. *Journal of Social Work, 58*(1), 9–20.

Koob, J., & Funk, J. (2002). Kolb's learning style inventory: Issues of validity and reliability. *Research on Social Work Practice, 12*(2), 293–308.

Krall, H. (2012). Training and research in supervision—An introduction. In H. Krall, J. Fürst, & P. Fontaine (Eds.), *Supervision in psychodrama* (pp. 201–206). Wiesbaden: Springer.

Krall, H., & Fürst, J. (2012). Supervision and evaluation: Objectives, practices and helpful aspects. In H. Krall, J. Fürst, & P. Fontaine (Eds.), *Supervision in psychodrama* (pp. 259–278). Wiesbaden: Springer.

Krall, H., Fürst, J., & Fontaine, P. (2012). Supervision in psychodrama–an introduction. In H. Krall, J. Fürst, & P. Fontaine (Eds.), *Supervision in psychodrama* (pp. 9–12). Wiesbaden: Springer.

Kramer, B. J., & Wrenn, R. (1994). The blending of andragogical and pedagogical teaching methods in advanced social work practice courses. *Journal of Teaching in Social Work, 10*(1/2), 43–64.

Landis, H. (2020). *Collective stories: The application of sociodrama with high school immigrant students. Social work with groups.* Advanced Online Publication. https://doi.org/10.1080/016 09513.2020.1811014.

Landy, R. J. (2017). The love and marriage of psychodrama and drama therapy. *The Journal of Psychodrama, Sociometry, and Group Psychotherapy, 65*(1), 33–40.

LaRocque, S. E. (2017). Group work education in social work: A review of the literature reveals possible solutions. *Journal of Social Work Education, 53*(2), 276–285.

Liberali, R., & Grosseman, S. (2015). Uso de Psicodrama em medicina no Brasil: Uma revisão de literatura. *Interface (Botucatu), 19*(54), 561–571.

Lu, Y. E., Ain, E., Chamorro, C., Chang, C., Feng, J. Y., Fong, R., & Yu, M. (2011).A new methodology for assessing social work practice: The adaptation of the objective structured clinical evaluation (SW-OSCE). *Social Work Education, 30*, 170–185.

MacGowan, M., & Vakharia, S. (2012). Teaching standards-based group work competencies to social work students: An empirical examination. *Research on Social Work Practice, 22*(4), 380–388.

Marineau, R. (2014). *Jacob Levy Moreno 1889–1974: Father of psychodrama, sociometry, and group psychotherapy.* Princeton, New Jersey: Psychodrama Press.

Maya, J., & Maraver, J. (2020). Teaching-learning processes: Application of educational psychodrama in the University setting. *International Journal of Environmental Research and Public Health, 17*(11), 3922.

McCarthy, M. (2010). Experiential learning theory: From theory to practice. *Journal of Business & Economics Research, 8*(5), 131–139.

McGovern, M., & Harmsworth, P. (2010). A taste of reflecting practice. *Journal of Family Therapy, 32*(4), 440–443.

McKinney, J., O'Conner, V., & Pruitt, D. (2018). Experiential learning through group work and theater. *Social Work with Groups, 41*(1–2), 49–59.

McLaughlin, D. E., Freed, P. E., & Tadych, R. A. (2006). Action methods in the classroom: Creative strategies for nursing education. *International Journal of Nursing Education Scholarship, 3*(1).

Michaels, T. J., & Hatcher, N. C. (1972). Sociodrama in the classroom: A different approach to learning. *The High School Journal, 55*(4), 151–156.

Mooradian, J. K. (2007). Simulated family therapy interviews in clinical social work education. *Journal of Teaching in Social Work, 27*(1/2), 89–104.

Mooradian, J. K. (2008). Using simulated sessions to enhance clinical social work education. *Journal of Social Work Education, 44*(3), 21–35.

Mor Barak, M. E., Travis, D. J., Pyun, H., & Xie, B. (2009). The impact of supervision on worker outcomes: A meta-analysis. *Social Service Review, 83*(1), 3–32.

Moreno, J. L. (1946). *Psychodrama* (Vol. 1). Beacon, NY: Beacon House Press.

Moreno, J. L. (1949). The spontaneity theory of learning. In R. B. Hass (Ed.), *Psychodrama and sociodrama in American education.* Beacon, NY: Beacon House Press.

Moreno, J. L. (1953). *Who shall survive? Foundations of sociometry, group psychotherapy and sociodrama* (2nd ed.). Beacon, NY: Beacon House.

Moreno, J. L. (1955). *Preludes to my autobiography.* Beacon, NY: Beacon House.

Moreno, J. L. (2011). *The Autobiography of J. L. Moreno (abridged).* United Kingdom: North-West Psychodrama Association.

Moreno, J. L. (2012a). *Preludes to my autobiography* (reprint of 1955 ed.). United Kingdom: North-West Psychodrama Association.

Moreno, J. L., & Moreno, Z. T. (1959). *Foundations of psychodrama* (Vol. II). Beacon, NY: Beacon House Press.

Moreno, Z. T. (2012b). *A message from Zerka. Psychodrama network news* (p. 5). American Society of Group Psychotherapy and Psychodrama, Fall 2012.

Munson, C. (2012). *Handbook of clinical social work supervision.* Birmingham, NY: Routledge.

Nery, M. D. P., & Gisler, J. V. T. (2019). Sociodrama: An active method in research, teaching and educational intervention. *Revista Brasileira de Psicodrama, 27*(1), 11–19.

Nicholas, M. W. (2017). The use of psychodrama and sociometry techniques in psychodynamic and other process groups. *International Journal of Group Psychotherapy, 67*(S1), S131–S140.

Nolte J. (2018) Psychodrama and creativity in education. In: Burgoyne, S. (Eds.), *Creativity in theatre. Creativity theory and action in education* (Vol. 2). Cham, Switzerland: Springer Publishing.

Ochs, P. (2020). Using action methods in clinical supervision: A journey from talk to action. *Social Work with Groups, Advanced Online Publication.* https://doi.org/10.1080/01609513.2020.1793057.

Ochs, P., & Webster, J. (2017). Family therapy supervision in action. *The Journal of Psychodrama, Sociometry, and Group Psychotherapy, 65*(1), 111–121.

Oudijk, R. (2007). A postmodern approach to psychodrama theory. In C. Baim, Clark, J. Burmeister, & M. Maciel, Manuela (Eds.), *Psychodrama: Advances in theory and practice* (pp. 139–150). New York: Routledge, Taylor & Francis Group.

Powell, J. Y., & Causby, V. D. (1994). From the classroom to the capitol-from MSW students to advocates: Learning by doing. *Journal of Teaching in Social Work, 9*(1/2), 141–154.

Propper, H. (2003). Psychodrama as experiential education: exploring literature and enhancing a cooperative learning environment. In J. Gershoni (Ed.), *Psychodrama in the 21st century: clinical and educational applications* (pp. 229–248). New York: Springer Publishing Company.

Pugh, G. L. (2014). Revisiting the pink triangle exercise: An exploration of experiential learning in graduate social work education. *Journal of Teaching in Social Work, 34*(1), 17–28.

Quinn, P., Jacobsen, M., & LaBarber, L. (1992). Utilization of group projects in teaching social work research methods: Benefits to students and faculty. *Journal of Teaching in Social Work, 6*(1), 63–76.

Ramsauer, S. (2007). Psychodramatische Supervision in der Sozialen Arbeit: Kleine Interventionen mit großer Wirkung. *Zeitschrift für Psychodrama und Soziometrie, 6*(2), 293–302.

Raschick, M., Maypole, D., & Day, P. (1998). Improving field education through Kolb learning theory. *Journal of Social Work Education, 34*(1), 31–42.

Rawlings, M. A. (2012). Assessing BSW student direct practice skill using standardized clients and self-efficacy theory. *Journal of Social Work Education, 48,* 553–576.

Rogers, C. (1961). *On becoming a person: A therapist's view of psychotherapy.* Boston, MA: Houghton Mifflin.

Sachdev, P. (1997). Cultural sensitivity training through experiential learning: A participatory demonstration field education project. *International Social Work, 40*(1), 7–25.

Schön, D. (1987). *Educating the reflective practitioner: Toward a new design for teaching and learning in the professions.* San Francisco, CA: Jossey-Bass.

Schreiber, J. C., & Minarik, J. D. (2018). Simulated clients in a group practice course: Engaging facilitation and embodying diversity. *Journal of Social Work Education, 54*(2), 310–323.

Semb, G. B., & Ellis, J. A. (1994). Knowledge taught in school: What is remembered? *Review of Educational Research, 64*(2), 253–286.

Shera, W., Muskat, B., Delay, D., Quinn, A., & Tufford, L. (2013). Using a group work practice standards inventory to assess the impact of a "social work practice with groups" course. *Social Work with Groups, 36*(2–3), 174–190.

Shulman, L. (1987). The hidden group in the classroom. *Journal of Teaching in Social Work, 1*(2), 3–31.

Shulman, L. (2010a). *Dynamics and skills of group counseling.* Belmont, CA: Cengage Learning.

Shulman, L. (2010b). *Interactional supervision* (3rd ed.). Washington, DC: NASW Press.

Siegel, D. J. (2012). *Developing mind: How relationships and the brain interact to shape who we are.* New York: Guilford Press.

Sobieski, C., & Dell'Angelo, T. (2016). Sociograms as a tool for teaching and learning: Discoveries from a teacher research study. *The Educational Forum, 80*(4), 417–429.

Specht, L. B., & Sandlin, P. K. (1991). The differential effects of experiential learning activities and traditional lecture classes. *Simulation & Gaming, 22*(2), 196–210.

Sternberg, P., & Garcia, A. (2000). *Sociodrama: Who's in your shoes?* Westport, CT: Praeger Publishers.

Strozier, A. L. (1997). Group work in social work education: What is being taught? *Social Work with Groups, 20*(1), 65–77.

Swiller, H. I. (2011). Process groups. *International Journal of Group Psychotherapy, 61*(2), 263–273.

Tabib, S. L. (2017). *Effective psychodrama supervision a grounded theory study on senior supervisors' perspectives.* Doctoral dissertation, Lesley University. Retrieved from https://digitalcommons.lesley.edu/expressive_dissertations/4/.

ter Avest, I. (2017). "I experienced freedom within the frame of my own narrative": The contribution of psychodrama techniques to experiential learning in teacher training. *International Review of Education, 63*(1), 71–86.

Truedley, M. B. (1944). Psychodrama and social case work. *Sociometry, 7,* 170–178.

Tully, G. (2015). The faculty field liaison: An essential role for advancing graduate and undergraduate group work education. *Social Work with Groups, 38*(1), 6–20.

Veiga, S., Bertão, A., & Franco, V. (2015). Sociodrama in the training of social educators: An exploratory research. *The Journal of Psychodrama, Sociometry, and Group Psychotherapy, 63*(1), 47–64.

Walters, R., & Baile, W. F. (2014). Training oncology professionals in key communication skills: Adapting psychodrama and sociodrama for experiential learning. *The Journal of Psychodrama, Sociometry, and Group Psychotherapy, 62*(1), 55–66.

Warkentin, B. (2017) Teaching social work with groups: Integrating didactic, experiential and reflective learning. *Social Work with Groups, 40*(3), 233–243.

Wehbi, S. (2011). Reflections on experiential teaching methods: Linking the classroom to practice. *Journal of Teaching in Social Work, 31*(5), 493–504.

Whiteman, V. L., & Nielsen, M. (1990). Drama in teaching survey research methods: An experimental evaluation. *Journal of Teaching in Social Work, 4*(2), 67–81.

Wiener, R. (1988). Sociodrama and management training. *Industrial and Commercial Training, 20*(4), 18–20.

Williams, A. (1995). *Visual and active supervision: Roles, focus, technique.* New York: W. W. Norton.

Williams, A. J. (1988). Action methods in supervision. *The Clinical Supervisor, 6*(2), 13–27.

Yalom, I. D., & Leszcz, M. (2005). *The theory and practice of group psychotherapy* (5th ed.). New York, NY: Basic Books.

Zastrow, C. (2001). *Social work with groups: using the classroom as a group leadership laboratory* (5th ed.). Pacific Grove, CA: Brooks/Cole.

Chapter 21
Conclusion—A Future Vision of Social Work with Moreno's Methods

Abstract This brief conclusion offers a new vision for the integration of Moreno's methods into the social work field. Moreno's triadic system, sociometry, psychodrama, and group psychotherapy, provides social workers with group work skills lacking in most social work curriculums but are essential for competent practice. This chapter is largely written in the form of a psychodramatic process which includes role reversing with a social work leader in the year 2074 at the 100th year anniversary of Jacob Moreno's death. This role reversal into an idealized future provides a reflection on how the social work field could benefit from the full integration of sociometry and psychodrama into its repertoire.

Keywords Future of psychodrama · Social work education · Social work field · Jacob Moreno · Psychodramatic letter

> Mankind needs to be educated; education means more than intellectual enlightenment, it isn't emotional enlightenment, it isn't insight only, it is a matter of the deficiency of spontaneity to use the available intelligence and to mobilize his enlightened emotions… it requires action research and action methods continuously modified and sharpened to meet new inner and outer environments. (Moreno, 1947, p. 11)

Moreno's (1947) statement on education begs us to consider if social work education has been "sharpened to meet new inner and outer environments" and provide high-quality education for the next generation of social workers. Increasingly, social workers are expected to facilitate group therapy in clinical settings without the educational background or training necessary to work competently upon graduation (Goodman, Knight, & Khudodov, 2014; Knight, 2017; Sweifach & Heft-Laport, 2008). The reliance on social work education's cultural conserve may result in the gradual loss of potential clinical students to other graduate programs (counseling, psychology, marriage and family therapy, creative arts therapies, etc.) that provide a more comprehensive clinical education and training in group work. A recent study in Israel even found creative arts therapists demonstrate higher job satisfaction than psychologists or social workers but lack a sense of collective self-esteem that comes with belonging to a fully recognized profession (Orkibi, 2019). It is time that social work education responds to the needs of social work practice with groups more fully embedding experiential methods, group work, creative arts therapies, and trauma therapy within the social work curriculums.

423

S. Giacomucci, *Social Work, Sociometry, and Psychodrama*, Psychodrama in Counselling, Coaching and Education 1,
https://doi.org/10.1007/978-981-33-6342-7_21

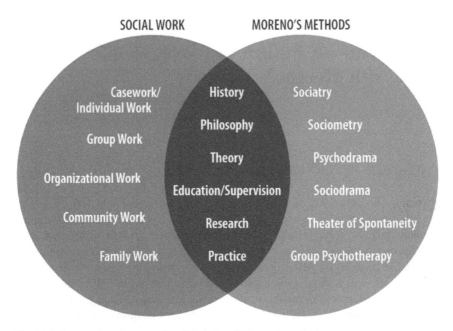

SOCIAL WORK   MORENO'S METHODS

Casework/   History   Sociatry
Individual Work
                 Philosophy   Sociometry
Group Work
                 Theory   Psychodrama
Organizational Work
                 Education/Supervision   Sociodrama

Community Work   Research   Theater of Spontaneity

Family Work   Practice   Group Psychotherapy

Fig. 21.1 Intersecting elements of social work and Moreno's methods

The learning of Moreno's triadic system would provide social workers with the needed knowledge and skills to be successful in their careers which will inevitably include working with groups (Giacomucci, 2019). The publication of this book will concretize and further integrate Moreno's methods into the social work profession. As more professionals are introduced to psychodrama, there will be a greater interest in conducting quality research to strengthen its research base. While this book focused largely on clinical applications of Moreno's methods, it is important to note that psychodrama and sociometry processes are applicable in non-clinical settings as well. Moreno's methods can help prepare the current generation of social workers to provide the next generation with competent psychodrama supervision and education in the field placement and the classroom.

The primary goal of this publication is to initiate dialogue and integration between the field of social work, sociometry, and psychodrama (see Fig. 21.1). The first few chapters of this book oriented upon the histories of psychodrama and social work; therefore, it is only fitting that the final chapter concern itself with the future of social work and Moreno's methods. Considering the content of this book, it seems appropriate to conclude with a psychodramatic process. In the following psychodramatic letter writing experiment, I have attempted to role reverse with a social work leader in an idealized future where Moreno's methods have been fully integrated into the social work field. This is of course a biased future projection based on my own vision where psychodrama and social work exist in a synergistic union. Perhaps in the year 2074, we can look back and see if any of this vision has materialized!

21.1 An Idealized Future of Social Work and Psychodrama

Dear Readers,

Today, May 14th, 2074, marks the 100th year since the death of Jacob Moreno. On this anniversary, let us remember Moreno's contributions and celebrate how his legacy continues to live on. Moreno is remembered as many things including the founder of psychodrama and sociometry, a pioneer of group therapy and social network theory, and even "the man who brought laughter into psychiatry" as his tombstone reads.

Much has transpired in the past century as it relates to the evolution of Moreno's methods, and especially as it concerns us in the field of social work. About 50 years ago, social workers' interest in sociometry and psychodrama increased significantly due a realization of the need for more group work training and the outpouring of research on the effectiveness of body-oriented and creative arts therapies in the treatment of trauma-related issues. In the 2020s, an influx of new social work publications on Moreno's methods emerged with a special journal edition in *Social Work with Groups*. Psychodrama and sociometry found a home within the non-deliberative tradition of social work with groups. The larger movements in the social work field focused on social justice, trauma-informed work, strengths-based approaches, and emphasizing the creative arts modalities seemed to intersect at the point of sociometry and psychodrama.

I know it is hard to believe, but in the early 2000s, few social workers were trained in sociometry or psychodramatic methods and their existence was unknown to many. The psychodrama community, finding itself isolated from other professional fields, made an increased effort to collaborate with social workers—in addition to counselors, psychologists, educators, lawyers, coaches, and religious leaders.

In the early 2000s, the practices of social workers, counselors, and psychologists—as well as social group workers, group counselors, group psychologists, and group psychotherapists—had become almost identical. Social workers were losing their unique identity in group work. While working together with other professions is important, we also needed to differentiate ourselves as social workers and social group workers. The adoption of sociometric and psychodramatic philosophy, theory, and practices into our field helped us to distinguish ourselves from counselors and psychologists while remaining in integrity with our core values. The social work with groups field has been revitalized with an influx of new sociometric and psychodramatic ideas while also helping the psychodrama community to modernize and validate their methods. Social workers, utilizing their professional training in research and social justice, have developed new ways of using sociometry and psychodrama techniques which emphasize Moreno's vision of Sociatry while conforming to the standards of evidence based practice.

The field of psychodrama, which had largely failed to professionalize in the USA, integrated into academia with the help of many social workers. MSW concentrations in psychodrama sociatry developed in the 2030s, and later, a doctoral degree in psychodrama and sociatry was established with CSWE accreditation. The psychodrama MSW concentrations helped to train social work practitioners as they entered the field using Moreno's methods while the doctoral program created scholars and researchers of Moreno's methods.

Social work educators regularly integrate experiential teaching components including sociometry and role-play into their social work courses which keep students actively engaged in the learning process. Many students are initially attracted to social work degree programs because they know they will not spend multiple years sitting through lectures or PowerPoint presentations, instead they will be active partici- pants in the classroom. Rather than being treated as students, they are empowered to become student-instructors in the learning experience.

Sociometry and psychodrama have enhanced social work practice at the micro- , mezzo-, and macrolevels. Social work caseworkers now regularly employ the sociogram, social atom, and role atom tests as non-pathologizing assessment tools that emphasize our person-in-environment perspective. With these sociometric tools, we are now able to more fully work from a biopsychosocial –spiritual approach beginning with our assessments.

Social group workers, equipped with sociometry and psychodrama interventions, have mastered the art of working with the group-as-a-whole and cultivating mutual aid . In the past, we had been critiqued for doing individual therapy in group settings. Now, we fully integrate group methods to that produce both intrapsychic and inter- personal change while addressing psychodynamic and sociodynamic experience. It may be hard to believe, but years ago social workers could obtain an MSW degree without ever taking a course in group work. Since then, the CSWE requirements have changed and require group work training. Many agencies have come to prefer MSW interns over other interns due to the noticeable difference in their group facilitation competencies.

Many clients actively seek out clinical social workers for psychotherapy after finding talk therapy to be ineffective or unhelpful. Programs that work with young adults or people with addiction or trauma-related issues have come to prefer clinical social workers due to their use of experiential therapy and their clients' positive feedback regarding it. The neuroscience research supporting experiential methods for the treatment of trauma and other mental health conditions continues to pile up.

Macrosocial workers have incorporated the tools of sociometry and sociodrama into community social work practice. Rather than falling into the trap of becoming agents of social control, macroworkers center their work around the philosophy of empowering community members and advocating for social change. Sociodrama and role-playing techniques have become standard practice within community spaces to resolve intergroup conflict and role train community members to advocate on their own behalf. Sociometric tools and social network instruments are actively used to promote more democratic and inclusive organizations and societies.

Social workers employ experiential methods in their supervision of other social workers and in agency contexts. Staff meetings and supervision groups, which previously relied on group discussion or individual case presentations, now encom- pass experiential processes including sociometry and role-playing. Treatment teams operate with more cohesion, connection, and collaboration than previously. The regular use of role reversal has helped social work supervisees better understand their clients' experiences when offering case presentations.

It is no secret that many of us choose the social work fields, or other helping professions, because of our own personal experiences with trauma, mental health issues, or oppression. Over the years, it became clearer that this was both a noble motivating factor but also the source of much countertransference, projection, and dysfunction in our field. The use of psychodramatic processes in social work education, supervision, training, and professional development seems to also have challenged emerging social workers to reflect on their own unresolved emotional issues and work through them. This has substantially improved the collective integrity of our field.

The social work core values have not changed, but we have systematically become better at embodying them and putting them into action within all areas of the field—education, training, supervision, clinical practice, casework, group work, community work, and organizational leadership. Social workers maintain committed to working with competency, integrity, service while emphasizing social justice, the importance of relationships, and the dignity and worth of every person. Morenean philosophy, theory, and practices have helped us to strengthen these axiological commitments and solidify our collective identity as social workers.

Though Dr. Moreno (see Fig. 21.2) never identified himself as a social worker, his career embodies that of one. He worked with oppressed and marginalized communities, groups, and individuals while creating larger societal changes which have had a lasting impact on society, education, group therapy, and social work. For this, we

Fig. 21.2 Jacob Moreno in 1942 in Chicago. Reprinted with permission from Figusch (2014)

recognize him as a pioneer of the social work field and honor him on the 100th anniversary of his death . Thank you.

References

Figusch, Z. (2014). *The JL Moreno memorial photo album.* London: lulu.com

Giacomucci, S. (2019). *Social group work in action: A sociometry, psychodrama, and experiential trauma therapy curriculum* (Doctorate in Social Work (DSW) Dissertations. 124. ProQuest Dissertations and Theses). https://repository.upenn.edu/cgi/viewcontent.cgi?article=1128&context=edissertations_sp2.

Goodman, H., Knight, C., & Khudododov, K. (2014). Graduate social work students' experiences with group work in the field and the classroom. *Journal of Teaching in Social Work, 34*(1), 60–78.

Knight, C. (2017). Social work students' experiences with group work in the field practicum. *Journal of Teaching in Social Work, 37*(2), 138–155.

Moreno, J. L. (1947). *The future of man's world.* Beacon, NY: Beacon House Press.

Orkibi, H. (2019). Creative arts therapists report lower collective self-esteem but higher job satisfaction than other professionals. *Art Therapy, 36*(2), 98–102.

Sweifach, J., & LaPorte, H. (2008). Why did they choose group work: Exploring the motivations and perceptions of current MSW students of group work. *Social Work with Groups, 31*(3/4), 347–362.

Index

A

Act hunger, 103, 104, 178, 271, 282
Action insights, 104
Action theory, 56, 63, 114
Activism, 4, 42, 117, 263, 293, 356, 373–376, 388
Addams, Jane, 399
Addiction, 56, 179, 192, 195, 216, 219, 220, 227, 257, 258, 260, 263, 264, 284, 317–319, 351, 359, 379, 381, 387, 426
Addictions treatment, 86, 140, 257, 317
Adverse childhood experiences, 129
Aesthetic distance, 260, 262, 283, 291, 292, 375, 386
Alcoholics Anonymous, 179, 352
American Board of Examiners in Sociometry, Psychodrama, and Group Psychotherapy, 2, 43, 74, 84, 197, 297, 396, 401
American Group Psychotherapy Association (AGPA), 34, 43
American Psychological Association, 44, 45, 188
American Psychiatric Association, 32, 128, 133, 137, 348
American Society of Group Psychotherapy & Psychodrama (ASGPP), 32, 34, 43, 44, 294, 394, 396
American Sociological Society, 40
Amygdala, 148, 150, 156
Anxiety, 61, 134, 192–195, 222, 238, 240, 260, 263, 286, 313, 318, 325, 331–334, 336, 340, 359, 382, 386, 407, 412, 415
Aristotle, 76, 105, 374
Art therapy, 22, 56, 130, 225, 324

Association for the Advancement of Social Work with Groups (AASWG), 19
Attachment theory, 56, 135
Audience, 6, 37, 105, 109, 111, 112, 114, 116, 157, 173, 240, 243, 248, 256, 272, 277–279, 281, 284, 287, 288, 292, 300, 301, 324, 326, 374, 376–378
Autobiography of a Genius, 10, 45, 57, 176
Autodrama, 295, 296
Autonomous healing center, 60, 72, 156, 174, 284, 294, 295, 302
Auxiliary ego, 36, 63, 109, 111, 112, 256, 258, 329
Axiodrama, 295, 297

B

Beacon, 38, 39, 109, 344, 351
Beacon Hill Sanitarium. *See* Moreno Sanitarium
Behaviorism, 64, 118, 177
Bibliodrama, 291, 295, 297
Biopsychosocial, 9, 55, 64, 67, 103, 151, 189, 238, 278, 299, 426
Boal, Augusto, 300, 375
Brain stem, 148, 150, 156
Bryn Mawr College, 2, 45, 90, 394
Buber, Martin, 86
Burrow, Trigant, 32

C

Canon of Creativity, 61, 114, 237
Casework, 18, 19, 23, 33, 166, 173, 309, 320, 341, 349, 427

© The Editor(s) (if applicable) and The Author(s) 2021
S. Giacomucci, *Social Work, Sociometry, and Psychodrama*, Psychodrama in Counselling, Coaching and Education 1,
https://doi.org/10.1007/978-981-33-6342-7

CPSIA information can be obtained
at www.ICGtesting.com
Printed in the USA
BVHW011120270221
601300BV00011B/238